# ERISA Survey of Federal Circuits

**Brooks R. Magratten, Editor**

## Second Edition

**AMERICAN BAR ASSOCIATION**
**Defending Liberty**
**Pursuing Justice**

**TORT TRIAL & INSURANCE PRACTICE SECTION**
**HEALTH AND DISABILITY INSURANCE LAW COMMITTEE**

Printed in the United States of America

11 10 09 08 07   5 4 3 2 1

**Library of Congress Cataloging-in-Publication Data**

ERISA survey of federal circuits / edited by Brooks R. Magratten.—2nd ed.
    p.  cm.
    Includes bibliographical references and index.
    ISBN 978-1-59031-821-8
    1. Pension trusts—Law and legislation—United States. 2. United States. Employee Retirement Income Security Act of 1974. 3. Actions and defenses—United States. I. Magratten, Brooks R., 1961– II. American Bar Association. Tort Trial and Insurance Practice Section.

KF3512.E725 2007
344.7301'252—dc22

2007011914

# Contents

CHAPTER 2
**Second Circuit   31**
*David J. Burke*
*Steven B. Getzoff*
*Helen M. Kemp*
*Randi F. Knepper*
*Allan M. Marcus*
*Amy Zinser*

*CHAPTER 3*
**Third Circuit   61**
*Joshua Bachrach*
*Randi F. Knepper*
*Patricia M. McIntire*

*CHAPTER 4*
**Fourth Circuit   91**
*Bryan D. Bolton*
*Cheryl A. C. Brown*
*George K. Evans Jr.*
*E. Ford Stephens*
*Erna A. P. Womble*

CHAPTER 5
**Fifth Circuit   151**
*Jennifer M. Lawrence*
*Virginia N. Roddy*
*Kelly D. Simpkins*
*Stephen W. Smith*

*CHAPTER 6*
**Sixth Circuit   175**
*Robert D. Anderle*
*Craig R. Carlson*
*Leigh M. Chiles*
*Kristi R. Gauthier*
*S. Russell Headrick*
*Michael Shpiece*

CHAPTER 7
**Seventh Circuit   201**
*Michael Brown*
*Mark D. Debofsky*
*Mark E. Schmidtke*

*CHAPTER 8*
**Eighth Circuit   221**
*Clark H. Cole*
*Matthew Shorey*
*Terrance J. Wagener*

*CHAPTER 10*
**Tenth Circuit   279**
*Michael S. Beaver*
*Trent A. Howell*
*David N. Kelley*
*Scott M. Petersen*

*CHAPTER 11*

**Eleventh Circuit    307**

*Russell Buhite*
*H. Sanders Carter Jr.*
*Nikole M. Crow*
*Tiffany D. Downs*
*Stacia L. Guthrie*
*Maggie Marrero-Ladik*
*Douglas L. Oppenheimer*
*Anthony H. Pelle*
*Aaron E. Pohlmann*
*Joelle C. Sharman*

## CHAPTER 12

## D.C. Circuit    355

*James L. Marketos*
*Glenn Merten*
*Robin Sanders*

# Foreword

This book is a project of the Health and Disability Insurance Law Committee of the Tort, Trial and Insurance Practice Section of the American Bar Association. The Committee consists of practitioners representing plaintiffs and defendants nationwide in health and disability insurance cases. This book, however, is intended to address a wide variety of substantive and procedural issues that arise in ERISA litigation.

For the original volume, *ERISA Survey of Federal Circuits,* published in 2005, Committee volunteers from each of the federal circuits agreed to write on several substantive and procedural issues regarding the Employee Retirement Income Security Act of 1974. These volunteers were organized into teams and asked to write on the law of their respective circuits according to the following outline:

I. What Constitutes an ERISA Plan?
 ■ What rules or tests does your circuit apply to determine if an employee welfare benefit plan exists?
 ■ How does your circuit define "employees" for ERISA purposes?
 ■ How has your circuit interpreted the "safe harbor" regulation?
 ■ How much employer involvement is required to sustain an employee welfare benefit plan?
 ■ Treatment of multiple employer trusts or welfare agreements?
 ■ Treatment of individual business owners?

II. Preemption
 ■ Using the analytical framework established in *Pilot Life* and *Ward,* what is the scope of ERISA preemption as defined by your circuit?
 ■ Preemption of managed-care claims?
 ■ Preemption of malpractice claims?
 ■ State independent review statutes?

III. Exhaustion of Administrative Remedies
 ■ Is exhaustion an absolute requirement?
 ■ Does your circuit recognize a futility exception? Other exceptions?
 ■ What are the consequences of a plaintiff's failure to exhaust?
 ■ How many levels of administrative review are required?
 ■ Can a defendant waive a failure-to-exhaust defense?

IV. Standard of Review
- What kind of plan language satisfies *Firestone* criteria?
- What standards of review does your circuit apply in ERISA cases? Does it apply a sliding scale in certain circumstances?
- How does a conflict of interest or procedural irregularities affect the standard of review?
- What evidence is required to establish a conflict of interest? Can a conflict be implied?
- What factors, other than plan language or a conflict, can affect the standard of review?
- Effect of state insurance laws on standard of review?
- Possible impact of ERISA regulations on standard of review?

V. Rules of Plan Interpretation
- Subject to federal common law?
- Does your circuit apply *contra proferentem?* Under what circumstances?
- Is an administrator's interpretation of a plan entitled to deference?
- Other rules of plan or contract interpretation?
- Effect of plan amendments on pending claims, both substantive and procedural?

VI. Discovery
- Does your circuit recognize limitations on discovery in ERISA cases? Does it depend on the standard of review?
- Is discovery permitted to prove conflict of interest or degree of conflict of interest?

VII. Evidence
- Is the scope of evidence under a deferential standard of review limited to the administrative record?
- Under de novo review?
- Under what circumstances will a court look beyond the administrative record?
- What if there is a dispute over the composition of the administrative record?
- What is the evidentiary value, if any, of Social Security determinations?

VIII. Procedural Aspects of ERISA Practice
- Are ERISA cases typically resolved on summary judgment?
- Have there been any reported ERISA trials?
- Are jury trials permitted under any circumstances?
- Has your circuit developed any special procedures for ERISA benefit cases?

IX. Fiduciary Liability Claims
- Who is a fiduciary?
- How does your circuit define fiduciary duties?
- Does fiduciary liability arise in the context of health and disability claims?

- Remedies for breach of fiduciary duties?
- Does your circuit allow claims for contribution and indemnity among fiduciaries?
- Does your circuit recognize ERISA claims against nonfiduciaries?

X. Attorneys' Fees
- What are your circuit's stated criteria for awarding attorney's fees under 29 U.S.C. §1132(g)?
- Have fees been awarded to plan fiduciaries?
- How are fees calculated?

XI. ERISA Regulations
- Cases interpreting current regulations?
- Cases interpreting old regulations that may form a basis for interpreting current regulations?

XII. Cases Interpreting ERISA Statutes of Limitation

XIII. Subrogation Litigation
- How has your circuit handled subrogation claims after *Great-West Life v. Knudson?*

XIV. Miscellaneous
- Has your circuit developed any unique substantive or procedural rules for ERISA benefit cases?
- Has your circuit developed a unique approach to common policy-based defenses such as mental/nervous conditions, residual versus total disability, and so forth?
- Does your circuit favor or disfavor ERISA class actions? Have class actions been certified in ERISA cases?
- Any unusual or unique rulings concerning jurisdiction or removal?

The resulting compendium provided a convenient reference of the law of various circuits to the ERISA practitioner. This volume is an update, current as of February, 2007. The outline addresses issues that frequently arise in the prosecution and defense of claims for ERISA-regulated benefits. As you will see, circuits can vary significantly in their approach to substantive and procedural ERISA issues.

Many thanks to the contributing authors, who are identified at the beginning of their respective chapters. These individuals devoted significant time and effort to make this compendium a valuable publication. Thanks are also due to my assistant, Melaine Gosetti, who devoted long hours to this project.

The Committee may produce additional updates as ERISA law continues to evolve. We welcome comments from readers on the content and format of this volume.

Brooks Magratten

# About the Editor

Brooks R. Magratten is a partner in the Providence, Rhode Island, law firm of Vetter & White. He represents insurers and fiduciaries in life, health, disability, and ERISA litigation in New England. He is the former Chair of the Health and Disability Insurance Law Committee of the Tort Trial and Insurance Practice Section (TIPS) of the ABA and is the Vice Chair of DRI's Life, Health & Disability Committee. Mr. Magratten is a frequent author and lecturer on life, health, disability insurance, and ERISA topics.

# About the Authors

## FIRST CIRCUIT

Joseph M. Hamilton
Kristina H. Allaire
Mirick O'Connell
100 Front Street
Worcester, MA 01603
(508) 791-8500

Byrne J. Decker
Geraldine G. Sanchez
Pierce Atwood, LLP
One Monument Square
Portland, ME 04101
(207) 791-1100

Brooks Magratten
Hinna Upal
Vetter & White
20 Washington Place
Providence, RI 02903
(401) 421-3060

## SECOND CIRCUIT

Steven B. Getzoff
Allan M. Marcus
Lester Schwab Katz &
    Dwyer, LLP
120 Broadway, 38th Floor
New York, NY 10271
(212) 341-4345

Helen M. Kemp
David J. Burke
Amy Zinser
Robinson & Cole, LLP
280 Trumbull Street
Hartford, CT 06103
(860) 275-8235

Randi F. Knepper
McElroy Deutsch Mulvaney &
    Carpenter, LLP
1300 Mt. Kemble Avenue
P.O. Box 2075
Morristown, NJ 07962-2075
(973) 993-8100

## THIRD CIRCUIT

Randi F. Knepper
Patricia McIntire
McElroy Deutsch Mulvaney &
    Carpenter, LLP
1300 Mt. Kemble Avenue
P.O. Box 2075
Morristown, NJ 07962-2075
(973) 993-8100

Joshua Bachrach
Rawle & Henderson
One S. Penn Square
Philadelphia, PA 19107
(215) 575-4200

## FOURTH CIRCUIT

Bryan D. Bolton
Cheryl A. C. Brown
Funk and Bolton, P.A.
36 South Charles St.
12th Floor
Baltimore, MD 21201
(410) 659-7700

E. Ford Stephens
Christian & Barton, LLP
909 East Main Street
Suite 1200
Richmond, VA 23219
(804) 697-4124

Erna A. P. Womble
George K. Evans Jr.
Womble Carlyle
    Sandridge & Rice,
    PLLC
One West Fourth Street
Winston-Salem, NC
    27101
(336) 721-3723

## FIFTH CIRCUIT

Virginia N. Roddy
Jennifer M. Lawrence
Preaus Roddy & Assoc.
650 Poydras St., Suite 1650
New Orleans, LA 70130
(504) 523-2111

Kelly D. Simpkins
Wells Marble & Hurst, PLLC
317 E. Capitol Street
Jackson, MS 39205-0131
(601) 355-8321

Hon. Stephen W. Smith
United States Magistrate Judge
Southern District of Texas
Houston, TX 77002

## SIXTH CIRCUIT

Robert D. Anderle
Porter Wright Morris & Arthur
925 Euclid Avenue, Suite 1700
Cleveland, OH 44125
(216) 443-2554

Craig R. Carlson
Porter Wright Morris & Arthur
41 S. High St.
Columbus, OH 43215
(614) 227-2163

S. Russell Headrick
Leigh M. Chiles
Baker Donelson Bearman
    Caldwell & Berowitz
165 Madison Ave.
Memphis, TN 38103
(901) 525-2000

Michael Shpiece
Miller Shpiece & Tischler
26711 Northwestern Highway
Suite 200
Southfield, MI 48034
(248) 945-1040

Kristi R. Gauthier
Clark Hill, PLC
255 S. Old Woodward Ave.
Birmingham, MI 48009
(248) 642-9692

## SEVENTH CIRCUIT

Mark E. Schmidtke
Schmidtke Hoeppner
  Consultants LLP
103 E. Lincolnway
Valparaiso, IN 46384
(219) 464-4961

Michael Brown
Kightlinger & Gray, LLP
151 N. Delaware St., Ste. 600
Indianapolis, IN 46204-2599
(317) 968-8119

Mark D. DeBofsky
Daley, DeBofsky & Bryant
1 North LaSalle Street, Suite
  3800
Chicago, IL 60602
(312) 372-5200

## EIGHTH CIRCUIT

Terrance J. Wagener
Krass Monroe
8000 Norman Center Dr.
Suite 1000
Minneapolis, MN 55437-1178
(952) 346-1408

Clark H. Cole
Matthew Shorey
Armstrong Teasdale
One Metropolitan Square
Suite 2600
St. Louis, MO 63102
(314) 342-8037

## NINTH CIRCUIT

Linda M. Lawson
Frederic Esrailian
Meserve Mumper Hughes, LLP
300 S. Grand Avenue, Suite
  2400
Los Angeles, CA 90071-3185
(213) 620-0300

Horace W. Green
Green & Humbert
220 Montgomery Street,
  Suite 438
San Francisco, CA 94104
(415) 837-5433

Katherine Somervell
Bullivant Houser Bailey
888 SW Fifth Avenue, Suite 300
Portland, OR 97204
(503) 499-4454

## TENTH CIRCUIT

Michael S. Beaver
Holland & Hart LLP
8390 East Crescent Parkway,
    Suite 400
Greenwood Village, CO 80111
(303) 290-1631

Scott Petersen
David N. Kelley
Fabian & Clendenin, P.C.
215 South State Street, 12th
    Floor
Salt Lake City, UT 84111
(801) 531-8900

Trent A. Howell
Holland & Hart LLP
Jefferson Place
110 North Guadalupe, Suite 1
Santa Fe, NM 87504
(505) 988-4421

## ELEVENTH CIRCUIT

Russell Buhite
Maggie Marrero-Ladik
Fowler White Boggs &
    Banker
P.O. Box 1438
Tampa, FL 33601
(813) 222-1193

H. Sanders Carter Jr.
Nikole M. Crow
Tiffany D. Downs
Aaron E. Pohlmann
Joelle C. Sharman
Carter & Ansley LLP
1180 W. Peachtree Street
Suite 2300
Atlanta, GA 30309
(404) 965-4950

Anthony H. Pelle
Douglas L. Oppenheimer
Carlton Fields, P.A.
100 S.E. 2nd Street
Suite 4000
Miami, FL 33131
(305) 530-0050

## D.C. CIRCUIT

Glenn Merten
Robin Sanders
Ben Tompkins
Jorden Burt LLP
1025 Thomas Jefferson Street,
    N.W.
Suite 400 East
Washington, D.C. 20007
(202) 965-8100

James L. Marketos
Berliner Corcoran & Rowe
1101 Seventeenth Street, N.W.
Suite 1100
Washington, D.C. 20036
(202) 861-2338

# CHAPTER 1

# First Circuit

KRISTINA H. ALLAIRE
BYRNE J. DECKER
JOSEPH M. HAMILTON
BROOKS R. MAGRATTEN
GERALDINE G. SANCHEZ
HINNA UPAL

## I. What Constitutes an ERISA Plan?

The First Circuit has adopted the Eleventh Circuit's formulation with respect to what constitutes an ERISA (Employee Retirement Income Security Act of 1974) plan, and has broken down the statutory definition into the following five elements: (1) a plan, fund, or program (2) established or maintained (3) by an employer (4) for the purpose of providing medical, surgical, or hospital care, sickness, accident, disability, death, or unemployment or vacation benefits (5) to participants or their beneficiaries. *Wickman v. Nw. Nat'l Ins. Co.*, 908 F.2d 1077, 1082 (1st Cir. 1990), quoting *Donovan v. Dillingham*, 688 F.2d 1367, 1371 (11th Cir. 1982) (*en banc*).

### A. Determining the Existence of an Employee Welfare Benefit Plan

A "plan, fund or program" exists if "from the surrounding circumstances a reasonable person can ascertain the intended benefits, a class of beneficiaries, the source of financing, and the procedures for receiving benefits." *Wickman*, 908 F.2d at 1082, citing *Donovan*, 688 F.2d at 1373.

The First Circuit has held that a "plan" can be established or maintained through purchase of insurance; however, the purchase of insurance, standing alone, is not sufficient to establish a plan. *Wickman*, 908 F.2d at 1082. Where an employer purchases insurance for employees, "the crucial factor in determining if a 'plan' has been established is whether the purchase of the insurance policy constituted an

1

expressed intention by the employer to provide benefits on a regular and long term basis." *Id.* at 1083. "Similarly, whether a reasonable employee would perceive an ongoing commitment by the employer to provide employee benefits is an important consideration." *New England Mut. Life Ins. Co. v. Baig*, 166 F.3d 1 (1st Cir. 1999).

In *Baig*, 166 F.3d at 4, the court rejected an argument to the effect that an employer's reimbursement of premiums paid directly by the employee to the insurer was sufficient to establish a plan. The court went on to hold, however, that "when an employer deals directly with the insurer and actually purchases an insurance policy for an employee [as opposed to merely paying an employee enough to purchase his or her own insurance policy], there may be sufficient participation to meet the 'established or maintained' requirement under ERISA." *Id.*

The purchase of "a group policy or multiple policies covering a class of employees offers substantial evidence that a plan . . . has been established." *Wickman*, 908 F.2d at 1082. However, a plan is unlikely to be established where the purchase of insurance is an "isolated and aberrational incident." *Id.*

An employer's distribution of a handbook or summary plan description detailing ERISA rights is "strong evidence that the employer has adopted an ERISA regulated plan." *Id.* at 1083. However, "the absence of such documentation should not necessarily lead to a finding that there was no plan under ERISA." *Baig*, 166 F.3d at 5, n.6.

Any part of a benefits plan that addresses ERISA welfare benefits is governed by ERISA. *See Balestracci v. NSTAR Elec. & Gas Corp.*, 449 F.3d 224, 229 (1st Cir. 2006). In *Balestracci*, certain aspects of an early retirement plan were not governed by ERISA. *Id.* However, the court recognized that in a multifaceted early retirement plan, ERISA may govern only certain facets. *Id.* Disputes over those facets must be resolved under ERISA. *Id.*

In determining whether a plan has been established or maintained, the First Circuit will also consider Congress's dual purpose of reducing the threat of abuse or mismanagement and eliminating the threat of conflicting and inconsistent state and local regulation. *Demars v. Cigna Corp.*, 173 F.3d 443 (1st Cir. 1999). In *Demars* the court held that "conversion policies" do not implicate Congress's core concerns sufficiently to come within ERISA's purview. However, disputes concerning "conversion rights" under group policies are governed by ERISA, *id.* at 448, as are disputes arising from injuries maintained prior to the "conversion" when the original plan was still in place. *See Paul Revere Life Ins. Co. v. Bromberg*, 382 F.3d 33, 35 (1st Cir. 2004).

## B. Definition of "Employee" for ERISA Purposes

In *Kwatcher v. Mass. Serv. Employees Pension Fund*, 879 F.2d 957, 959–60 (1st Cir. 1989), the court held that a sole shareholder of a closely held corporation was an "employer" and therefore could not be an "employee" and thereby a "participant" in an ERISA plan. *Kwatcher*, however, was overruled by the Supreme Court. *See Yates v. Hendon*, 541 U.S. 1 (2004). In *Yates*, the court expressly rejected the *Kwatcher* court's holding that a "working owner" is not a "participant" in the company's ERISA benefits plan. *Id.* at 16. As the court noted, affording "participant" status to working owners promotes ERISA's purpose of establishing uniformity, by avoiding the anomaly of the same plan being governed by separate regimes. *Id.* at 17. *Yates* held that a working owner is a "participant" to the extent that the owner participates in a plan with other employees, but it leaves open the question of whether a plan that covers only the working owner is governed by ERISA.

Mere classification as a "common law" employee does not mandate coverage as a participant under an ERISA plan. *Edes v. Verizon Commc'ns, Inc.*, 417 F.3d 133, 137 (1st Cir. 2005). Instead, courts should look to the explicit plan language to determine which employees qualify as "participants" under an ERISA plan. *See id.*

## C. Interpretation of Safe Harbor Regulation

In *Johnson v. Watts Regulator*, 63 F.3d 1129 (1st Cir. 1995), the court held that an employer must satisfy all four "safe harbor" criteria in order to avoid ERISA. That is, to be exempt from ERISA a plan must meet the following four criteria, established by the Department of Labor at 29 C.F.R. §§ 2510.3-1(j): (1) no contributions are made by the employer or employee organization; (2) participation in the plan is completely voluntary; (3) the employer permits the insurer to publicize the program to its employees and collects premiums through payroll deduction and remits them to the insurer, but the employer does not endorse the plan; and (4) the employer receives no consideration for its administrative services other than reasonable compensation. Although the court specifically addressed only the "endorsement" factor, it held more generally that employer "neutrality" is key to safe harbor protection, but that remaining neutral does not require an employer to "build a moat around a program or to separate itself from all aspects of program administration." *Watts Regulator*, 63 F.3d at 1134. The issue of "endorsement" depends on whether "in light of all the surrounding facts and circumstances, an objectively reasonable employee would conclude on the basis of the employer's actions that the employer had not merely facilitated the program's availability but had exercised control over it or made it appear to be part and parcel of the company's own benefit package." *Id.* at 1135.

## D. Amount of Employer Involvement Required to Sustain an Employee Welfare Benefit Plan

With respect to specific actions, the *Watts* court held that as long as the employer "merely advises employees of the availability of group insurance, accepts payroll deductions, passes them on to the insurer, and performs other ministerial tasks that assist the insurer in publicizing the program, it will not be deemed to have endorsed the program." *Id.* at 1134. The court found that an employer's activities in terms of issuing certificates to covered employees, maintaining a list of insured persons, and assisting the insurer in securing appropriate claims documentation were merely "administrative tasks," and that the employer had no "role in the substantive aspects of program design and operation" and therefore had not "endorsed" the accidental death plan underwritten by the insurer. *See id.* at 1136.

## E. Treatment of Multiple Employer Trusts and Welfare Agreements

There are no published First Circuit cases addressing the issue of multiple employer trusts and welfare agreements.

## II. Preemption

### A. Scope of ERISA Preemption

The First Circuit has held that express preemption under ERISA "involves two central questions: (1) whether the plan at issue is an 'employee benefit plan' and (2) whether the cause of action 'relates to' this employee benefit plan," *McMahon v. Digital Equip. Corp.*, 162 F.3d 28, 36 (1st Cir. 1998). A state-law claim "relates to" an ERISA plan if "it has a connection with or reference to such a plan," *Carlo v. Reed Rolled Thread Die Co.*, 49 F.3d 790, 793 208 94 (1st Cir. 1995), or if "the trier of fact necessarily would be required to consult the ERISA plan to resolve the plaintiff's claims." *Harris v. Harvard Pilgrim Health Care*, 208 F.3d 274, 281 (1st Cir. 2000) ("state-law claims for unfair and deceptive trade practices are preempted by ERISA" because the court necessarily would have to refer to the plan to determine whether the defendant breached its duties). *See also Vartanian v. Monsanto Co.*, 14 F.3d 697 (1st Cir. 1994) (state law expressly preempted if "in order to prevail, [plaintiff] must plead, and the court must find, that an ERISA plan exists.").

A state law has a "connection with" an ERISA plan if it impedes ERISA's goal of achieving "nationally uniform administration of employee benefit plans." *Pharm. Care Mgmt. Ass'n v. Rowe*, 429 F.3d 294, 302 (1st Cir. 2005), quoting *N.Y. State Conference of Blue Cross & Blue Shield Plans v. Travelers Ins. Co.*, 514 U.S. 645, 657 (1995). ERISA will not preempt a state law that allows plan administrators freedom to structure plans similarly from state to state. *Id.* at 303. However, ERISA will preempt a law that establishes an "alternative enforcement mechanism for ERISA plan benefits" as long as that alternative enforcement mechanism affects relationships between "the [ERISA] plan, administrators, fiduciaries, beneficiaries, and employer." *Carpenters Local Union No. 26 v. U.S. Fid. & Guar. Co.*, 215 F.3d 136, 140–41 (1st Cir. 2000).

A state law "references" an ERISA plan if the existence of an ERISA plan is "essential" to the operation of the law. *See Rowe*, 429 F.3d at 304. If deletion of the reference to an ERISA plan in the statute would render that law "inoperable," the ERISA plan is "essential" to the law. *See id.* Therefore, ERISA will preempt state laws that either "single[] out ERISA plans for special treatment [or] depend[] on their existence as an essential part of its operation." *See Carpenters Local*, 215 F.3d at 145.

In both *Carlo v. Reed Rolled Thread Die*, 49 F.3d at 793–94, and *Vartanian v. Monsanto*, 14 F.3d at 700, the First Circuit held that state-law misrepresentation claims against employers/plan administrators concerning claimants' entitlement to benefits were expressly preempted because the court would necessarily be required to consult the plan in order to analyze plaintiffs' claims and/or compute the damages claimed by the plaintiffs. In *Golas v. Homeview, Inc.*, 106 F.3d 1 (1st Cir. 1997), the court refused to decide whether misrepresentation claims brought against an insurance broker/agent, prior to plaintiff's enrollment in a plan, were preempted. In *dicta*, the majority stated that the claims would be preempted under *Vartanian* if the defendant was an agent of the plaintiff's employer or the insurance company that issued and decided claims under the disability policy in question. *Id.* at 4, n.5. A concurrence would have found no preemption based on an assumption that the defendant was an independent broker and not an agent of an ERISA fiduciary. See *id*.

## B. Preemption of Managed-Care Claims

The First Circuit has followed the teachings of *Pilot Life Insurance Co. v. Dedeaux*, 481 U.S. 41 (1987), to the effect that ERISA's civil enforcement provisions were intended to be exclusive. *Danca v. Private Health Care Sys., Inc.*, 185 F.3d 1, 5 (1st Cir. 1999). Accordingly, state laws that constitute "alternative enforcement mechanisms" to ERISA or to ERISA plans are preempted. *Id*. "It therefore follows that state law tort suits that allege the improper processing of a claim for benefits under an ERISA covered plan . . . fall within the scope of [ERISA] § 502(a)" and are preempted, regardless of whether such claims otherwise might be "saved" under ERISA's insurance savings clause. *Id*.

In *Danca*, the court held that plaintiff's state-law claims based on the defendant HMO's decision to deny plaintiff's physician's recommendation for in-patient treatment were preempted pursuant to the principles articulated in *Pilot Life*. *Id*. at 6. The court held that although the allegedly negligent decision making could be characterized as medical in nature, "[w]hat matters, in our view, is that the conduct was indisputably part of the process used to assess a participant's claim for a benefit payment under the plan. As such, any state-law-based attack on this conduct would amount to an 'alternative enforcement mechanism' to ERISA's civil enforcement provisions contained in ERISA § 502(a). . . ." *Id*.

Similarly, in *Hotz v. Blue Cross & Blue Shield*, 292 F.3d 57, 61 (1st Cir. 2002), the court relied on *Pilot Life* to hold that plaintiff's "bad faith" claims under Massachusetts Chapters 93-A and 176D were preempted. The court held that these state statutes offered remedies "at odds" with those available under ERISA. *Id*. The court rejected the argument that *Unum Life Insurance Co. of America v. Ward*, 526 U.S. 358 (1999), somehow alters *Pilot Life's* holdings. *Id*. at 60–61.

These cases must be viewed in light of subsequent Supreme Court opinions in *Rush Prudential HMO, Inc. v. Moran*, 536 U.S. 355 (2002), and *Aetna Health, Inc. v. Davila*, 542 U.S. 200 (2004). In *Moran*, the Court held that an Illinois law requiring HMOs to provide services if a reviewing physician found such services medically necessary was not preempted under *Pilot Life*. 536 U.S. at 373–74. The Court held that the law did not provide a "new cause of action" or "new form of relief" and did not "enlarge the claim beyond the benefits available" in an action under ERISA. *Id*. at 379–80. In *Davila*, the Court rejected plaintiffs' attempts to use state law to remedy damages they claimed to have suffered as a result of the defendants' denial of plaintiffs' health care claims. 542 U.S. at 209. The Court held that the claims were preempted because plaintiffs could have brought claims for benefits under ERISA and plaintiffs' claims implicated no legal duties independent of ERISA. *Id*. at 213–14.

## C. Preemption of Malpractice Claims

In *McMahon v. Digital Equip. Corp.*, 162 F.3d 28 (1st Cir. 1998), plaintiff brought state-law claims for negligence against the administrator of her employer's short-term disability plan. Plaintiff tried to avoid preemption by characterizing her claims as malpractice claims. *Id.* at 38. Without discussing the underlying substantive issue, the First Circuit rejected plaintiff's analogy, stating as follows: "But [the administrator of the disibility plan] was not a managed care provider; it was not responsible for providing McMahon with medical care, but rather for determining whether McMahon was eligible for short-term disability leave. Whether [the administrator] performed this responsibility properly clearly 'relates to' the terms of Plan 502." *Id.*

### D. Other Preemption Issues

The *Hotz* case constitutes the only recent First Circuit savings clause jurisprudence. In *Hotz*, the court applied a two-pronged analysis, holding first that the state statutes in question did not come within the savings clause, and second that they were nonetheless preempted by conflict preemption principles as discussed above. 292 F.3d at 60–61. With respect to the savings clause analysis, the *Hotz* court found the clause inapplicable because the remedies provided by Massachusetts Chapter 93-A were not "unique" to the insurance industry but rather applied more generally to unfair commercial practices in any industry. *Id.* In so doing, the *Hotz* court applied the McCarran-Ferguson factors that have since been abandoned by the Supreme Court. *See Kentucky Ass'n of Health Plans, Inc. v. Miller*, 538 U.S. 329, 339–340 (2003). Although the *Hotz* court's savings clause analysis is subject to reexamination after *Miller*, the savings clause aspect of the case was rendered moot by the Supreme Court's confirmation in *Moran*, 536 U.S. at 373–74 and *Davila*, 542 U.S. at 209, that ERISA preempts state-law remedies that "supplement or supplant" ERISA's exclusive enforcement regime, regardless of the savings clause. Since the *Hotz* court held that the state statutes in question offered remedies "at odds" with ERISA, its belt-and-suspenders savings clause discussion is *dicta*.

In *Rowe*, 429 F.3d at 305, the First Circuit held that a state law imposing regulations on pharmacy benefits managers was not preempted under *Davila*. The court distinguished *Davila* on the grounds that the plaintiffs in that case brought suit only to rectify a wrongful benefits denial and that "all the parties in that case were part of the 'intricate web of relationships among the principal players in the ERISA scenario,'" i.e. participants, beneficiaries, and fiduciaries. *Id.* (Quoting *Carpenters Local Union No. 26 v. U.S. Fid. & Guar. Co.*, 215 F.3d 136, 141 (1st Cir. 2000)).

## III. Exhaustion of Administrative Remedies

### A. Is Exhaustion an Absolute Requirement?

Ordinarily, a claimant seeking benefits under an ERISA plan must exhaust administrative remedies prior to suing in federal court. *See Terry v. Bayer Corp.*, 145 F.3d 28, 36 (1st Cir. 1998); *Drinkwater v. Metro. Life Ins. Co.*, 846 F.2d 821, 825–26 (1st Cir. 1988). *See also Morais v. Cent. Beverage Corp. Union Employees Supp. Ret. Plan*, 167 F.3d 709, 712 n. 4 (1st Cir. 1999) (First Circuit adheres to well- established federal policy favoring exhaustion of administrative remedies in contract-based ERISA claims).

However, several district courts in the First Circuit have held that exhaustion of administrative remedies is unnecessary when the claims brought are based exclusively on statutory violations of ERISA itself. *Alexander v. Fujitsu Bus. Comm-c'n Sys., Inc.,* 818 F. Supp. 462, 471 (D.N.H. 1993); *United Paperworkers Int'l Union v. Int'l Paper Co.,* 777 F. Supp. 1010, 1017 (D. Me. 1991); *Treadwell v. John Hancock Mut. Life Ins. Co.,* 666 F. Supp. 278, 283–84 (D. Mass. 1987).

## B. Exceptions to the Exhaustion Requirement

Traditional exhaustion principles include an exception for instances "when resort to the administrative route is futile or the remedy inadequate." *Drinkwater,* 846 F.2d at 826; *accord Turner v. Fallon Cmty. Health Plan, Inc.,* 127 F.3d 196, 200 (1st Cir. 1997). However, a "blanket assertion, unsupported by any facts, is insufficient to call this exception into play." *Drinkwater,* 846 F.2d at 826; *Madera v. Marsh, USA, Inc.,* 426 F.3d 56, 62 (1st Cir. 2005); *Nieves Ayala v. Johnson & Johnson, Inc.,* 208 F. Supp. 2d 195, 199 (D.P.R. 2002); *Tarr v. State Mut. Life Assur. Co. of Am.,* 913 F. Supp. 40, 44 (D. Mass. 1996).

The inadequacy exception has been properly invoked where the relief sought is of an urgent nature, such as threat to the claimant's health or life. *Watts v. Organo-genesis, Inc.,* 30 F. Supp. 2d 101, 104 (D. Mass. 1998) ("A failure to exhaust 'is easily forgiven for good reason, and no reason is better than an imminent threat to life or health,'" quoting *Ezratty v. Puerto Rico,* 648 F.2d 770, 774 (1st Cir. 1981)).

## C. Consequences of Failure to Exhaust

The failure to exhaust administrative remedies is not a jurisdictional bar. *Sidou v. UnumProvident,* 245 F. Supp. 2d 207, 216 (D. Me. 2003). Rather, because ERISA itself does not specifically mandate exhaustion, courts apply the requirement as a matter of judicial discretion. *Tarr,* 913 F. Supp. at 44. The exhaustion doctrine has been held to serve important policy considerations, including (1) the reduction of frivolous litigation, (2) the promotion of consistent treatment of claims, (3) the provision of a nonadversarial method of claims settlement, (4) the minimization of costs of claims settlement, (5) a proper reliance on administrative expertise, and (6) the development of a complete record for review by the courts. *Terry,* 145 F.3d at 40; *Tarr,* 913 F. Supp. at 44. In noting these considerations, the First Circuit found that "[i]t would be anomalous if the same reasons which led Congress to require plans to provide remedies for ERISA claimants did not lead courts to see that those remedies are regularly utilized." *Terry,* 145 F.3d at 40.

When a complaint is dismissed solely on exhaustion grounds, it should be dismissed without prejudice as premature. *Rivera-Diaz v. Am. Airlines, Inc.,* 229 F.3d 1133 (1st Cir. 2000). Plaintiffs remain free to pursue their administrative remedies under the plan, and to return to court to assert any claims they may have once they have exhausted that process. *Id.; see also Belanger v. Healthsource of Maine,* 66 F. Supp. 2d 70, 74 (D. Me. 1999); *Snow v. Borden, Inc.,* 802 F. Supp. 550, 558 (D. Me. 1992).

## D. Minimum Number of Levels of Administrative Review

No First Circuit case has expressly decided how many levels of administrative review a claimant may be required to exhaust. The First Circuit has held, however, that a participant must attend the plan's internal appeals process as outlined in an employee benefit plan prior to bringing suit. *Terry v. Bayer Corp.*, 145 F.3d 28, 36 (1st Cir. 1998); *Drinkwater v. Metro. Life Ins. Co.*, 846 F.2d 821, 826 (1st Cir.), *cert. denied*, 488 U.S. 909 (1988).

### E. Can a Defendant Waive a Failure-to-Exhaust Defense?

The First Circuit has not addressed waiving a failure-to-exhaust defense in ERISA cases.

## IV. Standard of Review

### A. Plan Language

The First Circuit has interpreted *Firestone Tire & Rubber Co. v. Bruch*, 489 U.S. 101 (1989), to require that the plan convey "a clear grant of discretionary authority" in order for the court to invoke the deferential "arbitrary and capricious" standard of review. *See Recupero v. New England Tel. & Tel. Co.*, 118 F.3d 820, 828 (1st Cir. 1997) (requiring "some discretion" be given to out-of-court decision maker); *Diaz v. Seafarers Int'l Union*, 13 F.3d 454, 457 (1st Cir. 1994) (requiring "evidence" of discretionary authority). The "arbitrary and capricious" standard of review will still apply where the plan contains language conferring a grant of discretionary authority but the summary plan description does not contain such language. *See Fenton v. John Hancock Mut. Life Ins. Co.*, 400 F.3d 83, 90 (1st Cir. 2005).

In *Cooke v. Lynn Sand & Stone Co.*, the court found plan language insufficient where it "stated only that the administrator had exclusive control and authority over the Plan." 70 F.3d 201, 204 (1st Cir. 1995). By contrast, in *Terry v. Bayer Corp.*, 145 F.3d 28, 37 (1st Cir. 1998), the court held that language that "specifically allocates to the Company the right to find necessary facts, determine eligibility for benefits, and interpret the terms of the Plan" is sufficient to compel an arbitrary and capricious standard of review. In *Gannon v. Metropolitan Life Insurance Co.*, 360 F.3d 211, 213–14, n.1 (1st Cir. 2004), the plan specifically granted the plan administrator "discretionary authority to interpret the terms of the Plan and to determine eligibility for and entitlement to Plan benefits." This language was sufficient for the court to apply the arbitrary and capricious standard of review. *See id.*

In *Brigham v. Sun Life of Canada*, 317 F.3d 72, 81 (1st Cir. 2003), the court considered plan language stating that "[i]f proof is required, we must be provided with such evidence *satisfactory to us* as we may reasonably require under the circumstances" (emphasis in original). The court engaged in a review of cases from other circuits and stated that "with the possible exception of the Second Circuit *in dicta*, no federal appeals court has viewed the type of language at issue in this case as inadequate to confer discretion on the plan administrator." *Id.* at 82. The court ultimately based its decision to apply the arbitrary and capricious standard, however, on the fact that the plaintiff had waived any objection to an application of that standard. *Id.* The court made clear, however, that it agreed with the majority rule on the substantive issue. The court stated as follows:

Were we to consider ruling otherwise, we would undertake a thorough exploration of the issue. As matters stand, the widespread acceptance of the view that the language here triggers discretionary review assures us that adhering to our raise-or-waive rule results in no injustice in this case.

*Id.*

## B. Effect of Conflict of Interest or Procedural Irregularity

The First Circuit has addressed the issue of "conflict of interest" on several occasions and has held that a so-called "inherent conflict," without more, cannot change or heighten that standard. *See Wright v. R.R. Donnelley & Sons Co.*, 402 F.3d 67 (1st Cir. 2005); *Leahy v. Raytheon Co.*, 315 F.3d 11, 16 (1st Cir. 2002); *Pari-Fasano v. ITT Hartford Life & Acc.*, 230 F.3d 415 (1st Cir. 2000); *Doe v. Travelers Ins. Co.*, 167 F.3d 53 (1st Cir. 1999); *Doyle v. Paul Revere Life Ins. Co.*, 144 F.3d 181 (1st Cir. 1998); *see also Fenton v. John Hancock Mut. Life Ins. Co.*, 400 F.3d 83, 90 (1st Cir. 2005) (recognizing that a stricter standard of review applies only when the plan participant can show that the administrator was improperly motivated to make the adverse determination); *Glista v. Unum Life Ins. Co. of Am.*, 378 F.3d 113, 125–26 (1st Cir. 2004) ("The fact that Unum, the plan administrator, will have to pay Glista's claim out of its own assets does not change [the] standard of review.")

In *Doyle*, the claims administrator was not only the decision maker and the funding source, it was also a subsidiary of the employer/plan sponsor. *Doyle*, 144 F.3d at 184. The court noted that "any award of benefits would come out of Paul Revere's own pocket," and recognized that such an arrangement might give the appearance of a conflict of interest. *Id.* However, the court rejected the plaintiff's argument that because the plan administrator was also the source of funding, the court should conduct a de novo review of the administrator's denial of benefits. The court suggested "an important competing motive" that offset the appearance of a financial conflict: "having a benefit plan is to please employees, not to result in the employer's bad reputation." *Id.* Thus, the court explained that "an employer would not want to keep an overly tight-fisted insurer," so "the conflict is not as serious as might appear at first blush." *Id.*

With respect to the standard of review, the court "adher[ed] to the arbitrary and capricious principle, with special emphasis on reasonableness, but with the burden on the claimant to show that the decision was improperly motivated." *Id.* And the court held that a financial conflict does not exist merely because the plan administrator "decided which claims it would pay." *Id.*

In *Doe*, the First Circuit again acknowledged that "Travelers would pay the claim out of its own assets." *Doe*, 167 F.3d at 57. Travelers argued that "it is a very small claim payable out of very large assets," but the court noted that "small claims add up." *Id.* Nevertheless, the court again recognized that "Travelers can hardly sell policies if it is too severe in administering them," and reiterated that "the mere fact that an individual claim, if paid, would cost the decision maker something [does] not show that 'the decision was improperly motivated.'" *Id.*, quoting *Doyle*, 144 F.3d at 184. The court held that the plan administrator's "general interest in conserving its resources is [not] the kind of conflict that warrants" a heightened standard of review. *Id.* The court concluded that the "essential requirement of reasonableness" by which courts review benefit denials under the arbitrary and capricious standard "has substantial bite itself." *Id.* And while "[a]ny reviewing court is going to be aware that in the large, payment of claims costs [the administrator] money," where "the policy amply warns beneficiaries that [the administrator] retains reasonable discretion," the administrator's financial stake is not enough to invalidate the denial of a claim. *Id.*

In *Pari-Fasano* the First Circuit again recognized that "an insurer does have a conflict of sorts when a finding of eligibility means that the insurer will have to pay benefits out of its own pocket," but reiterated that "the market presents competing incentives to the insurer that substantially minimize the apparent conflict." *Pari-Fasano*, 230 F.3d at 418. Thus, even when the decision maker is the funding source, the arbitrary and capricious standard continues to apply. The court held that in the face of an allegation of financial conflict, the district court applied the correct analysis in terms of (1) recognizing that the reasonableness of the insurer's decision determines whether or not it constituted an abuse of the discretion vested in the insurer by the plan and (2) further recognizing that the possible existence of a conflict of interest would necessarily affect the court's determination of what was reasonable conduct by the insurer under the circumstances. The court correctly inquired whether the circumstances indicated an improper motivation on the part of ITT Hartford and, finding no such impropriety, proceeded to simply ensure that the termination decision was not objectively unreasonable in light of the available evidence. 230 F.3d at 419.

In *Leahy*, 315 F.3d at 16, the court held that "[t]o affect the standard of review . . . a conflict of interest must be real. A chimerical, imagined, or conjectural conflict will not strip the fiduciary's determination of the deference that would otherwise be due." The court went on to state as follows:

> If MetLife denies claims that Plan participants as a group view as valid, those employees will be inclined to withdraw from the Plan, thus reducing MetLife's role (and, presumably, its compensation). By the same token, if MetLife awards benefits that are viewed as undeserved, Plan participants will experience an increase in their premiums and thus be inclined to withdraw from the Plan (again reducing MetLife's role and remuneration). Either way, the structure of the Plan furnishes an incentive for MetLife to be unbiased in its handling of claims. This is telling, for courts should not lightly presume that a plan administrator is willing to cut off its nose to spite its face.

*Id.*

In *Wright*, the plaintiff acknowledged the precedent of *Pari-Fasano*, *Doe*, and *Doyle* related to inherent conflict of interest but argued that those cases "overstate[] the ability of market forces to minimize the apparent conflict." 402 F.3d at 75. The court noted that some other circuits have "rejected the market forces rationale" and have recognized a conflict of interest where an insurer also acts as the ERISA plan administrator. *Id.* at n.5. However, the court also found that other circuits did not have a "consistent approach" for adjusting the standard of review in these situations. *Id.* Further, absent "an opinion by the Supreme Court, an *en banc* decision of the Circuit, or statutory overruling," the court remained bound by the above precedent and refused to alter the standard of review. *Id.*

The court went on to evaluate the plaintiff's allegations of improper motivation on the part of the insurer/plan administrator in refusing benefits. *Id.* at 76–78. The court evaluated several factual situations that plaintiff claimed illustrated "improper motivation." *Id.* However, the court refused to find any behavior that indicated bad faith on the part of the insurer. *Id.* at 78. *See also Tsoulas v. Liberty Life Assurance Co. of Boston*, No. 05-2668, 2006 WL 1892248, at *4–5 (1st Cir. July 11, 2006) (reviewing and finding no merit in several factual allegations made by the plaintiff regarding plan administrator's improper motivation for terminating benefits). To date, the First Circuit has yet to consider a case involving allegations of "improper motivation" sufficient to affect the standard of review.

### C. Other Factors Affecting Standard of Review

Notwithstanding a proper grant of discretion under *Firestone*, the First Circuit has held that de novo review will nonetheless apply in the event of an improper delegation of that discretion. In *Rodriguez-Abreu v. Chase Manhattan Bank*, 986 F.2d 580 (1st Cir. 1993), the only decision makers referenced in the plan documents were "named fiduciaries." 986 F.2d at 584. The benefits decision was made, however, by a party (Chase) that was not a "named fiduciary." *Id.* And the plan documents contained no provision allowing "named fiduciaries" to delegate powers and duties, nor any provisions delegating any duties to Chase. *Id.* Accordingly, the court found a lack of appropriate delegation and reviewed the benefits decision de novo. *Id.*

In *Terry v. Bayer Corp.*, 145 F.3d 28, 37–38 (1st Cir. 1998), by contrast, the plan document gave authority to the plan administrator to "appoint one or more individuals to act on its behalf." An entirely different document established the existence of a "Committee" to "assist[] the Corporation in fulfilling its administrative duties." *Id.* at 38. And it was the committee that made the final determination. The court held that this was an effective delegation. *Id.*

## V. Rules of Plan Interpretation

### A. Application of Federal Common Law

Federal common law governs the interpretation of provisions in an ERISA benefit plan. *Filiatrault v. Comverse Tech., Inc.*, 275 F.3d 131, 134 (1st Cir. 2001); *Morais v. Cent. Beverage Corp.*, 167 F.3d 709, 711 (1st Cir. 1999). A plan is construed using "common-sense canons of contract interpretation" derived from general state-law principles. *Rodriguez-Abreu v. Chase Manhattan Bank, N.A.*, 986 F.2d 580, 585 (1st Cir. 1993).

Plan language is interpreted according to its plain meaning taken in context, and language is ambiguous only "'where an agreement's terms are inconsistent on their face or where the phraseology can support reasonable differences of opinion as to the meaning of the words employed and obligations undertaken.'" *Smart v. Gillette Co. Long-Term Disability Plan*, 70 F.3d 173, 178 (1st Cir. 1995), quoting *Fashion House, Inc. v. K Mart Corp.* 892 F.2d 1076, 1083 (1st Cir. 1989). *See also Unum Life Ins. Co. of Am. v. Cappello*, 278 F. Supp. 2d 228, 233–34 (D.R.I. 2003). "[W]hether an ERISA plan term is ambiguous is generally a question of law for the judge."

*Balestracci v. NSTAR Elec. & Gas Corp.*, 449 F.3d 224, 230 (1st Cir. 2006). In *Balestracci*, the First Circuit held that ambiguous plan language can support a finding of intention to vest lifetime ERISA benefits, rejecting the district court's rule that intention to vest retirement benefits be stated in clear and express terms. *Id.* at 231.

### B. Application of *Contra Proferentem*

The First Circuit has applied the rule of *contra proferentem* to ERISA cases only where the standard of review was de novo and the interpretation of an ambiguous provision of a plan funded by an insurance policy was at issue. *See Hughes v. Boston Mut. Life Ins. Co.*, 26 F.3d 264, 268 (1st Cir. 1994). In *Recupero v. New England Tel. & Tel. Co.*, 118 F.3d 820, 825 (1st Cir. 1997), the court cited authority in support of the proposition that *contra proferentem* would be inapplicable in cases in which the administrator was given discretionary authority to interpret plan terms, citing *Pagan v. NYNEX*, 52 F.3d 438, 442 (2d Cir. 1995). Nonetheless, the court has specifically held that *contra proferentem* does not apply to ERISA plans that are not funded by insurance policies. *Allen v. Adage, Inc.*, 967 F.2d 695, 701 n.6 (1st Cir. 1992). *See also Jorstad v. Conn. Gen. Life Ins. Co.*, 844 F. Supp. 46 (D. Mass. 1994).

### C. Deference Afforded to an Administrator's Interpretation of a Plan

The First Circuit has held that review of an administrator's plan interpretation is deferential and focuses on whether that interpretation was reasonable. *Terry v. Bayer Corp.*, 145 F.3d 28, 35–36 (1st Cir. 1998). Under an arbitrary and capricious standard, the court must decide "whether the administrator's action on the record before him was unreasonable." *Liston v. Unum Corp. Officer Severance Plan*, 330 F.3d 19, 24 (1st Cir. 2003). However, under a de novo standard, the court must decide "whether, upon a full review of the administrative record, the decision of the administrator was correct." *Orndorf v. Paul Revere Life Ins. Co.*, 404 F.3d 510, 518 (1st Cir. 2005). The court should independently review the record and "grant[] no deference to administrators' opinions or conclusions." *Id.*

## VI. Discovery

### A. Limitations on Discovery

Discovery is permitted in limited circumstances in the First Circuit. However, the party seeking discovery must overcome the strong presumption that the record on review is limited to what was before the administrator. *Orndorf v. Paul Revere Life Ins. Co.*, 404 F.3d 510, 520 (1st Cir. 2005), citing *Liston v. Unum Corp. Officer Severance Plan*, 330 F.3d 19, 23–24 (1st Cir. 2003). This rule applies to discovery regardless of whether the standard of review is de novo or deferential. *Orndorf*, 404 F.3d at 520.

In *Liston*, the First Circuit addressed the issue of judicial discretion to permit discovery in ERISA denial-of-benefits cases when the stated objective of discovery is to supplement the record with evidence pertaining to claims other than the one being reviewed. According to the court, "some very good reason is needed to overcome the strong presumption that the record on review is limited to the record before the administrator." *Liston*, 330 F.3d at 23. In a denial-of-benefits claim, "the central issue must always be what the plan promised . . . and whether the plan delivered." *Id.* at 25. However, the court recognized that the treatment afforded to similarly situated individuals can be an appropriate topic for discovery "in some cases." *Id.*

Whether or not discovery may be permitted "turns on the nature of the challenge to the decision." *Id.* Where the challenge is to the procedure used to reach the decision, personal bias by the plan administrator, or prejudicial procedural irregularity, discovery may be permitted. Also, discovery may be needed to explain a key item, such as the duties of a claimant's occupation, if omitted from the record. *Id.* at 519–20; *Liston*, 330 F.3d 9, 23–24; *Doe v. Travelers Ins. Co.*, 167 F.3d 53, 57–58 (1st Cir. 1999).

Courts in the First Circuit have allowed the plaintiff limited discovery "to determine whether the fiduciary or administrator fulfilled his fiduciary role in obtaining the necessary information in order to make his determination, whether the persons who assisted in compiling the record followed the proper procedure, as well as whether the record is complete." *Ardolino v. Metro. Life Ins. Co.*, No. 00-12115 2001 U.S. Dist. LEXIS 14318 *6–11 (D. Mass. 2001) (allowing discovery to determine the parameters of the administrative record, and the policy, procedures, training, and experience that the plan administrator relied upon in denying the claim). *See also Glista v. Unum Life Ins. Co. of Am.*, 378 F.3d 113 (1st Cir. 2004) (district court allowed discovery of policy and procedures manuals and training manuals and limited depositions regarding whether the insurer failed to follow its own guidelines); *Recupero v. New England Tel. & Tel. Co.*, 118 F.3d 820, 834–35 (1st Cir. 1997) (before deciding a disputable factual issue about the record, a trial judge should give the parties an opportunity to discover evidence bearing on the issue); *Lowell v. Drummond*, No. 03-244-P-S 2004 U.S. Dist. LEXIS 3326, at *8 (D. Me. 2004) (allowing limited discovery regarding the content of the record and contractual relationship between the contract administrator and the plan administrator); *Cannon v. Unum Life Ins. Co. of Am.*, 219 F.R.D. 211, 216 (D. Me. 2004) (requiring defendant to produce documents regarding internal policies and procedures relied upon in denying claim and administrative precedent on other claims regarding related illnesses).

Discovery in an ERISA case is not open ended. ERISA's goal of speedy adjudication, in addition to the limitation of review on the merits to the record, operates to circumscribe discovery. Discovery related to new evidence outside the administrative record, such as newly uncovered medical opinions that the plaintiff is disabled, is improper. *Orndorf*, 404 F.3d at 518; *Doe*, 167 F.3d at 58. "Plaintiff is not entitled to engage in discovery which could have or should have been presented to the administrator prior to action on the ERISA claim." *Ardolino*, 2001 U.S. Dist. LEXIS 14318, at *6–11.

### B. Discovery and Conflict of Interest

No reported First Circuit decision has decided whether discovery can be conducted to investigate or establish a conflict of interest. The Districts of Massachusetts and Puerto Rico have both addressed the possibility of such discovery. The District of Massachusetts has allowed for it on at least one instance and prohibited it in another. *See Denmark v. Liberty Life Assurance Co. of Boston*, No. 04-12261 2005 U.S. Dist.

LEXIS 27180 (D. Mass. 2005) (allowing discovery of insurer's relationship with medical review company to demonstrate improper motivation); *Downey v. Aetna Life Ins. Co.*, No. 02-10103 2003 U.S. Dist. LEXIS 8150 (D. Mass. 2003) (refusing to allow discovery regarding conflict of interest); *Gonzalez-Rivera v. Citibank, N.A.*, 260 F. Supp. 2d 350 (D.P.R. 2003) (refusing to allow discovery regarding conflict of interest).

In *Denmark*, the court allowed the plaintiff to conduct limited discovery regarding the financial relationship between Liberty and NMR, a medical review company that provided Liberty with a physician to review the plaintiff's medical records. *Denmark*, 2005 U.S. Dist. LEXIS 27180, at *35–36. Specifically, the court ordered Liberty to produce certain documents requested by the plaintiff and to answer plaintiff's interrogatory questions about the number of files that Liberty had referred to NMR. *Id*. The court also ordered Liberty to stipulate to the number of cases where NMR has accepted a claim. *Id*. at 36.

Conversely, in *Downey*, the court refused to allow discovery regarding the alleged conflict of interest. The defendant, Aetna, did not dispute that it was both a plan fiduciary and payor of claims against the plan. The court concluded that because "the conflict [of interest] has already been acknowledged" by Aetna and the standard of review is unchanged by the allegation of conflict of interest, the discovery of material pertinent to the conflict is unlikely to defeat summary judgment. *Downey*, 2003 U.S. Dist. LEXIS 8150, at *35.

## VII. Evidence

### A. Scope of Evidence under Standards of Review

In the First Circuit, the general rule is that the scope of evidence is limited to the administrative record, regardless of whether the standard of review is de novo or deferential. *Orndorf v. Paul Revere Life Ins. Co.*, 404 F.3d 510, 518 (1st Cir. 2005); *Liston v. Unum Corp. Officer Severance Plan*, 330 F.3d 19 (1st Cir. 2003). In 2003, the First Circuit held in *Liston* that under the arbitrary and capricious standard, the focus of judicial review is ordinarily limited to the record before the plan administrator and at least some very good reason is needed to overcome that presumption. *Liston*, 330 F.3d at 24. It is almost inherent in the idea of reviewing an agency or other administrative action for reasonableness; how could an administrator act unreasonably by ignoring information never presented to it? *Id*. at 23. Review of the ultimate conclusion of whether the evidence supports the finding of a disability does not itself warrant introduction of new evidence about historical facts. *Orndorf*, 404 F.3d at 518. Previously unavailable medical evidence offered for the first time during litigation is inadmissible. *Doe v. Travelers Ins. Co.*, 167 F.3d 53, 57 (1st Cir. 1999); *Burchill v. Unum Life Ins. Co. of Am.*, 327 F. Supp. 2d 41 (D. Me. 2004) (medical evidence that plaintiff's condition worsened after the final denial of the claim need not be considered by insurer).

In 2005, the First Circuit expanded this ruling to cases reviewed under de novo and expressly held that it would offend interests of finality and exhaustion of administrative procedures required by ERISA to shift the focus from that decision to a moving target by presenting extra-administrative-record evidence going to the sub-stance of the decision. Review of the ultimate conclusion of whether the evidence supports the finding does not warrant calling as witnesses those persons whose opin-ions and diagnosis or expert testimony and reports are in the administrative record. *Orndorf*, 404 F.3d at 519.

Both *Liston* and *Orndorf* held that "[t]here may be times where it is appropriate for courts to hear new evidence." For example, where the challenge is not to the merits of the decision to deny benefits but to the procedure used to reach the deci-sion, outside evidence may be of relevance. *Id.* Evidence outside the administrative record might be relevant to a claim of personal bias by a plan administrator or preju-dicial procedure irregularity in the ERISA administrative review procedures. *Id.* at 520. Also, evidence may be relevant to explain a key item, such as the duties of the claimant's position, if it was omitted from the administrative record. *Id.*

### B. Evidentiary Value of Social Security Determinations

Although a determination of disability by the Social Security Administration can be relevant evidence, the mere existence of a Social Security disability award has no binding effect on a plan's decision to discontinue benefits. *Gannon v. Metro. Life Ins. Co.*, 360 F.3d 211, 215 (1st Cir. 2004); *Pari-Fasano v. ITT Hartford Life & Acc. Ins. Co.*, 230 F.3d 415, 420 (1st Cir. 2000); *Doyle v. Paul Revere Life Ins. Co.*, 144 F.3d 181, 187 (1st Cir. 1998); *see also Chandler v. Raytheon Employees Disability Trust*, 53 F. Supp. 2d 84, 91 (D. Mass.), *aff'd*, 229 F.3d 1133 (1st Cir. 2000), *cert. denied*, 531 U.S. 1114 (2001). The criteria for determining eligibility for Social Security disability benefits are substantially different from the criteria established by many, if not most, insurance plans. *Pari-Fasano*, 230 F.3d at 420. "Consequently, although a related Social Security benefits decision might be relevant to an insurer's eligibility decision, it should not be given controlling weight, except perhaps in the rare case in which the statutory criteria are identical to the criteria set forth in the insurance plan." *Id.*

In *Gannon*, the Social Security Administration made specific findings that were highly relevant to MetLife's determination of Gannon's eligibility for disability ben-efits. Most significantly, the Social Security Administration found that Gannon's condition was "not severe enough to keep [her] from working," thereby providing some independent evidence that Gannon no longer met the plan's definition of "dis-abled." The First Circuit held that MetLife was therefore entitled to rely on the Social Security Administration's denial of Gannon's claim for Social Security dis-ability benefits in its consideration of Gannon's claim for disability benefits under the plan. *Gannon*, 360 F.3d at 215.

### C. Other Evidence Issues

If a dispute arises as to what constitutes the record, the court makes the final deci-sion. *Recupero v. New England Tel. & Tel Co.*, 118 F.3d 820, 831–32 (1st Cir. 1997). The district court may take "evidence on motion or convene a non-jury 'trial' in order to develop a 'record' suitable for judicial review of a challenged out of court decision." *Id.* at 833. A court may also convene either of these kinds of proceedings to determine whether the record is complete and, if not, what additional supplementation is appropriate. *Id.* at 834. Where the court determines that the record is incomplete and admits supplemental evidence, it may remand the case back to the insurer for a full and fair review. *Urso v. Prudential Ins. Co. of Am.*, No. 03-024 2004 U.S. Dist. LEXIS 23930 (D. N.H. 2004).

In the First Circuit the insured has the duty to produce affirmative evidence of total disability. *DiGregorio v. PricewaterhouseCoopers Long Term Disability Plan*, No. 03-11191 2004 U.S. Dist. LEXIS 15485 (D. Mass. 2004). It is insufficient to simply challenge the sufficiency of the insurer's evidence. *Id.*

## VIII. Procedural Aspects of ERISA Practice

### A. Methods of Adjudication

The First Circuit has expressly ruled that in an ERISA case where review is based only on the administrative record before the plan administrator and an ultimate conclusion as to disability is to be drawn from the facts, summary judgment is the vehicle for deciding the issues, regardless of whether the standard of review is de novo or deferential. *Orndorf v. Paul Revere Life Ins. Co.*, 404 F.3d 510, 517 (1st Cir. 2005). However, normal summary judgment standards do not apply. "This means that the non-moving party is not entitled to the usual inferences in its favor." *Id.* The First Circuit leaves open the possibility that in instances where the court determines that additional discovery or evidence is warranted, another form of adjudication may be appropriate. See *Recupero v. New England Tel. & Tel. Co.*, 118 F.3d 820, 831 (1st Cir. 1997) (expressly refusing to rule that jury trials are never available for ERISA benefits claims). However, trial is not warranted just because of the existence of conflicting medical opinions. *Orndorf*, 404 F.3d at 519.

### B. Reported ERISA Trial

There have been rare occasions in the First Circuit where claims for benefits under ERISA have resulted in a bench trial. *See, e.g., Doe v. Travelers*, 167 F.3d 53 (1st Cir. 1999) (four-day bench trial held on ERISA claim for benefits); *Janeiro v. Urological Surgery Prof'l Ass'n*, 457 F.3d 130 (1st Cir. 2006) (three-day bench trial held on ERISA claim for pension benefits). However, *Orndorf v. Paul Revere Life Ins. Co.*, 404 F.3d 510, 517 (1st Cir. 2005), now makes clear that summary judgment is the appropriate vehicle for deciding cases where review is based only on the administrative record that was before the plan administrator.

### C. Special Procedures for ERISA Benefit Cases

The First Circuit has not adopted any formal procedures specifically for ERISA benefit cases that are used uniformly throughout the circuit. However, some district court judges issue a preliminary order regulating ERISA proceedings. For example, in the District of Massachusetts, Judge Woodlock sitting in Boston and Magistrate Judge Neiman in Springfield have issued such orders formalizing the procedure in ERISA cases. Their orders are virtually identical. The order specifies that the judge will assume that the matter is reviewed under the abuse of discretion standard of review unless good cause is shown for applying the de novo review. In addition, the order sets parameters for filing the record with the court, specific procedures for resolving disputes about the record, and procedures for requesting discovery related to supplementing the record. Finally, the judges require that the case be resolved on motions for summary judgment unless a party shows cause for holding a trial or evidentiary hearing.

## IX. Fiduciary Liability Claims

### A. Definition of Fiduciary

In the First Circuit the fiduciary duties imposed by ERISA apply only to those people or entities properly classified as fiduciaries. *Beddall v. State Street Bank & Trust Co.*, 137 F.3d 12, 18 (1st Cir. 1998). Fiduciary status does not depend on whether one is titled "plan administrator." *See Boucher v. Williams*, 13 F. Supp. 2d 84, 91 (D. Me. 1998). The court will look at the plan document to determine whom it designates as the fiduciary. *Dall v. Chinet Co.*, 33 F. Supp. 2d 26, 38 (D. Me. 1998).

In addition to named fiduciaries, ERISA extends fiduciary status to functional fiduciaries—persons who act as fiduciaries. *Beddall*, 137 F.3d at 18. However, the mere exercise of physical control or the performance of mechanical administrative tasks generally is insufficient to confer fiduciary status. *See Cottrill v. Sparrow, Johnson & Ursillo, Inc.*, 74 F.3d 20, 21–22 (1st Cir. 1996); *Green v. ExxonMobil Corp.*, 413 F. Supp. 2d 103, 110–11 (D. R.I. 2006). Because one's fiduciary responsibility under ERISA is directly and solely attributable to the possession or exercise of discretionary authority, fiduciary liability arises in specific increments correlated to the vesting or performance of particular fiduciary functions in service of the plan, not in broad, general terms. *Beddall*, 137 F.3d at 18.

When the plan administrator retains discretion to decide disputes, a third-party service provider is not a fiduciary of the plan and thus not amenable to a suit under 29 U.S.C. § 1132(a)(1)(B). *Terry v. Bayer Corp.*, 145 F.3d 28, 35 (1st Cir. 1998); *Maine Coast Memorial Hosp. v. Sargent*, 369 F. Supp. 2d 61, 64 (D. Me. 2005). Indeed, the power to act for a plan and institute plan policies is essential to the status of a fiduciary under ERISA. *Santana v. Deluxe Corp.*, 920 F. Supp. 249, 254 (D. Mass. 1996). Making recommendations regarding plan administration is not indicative of fiduciary status. *Id.* Attorneys, accountants, auditors, actuaries, and others who render their professional services to an employee benefit plan are not fiduciaries unless there is a showing of control of the management of the plan's assets, investment advice for a fee, or a discretionary responsibility over the administration of the plan. *Toomey v. Jones*, 855 F. Supp. 19, 23 (D. Mass. 1994). Persons processing claims, applying plan eligibility rules, communicating with employees, and calculating benefits are also not fiduciaries. *Id.*

### B. Definition of Fiduciary Duties

The First Circuit follows the general rule that a "fiduciary must, among other things, follow a 'prudent man standard of care.'" *Watson v. Deaconess Waltham Hosp.*, 298 F.3d 102, 109 (1st Cir. 2002), citing 29 U.S.C. § 1104(a)(1). "A fiduciary may be liable to the plan for violations of this duty." *Id.*, citing 29 U.S.C. § 1109. "In addition, an individual plan participant or beneficiary may bring suit for equitable relief for breach of fiduciary duty under ERISA's so-called 'catch all' provision, 29 U.S.C. § 1132(a)(3)." *Id.*

"ERISA's specific statutory duties are not meant to be exhaustive of a fiduciary's obligations; federal courts are expected to flesh out ERISA's general fiduciary duty clause, 29 U.S.C. § 1104(a)." *Barrs v. Lockheed Martin Corp.*, 287 F.3d 202, 207 (1st Cir. 2002).

For instance, the First Circuit held there was no breach of fiduciary duty by a hospital where there was no evidence of "bad faith, concealment, or fraud." *Watson*, 298 F.3d at 114. *See also Alves v. Harvard Pilgrim Health Care, Inc.*, 204 F. Supp. 2d 198, 214 (D. Mass. 2002) (no evidence of the usual hallmarks of breach of fiduciary duty: intentional misrepresentation, bad faith, failure to protect the financial integrity of the plan, or a failure to provide material information in response to a direct inquiry).

Fiduciaries have a duty to inform beneficiaries of material facts about the plan. *Watson*, 298 F.3d at 115. However, that affirmative fiduciary duty is subject to two limitations: (1) "a duty only arises if there was some particular reason that the fiduciary should have known that his failure to convey the information would be harmful" and (2) "fiduciaries need not generally provide individualized unsolicited advice." *Id.* "Absent a promise or misrepresentation, the courts have almost uniformly rejected claims by plan participants or beneficiaries that an ERISA administrator has to volunteer individualized information. . . ." *Barrs*, 287 F.3d at 207. However, if a specific commitment is made by an employer to notify a beneficiary about a particular event relating to plan benefits, the First Circuit has found it "at least arguable" that the employer breaches its fiduciary duty if it fails to do so. *Id.* at 210.

An employer also has "a fiduciary duty not to mislead an employee as to the prospective adoption of a plan under serious consideration." *Vartanian v. Monsanto Co.*, 14 F.3d 697, 702 (1st Cir. 1994).

### C. Fiduciary Liability in the Context of Health and Disability Claims

The First Circuit has held breach of fiduciary duty claims cannot stand where adequate relief is available under a claim for benefits. *Turner v. Fallon Cmty. Health Plan, Inc.*, 127 F.3d 196, 200 (1st Cir. 1997); *LaRocca v. Borden, Inc.*, 276 F.3d 22, 28 (1st Cir. 2002).

### D. Remedies for Breach of Fiduciary Duty

Fiduciaries who fail to fulfill their responsibilities are "personally liable to make good to [the] plan any losses to the plan resulting from . . . such breach." *Beddall v. State Street Bank & Trust Co.*, 137 F.3d 12, 18 (1st Cir. 1995).

The only situations in which an individual may bring a claim against a fiduciary are (1) on behalf of the plan or (2) when equitable relief is sought. *Watson v. Deaconess Waltham Hosp.*, 298 F.3d 102, 109 (1st Cir. 2002). Individuals cannot obtain compensatory or punitive damages for breach of fiduciary duty. *Watson v. Deaconess Waltham Hosp.*, 141 F. Supp. 2d 145, 150 (D. Mass. 2001).

In some instances the First Circuit permitted an award of restitution to the plaintiff in order to prevent unjust enrichment. *See Kwatcher v. Mass. Serv.*

*Employees Pension Fund*, 879 F.2d 957 (1st Cir. 1989). However, the court has recently noted the uncertainty surrounding whether a claim for reinstatement of benefits or equitable restitution can be classified as a request for equitable relief, *Barrs v. Lockheed Martin Corp.*, 287 F.3d 202, 206 (1st Cir. 2002), in light of the recent Supreme Court holding in *Great-West Life & Annuity Ins. Co. v. Knudson*, 534 U.S. 204 (2002). *But see Sereboff v. Mid Atlantic Medical Services*, 126 S. Ct. 1869 (2006).

### E. Contribution and Indemnity Claims among Fiduciaries

There is no express provision for contribution under ERISA. Although the First Circuit has not spoken on the issue, district courts have found that a claim for contribution and indemnity can be implied by relying on a court's ability to develop equitable remedies from federal common law. *Duncan v. Santaniello*, 900 F. Supp. 547, 550, 551 (D. Mass. 1995). *See also Reich v. Rowe*, 20 F.3d 25, 33 (1st Cir. 1994) (allowing federal common law cause of action where the remedy is designed and directed toward recovering plan assets). In *Duncan*, the district court held that former fiduciaries were able to maintain a claim for contribution and indemnity because it serves to enhance the enforcement of fiduciary responsibilities by making all fiduciaries ultimately accountable for harm done to the plan. *Duncan*, 900 F. Supp. at 551.

### F. ERISA Claims Against Nonfiduciaries

"ERISA contemplates actions against an employee benefit plan and the plan's fiduciaries. With narrow exception, however, ERISA does not authorize actions against nonfiduciaries of an ERISA plan." *Terry v. Bayer Corp.*, 145 F.3d 28, 35 (1st Cir. 1998). For example, in *Reich v. Rowe*, 20 F.3d 25, 29 (1st Cir. 1994), the court found that nonfiduciary liability was limited to those "who commit violations of ERISA or who are engaged in an 'act or practice' proscribed by the statute" and does not extend to nonfiduciaries merely because they knowingly participate in a fiduciary breach. *Id.* In *Rowe*, the court expressed its concern "that extending the threat of liability over the heads of those who only lend professional services to a plan without exercising any control over, or transacting with, plan assets will deter such individuals from helping fiduciaries navigate the intricate financial and legal thicket of ERISA." *Id. See also Toomey v. Jones*, 855 F. Supp. 19, 25 (D. Mass. 1994).

# X. Attorneys' Fees

## A. Criteria for Awarding Attorneys' Fees

The First Circuit applies a five-factor test to determine whether attorneys' fees should be awarded. *Cottrill v. Sparrow, Johnson & Ursillo, Inc.*, 100 F.3d 220, 225 (1st Cir. 1996); *Janeiro v. Urological Surgery Prof'l Ass'n*, 457 F.3d 130 (1st Cir. 2006). This test is a "flexible one. . . . Not every factor must be considered in each case, . . . and [] no one [factor] should be dispositive." *Gray v. New England Tel. & Tel. Co.*, 792 F.2d 251, 258 (1st Cir. 1986). The five factors are

(1) the degree of bad faith or culpability of a losing party; (2) the ability of such party to personally satisfy an award of fees; (3) whether such an award would deter other persons acting under similar circumstances; (4) the amount of benefit to the action as conferred on the members of the pension plan; and (5) the relative merits of the parties' positions.

*Id.* at 257–58. An award of attorneys' fees under ERISA is not automatic and there is no presumption of attorneys' fees in favor of the prevailing party. Where the case on the merits is a close one, attorneys' fees are frequently denied. *See Vickers v. Principal Mut. Life Ins. Co.*, 993 F. Supp. 19 (D. Mass. 1998); *Janeiro*, 2006 U.S. App. LEXIS 20131.

The decision to award attorneys' fees is solely within the discretion of the trial judge. *See Lodge v. Shell Oil Co.*, 747 F.2d 16, 20 (1st Cir. 1984). Thus, if the district court applies the correct standard, the First Circuit will review the grant or denial of attorneys' fees in ERISA cases "solely for abuse of discretion." *Cottrill*, 100 F.3d at 223, 227. The court will disturb such rulings only if based on the record it finds that the district court "indulged in a serious lapse in judgment." *Twomey v. Delta Airlines Pilots Pension Plan*, 328 F.3d 27, 33 (1st Cir. 2003); *Janeiro*, 2006 U.S. App. LEXIS 20131.

However, the courts are clear that fees are recoverable only for the time spent on the litigation. "[A]ttorney's fees are categorically unavailable for expenses incurred while exhausting administrative remedies." *Warren v. Cochrane*, 257 F. Supp. 2d 321, 324 (D. Me. 2003) (also refusing to award attorneys' fees charged for clerical tasks and other charges the court deemed excessive); *Choi v. Mass. Gen. Physicians Org.*, 66 F. Supp. 2d 251 (D. Mass. 1999); *Torres-Negron v. Ramallo Bros. Printing, Inc.*, 203 F. Supp. 2d. 120 (D.P.R. 2002). However, a court may award attorneys' fees incurred for the litigation costs even if the case is resolved prior to a judgment on the merits. In *Doe v. Raytheon Co.*, No. 00-12545 (D. Mass. 2002), the insurer reinstated benefits shortly after suit was commenced. The court awarded attorneys' fees for the litigation.

Attorneys' fees are also available to the prevailing party who successfully defends a judicial appeal. *Cook v. Liberty Life Assur. Co. of Boston*, 334 F.3d 122, 123–24 (1st Cir. 2003). In determining whether to award attorneys' fees to the prevailing party on an appeal, the court will apply the same five-factor test. However, these factors are applied to the applicant's "conduct during the appeal rather than the conduct that brought [the] benefit dispute into court or to conduct before the trial court," so as not to "deter a plausible but ultimately unsuccessful appeal." *Id.* at 124.

### B. Fees Awarded to Plan Fiduciaries

The First Circuit recognizes that attorneys' fees are available to a prevailing defendant as well as a plaintiff. The same five-factor test is used regardless of which party prevails. *Gray v. New England Tel. & Tel. Co.*, 792 F.2d 251, 258 (1st Cir. 1986). The First Circuit has rejected arguments that a different test should apply to prevailing defendants because the second, third, and fourth factors have no bearing in evaluating a case where the defendant prevails. *Id.* Even if applying the five-factor test favors prevailing plaintiffs, the First Circuit holds that this result is in line with the purposes of ERISA to protect the interests of plan beneficiaries and participants. *Id.* at 258–59. Factors may simply not weigh equally where defendants rather than plaintiffs seek fees. *Id.*

### C. Calculation of Attorneys' Fees

Once a court determines that attorneys' fees are warranted under the test set forth in *Gray v. New England Tel. & Tel. Co.*, 792 F.2d 251, 258 (1st Cir. 1986), the determination of reasonable fees is within the discretion of the trial court. The First Circuit has stated that where the relevant statute does not provide an alternate method for calculating reasonable attorneys' fees, the "lodestar" method should be used. *Tenn. Gas Pipeline Co. v. 104 Acres of Land*, 32 F.3d 632, 634 (1st Cir. 1994). A court arrives at the lodestar by determining the number of hours productively spent on the litigation and multiplying those hours by reasonable hourly rates." *In re San Juan DuPont Plaza Hotel Fire Litig.*, 56 F.3d 295, 305 (1st Cir. 1995). Once established, the lodestar represents a presumptively reasonable fee, although it is subject to upward or downward adjustments. *Lipsett v. Blanco*, 975 F.2d 934, 937 (1st Cir. 1992); *Radford Trust v. First Unum Life Ins. Co.*, 399 F. Supp. 2d 3 (D. Mass. 2005).

# XI. ERISA Regulations

In November of 2000, the Department of Labor modified ERISA regulations on claims procedure. The revised regulations, which apply to claims filed after January 1, 2002, establish shorter time frames for benefits determinations than those contained in the earlier version of the regulations. *See* 29 C.F.R. § 2560.503-1(f)(3). Appeals of claims filed before the effective date are governed by the old regulations. However, many cases decided on claims filed prior to January 1, 2002, may form a basis for interpreting current regulations.

- **29 C.F.R. § 2509.75:** *Kling v. Fidelity Mgmt. Trust Co.*, 323 F. Supp. 2d 132, 146 (D. Mass. 2004) (citing regulation, duty to monitor is a responsibility of a fiduciary who has appointed other fiduciaries, therefore corporations may be held vicariously liable for the actions of their employees); *DiGregorio v. PricewaterhouseCoopers*, 03-11191-DPW 2004 WL 1774566, at *17 (D. Mass.) (where a service provider had sufficient responsibilities to qualify as a fiduciary); *Pegram v. Herdrich*, 530 U.S. 211, 236 (2000) (physician's mixed administrative decisions regarding eligibility were not fiduciary decisions under ERISA); *Terry v. Bayer Corp.*, 145 F.3d 28, 35–36 (1st Cir. 1998) (citing regulation, holding that intermediate party who made a nonfinal decision to terminate benefits did not have any inherent discretionary authority or control over the plan and was not a fiduciary); *Beddall v. State Street Bank & Trust Co.*, 137 F.3d 12 (1st Cir. 1998) (citing regulation, court concludes that bank was not a fiduciary with respect to misevaluation of plan's real estate investments); *Torchetti v. Int'l Bus. Machs. Corp.*, 986 F. Supp. 49, 51 (D. Mass. 1997) (holding that the director/CEO was not a fiduciary without an express delegation of discretion); *Santana v. Deluxe Corp.*, 920 F. Supp. 249, 254–58 (D. Mass. 1996) (where a plan has contracted with a third party to provide claims processing and other administrative services to the plan, but has retained discretion to decide disputed claims, the service provider is not a fiduciary); *Toomey v. Jones*, 855 F. Supp. 19, 24–25 (D. Mass. 1994) (pension fund consulting company did not attain fiduciary status when it advised plan to stop paying cash dividend); *Pension Plan of Pub. Serv. Co. of N.H. v. KPMG Peat Marwick*, 815 F. Supp. 52 (D.N.H. 1993) (attorneys, accountants, actuaries, and consultants performing their usual professional functions will ordinarily not be considered fiduciaries); *Norton Co. v. John Hancock Mut. Life Ins. Co.*, 87-0084 87-0136 1992 WL 237410 (D. Mass. 1992) (employer is a fiduciary to the extent it selects and retains plan fiduciaries).

- **29 C.F.R. § 2509.95-1:** *Blossom v. Bank of N.H.*, 02-573-JD 2004 WL 1588307, at *4 (D.N.H.) (citing regulation, employers decision to purchase annuity plan to pay for employee's monthly benefit did not create an ERISA plan and the plan's liability is transferred to the annuity provider).
- **29 C.F.R. § 2510.3-1(a):** *McCoy v. Mass. Inst. of Tech.*, 950 F.2d 13, 21–22 (1st Cir. 1991), *cert. denied*, 504 U.S. 910 (1992) (court labels "unpersuasive" the argument that regulation's failure to include plans granting benefits under 29 U.S.C. § 186(c)(9) [money or things of value paid to a plant, area, or industrywide labor management committee] excludes such plans from ERISA coverage); *LaChapelle v. Fechtor, Detwiler & Co.*, 901 F. Supp. 22 (D. Me. 1995) (regulation makes clear that a simplified employee pension–individual retirement account is not a welfare plan); *Riofrio Anda v. Ralston Purina Co.*, 772 F. Supp. 46, 51 (D.P.R. 1991), *aff'd*, 959 F.2d 1149 (1st Cir. 1992) (promise to reimburse relocation expenses not an employee welfare benefit plan); *Panto v. Moore Bus. Forms, Inc.*, 676 F. Supp. 412, 413–14 (D.N.H. 1988) (state claims relating to employer's failure to pay severance benefits found to be ERISA preempted); *Adam v. Joy Mfg. Co.*, 651 F. Supp. 1301 (D.N.H. 1987) (severance pay plan found to be an employee welfare benefit plan subject to ERISA).
- **29 C.F.R. § 2510.3-1(b):** *Woods v. Berry, Fowles & Co.*, 01-CV-37-B-C 2001 WL 1602055, at *10 (D. Me.) (citing regulation, the "payroll practice exception" did not exempt the plan from ERISA because, although the premiums were paid from general assets, they were ongoing and long-term payments); *McMahon v. Digital Equip. Corp.*, 162 F.3d 28 (1st Cir. 1998) (accident and sickness plan and salary continuation plan held not to be "payroll practices" exempt from ERISA coverage); *Woods v. Berry, Fowles & Co.*, 01-CV-37-B-C 2001 WL 1602055 (D. Me. 2001) (employer's life insurance premium payments were ongoing, long-term, and not compensation and therefore life insurance coverage was not a "payroll practice"); *In re Palmos Del Mar Props., Inc.*, 932 F. Supp. 36 (D.P.R. 1996) (holding that overtime and sick leave pay, paid at employee's normal rate of compensation, out of employer's general assets and without additional compensation or conditions, was a pay-

roll practice exempt from ERISA); *Rosario-Cordero v. Crowley Towing & Trans. Co.*, 850 F. Supp. 98 (D.P.R. 1994) (vacation benefits paid from trust fund, and not employer's general assets, did not constitute a payroll practice); *LePage Bakeries v. N.H. Labor Comm'r*, C-94-63-L 1994 WL 269288 (D.N.H. 1994) (sick leave and vacation wages, paid from employer's general assets, were exempted from ERISA as a payroll practice).

- **29 C.F.R. § 2510.3-1(j):** *Desrosiers v. Hartford Life & Accident Ins. Co.*, 354 F. Supp. 2d 119, 125 (D.R.I. 2005) (citing regulation, ERISA applied when DOJ promoted a private welfare plan for its employees because the safe harbor requirement of neutrality was not met); *Demars v. Cigna Corp.*, 173 F.3d 443 (1st Cir. 1999) (fact that conversion policy falls within scope of safe harbor regulation is a factor the court considers in concluding that conversion policy is not subject to ERISA); *New England Mut. Life Ins. Co., Inc. v. Baig*, 166 F.3d 1 (1st Cir. 1999) (court considers safe harbor factors in concluding that a physician's individual disability policy was not subject to ERISA); *Johnson v. Watts Regulator Co.*, 63 F.3d 1129 (1st Cir. 1995) (court focused on safe harbor regulation requirements in concluding that employer did not endorse benefit program and in concluding that such program was not subject to ERISA); *Sorel v. CIGNA*, 94-098-JD 1994 WL 605726 (D.N.H. 1994) (employer who facilitated plan orientation program and recommended that employees enroll in benefit plan did more than merely advertise plan, and therefore plan fell outside safe harbor).

- **29 C.F.R. § 2510.3-1(k):** *Cuoco v. Nynex, Inc.*, 722 F. Supp. 884, 887 (D. Mass. 1989) (scholarship benefits payable to child of former employee were to be made solely from general assets of employer and were not included under an employee welfare benefit plan).

- **29 C.F.R. § 2510.3-2(c):** *Rivera Sanfeliz v. Chase Manhattan Bank*, 349 F. Supp. 2d 240, 247 (D.P.R. 2004) (payments made as bonuses are generally not pension plans).

- **29 C.F.R. § 2510.3-2(d)(1):** *In re Printy*, 171 B.R. 448, 450 (Ban. D. Mass. 1994) (an IRA is not established or maintained by an employer and generally is not covered by ERISA).

- **29 C.F.R. § 2510.3-2(g):** *United Steel Workers of Am. v. Newman-Crosby Steel, Inc.*, 822 F. Supp. 862, 868 (D.R.I. 1993) (supplemental pension benefits found not to be cost-of-living adjustments under regulation).

- **29 C.F.R. § 2510.3-21(c):** *Stein v. Smith*, 270 F. Supp. 2d 157, 170 (D. Mass. 2003) (citing regulation, an officer acting as an investment advisor may have fiduciary liability); *Dudley Supermarket, Inc. v. Transamerica Life Ins. & Annuity Co.*, 302 F.3d 1, 3 (1st Cir. 2002) (citing regulation, finding Transamerica was a fiduciary rendering investment advice and not a mere professional service provider).

- **29 C.F.R. § 2510.3-21(e)(2):** *Drolet v. Healthsource, Inc.*, 968 F. Supp. 757, 761 (D.N.H. 1997) (citing regulation, court notes that allegations of defendant's control over a plan was a sufficient foundation for stating a claim of fiduciary violations); *Toomey v. Jones*, 855 F. Supp. 19, 24–25 (D. Mass.

1994) (pension fund consulting company did not attain fiduciary status when it advised plan to stop paying cash dividend).

- **29 C.F.R. § 2510.3-3:** *Yates v. Hendon*, 541 U.S. 1 (2004) (citing regulation, the Court held that there is no categorical barrier against working owners participating in ERISA plans).
- **29 C.F.R. § 2510.3-3(a) and (d):** *Blossom v. Bank of N.H.*, 2005 WL 1588307 (D.N.H.) (citing regulation, when employer purchased an annuity it did not constitute an "employee benefit plan" as it had sold its obligations under the plan).
- **29 C.F.R. § 2510.3-101:** *Patient Advocates, LLC v. Prysunka*, 316 F. Supp. 2d 46, 48 (D. Me. 2004) (DOL definition of "plan assets" is not exhaustive but beneficiaries' personal data was not considered plan assets absent evidence of economic value).
- **29 C.F.R. § 2520.102-2(a):** *Caradonna v. Compaq Computer Corp.*, 98-701-B 2000 WL 1507454 (D.N.H. 2000) (court concludes that benefits book failed to satisfy categories of information required in a summary plan description).
- **29 C.F.R. § 2520.102-3:** *Alves v. Harvard Pilgrim Health Care, Inc.*, 204 F. Supp. 2d 198 (D. Mass. 2002), *aff'd*, 316 F.3d 290 (1st Cir. 2003) (noting that there is no statutory or regulatory requirement to disclose costs of prescription medications to plan); *Caradonna v. Compaq Computer Corp.*, 98-701-B 2000 WL 1507454 (D.N.H. 2000) (court concludes that benefits book failed to satisfy categories of information required in a summary plan description); *United Paperworkers Int'l Union v. Int'l Paper Co.*, 777 F. Supp. 1010, 1019 (D. Me. 1991) (administrator failed to meet summary plan description requirements and therefore plan, as written, had no proper claim procedure).
- **29 C.F.R. § 2520.102-4:** *Dall v. Chinet Co.*, 33 F. Supp. 2d 26, 44 n.12 (D. Me. 1998), *aff'd*, 201 F.3d 426 (1st Cir. 1999) (noting that administrator may issue separate summary plan descriptions for separate classes of employees so long as the descriptions adequately give notice of the coverage of other classes under another summary.)
- **29 C.F.R. § 2520.104(b)(1):** *Barrs v. Lockheed Martin Corp.*, 287 F.3d 202, 207 (1st Cir. 2002) (citing regulation, employer had no reporting and disclosure duty in welfare benefit plan); *Kenna v. Hartford Life & Accident Ins. Co.*, 04-CV-232-SM 2005 WL 2175158, at *16 (D.N.H.) (citing regulation, plan administrator was the only party responsible to provide summary plan description); *Heller v. Cap Gemini Ernst & Young Welfare Plan*, 396 F. Supp. 2d 10, 20 (D. Mass. 2005) (citing regulation, while measures reasonably calculated to provide "actual receipt" of materials is mandated, technical violations of notice provisions generally do not give rise to substantive remedies absent exceptional circumstances).
- **29 C.F.R. § 2560.503-1:** *Black & Decker Disability Plan v. Nord*, 538 U.S. 822, 825 (2003) (treating physicians' opinions are not accorded extra respect under ERISA, unlike the Social Security Administration's treating physician rule).

- **29 C.F.R. § 2560.503-1(f):** *Cole v. Central States Se. & Sw.*, 101 Fed. Appx. 840, 2004 WL 1335920, at *1 (1st Cir. 2004) (letter satisfied notice requirements although sparse; no requirement to give reasoning behind specific reasons for denial); *Glista v. Unum Life Ins.*, 378 F.3d 113, 128–29 (1st Cir. 2004) (citing regulation, limiting basis for denial of benefits to those actually communicated to beneficiary); *Doe v. Travelers Ins. Co.*, 167 F.3d 53 (1st Cir. 1999) (claimant's request for a medical examiner's report did not impose duty on administrator to produce mental health guidelines); *Terry v. Bayer Corp.*, 145 F.3d 28, 38–39 (1st Cir. 1998) (regulation does not require administrator to advise claimant what information is needed to win his appeal, only that which is needed to perfect the claim); *Tavares v. Unum Corp.*, 17 F. Supp. 2d 69, 78 (D.R.I. 1998) (administrator's letter notifying participant of termination of benefits failed to satisfy requirements under the regulation); *I.V. Servs. of Am., Inc. v. Inn Dev. & Mgmt., Inc.*, 7 F. Supp. 2d 79, 87 (D. Mass. 1998), *aff'd*, 182 F.3d 51 (1st Cir. 1999) (court cites regulation noting that while a deficient denial notice may excuse a claimant's failure to exhaust administrative remedies, it did not excuse plaintiff's failure to sue within the limitations period); *Smart v. Gillette Co. Long-Term Disability Plan*, 887 F. Supp. 383 (D. Mass.), *aff'd*, 70 F.3d 173 (1st Cir. 1995) (ERISA requires only that a plan notify claimant of reasons under the terms of the plan for its denial of a request for benefits); *Perez-Rodriguez v. Citibank, N.A.*, 93-2364CCC 1995 WL 116353 (D.P.R. 1995) (denial letters that failed to advise claimant of specific reasons for claim denial did not satisfy regulatory requirements); *Jorstad v. Conn. Gen. Life Ins. Co.*, 844 F. Supp. 46 (D. Mass. 1994) (court, citing regulation, concludes that information in administrator's denial letters satisfied requirements of 29 U.S.C. § 1133); *McLean Hosp. Corp. v. Lasher*, 819 F. Supp. 110, 124–26 (D. Mass. 1993) (insufficiency of notice of denial of claim excused claimant from exhausting administrative remedies); *DePina v. Gen. Dynamics Corp.*, 674 F. Supp. 46, 50 (D. Mass. 1987) (denial letter failed to provide specific reasons for claim denial, failed to reference specific plan provision upon which denial was based, and failed to provide adequate information for seeking administrative review).
- **29 C.F.R. § 2560.503-1(g):** *Bard v. Boston Shipping Ass.*, 471 F.3d at 240 (administrative appeal procedures failed to comport with regulatory requirements, entitling participant to an award of benefits); *Denmark v. Liberty Assur. Co.*, 04-12261-DPW 2005 WL 3008684, at *15 (D. Mass.) (citing old 1977 regulation and amended regulations as not requiring administrators of disability policies to afford more than one level of internal review); *Madera v. Marsh*, 426 F.3d 56, 62 (1st Cir. 2005) (failure to give written notice of denial is not a defense to failure to exhaust remedies when a formal claim was never made and there was no evidence of futility).
- **29 C.F.R. § 2560.503-1(h):** *Bard v. Boston Shipping Ass.*, 471 F.3d 229, 239 (1st Cir. 2006) (awarding disability pension benefits in part because denial letter lacked specificity); *Davey v. Life Ins. Co. of N. Am.*, CV-05-126-PB 2006 WL 1644690, at *14 (D.N.H.) (ERISA does not require consultation with the

same medical advisor at different levels of appeal, and regulations suggest that deference should not be given to prior adverse benefit determination); *Krodel v. Bayer Corp.*, 345 F. Supp. 2d 110, 115 (D. Mass. 2004) (deferential review violated ERISA, and numerous violations of regulations resulting in a procedurally inadequate review, may be remanded for reconsideration by the administrator; *Aetna Health v. Davila*, 542 U.S. 200, 220 (2004) (unlike *Pegram*'s mixed treatment and eligibility decisions, regulations strongly imply that benefit determinations involving medical judgments made by doctors are actions by plan fiduciaries); *Cannon v. Unum Life Ins. Co. of Am.*, 219 F.R.D. 211 (D. Me. 2004) (court, citing regulation, held that claimant was entitled to production of complete record of administrative review); *Glista v. Unum Life Ins. Co. of Am.*, 01-10202-GAO 2003 WL 22282175, at *7 (D. Mass. 2003) (court, noting regulation, held that claim administrator must disclose all documents relevant to a beneficiary's claim for benefits, "including the plan's statement of policy or guidance concerning the denied benefit, regardless of whether the administrator relied upon that policy in making the benefit determination."); *Sidou v. UnumProvident Corp.*, 245 F. Supp. 207, 216 (D. Me. 2003) (administrative appeal deemed denied when decision not rendered within 120 days).

- **29 C.F.R. § 2560.503-1(i):** *Schmir v. Prudential Ins. Co. of Am.*, 03-187-P-S 2003 WL 22466168, at *3 (D. Me. 2003) (untimely denial letter did not preclude claimant's appeal from being deemed denied).
- **29 C.F.R. § 2560.503-1(j):** *Sheckley v. Lincoln Nat'l Corp. Employees' Retirement Fund*, 04-109-P-C 2004 WL 2905347, at *5 (D. Me. 2004) (only requirement for notice after the denial of internal appeal is that it must state that claimant has a right to bring an action under ERISA).
- **29 C.F.R. § 2560.503-1(m):** *Glista v. Unum Life Ins. Co. of Am.*, 01-10202-GAO 2003 WL 22282175, at *7 (D. Mass. 2003) (court, noting regulation, held that claim administrator must disclose all documents relevant to a beneficiary's claim for benefits, "including the plan's statement of policy or guidance concerning the denied benefit, regardless of whether the administrator relied upon that policy in making the benefit determination.").
- **29 C.F.R. § 2619.26:** *Cooke v. Lynn Sand & Stone Co.*, 70 F.3d 201 (1st Cir. 1995) (court, citing regulation, concludes that discount rate applied to lump-sum payout from terminated pension plan was reasonable).

## XII. Cases Interpreting ERISA Statutes of Limitation

"Because Congress did not provide a statute of limitations in the ERISA statute for section 510 claims, federal courts must apply the limitations period of the state-law cause of action most analogous to the federal claims." *Muldoon v. C.J. Muldoon & Sons*, 278 F.3d 31, 32 (1st Cir. 2002) (citing *Wilson v. Garcia*, 471 U.S. 261 (1985)). In *Muldoon* the First Circuit held that Section 510 claims for benefits are most analogous to state-law actions for wrongful termination or retaliatory discharge. *Muldoon*, 278 F.3d at 32. The court affirmed the Massachusetts district court's application of the three-year statute of limitations for torts, instead of the six-year statute of limitations for general contracts, finding that the cause of action accrued on the date that the plaintiff alleged he was wrongfully terminated. *Id.*; *see also Edes v. Verizon Commc'ns, Inc.*, 288 F. Supp. 2d. 55 (D. Mass. 2003) (Section 510 claims are governed by Massachusetts' three-year limitations period for torts and "the fact that plaintiffs did not realize their injuries were actionable does not affect the date of accrual"); *but see Hubert v. Medical Info. Tech. Inc.*, 05-10269-RWZ 2006 WL 721540 (D. Mass.) (when a plaintiff sues for benefits that are "incidents of the plaintiff's employment," and are provided "under an employment contract . . . the appropriate statute of limitations is six years.").

Consistent with *Muldoon*, courts in the First Circuit have looked to analogous state statutes of limitation. *See, e.g., Skipper v. Claims Servs. Int'l*, 213 F. Supp. 2d 4, 6 (D. Mass. 2002). A Puerto Rico 15-year residual contract limitations period (*Martinez v. Johnson & Johnson Baby Products, Inc.*, 184 F. Supp. 2d 157 (D.P.R. 2002)), a Maine six-year state limitations period for all civil actions (*Bolduc v. Nat'l Semiconductor Corp.*, 35 F. Supp. 2d 106 (D. Me. 1998)), a New Hampshire three-year limitations period for breach of contract (*Lund v. Citizens Fin. Group, Inc.*, CV97-183-M 1999 WL 814341, at *5 (D.N.H. 1999)), and a Massachusetts six-year breach of contract limitations period (*Keiffer v. Shaw Group Inc.*, 2006 WL 1982684*3 (D. Mass.) *Salcedo v. John Hancock Mut. Life Ins. Co.*, 38 F. Supp. 2d 37, 40 (D. Mass. 1998)) have been applied to 29 U.S.C § 1132(a)(1)(B) benefit claims.

The court in *Pierce v. Metropolitan Life Insurance Co.* held that an action for wrongful termination of disability benefits would be subject to New Hampshire's three-year limitations period for installment contracts. It held that even though MetLife's termination of benefits occurred more than three years prior to suit, plaintiff was not barred from seeking to recover benefit payments for the three years prior to filing suit. 307 F. Supp. 2d 325, 333 (D.N.H. 2004).

Courts within the circuit have disagreed about when a limitations period begins to accrue in an ERISA benefits case. The court in *Salcedo*—an action challenging the termination of disability benefits—held that the limitations period did not accrue until after the claimant had exhausted administrative remedies. 38 F. Supp. 2d at 43. Other courts have applied a discovery rule in which limitations periods have been deemed to run when the claimant first gets clear and unequivocal notice of an adverse claim determination. *See, e.g., Hubert v. Medical Info. Tech. Inc.*, 05-10269-RWZ 2006 WL 721540, at *5 (D. Mass) (consistent with federal discovery rule, the general rule in an ERISA action is that a cause of action accrues after a claim of benefits has been made and has been formally denied); *Laurenzano v. Blue Cross & Blue Shield of Mass., Inc. Retirement Income Trust*, 134 F. Supp. 2d 189, 208–09 (D. Mass. 2001). The district of Maine, in *McLaughlin v. Unum Life Ins. Co. of Am.*—an action brought to challenge an administrator's determination that plaintiff's claim was subject to a mental/nervous limitation—held that the limitations period began to run when the claimant first clearly and unequivocally repudiated the plaintiff's claim. 224 F. Supp. 2d 283, 287–90 (D. Me. 2002). *See also Lund*, 1999 WL 814341, at *7; *Bolduc*, 35 F. Supp. 2d at 118–20.

The First Circuit has held that while a technically deficient notice of denial or termination of benefits may excuse a participant's failure to exhaust administrative remedies, it may not toll the limitations period. *I.V. Servs. of Am., Inc. v. Inn Dev. & Mgmt., Inc.*, 182 F.3d 51, 57 (1st Cir. 1999).

The First Circuit requires that ERISA "claims based on a breach of fiduciary duty must be brought within six years of the 'latest date on which the fiduciary could have cured the breach or violation,' *and* within three years of the date on which the plaintiff had actual knowledge of the breach." *Watson v. Deaconess Waltham Hosp.*, 298 F.3d 102, 117 (1st Cir. 2002) (emphasis in original). In *Edes v. Verizon Communications Inc.*, the First Circuit found that plaintiffs obtained "actual knowledge" on the date they got their paychecks and realized they were misclassified, rejecting the argument that a continuing breach would toll the limitations period. *Edes v. Verizon Commc'ns, Inc.*, 417 F.3d 133 (1st Cir. 2005). In *Kling v. Fidelity Management Trust Co.*, the court held that the evidence was insufficient, under both the "legal claims" and the "underlying facts" approaches, to determine whether the plaintiff had "actual knowledge." 323 F. Supp. 2d 132 (D. Mass. 2004). Furthermore, the court stated, "it is not enough that [plaintiffs] had notice that something was awry; [plaintiffs] must have had specific knowledge of the actual breach of duty upon which [they sue]." *Id.* at 137 (citing *Brock v. Nellis*, 809 F.2d 753, 755 (11th Cir. 1987)).

The First Circuit has construed the limitations period for breach of fiduciary duty claims, 29 U.S.C. § 1113, as incorporating the federal doctrine of "fraudulent concealment." *J. Geils Band Employee Benefit Plan v. Smith Barney Shearson, Inc.*, 76 F.3d 1245, 1252 (1st Cir. 1996); *Watson*, 298 F.3d. at 118 ("In cases with fraud or concealment ERISA provides an alternate statute of limitations of six years from the date the plaintiff discovers the breach."). Under this construction, the limitations period may begin to run when a plaintiff actually or constructively discovers the acts or omissions giving rise to the cause of action. *Id.* at 1254. The court noted that a plaintiff must exercise reasonable diligence in asserting its rights. The limitations period may indeed begin to run on a plaintiff lacking actual knowledge of a claim if that plaintiff should have known of the claim in the exercise of reasonable diligence. *Id.*

Finally, courts within the First Circuit have split on whether to apply limitations periods set by contract, indicating that the outcome of this issue is highly fact-specific. *Compare Skipper*, 213 F. Supp. 2d at 6, 7 (plan language requiring suit to be filed within "two years from the time written proof of loss is required to be given" ambiguous and therefore unenforceable) *with Alcorn v. Raytheon Co.*, 175 F. Supp. 2d 117, 121–23 (D. Mass. 2001) (court enforced plan language requiring that suit be filed "within three (3) years after expiration of the time permitted under the Plan for furnishing proof of disability."). The New Hampshire district court held a plaintiff's claim was time-barred because of the limitations provision provided in the plan, requiring that "legal action . . . must be brought . . . within one year from the date the cause of action arose." *Ayotte v. Matthew Thornton Health Plan Inc.*, 2004 WL 1447875 (D.N.H.).

## XIII. Subrogation Litigation

The First Circuit has not yet addressed the impact of *Great-West Life & Annuity Ins. Co. v. Knudson*, 534 U.S. 204 (2002), or *Sereboff v. Mid Atlantic Medical Servs., Inc.*, 126 S. Ct. 1869 (2006), on benefit overpayment or subrogation litigation in ERISA cases.

In *Sereboff*, the U.S. Supreme Court affirmed the Fourth Circuit's holding that Mid Atlantic Medical Services sought equitable relief when it sued a beneficiary for reimbursement of medical expenses paid by the ERISA plan after the beneficiary had recovered for its injuries from a third party, and the funds were set aside by the court during the settlement proceedings. The question facing the Court was whether the relief sought was "equitable in the days of the divided bench." 126 S. Ct. at 1870–71. The Court distinguished *Knudson*, where the relief sought was "not equitable—the imposition of a constructive trust or equitable lien on particular property—but legal—the imposition of personal liability for the benefits that [Great-West] conferred upon [Knudson]." *Id.* at 1874 (citing *Knudson*, 534 U.S. 204 at 212). Here, the Court held that Mid Atlantic's claims were equitable because it sought specifically identifiable funds that were set aside and preserved from the proceeds of beneficiaries' settlement with the third-party tortfeasors. *Id.* at 1874.

The district court of Maine, in *Mank v. Green*, 297 F. Supp. 2d 297 (D. Me. 2003), preliminarily enjoined a plan participant from disbursing funds from a settlement with a third-party tortfeasor because those funds were specifically identifiable and could be awarded to the plan administrator under the plan's subrogation provision.

After a hearing on cross-motions for summary judgment, the court ordered the participant to pay to the plan those funds that were subject to the injunction and could be identified to the third-party settlement. While the plan administrator asked the court to equitably trace other funds from the settlement through a series of transactions to the pockets of the participant's counsel, the court concluded that the trail was too long and tenuous for the type of equitable lien contemplated by *Knudson*. *Mank v. Green*, 2004 WL 1516530 (D. Me. 2004).

## XIV. Miscellaneous

### A. Unique Substantive or Procedural Rules for ERISA Cases

The First Circuit generally has not adopted unique substantive or procedural rules for ERISA benefit cases. Most cases are resolved on summary judgment. The First Circuit has not recognized exceptions to the general rule that 29 U.S.C. § 1132(a)(1)(B) cases are not tried by jury. Where there are disputes about the composition of the administrative record, the First Circuit has suggested that such disputes may be resolved by motion or a nonjury trial. *Recupero v. New England Tel. & Tel. Co.*, 118 F.3d 820, 833–34 (1st Cir. 1997).

The First Circuit has addressed the issue of alleged ERISA violations against an employee stock ownership plan (ESOP), holding that the participants stated a cause of action against the employer for breach of fiduciary duty. *Lalonde v. Textron, Inc.*, 369 F.3d 1 (1st Cir. 2004). The court acknowledged the difficulties an ESOP fiduciary faces in reconciling the ESOP goal of employee ownership (where the goal is not to guarantee retirement funds and assets are invested at a greater risk than typical diversified ERISA plans) and ERISA's rigorous fiduciary obligations. *Lalonde*, 369 F.3d at 5. However, the court vacated the lower court, holding that the plaintiffs asserted enough facts to withstand dismissal under Federal Rule of Civil Procedure 12(b)(6). *Id.* at 6–7.

The district court of Puerto Rico held that the existence of contradictory medical reports did not defeat a finding of sufficient evidence for the plan administrator's decision to deny benefits. *Olivera v. Bristol Labs.*, 03-2195(HL) 2006 WL 897972, at *9 (D.P.R.) (citing *Doyle v. Paul Revere Life Ins. Co.*, 144 F.3d 181 (1st Cir. 1988)). Where the plaintiff's treating physicians found total disability but the independent medical consultants did not find total disability, the court held that the plan administrator's decision to deny benefits was based upon sufficient and substantial evidence, even if one viewpoint was credited over another. *Id.*

### B. Unique Approach to Common Policy-Based Defenses

The First Circuit has developed no unique approaches to common policy-based defenses.

The district court of Massachusetts permitted an ERISA fiduciary to file an interpleader action in lieu of exercising its lawful discretion to designate a beneficiary for certain life insurance proceeds. *Forcier v. Forcier*, 406 F. Supp. 2d 132, 135 (D. Mass. 2005). The court rejected the "reverse exhaustion" argument, allowing MetLife to have the court make its decision instead. *Forcier*, 406 F. Supp. 2d at 141. The court reasoned that making MetLife choose between potential beneficiaries would only prolong litigation, requiring the parties to expend additional attorneys' fees and resources because the "losing" party would file suit anyway. *Id.* at 142. The court awarded MetLife $5,000 in attorneys' fees and costs from the proceeds and dismissed it as a party. *Id.* at 139.

In the bench trial to determine who was the beneficiary under the policy, since none was named, the court took a practical approach, rejecting the spouse in favor of the decedent's living parents. *Id.* at 149–50. Although the decedent was still technically married when he committed suicide, the final divorce decree was signed and it was only a matter of weeks before its effective date. *Id.* at 147.

### C. Other Miscellaneous Issues

Class actions have been certified in ERISA cases in the First Circuit, provided the requirements of Federal Rule of Civil Procedure 23 are met. *See, e.g., Carrier v. JPB Enters., Inc.*, 206 F.R.D. 332 (D. Me. 2002). The circuit court will review orders granting or denying class actions for abuse of discretion. *Tilley v. TJX Cos., Inc.*, 345 F.3d 34, 39 (1st Cir. 2003), citing *Waste Mgmt. Holdings, Inc. v. Mowbray*, 208 F.3d 288, 295 (1st Cir. 2000).

In *Lalonde v. Textron, Inc.*, 418 F. Supp. 2d 16, 22 (D.R.I. 2006), on remand from the First Circuit, the district court held that plaintiffs who were seeking class certification had no standing to bring action. The district court of Rhode Island held that the former employees were not "participants" when they had neither (1) a reasonable expectation of returning to covered employment nor (2) a colorable claim to vested benefits. *Lalonde*, 418 F. Supp. 2d at 22.

# CHAPTER 2

# Second Circuit

DAVID J. BURKE
STEVEN B. GETZOFF
HELEN M. KEMP
RANDI F. KNEPPER
ALLAN M. MARCUS
AMY ZINSER

## I. What Constitutes an ERISA Plan?

### A. Determining the Existence of an Employee Welfare Benefit Plan

The Second Circuit has held that an ERISA (Employee Retirement Income Security Act of 1974) plan is established if "from the surrounding circumstances a reasonable person can ascertain intended benefits, a class of beneficiaries, the source of financing, and procedures for receiving benefits." *Grimo v. Blue Cross/Blue Shield of Vt.,* 34 F.3d 148, 151 (2d Cir. 1994), quoting *Donovan v. Dillingham,* 688 F.2d 1367, 1373 (11th Cir. 1982). A plan can be established without a formal written instrument, so long as the essential functions are present. *Grimo,* 34 F.3d at 151. *See also Gilbert v. Burlington Indus., Inc.,* 765 F.2d 320, 323–25 (2d Cir. 1985), *aff'd,* 477 U.S. 901 (1986) (noncompliance with ERISA's disclosure and claims procedure requirements did not preclude establishment of ERISA plan). Some of the essential functions of a plan can be ascertained from sources outside the plan, such as an insurance company's procedure for processing claims. *Grimo,* 34 F.3d at 151.

As to the question of whether an employer's involvement was enough to have "established or maintained" the plan, the Second Circuit has held that the employer's purchase of a group policy of insurance, while not conclusive, offers substantial evidence that a plan has been established. *Id.* A "minimal ongoing administrative

31

scheme" is all that is needed to establish a plan. *Garrett v. Veterans Mem'l Med. Ctr.,* 821 F. Supp. 838, 840 (D. Conn. 1993). However, the Second Circuit has held that an insurance program was not governed by ERISA where the employer made irregular contributions to the insurance costs for only some of its employees, reasoning that the insurance program was not "maintained" by the employer. *See Grimo,* 34 F.3d at 153. In addition, in *Devlin v. Transportation Communications International Union,* 175 F.3d 121, 127 (2d Cir. 1999), the Second Circuit held that an employer's death benefit fund that paid $300 to an employee's survivors was not an employee welfare benefit plan subject to ERISA because the regulations exclude "small gifts" made in remembrance of deceased employees.

### B. Definition of "Employee" for ERISA Purposes

If no employees are participants in a plan, the plan is not governed by ERISA. *See, e.g., Rand v. Equitable Life Assur. Soc. of U.S.,* 49 F. Supp. 2d 111, 116–17 (E.D.N.Y. 1999) (group disability insurance policy issued to chiropractor and partner was not an employee benefit plan covered by ERISA since no employees of the practice were covered and the sole beneficiaries of policy were the owners of the practice).

The Eastern District of New York has held that a commodities floor broker who was a member of a mercantile exchange, and who received coverage under a group long-term disability plan sponsored by the exchange, was not an employee of the exchange and, as such, ERISA was inapplicable to his claim for benefits. *Rafferty v. New York Mercantile Exchange Long-Term Disability Plan,* 133 F. Supp. 2d 158, 161–62 (E.D.N.Y. 2000). Moreover, the District Court of Connecticut held that employees of an acquired company were not "employees" of the acquiring company until completion of the sale; thus, the acquiring company did not have the fiduciary duty under ERISA to provide employees of the acquired company with information regarding benefits the acquiring company was planning to offer. *Flanigan v. Gen. Elec. Co.,* 93 F. Supp. 2d 236, 259–60 (D. Conn. 2000).

With respect to the statutory exceptions to plans that are governed by ERISA, the Second Circuit has held that an employee benefit plan established by a railroad is exempt from ERISA pursuant to the governmental exception where the railroad is an agency or instrumentality of a political subdivision of a state. *See Rose v. Long Island R. R. Pension Plan,* 828 F.2d 910, 914–21 (2d Cir. 1987). A plan maintained outside the United States may be deemed an ERISA plan, unless it is primarily for the benefit of persons substantially all of whom are nonresident aliens. *Lefkowitz v. Arcadia Trading Co.,* 996 F.2d 600, 602 (2d Cir. 1993).

### C. Interpretation of Safe Harbor Regulation

Courts within the Second Circuit interpret the "safe harbor" regulation, 29 C.F.R. § 2510.3-1(j), in conformity with its interpretation by other circuits. *See Grimo v. Blue Cross/Blue Shield of Vt.,* 34 F.3d 148, 152 (2d Cir. 1994). The safe harbor regulation provides that if all four of the following criteria are met, a group insurance program will be excluded from ERISA coverage:

1. No contributions are made by an employer or employee organization;
2. Participation in the program is completely voluntary for employees or members;

3. The sole functions of the employer or employee organization with respect to the program are, without endorsing the program, to permit the insurer to publicize the program to employees or members, and to collect premiums through payroll deductions or dues checkoffs and remit them to insurer; and

4. The employer or employee organization receives no consideration in the form of cash or otherwise in connection with the program, other than reasonable compensation, excluding any profit, for administrative services actually rendered in connection with payroll deductions or dues checkoffs.

For example, where an employer pays any portion of the premium for an insurance program, the program will not fall within the safe harbor. *See, e.g., Adler v. Unicare Life & Health Ins. Co.,* 2003 WL 22928653, at *4 (S.D.N.Y. Dec. 10, 2003) (insurance plan fails to meet safe harbor exception where employer contributes certain percentage of employees' premiums); *DiMaria v. First Unum Life Ins. Co.,* 2003 WL 21018819, at *4 (S.D.N.Y. May 6, 2003) (where physician employer, a sole practitioner, paid for group disability insurance premiums with personal check, safe harbor criteria not satisfied). Several district courts have held that subsection (3) of the safe harbor regulation is not satisfied when an employee can reasonably conclude that the employer had not merely facilitated the program's availability but had exercised some administrative control over it to make it appear to be part of the employer's benefit plan. *See, e.g., Cronin v. Zurich Am. Ins. Co.,* 189 F. Supp. 2d 29, 35 (S.D.N.Y. 2002). In *Cronin,* the Southern District of New York held that subsection (3) of the regulation was not satisfied where the employer (1) considered the "Voluntary Accident Insurance Plan" an ERISA plan (it distributed summary plan description and filed IRS Form 5500); (2) negotiated policy provisions; (3) was named as "plan administrator" in the summary plan description; (4) processed claim forms and provided guidance in completing forms; (5) exercised control over enrollment and eligibility requirements; and (6) offered the Voluntary Policy along with other plans in its overall program of employee benefits. *Id.,* 189 F. Supp. 2d at 35–36; *see also Sanfilippo v. Provident Life & Cas. Ins. Co.,* 178 F. Supp. 2d 450, 456 (S.D.N.Y. 2002) (holding that policy does not come within safe harbor exemption where policy describes itself as providing benefits under employer's plan and includes ERISA-specific notices).

## D. Amount of Employer Involvement Required to Sustain an Employee Welfare Benefit Plan

See cases discussed in subsections A and C above.

## E. Treatment of Multiple Employer Trusts and Welfare Agreements

The Second Circuit applies the same criteria to establish the existence of a welfare benefit plan to multiple employer trusts and welfare agreements (MEWAs) as it does to single-employer plans. *See Atlantic Health Benefits Trust v. Googins,* 2 F.3d 1, 3 (2d Cir. 1993). Cases in the Second Circuit have focused on the issue of whether states may regulate MEWAs as insurance companies under 29 U.S.C. § 1144(b)(6)(A). *Id.,* 2 F.3d at 4–6; *USA for Healthcare Benefit Trust v. Googins,* 1998 WL 136169, at *3–5 (D. Conn. Mar. 16, 1998).

## II. Preemption

### A. Scope of ERISA Preemption

The scope of ERISA preemption in the Second Circuit is "fundamentally a question of congressional intent." *Gerosa v. Savasta & Co.,* 329 F.3d 317, 323 (2d Cir.), *cert. denied,* 124 S. Ct. 435, 540 US 967 (2003). In *Gerosa,* the Second Circuit held that Congress intended ERISA preemption to be limited to those laws that would interfere with ERISA's primary goal of protecting the interests of participants in employee benefit plans and their beneficiaries. *Id.* For this reason, the key focus in any preemption analysis is whether the state law in question affects the relationship among the core ERISA entities: beneficiaries, participants, administrators, employers, trustees, fiduciaries, and the plan itself. *Id.* at 324. Also integral to the analysis is whether the state law conflicts with central ERISA functions, including, inter alia, determining benefit eligibility, the amount of benefits, or the means of securing unpaid benefits. *Id.* State laws affecting interactions among core ERISA entities with respect to central ERISA functions are likely to be preempted whereas those involving relationships between ERISA and non-ERISA entities (such as a plan's arrangement with an outside actuarial firm) are not. *Id.* at 328 (recognizing that "ERISA does not create a 'fully insulated legal world' for plans; they must deal with outsiders, such as landlords or debt-collectors, under the same diverse hodge-podge of state law as any other economic actor.").

The Second Circuit recently restated with approval *Gerosa*'s holding that "state laws that would tend to control or supersede central ERISA functions—such as state laws affecting the determination of eligibility for benefits, amounts of benefits, or means of securing unpaid benefits—have typically been found to be preempted." *Hattem v. Schwarzenegger,* 449 F.3d 423, 2006 U.S. App. LEXIS 12819, at *19–20 (2d Cir. 2006) (citing *Gerosa,* 329 F.3d at 327).

The Second Circuit has long described complete preemption as having two separate components. *See Cicio v. Does,* 321 F.3d 83, 92–94 (2d. Cir. 2003) (*Cicio I*), *vacated,* 2004 U.S. LEXIS 4579 (U.S. 2004); *Romney v. Lin,* 94 F.3d 74, 78 (2d Cir. 1996), *reh'g denied,* 105 F.3d 806 (2d Cir.), *cert. denied,* 522 U.S. 906 (1997). First, the reviewing court determines whether the state law conflicts with ERISA—i.e., whether the state law relates to an ERISA plan. *Cicio I,* 321 F.3d at 93 (citing 29 U.S.C. § 1144(a)). "A state law relates to an ERISA plan if it has a connection with or reference to such a plan." *Id.* (citations omitted). Second, the court determines whether the cause of action is "within the scope of the civil enforcement provisions of ERISA § 502(a)." *Id.,* quoting 29 U.S.C. § 1132(a). This requirement is met if the state law acts as an alternative enforcement mechanism to ERISA by "seek[ing] to vindicate rights already protected by § 502(a)." *Id.* at 94. If both of these conditions are satisfied, the state law is completely preempted and the action is subject to removal and dismissal under ERISA. *Id.* at 93.

Recently, the Second Circuit revisited its preemption analysis following the U.S. Supreme Court's decision in *Aetna Health Inc. v. Davila,* 542 U.S. 200 (2004), and the subsequent order vacating *Cicio v. Does,* 2004 U.S. LEXIS 4579. As more fully discussed in the following section, *Davila* was factually similar to *Cicio* in that both cases addressed whether ERISA preempts state-law medical malpractice claims brought against managed care organizations (MCOs). *Davila,* 542 U.S. at 203–205; *Cicio I,* 321 F.3d at 100–04. However, in addition to finding that ERISA completely preempts state-law medical malpractice claims against most MCOs, the Supreme Court in *Davila* set out one of the most comprehensive analyses of ERISA preemption to date. *Davila,* 542 U.S. at 206–221. Interestingly, the Supreme Court held that a state claim is both removable and completely preempted solely under ERISA § 502 "if [the state law] provides a separate vehicle to assert a claim for benefits outside of, or in addition to, ERISA's remedial scheme" regardless of whether the law is saved from preemption under § 514. *Id.* at 217–218.

After the Supreme Court vacated and remanded *Cicio,* the Second Circuit vacated its earlier decision and affirmed the district court's dismissal of the plaintiff's complaint. *Cicio v. Does,* 385 F.3d 156 (2d Cir. 2004) (*Cicio II*). The Second Circuit noted that the Supreme Court's reasoning in *Davila* "fatally undermine[d]" the holding in *Cicio I. Cicio II,* 385 F.3d at 158. The Second Circuit recognized in *Cicio II* that *Davila* required dismissal of state medical malpractice claims against ERISA plan providers. *Id.*

*Davila*'s holding appeared to contradict the Second Circuit's long-standing two-step analysis requiring application of *both* §§ 502 *and* 514 before a state-law claim would be removable and completely preempted under ERISA. *Cicio I,* 321 F.3d 92–94; *Romney,* 94 F.3d at 78. However, the Second Circuit has not addressed the issue of whether *Davila*'s analysis supersedes the two-step method, and has in at least one instance since *Davila* relied on the two-step analysis. *DaPonte v. Manfredi Motors, Inc.,* 157 Fed. Appx. 328, 330, 2005 U.S. App. LEXIS 19948, at * 4, 35 Empl. Benefits Cas. (BNA) 2589 (2d Cir. 2005) (analyzing the plaintiff's claim using the two-step method); *see also Strohmeyer v. Metro. Life Ins. Co.,* 365 F. Supp. 2d 258, 260 (D. Conn. 2005) ("The determination of whether a state law is preempted by ERISA requires two prongs of analysis.") *But see NYU Hosps. Center-Tisch v. Local 348 Health & Welfare Fund,* 2005 U.S. Dist. LEXIS 256, at *5–6, 34 Employee Benefits Cas. (BNA) 2339 (S.D.N.Y. 2005) (noting that *Davila* "reformulated" the Second Circuit's traditional two-step inquiry).

### B.  Preemption of Managed-Care Claims

In *Cicio,* the plaintiff brought multiple state-law claims against the defendant health maintenance organization alleging that the HMO wrongfully denied authorization for a requested medical service. *Cicio I,* 321 F.3d 83. Plaintiff alleged that (1) the HMO's benefit determination was untimely ("timeliness claims");[1] (2) the HMO misrepresented the availability of benefits under the plan ("misrepresentation claims");[2] and (3) the HMO's denial of the benefit was based upon a negligent medical decision ("medical malpractice claims"). *Id.* at 90. The district court found that each of plaintiff's eighteen counts was preempted by ERISA. *Id.* at 89. Plaintiff appealed. *Id.*

Plaintiff's timeliness claims were based on a New York law requiring HMOs to render medical benefit determinations within one business day after receiving all necessary information relating to the request. *Id.* at 95 (citing N.Y. PUB. HEALTH

LAW § 4903(3)). The Second Circuit held that the New York law conflicts with regulations issued by the Secretary of Labor setting forth time frames for responding to requests for services and thus has an "effect on the primary administrative functions of benefit plans." *Id.* at 95, citing *Aetna Life Ins. Co. v. Borges,* 869 F.2d 142, 146 (2d Cir.), *cert. denied,* 493 U.S. 811 (1989). The Second Circuit also held that plaintiff's timeliness claims acted as an alternative mechanism for enforcing the rights already available under ERISA § 502, namely the right to ensure timely benefit determinations through injunctive relief. *Id.* at 95–96. Accordingly, plaintiff's timeliness claims were completely preempted. *Id.* at 95.

The Second Circuit also found that plaintiff's misrepresentation claims related to the existence or extent of benefits available under the plan and thereby conflicted with ERISA. *Id.* at 96. The claims also acted as an alternative enforcement mechanism in that they sought to vindicate rights accruing under the plan's terms. *Id.* Because ERISA § 502(a)(1)(B) allows recovery of benefits due under a plan, plaintiff's misrepresentation claims were deemed to be within the scope of ERISA's civil enforcement provisions. *Id.* Based on these findings, the Second Circuit held that plaintiff's misrepresentation claims were completely preempted. *Id.* at 96–97; *see also Wiggin v. Bridgeport Hosp.,* 2003 U.S. Dist. LEXIS 10509, at *5–6 (D. Conn. 2003) (granting defendants' motion to dismiss plaintiffs' fraud and misrepresentation claims based on defendants' statements concerning the availability of benefits under the plan).

### C. Preemption of Malpractice Claims

Prior to *Davila,* the Second Circuit found that state medical malpractice law involves the application of duties of conduct that are defined outside of ERISA. *Cicio I,* 321 F.3d at 99–100. The Second Circuit reasoned that, because the plaintiff's malpractice claim was based on the medical component of the MCO's mixed eligibility and treatment decision, the claim did not "relate to" the plan. *Id.* at 104. Accordingly, the plaintiff's medical malpractice claim was not preempted. *Id.*

However, the Supreme Court vacated *Cicio* based upon its decision in *Davila.* 542 U.S. 200. *Davila* involved two consolidated cases from the Fifth Circuit (*Aetna Health Inc. v. Davila* and *Cigna Healthcare of Texas Inc.*) wherein plaintiffs asserted medical malpractice-type claims against ERISA plan administrators based on the allegedly wrongful denial of benefits. *Id.* at 204. Specifically, plaintiffs stated claims under the Texas Health Care Liability Act (THCLA) alleging that the defendants violated the statutorily imposed duty of ordinary care in making their health insurance benefit determinations. *Id.* In a unanimous decision, the Supreme Court held that the plaintiffs' causes of action fell within the scope of ERISA § 502 and were completely preempted as alternative remedies to ERISA's civil enforcement provisions. *Id.* at 214. The Supreme Court rejected plaintiffs' argument that THCLA was saved from preemption as a law regulating insurance, finding instead that "a state cause of action that provides an alternative remedy to those provided by the ERISA civil enforcement mechanism conflicts with Congress' clear intent to make the ERISA mechanism exclusive" regardless of whether the underlying state law was saved from preemption under ERISA § 514. *Id.* at 214 n.4, citing *Ingersoll-Rand Co. v. McClendon,* 498 U.S. 133, 142 (1990).

The Second Circuit has not applied *Davila* to a medical malpractice claim at the time of this publication. Prior to *Davila,* however, one district court applied *Cicio* in a way that seemed to anticipate the Supreme Court's newly pronounced preemption analysis. In a case involving a plan's utilization management (UM) agent as opposed to an HMO, the U.S. District Court for the Southern District of New York found that plaintiff's medical malpractice claim was completely preempted despite the Second Circuit's decision in *Cicio. Rubin-Schneiderman v. Merit Behavioral Care Corp,* 2003 U.S. Dist. LEXIS 14811, at *5 (S.D.N.Y. 2003), *appeal docketed,* No. 03-9111-CV (2d Cir. Oct. 23, 2003). The court began its analysis by reviewing the plan's brochure and the correspondence between the UM agent and the plaintiff's treating physician. *Id.* at *3 n.1 and *5. Based on these documents, the court found that the relationship between the plaintiff and the UM agent did not give rise to a duty of care outside of ERISA. *Id.* at *5. *See also id.* at *2–3 (distinguishing the role of a UM agent from that of an HMO, which, in some cases, may have a physician-patient relationship with a member).

The *Rubin-Schneiderman* court held that, even under *Cicio,* ERISA continues to preempt medical negligence claims brought against entities "which never sought to undertake responsibility for its insureds' treatment." *Id.,* citing *Marks v. Watters,* 322 F.3d 316, 324 (4th Cir. 2003). This decision appears consistent with *Davila,* which suggested that liability beyond ERISA may still exist if the defendant is responsible for both treating the plaintiff and making benefit determinations. *Davila,* 542 U.S. at 220–224.

### D. Other Preemption Issues

The Second Circuit has held that state-law malpractice claims brought by plan fiduciaries against the plan's outside actuary are not preempted. *Gerosa,* 329 F.3d 317; *see Cicio I,* 321 F.3d at 103–04 (noting that ERISA's goal of promoting the interests of plan beneficiaries does not mandate "the elimination of protective standards of professional conduct"). In reaching this conclusion, the Second Circuit applied the general principle that Congress intended preemption to apply among core ERISA entities to further ERISA's central purpose of protecting the interests of plan beneficiaries. *Id.* at 328. The state-law claims in *Gerosa* were brought by the plan's fiduciary (core ERISA entity) against an outside consultant (noncore ERISA entity). *Id.* The court also held that the claims were aimed at furthering the interests of the plan's participants by seeking monetary damages to offset the losses allegedly caused by the defendant's negligence and that no ERISA purpose would be served by preempting the claims. *Id.* Accordingly, the Second Circuit found that the plan's state-law claims were not preempted.

## III.  Exhaustion of Administrative Remedies

### A.  Is Exhaustion an Absolute Requirement?

The Second Circuit recognizes the "firmly established federal policy favoring exhaustion of administrative remedies in ERISA cases." *Kennedy v. Empire Blue Cross & Blue Shield,* 989 F.2d 588, 594 (2d Cir. 1993). The exhaustion requirement, the court has stated, encourages that administrative claim procedures established by plans be followed, and facilitates the full development of the administrative record should the claim be litigated. *Id.* The Second Circuit has recently held, however, that failure to exhaust administrative remedies is not a jurisdictional bar to bringing an action, but rather an affirmative defense that is waived if not asserted. *See Paese v. Hartford Life & Accident Ins. Co.,* 449 F.3d 435, 445–56 (2d Cir. 2006). Exhaustion "requires only those administrative appeals provided for in the relevant plan or policy." *Kennedy,* 989 F.2d at 594. One district court has held that where the plan handbook stated only that a participant "may" seek review of a denied claim, exhaustion was not required. *Sibley-Schreiber v. Oxford Health Plans (N.Y.), Inc.,* 62 F. Supp. 2d 979, 985–89 (E.D.N.Y. 1999).

### B. Exceptions to the Exhaustion Requirement

A plaintiff must make a "clear and positive" showing of futility to avoid the exhaustion requirement. *Kennedy v. Empire Blue Cross & Blue Shield,* 989 F.2d at 594; *Davenport v. Harry N. Abrams, Inc.,* 249 F.3d 130, 133 (2d Cir. 2001). *See also Stewart v. NYNEX Corp.,* 78 F. Supp. 2d 172, 183 (S.D.N.Y. 1999) (finding that denial of one class member's claim appeal was sufficient for "clear and positive" showing that exhaustion by other class members would be futile).

In *Paese,* the court held that where the administrator did not distinguish between the "own occupation" and "any occupation" periods of disability in denial letters, the plan was estopped from asserting plaintiff's failure to exhaust remedies for the "any occupation" phase of disability. 449 F.3d at 447–48. In *Nichols v. Prudential Insurance Co. of America,* 406 F.3d 98 (2d Cir. 2005), the Second Circuit held that an ERISA plan administrator's failure to comply with regulatory deadlines governing appeals of adverse benefit determinations rendered the claimant's administrative remedies exhausted. 406 F.3d at 106. At least one district court has held that an employee's failure to adhere to administrative review deadlines may be excused on the grounds of equitable estoppel. *See Tiger v. AT&T Techs. Plan,* 633 F. Supp. 532, 534 (E.D.N.Y. 1986). *See also Chapman v. Choicecare Long Island Long Term Disability Plan,* 288 F.3d 506, 512–14 (2d Cir. 2002) (suggesting without deciding that equitable tolling of administrative review deadlines might be appropriate where mental illness of participant prevented pursuit of appeal). Where a plaintiff failed to appeal the denial of his disability benefits claim within sixty days, but argued that the administrator should be estopped from asserting exhaustion since it had taken over 180 days to issue an initial claim denial, the court held that plaintiff's failure to file a timely appeal was not excused, since he could have appealed after the 180-day period had expired. *Holm v. First UNUM Life Ins. Co.,* 7 Fed. Appx. 40, 41–42 (2d Cir. 2001).

### C. Consequences of Failure to Exhaust

Failure to exhaust remedies is an affirmative defense but not a jurisdictional bar to bringing an action. *See Paese,* 449 F.3d 435, 445–56 (2d Cir. 2006). Although the Second Circuit has not yet addressed whether exhaustion is required for statutory ERISA claims, some district courts have held that it is not. *See, e.g., MacKay v. Rayonier, Inc.,* 25 F. Supp. 2d 47, 50 (D. Conn. 1998) (exhaustion not required for § 510 claims); *Gray v. Briggs,* 1998 WL 386177, at *7 (S.D.N.Y. 1998) (no exhaustion requirement for ERISA claims alleging statutory violation rather than denial of benefits); *DePace v. Matsushita Elec. Corp.,* 257 F. Supp. 2d 543, 557 (E.D.N.Y. 2003) (same).

### D. Minimum Number of Levels of Administrative Review

The Second Circuit does not require a plan to provide more than the single appellate review mandated by ERISA.

### E. Can a Defendant Waive a Failure-to-Exhaust Defense?

The Second Circuit has not addressed this issue.

## IV. Standard of Review

### A. Plan Language

The Second Circuit has held that when a plan confers upon a plan administrator discretionary authority to determine eligibility for benefits or construe plan terms, "we will not disturb the administrator's ultimate conclusion unless it is 'arbitrary or capricious,'" i.e., "'without reason, unsupported by substantial evidence or erroneous as a matter of law.'" *Pagan v. NYNEX Pension Plan,* 52 F.3d 438, 441–42 (2d Cir. 1995). As to what plan language is sufficient to confer discretionary authority, the Second Circuit has recognized that "magic words" like "discretion" or "deference" are not necessarily required. *Jordan v. Ret. Comm. of Rensselaer Polytechnic Inst.,* 46 F.3d 1264, 1271 (2d Cir. 1995); *Kinstler v. First Reliance Standard Life Ins. Co.,* 181 F.3d 243, 251 (2d Cir. 1999). The Second Circuit has found that the following language is sufficient to confer discretionary authority on an administrator:

- "[T]he trustees shall determine any questions arising under the plan" (*O'Shea v. First Manhattan Co. Thrift Plan & Trust,* 55 F.3d 109, 112 (2d Cir. 1995).
- Fiduciaries authorized to "determine conclusively . . . all questions arising in the administration of the Plan" (*Pagan v. NYNEX Pension Plan,* 52 F.3d at 441).
- Trustees to be "sole judge" of plan interpretation and applicant's entitlement to benefits (*Jiras v. Pension Plan,* 170 F.3d 162, 164, 166 (2d Cir. 1999)).
- "[The] decision of Pension Committee regarding whether or not a person is disabled is final and binding" (*Neely v. Pension Trust Fund,* 2003 WL 21143087, at *7 (E.D.N.Y. 2003)).
- Trustees had authority to "resolve all disputes and ambiguities relating to the interpretation of the Plan" (*Ganton Techs., Inc., v. Nat'l Indus. Group Pension Plan,* 76 F.3d 462, 466 (2d Cir. 1996)).

The following plan language has been held not to be sufficient to confer discretion:

- Participant must submit "satisfactory proof to us" (*Kinstler v. First Reliance Standard Life Ins. Co.,* 181 F.3d 243, 251–52 (2d Cir. 1999).
- Discretion to establish initial terms of plan (*Masella v. Blue Cross & Blue Shield of Conn., Inc.,* 936 F.2d 98, 103 (2d Cir. 1991)).

## B. What Standard of Review Applies?

When a plan confers discretionary authority to its fiduciaries, the arbitrary and capricious standard of review applies. *See Pagan v. NYNEX Pension Plan,* 52 F.3d 438, 441 (2d Cir. 1995); *Murphy v. IBM Corp.,* 23 F.3d 719, 721 (2d Cir.), *cert. denied,* 115 S. Ct. 204 (1994). The district court's review of an administrator's claim determination under the arbitrary and capricious standard is narrow in scope and highly deferential. The Second Circuit has explained: "[W]e may overturn a decision and deny benefits only if it was 'without reason, unsupported by substantial evidence or erroneous as a matter of law.' . . . [W]e are not free to substitute our own judgment for that of the [administrator] as if we were considering the issue of eligibility anew." *Pagan,* 52 F.3d at 442 (citations omitted). *See also Jordan v. Ret. Comm. of Rensselaer Polytechnic Inst.,* 46 F.3d 1264, 1271 (2d Cir. 1995) ("The arbitrary and capricious standard of review is highly deferential to a plan administrator. . . . The Court may not upset a reasonable interpretation by the administrator."); *Scannell v. Metro. Life Ins. Co.,* 2003 WL 2722954, at *4 (S.D.N.Y. Nov. 18, 2003) ("[administrator's] decision will be upheld unless it is not grounded on *any* reasonable basis. The reviewing court need only assure that the administrator's decision falls somewhere on a continuum of reasonableness—even if on the low end.") (emphasis in original; internal citations omitted).

## C. Effect of Conflict of Interest or Procedural Irregularity

If a plan administrator is granted discretionary authority, evidence of a potential conflict of interest on the part of the administrator is not sufficient to alter the arbitrary and capricious standard. *See Sullivan v. LTV Aerospace & Defense Co.,* 82 F.3d 1251, 1255–56, 1259 (2d Cir. 1996). It is the plaintiff's burden to prove that the administrator was in fact influenced by an actual conflict of interest in rendering the decision at issue. *Id.* at 1259. If such proof is presented, the deferential standard drops away and review is de novo. (There is no "sliding scale" of deference in Second Circuit law.) The Second Circuit has prescribed a two-part test: "[f]irst, whether the determination made by the administrator is reasonable, in light of possible conflicting interpretations of the plan; second, whether the evidence shows that the administrator was in fact influenced by such conflict." *Id.* at 1255–56; *Whitney v. Blue Cross & Blue Shield,* 106 F.3d 475, 477 (2d Cir. 1997). *See also Alakozai v. Allstate Ins. Co.,* 2000 WL 325685, at *7 (S.D.N.Y. 2000) (beneficiary must present material, probative evidence of actual conflict of interest).

Failure to comply with ERISA regulations may alter the standard of review. In *Nichols v. Prudential Insurance Co. of America,* 406 F.3d 98 (2d Cir. 2005), the Second Circuit held that an ERISA-plan administrator's failure to comply with regulatory deadlines for claims determinations resulted in the claim being "deemed denied." Even though the plan may contain a grant of discretionary authority, the Second Circuit explained, the court's review of a "deemed denied" claim is de novo because inaction is not a valid exercise of discretion. 406 F.3d at 109. The *Nichols* court did not decide the question of whether substantial compliance as compared to strict compliance with regulatory deadlines is sufficient to avoid de novo review. *Id.* at 109–10.

## D. Other Factors Affecting Standard of Review

Among other factors that can affect the standard of review is whether discretionary authority has been properly delegated to the entity or person making the benefit determination. Thus, where a plan granted discretion to a named fiduciary, but did not permit such discretion to be delegated, a claim decision made by an unrelated subcommittee was held reviewable de novo. *Rubio v. Chock Full O'Nuts Corp.,* 254 F. Supp. 2d 413, 423 (S.D.N.Y. 2003). Where the plan does not explicitly "name" its claims administrator as a fiduciary, but describes the administrator's specific fiduciary functions (such as making final claim determinations), a provision conferring discretionary authority on "other plan fiduciaries" is sufficient to confer discretionary authority on the claims administrator. *See Winkler v. Metro. Life Ins. Co.,* 2004 WL 1687202, at *2–3 (S.D.N.Y. July 27, 2004), *reh'g denied,* 340 F. Supp. 2d 411 (S.D.N.Y. 2004).

A grant of discretionary authority contained only in the summary plan description (rather than in the plan document or group policy) has been held to be effective. *See Murphy v. IBM Corp.,* 23 F.3d 719, 721 (2d Cir. 1994); *Scannell v. Metro. Life Ins. Co.,* 2003 WL 22722954, at *4 (S.D.N.Y. 2003). In *Gibbs v. CIGNA Corp.,* 440 F.3d 571 (2d Cir. 2006), the Second Circuit held that the summary plan description in effect at the time disability benefits "vested" (i.e., at the time the participant became disabled) was the governing document for purposes of determining the applicable standard of review. 440 F.3d at 576–77. A plan's grant of discretion, the court noted, affects the substance of a participant's benefits. *Id.* at 577–78.

# V. Rules of Plan Interpretation

## A. Application of Federal Common Law

The Second Circuit interprets an ERISA plan "as a whole, giving terms their plain meanings." *Fay v. Oxford Health Plan,* 287 F.3d 96, 104 (2d Cir. 2002). *See also Perreca v. Gluck,* 295 F.3d 215, 223 (2d Cir. 2002) (unambiguous language in ERISA plan interpreted and enforced "in accordance with its plain meaning") (citation omitted).

## B. Application of *Contra Proferentem*

The Second Circuit has incorporated the *contra proferentem* rule of contract construction (construing ambiguities in plan language against the drafter) into the federal common law of ERISA. However, the rule applies only when the court's review is de novo. *See Fay,* 287 F.3d at 104; *IV Servs. of Am. Inc. v. Trustees of Am. Consulting Eng'rs Council Trust Fund,* 136 F.3d 114, 121 (2d Cir. 1998); *Pagan v. NYNEX Pension Plan,* 52 F.3d 438, 443 (2d Cir. 1995).

## C. Deference Afforded to an Administrator's Interpretation of a Plan

If the administrator is granted discretionary authority, its interpretation of a plan term is to be given deference. The Second Circuit has stated that "[w]hen both the plan administrator and a spurned claimant 'offer rational, though conflicting, interpretations of plan provisions, the [administrator's] interpretation must be allowed to control.'" *Pulvers v. First Unum Life Ins. Co.,* 210 F.3d 89, 92–93 (2d Cir. 2000), quoting *O'Shea v. First Manhattan Thrift Plan & Trust,* 55 F.2d 109, 112 (2d Cir. 1995). However, "where the administrator 'impose[s] a standard not required by the plan's provisions, or interpret[s] the plan in a manner inconsistent with its plain words, . . . [its] actions may well be found to be arbitrary and capricious.'" *Pulvers,* 210 F.3d at 93, quoting *O'Shea,* 55 F.3d at 112. Nevertheless, courts have held that it is not unreasonable for a fiduciary with discretionary authority to require objective medical evidence as proof of disability. *See Scannell v. Metro. Life Ins. Co.,* 2003 WL 22722954, at *5 (S.D.N.Y. Nov. 18, 2003); *Alakozai v. Allstate Ins. Co.,* 2000 WL 325685, at *7 (S.D.N.Y. Mar. 28, 2000).

### D.  Other Rules of Plan or Contract Interpretation

There are no other rules of plan or contract interpretation.

## VI.  Discovery

### A.  Limitations on Discovery

Because the Second Circuit has held that the court's scope of evidentiary review in an ERISA plan benefits case is generally limited to the administrative record (see Section VII, below), most district courts have held that discovery is narrowly limited to such matters as determining the completeness of the claim file or clarifying codes or abbreviations found therein. *See, e.g., Maida v. Life Ins. Co. of N.A.,* 949 F. Supp. 1087, 1091 (S.D.N.Y. 1997) (holding that employee challenging plan administrator's denial of benefits was not entitled to depose claim adjuster where employee made no showing of how adjuster's testimony might be expected to raise material issue of fact). The parameters of permissible discovery are not strictly fixed, however. Even in *Miller v. United Welfare Fund,* 72 F.2d 1066 (2d Cir. 1995), where the Second Circuit announced that the court's review under the arbitrary and capricious standard is limited to the administrative record, and held that the district court had erred in considering extrinsic evidence (*see id.* at 1071) the court relied on the deposition testimony of the fund's administrator as support for its conclusion that the trustees' decision was arbitrary and capricious. *Id.* at 1072. *See also Nagele v. Elec. Data Sys. Corp.,* 193 F.R.D. 94, 103–05 (W.D.N.Y. 2000) (holding that standard discovery devices under rules of civil procedure are available in ERISA plan benefits cases to determine completeness and meaning of administrative record).

### B.  Discovery and Conflict of Interest

Limited discovery may be permitted on the issue of whether an administrator's decision was influenced by a conflict of interest. "On such an issue," the Second Circuit has commented, "which is distinct from the reasonableness of the plan administrator's decision, the district court will not be confined to the administrative record." *Zervos v. Verizon N.Y., Inc.,* 252 F.3d 163, 174 (2d Cir. 2001). *See also Samedy v. First UNUM Life Ins. Co. of Am.,* 2006 WL 624889, at *2 (E.D.N.Y. May 10, 2006) (granting some limited discovery to assist in determining whether actual conflict of interest influenced claim decision); *Sheehan v. Metro. Life Ins. Co.,* 2002 WL

1424592, at *4 (S.D.N.Y. 2002) (concluding that proper subject for discovery was whether plan administrator was conflicted when it terminated plaintiff's benefits). In a recent case where plaintiff argued that she should have been permitted to conduct discovery on the conflict of interest issue, however, the Second Circuit, while noting the propriety of such discovery in some cases, affirmed the district court's denial of discovery where plaintiff did not show "good cause" for her request. *See Wagner v. First Union Life Ins. Co.*, 2004 WL 1303637, at *1 (2d Cir. 2004).

## VII. Evidence

### A. Scope of Evidence under Standards of Review

The Second Circuit's review has held that when the arbitrary and capricious standard of review applies, a district court is limited in the scope of its evidentiary review and may consider only the administrative record that was before the fiduciary at the time of its claim decision. *Miller v. United Welfare Fund*, 72 F.3d 1066, 1071 (2d Cir. 1995). The court explained, "This rule is consistent with the fact that nothing 'in the legislature history suggests that Congress intended that federal district courts would function as substitute plan administrators' and with the ERISA 'goal of prompt resolution of claims by the fiduciary.'" *Id.* at 1071, quoting *Perry v. Simplicity Eng'g*, 900 F.2d 963, 967 (6th Cir. 1990).

Consequently, the Second Circuit has held on multiple occasions that district courts erred in considering evidence outside the administrative record. *See, e.g., Zervos v. Verizon N.Y., Inc.*, 277 F.3d 635, 646 (2d Cir. 2002) (holding that district court erred in considering testimony of insurer's experts that had not been before administrator at time of its claim decision); *Krizek v. Cigna Group Ins.*, 345 F.3d 91, 99–100 (2d Cir. 2003) (vacating decision of district court, which expressly considered plaintiff's demeanor during testimony at trial in upholding denial of benefits); *see also Klecher v. Metro. Life Ins. Co.*, 2003 WL 21314033, at *7 (S.D.N.Y. 2003) (rejecting consideration of affidavits of co-workers offered in support of plaintiff's summary judgment motion on her benefits claim, since affidavits not part of administrative record).

When the de novo standard of review is applied, the Second Circuit has held that additional evidence may be considered in reviewing an issue of plan interpretation. *See Masella v. Blue Cross & Blue Shield of Conn. Inc.*, 936 F.2d 98, 103–05 (2d Cir. 1991). In *DeFelice v. American International Life Assurance Co. of New York*, 112 F.3d 61 (2d Cir. 1997), the Supreme Court held that when conducting a de novo review of factual issues, it is within the discretion of the court to admit evidence not available at the administrative level if "good cause" is shown. *Id.* at 67. A "demonstrated conflict of interest" on the part of the administrator is an example of "good cause" warranting the introduction of additional evidence. *Id.* Moreover, the Second Circuit noted, "the plaintiff need not demonstrate that the conflict caused her actual prejudice in order for the court to consider the conflict to be 'good cause.'" *Id.* In *Locher v. Unum Life Insurance Co. of America*, 389 F.3d 288 (2d Cir. 2004), the Second Circuit clarified its holding in *DeFelice,* stating that a potential conflict of interest (such as where the claims reviewer and claims payor are the same entity) does not per se establish "good cause" to consider evidence outside the administrative reward. 289 F.3d at 294–95. The Second Circuit cautioned that "a finding of a conflicted administrator alone should not be translated *necessarily* into a finding of good cause." *Id.* at 296 (emphasis in original). In *Locher,* the Second Circuit nevertheless upheld the district court's finding of good cause to consider evidence outside the administrative record based upon the insurer/administrator's inadequate claim review procedures. *Id.* The incompleteness of an administrative record may also constitute "good cause" for admitting additional evidence. *See Zervos,* 277 F.3d at 646–47; *see also Juliano v. Health Maint. Org. of N.J.,* 221 F.3d 279 (2d Cir. 2000) (holding that failure of HMO to state in denial letter that reason for denial was lack of proof of medical necessity was "good cause" to admit additional evidence on that issue).

The plaintiff bears the burden of demonstrating "good cause" to expand the administrative record. *See Krizek,* 345 F.3d at 98. The Second Circuit has held that the plaintiff must allege facts "with sufficient specificity" to support the existence of "good cause" to admit evidence beyond the administrative record. *Id.* at 98 n.2. The Second Circuit has further commented that a district court should not exercise its discretion to expand the record in cases where a party fails to demonstrate "beyond mere speculation or conjecture" that the administrative record is inadequate. *Id.,* citing *Hotaling v. Teachers Ins. Annuity Ass'n of Conn.,* 62 F. Supp. 2d 731, 738 (N.D.N.Y. 1999).

Even when "good cause" is shown to exist, "the decision whether to consider information outside the administrative record is a discretionary one." *Critchlow v. First Union Life Ins. Co. of Am.,* 340 F.3d 130, 133 n.2 (2d Cir. 2003), *withdrawn and vacated on reconsideration on other grounds,* 378 F.3d 246 (2d Cir. 2004). For example, in *Suozzo v. Bergreen,* 2003 WL 22387083, at *4–5 (S.D.N.Y. 2003), the court concluded that even if the existence of a conflict of interest constituted "good cause," it would not exercise its discretion to expand the administrative record because the reason that the proffered evidence was not in the record was the claimant's failure to contest the administrator's reliance on a certain "model" plan amendment. *See also Critchlow v. First Union Life Ins. Co. of Am.,* 198 F. Supp. 2d 318, 322 (W.D.N.Y. 2002) (refusing to admit additional evidence because plaintiff offered no good reason why she could not have submitted such evidence to administrator before it rendered its decision), *aff'd,* 340 F.3d 130 (2d Cir. 2003); *Kaus-Rogers v. Union Life Ins. Co. of Am.,* 2004 WL 1166640, at *3–4 (W.D.N.Y. 2004) (holding that denial letter's technical noncompliance with ERISA's notice regulations did not justify admission of evidence outside administrative record); *Muller v. First Union Life Ins. Co. of Am.,* 166 F. Supp. 2d 706, 711 (N.D.N.Y. 2001) (concluding that plaintiff had not demonstrated "good cause" because she failed to state why additional evidence could not have been submitted during two-and-one-half-year administrative claim process).

However, in *Sheehan v. Metropolitan Life Insurance Co.,* 2003 WL 22290230, at *3 (S.D.N.Y. 2003), the district court granted the employee's motion to supplement the administrative record with additional medical reports, finding that "good cause" existed because plaintiff's treating physicians were not afforded an opportunity to review video surveillance tapes prior to MetLife's termination of his benefits.

## B. Evidentiary Value of Social Security Determinations

While an award of benefits by the Social Security Administration may be considered by an ERISA administrator if included in the administrative record, courts within the Second Circuit have held that the Social Security determination is not binding on a plan. *See, e.g., Billinger v. Bell Atlantic,* 240 F. Supp. 2d 274, 285 (S.D.N.Y. 2003) (holding that the decision of the Social Security Administration granting disability benefits is "but one piece of evidence [to be considered by plan administrator], and is far from determinative"); *Martin v. E.I. DuPont de Nemours,* 999 F. Supp. 416, 424 (W.D.N.Y. 1998) (holding that while a favorable determination by the Social Security Administration may be considered, it is not binding on the plan); *Pagan v. NYNEX Pension Plan,* 846 F. Supp. 19, 21 (S.D.N.Y. 1994) (same), *aff'd,* 52 F.3d 438 (2d Cir. 1995). Likewise, the definition of disability utilized in the Social Security Administration's determination is not binding on an ERISA plan. *See Kocsis v. Standard Ins. Co.,* 142 F. Supp. 2d 241, 255 (D. Conn. 2001). *See also Kunstenaar v. Conn. Gen. Life Ins. Co.,* 902 F.2d 181, 184 (2d Cir. 1990) (holding that statutory definitions of "disability," such as one used by the Social Security Administration, are not binding on ERISA plans).

# VIII. Procedural Aspects of ERISA Practice

## A. Methods of Adjudication

The procedural aspect of litigating an ERISA case in the Second Circuit is both relatively simple and strangely complex, depending on the standard of review. If the facts of the case warrant, a motion for summary judgment under Rule 56 of the Federal Rules of Civil Procedure is entirely appropriate for a case governed by ERISA. *See Fay v. Oxford Health Plan,* 287 F.3d 96 (2d Cir 2002); *Todd v. Aetna Health Plans,* 31 Fed. Appx. 13 (2d Cir. 2002) (both affirming summary judgment motions). As the court's review of a claim determination is limited to the administrative record where the arbitrary and capricious standard of review applies with respect to a motion for summary judgment, the district court does not review the record to determine if there is an issue of fact but rather "sits in effect as an appellate court to determine whether the denial of ERISA benefits was arbitrary and capricious." *Rizk v. Long Term Disability Plan of the Dun & Bradstreet Corp.,* 862 F. Supp. 783, 791 (E.D.N.Y. 1994).

To distinguish this type of summary judgment motion from the more traditional Rule 56 "issue of fact" motion, some litigants have styled an ERISA motion as a "motion for judgment on the administrative record" regardless of whether the standard of review is arbitrary and capricious or de novo. *See Casey v. First Unum Life Ins. Co.,* 2004 U.S. Dist. LEXIS 5304 (N.D.N.Y. 2004) (granting motion for judgment on the administrative record); *see also Henar v. First Unum Life Ins. Co.,* 2002 U.S. Dist. LEXIS 17585 (S.D.N.Y. 2002) (plaintiff's motion for judgment on the administrative record granted).

The Second Circuit has noted that a motion for judgment on the administrative record "[is] a motion that does not appear to be authorized in the Federal Rules of

Civil Procedure." *Muller v. First Unum Life Ins. Co.*, 341 F.3d 119, 124 (2d Cir. 2003). However, the court stated that such a motion could be converted into a Rule 56 motion for summary judgment by the district court or in cases where a district court had *already denied* summary judgment. The Second Circuit held that a motion for judgment on the administrative record could be equated to a request for a bench trial "on the papers," with the district court acting as the finder of fact and that this form of bench trial was entirely proper. *Id.,* citing *Connors v. Conn. Gen. Life Ins. Co.,* 272 F.3d 127, 134 (2d Cir. 2001).

If a court denies summary judgment, it generally remands the case back to the administrator for further review in accordance with its findings. Remand is the proper step to take "if upon review a district court concludes that the [trustee's or administrator's] decision was arbitrary and capricious." *Miller v. United Welfare Fund,* 72 F.3d 1066, 1071 (2d Cir. 1995). For example, in the case of *Peterson v. Continental Casualty Co.,* the district court denied full summary judgment but held that Continental improperly defined Peterson's regular occupation as the position created by CBS to accommodate Peterson's disability. Because Continental evaluated Peterson's claim against the wrong occupation, the district court remanded the claim back to the claim administrator to determine whether Peterson's medical condition—evaluated against the duties of his "regular occupation" rather than his temporary accommodation—rendered him eligible for benefits under the terms of the long-term plan. *See Peterson v. Cont'l Cas. Co.,* 77 F. Supp. 2d 420, 429 (S.D.N.Y. 2000).

Under an arbitrary and capricious review, a district court also has the discretion to order that benefits be paid or reinstated if it concludes that no new evidence or consideration would produce a reasonable conclusion permitting denial of the claim or if "remand would otherwise be a 'useless formality.'" *See Miller,* 72 F.3d at 1071.

District courts within the Second Circuit have apparently accepted *Muller*'s premise that a court can either treat a motion for judgment on the administrative record as a Rule 56 motion for summary judgment or as a motion for a bench trial "on the papers," depending on the status of the case. *See Kaus-Rogers v. Unum Life Ins. Co. of Am.,* 2004 U.S. Dist. LEXIS 9797 (W.D.N.Y. 2004), citing *Muller,* 341 F.3d at 124; *see also Casey,* 2004 U.S. Dist. LEXIS 5304 (granting motion for judgment on the administrative record); *Charles v. First Unum Life Ins. Co.,* 2004 U.S. Dist. LEXIS 9307 (W.D.N.Y. 2004) (treating a motion for "judgment based on the administrative record" as a motion for summary judgment under Rule 56(c)).

If the court treats the motion as a request for a "bench trial on the papers," the district court has an obligation to make explicit findings of fact and conclusions of law explaining the reasons for its decision as well as "judge the credibility of witnesses," FED. R. CIV. P. 52(a). If the district court does not make explicit findings of fact or conclusions of law in support of its denial of a claim, the Second Circuit must vacate and remand back to the district court and has done so in ERISA cases. *See, e.g., Sullivan,* 82 F.3d at 1261; *Grimo v. Blue Cross/Blue Shield of Vt.,* 34 F.3d 148, 152–53 (2d Cir. 1994). The court's factual findings will be subject to review for "clear error" on appeal and the legal conclusions reviewed de novo. *See LoPresti v. Terwilliger,* 126 F.3d 34, 39–40 (2d Cir. 1997).

Under the de novo standard of review, the question before the court is not whether the administrator abused its discretion but instead whether the plaintiff has presented sufficient evidence to demonstrate that he or she is entitled to benefits under the policy. If the case is not resolved on summary judgment, the court then becomes the fact finder in a procedure sometimes referred to as an ERISA trial de novo. There is a conflict among the district courts within the Second Circuit as to the appropriate method of de novo review. For example, the following types of proceedings have been utilized for a de novo "trial":

- Bench trial on the record supplemented with witness testimony. *Locher v. Unum Life Ins. Co. of Am.,* 2002 U.S. Dist. LEXIS 3745 (March 2002) (three-day bench trial was held).
- "Summary" bench trial based upon written submissions outside of the administrative record. *Schwartz v. Oxford Health Plans, Inc.,* 175 F. Supp. 2d 581 (S.D.N.Y. 2001); *Meyer v. Ins. Co. of Am.,* 1998 WL 709854 (S.D.N.Y. 1998).
- A de novo review of the administrative record without submission of any additional evidence. *Connors v. Conn. Gen. Life Ins. Co.,* 2000 U.S. Dist. LEXIS 12962 (S.D.N.Y. Sept. 8, 2000); *Moore v. INA Life Ins. Co.,* 66 F. Supp. 2d 378 (E.D.N.Y. 1999).

As should be clear from the foregoing, the scope of an ERISA trial varies, and it is difficult to reach a uniform conclusion about the appropriate method for court review of a benefits decision under the de novo standard of review. The evidence before the court will be generally limited to the administrative record unless the court determines that additional evidence is necessary to conduct an adequate de novo review. *See Zervos v. Verizon N.Y., Inc.,* 277 F.3d 635, 646 (2d Cir. 2002) ("Even where the district court exercises de novo review of the plan administrator's determination, the district court 'ought not' to accept additional evidence absent 'good cause.'" (quoting *DeFelice,* 112 F.3d at 66)). Once again, the court's role is to provide, in effect, a bench trial with the judge acting as the finder of fact. *Muller,* 341 F.3d at 124.

### B. Reported ERISA Trials

Under *Sullivan,* regardless of the standard of review, there is no right to a jury trial on an ERISA benefits claim in the Second Circuit. *See Sullivan v. LTV Aerospace & Def. Co.,* 82 F.3d 1251, 1257 (2d Cir. 1996); *see also DeFelice v. Am. Int'l Life Assurance Co. of N.Y.,* 112 F.3d 61, 66 (2d. Cir. 1997). The basis of the decision is that the Second Circuit has held that ERISA actions are equitable, not legal, in nature. *Id.*

Recent Supreme Court jurisprudence has raised the specter of the possibility of a right to a jury trial with regard to breach of fiduciary duty claims under ERISA. Since the Supreme Court's decision in *Great-West Life & Annuity Ins. Co. v. Knudson,* 534 U.S. 204 (2002), which revived the distinction between suits in law and equity, *Knudson,* 534 U.S. at 212–13, courts have struggled to classify claims as legal or equitable and treat them accordingly. *See, e.g., Pereira v. Farace,* 413 F.3d 330, 340 (2d Cir. 2005) ("[T]he Supreme Court's decision [in *Knudson*] . . . reconfigured the legal landscape of restitution."). In *Pereira,* a non-ERISA case, the Second Circuit held that an action for breach of fiduciary duty sounded in law, not equity, and as such, there was a right to a jury trial. *Pereira,* 413 F.3d at 341. The combination of *Knudson* and *Pereira* has led to speculation that the Second Circuit's holding in *Sullivan* may be on tremulous grounds with regard to breach of fiduciary claims, but at present, courts in the Second Circuit continue to rely on *Sullivan. See Allison v. UNUM,* 2005 U.S. Dist. LEXIS 3465, at *41 (E.D.N.Y. 2005) ("This court finds that [*Knudson*] has not changed the law in this District regarding jury trials in ERISA actions."); *Peck v. Aetna Life Ins. Co.,* 2005 U.S. Dist. LEXIS 35605 at *11–13 (D. Conn. 2005) (*Knudson* does not change Second Circuit precedent that there is no right to a jury trial in a suit brought under ERISA).

Although jury trials are not conducted, the longstanding tradition in common law courts is that a trial court may consult with an advisory jury during a bench trial as long as the court retains the ultimate responsibility for findings of fact and conclusions. FED. R. CIV. P. 39(c); *Lumbermens Mut. Cas. Co. of Ill. v. Timms & Howard, Inc.,* 108 F.2d 497 (2d Cir. 1939); WRIGHT & MILLER, FEDERAL PRACTICE & PROCEDURE: CIVIL 2d § 2335 (1990). Although there appears to have been two such advisory juries allowed in the ERISA context in the Second Circuit, the "advisory jury" was deemed "advisory" only *after* the jury had heard the case and the Second Circuit had ruled that there was no right to a jury trial in ERISA cases.

The district court in *Sullivan* permitted a jury trial. On appeal, the Second Circuit held that jury trials were not permitted in ERISA. Rather than remanding the case for a new "bench" trial, the Second Circuit chose to view the jury in *Sullivan* as an advisory jury and remanded the case to the district court, with instructions to explain how the findings were made. *Sullivan,* 82 F.2d at 1261. In *DeFelice,* the case was tried before a jury prior to the *Sullivan* decision being issued. In its opinion, the Second Circuit noted that based upon its decision in *Sullivan,* DeFelice did not have a right to have her claim tried by a jury; however, because she had already received a jury trial, the question was more properly stated in the inverse: Did defendant American International have a right to a bench trial? It held that the defendant did have this right as the claim was equitable in nature. Once again, rather than ordering that a new trial be conducted, the Second Circuit treated the jury as if it was an advisory jury and remanded the case to the district court with instructions to make its own factual findings and conclusions. *DeFelice,* 112 F.3d at 66. The Second Circuit in *DeFelice* recognized: "With regard to the role of the jury in this case, we note, as did *Sullivan,* the longstanding tradition in common law courts that a trial court may consult with an advisory jury during a bench trial so long as the court retains the ultimate responsibility for findings of fact and conclusions." *Id.* at 65, apparently giving lukewarm support to the proposition that a bench trial with an advisory jury was appropriate in an ERISA matter. However, factually speaking, the only times advisory juries were used in Second Circuit ERISA cases was when a jury had been allowed, pre-*Sullivan,* in the first place. There are no Second Circuit or district court cases post-*DeFelice* noting that an advisory jury was used in an ERISA matter.

## IX.  Fiduciary Liability Claims

### A.  Definition of Fiduciary

An individual or entity who has any discretionary authority or discretionary control respecting management or administration of an ERISA plan or control over disposition of its assets is a fiduciary. A person who renders investment advice for direct or indirect compensation is also a fiduciary. 29 U.S.C. § 1002(21)(A). ERISA permits an ERISA fiduciary to wear "two hats," for example, as employer and fiduciary. *Varity Corp. v. Howe,* 516 U.S. 489, 498 (1996); *Engler v. Cendant Corp. & Int'l Bus. Machs. Corp.,* 2006 WL 1408583, *7 (E.D.N.Y. 2003). Courts will look not just at titles or formal job descriptions but at the actual daily operation of the plan and the activities such operation entails. *Blatt v. Marshall & Lassman,* 812 F.2d 810, 812 (2d Cir. 1987); *Yurevich v. Sikorsky Aircraft Div., United Techs. Corp.,* 51 F. Supp. 2d 144, 151 (D. Conn. 1999); *Cerasoli v. Xomed, Inc.,* 47 F. Supp. 2d 401, 407 (W.D.N.Y. 1999).

In sum, ERISA defines a fiduciary "in functional terms of control and authority over the plan." The "threshold question" in an action charging breach of a fiduciary duty under ERISA "is not whether the actions of some person employed to provide services under a plan adversely affected a plan beneficiary's interest, but whether that person was acting as a fiduciary (that is, performing a fiduciary function) when taking the action subject to complaint." *In re Worldcom, Inc. ERISA Litig.,* 263 F. Supp. 2d 745, 757 (S.D.N.Y. 2003) (citations omitted).

### B.  Definition of Fiduciary Duties

There are four specific duties imposed upon fiduciaries, who must act solely in the interests of participants and beneficiaries. Fiduciaries must act (1) for the exclusive purpose of providing benefits to participants and beneficiaries and defraying reasonable expenses of administering the plan; (2) with the care, skill, prudence, and diligence under the circumstances then prevailing that a prudent person acting in a like capacity and familiar with such matters would use in the conduct of an enterprise of like character and with like aims; (3) by diversifying the investments of a plan to minimize risks of large losses; and (4) in accordance with plan documents. ERISA § 404(a)(1)(A)–(D).

The Second Circuit recently held that reliance upon erroneous information will not necessarily be considered a breach of fiduciary duty. *Hart v. Equitable Life Assurance Soc'y,* 75 Fed. Appx. 51, 2003 U.S. App. Lexis 19397 (2d Cir. 2003). A plan fiduciary may rely upon information furnished by persons who perform ministerial functions for a plan as long as the fiduciary acted prudently in the selection and retention of such person. Prudence in such a situation would entail having no reason "in the exercise of ordinary care . . . to doubt the competence, integrity or responsibility of such persons." *Id.* at *2 (citations omitted).

However, in a more recent case, the U.S. District Court for the District of Connecticut made it clear that misrepresenting to employees facts concerning a company's intentions to offer special retirement plans was a breach of fiduciary duty where the fiduciary knowingly and significantly deceived "a plan's beneficiaries in order to save the employer money at the beneficiaries' expense." *Broga v. Ne. Utils.*, 315 F. Supp. 2d 212, 255 (D. Conn. 2004), quoting *Varity Corp. v. Howe,* 516 U.S. 489, 506 (1996). The court held that the defendant had deliberately withheld critical information from employees, "including those charged with counseling other employees about retirement." *Id.* at 243.

Although the key to determining if a person is a fiduciary is whether his duties include discretion and are not merely ministerial, such a person need not have absolute discretion with respect to a benefit plan to be considered a fiduciary. *Blatt,* 812 F.2d at 812. A person or entity need only have "sufficient control over at least a part of the [plan] assets to create a fiduciary relationship." *New York State Teamsters Council Health & Hosp. Fund v. Centrus Pharmacy Solutions,* 235 F. Supp. 2d 123, 126 (N.D.N.Y. 2002), citing to *United States v. Glick,* 142 F.3d 520, 528 (2d Cir. 1998). "[F]iduciary status exists with respect to any activity enumerated in the statute over which the entity exercises discretion or control." *Blatt* at 812.

## C. Fiduciary Liability in the Context of Health and Disability Claims

There are numerous Second Circuit cases that hold that fiduciary liability may arise in the context of health and disability claims. *See, e.g., Dobson v. Hartford Fin. Servs.,* 196 F. Supp. 2d 152, 165–74 (D. Conn. 2002); *Am. Med. Ass'n. v. United Healthcare Corp.,* 2002 WL 31413668 (S.D.N.Y. 2002); *Geller v. County Line Auto Sales, Inc.,* 86 F.3d 18 (2d Cir. 1996); *Sunderlin v. First Reliance Standard Life Ins. Co.,* 235 F. Supp. 2d 222 (W.D.N.Y. 2002); *Engler v. Cendant Corp. & Int'l Bus. Machs. Corp.,* 2006 WL 1408583, *7 (E.D.N.Y. 2003).

## D. Remedies for Breach of Fiduciary Duty

With regard to remedies against fiduciaries, § 409 of ERISA provides that any fiduciary who breaches any imposed responsibilities, obligations, or duties "shall be personally liable to make good . . . on any losses to the plan resulting from each such breach, and to restore to such plan any profits of such fiduciary . . . and shall be subject to such other equitable or remedial relief as the court may deem appropriate; including removal of such fiduciary." This section is enforced through § 502(a)(2), which authorizes the Secretary of Labor or any participant, beneficiary, or fiduciary to seek appropriate relief. The type of relief available under this section is categorized only as "appropriate" and is not limited to equitable relief. The plan is not authorized by this section to seek relief on its own behalf. Actions under this section may be brought only against plan fiduciaries. *Geller v. County Auto Sales, Inc.,* 86 F.3d 18, 20–22 (2d Cir. 1996). There is no private cause of action that may be brought by participants under this section. Such actions may be brought only on behalf of the plan itself. *Mass. Mut. Life Ins. Co. v. Russell,* 473 U.S. 134, 140–41 (1985).

There is, however, a private cause of action against a fiduciary (or other persons) under § 502(a)(3) for equitable relief, and in the Second Circuit such a claim may be made even though a claim has also been made to recover plan benefits under § 502(a)(1)(B). *Devlin v. Empire Blue Cross & Blue Shield,* 274 F.3d 76, 89–90 (2d Cir. 2001). Although only injunctive and other appropriate equitable relief is authorized under § 502(a)(3), a recent case from the District of Connecticut held that an award of interest, or disgorgement of the fiduciary's profits, for delayed payment of benefits under a long-term disability plan may be available as an equitable remedy. *Dobson v. Hartford Fin. Servs.,* 196 F. Supp. 2d 152, 165–74 (D. Conn. 2002). *See also Am. Med. Ass'n v. United Healthcare Corp.,* 2002 WL 31413668, at *7. Restitution is also available as an equitable remedy under § 502(a)(3) where the defendant wrongfully obtained a benefit, or had passively received a benefit, which the retention of would be unconscionable. *Geller,* 86 F.3d at 22.

### E.  Contribution and Indemnity Claims among Fiduciaries

The Second Circuit permits contribution and indemnification claims among cofiduciaries. *Smith v. Local 819 I.B.T. Pension Plan,* 291 F.3d 236, 240–41 (2d Cir. 2002) (although Congress created no explicit cause of action for contribution or indemnity, court's reading of ERISA is that Congress intended to develop federal common law based upon principles of trust law). *See also Sunderlin v. First Reliance Standard Life Ins. Co.,* 235 F. Supp. 2d 222, 236–38 (W.D.N.Y. 2002) (concerning denial of long-term disability payments). However, "ERISA does not provide a cofiduciary with a statutory claim against a cofiduciary." *GCO Servs., LLC,* 324 B.R. 459, 464 (S.D.N.Y. 2005). "Knowing conduct is a prerequisite for cofiduciary liability under ERISA." *Polaroid ERISA Litig.,* 362 F. Supp. 2d 461, 470 (S.D.N.Y. 2005); *Prentiss v. Wasley Prods., Inc.,* 2005 WL 563091, at *3 (D. Conn. 2005); *In re Worldcom, Inc. ERISA Litig.,* 354 F. Supp. 2d 423, 445 (S.D.N.Y. 2005).

### F.  ERISA Claims against Nonfiduciaries

The Second Circuit has held that a nonfiduciary may be a proper defendant under § 502(a)(3) if it would be a proper defendant under "'the common law of trusts.'" *Carlson v. Principal Fin. Group,* 320 F.3d 301, 307–08 (2d Cir. 2003), quoting *Harris Trust & Savs. Bank v. Salomon Smith Barney, Inc.,* 530 U.S. 238, 246 (2000). A nonfiduciary may be liable where the nonfiduciary is "a transferee of ill-gotten trust assets . . . , and then only when the transferee . . . knew or should have known of the existence of the trust and the circumstances that rendered the transfer in breach of the trust." *Carlson,* 320 F.3d at 308, quoting *Harris,* 230 U.S. at 251. *See also Lee v. Burkhart,* 991 F.2d 1004, 1010 (2d Cir. 1993) (claim involving health benefits). *But see Smith v. Champion Int'l Corp.,* 220 F. Supp. 2d 124 (D. Conn. 2002) (corporation that employer hired to obtain evidence and information to use to deny or terminate long-term disability benefits was a nonfiduciary and could not be held liable under ERISA.) "Nothing in the statute, however permits a nonfiduciary to be held liable for breaches of fiduciary duties by others. . . ." Nor is there an implied cause of action under the theory of *respondeat superior. In re AOL Time Warner, Inc. Secs. & "ERISA" Litig.,* 2005 WL 563166, at *4 n.5 (S.D.N.Y. 2005).

## X.  Attorneys' Fees

### A.  Criteria for Awarding Attorneys' Fees

The Second Circuit has held that ERISA's attorneys' fee provision should be liberally construed to protect the statutory purpose of vindicating retirement rights. *Chambless v. Masters, Mates & Pilots Pension Plan,* 815 F.2d 869, 872 (2d Cir. 1987).

The Second Circuit has aligned with the majority of the circuits in holding that the decision of whether to award attorneys' fees in an ERISA action is ordinarily based on five factors: (1) the degree of the offending party's culpability or bad faith; (2) the ability of the offending party to satisfy an award of attorneys' fees; (3) whether an award of fees would deter other persons from acting similarly under like circumstances; (4) the relative merits of the parties' positions; and (5) whether the action conferred a common benefit on a group of plan participants. *Chambless,* 815 F.2d at 871; *Miller v. United Welfare Fund,* 72 F.3d 1066, 1074 (2d Cir. 1995); *Salovaara v. Eckert,* 222 F.3d 19, 27–28 (2d Cir. 2000).

An award of attorneys' fees is not automatic and rests within the discretion of the trial court. A court may decline to award fees to a plaintiff if it finds that the defendant acted neither oppressively nor in bad faith. *Miller,* 72 F.3d at 1066; *Lucaskevge v. Mollenberg,* 11 Empl. Benefits Cas. (BNA) 1355 (W.D.N.Y. 1989); *Leyda v. Allied Signal, Inc.,* 322 F.3d 199 (2d Cir. 2003) (denying fees where defendant's actions were not unreasonable and where resolution of the case was close). Similarly, that a defendant's position on coverage is subsequently held to be incorrect does not automatically warrant an award of attorneys' fees. *Lauder v. First Unum Life Ins. Co.,* 284 F.3d 375, 382–83 (2d Cir. 2001). In reviewing the *Chambless* factors with regard to the "common benefit" criterion, the Second Circuit has held that a district court should also consider if any legal precedent was established by the litigation and "whether the legal precedent established by [this] case and the benefits that precedent might confer on another plan participants make an award of attorney fees appropriate." *Chapman v. Choicecare Long Island Long Term Disability Income Plan,* 2005 U.S. App. LEXIS 29193, at *7 (2d Cir. 2005).

In the Second Circuit, a court's authority to award fees is generally limited to fees incurred subsequent to litigation and any court-ordered remand. *Peterson v. Cont'l Cas. Co.,* 282 F.3d 112, 119 (2d Cir. 2002) (holding that fees may be awarded during a court-ordered remand; however, fees may not be awarded for work performed during the original administrative review of the claim, which occurred prior to the litigation). Where administrative proceedings are not ordered by the court, fees could be awarded for time devoted to such proceedings if the work was "useful and of the type ordinarily necessary" to secure the final result obtained from the litigation. *Trs. of the Eastern States Health & Welfare Fund v. Crystal Art Corp.,* 2004 U.S. Dist. LEXIS 8932 (S.D.N.Y. 2004); *but cf. Aminoff v. Ally & Gargano Inc.,* 20 Empl. Benefits Cas. (BNA) 2172, 1996 U.S. Dist. LEXIS 17372 (S.D.N.Y. 1996) (holding that plaintiffs could not recover attorneys' fees incurred in settling a pension fund dispute where no litigation was ever instituted).

At least one district court has held that awarding attorneys' fees to a competing claimant is inappropriate in an interpleader action brought by plan fiduciaries faced with competing claims to plan benefits. *Lucaskevge,* 11 Empl. Benefits Cas. (BNA) at 1355 (noting that an award to the prevailing claimant would be a likely abuse of discretion in that the plan fiduciaries had not acted in bad faith but in fact had acted in a laudatory manner).

## B. Fees Awarded to Plan Fiduciaries

Citing 29 U.S.C. § 1132(g)(1), the Second Circuit has acknowledged that a court has discretion to award attorneys' fees and costs to either party in an ERISA action and that the five-factor test is applicable regardless of which party seeks attorneys' fees. *See* 29 U.S.C. § 1132(g)(1); *Anita Founds., Inc. v. ILGWU Nat'l Ret. Fund,* 902 F.2d 185, 188–89 (2d Cir. 1990).

The Second Circuit has been willing to uphold an award of attorneys' fees to successful defendants when the factors balance in favor of doing so, such as where a plaintiff acts in bad faith or pursues a meritless claim. *See, e.g., Seitzman v. Sun Life Ins. Co. of Canada, Inc.,* 311 F.3d 477, 485 (2d Cir. 2002) (approving a fee award to a defendant insurance company where evidence indicated that the plaintiff, a physician who sought long-term disability benefits under an ERISA plan, had falsified testimony and otherwise acted in bad faith); *Anita Founds., Inc.,* 902 F.2d at 189–91 (upholding fee award where, inter alia, plaintiffs did not demonstrate a colorable legal position and brought suit in direct contravention to previous settlement agreements); *Salovaara v. Eckert,* 222 F.3d 19, 31–32 (2d. Cir. 2000) (indicating it would affirm a defendant's fee award if the plaintiff acted in bad faith). However, the Second Circuit has also held that "the bad faith prong is not automatically dispositive of a claim for attorney fees." *Chapman,* 2005 U.S. App. LEXIS 29193, at *7.

## C. Calculation of Attorneys' Fees

In the Second Circuit, "the lodestar method is ordinarily the starting point in determining the amounts of fees that may be awarded." *Seitzman,* 311 F.3d at 487. It is calculated by multiplying together two figures: "(1) the reasonable hourly rate; and (2) the number of hours reasonably expended." *Id.* The fee award may not "reflect work done only in connection with unrelated claims on which the party did not succeed." *Id.* at 487. Further, the compensable time must be "neither excessive nor duplicative." *Id.*

The party requesting the fee award bears the evidentiary burden for establishing an appropriate rate and documenting the time reasonably expended, but in the Second Circuit the "district judge may rely in part on his or her own knowledge of hourly rates charged in [the] community and is not limited to the submitted evidence of prevailing rates." *Chambless,* 885 F.2d at 1059. The flexibility of the standard allows for different rates, depending on the lawyer, the firm, and the court's assessment of the attorney's skill and success; however, only work properly done by attorneys may be compensated at attorney rates. The Second Circuit has stated that an attorney's status as a solo practitioner is not by itself a valid reason to reduce the hourly rate. *McDonald v. Pension Plan of the NYSA-ILA Pension Trust Fund,* 2006 U.S. App. LEXIS 13965, at *13 n.6 (2d Cir. 2006).

In *McDonald,* the Second Circuit expressed its strong disapproval of the district court's use of a "blended hourly rate" to calculate attorney's fees for a solo practitioner and to distinguish between work that could have been done by a hypothetical junior associate and work that could only have been done by the solo practitioner himself. *Id.* at *14. The Second Circuit noted, "The application of a blended hourly rate in calculating the lodestar figure has not been endorsed in our decisions, and it appears never to have been applied to a solo practitioner by any court in this Circuit." *Id.* at *15. The court further stated, "There is simply no support for the proposition that a district court can decide what legal tasks could have been done by a hypothetical associate attorney . . . in order to calculate a blended hourly rate." *Id.* at *17–18. The court suggested, though, that it would be acceptable to use different hourly rates for different litigation tasks rather than a blended hourly rate. *Id.* at *19.

Courts have refused to reimburse solo practitioners for secretarial and clerical services. *New York State Teamster Conf. Pension & Ret. Fund v. UPS,* 32 Empl. Benefits Cas. (BNA) 1711, 2004 U.S. Dist. LEXIS 3062, at *22 (N.D.N.Y. 2004). Instead, the rule in the Second Circuit is that attorneys will be reimbursed only for "those reasonable out-of-pocket expenses incurred by the attorney . . . which are normally charged fee-paying clients." *Reichman v. Bonsignore, Brignati & Mazzotta P.C.,* 818 F.2d 278, 283 (2d Cir. 1983); *see also Onandaga County Laborers' Health & Welfare, Pension, Annuity, & Training Funds v. Maxim Const. Servs. Corp.,* 2006 U.S. Dist. LEXIS 39698, at *14 (N.D.N.Y. 2006) ("[C]osts associated with lodging, meals, transportation, photocopying, postage, long distance telephone charges, and facsimiles are reasonable out-of-pocket expenses and thus recoverable.") (citation omitted). *But see Morin v. Nu-Way Plastering, Inc.,* 2005 U.S. Dist. LEXIS 37867, at *14 (E.D.N.Y. 2005) (holding that "the cost of transportation is not incidental to the representation and thus not reimbursable.").

The magistrate judge in *Morin* also dismissed costs for computer-assisted legal research, since computerized research "is merely a substitute for an attorney's time that is compensable under an application for attorney's fees and is not a separately taxable cost." *Id.* at *14–15 (citing *United States ex rel. Evergreen Pipeline Constr. Co. v. Merritt Meridian Constr. Corp.,* 95 F.3d 153, 173 (2d Cir. 1996)); but see *Arbor Hill Concerned Citizens Neighborhood Ass'n v. County of Albany,* 369 F.3d 91, 98 (2d Cir. 2004) (holding that use of online research services likely reduces the number of hours required for an attorney's manual search, thereby lowering the lodestar, and that in the context of a fee-shifting provision, the charges for such online research may properly be included in a fee award.)

Once a court has calculated the lodestar figure, it has broad discretion to alter the award as appropriate. Reasons for adjusting the lodestar amount include "(1) the time and labor required; (2) the novelty and difficulty of the questions; (3) the skill requisite to perform the legal service properly; (4) the preclusion of other employment by the attorney due to acceptance of the case; (5) the customary fee; (6) whether the fee is fixed or contingent; (7) time limitations imposed by the client or the circumstances; (8) the amount involved and the result obtained; (9) the experience, reputation and ability of the attorneys; (10) the 'undesirability' of the case; (11) the nature and length of the professional relationship with the client; and (12) awards in similar cases." *U.S. Football League v. Nat'l Football League,* 887 F.2d 408, 415 (2d Cir. 1989), *cert. denied,* 493 U.S. 1071 (1990).

Courts have reduced fees when they have found the documentation of expenses or the evidence of reasonable fees insufficient. *ILGWU Nat'l Ret. Fund v. ESI Group,*

*Inc.,* 2003 U.S. Dist. LEXIS 626, at *9 (S.D.N.Y. 2003); *McDonald,* 2002 U.S. Dist. LEXIS 15908, at *8. The magistrate judge in *Morin* noted that the number of hours that the plaintiff's attorneys spent working on the case was "not unreasonable," but reduced the attorneys' fees claimed by 25 percent because "some greater economy of time might have been used." *Morin,* 2005 U.S. Dist. LEXIS 37867, at *9. The magistrate judge further noted that although some "overlap of efforts" often occurs in litigation, the "potential overlap is of particular concern when five attorneys and a paralegal work on a single case." *Id.* She also reduced by 25 percent the fees charged in the case by an auditing firm, citing the same concerns about economy of time and overlap of efforts. *Id.* at *13. Finally, in the rare case when fees have been awarded to successful defendants, reductions have been made based on the plaintiff's "ability to pay, and the need to avoid over-deterrence." *Seitzman,* 311 F.3d at 487.

### D. Who May Be Reimbursed for Attorneys' Fees

Generally, participants, beneficiaries, and plan fiduciaries may be reimbursed for attorneys' fees. In a recent case in the Southern District of New York, the court held that an individual's estate that was not named as the beneficiary prior to the participant's death was not a "beneficiary" for ERISA purposes and could not recover attorneys' fees. *Uon Suk Park v. Trustees of the 1199 SEIU Health Care Employees Pension Fund,* 418 F. Supp. 2d 343, 350–51 (S.D.N.Y. 2005). In *Uon Suk Park,* the deceased was a participant in an ERISA plan that awarded pension benefits only to surviving spouses unless the participant and his or her spouse both completed paperwork allowing the benefits to be paid to a third party. *Id.* at 348–49. The deceased participant apparently had wanted her pension benefits to be paid to her children upon her death, but failed to complete the requisite paperwork. Upon her death, her estate brought suit against the ERISA administrator seeking benefits. *Id.* at 349. The court granted summary judgment to the plan, holding that the estate was not the beneficiary and thus did not have standing to sue under ERISA. *Id.* at 352, 360. The court also granted summary judgment with respect to the estate's claim for attorneys' fees, saying that the *Chambless* factors, which weighed against the award of fees as the estate was not a beneficiary and did not have standing to sue, rendered its position meritless. *Id.* at 359.

## XI. ERISA Regulations

Within the Second Circuit, the consequence of a violation of the ERISA regulations with respect to deficient summary plan descriptions (SPD) is dependent upon the participant's ability to demonstrate prejudice: A plan participant or beneficiary must demonstrate that he or she was likely to have been harmed as a result of a deficient summary plan description. "Where a participant makes this initial showing, however, the employer may rebut it through evidence that the deficient SPD was in effect a harmless error." *Burke v. Kodak Ret. Income Plan,* 336 F.3d 103, 113 (2d Cir. 2003). In *Burke,* the plan required an affidavit of domestic partnership for a partner to be eligible for benefits, but the affidavit was not mentioned in the summary plan description. The court held that the documents were inconsistent and that the summary plan description controlled and that Burke was prejudiced as a result of the same. However, the plan administrators were able to rebut this presumption by demonstrating a lack of detrimental reliance, namely that the Burkes had decided not to apply for domestic partnership status.

In *Nichols v. Prudential Insurance Co. of America,* 306 F. Supp. 2d 418 (S.D.N.Y. 2004), the Southern District of New York held that it would not penalize a claim administrator for its technical noncompliance with the sixty-day deadline to render a determination on appeal. *See also Pava v. Hartford Life & Accident Ins. Co.,* 2005 WL 203912, at *8–10. 29 C.F.R. § 2560.503-1(h)(2)(i) provides sixty days for the administrator to render a claim determination on appeal or request additional time. Sixty-six days after the appeal was received, Prudential sent a letter to Nichols advising that it was reviewing her claim and a decision would be rendered within thirty days. *Nichols,* 306 F. Supp. 2d at 420. Thereafter, Prudential sent two subsequent letters, first advising that the appeal was pending receipt of medical records from Nichols' treating physicians and then that it was pending the outcome of an independent medical examination. Nichols refused to attend the independent medical examination, advising that the time allotted by the regulations had expired and as such she was seeking judicial review. The Southern District of New York held that it would not penalize Prudential's technical noncompliance with the deadlines, as "Prudential's own solicited communications with Nichols beginning just one week after the expiration of the sixty-day deadline evidenced a good-faith effort to resolve Nichols' appeal and constituted substantial compliance with the regulations." *Id.* at 424. The court further held that Nichols's proceeding to court with notice that Prudential was actively reviewing her appeal contradicted the spirit of the deadline. *Id.* at 424. The court remanded the matter to Prudential, providing it thirty days to render a claim determination.

The Second Circuit has held that denial letters must notify members what information is necessary to obtain benefits and how to effectively protest a decision. *Juliano v. Health Maint. Org. of N.J., Inc.,* 221 F.3d 279, 287 (2d Cir. 2000). "Substantial compliance with the regulations may suffice absent strict compliance with the standards." *Burke,* 336 F.3d at 107–09. "Substantial compliance means that the beneficiary was 'supplied with a statement of reasons that, under the circumstances of the case, permitted a sufficiently clear understanding of the administrator's position to permit effective review.'" *Cook v. New York Times Co. Long Term Disability Plan,* 2004 WL 203111, at *6 (S.D.N.Y. 2004), quoting *Halpin v. W.W. Grainger, Inc.,* 962 F.2d 685, 690 (7th Cir. 1992). In *Cook,* the Southern District adopted the standard that "[t]he existence of substantial compliance should be determined in light of the core requirements of a full and fair review, which includes 'knowing what evidence the decision-maker relied upon, having an opportunity to address the accuracy and reliability of that evidence, and having the decisionmaker consider the evidence submitted by both parties prior to reaching and rendering his decision.'" *Id.* at *6, quoting *Brown v. Ret. Comm'n of Briggs & Stratton Ret. Plan,* 797 F.2d 521, 534 (7th Cir. 1986). The court held that determining whether there was substantial compliance requires a multistep fact-intensive inquiry as to what was communicated to the plaintiff in the letters informing her of the denial. The court adopted the following test:

> In sum, in order to evaluate the adequacy of notice in an internal ERISA appeal, a reviewing court must look first to what information is communicated to the claimant in the denial of the claim or appeal in question, and to what information the claimant submits in response. Then, it must determine whether the subsequent denial of the appeal is consistent with the rationale given in the first denial notice, representing a fair evaluation that the appeal is still insufficient, or whether it impermissibly relies upon additional factors that were never communicated to the claimant. Accordingly, each of the plaintiff's claims/appeals and defendant's subsequent determinations will be considered in turn in light of ERISA requirements.

*Cook* at *7. In *Cook,* the court held that the plan failed to give an employee a meaningful opportunity to correct the deficiencies in her claim where her claim was for chronic fatigue syndrome and the decision was rendered based upon her failure to meet the requirements of the Centers for Disease Control, but the plan did not provide her with a copy of those requirements. *Id.* at *4.

## XII. Cases Interpreting ERISA Statutes of Limitation

In situations where ERISA does not prescribe a limitation period, the Second Circuit will utilize the most analogous state limitation statute. *See, e.g., Miles v. New York State Teamsters Conference Pension & Ret. Fund Employee Pension Benefit Plan,* 698 F.2d 593 (2d Cir. 1983). However, if the ERISA plan contains an express limitation period, that limitation period will be enforced. *Manginaro v. Welfare Fund of Local 771,* 21 F. Supp. 2d 284, 306 (S.D.N.Y. 1998). "Although state law determines the limitations period, federal law governs the accrual date for a claim under ERISA. The cause of action accrues where there has been a repudiation by the fiduciary that is clear and made known to the beneficiary." *Carey v. Int'l Bhd. of Elec. Workers Local 373 Pension Plan,* 201 F.3d 44, 47 (2d Cir. 1999),citing to *Miles.* A cause of action begins to accrue where there is a clear repudiation by the plan that is known or should have been known by the plaintiff regardless of whether the plaintiff has filed a formal application for benefits. *Id.* There is a lack of consensus within the Second Circuit as to whether all administrative remedies need to be exhausted prior to the cause of action accruing. *See Paterson Priori v. Unum Life Ins. Co.,* 848 F. Supp. 1102, 1106–07 (E.D.N.Y. 1994) (holding that a cause of action begins to accrue upon the initial denial); *Mitchell v. Shearson Lehman Bros., Inc.,* 1997 WL 277381, at *3 (S.D.N.Y. 1997) (holding that a cause of action does not accrue until administrative remedies are exhausted, reasoning "[s]o long as internal remedies are available to the plaintiff, the possibility means that the insurance company or plan will grant the claim—i.e., there has been no final decision and resort to a court is premature"). The clear repudiation standard is inapplicable to breach fiduciary duty claims. *See Jeffries v. Pension Trust Fund of the Pension of Hospitalization &*

*Benefits Plan,* 172 F. Supp. 2d 389 (S.D.N.Y.); *DeVito v. Pension Plan of Local 819,* 975 F. Supp. 258 (S.D.N.Y. 1997).

## XIII. Subrogation Litigation

*Knudson* has had a great impact on Second Circuit law of subrogation and the right to recover monetary relief. In particular, prior to *Great-West Life & Annuity Insurance Co. v. Knudson,* 534 U.S. 204 (2002), the Second Circuit had held on multiple occasions that there is a right to recovery against both fiduciaries and nonfiduciaries who knowingly participate in a plan fiduciary's breach of duties. *See Strom v. Goldman Sachs & Co.,* 202 F.3d 138, 144–45 (2d Cir. 1999) (with respect to an individual's right to recover against a fiduciary); *Diduck v. Kaszycki & Sons Contractors, Inc.,* 974 F.2d 270 (2d Cir. 1992) (with respect to the right to recover against a nonfiduciary). However, *Knudson* resulted in the Second Circuit's reversal of its position on these issues. In particular, in *Gerosa v. Savasta & Co., Inc.,* 329 F.3d 317 (2d Cir. 2003), the Second Circuit held that there is no right to recover against a nonfiduciary (the plan's actuaries) for producing incorrect actuarial statements. The Second Circuit reasoned that if such a cause of action was not preempted by the Supreme Court's decision in *Mertens v. Hewitt Associates,* 508 U.S. 248 (1993) (holding that such claims for consequential damages are not permitted by ERISA's exclusive remedy scheme), it most certainly was preempted by the Supreme Court's decision in *Knudson,* as "the monies sought by the Plaintiffs were never in Savasta's possession; rather, they are simply consequential damages resulting from Savasta's alleged negligence." *Id.* at 322; *see also Yoon v. Fordham Univ. Faculty & Admin. Ret. Plan,* 2004 WL 3019500 (S.D.N.Y. Dec. 29, 2004).

Thereafter, the Southern District of New York considered the issue of whether individuals can bring a suit for monetary relief under 29 U.S.C. § 1132(a)(3). *Bona v. Barasch,* 2003 WL 1395932 (S.D.N.Y. 2003). The court held that *Knudson* precluded such relief. In doing so, the Southern District rejected the Second Circuit's pre-*Knudson* decision in *Strom,* which held that breach of fiduciary duty claims were always equitable in nature. *See Strom,* 202 F.3d 138. The Southern District held that post-*Knudson* the issue is not whether a claim for breach of fiduciary duty is asserted, but rather, "in determining whether monetary relief in a particular case can be classified as equitable restitution, the crucial question under [*Knudson*] is whether a suit seeks to 'restore the plaintiff particular funds or property in the defendant's possession.'" *Bona,* 2003 WL 1395932, at *11, quoting *Knudson,* 534 U.S. at 214. In *Strom,* the Second Circuit held that a potential beneficiary could maintain a breach of fiduciary duty claim against a fiduciary for failing to submit an application for life insurance to the plan's insured. Post-*Knudson,* in a case factually similar but far less sympathetic, the Southern District of New York held that *Knudson* repudiated *Strom* and its reasoning. *See Kishter v. Principal Life Ins. Co.,* 186 F. Supp. 2d 438, 444–45 (S.D.N.Y. 2002).

In contrast, in *Gaunlett v. Webb,* 2003 WL 22079536 (Conn. Super. Ct. 2003), the Connecticut Superior Court sought to limit the holding in *Knudson.* The court held that Connecticut's "No Collateral Source Rule," General Statute § 52-225 (preventing subrogation from amounts recovered in litigation, inclusive of subrogation for costs of hospital, mental, dental, and other healthcare services), was preempted by ERISA. However, the court refused to consider the issue of whether *Knudson* precluded subrogation of monetary relief as a result of a lawsuit, holding that the issue was not ripe as the money had not yet been distributed to plaintiff. The deciding court reasoned that permitting state collateral source rules to apply to ERISA plans would create inconsistencies in ERISA law and consequently subrogation *should* be permitted in ERISA matters. In particular, the court noted that the purpose of permitting collateral source deductions from money recovered in litigation is to prohibit double recovery. Welfare plans pay benefits on "strict reliance on a written promise of both the Welfare Fund participant and the participant's attorney to reimburse the Welfare Fund from any subsequent recovery." *Id.* at *6. The court opined that by preventing such recoveries the tortfeasor could seek a collateral source reduction from contributions from ERISA plans, which Congress did not intend.

In contrast, the Southern District of New York has held that *Knudson* precludes subrogation recovery of health care benefits regardless of whether the participant is in the possession of the fund at the time the lawsuit is brought and resolved. *Primax Recoveries, Inc. v. Carey,* 247 F. Supp. 2d 337 (S.D.N.Y. 2002).

## Notes

1. The plaintiffs in *Davila* did not assert a timeliness or misrepresentation claim in their case. Accordingly, it is not likely that the *Davila* decision will have any impact on the Second Circuit's analysis of this type of claim.

2. Supra.

# CHAPTER 3

# Third Circuit

JOSHUA BACHRACH
RANDI F. KNEPPER
PATRICIA M. McINTIRE

## I.  What Constitutes an ERISA Plan?

### A.  Determining the Existence of an Employee Welfare Benefit Plan

There are few cases in the Third Circuit that address the question of what constitutes an ERISA (Employee Retirement Income Security Act of 1974) plan. As a result, many of the district courts that have been called upon to answer this question rely on cases from other jurisdictions. One of the few decisions from the Third Circuit to address this topic is *Smith v. Hartford Insurance Group,* 6 F.3d 131 (3d Cir. 1993). In *Smith,* the Third Circuit adopted the Eleventh Circuit's test to determine whether a "plan" exists. *See Donovan v. Dillingham,* 688 F.2d 1367, 1373 (11th Cir. 1982). Under this test, the court looks to whether a reasonable person could identify the intended benefits, class of beneficiaries, source of financing for the plan, and procedures for receiving benefits based on the surrounding circumstances. *Smith,* 6 F.3d at 136. *See also Deibler v. United Food & Commercial Workers' Local Union 23,* 973 F.2d 206, 209 (3d Cir. 1992).

The Third Circuit recognizes that a plan may exist even if there is no formal written document. *Smith,* 6 F.3d at 136; *Deibler,* 973 F.2d at 209. An employer's express intention to provide benefits on a regular and long-term basis is a "crucial" factor in deciding whether a plan exists. *Gruber v. Hubbard Bert Karle Weber, Inc.,* 159 F.3d 780, 789 (3d Cir. 1998).

### B.  Definition of "Employee" for ERISA Purposes

There are times when the court must decide when an individual is an "employee" for purposes of ERISA coverage. This issue typically involves whether the person is an independent contractor or a covered employee. In *Nationwide Mutual Insurance Co. v. Darden*, 503 U.S. 318 (1992), the court adopted the common-law test for determining whether an individual qualified as an "employee" under ERISA. The factors to be considered include the hiring party's right to control the manner and means by which the work is accomplished, the skill required, the source of the instrumentalities and tools, the location of the work, the duration of the relationship between the parties, whether the hiring party may assign additional projects to the hired person, the extent of the hired person's discretion over how and when to do the work, the method of payment, the hired person's ability to hire and pay assistants, whether the work is part of the regular business of the hiring party, the nature of the hiring party's business, whether employee benefits are provided, and how the hired party is treated for tax purposes. *Darden*, 503 U.S. at 323–24. *See also Bauer v. Summit Bancorp*, 325 F.3d 155, 160 (3d Cir. 2003).

Since the *Darden* decision, courts within the Third Circuit have considered this issue in the ERISA context. In *Schwartz v. Independence Blue Cross*, 299 F. Supp. 2d 441 (E.D. Pa. 2003), the court held that a computer programmer who worked exclusively on the premises of the plan sponsor but was paid by a separate company was not an "employee" but an independent contractor. Also, in *Holtzman v. World Book Co.*, 174 F. Supp. 2d 251, 256 (E.D. Pa. 2001), the court stated that the classification of the individual as an independent contractor, while not dispositive, is a strong indicator of the individual's status.

In *Yates v. Hendon*, 541 U.S. 1 (2004), the Supreme Court resolved a split in the circuits as to whether a working owner may qualify as a participant in an employee benefit plan under ERISA. In *Yates*, the Supreme Court held that the working owner of a company may qualify as a participant in the plan resulting in the applicability of ERISA if the plan covers one or more employees other than the business owner or his or her spouse. *Id.* If no other employees are participants in the plan, ERISA does not apply. *Matinchek v. John Alden Life Ins. Co.*, 93 F.3d 96, 102 (3d Cir. 1996). There is a regulation stating that a spouse cannot be considered an employee of the company or partnership for purposes of ERISA. 29 C.F.R. § 2510.3-3. The Third Circuit has held that based on its plain language, this regulation does not apply to children of owners. *Leckey v. Stefano*, 263 F.3d 267, 270–72 (3d Cir. 2001). Because there were two employees who were not covered by the regulation, all claims under the plan were controlled by ERISA. *Id.*

### C. Interpretation of Safe Harbor Regulation

The Department of Labor promulgated a regulation as to what does not constitute an ERISA plan, which is commonly referred to as ERISA's "safe harbor" regulation. *See* 29 C.F.R. § 2510.3-1(j). To be exempt from ERISA and fall under the safe harbor regulation a plan must meet all of the following criteria: (1) no contributions are made by the employer or employee organization; (2) participation in the plan is completely voluntary; (3) the employer permits the insurer to publicize the program to its employees and to collect premiums through payroll deduction and remit them to the insurer but does not itself endorse the plan; and (4) the employer receives no consideration for its administrative services other than reasonable compensation. *Id.* *See also Schneider v. Unum Life Ins. Co. of Am.*, 149 F. Supp. 2d 169 (E.D. Pa.

2001). For the safe harbor regulation to apply, all four of the criteria must be satisfied. *Murdock v. Unum Provident Corp.,* 265 F. Supp. 2d 539, 540 (W.D. Pa. 2002).

The most often litigated issue is whether the employer "endorsed" the plan.
Courts have held that there is endorsement when an employer presents the plan to its
employees as being a part of its benefit package. *Shiffler v. Equitable Life Assurance
Soc'y of the U.S.,* 663 F. Supp. 155 (E.D. Pa. 1986), *aff'd,* 838 F.2d 78 (3d Cir.
1988). In *Schneider,* the court found endorsement based on the fact that the
employer's logo was placed on the plan and it was referred to as being part of the
employee benefit package. *Schneider,* 149 F. Supp. 2d at 181.

An employer will not be deemed to have endorsed the plan when it simply
makes the employees aware of the opportunity to obtain the coverage but does not
identify the plan as being its own program or part of another program offered by the
employee. *Bagden v. Equitable Life Assurance Soc'y of the U.S.,* 1999 WL 305518
(E.D. Pa. 1999). Likewise, in *Byard v. QualMed Plans for Health, Inc.,* 966 F. Supp.
354 (E.D. Pa. 1997), the court concluded that the employer did not endorse the plan
since the employees had the right to select coverage from a number of options.

The ERISA statute also exempts from its coverage governmental plans and
church plans. *See* 29 U.S.C. § 1003. The governmental plan exception includes plans
that are established by political subdivisions, agencies, or instrumentalities. 29 U.S.C.
§ 1002(32). Courts have taken different approaches to deciding if an entity falls
within these undefined categories and are therefore subject to the exception to
ERISA. In *Krupp v. Lincoln University,* 663 F. Supp. 289, 292 (E.D. Pa. 1987), the
court looked to whether the organization was one that was traditionally characterized
as being governmental. *Krupp,* 663 F. Supp. at 292. Similarly, in *Zarilla v. Reading
Area Community College,* 1999 WL 554609 (E.D. Pa. 1999), the court's focus was
on whether the employer functioned like a governmental agency or a private-sector
employer. A different test was employed by the court in *Poitier v. Sun Life of
Canada,* 1998 WL 754980 (E.D. Pa. 1998). There, the court considered an entity to
be a political subdivision if it was either created directly by the state or was administered by individuals who were responsible to public officials or the general electorate.

There are no significant Third Circuit decisions or decisions by the district
courts within it that address what constitutes a church plan.

### D. Amount of Employer Involvement Required
### to Sustain an Employee Welfare Benefit Plan

There are no unique cases from the Third Circuit addressing the issue of the amount
of employer involvement necessary to establish that a plan is governed by ERISA.
District courts addressing this issue within the Third Circuit often cite to the decision from the First Circuit in *Johnson v. Watts Regulator Co.,* 63 F.3d 1129 (1st Cir.
1995). *See, e.g., Byard v. Qualmed Plans for Health, Inc.,* 966 F. Supp. 354, 359
(E.D. Pa. 1997); *Murdock v. Unum Provident Corp.,* 265 F. Supp. 2d 539, 543 (W.D.
Pa. 2002), *Schneider v. Unum Life Ins. Co. of Am.,* 149 F. Supp. 2d 169 (E.D. Pa.
2001). Under *Johnson,* an employer's involvement will be sufficient to have endorsed
the plan if an objectively reasonable person would conclude that the employer made
the program appear to be part of its own benefit package based on all of the surrounding facts and circumstances. *Johnson,* 63 F.3d at 1135.

In *Schneider*, the court held that ERISA applied even though the employer took no part in the plan's administration because it allowed its logo to be printed on promotional materials that referred to the plan as being its own. *Schneider*, 149 F. Supp. 2d at 181. Likewise, in *Shiffler v. Equitable Life Assurance Society*, 663 F. Supp. 155, 161 (E.D. Pa. 1986), *aff'd*, 838 F.2d 78 (3d Cir. 1988), the court concluded that an ERISA plan existed based on the employer's presentation of the plan to its employees as being part of the employer's benefits package. However, courts are more likely to find that the employer's involvement is insufficient to conclude that ERISA applies when an employer offers different coverage options to its employees. *Murdock*, 265 F. Supp. 2d at 545; *Byard*, 966 F. Supp. at 360.

The district court in *Post v. Hartford Insurance Co.*, 2005 WL 424945 (E.D. Pa. 2005), had no difficulty in finding that there was endorsement of the plan based upon the following facts: the policy was issued to the employer, not individual employees; the employer limited participation to full-time employees; the employer characterized the coverage as being governed by ERISA when it annually filed Form 5500 documents that are required only of ERISA plans; and the cover page of the summary plan description included the employer's name. Collectively, these actions were held to "show a level of involvement by the employer above the limits of the third provision of ERISA's safe harbor." *Id.*

### E.  Treatment of Multiple Employer Trusts and Welfare Agreements

At times, an employer will join other employers in offering benefits to employees under a multiemployer trust. Not all of these trusts are governed by ERISA. *See Gruber v. Hubbard Bert Karle Weber, Inc.*, 159 F.3d 780, 785 (3d Cir. 1998). Courts look to two factors in deciding whether a particular multiemployer plan is governed by ERISA. First, the court will look to whether the individual employers are involved in the administration of the plan. *Atl. Health Care Benefits Trust v. Foster*, 809 F. Supp. 365, 372 (M.D. Pa. 1992). Second, the court will look to whether the employers participating in the trust have a common interest other than their participation in the plan.

Classification as a multiemployer trust under ERISA has both advantages and risks. Under the Multiemployer Pension Plan Amendments Act of 1980, 29 U.S.C. § 1301, all businesses are treated as a single employer. Based on this language, ERISA would apply to a claim by a participant of the multiemployer trust who is the owner of a business and has no other employees. As explained in Section I.B, this would not be the case if the plan covered only the owner and/or a spouse. Because all members are treated as a single employer, each member is potentially liable for withdrawal liability for any other member of the group. *Flying Tiger Line v. Teamsters Pension Trust Fund*, 830 F.2d 1241, 1244 (3d Cir. 1987).

## II.  Preemption

### A.  Scope of ERISA Preemption

Third Circuit authority is in line with the Supreme Court decision in *Pilot Life Insurance Co. v. Dedeaux*, 481 U.S. 41 (1987), with regard to the issue of preemption. *See, e.g., Joyce v. RJR Nabisco Holdings Corp.*, 126 F.3d 166, 171 (3d Cir. 1997). Courts within the Third Circuit have likewise expressly recognized that the purpose of the broad preemption clause is "to ensure plans and plan sponsors that they would be subject to a uniform body of benefit law, minimizing the administrative and financial burden of complying with the conflicting requirements of the various states." *See, e.g., Jorgensen v. Prudential Ins. Co. of Am.*, 852 F. Supp. 255, 260–61 (D.N.J. 1994). The Supreme Court has firmly established that a state law "relates to" an ERISA plan "if it has a connection with or reference to such a plan." *Egelhoff v. Egelhoff*, 532 U.S. 141, 147 (2001); *see also Keystone Chapter, Assoc. Builders & Contractors, Inc. v. Foley*, 37 F.3d 945, 954–55 (3d Cir. 1994). A "state law relates to an ERISA plan if among other things, the rights or restrictions" created by the state law "are predicated on the existence of . . . an [ERISA] plan." *Ragan v. Tri-County Excavating, Inc.*, 62 F.3d 501, 510–11 (3d Cir. 1995); *Ingersoll-Rand Co. v. McClendon*, 498 U.S. 133, 142 (1990); *Aetna Health Inc. v. Davila*, 542 U.S. 200 (2004) (state bad-faith claims are foreclosed by ERISA's civil enforcement scheme). Courts within the Third Circuit have repeatedly given the preemption provision of ERISA a sweeping scope. *Barber v. Unum Life Ins. Co. of Am.*, 383 F.3d 134 (3d Cir. 2004) (holding that Pennsylvania's bad-faith statute was preempted); *see also Post v. Hartford Ins. Co.*, 2005 WL 424945 (E.D. Pa. 2005); *Gilbertson v. Unum Life Ins. Co. of Am.*, 2005 WL 1484555 (E.D. Pa. 2005); *Wells v. Genesis Health Venture, Inc.*, 2005 WL 2455371 (E.D. Pa. 2005); *see, e.g., Pane v. RCA Corp.*, 868 F.2d 631 (3d Cir. 1989) (state causes of action for breach of contract and tort were preempted); *Benvenuto v. Conn. Gen. Life Ins. Co.*, 643 F. Supp. 87 (D.N.J. 1986) (state common-law causes of action for breach of contract, fraud, and negligent mishandling of an insurance claim against an insurer under a policy of group health insurance were preempted by ERISA).

## B. Preemption of Managed-Care and Malpractice Claims

The Third Circuit case law with respect to preemption of managed-care malpractice claims was preempted by the Supreme Court's decision in *Aetna Health Inc. v. Davila*, 542 U.S. 200 (2004). Prior to *Davila*, the Third Circuit drew a distinction on the issue of quality of care as opposed to quantum of benefits received. *Lazorko v. Pa. Hosp.*, 237 F.3d 242 (2000); *In re U.S. Healthcare, Inc.*, 193 F.3d 151 (3d Cir. 1999); *Dukes v. U.S. Healthcare, Inc.*, 57 F.3d 350 (3d Cir. 1995). In *Dukes*, the seminal case on point, the Third Circuit held, "patients enjoy the right to be free from medical malpractice regardless of whether or not their medical care is provided through an ERISA plan." *Id.* at 357. However, the Third Circuit explicitly recognized "that the distinction between the quantity of benefits due under a welfare plan and the quality of those benefits will not always be clear in situations . . . where the benefit contracted for is healthcare services rather than money to be paid for such services." *Id.* at 358. Thereafter, the Third Circuit held that when a health maintenance organization (HMO) arranges medical treatment and services either directly or through contracts with hospital doctors and nurses, it is acting not in its capacity as plan administrator but as a provider of health care, and related claims are not preempted by ERISA. *In re U.S. Healthcare*, 193 F.3d at 162. In particular, the Third Circuit held that an HMO may be precariously liable for physicians in a hospital's negligence in discharging a newborn within twenty-four hours, which was not completely preempted by ERISA, nor was a claim for negligence with respect to policies in this regard. *Id.* Thereafter, the Third Circuit held that a claim for imposing financial disincentives on treating physicians that discouraged the treating physician from recommending additional treatment was also not completely preempted by ERISA. *Lazorko v. Pa. Hosp.,* 237 F.3d 242 (3d Cir. 2000). Thus, prior to *Davila,* whether or not a claim for medical malpractice and/or an HMO's policy is or is not preempted was very much dependent upon how the complaint was written. These decisions, however, were and have since been clearly overruled by *Davila,* which makes clear that such claims are foreclosed by ERISA's civil enforcement scheme even when the complaint alleges negligent conduct. *See DiFelice v. Aetna U.S. Healthcare,* 346 F.3d 442 (3d Cir. 2003); *Brown v. Weiner,* 2005 WL 2665649 (E.D. Pa. 2005); *Pascack Valley Hosp. v. Local 464A Welfare Reimbursement Plan,* 388 F.3d 393 (3d Cir. 2004) (complete preemption applies when the plaintiff could have brought its claims under ERISA and no other legal duty independent of ERISA is implicated by the defendant's actions).

## C. Other Preemption Issues

Consistent with the Supreme Court authority on point, the Third Circuit has continually and consistently held that all damages beyond those permitted by ERISA's exclusive remedy scheme are preempted by ERISA. *See, e.g., Barber v. Unum Life Ins. Co. of Am.,* 383 F.3d 134 (3d Cir. 2004); *Cox v. Keystone Carbon Co.,* 894 F.2d 647 (3d Cir. 1990); *Cox v. Keystone Carbon Co.,* 861 F.2d 390 (3d Cir. 1988); *Pane v. RCA Corp.,* 868 F.2d 631 (3d Cir. 1988); *McBride v. Hartford Life & Accident Ins. Co.,* 2006 WL 279113 (E.D. Pa. 2006) (RICO claims dismissed).

## III. Exhaustion of Administrative Remedies

### A. Is Exhaustion an Absolute Requirement?

Section 503 of ERISA requires plans to provide claimants with a "full and fair review" of a claim denial. 29 U.S.C. § 1133. Although the ERISA statute does not explicitly require that a beneficiary exhaust the internal plan reviews before filing a lawsuit, this requirement has been enforced by courts. *D'Amico v. CBS Corp.,* 297 F.3d 287, 291 (3d Cir. 2002). However, not all types of claims require the exhaustion of plan remedies. A claimant seeking to enforce the terms of a benefit plan must exhaust all plan remedies, whereas one asserting rights under the ERISA statute is not required to do so. *Id.* The Third Circuit has also left open the possibility that exhaustion of administrative remedies is not required when the claim is for breach of fiduciary duties under § 404 of ERISA. *Id.* If the claim for breach of fiduciary duties is in actuality one for plan benefits, however, exhaustion will be required. *Id.; Harrow v. Prudential Ins. Co. of Am.,* 279 F.3d 244, 255 (3d Cir. 2002); *Engers v. AT&T,* 428 F. Supp. 2d 213 (D.N.J. 2006) (exhaustion requirement applied to the plaintiff's claim for breach of fiduciary duty because the "crux" of the claim was one for benefits under the plan).

## B. Exceptions to the Exhaustion Requirement

An exception to the exhaustion requirement exists when exhaustion would be futile. *Harrow,* 279 F.3d at 249; *Hendricks v. Edgewater Steel Co.,* 898 F.2d 385, 388 (3d Cir. 1990). A plaintiff arguing for waiver of the exhaustion requirement bears the burden of proving futility by a "clear and positive showing." *Harrow,* 279 F.3d at 249; *Brown v. Cont'l Baking Co.,* 891 F. Supp. 238, 241 (E.D. Pa. 1995). Factors that a court may consider in deciding whether exhaustion would be futile include whether the plaintiff diligently pursued the available administrative relief; whether the plaintiff acted reasonably in seeking immediate judicial review under the circumstances; whether there was a fixed policy of denying benefits; and whether the insurance company complied with its own internal administrative procedures. *Id.* at 250. *See also Berger v. Edgewater Steel,* 911 F.2d 911, 916–17 (3d Cir. 1990).

Exhaustion is also excused when the claimant demonstrates that he was refused meaningful access to the plan's administrative review procedures. *Tomczyscyn v. Teamsters, Local 115 Health & Welfare Fund,* 590 F. Supp. 211, 213 (E.D. Pa. 1984); *Brown v. Continental Baking Co.,* 891 F. Supp. 238, 241 (E.D. Pa. 1995). A final exception to exhaustion exists when the claimant proves that he is threatened with irreparable harm. *Tomczyscyn,* 590 F. Supp. at 213.

## C. Consequences of Failure to Exhaust

Courts within the Third Circuit have held that if a court dismisses a claim or grants summary judgment for failure to exhaust, it must do so without prejudice, granting the plaintiff the right to refile after exhausting the plan's administrative remedies. *D'Amico,* 297 F.3d at 294; *Carducci v. Aetna U.S. Healthcare,* 247 F. Supp. 2d 596, 610 (D.N.J. 2003). On September 8, 2006, the District Court of New Jersey decided *Baglione v. Clara Maas Medical Center, Inc.,* 2006 U.S. Dist. LEXIS 64251 (D.N.J. 2006) wherein Magistrate Judge Hayden administratively terminated plaintiff's complaint for disability retirement benefits, pending plaintiff's exhaustion of all plan appeals. In this recent opinion, the court granted plaintiff's motion to reopen the case, rejecting defendants' assertions that the cause of action is time-barred. Although the Third Circuit has not yet addressed the issue, the court concluded that the magistrate judge's administrative termination of the matter tolled the statute of limitations.

Courts have also held that exhaustion is still required even if the plan fails to notify the claimant of the guidelines for seeking review. *Tomczyscyn; see also Majka v. Prudential Ins. Co. of Am.,* 171 F. Supp. 2d 410, 416 (D.N.J. 2001). When a plan provides inadequate notice to a claimant about appeal rights under the plan, the proper remedy is to remand the claim for exhaustion of administrative remedies prior to judicial review. *Id; Dellavalle v. Prudential Ins. Co. of Am.,* 2006 WL 83449 (E.D. Pa. 2006).

## D. Minimum Number of Levels of Administrative Review

Some plans offer a second mandatory level of review before a claimant has exhausted administrative remedies and may file suit in federal court. Under the most recent ERISA claim regulations, when a plan offers multiple appeals, all appeals must be completed within the time requirement for a single appeal. 29 C.F.R. § 2561.503-1(h). At least one district court within the Third Circuit has not been strict in its enforcement of the exhaustion requirement for supplemental levels of review. *See Sprecher v. Aetna U.S. Healthcare, Inc.,* 2002 WL 1917711 (E.D. Pa. 2002). However, in *Schaffer v. Prudential Ins. Co. of America,* 301 F. Supp. 2d 383 (E.D. Pa. 2003), the court stated that the claimant had to exhaust all levels of administrative review prior to filing a lawsuit. In *Dellavalle v. Prudential Insurance Co. of America,* 2006 WL 83449 (E.D. Pa. 2006), the court held that the time limits for invoking the second appeal could not be enforced because of the plan's faulty notice.

### E.  Can a Defendant Waive a Failure-to-Exhaust Defense?

A defendant may waive the defense of failure to exhaust if it is not raised in the answer. One district court within the Third Circuit held that the failure to exhaust is an affirmative defense that must be raised in the answer to the complaint or it is waived. *McCoy v. Bd. of Trustees of the Laborers' Int'l Union,* 188 F. Supp. 2d 461, 468 (D.N.J. 2002). In *McCoy,* the court noted the prejudice to the plaintiff resulting from the plan's failure to raise the defense earlier. According to the court, had the plaintiff been made aware of the requirement sooner, he could have sought a stay and remand to allow for exhaustion. Based on the harm caused by the delay, the court held that the defense was waived. In *Engers v. AT&T,* 428 F. Supp. 2d 213 (D.N.J. 2006), the court held that the defendant did not waive the defense when it was not included in a motion to dismiss since it was raised as an affirmative defense prior to its inclusion in a motion for summary judgment.

## IV.  Standard of Review

### A.  Plan Language

The Third Circuit has long recognized that the denial of benefits under an ERISA qualified plan must be reviewed using a deferential standard where the plan administrator has discretion to interpret the plan and to decide whether benefits are payable. When the plan expressly provides such discretion, the fiduciary's exercise of discretion is judged by the arbitrary and capricious standard of review. *Firestone Tire & Rubber Co. v. Bruch,* 489 U.S. 101 (1989).

Likewise, the Third Circuit has recognized that an ERISA plan may implicitly confer discretionary authority upon a claim administrator. Courts within the Third Circuit have recognized that a plan need not expressly grant discretionary authority; rather, such discretion may be implied. *Luby v. Teamsters Health, Welfare & Pensions Trust Funds,* 944 F.2d 1176, 1180 (3d Cir. 1991); *McLain v. Metro. Life Ins. Co.,* 820 F. Supp. 169, 174 (D.N.J. 1993) ("discretion may be implied [by] the terms of the plan"); *Marx v. Meridian Bancorp., Inc.,* 32 Fed. Appx. 645 (3d Cir. 2002), *cert. denied,* 537 U.S. 885 (2002) (the discretion required to trigger the deferential arbitrary and capricious standard of review may be implied from the terms of the plan); *Sollon v. Ohio Cas. Ins. Corp.,* 396 F. Supp. 2d 560 (W.D. Pa. 2005) (no "magic words" such as "discretion is granted" need be expressed for the plan to accord the administrator discretion to interpret plan terms and determine eligibility).

To imply a grant of discretion, the language in the plan must indicate an intent to commit discretion to the plan administrator. *McLain,* 820 F. Supp. at 174. If the language of the plan is ambiguous, "the interpretation that is most favorable to the insured will be adopted." *Heasley v. Belden & Blake Corp.,* 2 F.3d 1249, 1257 (3d Cir. 1993).

The Third Circuit has recognized that an ERISA plan need not contain "magic words" for a court to determine that a plan confers discretionary authority upon the claim administrator. The Third Circuit has recognized the split among other federal circuits concerning whether a plan that requires "proof of loss" grants discretion to a plan administrator. District courts within the Third Circuit are also divided on this issue and, in particular, on whether a plan language requiring the submission of "satisfactory proof" grants discretionary authority to a plan administrator. *See Landau v. Reliance Standard Ins. Co.,* 1999 WL 46585 (E.D. Pa. 1999) (a plan stating that insured must submit "satisfactory proof of total disability to us" granted discretion to plan administrator); *but cf. Cannon v. Vanguard Group, Inc.,* 1998 WL 310663 (E.D. Pa. 1998) (a plan providing that "benefits will be paid monthly after we receive due written proof of loss" did not vest administrator with discretion).

In *Jones v. United States Life Insurance Co.,* it was held:

> The ERISA plan need not explicitly allocate discretionary authority to warrant an arbitrary and capricious review standard; such discretion may be impliedly conferred from the language employed. The requirement of satisfactory proof eligibility has been held to vest an administrator with sufficient discretion so as to justify an arbitrary and capricious standard of review.

12 F. Supp. 2d 383, 385 (D.N.J. 1998). Based upon the above, the Third Circuit has at least tacitly aligned itself with those circuits that will permit the conferring of discretionary authority based upon implicit grants of discretionary authority contained within plan documents. Furthermore, the Third Circuit may rely upon proof-of-loss provisions contained in group policies as sufficient to confer discretionary authority.

The Third Circuit has also held that in determining whether a plan confers discretionary authority upon the administrator, the courts should look at the plan in effect on the date the actual determination was made. *See Smathers v. Multi-Tool, Inc./Multi-Plastics, Inc. Employee Health & Welfare Benefit Plan,* 298 F.3d 191, 195–96 (3d Cir. 2002). In *Smathers,* the plan was amended to include discretionary authority after the insured's injury occurred and after the claim was submitted, but before the administrator made its actual determination. In doing so, the Third Circuit adopted the Ninth Circuit's approach in *Grosz-Salomon v. Paul Revere Life,* 237 F.3d 1154 (9th Cir. 2001). The Third Circuit, and courts within the circuit, held that while the rights of participants to coverage or benefits may vest at the time of the occurrence of an accident, the standard of review does not vest and, accordingly, the standard of review at the time the claim determination is rendered is relevant in determining what standard a court will apply. *Id; see also Sapovits v. Fortis Benefits Ins. Co.,* 2002 WL 31923047 (E.D. Pa. 2002); *Cherry v. BioMedical Applications of Pa.,* 397 F. Supp. 2d 609 (E.D. Pa. 2005).

## B.  What Standard of Review Applies?

In *Pinto v. Reliance Standard Life Insurance Co.,* 214 F.3d 377 (3d Cir. 2000), the Third Circuit adopted a sliding scale approach to the review of a conflicted administrator's determination. The Third Circuit applies the arbitrary and capricious standard, but accords less deference to a plan or claim administrator's decision in proportion to the perceived or actual conflict of interest. *Pinto,* 214 F.3d at 393.

In adopting the sliding scale approach, the Third Circuit made clear its expectation that "courts . . . consider the nature and degree of apparent conflicts with a view to shaping their arbitrary and capricious review of the benefits determinations of discretionary decision-makers." *Id.* Under the Third Circuit's approach, once a conflict is established, the district court should apply a lower level of deference, or a heightened standard, when reviewing the claim determination. The level of deference is determined along a sliding scale depending upon the relative degree of the structural conflict. In assessing the degree of conflict, a reviewing court may consider several factors such as (1) the sophistication of the parties; (2) the information accessible to the parties; (3) the exact financial arrangement between the insurer and the plan sponsor; and (4) the current status of the plan sponsor. Under such an analysis, the higher degree of structural conflict determined by the court would dictate a corresponding lower level of deference under the arbitrary and capricious standard of review. *Pinto,* 214 F.3d at 392. The burden of proof is on the plaintiff to show that a heightened standard of review is warranted. *See Marciniak v. Prudential Fin. Ins. Co. of Am.,* 2006 WL 1697010 (3d Cir. 2006) (burden of proof is on claimant to show that a heightened standard of review is warranted in a particular case); *Schlegel v. Life Ins. Co. of N. Am.,* 269 F. Supp. 2d 612, 617 (E.D. Pa. 2003) (same).

Having derived and adopted the sliding scale standard, the Third Circuit candidly admitted that it provides little or no guidance to the parties or the courts:

> We acknowledge that there is something intellectually unsatisfying, or at least discomforting, in describing our review as a "heightened arbitrary and capricious" standard. The locution is somewhat awkward. The routine legal meaning of an "arbitrary and capricious" decision is that used, quite understandably, by the district court: a decision "without reason, unsupported by substantial evidence or erroneous as a matter of law." Once the conflict becomes a "factor" however, it is not clear how the process required by the typical arbitrary and capricious review changes. Does there simply need to be more evidence supporting a decision, regardless of whether that evidence was relied upon?
>
> This is unsatisfying. Rather, once "factors" are introduced, arbitrary and capricious stop sounding like arbitrary and capricious and more like some form of intermediate scrutiny, which has no analogue in this field.

*Pinto,* 214 F.3d at 392. The court blamed its inability to fashion a workable standard on the Supreme Court's failure to squarely address the issue since *Firestone:*

> While we also find this explanation wanting, we can find no better method to reconcile *Firestone*'s dual commands to apply the arbitrary and capri-

cious standard, and integrate conflicts as factors in applying that standard, approximately calibrating the intensity of our review to the intensity of the conflict. While the approach of Professor [John H.] Langbein . . . and of the Eleventh Circuit would seem more compatible with the basic principles of trust law, and hence a better "fit," only the Supreme Court can undo the legacy of *Firestone.*

*Id.* at 393.

Since the decision in *Pinto,* several district courts within the Third Circuit have struggled with the above-noted problem. District courts reason that the amount of deference afforded to the claim administrator's decision is discernibly reduced only where there is evidence that the claim administrator's capacity for fairness was actually adversely affected by a conflict of interest. *See Lasser v. Reliance Standard Life Ins. Co.,* 146 F. Supp. 2d 619, 623 (D.N.J. 2001) ("it is also clear that the beginning point of *Pinto*'s sliding scale of heightened arbitrary and capricious review lies but a modest distance from the original standard, and that, absent other evidence of bias, the court should engage in no more than a modicum of additional scrutiny."); *Oslowski v. Life Ins. Co. of N. Am.,* 139 F. Supp. 2d 668, 675 (W.D. Pa. 2001) ("when applying the heightened arbitrary and capricious standard, we are deferential, but not absolutely deferential. . . . The greater the evidence of conflict on the part of the administrator, the less deferential our review must be"). Courts within the Third Circuit consider whether the claim determination is supported by the administrative record and its placement of the standard of review on the sliding scale. For example, in *Russell v. Paul Revere Life Insurance Co.,* 148 F. Supp. 2d 392 (D. Del. 2001), *aff'd,* 288 F.3d 78 (3d Cir. 2002), the court held that Paul Revere's initial payment of monthly benefits pending continued investigation and termination of those benefits only upon receipt of medical evidence contrary to a finding of disability was "inconsistent with a finding of bias on Paul Revere's part." *Id.* at 406. The court therefore applied a highly deferential standard of review. *Id; see also Oslowski,* 139 F. Supp. 2d at 676–77 (noting no procedural irregularities and no bias evident in factual assessment and applying deferential standard); *Vitale v. Latrobe Area Hosp.,* 420 F.3d 278 (3d. Cir. 2005) (holding that it was inappropriate to apply a heightened arbitrary and capricious standard of review to decisions made by a plan administrator where an employer (1) established an ERISA trust fund and (2) funded the plan where contributions were not directly influenced by individual benefits decisions).

Based upon the foregoing, the Third Circuit, while quick to presume the existence of a conflict of interest when an insurer both funds and administers the benefit plan, is more stringent with the evaporation of deference afforded the claim determination in the face of a conflict. The Third Circuit will not permit the existence of a conflict to change the standard of review from that of arbitrary and capricious to de novo.

## C. Effect of Conflict of Interest or Procedural Irregularity

The lead case on point in the Third Circuit is *Pinto v. Reliance Standard Life Insurance Co.,* 214 F.3d 377 (3d Cir. 2000). In *Pinto,* the Third Circuit held that when an insurer with discretionary authority both funds and administers the benefits afforded under an ERISA plan, the inherent structural conflict requires a court to modify the arbitrary and capricious standard applied to review its claim determination. The court began its analysis by citing the three typical structures utilized to administer an employee welfare benefit plan:

1. The employer funds the plan and pays an independent third party to interpret the plan;
2. The employer establishes a plan, ensures its liquidity, and creates an internal benefits committee to interpret the plan; or
3. The employer pays an independent insurance company to fund, interpret, and administer the plan.

*Pinto,* 214 F.3d at 383.

In *Pinto,* the Third Circuit was presented with and limited its ruling to the third situation, where an insurer both issues a policy of insurance that funds an ERISA plan (which plan affords discretion to the claim administrator) and serves as the claim administrator. The court held that such an arrangement "generally presents a conflict and thus invites a heightened standard of review." 214 F.3d at 383. In so holding, the Third Circuit explicitly rejected holdings from other circuit courts that require a participant to prove actual bias before finding a conflict to exist. The court also rejected converse holdings and reasoning of other circuit courts, which have held that such a circumstance necessarily presents an inherent conflict of interest warranting decreased deferential review. 214 F.3d at 387. Instead, the *Pinto* court recognized that the presence and extent of a conflict in such circumstances is dependent upon the relationship of the insurer to the plan sponsor or policyholder. For example, where the group policy is experience rated—that is, the premiums charged to the plan sponsor are adjusted based upon claims paid—the *Pinto* court noted that any apparent incentive for the insurer to deny claims in order to maximize profits would be reduced or eliminated.

The sole basis offered by the *Pinto* court for its perception of a "structural" conflict of interest is its assumption (without any basis in the record) that "the typical insurance company is structured such that its profits are directly affected by the claims it pays out and those it denies." *Pinto,* 215 F.3d at 388. Thereafter, the Third Circuit expanded its holding in *Pinto* to apply to situations in which an employer both funds and administers its own plan. *See Smathers v. Multi-Tool, Inc./Multi-Plastics, Inc. Employee Health & Welfare Plan,* 298 F.3d 191 (3d Cir. 2002). In *Smathers,* Multi-Tool funded its medical plan and maintained excess loss coverage through the Life Insurance Company of North America to pay claims in excess of its deductible (in the case of *Smathers,* the deductible was $30,000). The Third Circuit held that Multi-Tool would suffer direct financial harm if the claim was required to be paid, and accordingly, the company had an inherent conflict of interest that required that the sliding scale approach be applied. *Id.* at 199. *Sommer v. Prudential Ins. Co. of Am.,* 138 Fed. Appx. 426 (3d. Cir. 2005) (committee that employer created to serve as administrator of benefits plan was not operating under conflict of interest and as such no heightened review was warranted).

In 2004, the Third Circuit held "[o]ur precedents establish at least one more cause for heightened review: demonstrated procedural irregularity, bias, or unfairness in the review of the claimant's application for benefits." *Kosiba v. Merck & Co.,* 384 F.3d 58 (3d Cir. 2004). In *Kosiba,* the plan delegated discretionary authority to Merck to render claim determinations and construe the terms and provisions of the plan. Merck delegated the authority to Unum, which was permitted by the plan. Acknowledging that the Third Circuit had never before reduced deference based exclusively on the presence of procedural irregularity, the panel did so in this case, based solely upon Unum's and Merck's request that the plaintiff submit to an independent medical examination. *Id.* at 67–68. The panel held that this was a procedural bias, warranting "a moderately heightened arbitrary and capricious standard of review." *Id.* at 68. The petition for writ of certiorari, seeking that the Supreme Court of the United States review the decision, was denied.

In *Pinto*'s wake, the courts have not been hesitant to apply a heightened standard of review where the evidence demonstrates a reason to question the administrator's impartiality. *See, e.g., Goldstein v. Johnson & Johnson,* 251 F.3d 433 (3d Cir. 2001) (heightened arbitrary and capricious review is required when the beneficiary has put forth specific evidence of bias or bad faith in his own particular case); *Kosiba,* 384 F.3d at 66 (demonstrated procedural irregularity, bias, or unfairness in the review for benefits justifies heightened standard of review); *Stratton v. E.I. DuPont de Nemours & Co.,* 363 F.3d 250 (3d Cir. 2004) (applying heightened standard of review after applying Pinto factors); *Lemaire v. Hartford Life & Accident Ins. Co.,* 69 Fed. Appx. 88 (3d Cir. 2003) (failing to follow the plan's notification provisions and conducting self-serving paper reviews of medical files); *Friess v. Reliance Standard Life Ins. Co.,* 122 F. Supp. 2d 566 (E.D. Pa. 2000) (denying benefits based on inadequate information and lax investigation); *Patton v. Cont'l Cas. Co.,* 2005 WL 736595 (E.D. Pa. 2005) (procedural anomalies of failing to take into account medical evidence warranted heightened standard); *Ott v. Litton Indus., Inc.,* 2005 WL 1215958 (M.D. Pa. 2005) (moderately heightened arbitrary and capricious review applied to administrator's decision based on defendants' clear procedural violations of both applicable ERISA regulations and the plan at issue failing to provide a timely decision).

In the absence of a financial conflict or a procedural irregularity, however, the courts have refused to employ the moderately heightened standard of review to an administrator's decision. *Bill Gray Enter. Inc. Employee Health & Welfare v. Gourley,* 248 F.3d 206 (3d Cir. 2001) (unless specific evidence or bias or bad faith has been submitted, plans are reviewed under the traditional arbitrary and capricious review); *Skretvedt v. E.I. DuPont de Nemours & Co.,* 268 F.3d 167 (3d Cir. 2001) (physician involvement in decision making both in initial benefits denial and denial on appeal did not warrant heightened standard of review); *Sweeney v. Standard Ins. Co.,* 276 F. Supp. 2d 388 (E.D. Pa. 2003) (reliance on the review of non-treating physicians is not a procedural abnormality warranting a heightened level of scrutiny); *Vitale v. Latrobe Area Hosp.,* 420 F.3d 278, 283 (3d Cir. 2005); *Grossman v. Wachovia Corp.,* 2005 WL 2396793 (E.D. Pa. 2005); *Sarlo v. Broadspire Serv., Inc.,* 2006 WL 1933664 (D.N.J. 2006) (evidence in record contradicts assertion that increased scrutiny is warranted); *Burick v. Cement Masons Local 699 Pension,* 2005 WL 1868927 (D.N.J. 2005) (same); *Hunter v. Fed. Express Corp.,* 169 Fed. Appx. 697 (3d Cir. 2006); *Michaux v. Bayer Corp.,* 2006 WL 1843123 (D.N.J. 2006).

## D. Other Factors Affecting Standard of Review

Unlike other circuits, the courts within the Third Circuit have had no activity with respect to state insurance laws or the Department of Insurance interfering with the standard of review or discretionary language being included in policies of insurance issued within the Third Circuit. However, in a letter responding to a *New Jersey Law Journal* op-ed that criticized the inclusion of discretionary clauses in plans governed by ERISA, the director of New Jersey's Division of Insurance stated that discretionary clauses in group plans are prohibited by the regulations of the State of New Jersey. Donald Bryan, Director Division of Insurance N.J. Dept. of Banking & Insurance, *Voice of the Bar: Insurance Director Answers Critic of ERISA Discretionary Clauses,* 183 N.J.L.J. 449 (Feb. 13, 2006). While the courts have not addressed this issue head on, the District Court of New Jersey included it in a recent opinion. In *Sarlo v. Broadspire,* 2006 WL 1933664 (D.N.J. 2006), the plaintiff urged the court to apply a de novo standard of review, stating that the discretionary language of the plan was void because it "is prohibited by the regulations of the State of New Jersey." In support of his argument, plaintiff relied on the letter written by the director of New Jersey's Department of Insurance. The court, addressing the issue in a footnote, held that such a letter itself is not a law or regulation and cannot invalidate any contractual provision of the plan. The court further opined that the statutory authorities cited in the letter merely permit the New Jersey Department of Banking and Insurance to "disapprove" a group health insurance policy that had been submitted for approval on the grounds that the policy "contains provisions that are unjust, unfair, inequitable, misleading, contrary to law or to the public policy of this State." N.J. STAT. ANN. § 17B:27-49. However, the court held that nothing in the statute voids the discretionary clause in the plan at issue. Moreover, the court further noted that Sarlo's group insurance certificate specifically stated that it is governed by the laws of Delaware. Thus, there was a significant question, not addressed by Sarlo, whether New Jersey law is even the applicable law on this issue. *See generally Berg Chilling Sys. v. Hull Corp.,* 435 F.3d 455, 470 (3d Cir. 2006) (noting that the district court was correct to look to the law of the state chosen by the contracting parties to govern their agreement in determining whether a provision of the agreement was voided by statute). For these reasons, the court rejected Sarlo's argument that New Jersey law voids the clause at issue.

We expect that this issue will be addressed by the courts in the near future.

## V.  Rules of Plan Interpretation

### A.  Application of Federal Common Law

The Third Circuit has held that courts should follow federal common law to fill in any gaps in ERISA. *See Heasley v. Belden & Blake Corp.,* 2 F.3d 1249, 1257 n.8 (3d Cir. 1993); *Zienowicz v. Metro. Life Ins. Co.,* 204 F. Supp. 2d 339, 344 (D.N.J. 2002). Accordingly, as long as a state law is consistent with the purposes of ERISA, federal courts will adopt it as federal common law. *Heasley,* 2 F.3d at 1258; *Interna-*

*tional Union v. Skinner Engine Co.,* 188 F.3d 130, 138 (3d Cir. 1999); *Ryan by Capria-Ryan v. Fed. Express Corp.,* 78 F.3d 123, 129 (3d Cir. 1996).

## B. Application of *Contra Proferentem*

Under the de novo standard of review, the Third Circuit applies the doctrine of *contra proferentem. Heasley,* 2 F.3d at 1257; *Curcio v. John Hancock Mut. Life Ins. Co.,* 33 F.3d 226, 231 (3d Cir. 1994), *Cohen v. Standard Ins. Co.,* 155 F. Supp. 2d 346, 354 (E.D. Pa. 2001). Under this rule of contract interpretation, if language in an insurance contract is susceptible to two different interpretations, it is ambiguous and the court will follow the interpretation that is most favorable to the insured. *Heasley,* 2 F.3d at 1257.

## C. Deference Afforded to an Administrator's Interpretation of a Plan

The doctrine of *contra proferentem* has not been applied when the plan grants discretionary authority to the fiduciary to interpret a plan's terms. *Skretvedt v. E.I. DuPont de Nemours & Co.,* 368 F.3d 167, 177 (3d Cir. 2001); *Lasser v. Reliance Standard Life Ins. Co.,* 344 F.3d 381, 385–86 (3d Cir. 2003). Under the deferential standard of review, the court will accept the fiduciaries' interpretation as long as it is reasonable and not contrary to the language in the plan. *Id.* In *McElroy v. SmithKline Beecham Health & Welfare Benefits Trust,* 340 F.3d 139, 143 (3d Cir. 2003), the Third Circuit held that even though the plan language was ambiguous, the court "must defer to this interpretation [of the plan administrator] unless it is arbitrary and capricious."

In contrast to the cases cited above, in *McLeod v. Hartford Life & Accident Insurance Co.,* 372 F.3d 618 (3d Cir. 2004), the court stated that under the heightened standard of review, the court "must be especially mindful to insure that the administrator's interpretation of policy language does not unfairly disadvantage the policyholder."

## D. Other Rules of Plan or Contract Interpretation

At times courts will also accept extrinsic evidence when interpreting the language in the plan. In *Smith v. Hartford Insurance Group,* 6 F.3d 131, 139 (3d Cir. 1993), the Third Circuit considered extrinsic evidence of the party's understanding of the term that was in dispute. Extrinsic evidence includes the party's prior performance under the agreement. *Id.; see also Langer v. Monarch Life Ins. Co.,* 879 F.2d 75, 81 (3d Cir. 1989). According to *Smith,* evidence of prior performance under the policy may be used to demonstrate a latent ambiguity. In *Executive Benefit Plan Participants v. New Valley Corp.,* 89 F.3d 143, 150 (3d Cir. 1996), the Third Circuit held that extrinsic evidence "must be considered" to clarify the meaning of a term once an ambiguity is found. The Third Circuit has cautioned that extrinsic evidence should not be used to create an ambiguity where none exists. *Gritzer v. CBS, Inc.,* 275 F.3d 291, 299 (3d Cir. 2002); *In re Unisys Corp. (Unisys I),* 58 F.3d 896, 904–06 (3d Cir. 1995). In *Unysis I,* the Third Circuit refused to consider extrinsic evidence because the language in the plan was unambiguous and did not allow the claims.

Often benefit plans are amended and the question arises as to which plan covers the particular claim. In *Confer v. Custom Engineering Co.,* 952 F.2d 34 (3d Cir. 1991), the Third Circuit held that coverage under the plan vests at the time of the loss and that a subsequent amendment limiting coverage cannot be applied retroactively. Many of the other circuits have reached the opposite conclusion, however, noting that under ERISA, only pension benefits vest, not welfare benefits.

In *Smathers v. Multi-Tool, Inc.,* 298 F.3d 191 (3d Cir. 2002), the holding in *Confer* was limited to substantive, not procedural, amendments to a plan. In *Smathers,* the claimant sought coverage for medical expenses. Following the loss, the plan was amended to grant the administrator discretionary authority. The claimant relied on *Confer* in arguing that he had a vested right to have his claim reviewed based on the terms contained in the earlier plan. The Third Circuit disagreed, stating that the plan amendment granting discretion applied to the claim since it did not change the coverage under the plan. *Smathers,* 298 F.3d at 195.

A frequently litigated issue concerns the right to lifetime benefits. While pension benefits automatically vest, welfare benefits do not unless such vesting is clearly and expressly stated in the plan. *Int'l Union v. Skinner Engine Co.,* 188 F.3d 130, 138–39 (3d Cir. 1999). A claimant bears the burden of proving that the employer intended the benefits to vest. *Id.* Additionally, when benefits are offered as part of a collective bargaining agreement (CBA), there is a presumption that they will expire when the CBA expires. *Id.*

## VI. Discovery

### A. Limitations on Discovery

Under the arbitrary and capricious standard of review, the court's review is limited to the record before the administrator, which cannot be supplemented during litigation. *Mitchell v. Eastman Kodak Co.,* 113 F.3d 433, 440 (3d Cir. 1997); *Kosiba v. Merck & Co.,* 384 F.3d 58, 67 (3d Cir. 2004). Nevertheless, when a reviewing court is deciding whether to employ the arbitrary and capricious standard or a more heightened standard of review, it may consider evidence of potential biases and conflicts of interest that are not in the administrator's record. *Id.; Pinto v. Reliance Standard Life Ins. Co.,* 214 F.3d 377, 392 (3d Cir. 2000).

> The Court and the parties have found no applicable authority that would support looking beyond the administrative record when deferentially reviewing a plan administrator's factual determination that a claimant is ineligible for benefits. The purpose in limiting the evidentiary scope of judicial review is to encourage the parties to resolve their disputes at the administrator's level. *See Vega v. National Life Ins. Servs., Inc.,* 188 F.3d 287, 300 (5th Cir. 1999). If district courts permitted claimants to present additional evidence in reviewing benefit determinations, "the administrator's review of claims [would] be circumvented." *Id.* ERISA's goal of providing plan participants and beneficiaries an expeditious and inexpensive method of resolving their disputes would be seriously impaired. *See Perry v. Simplicity Eng'g.,* 900 F.2d 963, 967 (6th Cir. 1990).

. . .

Limiting the review of evidence to that which was before the plan administrator at the time of its decision is thus not overly burdensome to claimants, minus exceptional circumstances.

*O'Sullivan v. Metro. Life Ins. Co.,* 114 F. Supp. 2d 303, 309–10 (D.N.J. 2000); *see also Oslowski v. Life Co. of N. Am.,* 139 F. Supp. 2d 668, 675–76 (W.D. Pa. 2001); *Lasser v. Reliance Standard Life Ins. Co.,* 130 F. Supp. 2d 616, 630 (D.N.J. 2001).

In *Lasser,* the District Court of New Jersey unequivocally held in its first opinion that discovery beyond the *Pinto* conflict of interest issues was "contrary to the law" and the court was limited to considering evidence beyond the administrative record only "in weighing the existence or extent of the conflict of interest and resulting possibility of bias of the administrator in deciding the claim." *Lasser,* 130 F. Supp. 2d at 627. However, in the second *Lasser* decision at the district court level it is obvious that the court considered evidence beyond the administrative record in rendering a decision as to whether the claim determination was arbitrary and capricious by considering an affidavit of the plaintiff along with requiring and considering testimony of the claims representative. *See Lasser,* 146 F. Supp. 2d at 619. The district court held a hearing under the guise of determining whether there was a conflict of interest but considered full-blown testimony on the issue of the basis of the claim determination. *Id.* The decision was affirmed by the Third Circuit without mention of whether the district court erred in considering such testimony in rendering its decision. *See Lasser v. Reliance Standard Life Ins. Co.,* 344 F.3d 381 (3d Cir. 2003).

The Third Circuit has made abundantly clear that, when reviewing a claim administrator's determination regarding benefits under an ERISA plan, a district court is limited to the well-developed record available to the administrator at the time of the final determination. *Mitchell,* 113 F.3d 433; *Abnathya v. Hoffman-La Roche, Inc.,* 2 F.3d 40 (3d Cir. 1993). Even where the de novo standard review applies, the Third Circuit has recognized that review should be limited to the well-developed record. Only where the district judge perceives deficiencies in the record should it exercise its discretion to entertain additional evidence. *Luby v. Teamsters Health, Welfare, & Pension Trust Funds,* 944 F.2d 1176 (3d Cir. 1991) (holding that district court may conduct de novo review based on record where record sufficiently developed); *see also Scheider v. Life Ins. Co. of N. Am.,* 820 F. Supp. 191 (D.N.J. 1993).

In *Luby,* the Third Circuit specifically held that "if the record on review is sufficiently developed, the district court may, in its discretion, merely conduct a de novo review of the record, . . . making its own independent benefit determination." In so holding, the *Luby* court reasoned that "plan administrators are not governmental agencies who are frequently granted deferential review because of their acknowledged expertise" in rendering benefit determinations. The court further recognized that courts are "better suited to hear evidence" than to develop evidence necessary to render such a determination. *Luby,* 944 F.2d at 1184–85.

The Third Circuit will allow additional evidence to be considered under a de novo review when the administrative record is not "sufficiently developed." However, an argument can be made, under appropriate circumstances, that de novo review should be restricted to the administrative record before the administrator at the time of its claim determination under review.

## B. Discovery and Conflict of Interest

The Third Circuit permits discovery as to whether a conflict of interest exists, limited to the following issues:

> The court may take into account sophistication of the parties, the information accessible to the parties, and the exact financial arrangement between the insurer and the company.

*Pinto v. Reliance Standard Life Ins. Co.,* 214 F.3d at 392. Despite permitted limited discovery on these issues, the court's review of the record is nonetheless limited to the administrative record before the administrator at the time of the claim determination. In *Otto v. Western Pennsylvania Teamsters & Employers Pension Fund,* 127 Fed. Appx. 17 (3d Cir. 2005), the plan participant argued that the magistrate should not have relied on two affidavits that were not part of the record before the plain administrator. The Third Circuit, in a footnote, stated that "evidence beyond the administrative record may in certain circumstances be relevant and admissible as to the issues that were not before the plan administrator—such as trustee conflict of interest, bias, or a pattern of inconsistent benefits decision." *Otto,* 127 Fed. Appx. at 21 n.7 (citing *Kosiba,* 384 F.3d at 69). However, the court found it unnecessary to decide whether the magistrate judge erred by reviewing affidavits outside of the administrative record, reasoning that "irrespective of the disputed evidence, the trustees' interpretation of the plan is reasonable." *Id.* In *O'Malley v. Sun Life Assurance Co. of America,* 2006 WL 182099 (D.N.J. 2006), the plaintiff, relying on *Otto,* argued that the court's review of the record was not limited to the administrative record, that the court should review additional documents in rendering its decision, and that she had a right to discovery, purporting that there was a pattern of inconsistent decisions. The court, however, found no evidence that defendant treated the plaintiff differently than any other beneficiary and therefore refused to consider any additional documents in its review of the record. *See also Delso v. Trustees of the Ret. Plan for Hourly Employees of Merck & Co.,* 2006 WL 2403940 (D.N.J. 2006) (additional discovery that branches beyond the evidence that was before the administrative committee when it made the decision being reviewed is not permitted); *Johnson v. UMWA Health & Ret. Funds,* 125 Fed. Appx. 400, 405 (3d Cir. 2005) (this court has made clear that the record for arbitrary and capricious review of ERISA benefits denial is the record made before the plan administrator, which cannot be supplemented during litigation).

It is important to note that the Third Circuit, in referring to the "sophistication of parties" in *Pinto,* was referring to the insurer and the policyholder, not the actual plan participant. Accordingly, discovery on issues concerning the actual claim review and any alleged bias on behalf of the claims handlers or medical and vocational personnel utilized in the claims review is completely irrelevant in considering whether a conflict of interest exists under the *Pinto* standard.

## VII. Evidence

### A. Scope of Evidence under Standards of Review

When a court reviews a plan's decision under the deferential standard of review, the court is limited to reviewing that evidence that was before the administrator at the time it rendered its decision. *See* Kosiba v. Merck & Co., 384 F.3d 58, 67 n.5 (3d Cir. 2004); *Mitchell v. Eastman Kodak Co.,* 113 F.3d 433, 440 (3d Cir. 1997); *Abnathya v. Hoffmann-La Roche, Inc.,* 2 F.3d 40, 45 n.8 (3d Cir. 1993). These materials include the evidence that was before the administrator at the time it originally decided the claim as well as any additional evidence that was submitted to the administrator and reviewed during any administrative appeal.

When a court reviews a plan's decision de novo, the court is not limited to the evidence that is contained in the administrative record. *Luby v. Teamsters Health, Welfare & Pension Trust Funds,* 944 F.2d 1176, 1184–85 (3d Cir. 1991). However, a court is not required to accept additional evidence while conducting a de novo review. If the court believes in its discretion that the record is sufficiently developed, the court may limit its de novo review to the administrative record. *Luby,* 944 F.2d at 1185; *Morris v. Paul Revere Ins. Group,* 986 F. Supp. 872, 882–83 (D.N.J. 1997).

### B. Evidentiary Value of Social Security Determinations

In disability claims, a participant may have been awarded Social Security disability benefits. In such cases, the participant may ask the court to place extra weight on this evidence. In *Pokol v. E.I. DuPont de Nemours & Co.,* 963 F. Supp. 1361, 1380 (D.N.J. 1997), the court held that an award of Social Security benefits is not binding on an ERISA plan. *See also Scarinci v. Ciccia,* 880 F. Supp. 359, 365 (E.D. Pa. 1995). The district court in *Russell v. Paul Revere Life Insurance Co.,* 148 F. Supp. 2d 392, 409 (D. Del. 2001), *aff'd,* 288 F.3d 78 (3d Cir. 2002), stated that the favorable ruling of the Social Security Administration had "no bearing" on whether the plan's denial of benefits was arbitrary and capricious.

In *Weinberger v. Reliance Standard Life Ins. Co.,* 54 Fed. Appx. 553 (3d Cir. 2002), the Third Circuit placed additional weight on the finding of the Social Security Administration. The decision in *Weinberger,* however, predated the Supreme Court's decision in *Black & Decker Disability Plan v. Nord,* 538 U.S. 822 (2003), in which the court noted key distinctions between the Social Security system and ERISA benefit plans. Therefore, the rationale in *Weinberger* no longer seems to be valid. Noting the different standard used in Social Security cases, the court in *O'Connell v. Unum Provident,* 2006 WL 288080 (D. N.J. 2006), stated that the award of Social Security benefits was of "little value." The same conclusion was reached in *Sollon v. Ohio Casualty Insurance Co.,* 2005 WL 2768948 (W.D. Pa. 2005).

A plan's treatment of the Social Security decision may also be considered as evidence regarding the degree of a conflict of interest. In *Pinto,* the Third Circuit accused the plan of denying the benefit claim based on the denial of the claimant's Social Security application yet refusing to award benefits later when the Social Security Administration reversed its decision. *Pinto,* 214 F.3d at 393. According to the court, this was evidence of a conflict. *Id.* The failure of the defendant to explain its disagreement with the Social Security decision was one of the factors that led the court in *Goletz v. Prudential Insurance Co. of America,* 425 F. Supp. 2d 540 (Del. 2006), to conclude that the denial was arbitrary and capricious.

### C. Other Evidence Issues

In *Lasser v. Reliance Standard Life Insurance Co.,* 344 F.3d 381, 385 (3d Cir. 2003), the court noted that the district court held a hearing on the extent of the conflict of interest and its effect on the standard of review. The court did not criticize the use of the hearing to obtain evidence regarding the conflict but did note that the trial court erroneously went further and accepted evidence regarding the claim. *See also Doyle v. Nationwide Ins. Co.,* 240 F. Supp. 2d 328, 336 (E.D. Pa. 2003) (allowing outside evidence to assist the court in setting the applicable standard of review under the *Pinto* sliding scale).

## VIII.  Procedural Aspects of ERISA Practice

### A.  Methods of Adjudication

The Third Circuit has not specifically addressed the issue of whether there exists a preferred procedure to be utilized by district courts when adjudicating ERISA cases. From a purely statistical standpoint, however, summary judgment represents the most often used and upheld procedure, especially under the arbitrary and capricious standard of review. *See, e.g., Skretvedt v. E.I. DuPont de Nemours & Co.,* 268 F.3d 167 (3d Cir. 2001) (reversing grant of summary judgment in favor of plan and remanding for entry of judgment in favor of participant); *Orvosh v. Program of Group Ins. for Salaried Employees of Volkswagen of Am., Inc.,* 222 F.3d 123 (3d Cir. 2000) (affirming summary judgment entered on behalf of plan administrator under arbitrary and capricious standard of review); *Pinto v. Reliance Standard Life Ins. Co.,* 214 F.3d 377 (3d Cir. 2000) (reversing entry of summary judgment on behalf of claim administrator because of the existence of issues of material fact); *Mitchell v. Eastman Kodak Co.,* 113 F.3d 433 (3d Cir. 1997) (affirming district court's grant of summary judgment in favor of plan participant under arbitrary and capricious standard of review).

### B.  Reported ERISA Trials

Notwithstanding the above, district courts within the Third Circuit have not limited adjudication of ERISA claims to summary judgment motions. For example, in *Lasser v. Reliance Standard Life Insurance Co.,* 146 F. Supp. 2d 619 (D.N.J. 2001), *aff'd,* 344 F.3d 381 (3d Cir. 2003), the district court ultimately determined that Reliance Standard's determination to deny long-term disability benefits was arbitrary and capricious, but only after conducting a bench trial requiring only that a claims representative testify. In an earlier reported decision denying cross-motions for summary judgment, the court specifically rejected Reliance Standard's argument that no plenary hearing was required and that summary judgment was appropriate because there was no dispute over the contents of the administrative record. *Lasser,* 130 F. Supp. 2d at 629. After conducting a bench trial, the district court reaffirmed the position long articulated by the Third Circuit that a court's inquiry must be limited to evidence that was before the administrator when determining whether a denial of benefits was arbitrary and capricious. *Lasser*, 146 F. Supp. 2d at 621. However, the court noted as follows with respect to its consideration of the claim administrator's testimony at trial concerning the various internal rules and conventions employed in rendering the claim determination:

> [The administrator's] understanding and these rules and conventions, while not part of the paper record, nonetheless form part of the matrix within which [he] made the decision affecting Dr. Lasser. Their soundness, *vel non,* provides important insight into whether and how [he] may have abused his discretion. Evidence of what [the claim administrator] considered and how he considered it is thus part of the "record" in the broader sense. Moreover, [his] testimony regarding the basis for the denial of benefits substantially mirrors the arguments of Reliance's counsel, as might be expected given that [the administrator] is himself an attorney. On this basis, the Court will consider certain of [the administrator's] trial testimony in relation to the underlying question of whether the denial of benefits was arbitrary and capricious.

*Id.* How far district courts within the Third Circuit, or the Third Circuit itself, will expand or contract this "matrix" remains to be seen.

Whether an ERISA case is adjudicated by way of summary judgment or trial, there is no right to a jury trial under ERISA itself. While ERISA is silent on the issue, virtually every circuit court has held that regardless of whether the action is for benefits under 502(a)(1)(B) or one for general equitable relief under 502(a)(3), the relief sought is equitable in nature, thus there is no right to a jury trial under ERISA or under the Seventh Amendment. *Cox v. Keystone Carbon Co.*, 894 F.2d 647 (3d Cir. 1990); *Pane v. RCA Corp.* 868 F.2d 631 (3d Cir. 1989).

## IX. Fiduciary Liability Claims

### A. Definition of Fiduciary

Fiduciary status is broadly construed. *Smith v. Hartford Ins. Group*, 6 F.3d 131, 141 (3d Cir. 1993). Fiduciary status can be obtained by being named as the fiduciary in the instrument establishing the plan, by being named as a fiduciary pursuant to the plan's procedures, or by falling under the statutory definition of a fiduciary. *Glaziers & Glassworkers v. Newbridge Sec.*, 93 F.3d 1171, 1179 (3d Cir. 1996).

According to the Third Circuit, discretionary authority is the "linchpin" of fiduciary status. *Curcio v. John Hancock Mut. Life Ins. Co.*, 33 F.3d 226, 233 (3d Cir. 1991). When the party performs only a ministerial role such as processing claims and calculating the benefits to be paid, it is not a fiduciary. *Confer v. Custom Eng'g Co.*, 952 F.2d 34, 37 (3d Cir. 1991).

Often the plan will name a corporation as the fiduciary. This does not mean that the individual officers of the corporation are fiduciaries who may be liable under ERISA. There can be fiduciary liability only if the officer has been delegated personal discretionary control over the administration of the plan. *Curcio*, 33 F.3d at 233.

Not all actions taken by a plan fiduciary are subject to ERISA liability. Fiduciary responsibility attaches only to those undertakings that are regulated by ERISA. *Walling,* 125 F.3d at 117. Amendments to the plan by the sponsor are not considered fiduciary acts. Fiduciary responsibility will attach only when the plan administrator exercises discretionary control over the administration of the plan. *Id.; Curcio,* 33 F.3d at 234 n.10; *Bennett v. Conrail Matched Savings Plan,* 168 F.3d 671, 679 (3d Cir. 1999).

As noted above, a plan sponsor may wear two hats. While a plan administrator wearing the hat of plan sponsor may be free to amend the plan, it must be careful in doing so. A plan sponsor who is also the administrator of the plan may not make material misrepresentations, whether intentional or not, regarding modifications to an employee pension or benefit plan since this may result in a breach of fiduciary duty. *Curcio,* 33 F.3d 226 at 238–39. In *Curcio,* the Third Circuit held that the plan breached its fiduciary duty when it made a material misrepresentation regarding the coverage available under a group accidental-death plan. *Curcio,* 33 F.3d at 235. *See also Kurz v. Phila. Elec. Co.,* 994 F.2d 136, 139 (3d Cir. 1993).

### B.  Definition of Fiduciary Duties

The Third Circuit recognizes a limited claim for breach of fiduciary duty based on a misrepresentation. To state such a claim, the plaintiff must allege that the defendant was acting in its capacity as a fiduciary, that the fiduciary made a misrepresentation, that the misrepresentation was material, and that the beneficiary relied on the misrepresentation to his detriment. *Romero v. Allstate,* 404 F.3d 212, 227 (3d Cir. 2005); *Burstein v. Ret. Plan, Allegheny Health,* 334 F.3d 365, 387 (3d Cir. 2003). In *Adams v. Freedom Forge Corp.,* 204 F.3d 475, 492 (3d Cir. 2000), the Third Circuit stated that a beneficiary has a valid claim for breach of fiduciary duty if he can prove that the employer, acting as a fiduciary, made a material representation that would confuse a reasonable beneficiary about his benefits or rights under the plan and the beneficiary acted on the misrepresentation to his detriment.

In *Horvath v. Keystone Health Plan East,* 333 F.3d 450 (3d Cir. 2003), the court rejected the plaintiff's claim that the plan breached its fiduciary duty by failing to disclose information regarding its physician incentives. *Horvath,* 333 F.3d at 462–63. The Third Circuit held that there is no duty under ERISA to disclose such information absent a request by the participant or evidence that the plan knew that the participant needed the information in order to make a decision regarding the coverage. *Id.*

### C.  Fiduciary Liability in the Context of Health and Disability Claims

In *McMahon v. McDowell,* 794 F.2d 100, 109 (3d Cir. 1986), the Third Circuit recognized that a claim for breach of fiduciary duty under ERISA "does not go to any individual plan participant or beneficiary, but inures to the benefit of the plan as a whole." The holding was based on the Supreme Court's decision in *Massachusetts Mutual Life Insurance Co. v. Russell,* 473 U.S. 134, 141 (1985), which held that the ERISA fiduciary duty requirements are meant to prevent "misuse of plan assets" and to "protect the entire plan, not individual participants." Citing to *McMahon,* in *Doyle v. Nationwide Insurance Co.,* 240 F. Supp. 2d 328, 349 (E.D. Pa. 2003), the district court concluded that a claimant may not bring a separate claim for breach of fiduciary duty based on the denial of disability benefits. *See also Byrd v. Reliance Standard Life Ins. Co.,* 160 Fed. Appx. 209, n.4 (3d Cir. 2005).

## D. Remedies for Breach of Fiduciary Duty

Courts are limited in the remedies that are available for a breach of fiduciary duty under ERISA. Relief is available only under Section 502(a)(3) of ERISA if it is equitable and there is no alternative remedy available under ERISA. *Ream v. Frey,* 107 F.3d 147, 152 (3d Cir. 1997). Two decisions from the Third Circuit allowed actions to recover interest on delayed payment of benefits based on breach of fiduciary duty. *Fotta v. Trs. of United Mine Workers of Am.,* 319 F.3d 612 (3d Cir.), *cert. denied,* 124 S. Ct. 468 (2003); *Skretvedt v. E.I. DuPont de Nemours & Co.,* 372 F.3d 193 (3d Cir. 2004). These decisions are in question based on the Supreme Court's decision in *Sereboff v. Mid Atlantic Medical Services, Inc.,* 126 S. Ct. 1869 (2006).

In *Curcio,* the court awarded as a remedy for the plan's breach of fiduciary duty the benefits that were claimed under the plan. The court based its decision on the theory of equitable estoppel. To succeed on such a claim, the court held, a plaintiff must prove that there was a material misrepresentation, reasonable and detrimental reliance on the representation, and extraordinary circumstances. *Curcio,* 33 F.3d at 235; *Smith v. Hartford Ins. Group,* 6 F.3d 131, 137 (3d Cir. 1993).

In *Bixler v. Central Pennsylvania Teamsters Health & Welfare Fund,* 12 F.3d 1292 (3d Cir. 1993), the plaintiff claimed that the plan made material misrepresentations that led her not to elect COBRA coverage. The court recognized that under Section 502(a)(3) of ERISA it could award "other equitable relief" based on a breach of fiduciary duty. According to the court, equitable relief includes an award of benefits based on a breach of fiduciary duty. The court further recognized not only that it is a breach of fiduciary duty to provide misinformation, but also that there is an affirmative duty to provide information to a claimant when the fiduciary knows that the silence might be harmful. *Bixler,* 12 F.3d at 1300.

An action under Section 502(a)(2) for breach of fiduciary duty must be brought on behalf of the plan as a whole. The statute does not allow a claimant to seek individual relief. *See Byrd v. Reliance Standard Life Ins. Co.,* 160 Fed. Appx. 209 n.4 (3d Cir. 2005). However, the Third Circuit has recognized a claim under this section of ERISA for a subset of plan participants. *In re Schering-Plough Corp. ERISA Litig.,* 420 F.3d 231, 233 (3d Cir. 2005).

## E. Contribution and Indemnity Claims among Fiduciaries

There is disagreement among the various circuit and district courts as to whether ERISA permits an action for contribution or indemnity against a cofiduciary. The Third Circuit has not provided an answer to this question. However, district courts within the Third Circuit have routinely recognized such claims. *Pressman-Gutman Co., Inc. v. First Union Nat'l Bank,* 2004 WL 1091048 (E.D. Pa. 2004); *Site-Blauvelt Engineers, Inc. v. First Union Corp.,* 153 F. Supp. 2d 707, 709–10 (E.D. Pa. 2001); *Green v. William Mason & Co.,* 976 F. Supp. 298, 300–01 (D.N.J. 1997); *Cohen v. Baker,* 845 F. Supp. 289, 291 (E.D. Pa. 1994). These courts recognized that even though ERISA does not explicitly provide for a right to contribution or indemnity among fiduciaries, this is a remedy that traditionally exists under the law of trusts. As stated by the Supreme Court in *Firestone Tire & Rubber Co. v. Bruch,* 489 U.S. 101, 110 (1989), when developing the federal common law of ERISA, federal courts are to utilize traditional trust-law principles. Accordingly, these courts have held that claims for contribution or indemnity are not preempted.

### F. ERISA Claims against Nonfiduciaries

In general, ERISA liability does not attach to a nonfiduciary. However, the Third Circuit has recognized that a nonfiduciary is a proper party in an action under ERISA when it is a party to a transaction that is prohibited under the statute. *Reich v. Compton,* 57 F.3d 270, 287 (3d Cir. 1995); *Marks v. Indep. Blue Cross,* 71 F. Supp. 2d 432, 437 (E.D. Pa. 1999).

A third-party administrator that performs only ministerial functions such as processing claims and calculating the benefits to be paid is not a fiduciary. *Confer v. Custom Eng'g Co.,* 952 F.2d 34, 37 (3d Cir. 1991). A third-party administrator without discretionary authority is not a fiduciary and not a proper defendant to a lawsuit under ERISA. *Briglia v. Horizon Healthcare Servs.,* 2005 WL 1140687 (D. N.J. 2005).

## X.  Attorneys' Fees

### A.  Criteria for Awarding Attorneys' Fees

The Third Circuit has enumerated five factors that must be considered when considering ERISA fee applications:

1. The offending parties' culpability or bad faith;
2. The ability of the offending parties to satisfy an award of attorneys' fees;
3. The deterrent effect of an award of attorneys' fees against the offending parties;
4. The benefit conferred on members of the pension plan as a whole; and
5. The relative merits of the parties' position.

*Ursic v. Bethlehem Mines,* 719 F.2d 670, 673 (3d Cir. 1983); *Anthuis v. Colt Indus. Operating Corp.,* 971 F.2d 999, 1011 (3d Cir. 1992). When ruling on an ERISA fee application, a district court must articulate its analysis and conclusions with respect to each of the five *Ursic* factors. *Fields v. Thompson Printing Co.,* 363 F.3d 259, 275 (3d Cir. 2004) (it is mandatory for a district court to consider and analyze all five *Ursic* factors); *Tomasko v. Ira H. Weinstock, P.C.,* 80 Fed. Appx. 779 (3d Cir. 2003) (case remanded to district court for failure to consider *Ursic* factors and provide sufficient analysis). There is no presumption with the Third Circuit that a successful plaintiff in an ERISA suit should receive an award of attorneys' fees. *See Ellison v. Shenango, Inc. Pension Bd.,* 956 F.2d 1268, 1273 (3d Cir. 1992). It is incumbent on the party seeking fees to establish the appropriateness of such an award. *Id.* at 1268.

The Third Circuit has recognized that "a party is not culpable merely because it has taken a position that did not prevail in litigation." *McPherson v. Employees' Pen-*

*sion Plan of Am. Re-Ins. Co., Inc.,* 33 F.3d 253 (3d Cir. 1994). Rather, culpable conduct is commonly understood to mean conduct that is

> Blamable; censurable; at fault; involving a breach of a legal duty or the commission of a fault . . . such conduct normally involves something more than simple negligence . . . [on the other hand it] implies that the act or conduct spoken of is reprehensible or wrong, but not that it involves malice or guilty purpose.

*Id.* at 257 (quotations omitted); *see also Skretvedt v. E.I. Du Pont de Nemours & Co.,* 262 F. Supp. 2d 366, 370 (D. De. 2003) (defendant's failure to provide information necessary for plaintiff to proceed with his claim, while not bad-faith conduct, was deemed improper and culpable conduct).

### B. Fees Awarded to Plan Fiduciaries

There is no case law within the Third Circuit addressing whether a prevailing defendant may recover attorneys' fees. However, a district court in New Jersey did award fees to an insurer in a situation where an action brought against the insurer, seeking damages under the New Jersey Law Against Discrimination (N.J. STAT. ANN. § 10:5-2.1), was deemed lacking in merit. *See Veneziano v. Long Island Pipe Fabrication & Supply Corp.,* 238 F. Supp. 2d 683 (D.N.J. 2002), *aff'd,* 79 Fed. Appx. 506 (3d Cir. 2003). Thus, courts within the Third Circuit may be amenable to granting attorneys' fees to an insurer in situations where an action brought is completely lacking in merit.

### C. Calculation of Attorneys' Fees

The party seeking attorneys' fees bears the burden of proving that the request for attorneys' fees is reasonable. To meet this burden, the fee petitioner must submit evidence supporting the hours worked and the rates claimed. *Hensley v. Eckehart,* 461 U.S. 424, 433 (1983).

> The first inquiry of the court should be into . . . how many hours were spent in what manner by which attorneys. . . . [A]fter determining . . . the services performed by the attorneys, the district court must attempt to value those services. This formulation suggests a twin inquiry into reasonableness: a reasonable hourly rate and a determination of whether it was reasonable to expend the number of hours in a particular case.

> \* \* \*

> [The district court] should also make a good faith effort to exclude from a fee request hours that are excessive, redundant or otherwise unnecessary, just as a lawyer in private practice ethically is obligated to exclude such hours from his fee submission.

*Ursic,* 719 F.2d at 676–77.

The Third Circuit prohibits courts from granting contingency-fee enhancements in cases involving federal fee-shifting statutes, including ERISA. *See, e.g., Brytus v. Spang & Co.,* 203 F.3d 238 (3d Cir. 2000).

## XI.  ERISA Regulations

The ERISA statute and its regulations contain claim procedures that must be followed when a claim is denied. *See* 29 U.S.C. § 1133; 29 C.F.R. § 2560.503-1. These require the plan administrator or fiduciary to provide the claimant with adequate written notice identifying the specific reasons for the claim denial and to offer the claimant a "full and fair review" of the adverse decision. *Id. See also Skretvedt v. E.I. DuPont de Nemours & Co.*, 372 F.3d 193 (3d Cir. 2004). These procedures ensure that a claimant knows the basis for the denial so that additional evidence may be submitted in support of the claim during the appeal and also so that courts reviewing a denial of benefits can perform "an informed and meaningful review" of the decision. *Id. See also Grossmuller v. Int'l Union, United Auto. Aerospace & Agric. Implement Workers of Am.*, 715 F.3d 853, 857–58 (3d Cir. 1983). Strict compliance with the ERISA regulations is not required. As long as the plan "substantially complies" with the regulations, it is sufficient. *See Russell v. Paul Revere Life Ins. Co.*, 148 F. Supp. 2d 392, 410 (D. Del. 2001).

The district court in *Schreibeis v. Retirement Plan*, 2005 WL 3447919 (W.D. Pa. 2005), concluded that the plan violated the regulation in two ways. First, the court found that the claimant did not receive a full and fair review because the appeal was decided prior to the plan's receipt of a medical report that was promised by the claimant. Second, the denial letter was deficient because it did not identify a doctor's report that was relied on in reaching the decision.

In *Scott v. Hartford Life & Accident Insurance Co.*, 2004 WL 1090994 (E.D. Pa. 2004), the court held that the plan's denial letter was deficient. According to the court, the denial letter simply stated that the medical records provided by the participant's doctors were inadequate but failed to identify what evidence would be necessary to establish a disability under the plan. The court was careful to state, however, that a plan is not required to provide the claimant with a "learned treatise on medical diagnostics, conduct an independent medical examination, sacrifice its contractual right to interpret the Policy, or give special deference to the views of [the claimant's] treating physicians." *Id.*

In *McElroy v. SmithKline Beecham Health & Welfare Benefits Trust Plan*, 340 F.3d 139 (3d Cir. 2003), the plaintiff claimed that the plan violated ERISA in the manner in which it reviewed the appeal. At issue was the plan's interpretation of an offset provision. The plaintiff asserted that he did not receive a full and fair review because his claim file was not submitted to the plan administrator when it made its decision. The court disagreed, noting that only those documents "submitted by the claimant" must be reviewed and the claimant never submitted his claim file to the plan administrator. *McElroy*, 340 F.3d at 144.

Courts have rejected the argument that a plan's reliance on a peer review report over an examining physician violates the regulation. *Dinote v. United of Omaha Life Ins. Co.*, 331 F. Supp. 2d 341, 347–49 (E.D. Pa. 2004); *Fahringer v. Paul Revere Ins. Co.*, 317 F. Supp. 2d 504, 517–18 (D.N.J. 2003); *Sweeney v. Standard Ins. Co.*, 276 F. Supp. 2d 388, 396–97 (E.D. Pa. 2003).

The regulation requires a plan to provide certain documents when requested by a claimant. The Third Circuit has held that the failure to produce these documents cannot give rise to a claim for statutory penalties under 29 U.S.C. § 1132(c). *Groves v. Modified Ret. Plan,* 803 F.2d 109, 117–18 (3d Cir. 1986); *Syed v. Hercules Inc.,* 214 F.3d 155, 162 (3d Cir. 2000). The statutory penalty provision applies only to requests for those documents required under the statute, not its regulations. *Id.*

Generally, when there has been a violation of the ERISA regulations, the remedy is to remand the claim to the plan for a "full and fair review." *Syed,* 214 F.3d at 162; *Russell,* 148 F. Supp. 2d at 410. However, when the evidence shows that the procedural violation was so significant that it tainted the review process, a court may find that the denial was arbitrary and capricious. *Scott,* 2004 WL 1090994; *Syed,* 214 F.3d at 162; *Doyle v. Nationwide Ins. Co.,* 240 F. Supp. 2d 328, 344 (E.D. Pa. 2003).

## XII.  Cases Interpreting ERISA Statutes of Limitation

In applying a statute of limitations in ERISA cases, where the ERISA statute does not set forth a period of limitations, the Third Circuit utilizes the most analogous state-law period of limitations. *See Anderson v. Consol. Rail Corp.,* 297 F.3d 242 (3d Cir. 2002); *Gluck v. Unisys Corp.,* 960 F.2d 1168, 1179 (3d Cir. 1992). However, what constitutes the most analogous state-law statute of limitations is a hotly debated issue. The Third Circuit has held that Pennsylvania's two-year statute of limitations for wrongful discharge is most analogous to claims for wrongful termination of benefits brought pursuant to 29 U.S.C. § 1140. *Anderson,* 297 F.3d 252. In Pennsylvania, with respect to a suit for benefits under 29 U.S.C. § 1132(a)(1)(B), the Pennsylvania four-year contract statute of limitation has been held to be applicable. *Thomas v. SmithKline Beecham Corp.,* 297 F. Supp. 2d 773 (E.D. Pa. 2003) (citing 42 PA. CONS. STAT. § 5525(8)). In contrast, in New Jersey, a three-year period of limitations applies. N.J. STAT. ANN. § 17B:27-33.

Of great importance with respect to period of limitations/statute of limitation cases is when the cause of action accrues. The Third Circuit has adopted the discovery rule with respect to when a cause of action accrues, meaning that a cause of action accrues when the claimant knew or should have known the claim existed. *See Gluck,* 960 F.2d 1168. The Third Circuit has adopted a two-prong test for actual knowledge that requires a showing that (1) plaintiff actually knew the breaching events occurred; and (2) the events support a claim of breach of fiduciary duty or violation of ERISA. *Int'l Union of Electronic, Elec., Salaried, Mach. & Furniture Workers, AFL-CIO v. Murata Erie N. Am., Inc.,* 980 F.2d 889, 900 (3d Cir. 1992); *Kurz v. Phila. Elec. Co.,* 96 F.3d 1544 (3d Cir. 1996); *Montrose Med. Group Participating Sav. Plan v. Bulger,* 243 F.3d 773 (3d Cir. 2001). A cause of action can accrue prior to an actual formal denial of a claim for benefits where there has been a clear repudiation by the fiduciary that has been made known to the beneficiary. *See Miller v. Forkes,* F.3d 2007 WL 210370 (3d Cir. Jan. 29, 2007) and *Thomas,* 297 F. Supp. 2d at 784. In *Miller,* the Third Circuit held that TT's cause of action accrued when his claim was approved and he began receiving benefits, as opposed to when he discovered that benefits were incorrectly calculated 16 years later and the insurer denied his claim for additional benefits.

## XIII.  Subrogation Litigation

In *Great-West Life & Annuity Insurance Co. v. Knudson*, 534 U.S. 204 (2002), the Supreme Court narrowly construed what may be considered "equitable relief" under ERISA § 502(a)(3). *Knudson* involved a claim for reimbursement by the plan for medical expenses. The plan sought reimbursement from the proceeds of a settlement from a third-party action. The Court held that ERISA does not allow the imposition of personal liability for the contractual obligation to pay money. The Court further held that the claim, which sought any funds rather than funds in the defendant's possession that in good conscience belonged to the plan, was an impermissible claim for legal relief rather than equitable relief.

After *Knudson*, there developed a split in the circuits as to whether a plan could ever pursue a subrogation action even when the funds were in an identifiable account. The Third Circuit avoided the issue entirely. A few district courts within the Third Circuit have addressed *Knudson*. In *Godshall v. Franklin Mint Co.*, 285 F. Supp. 2d 628 (E.D. Pa. 2003), the plaintiffs sought benefits as employees of the plan sponsor. They could not pursue their claims under Section 502(a)(1)(B) since they were not participants in the plan. Therefore, they argued that they should be allowed to proceed under Section 502(a)(3), which allows a claimant to seek equitable relief to redress a breach of fiduciary duty. Since the complaint specifically requested restitution and disgorgement, the court held that the claim was allowed under *Knudson*.

In *Carducci v. Aetna U.S. Healthcare*, 204 F. Supp. 2d 796 (D.N.J. 2002), the plaintiffs argued that their claim was for subrogation, which is not subject to ERISA. They cited to *Knudson* in support of the argument. The district court rejected this position. The court concluded that the plaintiffs' claim was in fact one for benefits under the plan. Therefore, Section 502(a)(1)(B) applied and the claim was not governed by state law.

Whether the plan could pursue a subrogation action was at issue in *Asbestos Workers Local No. 42 Welfare Fund v. Brewster*, 227 F. Supp. 2d 226 (D. Del. 2002). Brewster was injured in an automobile accident and received medical benefits from the plan. She later signed a subrogation agreement with the plan. Notwithstanding the subrogation agreement, her attorney disbursed to her all of the proceeds from the settlement of the third-party action less the attorney fees. The plan then filed suit. In an attempt to avoid the holding in *Knudson*, the plan argued that it was seeking to impose a constructive trust on the funds since they were disbursed to the participant, unlike *Knudson*. The plan also argued that the participant and her attorney were fiduciaries of the plan and could be held personally liable under ERISA. The court disagreed on both points. The district court found no real distinction between the claim of the plan and the claim in *Knudson*. The court also rejected the argument that the defendants were plan fiduciaries as contrary to the law.

In *Skretvedt v. E.I. DuPont de Nemours*, 372 F.3d 193 (3d Cir. 2004), the Third Circuit addressed the scope of equitable relief after *Knudson*. The plaintiff sought interest on delayed payment of benefits under two separate plans. Based on *Knudson*, the lower court decided that the claim for interest on delayed payment was not "appropriate equitable relief" and dismissed the claim. The Third Circuit disagreed and reversed the decision. The court held that *Knudson* did not preclude a claim for interest on delayed payment of benefits under § 502(a)(3)(B). The Third Circuit recognized that one form of equitable relief is a constructive trust. Citing to *Knudson,* the court explained that the purpose of a constructive trust is to disgorge any gain by the plan. Therefore, the court stated that a claimant may pursue an equitable action to disgorge the amount of actual gain, if any, made on the withheld benefits.

Based on the split in circuits, the Supreme Court once again addressed the scope of equitable relief, in *Sereboff v. Mid Atlantic Medical Services, Inc.,* 126 S. Ct. 1869 (2006). Unlike *Knudson,* where the plaintiff did not seek to impose a constructive trust, this was specifically requested by the plan. The court held that an equitable lien was created and a constructive trust could be imposed as soon as the funds passed to the participant. The court also stated that strict tracing was not required.

## XIV. Miscellaneous

Since its publication, courts within the Third Circuit have been applying the Supreme Court's opinion in *Black & Decker Disability Plan v. Nord,* 538 U.S. 822 (2003). In *Nord,* the Supreme Court held that the treating-physician rule applicable to a Social Security determination is not applicable in ERISA matters. The Third Circuit has specifically held that an administrator need not automatically accord special weight to the opinions of a claimant's physician and that a disagreement between the treating physician and a consulting physician does not amount to an arbitrary determination. *See Stratton v. E.I. DuPont de Nemours & Co.,* 363 F.3d 250 (3d Cir. 2004); *Cerneskie v. Mellon Bank Long Term Disability Plan,* 142 Fed. Appx. 555 (3d Cir. 2005). Courts within the circuit likewise have relied upon *Nord* in rendering similar opinions. *See e.g., Schlegel v. Life Ins. Co. of North Am.,* 269 F. Supp. 2d 612 (E.D. Pa. 2003) (reliance on conclusions of defendant's non-treating physicians over opinions of plaintiff's treating physician does not render denial of benefits arbitrary and capricious under ERISA); *Fahringer v. Paul Revere Ins. Co.,* 317 F. Supp. 2d 504 (D.N.J. 2003) (same); *Steele v. Boeing Co.,* 399 F. Supp. 2d 628 (E.D. Pa. 2005) (same); *Cord v. Reliance Standard Life Ins. Co.,* 362 F. Supp. 2d 480 (D. Delaware 2005) (insufficient evidence to show that defendant's interpretation of the available medical information was simply self-serving); *Brandenburg v. Corning Inc.,* 2006 WL 2136481 (W.D. Pa. 2006) (defendant not required to credit the opinion of plaintiff's treating physician over that of its own medical consultant); *Bowman v. Hartford Life Ins. Co.,* 2005 WL 2370852 (M.D. Pa. 2005) (defendant's use of medical consultant to evaluate the cumulative record was a sound method for resolving the conflicting medical evidence in the record); *Klimas v. Conn. Gen. Life Ins. Co.,* 2005 WL 4611913 (E.D. Pa. 2005) (plan administrator not obligated to have its consultants perform an exam of plaintiff rather than relying on the written submissions of plaintiff's treating physician).

Another issue uniquely handled by the Third Circuit is the treatment of subjective conditions. The Third Circuit has held that it is arbitrary and capricious to require objective proof of chronic fatigue syndrome, the court reasoning that such objective proof does not exist. *See Mitchell v. Eastman Kodak Co.,* 113 F.3d 433 (3d

Cir. 1997). However, the Third Circuit affirmed a district court opinion holding that while it may be arbitrary and capricious to require objective evidence of chronic fatigue syndrome, it is not arbitrary and capricious to require objective evidence of the symptoms of a subjective condition. *Nichols v. Verizon Commc'n, Inc.*, 2002 WL 31477114 (D.N.J. 2002), *aff'd,* 78 Fed. Appx. 209 (3d Cir. 2003). *See also Sarlo v. Broadspire*, 2006 WL 1933664 (D.N.J. 2006) (requesting objective evidence of subjective symptoms to establish a standard measurement of the extent of plaintiff's injury was not arbitrary and capricious).

# CHAPTER 4

# Fourth Circuit

BRYAN D. BOLTON
CHERYL A. C. BROWN
GEORGE K. EVANS JR.
E. FORD STEPHENS
ERNA A. P. WOMBLE

## I. What Constitutes an ERISA Plan?

### A. Determining the Existence of an Employee Welfare Benefit Plan

The Employee Retirement Income Security Act of 1974 (ERISA) is a comprehensive statute designed to promote the interests of employees and their beneficiaries by regulating the creation and administration of employee benefit plans. "Our inquiry into the existence of an 'employee benefit plan' must begin . . . with the language of the statute." *Madonia v. Blue Cross & Blue Shield of Va.,* 11 F.3d 444, 446 (4th Cir. 1993), *cert. denied,* 511 U.S. 1019 (1994). ERISA defines an employee benefit plan as either an "employee pension benefit plan" or an "employee welfare benefit plan." 29 U.S.C. § 1002(3). ERISA further defines an "employee welfare benefit plan" as

> any plan, fund, or program which was heretofore or is hereafter established or maintained by an employer or by an employer organization, or by both, to the extent that such plan, fund, or program was established or is maintained for the purpose of providing for its participants or their beneficiaries, through the purchase of insurance or otherwise, (A) medical, surgical, or hospital care or benefits, or benefits in the event of sickness. . . .

29 U.S.C. § 1002(1). Ultimately, "[t]he existence of an ERISA plan is a question of fact, to be answered in light of all the surrounding facts and circumstances from the

91

point of view of a reasonable person." *Custer v. Pan Am. Life Ins. Co.,* 12 F.3d 410, 417 (4th Cir. 1993) (citation omitted); *see also Provident Life & Accident Ins. Co. v. Cohen,* 137 F. Supp. 2d 631, 634 (D. Md. 2001) (citation omitted); *Barringer-Willis v. Healthsource N.C. Inc.,* 14 F. Supp. 2d 780, 782 (E.D.N.C. 1998) (citation omitted); *ELCO Mech. Contractors, Inc. v. Builders Supply Assoc. of W. Va.,* 832 F. Supp. 1054, 1057 (S.D.W. Va. 1993) (citation omitted).

In *Madonia,* the Fourth Circuit adopted the Eleventh Circuit's *Donovan* test to determine whether an employee benefit plan exists. The *Donovan* test divides the statutory definition of "employee benefit plan" into the following five elements: "(1) a plan, fund, or program (2) established or maintained (3) by an employer . . . (4) for the purpose of providing medical, surgical, hospital care or sickness . . . benefits (5) to participants or their beneficiaries." 11 F.3d at 446 (quoting *Donovan v. Dillingham,* 688 F.2d 1367, 1371 (11th Cir. 1982) (*en banc*)); *see also Provident Life,* 137 F. Supp. 2d at 634 (citation omitted); *Barringer-Willis,* 14 F. Supp. 2d at 782 (citation omitted); *Carbonell v. Nw. Mut. Life Ins. Co.,* 905 F. Supp. 308 (E.D.N.C. 1995) (citation omitted); *ELCO,* 832 F. Supp. at 1057.

## B. Definition of "Employee" for ERISA Purposes

In order to be a "participant" in an employee benefit plan, an individual must be an employee or former employee of the employer. 29 U.S.C. § 1002(7); *see West v. Murphy,* 99 F.3d 166, 169–70 (4th Cir. 1996) (refusing to apply Internal Revenue Code section to vary ERISA's definition of "participant" or its requirement of employer-employee relationship). ERISA defines "employee" as "any individual employed by an employer." 29 U.S.C. § 1002(6). In *Nationwide Mutual Insurance Co. v. Darden,* the Supreme Court found that this statutory definition is "completely circular and explains nothing" and therefore adopted "a common-law test for determining who qualifies as [an] employee under ERISA." 503 U.S. 318, 323 (1992) (footnote omitted).

In *Darden,* the Supreme Court rejected the Fourth Circuit's application of the term "employee" as that term is used in the ERISA context. *Id.* at 323–28. The Court stated that the determination of who qualifies as an "employee" under ERISA should be made according to common-law principles. *Id.* at 323–25. The Court adopted a test composed of thirteen factors:

> In determining whether a hired party is an employee under the general common law of agency, we consider the hiring party's right to control the manner and means by which the product is accomplished. Among other factors relevant to this inquiry are the skill required; the source of the instrumentalities and tools; the location of the work; the duration of the relationship between the parties; whether the hiring party has the right to assign additional projects to the hired party; the extent of the hired party's discretion over when and how long to work; the method of payment; the hired party's role in hiring and paying assistants; whether the work is part of the regular business of the hiring party; whether the hiring party is in business; the provision of employee benefits; and the tax treatment of the hired party.

*Id.* at 323–24 (citation omitted). The *Darden* Court also stated that "all incidents of the relationship must be assessed and weighed with no one factor being decisive." *Id.* at 324 (citation and quotation omitted).

Pursuant to statutory mandate, the Secretary of Labor issued regulations clarifying these definitions and filling in gaps left by Congress. The regulations clarify that the phrase "employee benefit plan" does not include any plan, fund, or program under which no "employees" are participants. 29 C.F.R. § 2510.3-3(b). The regulations then state:

> For the purposes of this section: (1) An individual and his or her spouse shall not be deemed to be employees with respect to a trade or business, whether incorporated or unincorporated, which is wholly owned by the individual and his or her spouse, and (2) A Partner in a partnership and his or her spouse shall not be deemed to be employees with respect to the partnership.

29 C.F.R. § 2510.3-3(c).

In *Madonia,* the Fourth Circuit clarified that although § 2510.3-3 does not modify the statutory definition of "employee" for all purposes, it is dispositive of whether a plan is covered by ERISA. 11 F.3d at 449–50. The dispute in *Madonia* centered on whether a health insurance policy purchased by a professional corporation that was wholly owned by the plaintiff's spouse qualified as an employee benefit plan under ERISA. *Id.* at 446–50. The plaintiff argued that no employee of the corporation met the statutory definition of "participant" because no employee, other than the sole shareholder, was covered by the policy at the time the litigation was removed to federal court. Addressing the issue of the sole shareholder of the corporation first, the Fourth Circuit, citing to § 2510.3-3(c), held that she could not be considered a participant for purposes of determining the existence of an employee benefit plan. *Id.* at 447–48.

The Fourth Circuit pointed out, however, that the other employees were "participants" because they were eligible for coverage under the insurance policy. *Id.* In doing so, the Fourth Circuit found that the regulation does not govern whether a sole shareholder can be a participant in an employee benefit plan once a plan has been determined to exist. *Id.* at 449–50. As explained in *Madonia,* a corporation's sole shareholder does not qualify as an employee/participant under § 2510.3-3 for purposes of determining, in the first instance, whether an "employee benefit plan" exists. The *Madonia* court, however, stressed that if a plan exists (which was the case because other nonowner employees received benefits under the plan), then a sole shareholder who constitutes a common-law employee can be a "participant" in the plan for the purpose of claiming benefits under ERISA. *Id.* at 448–50. In other words, if a plan exists, a corporate officer, who is an "employee" of the corporation within the common-law definition enunciated in *Darden,* may also be a "participant" in the company's employee benefit plan. *Cf. Heineman v. Bright,* 906 F. Supp. 306, 308–09 (D. Md. 1995) (finding that the policy at issue did not meet the statutory and regulatory requirements to be an employee benefit plan because no employees were covered by the policy).

The Fourth Circuit then concluded that sole shareholders could be participants in an employee benefit plan, thereby avoiding a situation in which two bodies of law governed a single corporation's employee benefit claims. *Madonia,* 11 F.3d at 450. The Fourth Circuit noted that

> [i]n enacting ERISA, Congress drafted its "most sweeping federal preemption statute" in order to achieve uniformity and consistency in the law governing employee benefits. Disallowing shareholders such as Dr. Madonia from being plan "participants" would result in disparate treatment of corporate employees' claims, thereby frustrating the statutory purpose of ensuring similar treatment for all claims relating to employee benefit plans.

*Id.* (citation omitted); *see also Barringer-Willis,* 14 F. Supp. 2d. at 782–83 (applying ERISA to an independent contractor because it would otherwise result in disparate treatment and thus frustrate the statutory purpose of ensuring similar treatment for all claims relating to employee benefit plans).

In *Carbonell,* the United States District Court for the Eastern District of North Carolina, applying the Fourth Circuit's rationale in *Madonia,* held that the plaintiff, as the sole shareholder of the professional corporation, was not a "participant" for purposes of determining whether the disability insurance policy constituted an ERISA-qualified employee welfare plan. 905 F. Supp. at 310–12. Unlike *Madonia,* where nonshareholder employees were eligible to receive a benefit under the plan at issue, no such benefits or benefit eligibility existed in *Carbonell.*

The *Carbonell* court found that the *Madonia* ruling "is further supported by the many circuit decisions construing the term 'participant' to exclude sole shareholders of corporations or owners of unincorporated businesses for the purposes of determining whether an employee welfare benefit plan exists under ERISA." *Id.* at 311 (citing Second, Fifth, and Sixth Circuit decisions). The district court further stated that the ruling "comports with the policy behind the enactment of ERISA . . . [because] Congress sought to protect employees, not employers, from the potential abuse and mismanagement of pension and benefit resources by employers." *Id.* (citation omitted); *but see Provident Life,* 137 F. Supp. 2d at 634–35 (allowing a 50 percent shareholder/employer to be considered a "participant").

In *Provident Life,* the United States District Court for the District of Maryland considered whether a 50-percent shareholder in a corporation can be considered an employee/participant. *See id.,* 137 F. Supp. 2d at 634–35. The *Provident Life* court noted that the Fourth Circuit in *Madonia* "broadly construed the definition of a 'plan' under ERISA to include a policy under which the only covered member of the company was its sole shareholder." *Id.* at 635. "Unlike the sole shareholder in *Madonia,* neither of the company's two 50-percent co-owners individually control[led] the plan." The district court stated that "the regulation limits its reach to individuals (and their spouses) who 'wholly' own a business." *Id.* at 635. The district court then stated that "[w]hile 'partner[s] in a partnership' also are excluded from the definition of employees under the regulation, no mention is made of a corporation's co-owners who are not married to each other." *Id.* Finding that both shareholders qualified as employees under the *Darden* test, the district court found that, since the shareholders are excluded by the regulation, they appear to satisfy the statutory definition of a participant at 29 U.S.C. § 1002(7). *Id.*

In *Raymond B. Yates, M.D., P.C., Profit Sharing Plan v. Hendon,* 541 U.S. 1 (2004), the Supreme Court considered whether a working owner of a business qualifies as a "participant" under an ERISA pension plan. In the underlying appeal, the Sixth Circuit held that such an owner would not qualify as a plan participant. Rejecting the Sixth Circuit's holding, the Supreme Court concluded that working owners may qualify as plan participants if the plan covers one or more employees who are not owners of the business or their spouses. *Id.* at 6. The Supreme Court looked to ERISA's text and relevant provisions of the Internal Revenue Code for guidance. *Id.* at 12–13. The Court observed that Title I assumes working owners may participate in ERISA plans. *Id.* at 15. The Court further observed that pursuant to Title IV, an employer may have a dual status as both the employer who established the plan and the employee who participates in the plan. *Id.* at 16. The Supreme Court then concluded that Congress intended that working owners qualify as plan participants under ERISA. *Id.* Echoing the concerns expressed in *Madonia,* the Supreme Court then noted that excepting working owners from coverage as plan participants under ERISA would generate confusion and be inconsistent with the congressional goal of national uniformity. *Yates,* 541 U.S. at 17 (citing *Madonia,* 11 F.3d at 450). The Court also noted that in a 1999 advisory opinion, the Department of Labor had similarly concluded that working owners may qualify as plan participants, and this agency view reflected a "body of experience and informed judgment" courts could rely on for guidance. *Yates,* 541 U.S. at 17–18 (citations omitted).

### C. Interpretation of Safe Harbor Regulation

"The Department of Labor has issued a regulation describing a 'safe harbor' which allows certain benefit plans to be exempt from ERISA, with the intended purpose of exempting from ERISA those arrangements in which employer involvement is completely absent." *Vazquez v. Paul Revere Life Ins. Co.,* 289 F. Supp. 2d 727, 731 (E.D. Va. 2001), citing 29 C.F.R. § 2510.3-1(j), 40 Fed. Reg. 34,526 (1975). The safe harbor provision excludes from the definition any "group or group-type insurance program offered by an insurer to employees or members of an employee organization if (1) no contributions are made by an employer or employee organization; (2) participation is voluntary; (3) the employer's function is limited to allowing the insurer to publicize the program and collect premiums through payroll deductions, and (4) the employer does not profit from the program." *Kerr v. United Teacher Assocs. Ins. Co.,* 313 F. Supp. 2d 617, 618–19 (S.D.W. Va. 2004) (citing 29 C.F.R. § 2510.3-1(j)). "[A]ll four of these conditions must be present for a plan to qualify for the safe harbor regulation." *Vazquez,* 289 F. Supp. 2d at 731. "This regulation is often used to determine 'whether a plan is "established or maintained" by an employer'" under the *Donovan* test. *Id.* (citation omitted); *see also Kerr,* 313 F. Supp. 2d at 618 (finding that "ERISA regulations attempt to clarify the meaning of 'established or maintained' by an employer").

In *Vazquez,* the United States District Court for the Eastern District of Virginia found that the plan at issue did not fall within the safe harbor provision, because the employer clearly endorsed the plan. *Id.* at 731–32. Although employees individually purchased and paid the premiums on their respective long-term disability policy with after-tax dollars, those premiums were subject to a 30 percent discount by account of the insurance company's arrangement with the employer. *Id.* at 731. The *Vazquez* court concluded that "[t]his arrangement constitutes endorsement because it basically belies a subsidy and *constructive* contributions to Plaintiffs' premium payments." *Id.* at 731–32 (emphasis in original). The district court further noted that the employer was required to approve an employee's plan before such employee could benefit from the 30 percent discount. *Id.* at 732. The district court also stated that although the policy was portable and an employee could benefit from it even after employment ended, the plaintiff failed to show that an employee who left would continue to receive the 30 percent discount. Thus, the discount appeared to be tied to employment. The district court then pointed out that the disability policy was part of an overall plan by the employer, which encompassed a basic policy and the supplemental employee policy. *Id.*

The purchase of every insurance contract, however, does not automatically establish the existence of an ERISA plan. *Custer,* 12 F.3d at 417. Under the safe harbor regulation, "if the employer merely facilitates the purchase of a group insurance policy paid for entirely by the employees, the employer is not establishing an 'employee benefit plan.'" *Id.* (citing 29 C.F.R. § 2510.3-1(j)). The courts have recognized, for example, that, in order "for an employee benefits program to come within the ambit of ERISA, the employer 'must do more than merely advertise the plan and collect the contributions; it must actively participate in the administration of the plan.'" *Gardner v. E.I. DuPont de Nemours & Co.,* 939 F. Supp. 471, 474 (S.D.W. Va. 1996) (quoting *ELCO,* 832 F. Supp. at 1057).

The Fourth Circuit, in *Casselman v. American Family Life Insurance Co. of Columbus,* Nos. 04-2370, 04-2378, 143 Fed. Appx. 507 (4th Cir. June 25, 2005), considered whether the safe harbor exception removed a plan from ERISA coverage. The Fourth Circuit found that the employer's selection of the type of employees eligible for the insurance program, review of the plans that would be offered, and retention of a consulting firm to investigate the quality of the insurer were sufficient to take the employer out of the safe harbor exception. *Id.* at 509–10 (quoting 29 C.F.R. 2510.3-1(j) (safe harbor exception allows employer only to publicize program and collect and remit payments)); *see also Hughes v. UnumProvident Corp.,* 2006 U.S. Dist. LEXIS 1400, at *12 (M.D.N.C. 2006) ("Even the slightest 'additional' functions performed by an employer in connection with a plan will trigger application of and preemption of state claims by ERISA.").

### D. Amount of Employer Involvement Required to Sustain an Employee Welfare Benefit Plan

In *Kerr,* the United States District Court for the Southern District of West Virginia further stated, "If an employer's only involvement in establishing or maintaining a plan is to allow an insurer to take premiums from employees' pay, this is not a sufficient basis to find that the program is an employee welfare benefits program for the purposes of ERISA." 313 F. Supp. 2d at 619 (citations omitted). Use of an employer's account to pay premiums and make monthly contributions to these premiums, however, has been held to establish an employee welfare benefit plan. *Id.* Thus, in principle, "[t]here must be some payment and manifestation of intent by the employer or employee organization to provide a benefit to the employees or the employees' beneficiaries of the type described in 29 U.S.C. § 1002(1)." *Custer,* 12 F.3d at 417.

In *Custer,* the Fourth Circuit found that the safe harbor provision did not apply because the ERISA plan was "established" by the employer. *See id.* at 417–18. The Fourth Circuit noted that, among other things, the employer obtained the group insurance policy at its president's direction for the benefit of the company's employees; the employer determined the benefits to be provided by the policy, negotiated the terms of the policy, and paid for one-half of the cost. The employer later canceled the policy and obtained a replacement policy when the employer became dissatisfied with the insurance company. *Id.* at 417; *cf. Kerr,* 313 F. Supp. 2d at 620 (holding group policy fell within the safe harbor provision because the defendant failed to show any involvement by employer except allowing the insurer to publicize its insurance and making payroll deductions).

### E. Treatment of Multiple Employer Trusts and Welfare Agreements

ERISA defines "employer" to mean "any person acting directly as an employer, or indirectly in the interest of an employer in relation to an employee benefit plan; and *includes a group or association of employers acting for the employer in such capacity.*" *Foster v. Int'l Ass'n of Entrepreneurs of Am. Ben. Trust,* 883 F. Supp. 1050, 1056 (E.D. Va. 1995) (citation omitted) (quoting 29 U.S.C. § 1002(5) (emphasis added)). The term "employer" also includes multiple employer welfare arrangements (MEWAs). A MEWA is an employee welfare benefit plan that offers or provides welfare benefits to employees of two or more employers. 29 U.S.C. § 1002 (40)(A)(i).

"The Department of Labor has articulated six factors by which to evaluate whether a purported association is in fact a *bona fide* association of employers within the meaning of ERISA: (1) how members are solicited; (2) who is entitled to participate and who actually participated in the association; (3) the process by which the association was formed; (4) the purposes for which it was formed and what, if any, were the preexisting relationships of its members; (5) the powers, rights, and privileges of employer-members; and (6) who actually controls and directs the activities and operations of the benefit program." Pension & Welfare Benefits Admin., U.S. Dep't of Labor, Multiple Employer Welfare Arrangements under the Employee Retirement Income Security Act: A Guide to Federal and State Regulation 9 (1992). The *Foster* court reiterated that "employer-members of the group or association that participate in the benefit program must, either directly or indirectly, exercise control over that program, both in form and in substance, in order to act as a bona fide employer group or association with respect to the benefit program." *Foster,* 883 F. Supp. at 1059.

The *Foster* court found that the plan established by the International Association of Entrepreneurs of America (IAEA) was not established or maintained by a bona fide association of employers. 883 F. Supp. at 1062; *compare with ELCO,* 832 F. Supp. at 1057 (finding that "[t]here exists no room for doubt the arrangement at issue was a MEWA," because "[t]he plan was established to provide health benefits to the employees of the [association]'s members"). First, the membership solicitation was "essentially indiscriminate and not focused on any particular type of employer or entrepreneur." "Second, membership in the association was opened to any employer considering himself an entrepreneur." Third, the evidence was unclear as to the makeup of the membership when the IAEA was incorporated. Fourth, the evidence was silent on why the IAEA was formed. Fifth, the evidence did not show that the IAEA's employer members actually exercised the requisite control over the plan. *Id.*

Since "[t]he statutory definition of MEWA is broader than the definition of employee welfare benefit plan (EWBP), ... [o]nly MEWAs that also constitute statutory EWBPs are governed by and regulated under ERISA." *ELCO,* 832 F. Supp. at 1056–57 (citations omitted). In *ELCO,* the district court applied the *Donovan* test to determine whether the multiple-employer plan at issue constituted an "employee benefit plan." *Id.* at 1057–58. The *ELCO* court ultimately determined that the multi-employer group failed to satisfy the "established or maintained" prong. *Id.*

Moreover, the *ELCO* court noted that there should be "some cohesive relationship between the provider of benefits and the recipient of benefits under the plan" in order for the multiemployer group to be considered an employer under § 1002(5). *Id.* at 1058. The district court agreed with the Eighth Circuit that "pertinent definitions require 'that the entity maintain the plan and the individuals that benefit from the plan be tied by a common economic representation interest, *unrelated to the provision of benefits.*'" *Id.* (emphasis in original) (citation omitted). The district court found that the plaintiff did not receive any other benefit from the multiemployer group other than receiving health insurance. The district court then noted that the relationship appeared "to be much like that between a private insurance company and the beneficiaries of a group insurance plan." As a result, the district court held that the plan did not constitute an "employee benefit plan." *Id.*

## II. Preemption

### A. Scope of ERISA Preemption

"ERISA preempts all state claims that 'relate to any employee benefit plan.'" *Madonia v. Blue Cross & Blue Shield of Va.,* 11 F.3d 444, 446 (4th Cir. 1993) (citing 29 U.S.C. § 1144(a)). ERISA's preemption clause specifically provides that "the provisions of [ERISA] shall supersede any and all State laws insofar as they may now or hereafter *relate to* an employee benefit plan." 29 U.S.C. § 1144(a) (emphasis added). In *Barringer-Willis,* the United States District Court for the Eastern District of North Carolina reiterated the Fourth Circuit's view that (1) "the force of ERISA's preemption is strong and its scope wide;" and (2) "Congress clearly intended to occupy the field and to exclude from the field any effort by the states to regulate ERISA matters." *Barringer-Willis v. Healthsource N.C. Inc.,* 14 F. Supp. 2d 780 (E.D.N.C. 1998), quoting *Custer v. Pan Am. Life Ins. Co.,* 12 F.3d 410, 418 (4th Cir. 1993).

"The phrase 'relates to' is given its common sense meaning," *Custer,* 12 F.3d at 418, as having "connection with or reference to such a plan." *Shaw v. Delta Air Lines, Inc.,* 463 U.S. 85, 96–97 (1983); *Stiltner v. Beretta U.S.A. Corp.,* 74 F.3d 1473, 1480 (4th Cir. 1996) (citation omitted), *cert. denied,* 519 U.S. 810 (1996); *PPG Indus. Pension Plan A (CIO) v. Crews,* 902 F.2d 1148, 1150 (4th Cir. 1990) (citation omitted); *Crews v. Long Term Disability Income Ins. for Employees of Lowe's Cos., Inc.,* 2000 WL 1811608, at *3 (W.D.N.C. 2000) (citations omitted); *Dykema v. King,* 959 F. Supp. 736, 739 (D.S.C. 1997) (citation omitted); *Jackson v. Roseman,* 878 F. Supp. 820, 823 (D. Md. 1995) (citations omitted).

ERISA's preemption clause does not encompass all state-law claims. Those actions that affect employee benefit plans in "too tenuous, remote or peripheral a manner" do not relate to the plan. *Shaw,* 463 U.S. at 100 n.21; *Dykema,* 959 F. Supp. at 739; *Jackson,* 878 F. Supp. at 823–24. As the Supreme Court recognized in *New York State Conference of Blue Cross & Blue Shield Plans v. Travelers Insurance Co.,* 514 U.S. 645 (1995), an expansive interpretation of the term 'relate to' would mean that "for all practical purposes preemption would never run its course." *Id.* at 655.

In *Travelers,* the Supreme Court further clarified the scope of ERISA's preemption clause by deciding to "go beyond the unhelpful text and the frustrating difficulty of defining its key term, and look instead to the objectives of the ERISA statute as a guide to the scope of the state law that Congress understood would survive." *Id.* at 656. The Supreme Court then reiterated the longstanding view that "[t]he basic thrust of ERISA's preemption clause . . . was to avoid multiplicity of regulation in order to permit the nationally uniform administration of employee benefit plans." *Id.* at 657. Moreover, ERISA was intended to "'protect . . . the interests of participants in employee benefit plans and their beneficiaries . . . by establishing standards of conduct, responsibility, and obligation for fiduciaries . . . and by providing for appropriate remedies, sanctions, and ready access to the Federal Courts.'" *Coyne & Delany Co. v. Selman,* 98 F.3d 1457, 1470 (4th Cir. 1996), quoting 29 U.S.C. § 1001(b). In light of ERISA's objectives, the Supreme Court explained that "Congress intended to preempt at least three categories of state law . . . : (1) laws that mandate employee benefit structures or their administration, (2) laws that bind employers or plan administrators to particular choices or preclude uniform administrative practices, and (3) laws that provide alternative enforcement mechanisms to ERISA's civil enforcement provisions. These three preemption categories are thus a guide for determining whether a particular state law relates to an ERISA plan." *Lippard v. UnumProvident Corp.,* 261 F. Supp. 2d 368, 374–75 (M.D.N.C. 2003) (citations omitted).

In *Stiltner,* the Fourth Circuit pointed out that courts have simply followed the Supreme Court's mandate in *Pilot Life Insurance Co. v. Dedeaux,* 481 U.S. 41 (1987), by uniformly holding that state-law claims of intentional infliction of emotional distress, based on the allegedly wrongful denial or termination of benefits under an ERISA plan, are preempted by ERISA. 743 F.3d at 1480; *see also Elmore v. Cone Mills Corp.,* 23 F.3d 855, 863 (4th Cir. 1994) (preempting state-law claims for breach of contract, fraud, unjust enrichment, breach of fiduciary duty, negligence, accounting, and conspiracy); *Powell v. Chesapeake & Potomac Tel. Co. of*

*Va.,* 780 F.2d 419, 421 (4th Cir. 1985) (state-law claims for intentional infliction of emotional distress, breach of contract, and breach of an implied covenant of good faith and fair dealing were preempted), *cert. denied,* 476 U.S. 1170 (1986); *Thomas v. Telemecanique, Inc.,* 768 F. Supp. 503, 506 (D. Md. 1991) (discharged employee's state-law emotional distress claim based on allegedly wrongful accusations that she had been defrauding her employer by collecting disability benefits from its ERISA plan to which she was not entitled was preempted by ERISA because "[t]he issue of whether the alleged conduct was extreme depends upon the parties' rights under the benefit plan"); *Lippard,* 261 F. Supp. 2d at 375 (plaintiff's claims for breach of contract, detrimental reliance, and estoppel relate to an employee benefit plan).

In *Chapman v. Health Works Med Group of West Virginia, Inc.,* 170 F. Supp. 2d 635 (N.D.W. Va. 2001), an employer allegedly made an oral promise that an employee's benefits under a disability plan would continue without interruption. After the employee suffered a disability and was denied insurance under the policy, the employee sued the employer for breach of contract, detrimental reliance, violation of good faith and fair dealing, fraud, and intentional conduct. *See id.* at 636–38. The United States District Court for the Northern District of West Virginia concluded that the state-law claims were preempted by ERISA. *See id.* at 639–40. In so holding, the district court stated that "[m]any circuits have held that ERISA preempts suits alleging breaches of oral promises or modifications of pension plans." *Id.* at 640 (citing Second, Fifth, Seventh, Eighth, and Eleventh Circuit precedent). The district court also relied on two recent Fourth Circuit rulings. In an unpublished decision, the Fourth Circuit found that "ERISA preempted state law claims for fraudulent inducement and negligent representation based on the employer's representations regarding plaintiff's retirement benefits during negotiations." *Id.* at 640, citing *Warren v. Blue Cross & Blue Shield of S.C.,* 129 F.3d 118 (4th Cir. 1997). The district court then noted that the Fourth Circuit in *Elmore* preempted state-law claims when the "employer had made representations in a letter to employees that were not incorporated in the formal plan documents." *Id.* (citing *Elmore,* 23 F.3d at 863).

## B. Preemption of Managed-Care Claims

Although "[c]ourts have consistently held that causes of action against an HMO that relate directly to the administration of claims or benefits under [an] employee benefit plan are preempted by ERISA," *Chaghervand v. Carefirst,* 909 F. Supp. 304, 309 (D. Md. 1995) (citation omitted), the courts struggle with the issue of whether ERISA preempts medical malpractice claims against an HMO under an ostensible agency or vicarious liability theory. These cases primarily hinge on whether the medical malpractice claim falls within the "complete preemption" exception to the well-pleaded complaint rule.

"Under the well-pleaded complaint rule, a cause of action 'arises under' federal law and removal is proper, only if a federal question is presented on the face of Plaintiff's properly pleaded complaint." *Dykema,* 959 F. Supp. at 739 (citation omitted). "[A] defendant cannot convert a plaintiff's state claim into a federal question solely on the basis of an asserted federal defense." *Lancaster v. Kaiser Found.*

*Health Plan of Mid-Atlantic States, Inc.,* 958 F. Supp. 1137, 1143 (E.D. Va. 1997), *Dykema,* 959 F. Supp. at 739 (citation omitted). Even the defense of preemption under 29 U.S.C. § 1144(a) is insufficient to permit removal to federal court. *Id.* Recognizing that the well-pleaded complaint might inappropriately close the federal courthouse doors to cases that merit removal, the Supreme Court created the doctrine of "complete preemption," allowing removal of an otherwise nonfederal action if the asserted state claim conflicts with a federal statutory scheme.

In the ERISA context, the Supreme Court determined that the "complete preemption" doctrine supports removal of state causes of action falling within the scope of ERISA's civil enforcement provision. *See Metro. Life Ins. Co. v. Taylor,* 481 U.S. 58, 65–67 (1987); *see also* 29 U.S.C. § 1132(a) (ERISA's civil enforcement provision).

As a practical purpose, the "complete preemption" doctrine dictates whether a state law is preempted under § 1144(a) as well. In *Lancaster,* the district court aptly stated:

> The fact that a plaintiff's claims may be preempted because they 'relate to' an ERISA plan . . . does not necessarily mean that they also fit within the scope of ERISA's civil enforcement provision. . . . Put another way, every state claim completely preempted by § [1132] is, *a fortiori,* related to ERISA.

958 F. Supp. at 1144. The *Lancaster* court further noted that:

> [I]t is now well accepted that the federal defense of ERISA preemption does not preempt professional malpractice actions. The Fourth Circuit . . . made clear that Congress did not intend to preempt traditional state based laws of general applicability that do not implicate the relations among traditional plan entities, including the principals, the employer, the plan, the plan fiduciaries, and the beneficiaries. Common law medical malpractice is quintessentially the province of state authority. There is simply no reason to believe that Congress—by enacting a statute designed to protect the interests of workers in their benefit plans—intended to remove the long-standing protection against medical negligence afforded by state malpractice law. Further, medical malpractice claims focus on whether a health care provider deviated from an adequate standard of care, not on the contents or administration of a particular ERISA benefit plan. Plaintiffs seek compensation for the purported malpractice and nothing more.

*Id.* at 1149 (footnotes omitted).

The United States District Court for the District of Maryland, in *Pomeroy v. Johns Hopkins Medical Services, Inc.,* 868 F. Supp. 110 (D. Md. 1994), was the first district court in the Fourth Circuit to address whether a medical malpractice claim against an HMO was preempted by ERISA. The district court concluded that the gravamen of the complaint was directed at the HMO's failure to properly administer the beneficiary's benefits and asserted the HMO's negligence as the primary cause of injury. The district court relied on *Dukes v. U.S. Health Care Systems of Pennsylvania,* 848 F. Supp. 39, 42 (E.D. Pa. 1994), *rev'd,* 57 F.3d 350 (3d Cir. 1995), in support of its conclusion that a medical malpractice claim against an HMO, whether couched in direct or vicarious liability terms, relates to the benefit plan. *See Pomeroy,* 868 F. Supp. at 113–14.

Significantly, after the decision in *Pomeroy,* the Third Circuit overturned the *Dukes* decision. In addition, the *Pomeroy* decision has been criticized by other district courts in the Fourth Circuit. In *Jackson v. Roseman,* 878 F. Supp. 820 (D. Md. 1995), for example, the court addressed whether a patient's state-law vicarious liability claim for medical malpractice sufficiently "related to" his employee benefit plan to require preemption. *Id.* at 823–26. The district court recognized that

> Courts are in disagreement . . . over whether ERISA preempts a beneficiary's medical malpractice claim against an HMO under an ostensible agency theory. Some courts reason that an action based on a theory of vicarious liability or ostensible agency would require a plaintiff to show that he looked to the HMO for medical care and that the HMO held out the supposedly negligent doctor or facility as its employee, thereby necessitating an examination of the benefits plan and consequently triggering ERISA preemption. Other courts take the opposite view. These courts begin with the principle that the term related to should be applied in a manner that is consistent with the policies of ERISA . . . [A] law relates to an ERISA plan if it is designed to affect such plans, singles them out for special treatment or predicates rights or obligations on the existence of such plans, impairs their ability to function simultaneously in different states, or effectively restricts such plans with regard to their structure, administration, reporting requirements, or choice of benefits. . . . Indeed, absent such a literal reading of ERISA's preemption provision, most, if not all, medical malpractice state claims brought by employees against plan providers would, on their face or by third party practice, be removable to federal court. This anomalous result would create [a] unique federalization of an entire class of state tort claims which, absent diversity, would be decided in state court.

*Id.* at 825–26 (citations and quotations omitted). The district court ultimately agreed with another district court decision in the Third Circuit that "reference to the plan, if any, will be necessary only for proving matters of agency, not of wrongful plan administration or of the withholding of promised benefits." *Id.* at 826. Based on this reasoning, the court found the claim for medical malpractice against the HMO was not preempted by ERISA. *Id.*

The United States District Court for the District of Maryland in *Chaghervand* reaffirmed the *Jackson* ruling, concluding that the patient's vicarious liability claim against an HMO was not preempted by ERISA. 909 F. Supp. at 309–12; *see also Dykema,* 959 F. Supp. at 739 (holding vicarious liability claim did not "relate to" ERISA plan). The district court reasoned that "while [an] agency claim may indeed require reference to the contents of the employee benefit plan to adduce evidence that the HMO held out a particular physician as its employee or agent, under the *Travelers* framework, this relation does not sufficiently implicate the underlying concerns of ERISA to warrant preemption." *Id.* at 312 (citation omitted). The court pointed out that such state-law claims do not "seek to recover benefits, enforce rights, or clarify future benefits under her employer benefit plan," nor does the claim "concern the administration or regulation of her employee benefit plan." *Id.* at 311.

In *Santitoro v. Evans,* 935 F. Supp. 733, 735–37 (E.D.N.C. 1996), the United States District Court for the Eastern District of North Carolina likewise found that vicarious and direct allegations of medical malpractice against an HMO were not preempted by ERISA. The district court stated:

> Plaintiffs' claims relate to the quality, rather than the quantity of benefits plaintiffs received under the plan. Plaintiffs do not assert claims against the . . . HMOs for wrongful denial or administration of benefits under the plans. To the contrary, they claim damages for Evans's alleged medical malpractice and other malfeasance related to the provision of those benefits. Thus, plaintiffs seek to hold defendants liable for breaches of duties related to medical care imposed by state tort law, rather than breaches of the duties contractually imposed by the plans.

*Id.* at 736; *see Lancaster v. Kaiser Found. Health Plan of Mid-Atlantic States, Inc.,* 958 F. Supp. 1137 (E.D. Va. 1997) (holding that preemption applies to state claims assailing the quantity of benefits received, but is unavailable where the quality of care is challenged); *see also Dykema,* 959 F. Supp. at 740 (claims attacking the quantity of services provided were preempted); *Prihoda v. Shpritz,* 914 F. Supp. 113 (D. Md. 1996).

In *Pegram v. Herdrich,* 530 U.S. 211 (2000), the Supreme Court considered an HMO's simultaneous duties as both an ERISA plan administrator and a health care provider: in acting as a plan administrator, an HMO functions as a plan fiduciary regulated by ERISA, but by providing treatment of a patient's medical conditions, the HMO also functions as a healthcare provider regulated by state malpractice jurisprudence. Analyzing this dual medical/administrative role of HMOs, the Supreme Court concluded that an HMO's activities can be placed in three categories: (1) pure administrative eligibility decisions, (2) mixed eligibility and treatment decisions, and (3) pure treatment decisions. *Id.* at 228–29. The *Pegram* Court concluded that mixed eligibility decisions by HMO physicians are not fiduciary decisions under ERISA. *See id.* at 231–33. In so holding, the Supreme Court reasoned that a mixed eligibility and treatment decision reduces such disputes to the stuff of state malpractice claims, not traditional breach of fiduciary duty claims. *Id.*

In *Marks v. Watters,* 322 F.3d 316 (4th Cir. 2003), the estate of a mental-health patient who committed suicide after murdering his wife and daughter and injuring his son brought suit against the healthcare providers involved in the patient's care, as well as the plan administrator and the utilization review case manager. The estate claimed that under *Pegram,* the state-law claims were not preempted by ERISA because the claims challenged mixed eligibility and treatment decisions. *Id.* at 322. The Fourth Circuit concluded the claims were preempted because the complaint attacked the administration of benefits rather than the quality of care received by the deceased. *Id.* at 326. The Fourth Circuit noted that the corporate utilization review agent did not treat patients; rather, it managed the patient's utilization of health care providers by others to accommodate the benefits of the plan. *Id.* at 325. Moreover, the individual case manager who was sued never provided treatment or made treatment decisions. *Id.* at 326.

## C. Preemption of Malpractice Claims

Professional malpractice claims are not preempted by ERISA. In *Custer v. Sweeney,* 89 F.3d 1156 (4th Cir. 1996), the Fourth Circuit held that ERISA does not preempt a state-law legal malpractice claim asserted by a trustee of and participant in an ERISA plan against a lawyer who provided services for the plan. The Fourth Circuit "did not believe that Congress intended ERISA to preempt state-law malpractice claims involving professional services to ERISA plans." *Id.* at 1167. Moreover, the Fourth Circuit noted that ERISA does not "evince a clear legislative purpose to preempt such traditional state-based laws of general applicability, and permitting professional malpractice claims would not undermine the congressional policies that underlie ERISA." *Id.*

In *Coyne & Delany Co. v. Selman,* the Fourth Circuit reaffirmed the *Sweeney* holding by ruling that a professional malpractice claim against designers of group health insurance plans was not preempted by ERISA because the claim did not "relate to" an employee benefit plan within the meaning of ERISA's preemption provision. 98 F.3d at 1470–72. The Fourth Circuit reiterated:

> Delany's malpractice claim against insurance professionals is a "traditional state-based law[ ] of general applicability [that does not] implicate the relations among the traditional ERISA plan entities," including the principals, the employer, the plan, the plan fiduciaries and the beneficiaries. There is no question that Delany's malpractice claim is rooted in a field of traditional state regulation. Common law professional malpractice, along with other forms of tort liability, has historically been a state concern. Moreover, a common law professional malpractice claim is "a generally applicable [law] that makes no reference to, or functions irrespective of, the existence of an ERISA plan." . . . However, the [professional malpractice] law at issue will have nothing to do with ERISA. The case will turn on legal duties generated outside the ERISA context, and the malpractice claim should not be preempted. As with this hypothetical case of lawyer malpractice, Delany's claim, although it may require the court to examine some provisions of an ERISA plan, turns on duties generated by Virginia common law.

*Id.* at 1471 (citations omitted).

## D. Other Preemption Issues

Notwithstanding the breadth of ERISA preemption, Congress did not intend to take from the states their ability to regulate the insurance industry. Congress, therefore, included the "savings clause," which preserves for state regulation any law that "*regulates insurance,* banking or securities." 29 U.S.C. § 1144(b)(2)(A) (emphasis added).

The Supreme Court has specified how a court must proceed to determine whether a particular statute regulates insurance within the meaning of ERISA. In

*Metropolitan Life Insurance Co. v. Massachusetts,* 471 U.S. 724, 739–47 (1985), the Supreme Court construed the savings clause to apply only to state laws regulating core insurance issues. Taking into account a complex state statutory scheme that regulated, among other things, the substantive content of health insurance policies, the Supreme Court held that state insurance regulations that mandate particular policy benefits are saved from preemption by the savings clause. The Supreme Court concluded that Congress intended to save from preemption only those state laws that regulate the traditional business of insurance to the extent that it involves contractual arrangements for protection against financial loss through the spreading of risk. *Id.*

To guide this inquiry, the Supreme Court followed a two-prong approach. First, the Court took a common-sense view of whether the law in question regulated insurance. Under the common-sense interpretation, a law must not just have an impact on the insurance industry, but must be specifically directed toward that industry. *Id.* at 740–42. Second, the Court looked at case law interpreting the phrase "business of insurance" in the McCarran-Ferguson Act. *Id.* at 742–44. These cases identified three criteria relevant to the determination of what falls within the business of insurance: (1) whether the challenged law had the effect of spreading risk, (2) whether it is integral to the policy relationship, and (3) whether it is specifically limited to the insurance industry. *Id.* at 743. Thus, a claim based on state law or regulation that regulates the "business of insurance" as defined by *Metropolitan Life*'s three-part test is saved from preemption by virtue of the savings clause.

The Supreme Court then applied its *Metropolitan Life* ruling in the case of *Pilot Life Insurance Co. v. Dedeaux,* 481 U.S. 41 (1987). In *Pilot Life,* an injured employee sued the insurance company that issued and administered his employer's disability plan, asserting improper acts in connection with the processing of a claim for benefits. *Id.* at 43–44. The suit was based on state common-law tort and contract principles. *Id.* After concluding that the plaintiff's claims against the insurance company for improper claim processing fell within ERISA's preemption clause, the Supreme Court then proceeded to determine whether such claims would be saved by the savings clause. *Id.* at 47–52. Applying the test enunciated in *Metropolitan Life,* the Supreme Court concluded that such claims were not made under state laws regulating the core insurance business and therefore were not saved by the savings clause. The *Pilot Life* Court reasoned that such actions are not directed at the insurance industry alone and do not relate to the spreading of the risk. *Id.* The Supreme Court ultimately concluded that an action for improper claim processing filed against an insurer is not "saved" from preemption under 29 U.S.C. § 1144(a). *Id.* at 51–52.

In *Custer,* the Fourth Circuit applied the *Pilot Life* holding to conclude that West Virginia's Unfair Trade Practices Act, which regulates insurance companies by prohibiting certain unfair trade and settlement practices, was not saved from preemption. 12 F.3d at 419–20. In *Custer,* plaintiffs claimed that the defendants "ha[d] been negligent, careless and irresponsible in their handling of the Plaintiffs' claims under the policy." *Id.* at 419. The Fourth Circuit reiterated that, under *Pilot Life* and its progeny, a state cause of action for improper claim processing filed against an insurer is not saved from preemption under § 1144(a). *Id.* at 420. The *Custer* court then concluded that plaintiffs' claims of improper claims processing and administration were also not saved from preemption by the savings clause. *Id.*

In *Tri-State Machine, Inc. v. Nationwide Life Insurance Co.,* 33 F.3d 309 (4th Cir. 1994), the Fourth Circuit reaffirmed its narrow construction of the savings clause to encompass only regulation of the core "business of insurance." *Id.* at 314–15. Although it recognized that the first section of the West Virginia statute specifically stated its purpose was to regulate trade practices in the business of insurance in accordance with the McCarren-Ferguson Act, the Fourth Circuit nonetheless concluded that the statute did not solely regulate the "business of insurance." *Id.* at 314. The Fourth Circuit pointed to a long list of prohibited acts in the marketing, sale, and administration of insurance under the West Virginia statute. Relying on the reasoning employed in *Custer,* the *Tri-State* court stated, "[T]his type of regulation is not unique to the business of insurance, and it does not target, at least in these provisions, the core business of insurance which involves contracts of protection under which risk is spread among policy holders." *Id.* at 314–15.

Subsequently, in *Unum Life Insurance Co. of America v. Ward,* 526 U.S. 358 (1999), the Supreme Court applied the framework established by *Pilot Life* and *Metropolitan Life* to determine whether California's notice-prejudice rule regulated insurance within the meaning of the savings clause. The Supreme Court rejected the insurer's argument that the notice-prejudice rule was not directed specifically at the insurance industry because it was merely an industry-specified application of general principles regarding forfeiture of contracts. *Id.* at 368–73. Although the Supreme Court agreed that the notice-prejudice rule was an application of the general contract maxim that the law abhors forfeiture, the Court held that the California notice-prejudice rule was unique and applied solely to insurance contracts. *Id.* at 370–71; *cf. Phoenix Mut. Life Ins. Co. v. Adams,* 30 F.3d 554, 561 (4th Cir. 1994) (ERISA preempted South Carolina's common-law doctrine of substantial compliance because the state law was not specifically directed toward the insurance industry). The Court also held that California's notice-prejudice rule regulated insurance when analyzed under the McCarren-Ferguson factors. *Id.* at 373–75. Recognizing that a state law need not satisfy all three of the factors in order to be deemed a state law that regulates insurance under ERISA, the Supreme Court stated that the factors are "checking points or 'guideposts, not separate essential elements . . . that must be satisfied' to save the State's law." *Id.* at 373–74 (citation omitted).

In *Coffman v. Metropolitan Life Insurance Co.,* 138 F. Supp. 2d 764, 766 (S.D.W. Va. 2001), a plaintiff argued the district court should reexamine the Fourth Circuit's holdings in *Custer* and *Tri-State* in light of the Supreme Court's recent decision in *Ward.* The district court in *Coffman* pointed out that some commentators, in fact, would agree that plaintiff's argument had some merit:

> *Pilot Life* did not consider any statutory unfair insurance practices claims. Arguably, state law claims arising from the violation of specific insurance regulations would fit within the ambit of the savings claims exception to preemption, particularly in light of the recent Supreme Court opinion in *Ward,* which clarifies the test for savings clause analysis.

*Id.* at 766–67 (citation omitted). Nevertheless, the district court refused to alter the force and effect of settled circuit law created in *Custer* and *Tri-State* because "neither *Ward*, nor the Court of Appeals *en banc*, have implicitly or explicitly overruled or otherwise delimited *Custer* or [*Tri-State*]." *Id.* at 767.

Recently, the Supreme Court clarified the test for determining the applicability of the savings clause. *See Ky. Ass'n of Health Plans, Inc. v. Miller*, 538 U.S. 329 (2003). In *Miller*, the Supreme Court reduced the inquiry to two factors: "First, the state law must be specifically directed toward entities engaged in insurance," and "[s]econd . . . the state law must substantially affect the risk pooling arrangement between the insurer and the insured." *Id.* at 341–42 (citations omitted). The Supreme Court made a clean break from the McCarren-Ferguson factors. *See id.* Instead, the *Miller* Court stated, "Rather than concerning itself with whether certain practices constitute 'the business of insurance,' ERISA 'asks merely whether a state law is a law . . . which regulates insurance, banking or securities.'" *Id.* at 340.

In *Singh v. Prudential Health Care Plan Inc.*, 335 F.3d 278, 284–87 (4th Cir.), *cert. denied*, 124 S. Ct. 924 (2003), the Fourth Circuit applied the analysis employed by the Supreme Court in *Miller* to determine whether the antisubrogation provisions in the Maryland HMO Act were saved from preemption. The insurer argued that because subrogation laws are not laws that regulate the business of insurance, the state provisions should not be saved from preemption. *Id.* at 285. The Fourth Circuit, applying the *Miller* test, noted that the inquiry under the savings clause was no longer whether the state law regulated the "business of insurance," but merely whether the law regulated insurance. *Id.* at 285–86. The Fourth Circuit ultimately concluded that the subrogation law fell within the ambit of the savings clause based on precedent created by the Supreme Court and the Fourth Circuit before the *Miller* decision. *Id.* at 286.

A state law regulating insurance may still be preempted if the remedies sought by the plaintiff conflict with ERISA's civil enforcement provisions. In *Singh*, the Fourth Circuit addressed this exception from the savings clause by citing the Supreme Court's recent ruling in *Rush Prudential HMO, Inc. v. Moran*, 536 U.S. 355 (2002):

> The Supreme Court has recognized a "limited exception from the savings clause" created by the overpowering reach of [1132(a)] of ERISA, in which Congress set forth the *exclusive* remedies available for claims relating to employee benefit plans. The Supreme Court concluded that State laws regulating insurance could be applied to ERISA plans, but only so long as doing so would not undermine the objectives of [1132(a)].

*Id.* at 287 (citations omitted). The *Singh* court stated that a state law would fall into this "limited exception" if the law either supplemented or supplanted ERISA's exclusive remedies. The Fourth Circuit ultimately found that because the law did not supplement or supplant the ERISA remedies, the subrogation prohibition remained "saved." *Id.* at 289.

ERISA goes a step further by limiting the savings clause with the deemer clause. The deemer clause provides that "[n]either an employee benefit plan . . . nor any trust established under such a plan shall be deemed to be an insurance company or other insurer . . . or to be engaged in the business of insurance . . . for the purposes of any law of any State purporting to regulate." 29 U.S.C. § 1144(b)(2)(B).

In *FMC Corp. v. Holliday,* 498 U.S. 52, 61–64 (1990), the Supreme Court held that, because of the deemer clause, ERISA preempted a state's antisubrogation provisions with respect to self-funded plans. In determining whether ERISA would preempt state law, the Supreme Court went to great lengths to distinguish insured and uninsured plans. *Id.* at 61–62. In *FMC Corp.,* the Supreme Court recognized that its decision resulted "in a distinction between insured and uninsured plans, leaving the former open to indirect regulation while the latter are not." *Id.* at 62. The Supreme Court ultimately concluded that the deemer clause exempts *"self-funded* ERISA plans from state laws . . . regulat[ing] insurance within the meaning of the saving clause." *Id.* at 61 (emphasis added). As a result, states may not deem self-funded employee benefit plans to be insurance companies or to be engaged in the business of insurance for purposes of direct state regulation. *See Singh,* 335 F.3d at 286 (concluding the plan was "insured" and, therefore, the deemer clause did not exempt the plan from state regulation); *Health Cost Controls v. Whalen,* 1996 WL 787163 (E.D. Va. 1996) (same); *cf. Eppard v. Builders Transp. Inc.,* 1993 WL 28813 (W.D. Va. 1993) (holding that self-funded plan was not subject to state regulation); *and Dillard v. Teamsters Joint Council No. 83 of Va. Health & Welfare Fund,* 1985 WL 17724 (W.D. Va. 1985) (same).

The mere purchase of insurance does not necessarily make the employee benefit plan an insured plan for ERISA purposes. In *Thompson v. Talquin Building Products Co.,* 928 F.2d 649 (4th Cir. 1991), the Fourth Circuit held that the purchase of stop-loss insurance does not convert a self-funded or self-insured employee benefit plan into a fully insured plan for preemption purposes. The Fourth Circuit pointed out that "[t]he stop-loss insurance does not pay benefits directly to participants, nor does the insurance company take over administration of the Plan at the point when the aggregate amount is reached." *Id.* at 653. The Fourth Circuit reasoned that the stop-loss insurance was to protect the employer from catastrophic losses rather than to provide accident and health insurance for the employees. The plan, therefore, was not insured for ERISA purposes. *Id.*

Since *Thompson,* the Fourth Circuit has consistently held that the presence of stop-loss coverage does not destroy a plan's self-funded status for ERISA preemption purposes. *Am. Med. Sec., Inc. v. Bartlett,* 111 F.3d 358 (4th Cir. 1997); *Tri-State,* 33 F.3d at 315; *Hampton Indus. Inc. v. Sparrow,* 981 F.2d 726 (4th Cir. 1992); *Sealy, Inc. v. Nationwide Mut. Ins. Co.,* 286 F. Supp. 2d 625 (M.D.N.C. 2003).

Federal courts also recently addressed whether independent review statutes are preempted by ERISA. In *Rush Prudential HMO, Inc. v. Moran,* 536 U.S. 355 (2002), the Supreme Court faced a challenge of an Illinois law requiring an external review by an independent medical expert of a health insurer's denial of coverage of a medical service as not being medically necessary. If the independent expert found that the service was medically necessary, the state law required the health insurer to pay for the service under the insurance policy. *Id.* at 359–61. The Supreme Court held that the law, even though it related to an employee benefit plan covered by

ERISA, was saved from preemption because it regulated insurance. *Id.* at 365–75. The Supreme Court also discussed whether the Illinois law fell within the limited exception to the savings clause. *Id.* at 375–86. The Supreme Court found the state law did not conflict with ERISA by supplementing or supplanting its civil enforcement scheme and thus remained "saved" from preemption by the savings clause. *Id.*

The United States District Court for the District of Maryland, in *Larsen v. Cigna Healthcare Mid-Atlantic, Inc.,* 224 F. Supp. 2d 998 (D. Md. 2002), was the first district court in the Fourth Circuit to discuss the potential effect of *Moran* on independent state statutes in its jurisdiction. In *Larsen,* the Maryland Insurance Commissioner brought an administrative enforcement action against HMOs under state statutes regulating an HMO's "utilization review." *Id.* at 1000–03. The HMOs removed the action and brought a separate claim for declaratory judgment that the statutes were preempted by ERISA. *Id.* Since there were pending state court actions seeking to enforce state statutes in which HMOs could assert the preemption argument, the district court held that abstention was appropriate. *Id.* at 1009–10. The district court reasoned:

> [T]he Court need only observe the current legal landscape to conclude that it is far from obvious whether Maryland's internal and external review laws are preempted. Very recently, the Supreme Court examined Illinois's independent review law, and concluded that the law (a) regulates insurance within the meaning of ERISA's saving clause, and (b) does not conflict with ERISA's civil enforcement scheme. In upholding the state law's validity, the Court recognized that numerous other states had crafted similar laws, and observed that "we do not believe that the mere fact that state independent review laws are likely to entail different procedures will impose burdens on plan administration that would threaten the object of 29 U.S.C. § 1132(a)." On the same day it decided [*Moran*], the Supreme Court vacated and remanded a Fifth Circuit case that had found Texas's independent review law preempted by ERISA. Certainly, Maryland's laws are not identical to Texas's or Illinois's, and they may yet be found to present "procedures so elaborate, and burdens so onerous, that they might undermine § 1132(a)." Also, the Supreme Court did not consider the possible preemption of internal review laws, which are at issue here. It would seem, however, that in light of such recent support for similar state laws by the highest court in the land, Plaintiffs' assertion of [the] "facially conclusive" preemption falls flat.

*Id.* at 1009 (citations omitted).

The Supreme Court recently held that claims arising under a statute imposing a duty of care on HMOs were preempted by ERISA. *See Aetna Health Inc. v. Davila,* 542 U.S. 200 (2004). In that consolidated action, plaintiffs alleged that their respective HMOs failed to exercise ordinary care in administering coverage decisions in violation of a duty imposed by the Texas Health Care Liability Act (THCLA), TEX. CIV. PRAC. & REM. CODE ANN. § 88.001–003 (2004 Supp. Pamphlet). *Davila,* 542 U.S. at 204–05. Rejecting plaintiffs' argument that their claims were not preempted, the Supreme Court reasoned:

[I]f a managed care entity correctly concluded, under the terms of the relevant plan, a particular treatment was not covered, the managed care entity's denial of coverage would not be a proximate cause of any injuries arising from the denial. Rather, the failure of the plan itself to cover the requested treatment would be the proximate cause. More significantly, the THCLA clearly states that "[t]he standards in Subsections (a) and (b) create no obligation on the part of the health insurance carrier, health maintenance organization, or other managed care entity to provide to an insured or enrollee treatment which is not covered by the health care plan of the entity." § 88.002(d). Hence, a managed care entity could not be subject to liability under the THCLA if it denied coverage for any treatment not covered by the health care plan that it was administering. Thus, interpretation of the terms of respondents' benefit plans forms an essential part of their THCLA claim, and THCLA liability would exist here only because of petitioners' administration of ERISA-regulated benefit plans. Petitioners' potential liability under the THCLA in these cases, then, derives entirely from the particular rights and obligations established by the benefit plans.

*Id.* at 212–13 (footnote omitted). The Court concluded that plaintiffs did not seek to remedy a violation of any legal duty independent of ERISA. *Id.* at 213–14. Rather, plaintiffs sought to rectify the denial of plan benefits. *Id.* Thus, their claims fell within the scope of ERISA.

The Supreme Court also rejected the argument that THCLA is saved from preemption because it is a law regulating insurance. *Id.* at 217. Applying ordinary principles of conflict preemption, the Court observed that even when a state law could be characterized as regulating insurance, it will be preempted if it provides a basis for seeking plan benefits outside of or in addition to the remedial scheme afforded by ERISA. *Id.* at 217–18.

Prior to *Davila,* the Fourth Circuit formulated a three-part test for determining whether a claim is completely preempted: (1) the claim must fall within the scope of an ERISA provision that can be enforced under 29 U.S.C. § 1132(a); (2) the claim must not be capable of resolution without an interpretation of the contract governed by federal law, i.e., an ERISA-governed employee benefit plan; and (3) the plaintiff must have standing under § 1132(a) to pursue its claim. *See Sonoco Prods. Co. v. Physicians Health Plan, Inc.,* 338 F.3d 366, 372 (4th Cir. 2003).

Relying on *Davila,* the District Court for the Southern District of West Virginia concluded that courts must consider two factors when determining whether a claim is completed preempted. *Radcliffe v. El Paso Corp.,* 377 F. Supp. 2d 558 (S.D.W. Va. 2005). First, the court should consider "whether the plaintiff could have originally brought his cause of action under ERISA's civil enforcement provisions." *Id.* at 562. If so, then the court should consider "whether the cause of action involves any independent legal duty on the part of the defendants." *Id.* The district court concluded that "[i]f the alleged liability is derived from or dependent upon the existence and administration of an ERISA-regulated benefit plan, then the state-law claims are not 'entirely independent of the federally regulated contract itself,' and are therefore preempted." *Id.* at 564.

The Fourth Circuit also considered ERISA preemption in the context of (i) a breach of contract claim, and (ii) a labor and employment statute. *Gresham v. Lumbermen's Mutual Casualty Co.*, 404 F.3d 253 (4th Cir. 2005), involved a breach of contract claim. There, the court stated that "what triggers ERISA preemption is not just any indirect effect on administrative procedures but rather an effect on the primary administrative functions of benefit plans, such as determining an employee's eligibility for a benefit and the amount of that benefit." *Id.* at 258 (citation omitted). Addressing preemption, the Fourth Circuit veered from dicta in *Stiltner v. Beretta U.S.A. Corp*, 74 F.3d 1473 (4th Cir. 1996) (*en banc*), in which it indicated that a breach of contract claim was likely preempted because the purpose of the claim was to recover ERISA plan benefits. *See Gresham*, 404 F.3d at 259 (citing *Stiltner*, 74 F.3d at 1480). The *Gresham* court determined that plaintiff's claims were not preempted, because the employer promised to pay severance in an amount greater than that provided by the underlying ERISA plan. Thus, the breach of contract claim was separate and independent from ERISA and the ERISA plan. *Id.*

In *Retail Industry Leaders Ass'n. v. Fielder*, Nos 06-1840, 06-1901, 2007 U.S. App. LEXIS 920, 39 Emp. Ben. Cas. (BNA) 2217 (4th Cir. Jan. 17, 2007), the Fourth Circuit found Maryland's Fair Share Health Care Fund Act, a labor and employment statute, to be preempted by ERISA. The Act, which only applied to certain large employers, sought to require Wal-Mart to spend 8 percent of its total payroll on health insurance. If Wal-Mart failed to meet this threshold, then Wal-Mart would pay the difference to the State of Maryland. In a 2-1 decision, the Fourth Circuit found that Act preempted by ERISA because it would force employers, including Wal-Mart, which was a member of the Retail Association that initiated this action, to change how they structure employee benefit plans. *Id.* at *48. Since the Act regulated the provision of healthcare benefits, it had sufficient "connection with" the ERISA plans to fall within the ERISA preemption. *Id.*

## III. Exhaustion of Administrative Remedies

### A. Is Exhaustion an Absolute Requirement?

In the Fourth Circuit, an ERISA claimant is required to exhaust plan remedies before pursuing an action to recover benefits pursuant to 29 U.S.C. § 1132. *See Hickey v. Digital Equip. Corp.*, 43 F.3d 941, 945 (4th Cir. 1995); *Makar v. Health Care Corp.*, 872 F.2d 80, 82 (4th Cir. 1989). In *Makar*, appellant Dorothy Makar sought reimbursement from her HMO for hospitalization and treatment at an out-of-plan hospital. Her husband, appellant Anthony Makar, similarly sought reimbursement from his employer's group health insurance plan. *Id.* at 81–82. The Makars, however, failed to file a written grievance as required by Mrs. Makar's plan or to pursue the appeal procedures provided by Mr. Makar's plan. *Id.* at 82. The Fourth Circuit observed that the exhaustion requirement is based on ERISA's text and structure, which mandates internal dispute resolution procedures for plan participants. *Id.* at 83. The court also recognized that the exhaustion requirement conserves judicial resources by reducing frivolous claims, minimizing the cost of dispute resolution, and allowing a court to analyze a fully developed record if litigation is required. *Id.* at 82–83.

## B. Exceptions to the Exhaustion Requirement

The general rule requiring exhaustion of plan remedies is applied as a matter of judicial discretion, which includes the discretion to excuse nonexhaustion. *See Nessell v. Crown Life Ins. Co.,* 92 F. Supp. 2d 523, 528–29 (E.D. Va. 2000). In the exercise of this discretion, courts in the Fourth Circuit have recognized two exceptions to the exhaustion requirement. *See Vogel v. Independence Fed. Sav.,* 728 F. Supp. 1210, 1223 (D. Md. 1990). First, failure to exhaust plan remedies will be excused if it appears that pursuit of the internal appeals process would be futile. *See Makar,* 872 F.2d at 83 (recognizing futility as exception to exhaustion requirement); *Fulk v. Hartford Life Ins. Co.,* 839 F. Supp. 1183, 1186 (M.D.N.C. 1993) (appeal to plan would be futile because denial was not based on any medical opinion or factual dispute resolvable by appeal); *Vogel,* 728 F. Supp. at 1223 (even if plaintiffs had not exhausted administrative remedies, their failure would be excused because alleged conduct of defendants indicates there was no reason to believe defendants would change position). Second, exhaustion will be excused if it appears that the plaintiff would have been denied meaningful access to the plan procedures. *See Suntrust Bank v. Aetna Life Ins. Co.,* 251 F. Supp. 2d 1282, 1289–90 (E.D. Va. 2003); *Nessell,* 92 F. Supp. 2d at 523; *Vogel,* 728 F. Supp. at 1223; *see also Makar,* 872 F.2d at 83 (rejecting exhaustion argument because "no findings of futility and appellants [made no showing] that they would be denied access to the claims procedures provided by [their ERISA plans]").

A clear and positive showing of futility is needed in order to suspend the exhaustion requirement. *See Hickey,* 43 F.3d at 945; *Makar,* 872 F.2d at 83; *Nessell,* 92 F. Supp. 2d at 529; *O'Bryhim v. Reliance Standard Life Ins. Co.,* 997 F. Supp. 728, 731 (E.D. Va. 1998) (plaintiff made clear and positive showing of futility because individuals who reviewed decision on remand also would be reviewing appeal to that decision). Bare allegations of futility, however, will not be substituted for the clear and positive showing mandated by the courts. *See Makar,* 872 F.2d at 83 (plaintiffs alleged, without any supporting evidence, that any attempt to pursue plan remedies would have been futile). Such unsupported allegations, therefore, are insufficient to circumvent the exhaustion requirement. *Id.; see also Hickey,* 43 F.3d at 945 (rejecting plaintiffs' allegation that remand for purpose of exhausting plan remedies was "mere formality if not a charade").

In *Nessell,* the plaintiff's sworn statement, which was not contradicted by the insurer, was sufficient to support waiver of the exhaustion requirement based on both exceptions. *Id.,* 92 F. Supp. 2d at 529. Specifically, the United States District Court for the Eastern District of Virginia concluded that an administrative appeal would have been futile because the insurer advised Nessell that any attempt to pursue an appeal through the plan would be unsuccessful. *Id.* (claims adjudicator advised plaintiff that (1) claim decision was final and irrevocable, and (2) insurer would not consider any further appeals). The district court also concluded that Nessell was denied meaningful access to the plan's internal review process because the insurer failed to provide her with a requested copy of the independent medical examiner's report upon which it had relied in rendering the claim decision. *Id.* (claims adjudicator refused to turn over requested medical reports and plan documents).

In contrast, the United States District Court for the Northern District of West Virginia rejected the plaintiffs' argument that the exhaustion requirement had been waived by the employer's failure "to advise employees in writing of the denial of the claim for . . . benefits and to apprise employees of their rights to seek review of such denial." *See Kern v. Verizon Commc'ns, Inc.,* 381 F. Supp. 2d 532, 537 (N.D.W. Va. 2005). The district court noted that "pursuit and exhaustion of internal Plan remedies is an essential prerequisite to judicial review of an ERISA claim for denial of benefits." *Id.* at 536 (citation omitted). The court further observed, "Circuit courts have refused to waive the exhaustion requirement in ERISA cases where the claimant was not adequately informed of claims procedures." *Id.* at 537 (citations omitted). Thus, the district court refused to waive the "strict requirement of exhaustion." *Id.*

Further, although the Fourth Circuit applies the exhaustion requirement in ERISA actions to recover plan benefits, it does not require exhaustion of plan remedies in actions involving a breach of fiduciary duty claim pursuant to 29 U.S.C. § 1104 and 1106. *See Smith v. Sydnor,* 184 F.3d 356, 364–65 (4th Cir. 1999) (judicially created exhaustion requirement not applicable to claims for breach of fiduciary duty); *Hall v. Tyco Int'l Ltd.,* 223 F.R.D. 219 (M.D.N.C. 2004) (holding exhaustion requirement inapplicable to breach of fiduciary duty claim based on employer's failure to comply with notice requirements mandated by ERISA); *Suntrust Bank v. Aetna Life Ins. Co.,* 251 F. Supp. 2d at 1287 (exhaustion requirement is expressly directed toward denial of benefits claims, and not breach of fiduciary duty claims). The Fourth Circuit's reasoning is twofold. First, the exhaustion requirement is derived, in part, from ERISA's statutory mandate that employee benefit plans must provide an internal review process for appealing denials of plan benefits. *See Smith v. Sydnor,* 184 F.3d at 364. A similar premise does not exist for statutory claims involving a violation of ERISA. *Id.* at 364–65 (plan in dispute did not include provision for handling statutory claims, which further supported position that exhaustion is not required for non–benefit-related claims). Second, a claim alleging a violation of a statutory provision under ERISA falls within the expertise of the judiciary, and, therefore, is distinguishable from a claim for benefits, which implicates the expertise of a plan fiduciary. *Id.* at 365. The policy considerations in favor of exhaustion, therefore, are not present in a claim for breach of fiduciary duty where no deference is given to the plan fiduciary's expertise. *See id.*

Significantly, a plaintiff cannot circumvent the exhaustion requirement through artful pleading. *See Smith v. Sydnor,* 184 F.3d at 362; *Suntrust Bank,* 251 F. Supp. 2d at 1287–88. The Fourth Circuit, therefore, requires that a plaintiff exhaust plan remedies before bringing an action for breach of fiduciary duty if the basis for the action is the denial of plan benefits or the action is closely related to the plaintiff's claim for benefits. *See Smith v. Sydnor,* at 362. A breach of fiduciary duty claim is an artfully pled claim for benefits where the resolution of the claim depends on an interpretation and application of plan provisions rather than an interpretation and application of ERISA's statutory provisions. *Id.* Claims related to the validity and effectiveness of assignment and/or beneficiary change forms, for example, were subject to the exhaustion requirement because they were inextricably linked to a claim for benefits and the only relief sought was payment of the policy proceeds. *See Suntrust*

*Bank,* 251 F. Supp. 2d at 1288 (exhaustion requirement applied but was waived based upon denial of meaningful access).

## C. Consequences of Failure to Exhaust

Once a court determines the exhaustion requirement is applicable and the plan participant has failed to pursue and exhaust plan remedies, it may dismiss the ERISA claim without prejudice so that the participant may pursue the plan remedies. *See Makar,* 872 F.2d at 83; *Nessell,* 92 F. Supp. 2d at 528 (claim involving benefit amount dismissed without prejudice to refile after exhaustion of plan's internal appeals procedure). The court also may stay the case, remanding the claim to the plan administrator or plan fiduciary to permit further consideration in accordance with the plan's remedies. *See Hickey,* 43 F.3d at 945.

The United States District Court for the District of South Carolina encountered the issue of whether to dismiss or remand an action involving failure to exhaust plan remedies. *See Gayle v. Flexible Benefit Plan/United Parcel Serv. Long Term Disability Plan,* 318 F. Supp. 2d 328 (D.S.C. 2004), *aff'd,* 401 F.3d 222 (4th Cir. 2005). The plaintiff asserted two claims in an action related to the denial of plan benefits. *See Gayle,* 318 F. Supp. 2d at 330. The first claim sought remand to the plan, with an order requiring that the plan allow plaintiff to exhaust plan remedies. The second claim sought judicial review of any subsequent denial made after the review on remand. *Id.* The district court recognized that it could not satisfy its obligation to enforce the terms of the written plan without holding the plaintiff to the time frames for filing appeals as set forth in the plan. *Id.* at 331 (plan provided that first-level appeal must be made within 180 days of denial of benefits and second-level appeal must be made within sixty days of denial of benefits). Consequently, the court dismissed the first claim with prejudice because the plaintiff had failed to comply with the plan's time-frame requirements. In addition, although the second claim was dismissed without prejudice because it was not a decision on the merits, the court recognized that the ultimate effect would likely be the equivalent of a dismissal with prejudice. *Id.*

Affirming the district court's decision, the Fourth Circuit addressed plaintiff's equitable tolling argument. The Fourth Circuit concluded that the principles of equitable tolling were not justified where a party failed to comply with the deadlines and internal procedures of an ERISA plan. *See Gayle v. United Parcel Serv.,* 401 F.3d 222, 227 (4th Cir. 2005). The court further concluded the exhaustion requirement would be useless if a party were allowed to wait for the internal deadlines to pass and then file a lawsuit. *Id.* at 229.

A failure to exhaust administrative remedies in accordance with an ERISA plan's time parameters also may result in summary judgment in favor of the plan. *Wheeless v. Wal-Mart Stores, Inc. Assoc. Health & Welfare Plan,* 39 F. Supp. 2d 577 (E.D.N.C. 1998). In *Wheeless,* the Wal-Mart plan denied claims for medical benefits, advising Wheeless that he had ninety days to file an appeal. *Id.* at 579. Wheeless filed a written appeal after the ninety-day period expired, and the plan denied the appeal for failure to timely pursue and exhaust the plan's administrative remedies. *Id.* at 581–82 (appeal letter filed 255 days after plaintiff was advised that his claim was denied). Concluding that the plan's denial based on the untimeliness of the appeal was not an abuse of discretion, the district court granted the plan's motion for summary judgment. *Id.*

### D. Minimum Number of Levels of Administrative Review

Courts in the Fourth Circuit have not specified a minimum number of levels of administrative review that must be exhausted before an action may be filed.

### E. Can a Defendant Waive a Failure-to-Exhaust Defense?

Courts in the Fourth Circuit have not specifically addressed the issues of how many levels of the appeals process must be exhausted or whether a defendant may waive the exhaustion requirement. The factual posture of *Hickey*, however, indicates that the Fourth Circuit would allow a defendant to waive all or a portion of a plan's appeal process. In *Hickey*, the district court remanded the case to the plan administrator in order for plaintiffs to exhaust their administrative remedies. *Id.*, 43 F.3d at 945. Although the plan provided for a two-level appeal process, the parties agreed to skip the first level and proceed directly to the second level of review. *Id.* In its discussion of the case, there is no indication the Fourth Circuit would object to a multilevel process or the waiver of the exhaustion requirement with respect to one or more of such levels of review.

## IV. Standard of Review

To determine the appropriate standard of review for reviewing a benefits decision, the Fourth Circuit employs a three-step approach. First, the court decides de novo whether the plan's language confers discretion on the administrator to determine eligibility for benefits or construe plan terms. *Feder v. Paul Revere Life Ins. Co.*, 228 F.3d 518, 522 (4th Cir. 2000). Second, if the plan confers discretion, the court decides de novo whether the administrator acted within the scope of the discretion conferred by the plan. Third, if the administrator acted within the scope of that discretion, the court reviews the benefit decision for an abuse of discretion. *Id.*

### A. Plan Language

"[T]here are obviously no magic words required to trigger the application of one or another standard of judicial review." *De Nobel v. Vitro Corp.*, 885 F.2d 1180, 1187 (4th Cir. 1989). The Fourth Circuit, therefore, gives deference to the fiduciary's decision as long as it appears from the face of the plan documents that the plan fiduciary is authorized to determine eligibility for plan benefits and construe plan language. *See id.; Rego v. Westvaco Corp.*, 319 F.3d 140, 146–47 (4th Cir. 2003). Indeed, an explicit grant of discretionary authority is not required, and a plan's provisions can create discretion by implication if the plan documents indicate a clear intention to delegate final authority for benefit determinations to the plan fiduciary. *See Rego*, 319 F.3d at 146; *Feder*, 228 F.3d at 523 (benefit decision not entitled to deference because insurer was not exercising discretion in ascertaining eligibility for benefits); *Boyd v. Tr. of the United Mine Workers Health & Ret. Funds*, 873 F.2d 57, 59 (4th

Cir. 1989) (trustees of a pension plan had discretionary authority because they had the power of "full and final determinations as to all issues concerning eligibility for benefits" and "are authorized to promulgate rules and regulations to implement [the] Plan").

In *Rego,* for example, the court found discretionary authority because the plan documents (1) instructed the plan administrator "to adopt such procedures and rules as he deems necessary or advisable to administer the Plan," and (2) provided that the plan administrator was responsible for the "determination of participants' eligibility to receive benefits" and the "determination of appeals of denied claims." 319 F.3d at 147 (quoting plan provisions). The Fourth Circuit also found discretionary authority under a plan providing that the plan fiduciary was authorized to "construe the terms of the Plan and resolve any disputes which may arise with regard to the rights of any persons under the terms of the Plan." *United McGill Corp. v. Stinnett,* 154 F.3d 168, 171 (4th Cir. 1998). In contrast, the court determined that discretionary authority did not exist even though a plan provided that (1) "written notice of a claim for disability must be given to [the insurer]," (2) "written proof should establish facts about the claim such as occurrence, nature and extent of the disability, injury or sickness or the loss involved," (3) the insurer had the "right to require additional written proof to verify the continuance of any disability," and (4) the insurer had the right to "request this additional proof as often as [it feels] is necessary, within reason." *Feder,* 228 F.3d at 523–24.

## B. What Standard of Review Applies?

If the court finds that a plan confers discretionary authority on a plan fiduciary, a decision denying plan benefits will be reviewed for an abuse of discretion. *See Ellis v. Metro. Life Ins. Co.,* 126 F.3d 228, 232 (4th Cir. 1997). *See also Booth v. Wal-Mart Stores, Inc.,* 201 F.3d 335, 341 (4th Cir. 2000) ("First, we continue to recognize that an 'arbitrary and capricious' standard is more deferential to the fiduciary than is an 'abuse of discretion' standard. And second, we affirm that the abuse of discretion standard, not the arbitrary and capricious standard, is the appropriate one for judicial review of a fiduciary's discretionary decision under ERISA."). Applying this deferential standard, the decision will not be disturbed if it is reasonable, even if the court would have reached a different conclusion independently. *Id.* A decision is reasonable if it results from a deliberate, principled reasoning process and is supported by substantial evidence. *Id.; Brogan v. Holland,* 105 F.3d 158, 161 n.2 (4th Cir. 1997). The court considers several factors to determine whether the administrator abused its discretion. *See Booth,* 201 F.3d at 342–43; *Brogan,* 105 F.3d at 161; *Lockhart v. United Mine Workers of Am. 1974 Pension Trust,* 5 F.3d 74, 77 (4th Cir. 1993); *de Nobel v. Vitro Corp.,* 885 F.2d at 1188. The court considers, for example, whether the administrator's interpretation of the plan is consistent with plan goals and whether the interpretation might render some plan language meaningless or internally inconsistent. The court also considers whether the interpretation conflicts with the procedural and substantive requirements of ERISA. Other considerations that guide the court's analysis are whether the disputed provisions have been consistently applied and whether the interpretation is contrary to the plan's clear language. *De Nobel,* 885 F.2d at 1188.

## C. Effect of Conflict of Interest or Procedural Irregularity

A caveat to the abuse of discretion standard is that when a plan fiduciary operates under a conflict of interest, the court will give some deference to the decision, but the deference will be lessened to the extent necessary to neutralize any undue influence resulting from the conflict. *Hickey,* 43 F.3d at 946. Significantly, less deference does not mean that the court deviates from the abuse of discretion standard. *Ellis,* 126 F.3d at 233. In other words, the court reviews the decision to determine whether it is consistent with a decision made by a fiduciary acting free of any conflict of interest. The more incentive there is for the fiduciary to benefit itself by a particular interpretation of the plan, the more objectively reasonable the decision must be and the more substantial the supporting evidence must be. *Id.*

The fact that a plan fiduciary has ties to the contributor funding the plan does not create a per se conflict of interest. *Hickey,* 43 F.3d at 946; *de Nobel,* 885 F.2d at 1191–92 (refusing to presume bias where fiduciaries of self-funded pension plan also served as employees of plan's sponsor). The Fourth Circuit, however, generally finds a conflict of interest if the fiduciary both administers the plan and pays for the benefits. *See Bedrick v. Travelers Ins. Co.,* 93 F.3d 149, 151–52 (4th Cir. 1996) (conflict created where insurer funds and administers plan); *Bernstein v. CapitalCare, Inc.,* 70 F.3d 783, 788 (4th Cir. 1995) (conflict existed where HMO plan was insured and administered by the same fiduciary); *Hickey,* 43 F.3d at 946 (conflict found because employer administered and funded plan). The determining factor is whether the fiduciary's exercise of discretion has a direct financial effect on the fiduciary. *See Bedrick,* 93 F.3d at 151–52 (insurer was subject to financial consequences and reaped financial benefits of its coverage decisions); *Hickey,* 43 F.3d at 946 (employer would receive financial benefit from its denial of benefits); *Doe v. Group Hosp. & Med. Servs.,* 3 F.3d 80, 86 (4th Cir. 1993) (insurer exposed to financial risk for claims made in excess of actuarial norm).

In *Doe,* Blue Cross & Blue Shield insured and administered an ERISA plan in exchange for a fixed premium. *Id.* at 86. Presuming that the premium was based on actuarial data, the court noted that the payment of claims was funded by the premiums collected and that Blue Cross & Blue Shield bore the financial risk for claims exceeding the actuarial norm. The insurer's profit, therefore, depended on whether the claims allowed exceeded the assumed risks. Consequently, there was an inherent conflict of interest because the denial of a claim by Blue Cross & Blue Shield promoted the potential for its own profit. *Id.* Based on this analysis, the Fourth Circuit held that "when a fiduciary exercises discretion in interpreting a disputed term of the contract where one interpretation will further the financial interests of the fiduciary, [the court] will not act as deferentially as would otherwise be appropriate." *Id.* at 87.

Although the Fourth Circuit has not directly addressed the issue of the effect of procedural irregularities on the standard of review, the United States District Court for the Eastern District of Virginia succinctly stated, "The correct view for interpreting 'deemed denied' provisions is that 'the mere presence of a procedural irregularity is not enough to strip a plan administrator of the deferential standard of review." *See Wertheim v. Hartford Life Ins. Co.,* 268 F. Supp. 2d 643, 664 (E.D. Va. 2003). Procedural irregularities, therefore, do not justify substituting a de novo standard of review for the abuse of discretion standard. *See id.* at 663–64 (construing effect of "deemed denial" on standard of review). Rather, if the plan administrator fails to comply with ERISA's procedural requirements, the appropriate remedy is to remand to the administrator so that a full and fair review can be conducted. *See Weaver v. Phoenix Home Life Mut. Ins. Co.,* 990 F.2d 154, 159 (4th Cir. 1993); *see also Berry v. Ciba-Geigy Corp.,* 761 F.2d 1003, 1007 n.4 (4th Cir. 1985) (instructing district court to remand to plan administrator if court found the plan failed to comply with ERISA regulations).

Remand to the plan administrator, however, is unnecessary if the evidence clearly establishes that the administrator abused its discretion. *See Weaver,* 990 F.2d at 159 (insurer's admission that it did not know basis for claim denial evidenced an abuse of discretion, thereby allowing court to dispense with remand). Remand also appears to be unnecessary if there is no causal connection between the procedural irregularities and the final claim determination. *See Ellis,* 126 F.3d at 128–39 (although administrator did not technically comply with ERISA's procedural regulations, remand was pointless because review was substantively full and fair).

### D. Other Factors Affecting Standard of Review

Significantly, although the deferential standard of review afforded to ERISA plan administrators and fiduciaries is well established in federal courts, there are state laws that invalidate the deferential standard. In 1998, for example, the Maryland legislature enacted a comprehensive regulatory scheme that established benefit determination standards for health insurers and provided claimants with an external administrative remedy when benefits are denied. *See* MD. CODE ANN., INS. II §§ 15-10A-01 to 15-10C-04. The Maryland regulation established standards for utilization review (an internal process health insurers employ to make initial benefit determinations), required health insurers to maintain an internal grievance procedure for insureds to dispute benefit determinations, and provided insureds with an external review process through the Maryland Insurance Administration. *Id.* The statutorily mandated external review process empowered the Maryland Insurance Commissioner to (1) determine whether a health insurer improperly denied benefits, (2) order the insurer to provide the disputed benefits, and (3) impose penalties against insurers, including fines, for improper denial of health care benefits. *Id.*

Under the statute, the Insurance Commissioner's external review is de novo; thus, no deference is given to the insurer's utilization review determination or internal grievance decision. In fact, the Insurance Commissioner may rely upon the advice of an independent review organization or a medical expert of his choice. *See* MD. CODE ANN., INS. II § 15-10A-03(d). Further, "the Commissioner may consider all of the facts of the case and any other evidence that the Commissioner or designee of the Commissioner considers appropriate." *Id.* at § 15-10A-03(e)(2). In addition, the health insurer shall have the burden of persuasion that its adverse decision is correct. *See id.* at § 15-10A-03(e)(1). Thus, the Maryland statute and similar statutes in other states appear to abolish the deferential standard of review by displacing judicial review under 29 U.S.C. § 1132(a).

Courts have concluded that the Maryland statute and similar statutes in other states are not preempted by ERISA. *See Moran,* 536 U.S. at 365–75 (Illinois independent review statute not preempted by ERISA); *Larsen,* 224 F. Supp. 2d at 1009–10 (abstaining from rendering conclusion, but noting Maryland's internal and external review statutes not necessarily preempted by ERISA); *but see Aetna v. Davila,* 542 U.S. 212–14 (claims under Texas Health Care Liability Act were preempted by ERISA). Thus, the law appears somewhat unsettled on whether state statutes modifying the deferential standard of review by displacing judicial review are preempted by ERISA.

## V. Rules of Plan Interpretation

### A. Application of Federal Common Law

When interpreting the provisions of an ERISA plan, courts are guided by federal common law. *See Baker v. Provident Life & Accident Ins. Co.,* 171 F.3d 939, 942 (4th Cir. 1999); *United McGill Corp. v. Stinnett,* 154 F.3d 168, 171–72 (4th Cir. 1998); *see also Mass. Mut. Life Ins. Co. v. Russell,* 473 U.S. 134, 156 (1985) (noting legislative history demonstrates Congress intended federal courts to develop federal common law to deal with issues involving rights and obligations under ERISA plans). Federal common law, however, may not be used to override the express terms of the plan. *See Baker,* 171 F.3d at 942 (language of plan is paramount to its interpretation); *United McGill,* 154 F.3d at 172–73 ("[W]e are bound to enforce the contractual provisions as drafted."). Rather, the Fourth Circuit requires that the plain language of the plan be enforced in accordance with "its literal and natural meaning." *See United McGill,* 154 F.3d at 172 (one of ERISA's primary functions is to ensure integrity of written plan). Thus, the Fourth Circuit uses and applies ordinary principles of contract law and enforces an ERISA plan's plain language in its ordinary sense. *See Bynum v. CIGNA Healthcare of N.C., Inc.,* 287 F.3d 305, 313 (4th Cir. 2002).

### B. Application of *Contra Proferentem*

If a court finds a plan term is ambiguous, it applies the doctrine of *contra proferentem* and construes the ambiguity against the drafter of the plan and in accordance with the reasonable expectations of the insured. *See Bynum,* 287 F.3d at 313–14; *Bailey v. Blue Cross & Blue Shield,* 67 F.3d 53, 57–58 (4th Cir. 1995); *Doe v. Group Hosp. & Med. Servs.,* 3 F.3d 80, 88–89 (4th Cir. 1993) (principle of construing ambiguity against drafting party may be applied when determining whether decision was made solely for benefit of plan participants). The application of this doctrine appears to become especially significant when a court is using a less deferential standard of review. *See Bailey,* 67 F.3d at 58. In *Bailey,* the court determined the plan's exclusionary language was ambiguous and construed the ambiguity against the insurer. *Id.* at 57–58. Noting that the insurer's discretionary interpretation was entitled to less deference than it might otherwise apply, the court concluded that the denial of coverage was improper. *Id.* at 58; *see also Doe,* 3 F.3d at 88–89 (contract construed for benefit of plan participants because, inter alia, discretionary interpretation was subject to less deferential standard).

### C. Deference Afforded to an Administrator's Interpretation of a Plan

The general rule is that if the plan administrator has discretion to construe plan terms, a court must accept its definition unless there is an abuse of discretion. *See*

*Bynum*, 287 F.3d at 313. Courts may reference several sources, including state and federal law, to determine whether the administrator's interpretation of an undefined plan term is reasonable. *See Baker,* 171 F.3d at 942. Baker, who was driving while intoxicated, collided head-on into another car, killing its driver. He pleaded guilty to, inter alia, involuntary manslaughter and driving while impaired. *Id.* at 941 (involuntary manslaughter is a felony under North Carolina law, and driving while impaired is a misdemeanor). The ERISA plan insuring Baker provided that benefits would not be paid for medical treatment if the illness or injury "is due to voluntary participation in a felony." *Id.* (quoting plan language). The Fourth Circuit examined the reasonableness of the plan's interpretation of the term "voluntary," relying on federal cases and North Carolina state court cases adjudicating the closely analogous area of accidental death benefits. *Id.* at 942. The court noted that, under federal and North Carolina law, the general rule is that the natural or probable consequence of an act or course of action is not an accident, and the insured should be held to have intended the result. *Id.* The court, therefore, concluded the denial of benefits was reasonable because Baker voluntarily drank too much, voluntarily drove while drunk, and should reasonably have foreseen the result of his acts. *Id.* at 942–43.

Significantly, the deferential standard is unlikely to be afforded if the plan fails to define a crucial term prior to the claim denial. *See Bynum,* 287 F.3d at 313. In *Bynum,* the insurer failed to define relevant plan terms throughout the administrative handling of the claim. The Fourth Circuit held that the failure to define the disputed plan term prior to the claim denial constituted an abuse of discretion. The district court, therefore, did not err in declining to defer to the insurer's after-the-fact definition. *Id.*

The Fourth Circuit also refused to afford "substantial deference" to a decision by a conflicted plan administrator simply because the claim was insubstantial in *Carolina Care Plan, Inc., v. McKenzie,* 467 F.3d 383 (4th Cir. 2006). According to the court, the consistent denial of small claims, by a conflicted administrator, can still have a large financial impact over time. For this reason, regardless of the value of the claim at issue, a decision by a conflicted administrator "demands diminished deference." *Id.* at 387.

### D. Other Rules of Plan or Contract Interpretation

Plan interpretation may involve the terms of plan amendments in addition to the terms of the original plan. Significantly, benefits under welfare benefit plans, such as health care and severance benefit plans, are not vested benefits. *See Wheeler v. Dynamic Eng'g, Inc.,* 62 F.3d 634, 637 (4th Cir. 1995) (health care plan exempt from ERISA's statutory vesting requirements); *Doe,* 3 F.3d at 84 (no vesting of health care benefits provided under ERISA plan); *Sejman v. Warner-Lambert Co.,* 889 F.2d 1346, 1348–49 (4th Cir. 1990) (no vesting of severance benefits, which were contingent and not accrued). The employer, therefore, may modify or withdraw plan benefits at any time. *Id.* To be effective, any amendment must be made in compliance with ERISA's requirements and the terms of the plan. *See Doe,* 3 F.3d at 84 (contract validly amended and insurer could base claim decision on language of amendment). In addition, because vesting may occur based on the plan terms, the amendment may not apply to all claims under the plan. *See Wheeler,* 62 F.3d at 637–38.

In *Wheeler,* the plan administrator denied a claim for high-dose chemotherapy with peripheral stem cell rescue (HDC/PSCR), a cancer treatment that involved a four-step process. *Id.* at 637. The plan administrator based its denial on a January 1, 1994, plan amendment that eliminated coverage for this treatment. In its analysis of the claim denial, the Fourth Circuit considered whether Wheeler's coverage for the HDC/PSCR treatment vested under the terms of the prior plan. *Id.* at 637–38. If so, then the amendment would be ineffective because a subsequent amendment could not apply retroactively to exclude coverage that was already vested. Applying a de novo standard of review, the court held that (1) if a medical insurance policy insures against illness, coverage for medical costs arising from an illness vests when that illness occurs; and (2) if a medical insurance policy insures against expenses, coverage vests when expenses are incurred. *Id.* Wheeler's plan provided coverage for medical expenses, but it did not define the term "incurred." *Id.* at 639. Analyzing the law of various state and federal courts, the Fourth Circuit concluded that an insured "incurs" all expenses stemming from a multistep medical procedure when the insured arranges for and begins the treatment. *Id.* The expenses were incurred and coverage for them was vested under the prior plan when Wheeler began the HDC/PSCR treatment on December 15, 1993. *Id.* Thus, the amended plan, which became effective January 1, 1994, did not retroactively exclude coverage, and the remaining steps in the HDC/PSCR treatment were covered in accordance with the prior plan terms. *Id.* at 640–41.

## VI. Discovery

### A. Limitations on Discovery

While the Fourth Circuit has not comprehensively addressed the scope of discovery in ERISA actions in a published decision, district courts within the circuit have been guided by the evidentiary rules set forth in *Quesinberry v. Life Insurance Co. of North America,* 987 F.2d 1017, 1021–27 (4th Cir. 1993). *Quesinberry* held that a district court reviewing a denial of benefits de novo may consider evidence outside the administrative record in its discretion, but "only when circumstances clearly establish that additional evidence is necessary to conduct an adequate *de novo* review of the benefit decision." *Id.* at 1025. The court cautioned that "[i]n most cases, where additional evidence is not necessary for adequate review of the benefits decision, the district court should look only at the evidence that was before the plan administrator or trustee at the time of determination." *Id.* The court of appeals elaborated in *Sheppard & Enoch Pratt Hosp., Inc. v. Travelers Ins. Co.,* 32 F.3d 120, 125 (4th Cir. 1994):

> Thus, although it may be appropriate for a court conducting a de novo review of a plan administrator's action to consider evidence that was not taken into account by the administrator, the contrary approach should be followed when conducting a review under the abuse of discretion standard.

Several recent unpublished decisions from the Fourth Circuit provide guidance regarding the limitation of discovery in an action to challenge the denial of benefits governed by the abuse of discretion standard. In *Donnell v. Metropolitan Life Insurance Co.,* 165 Fed. Appx. 288, 2006 WL 297314 (4th Cir. 2006), the court of appeals sustained the trial court's denial of benefits following review for an abuse of discretion. The plaintiff contended on appeal that she should have been permitted to conduct discovery regarding the insurer's conflict of interest. The court concluded that the district court's decision was proper "even under the least deferential version of our modified abuse of discretion standard," so that such evidence could not change the outcome. The court added:

> Where, as here, a court reviews an administrator's decision under a deferential standard, discovery and introduction of extrinsic evidence pertaining to the "mental processes of the plan's administrator" are generally, if not uniformly, disallowed.

*Id.* at *9.

In another action in which the denial of benefits was reviewed for an abuse of discretion, the court sustained the trial court's decision denying discovery as to a previous business relationship between the defendant insurer and a vocational expert upon whose report the denial was, in part, based. *Abromitis v. Cont'l Cas. Co.,* 114 Fed. Appx. 57, 2004 WL 2491367 (4th Cir. 2004). The court of appeals endorsed the trial court's analysis distinguishing the conflict of interest between a claimant and administrator, which is relevant, from the incidental possibility of a conflict of interest between the claim administrator and its employees and consultants, which is not. The court noted that a relevant inquiry might be whether the vocational survey contained inaccurate information, undermining the decision. *Id.* at *4, n.2. (The footnote does not address whether, to be admissible, such evidence must be offered during the administrative process.)

Some Fourth Circuit opinions reflect that discovery did take place at the district court level even though the claim fiduciary had discretionary authority. *See, e.g., Bedrick v. Travelers Ins. Co.,* 93 F.3d 149, 153 (1996), *Bernstein v. CapitalCare, Inc.,* 70 F.3d 783, 790 (1995). These cases do not, however, address the propriety of such discovery and in each case, the parties apparently had agreed to engage in discovery.

A number of district court decisions have addressed specific discovery issues. Typically, in an action challenging an insurer's denial of benefits under the "modified abuse of discretion" standard, no discovery has been allowed beyond production of the policy, plan, and administrative record. *See, e.g., Briggs v. Marriott Int'l, Inc.,* 368 F. Supp. 2d 461, 467, n. 4 (D. Md. 2005), *Sawyer v. Potash Corp. of Sask.,* 417 F. Supp. 2d 730, 737–38 (E.D.N.C. 2006). However, discovery into the claim process, may, in an appropriate case, be permissible. *Korotynska v. Metro. Life Ins. Co.,* 2005 WL 991003, at *4, n.4 (D. Md. 2005). Further, some discovery has been found necessary to address specific issues, such as whether a plan existed. *Hall v. Standard Ins. Co.,* 2005 WL 348266 (W.D. Va. 2005).

In other types of ERISA cases, such as claims for breach of fiduciary duty or interference with ERISA rights, standard discovery procedures usually apply. *E.g.,*

*O'Donnell v. Biolife Plasma Services, L.P.,* 384 F. Supp. 2d 971 (S.D.W. Va. 2005). However, even in such cases, it may be appropriate to limit discovery. *See, e.g., Schaffer v. Westinghouse Savannah River Co.,* 135 Fed. Appx. 568, 2005 WL 567812, at *3 (4th Cir. 2005).

Some district courts within the circuit, including the Western District of Virginia and the District of South Carolina, have implemented standardized procedures for handling ERISA benefit actions with special case management plans. Such standardized pretrial procedures, which direct production of the policy and administrative record and set out a briefing schedule for dispositive motions, contemplate no discovery, at least in abuse of discretion cases.

## B. Discovery and Conflict of Interest

In *Booth v. Wal-Mart Stores, Inc.,* 201 F.3d 335, 342–43 (4th Cir. 2000), the court identified certain factors to be considered when determining whether a fiduciary's discretionary denial of benefits should be set aside, including "the fiduciary's motives and any conflict of interest it may have." In cases involving a claimant's entitlement to benefits, and in which the claim fiduciary is not an insurer, discovery may be necessary in order to analyze whether, and to what extent, a conflict of interest exists. In *Colucci v. Agfa Corp. Severance Pay Plan,* 431 F.3d 170 (4th Cir. 2005), the court of appeals approved the denial of severance pay under a plan providing discretionary authority to the employer. The court rejected a contention that deference should be modified simply upon a showing that the administrator also provides funding for the plan. The court of appeals differentiated between employer-funded plans and those funded by an insurance policy, where the parties' relationships and interests are spelled out by the insurance policy itself:

> But the simple and commonplace fact that a plan administrator is also its funder is not enough to support a finding of a conflict of interest that would cause an adjustment to our deference. . . . The circumstances under which we have suggested a conflict of interest might arise are when a plan is managed by its insurer, whose revenue comes from fixed premiums paid by the plan's sponsor. In such a case, we were willing to assume that the insurer-administrator's profit motives unavoidably factored into its decision to accept or deny plan members' claims.

*Id.* at 179. The holding suggests that discovery should not normally be necessary to evaluate the conflict of interest between a plan claimant and an insurer, because that relationship is set out in the policy, but it may be appropriate when the plan is not insured.

*Donnell v. Metropolitan Life Insurance Co.,* 165 Fed. Appx. 288, 2006 WL 297314, at *9 (4th Cir. 2006), affirms one of several decisions from the Eastern District of Virginia in which the court rejected a contention that claimant is entitled to conduct discovery in an abuse of discretion case regarding the degree of conflict by the fiduciary. When the plan is insured, the nature of the conflict is clear, and that fact is to be taken into account on review. *See also Stanley v. Metro. Life Ins. Co.,* 2004 WL 329386 (E.D. Va. 2004); *Burkhart v. Metro. Life Ins. Co.,* 2003 WL

21655486 (E.D. Va. 2003). In those cases claimants had contended that *Booth* permitted limited discovery, and noted that discovery had been permitted in *Bedrick*. The district court observed that neither decision addressed the propriety of discovery. The review must be from the record itself:

> Plaintiff is mistaken in her assertion that she is entitled to discovery of the administrator's "knowledge" at the time MetLife evaluated the claim. Discovery into MetLife's thought process is prohibited.

*Stanley,* at *3.

In *DiCamillo v. Liberty Life Assurance Co.,* 287 F. Supp. 2d 616 (D. Md. 2003), plaintiff contended that summary judgment was not proper because he had not been permitted to conduct discovery. The court observed that "discovery would be entirely unnecessary on the merits of Liberty Life's decision since my review of the administrator's decision should be based on the record before the administrator." *Id.* at 627. Plaintiff, however, contended that he should be permitted to conduct discovery regarding similarly situated claimants and regarding payments to medical consultants in this and other cases. The court was unwilling to permit such discovery in the absence of "credible allegations that he was treated unfairly vis-à-vis other claimants or that the medical consultants are so beholden to a defendant that they have lost their professional independence." The court, however, was "not prepared to say that such discovery should never be permitted." *Id.* at 627–28.

# VII. Evidence

## A. Scope of Evidence under Standards of Review

### 1. Abuse of Discretion Standard

When a district court in the Fourth Circuit reviews an ERISA plan administrator's decision under the abuse of discretion standard, the court must assess the reasonableness of the administrator's decision based upon the facts known to the administrator at the time. Evidence outside the administrative record may not be considered. *Elliott v. Sara Lee Corp.,* 190 F.3d 601, 608 (4th Cir. 1999); *Bernstein v. Capital-Care, Inc.,* 70 F.3d 783, 788 (4th Cir. 1995); *Sheppard & Enoch Pratt Hosp.,* 32 F.3d 120, 125 (4th Cir. 1994). If the court believes the administrator lacked adequate evidence upon which to base a decision, the court should remand the claim to the administrator for a new determination rather than considering additional evidence. *Elliott,* 190 F.3d at 609; *Sheppard,* 32 F.3d at 125; *Berry v. Ciba-Geigy Corp.,* 761 F.2d 1003, 1008 (4th Cir. 1985). The district court may also exercise its discretion to remand a claim where there are multiple issues and an inadequate record to review. *Elliott,* 190 F.3d at 609; *Quesinberry v. Life Ins. Co. of N. Am.,* 987 F.2d 1017, 1025 n.6 (4th Cir. 1993). However, "remand should be used sparingly." *Elliott,* 190 F.3d at 609; *Berry,* 761 F.2d at 1008.

Accordingly, a party may not supplement the administrative record with reports created more than a year after the denial on appeal. *Sawyer v. Potash Corp. of Sask.,* 417 F. Supp. 2d 730 (E.D.N.C. 2006). An affidavit identifying the administrative record is admissible, but documents such as Social Security findings and letters between counsel, which were not part of the administrative record, are not. *Anderson v. Sara Lee Corp.,* 348 F. Supp. 2d 618 (W.D.N.C. 2004). The district court in *Barnes v. Bell South Corp.,* 2003 WL 22231261 (W.D.N.C. 2003), addressed a contention by plaintiff that he be permitted to supplement the administrative record by adding evidence submitted to the administrator after its final appeal decision but before suit. Finding no Fourth Circuit precedent to permit such supplementation, the court declined to permit modification of the record. *Id.* at *10. However, in *Brodish v. Federal Express Corp.,* 384 F. Supp. 2d 827 (D. Md. 2005), the court found that materials relating to the administrator's refusal to reconsider the claim six months after the denial on appeal, but before suit, should be considered part of the administrative record.

Further, even under the abuse of discretion standard, it may be appropriate to admit evidence regarding the parties' relationship to analyze properly any conflict of interest. *Colucci v. Agfa Corp. Severance Pay Plan,* 431 F.3d 170 (4th Cir. 2005).

### 2. De Novo Standard

When a district court employs the de novo standard to review an ERISA claim denial, the court may in its discretion consider evidence that was not before the plan administrator. *Elliott,* 190 F.3d at 609 n.6; *Quesinberry,* 987 F.2d at 1025. The district court should consider such additional evidence only when it is necessary to conduct an adequate de novo review of the decision. The Fourth Circuit has described certain exceptional circumstances that may warrant exercise of the court's discretion to allow additional evidence. This list is not exhaustive, but is rather a guide for district courts faced with motions to introduce evidence not previously presented to the plan administrator. *Quesinberry,* 987 F.2d at 1027. Examples cited are

> claims that require consideration of complex medical questions or issues regarding the credibility of medical experts; the availability of very limited administrative review procedures with little or no evidentiary record; the necessity of evidence regarding interpretation of the terms of the plan rather than specific historical facts; instances where the payor and the administrator are the same entity and the court is concerned about impartiality; claims which would have been insurance contract claims prior to ERISA; and circumstances in which there is additional evidence that the claimant could not have presented in the administrative process.

*Id.* In determining whether to admit additional evidence, the court "should address why the evidence proffered was not submitted to the plan administrator." *Id.*

Admission of such evidence may be appropriate if "administrative procedures do not allow for or permit the introduction of the evidence." Such evidence must not be admitted where it is only "cumulative of the evidence presented to the plan administrator, or is simply better evidence than the claimant mustered for the claim review." *Elliott,* at 609 n.6; *Quesinberry,* at 1027.

In most cases, the district court should consider only the evidence that was before the plan administrator at the time of the determination. *Quesinberry,* at 1025.

For example, it was not an abuse of discretion for the trial court to deny consideration of a supplemental analysis of a toxicology report that could have been added to the administrative record. *Moore v. UnumProvident Corp.,* 116 Fed. Appx. 416, 2004 WL 2538211 (4th Cir. 2004).

## B. Evidentiary Value of Social Security Determinations

The Fourth Circuit has stated that it is not an abuse of discretion for a plan fiduciary to deny disability benefits where conflicting medical reports were presented. *Elliott,* 190 F.3d at 606; *Ellis v. Metro. Life Ins. Co.,* 126 F.3d 228, 234 (4th Cir. 1997). Social Security determinations and other findings from an administrative law judge should be considered as evidence by the administrator, but they are not determinative. A plan administrator is under no obligation to weigh Social Security determinations more favorably than other evidence unless the plan expressly declares that Social Security determinations are binding on the plan. *Elliott,* 190 F.3d at 608. *See also Smith v. Cont'l Cas. Co.,* 369 F.3d 412, 418–19 (4th Cir. 2004) (in reversing the district court decision in favor of claimant, the court held it was error to utilize Social Security procedures for purpose of evaluating a disability claim under an employer-sponsored plan). However, a district court may conclude that a favorable Social Security decision "should be given significant weight" in evaluating whether the denial of disability benefits constituted an abuse of discretion. *Hines v. Unum Life Ins. Co. of Am.,* 110 F. Supp. 2d 458, 468 (W.D. Va. 2000). *See also Brogan v. Holland,* 105 F.3d 158, 163 n.6 (4th Cir. 1997) (determination of administrative law judge in state workers' compensation proceeding may be considered when evaluating claim for disability retirement benefits).

Despite the long-standing Fourth Circuit precedent holding that Social Security determinations of disability are not entitled to special weight, and the holding of the Supreme Court in *Black & Decker Disability Plan v. Nord,* 538 U.S. 822 (2003), district courts continue to encounter such arguments from litigants. *See, e.g., McCready v. Standard Ins. Co.,* 417 F. Supp. 2d 684, 702 (D. Md. 2006) (reiterating that a disability finding by Social Security does not mandate a finding of disability under a plan). However, Social Security findings may provide relevant factual information. For example, in *Smith v. A.T. Massey Coal Co.,* 2006 WL 285985, at *7 (S.D.W. Va. 2006), the Social Security Administration had concluded that plaintiff had residual sedentary work capacity, which was consistent with the basis of denial of benefits under the disability plan at issue. The court noted that while plaintiff was receiving Social Security disability benefits, his award supported a finding that he was not entitled to benefits under the disability plan.

## C. Other Evidence Issues

In *Booth v. Wal-Mart Stores, Inc.,* 201 F.3d 335, 342–43 (4th Cir. 2000), the court discussed certain factors to be evaluated in determining whether the denial of a discretionary benefit should be reversed for abuse of discretion. *Booth* involved an appeal by the defendant plan following a bench trial, which had resulted in a finding that the plan administrator did abuse its discretion. At trial, plaintiff was not permitted to introduce evidence on the merits that had not been presented to the administrative committee. *Id.* at 339, n.1. The court of appeals reversed. It found, from the record, that the administrator had not abused its discretion. Whether the court of appeals relied upon the administrative record itself or upon evidence presented at trial relating to the administrative process is unclear from the opinion.

## VIII. Procedural Aspects of ERISA Practice

### A. Methods of Adjudication

Many reported ERISA cases comprise decisions reviewing the denial of benefits under an abuse of discretion standard, normally resolved by summary judgment. In *Phelps v. C.T. Enterprises, Inc.,* 394 F.3d 213 (4th Cir. 2005), the court of appeals commented that such cases did, in fact, involve a modified summary judgment procedure, noting the discussion in *Wilkins v. Baptist Healthcare Systems, Inc.,* 150 F.3d 609, 617 (6th Cir. 1998). It is appropriate in some cases to sustain the denial of benefits as a matter of law on summary judgment, even if the de novo standard is applied. *See Gallagher v. Reliance Standard Life Ins. Co.,* 305 F.3d 264 (4th Cir. 2002).

The Fourth Circuit has expressly ruled that a jury trial is inappropriate in an action brought under ERISA. *See Biggers v. Wittek Industries, Inc.,* 4 F.3d 291 (4th Cir. 1993); *Berry v. Ciba-Geigy,* 761 F.2d 1003 (4th Cir. 1985). More recently, *Phelps* observed that claims alleging breach of fiduciary duty require no special procedure, except that they must be resolved by the court rather than by jury because the equitable relief provision of ERISA does not provide the right to jury trial. *Phelps* does not address the possible impact of the Seventh Amendment, relying upon the court's prior ruling in *Berry v. Ciba-Geigy Corp.* If ERISA and non-ERISA claims are brought jointly, only the non-ERISA claims are to be presented to the jury. *Varghese v. Honeywell Int'l, Inc.,* 424 F.3d 411, 415, n.5 (4th Cir. 2005).

A majority of district courts in the Fourth Circuit has found that jury trials are not available in ERISA actions. *See, e.g., Bursell v. Gen. Elec. Co.,* 243 F. Supp. 2d 460 (E.D.N.C. 2003); *Tingler v. Unum Life Ins. Co. of Am.,* 2003 U.S. Dist. LEXIS 5455 (S.D.W. Va. 2003); *Farrie v. Charles Town Races, Inc.,* 901 F. Supp. 1101, 1106–07 (N.D.W. Va. 1995); *Abels v. Kaiser Aluminum & Chemical Corp.,* 803 F. Supp. 1151, 1153–54 (S.D.W. Va. 1992); *Quesinberry v. Individual Banking Group, Acc. Ins.,* 737 F. Supp. 38, 41 (W.D. Va. 1990), *aff'd in part, rev'd in part,* 987 F.2d 1017 (4th Cir. 1993); *Wise v. Dallas & Mavis Forwarding Co.,* 751 F. Supp. 90, 92 (W.D.N.C. 1990).

Despite such precedent, there are a few district court opinions that have reached the opposite conclusion. These cases were decided after *Biggers* and *Berry,* but before *Phelps.* For example, in *Hulcher v. United Behavioral System, Inc.,* 919 F. Supp. 879 (E.D. Va. 1995), the district court held that a jury trial is permitted under 29 U.S.C. § 1132(a)(1)(B) for a participant's benefit claim under ERISA. The court reasoned that although the claim arose under ERISA, both the nature of the issue to be tried and the nature of the remedy sought were most closely analogous to an action in contract. *See also Vaughn v. Owen Steel Co.,* 871 F. Supp. 247 (D.S.C.

1994). More recently, in *Lamberty v. Premier Millwork & Lumber Co.,* 329 F. Supp. 2d 737 (E.D. Va. 2004), the court concluded that the Constitution provides a right to jury trial on a claim for breach of fiduciary duty, relying upon recent Supreme Court decisions.

Some district courts have refused to follow *Hulcher. See Lawrence v. Cont'l Cas. Co.,* 1998 U.S. Dist. LEXIS 15108 (M.D.N.C. 1998); *Ellis v. Metro. Life Ins. Co.,* 919 F. Supp. 936 (E.D. Va. 1996). Other district courts have questioned its ruling, but concluded that a jury trial was not available after following its analysis. *Allison v. Cont'l Cas. Ins. Co.,* 953 F. Supp. 127, 129 (E.D. Va. 1996). In addition, one district court found that neither *Berry* nor *Biggers* was dispositive and concluded that:

> Every claim under ERISA § 1132(a)(1)(B) merits individual analysis under the Seventh Amendment. This inquiry can be quickly disposed of in many instances, where analysis reveals a § 1132(a)(1)(B) action to be clearly equitable. Nevertheless, *Firestone* and the Seventh Amendment mandate examination of individual ERISA claims to recover benefits in order to assess whether a particular claim is legal thereby entitling claimant to a jury trial.

*Williams v. Unum Life Ins. Co. of Am.,* 940 F. Supp. 136, 141 (E.D. Va. 1996). However, this portion of the *Williams* decision apparently has not been followed by any other district court in the Fourth Circuit. *But see Colonial Williamsburg Found. v. Blue Cross & Blue Shield,* 909 F. Supp. 386, 390–91 (E.D. Va. 1995) (for a similar analysis).

### B. Reported ERISA Trials

In actions for breach of fiduciary duty, trials should follow the same procedure as other bench trials. *See, e.g. Meyer v. Berkshire Life Ins. Co.,* 250 F. Supp. 2d 544 (D. Md. 2003), *aff'd,* 372 F.3d 261 (4th Cir. 2004). However, remarkably little guidance exists regarding the procedure to be followed in an action for recovery of benefits, where the administrative record is the source of most, or all, admissible evidence. It is sometimes difficult to determine from the appellate decision exactly what procedure was employed by the trial court. For example, in *Booth v. Wal-Mart Stores, Inc.,* 201 F.3d 335 (4th Cir. 2000), the court of appeals reversed the trial court's decision, at a bench trial, that the claim committee had abused its discretion. The trial court opinion is unreported. Accordingly, it is unclear how the district court handled the case procedurally. In *Newman v. Prudential Insurance Co. of America,* 367 F. Supp. 2d 969 (E.D. Va. 2005), the court elaborated on the nature of a bench trial in which a claim denial is to be reviewed de novo. After addressing the analyses of other circuits, particularly the Sixth Circuit, the court outlined the procedure it considered appropriate in an ERISA bench trial for recovery of benefits; it would make findings of fact and conclusions of law from the existing administrative record, unless supplemental material is admissible under the narrow guidelines of *Quesinberry v. Life Insurance Co. of North America,* 987 F.2d 1017 (4th Cir. 1993).

Although most decisions reviewing a claim under the abuse of discretion standard are reached through dispositive motions, some courts have concluded that a trial is necessary to resolve material issues of fact. *See, e.g., Watson v. Unum Life Ins. Co. of Am.*, 126 Fed. Appx. 604, 2005 WL 665055 (4th Cir. 2005) (sustaining a district court bench trial finding that defendant had not abused its discretion); *Eubanks v. Prudential Ins. Co. of Am.*, 336 F. Supp. 2d 521 (M.D.N.C. 2004). In *Harvey v. Astra Merck Inc. Long Term Disability Plan*, 348 F. Supp. 2d 536 (M.D.N.C. 2004), the court concluded that summary judgment could not be granted to either party because there were issues of fact as to the insurer's motives and the extent to which the conflict of interest affected the claim decision. As discussed above, however, evidence regarding a conflict of interest may be necessary only if the plan is not insured. *See Colucci v. Agfa Corp. Severance Pay Plan*, 431 F.3d 170 (4th Cir. 2005) (noting that an insurer's conflict of interest is usually self-apparent). When an employer-administered plan is involved, evidence as to a potential conflict of interest would normally be admissible. *Id.* at 179–80.

A survey of reported opinions disclosed relatively few recent ERISA bench trials in actions to recover plan benefits. *See, e.g., Danz v. Life Ins. Co. of N. Am.*, 215 F. Supp. 2d 645 (D. Md. 2002) (bench trial of claims for group life insurance benefits denied on grounds that preexisting heart condition substantially contributed to death); *Johnson v. Gen. Am. Life Ins. Co.*, 178 F. Supp. 2d 644 (W.D. Va. 2001) (bench trial involving disability benefits terminated under mental illness limitation); *Bynum v. Cigna Healthcare of N.C., Inc.*, 287 F.3d 305 (4th Cir. 2002) (appeal from district court bench trial involving claim for benefits under ERISA health plan); *Johannssen v. Dist. No. 1—Pacific Coast Dist., Meba Pension Plan*, 292 F.3d 159 (4th Cir. 2002) (appeal from bench trial involving challenge to benefit termination under amendment to pension plan); *Myers v. Hercules, Inc.*, 253 F.3d 761 (4th Cir. 2001) (appeal from district court bench trial involving claim for benefits under disability plan). Most of these trials were de novo reviews of claim denials. However, in *Bynum* the parties agreed to a bench trial even though the case was to be decided under the abuse of discretion standard.

## C. Special Procedures for ERISA Benefit Cases

Though the Fourth Circuit has not adopted special procedures for ERISA actions, some district courts have implemented expedited procedures for the handling of ERISA actions. For example, case management orders used by some courts in the District of South Carolina require responses to special interrogatories designed to identify preemption issues, and call for expedited production of the administrative record and policy.

# IX. Fiduciary Liability Claims

## A. Definition of Fiduciary

In *Custer v. Pan American Life Insurance Co.*, 12 F.3d 410, 418 n.3 (4th Cir. 1993), the Fourth Circuit observed that "the concept of a fiduciary under ERISA is broader than the common law concept of a trustee." An ERISA fiduciary includes those specifically named as fiduciaries in the plan instrument and those who, pursuant to a procedure specified in the plan, are identified as fiduciaries. *Custer v. Sweeney*, 89

F.3d 1156, 1161 (4th Cir. 1996) (citing 29 U.S.C. § 1102(a)(2)). Equally important, a fiduciary is "any individual who de facto performs specified discretionary functions with respect to the management, assets, or administration of a plan." *Id.*

"The statutory language plainly indicates that the fiduciary function is not an indivisible one." *Coleman v. Nationwide Life Ins. Co.,* 969 F.2d 54, 61 (4th Cir. 1992) (holding that insurance company did not have fiduciary duty to notify beneficiary that her benefits were at risk due to employer's nonpayment of premiums, as insurance company had not assumed such duty under the terms of the plan or by voluntarily undertaking to inform beneficiaries). "Fiduciary status under ERISA is not 'an all-or-nothing concept.'" *Sweeney,* 89 F.3d at 1162 (quoting *Coleman*). Relying upon the language of 29 U.S.C. § 1002(21)(A), the Fourth Circuit has held that "a party is a fiduciary only as to the activities which bring the person within the definition." *Id.*

Because fiduciary status is often based upon a finding that the party had discretionary authority as to the specific act at issue, determination of fiduciary status often turns on facts specific to a particular case rather than on broad guidelines. For example, although an attorney is a fiduciary to his or her client, the Fourth Circuit has held that mere representation of an ERISA plan by an attorney "does not make the attorney an ERISA fiduciary because legal representation of ERISA plans rarely involves the *discretionary authority* or control required by the statute's definition of 'fiduciary.'" *Sweeney,* 89 F.3d at 1162 (emphasis added). Furthermore, "a plan sponsor does not become a fiduciary by performing settlor-type functions such as establishing a plan and designing its benefits." *Coyne & Delany Co. v. Selman,* 98 F.3d 1457, 1465 (4th Cir. 1996).

In *Estate of Weeks v. Advance Stores Co., Inc.,* 99 Fed. Appx. 470, 2004 WL 1191792 (4th Cir. 2004), the court of appeals affirmed dismissal of a claim against an individual human resource manager based on her purported misrepresentations regarding continuation of life coverage. The record established that the individual defendant did not have discretionary authority or control with respect to the administration of the plans at issue, nor was she a named fiduciary. In *Adams v. Brink's Co.,* 420 F. Supp. 2d 523 (W.D. Va. 2006), the court carefully parsed specific allegations of misrepresentation against each individual defendant in dismissing various claims for breach of fiduciary duty. The claims arose out of purported representations made by employees of an acquiring corporation regarding the anticipated effect of a future merger on the plaintiffs' pension coverage. The court addressed the fiduciary status of each individual defendant as it related to the specific representations at issue.

In *In re Mutual Funds Investment Litigation,* 403 F. Supp. 2d 434 (D. Md. 2005), a multidistrict class action proceeding, plaintiffs alleged retirement account losses resulting from the purported knowledge of fiduciaries regarding investments in mutual funds tainted by late trading and market timing problems. The court granted a motion to dismiss as to some defendants (with leave to amend), holding that certain allegations were insufficient to plead fiduciary status. Because corporate officers and directors are not fiduciaries simply by virtue of their corporate positions, the complaint must allege specific facts demonstrating fiduciary status. *Id.* at 445–47.

When a claim administrator has a limited role in processing claims, and does not have discretionary authority, the administrator is not an ERISA fiduciary. *Healthsouth Rehabilitation Hosp. v. Am. Nat'l Red Cross,* 101 F.3d 1005, 1009 (4th Cir. 1996). *See also Haidle v. Chippenham Hosp. Inc.,* 855 F. Supp. 127 (E.D. Va. 1994) (holding that insurance company was not an ERISA fiduciary where it provided claims processing and other administrative services with respect to medical benefits plan subject to review and modification by plan administrator).

An employer's status as an fiduciary is a frequently litigated issue. In *Phelps v. C.T. Enterprises,* 394 F.3d 213 (4th Cir. 2004), the court of appeals reversed summary judgment dismissing claims against defendants for their alleged failure to apply funds withdrawn from payroll to a health plan. When an employer is to remit employee funds to the claim administrator, the employer is usually a fiduciary in that activity. *Id.* at 219–20. In *U.S. Steel Mining Co., Inc. v. District 17, United Mine Workers of America,* 897 F.2d 149, 152 (4th Cir. 1990), the court of appeals determined that an employer exercised "sufficient discretionary authority respecting the administration of the plan" and was therefore a fiduciary when, pursuant to a state court injunction, the employer arranged for a pension fund to continue providing medical insurance coverage. Thus, the employer had standing as a fiduciary to seek restitution from those plan participants who benefited from the injunction under 29 U.S.C. § 1132(a)(3).

The court of appeals has held that an employer whose role included that of a plan administrator was an ERISA fiduciary. *Shade v. Panhandle Motor Serv. Corp.,* 1996 WL 386611 (4th Cir. 1996). In *Shade,* the employer plan administrator breached its duty to a plan participant by failing to inform him of a change in his medical insurance coverage status, and in failing to correct its mistake once it learned the participant was not among the covered employees under a new plan. *Id. See also Broadnax Mills, Inc. v. Blue Cross & Blue Shield of Va.,* 867 F. Supp. 398 (E.D. Va. 1994) (holding that both employer and insurer were fiduciaries because they both had discretionary authority—the employer to maintain the plan and the insurer to administer and manage the plan—in a dispute regarding stop-loss coverage). However, an employer does not have fiduciary duties with respect to its actions in creating a plan. *Elmore v. Cone Mills,* 23 F.3d 855, 862 (4th Cir. 1994).

## B. Definition of Fiduciary Duties

The Fourth Circuit has stated that ERISA's fiduciary responsibility provisions represent a codification of the common law of trusts. *Griggs v. E.I. DuPont de Nemours & Co.,* 237 F.3d 371, 380 (4th Cir. 2001); *Faircloth v. Lundy Packing* Co., 91 F.3d 648, 656 (4th Cir. 1996). Accordingly, "ERISA commands undivided loyalty to plan participants" at all times, including situations in which the fiduciary may have a conflict of interest, such as an insured health plan, where, in exchange for premiums from the employer, the insurer processes and pays claims, and acts as the plan administrator. *Bedrick v. Travelers Ins. Co.,* 93 F.3d 149, 154 (4th Cir. 1996). ERISA fiduciaries must "discharge their responsibilities 'with the care, skill, prudence, and diligence under the circumstances then prevailing that a prudent man would use.'" *Bidwill v. Garvey,* 943 F.2d 498, 507 (4th Cir. 1991) (quoting 29 U.S.C.

§ 1104(a)(1)(B)). ERISA further "requires plan fiduciaries to discharge their duties with respect to a plan 'in accordance with the documents and instruments governing the plan.'" *Faircloth,* 91 F.3d at 658 (quoting 29 U.S.C. § 1104(a)(1)(D)).

Claims alleging breach of fiduciary duty often relate to purported misrepresentations regarding benefits. When a participant makes a specific inquiry related to an early retirement election, an ERISA fiduciary has an "obligation 'not to misinform employees through material misrepresentations and incomplete, inconsistent or contradictory disclosures.'" *Griggs,* 237 F.3d at 380 (quoting *Harte v. Bethlehem Steel Corp.,* 214 F.3d 446, 452 (3rd. Cir. 2000)). Although there is no "general duty" that a fiduciary "ascertain on an individual basis whether each beneficiary understands the collateral consequences of his or her particular election," if "an ERISA fiduciary . . . knows or should know that a beneficiary [is acting] under a material misunderstanding of plan benefits that will inure to his detriment," the fiduciary "cannot remain silent," particularly if the misunderstanding is the result of "the fiduciary's own material representations or omissions." *Id.* at 381. In some circumstances, a fiduciary must inform a beneficiary of a change in coverage status. *Shade,* 1996 WL 386611 (4th Cir. 1996).

ERISA requires that a fiduciary diversify the plan's investments unless circumstances dictate that it is not prudent to do so. *Reich v. Walter W. King Plumbing & Heating Contractor, Inc.,* 98 F.3d 147, 152 (4th Cir. 1996) (citing 29 U.S.C. § 1104(a)(1)(C)). However, a fiduciary is not required to select the best investment option. *Riley v. Murdock,* 1996 WL 209613 (4th Cir. 1996) (rejecting Department of Labor argument that the proper standard would require an ERISA fiduciary to select the safest available annuity to assure payment of the benefits that a plan promises to its participants).

In *Atwater v. Nortel Networks, Inc.,* 388 F. Supp. 2d 610 (M.D.N.C. 2005), the court concluded that an insurer administrator of a life plan had a fiduciary duty to initiate an interpleader action to determine the proper recipient of death benefits when the named beneficiary was a suspected slayer of the insured. Thus, following conviction of the named beneficiary for murder, the plan was liable for payment of death benefits to the alternative beneficiary, subject to consideration of defendants' defenses of waiver and estoppel.

### C. Fiduciary Liability in the Context of Health and Disability Claims

Claims for breach of fiduciary duty in connection with ERISA plans have arisen in a variety of contexts. Most common, of course, are claims for plan benefits against a fiduciary under 29 U.S.C. § 1132(a)(1)(B). Whether a claim adjudicator has abused its discretion must be assessed with reference to its fiduciary duties. The court of appeals has stated that "[a] fiduciary with a conflict of interest must act as if he is 'free' of such a conflict. . . . 'Free' is an absolute, meaning that there is no balancing of interests; ERISA commands undivided loyalty to plan participants." *Bedrick v. Travelers Ins. Co.,* 93 F.3d 149, 154 (4th Cir. 1996).

The availability of a claim for benefits normally precludes a claim for equitable relief under 29 U.S.C. § 1132(a)(3). *Dwyer v. Metro. Life Ins. Co.,* 2001 WL 94749 (4th Cir. 2001). *See also Sawyer v. Potash Corp. of Sask.,* 417 F. Supp. 2d 730, 745

(E.D.N.C. 2006); *Hughes v. UnumProvident Corp.,* 2006 WL 51170 (M.D.N.C. 2006). However at least one decision has questioned the wisdom of that rule. *Korotynska v. Metro. Life Ins. Co.,* 2005 WL 991003, at *3–4 (D. Md. 2005).

In *Marks v. Watters,* 322 F.3d 316, 326 (4th Cir. 2003), the court addressed claims relating to the death of the insured. Applying *Pegram v. Herdrich,* 530 U.S. 211, 120 S. Ct. 2143 (2000), the court found that the state-law claims against the plan administrator and case manager were preempted because they related to plan administration rather than treatment. The court concluded that the factual record did not support a claim that the plan administrator and case manager breached a fiduciary duty under ERISA where the insured, who had been released from a mental health facility, murdered his family and subsequently committed suicide.

In *Coyne & Delany Co. v. Selman,* 98 F.3d 1457 (4th Cir. 1996), the court of appeals addressed claims brought by an employer alleging that defendant plan administrator had improperly designed its group health plan and failed to obtain proper replacement coverage. The court ruled that the employer was a fiduciary with standing to assert ERISA claims because of its power to appoint and remove the plan administrator. Because the plan had paid $160,000 to cover a portion of a nonparticipant's medical expenses, it was entitled to proceed on its ERISA claim. Further, the employer's state-law malpractice claims were deemed not to be preempted. However an employer may not bring an action against a fiduciary to obtain benefits for an employee; such action must be brought by a plan participant or beneficiary. *Coyne & Delany Co. v. Blue Cross & Blue Shield of Va., Inc.,* 102 F.3d 712 (4th Cir. 1996).

In *Barron v. Unum Life Insurance Co. of America,* 260 F.3d 310, 316 (4th Cir. 2001), the Fourth Circuit held that an insurer's fiduciary responsibility as administrator of a disability plan prohibited denial of a disability claim because of a release signed by the claimant while employed at another company that coincidentally had used the same insurer for administration of its disability plan. The court concluded that reliance on the release was not consistent with the insurer's duties to the second plan.

The failure of an employer or its officers to apply funds to a health plan may give rise to fiduciary liability. *Phelps v. C.T. Enterprises,* 394 F.3d 213, 219–20 (4th Cir. 2004). An insurer, as fiduciary, may bring an action seeking declaratory judgment and other relief, although it may not recover on its claims alleging unjust enrichment for repayment of benefits already paid. *Provident Life & Accident Ins. Co. v. Cohen,* 423 F.3d 413 (4th Cir. 2005).

## D. Remedies for Breach of Fiduciary Duty

"Section 502(a) provides the exclusive statement of civil actions available under ERISA to the Secretary of Labor, participants, beneficiaries, and fiduciaries." *Coyne & Delany Co. v. Blue Cross & Blue Shield of Va., Inc.,* 102 F.3d 712, 714 (4th Cir. 1996). *See also Singh v. Prudential Health Care Plan, Inc.,* 335 F.3d 278, 292 (4th Cir. 2003).

The Supreme Court has held that only equitable relief is available under 29 U.S.C. § 1132(a)(3). *Mertens v. Hewitt Assocs.,* 508 U.S. 248, 256–59 (1993). Extra-contractual and punitive damages are not recoverable under 29 U.S.C. § 1132(a)(1)–(3). *Darcangelo v. Verizon Commc'ns, Inc.,* 292 F.3d 181, 195 (4th Cir. 2002); *Coleman v. Nationwide Life Ins. Co.,* 969 F.2d 54, 60 n.2 (4th Cir. 1992). A claim for punitive damages for breach of fiduciary duty was dismissed following a thorough analysis in *Openshaw v. Cohen, Klingenstein & Marks, Inc.,* 320 F. Supp. 2d 357, 361–62 (D. Md. 2004).

A plan participant may not recover compensatory damages under ERISA for alleged breach of fiduciary duties for failure to follow a plan participant's investment instructions, nor may such a claim for damages be characterized as "other appropriate equitable relief" under 29 U.S.C. § 1132(a)(3). *LaRue v. De Wolfe, Boberg & Assocs., Inc.,* 450 F.3d 570 (4th Cir. 2006).

Reinstatement or return of an employee plan participant to his preelection position may be an appropriate remedy under ERISA's "other appropriate equitable relief" provision at § 1132(a)(3)(B). *Griggs v. E.I. DuPont de Nemours & Co.,* 237 F.3d 371, 384 (4th Cir. 2001). Equitable relief for breach of a fiduciary duty may, in appropriate circumstances, include monetary relief where rescission of the plaintiff's earlier retirement decision was impossible due to the passage of time. *Griggs v. E.I. DuPont de Nemours & Co.,* 385 F.3d 440 (4th Cir. 2004). In *Griggs,* plaintiff sought relief for allegedly negligent advice that had led him to accept a lump-sum early retirement benefit, with adverse tax consequences, rather than an annuity. In its 2004 ruling, the court of appeals modified the remedy granted by the trial court following the earlier appeal, reducing the relief awarded to plaintiff because of plaintiff's delay in pursuing his claim.

Appropriate relief for breach of fiduciary duty may include removal of the plan fiduciaries. *Chao v. Malkani,* 452 F.3d 290, (4th Cir. 2006). In *Faircloth v. Lundy Packing Co.,* 91 F.3d 648, 659 n.6 (4th Cir. 1996), the court stated that "[r]emoval of trustees is appropriate when the trustees have engaged in repeated or substantial violations of their fiduciary duties under ERISA."

### E. Contribution and Indemnity Claims among Fiduciaries

The Fourth Circuit has not addressed the issue of contribution and indemnity claims among fiduciaries. A split of authority exists among the district courts. In *Cooper v. Kossan,* 993 F. Supp. 375, 377 (E.D. Va. 1998), the court recognized the right to seek contribution among co-fiduciaries. Noting a split among the Circuit Courts of Appeals, the court adopted the reasoning of the Court of Appeals for the Second Circuit by quoting *Chemung Canal Trust Co. v. Sovran Bank/Maryland,* 939 F.2d 12, 16 (2d Cir. 1991):

> There is no reason why a single fiduciary who is only partially responsible for a loss should bear its full brunt. Full responsibility should not depend on the fortuity of which fiduciary a plaintiff elects to sue.

In *Narda v. Rhode Island Hospital Trust National Bank,* 744 F. Supp. 685 (D. Md. 1990), the district court concluded that there is no right to indemnification or contribution among culpable fiduciaries. The court concluded:

> It thus appears that the failure to include the rights of contribution and indemnity in ERISA was intended by Congress and the omission of those

rights is not an unaddressed detail or gap to be filled by a federal common law.

*Id.* at 697. Accordingly,

[T]he directive to develop a federal common law under ERISA does not include the right to infer common law rights of contribution and indemnity when the language and structure of the statute leads to a contrary intent.

*Id.* at 698. In *Openshaw v. Cohen, Klingenstein & Marks, Inc.,* 320 F. Supp. 2d 357, 363–64 (D. Md. 2004), the court dismissed a counterclaim against plaintiff trustees for contribution. The court noted that there was no statutory basis for such a claim under ERISA.

### F. ERISA Claims against Nonfiduciaries

Some district courts within the Fourth Circuit have viewed ERISA claims against nonfiduciaries as cognizable claims while others have not. For example, in *Pension Benefit Guaranty Corp. v. Ross,* 781 F. Supp. 415, 418 (M.D.N.C. 1991), the court observed that in *Pension Benefit Guaranty Corp. v. Ross,* 733 F. Supp. 1005 (M.D.N.C. 1990), the court had found that the essential elements of a claim against a nonfiduciary "for participation in a fiduciary's breach are '(1) an act or omission which furthers or completes the breach of trust by the trustee; and (2) knowledge at the time that the transaction amounted to a breach of trust or the legal equivalent of such knowledge.'"

Similarly, in *Atwood v. Burlington Industries Equity Inc.,* 1994 WL 698314 (M.D.N.C. 1994), the court denied defendants' motions to dismiss plaintiff's ERISA claim against the defendants for their role in a prohibited transaction with a fiduciary. *Id.* at *17. The court stated that "should Plaintiffs be able to prove that the [fiduciary] violated § 1106(a), Plaintiffs may be able to recover in equity against the remaining Defendants as parties in interest; that is, under 29 U.S.C. § 1132(a)(3), the remaining Defendants could be ordered to provide restitution to the Plan and/or disgorge any profits derived from their misuse of Plan assets." *Id.* at *12.

However, in *Colleton Regional Hospital v. MRS Medical Review Systems, Inc.,* 866 F. Supp. 891 (D.S.C. 1994), the court, without stating whether a nonfiduciary could ever be liable, refused to allow equitable relief against a nonfiduciary who knowingly participated in a fiduciary's breach. Stating that the issue was not properly before it, and citing *Mertens v. Hewitt Associates,* 508 U.S. 248 (1993), and *Custer v. Pan American Life Insurance Co.,* 12 F.3d 410, 419 (4th Cir. 1993), the court observed that "[n]either the Supreme Court nor the Fourth Circuit [has] resolved [the] issue" of whether plaintiffs could plead a cause of action for equitable relief against a nonfiduciary. *Id.* at 895 n.3.

*In re Mutual Funds Investment Litigation,* 403 F. Supp. 2d 434, 447, n.15 (D. Md. 2005), addressed a contention that the doctrine of *respondeat superior* could provide the basis of fiduciary liability for certain business entities due to misconduct by employees who were plan fiduciaries. The court reasoned that when an individual acts on behalf of the plan, he is not acting on behalf of his corporate employer, and thus does not create derivative ERISA liability for the employer unless the employer is otherwise a fiduciary "as to the functions performed by its agents." *Id.* However, in *Meyer v. Berkshire Life Insurance Co.,* 250 F. Supp. 2d 544, 563 n.27 (D. Md. 2003), *aff'd,* 372 F.3d 261 (4th Cir. 2004), the court observed that although the Fourth Circuit had not "squarely address[ed] the issue of vicarious liability under ERISA," the doctrine may serve to impose ERISA liability on a nonfiduciary principal stemming from actions of its fiduciary agent. *Id.* Because the insurer defendant admitted fiduciary status, the court was not required to determine whether it was derivatively liable.

# X. Attorneys' Fees

## A. Criteria for Awarding Attorneys' Fees

The leading Fourth Circuit case regarding the award of attorneys' fees in ERISA actions is *Quesinberry v. Life Insurance Co. of North America,* 987 F.2d 1017 (4th Cir. 1993). *Quesinberry* reaffirmed a "five-factor test to be used by the district court in exercising its discretion" under 29 U.S.C. § 1132(g), first adopted in *Reinking v. Philadelphia American Life Insurance Co.,* 910 F.2d 1210, 1217–18 (4th Cir. 1990). Those factors are

- The degree of opposing parties' culpability or bad faith;
- The ability of opposing parties to satisfy an award of attorneys' fees;
- Whether an award of attorneys' fees against the opposing parties would deter other persons acting under similar circumstances;
- Whether the parties requesting attorneys' fees sought to benefit all participants and beneficiaries of an ERISA plan or to resolve a significant legal question regarding ERISA itself; and
- The relative merits of the parties' positions.

*Quesinberry,* 987 F.2d at 1029. The court emphasized that this "is not a rigid test, but rather provides general guidelines for the district court in determining whether to grant a request for attorneys' fees." Not every factor will apply in every case, and in some cases, other considerations may be relevant. *Id.* The suggestion that the earlier *Reinking* decision established a presumption in favor of awarding fees to the prevailing party was expressly rejected. *Id.* at 1029–30. However, fees cannot be awarded to a nonprevailing party. *Martin v. Blue Cross & Blue Shield of Va., Inc.,* 115 F.3d 1201, 1209–10 (4th Cir. 1997). The failure of the district court to address those factors in awarding fees usually precludes review, requiring remand. *Denzler v. Questech, Inc.,* 80 F.3d 97, 104 (4th Cir. 1996).

Of the listed factors, the element of "bad faith" is sometimes seen as the most important. *Hines v. Unum Life Ins. Co. of Am.,* 110 F. Supp. 2d 458, 469 (W.D. Va. 2000). A finding of bad faith may not be necessary for an award of attorneys' fees. *Davidson v. Kemper Nat'l Servs., Inc.,* 231 F. Supp. 2d 446, 454–55 (W.D. Va. 2002).

In *Carolina Care Plan Inc. v. McKenzie,* 467 F.3d 383 (4th Cir. 2006), the court sustained the trial court's finding that the administrator had abused its discretion in denying benefits, but reversed a discretionary award of attorneys' fees. While the trial court had specifically addressed the *Quesinberry* factor, the Court of Appeals concluded that undue weight had been given the "bad faith" factor, whereas "the record contains *no* evidence of bad faith or culpability." *Id.* at 390. The opinion makes clear that "a court cannot rely solely on an administrator's improper denial of coverage on a single claim to support an award of fees to a claimant." *Id.* at 391.

In *Hensley v. International Business Machines Corp.,* 123 Fed. Appx. 534, 2004 WL 2857576 (4th Cir. 2004), the court reversed the district court's decision that the insurer had abused its discretion in denying benefits, and likewise reversed an attorneys' fee award for plaintiff. Rather than relying upon the rule that the party must prevail to recover fees, as set out in *Martin,* the court of appeals specifically addressed the five *Quesinberry* factors, and concluded that the district court had abused its discretion because the factors on which it had relied related to the parties' relative positions and culpability. Therefore, the reversal of a benefit award on appeal rendered the district court's fee analysis erroneous. As discussed in *Griggs v. E.I. DuPont de Nemours & Co.,* 385 F.3d 440 (4th Cir. 2004), a plaintiff who obtains relief is normally a "prevailing party," even if the relief is of limited practical value. A claimant may be entitled to recover fees as a prevailing party even if the only relief awarded is remand to the administrator for reconsideration. *Clark v. Metro. Life Ins. Co.,* 384 F. Supp. 2d 894, 897 (E.D. Va. 2005).

## B. Fees Awarded to Plan Fiduciaries

While most fee awards are against fiduciaries, district courts within the circuit have sometimes awarded fees to a fiduciary forced to defend claims or contentions unsupported by law or fact. *E.g., Devine v. Am. Benefits Corp.,* 27 F. Supp. 2d 669, 677–78 (S.D.W. Va. 1998). Fees have also been awarded against a claimant's attorney in favor of the fiduciary. *Childers v. Medstar Health,* 289 F. Supp. 2d 714, 718 (D. Md. 2003). In affirming the district court's denial of a fee claim against a losing claimant in an interpleader, based upon a *Quesinberry* analysis, the court of appeals acknowledged the possibility of such a fee award. *Pettit v. Metro. Life Ins. Co.,* 164 F.3d 857, 865–66 (4th Cir. 1998).

In *Mid Atlantic Medical Services, LLC v. Sereboff,* 407 F.3d 212 (4th Cir. 2005), *aff'd on other grounds,* 126 S. Ct. 1869 (2006), the court of appeals affirmed the district court's ruling permitting plaintiff to recover on its subrogation claim. However, it reversed a fee award to plaintiff and remanded for reconsideration, because of the trial court's failure to adequately consider "judicially recognized factors" in its determination. Failure to address each of those factors separately constituted an abuse of discretion. In *Essex v. Randall,* 2005 WL 600335 (D. Md. 2005), the court determined that fees should be awarded to the trustees of a health and welfare fund in an action to enforce a subrogation agreement. While the court's decision was based on an express provision of the agreement, it further concluded that a fee award was proper based upon the five *Quesinberry* factors.

## C. Calculation of Attorneys' Fees

If the district court, in its discretion, determines that fees should be awarded, the court must first determine an appropriate "lodestar" figure by multiplying a reasonable number of hours times a reasonable hourly rate. *Brodziak v. Runyon,* 145 F.3d 194, 196 (4th Cir. 1998). Quoting from earlier decisions, *Brodziak* further declared that in determining what rate and time are reasonable, the following factors should be taken into account:

> (1) The time and labor expended; (2) the novelty and difficulty of the questions raised; (3) the skill required to properly perform the legal services rendered; (4) the attorney's opportunity costs in pressing the instant litigation; (5) the customary fee for like work; (6) the attorney's expectations at the outset of the litigation; (7) the time limitations imposed by the client or circumstances; (8) the amount in controversy and the results obtained; (9) the experience, reputation and ability of the attorney; (10) the undesirability of the case within the legal community in which the suit arose; (11) the nature and length of the professional relationship between attorney and client; and (12) attorneys' fees awards in similar cases.

*Id. Brodziak* held that the district court had abused its discretion by awarding a percentage of the lodestar fee equal to the percentage of claims upon which plaintiff had prevailed. Instead of such a mechanical approach, the trial court "should consider the relationship between various claims raised by Brodziak and the degree of overall success obtained in determining an appropriate amount of fees and costs." *Id.* at 197.

A party may not recover fees incurred during the administrative process. *Rego v. Westvaco,* 319 F.3d 140, 150 (4th Cir. 2003). Fees may include time spent in preparing the fee petition. *Trimper v. City of Norfolk, Va.,* 58 F.3d 68, 77 (4th Cir. 1995). The court of appeals may determine that fees should be awarded in connection with an appeal. *Denzler,* 80 F.3d at 104–05. The issue may also be remanded to the trial court. *Cox v. Reliance Standard Life Ins. Co.,* 235 F. Supp. 2d 481 (E.D. Va. 2002).

When fees are awarded, they normally should be reduced to take into account the failure to prevail on some claims. *Clark,* 384 F. Supp. 2d at 897, 901. Thus partial reversal on the merits generally requires reconsideration of any fee award. *Mitchell v. Fortis Benefits Ins. Co.,* 163 Fed. Appx. 183, 2005 WL 1793641, at *11 (4th Cir. 2005). Fee awards must be based upon reasonable, rather than actual, rates and time for the work performed. *Essex,* 2005 WL 600335.

## XI. ERISA Regulations

29 U.S.C. § 1133 of ERISA requires:

> In accordance with regulations of the Secretary, every employee benefit plan shall—
>
> (1) provide adequate notice in writing to any participant or beneficiary whose claim for benefits under the plan has been denied, setting forth the

specific reasons for such denial, written in a manner calculated to be understood by the participant, and

(2) afford a reasonable opportunity to any participant whose claim for benefits has been denied for a full and fair review by the appropriate named fiduciary of the decision denying the claim.

The regulations of the Secretary pertaining to claims procedure are set forth in 29 C.F.R. § 2560.503-1, and the current regulations went into effect on January 1, 2002, for non-group health plans. *See* 29 C.F.R. § 2560.503-1(o). There have been only a few cases on post-January 1, 2002, claims pertaining to the new claims procedures.

In *Saunders v. Verizon Communications, Inc.,* 2006 U.S. Dist. LEXIS 40296 (N.D. W. Va. 2006), the court observed that 29 C.F.R. § 2650.503-1(l) requires that a claimant be deemed to have exhausted her administrative remedies if the employee benefit plan fails to establish and follow claims procedures consistent with the requirements of that section. The court in *Sawyer v. Potash Corp.,* 417 F. Supp. 2d 730, 744 (E.D.N.C. 2006), held that the notice provisions of 29 C.F.R. § 2560.503-(1)(h)(2) do not give a claimant the right to appear before an appeal committee or to present oral testimony. Nor is there any apparent proscription against a plan administrator's use of new information on appeal in support of its denial of a claim; a plan administrator is not limited to the information and plan provisions considered in the initial review. *Hall v. Metro. Life Ins. Co.,* 398 F. Supp. 2d 494, 500 (W.D. Va. 2005). Also, "Nothing in the Regulations requires that the entire appeals process be explicitly laid out in the Plan summary; referral to the denial letter is an appropriate means by which 'to apprise the plan's participants and beneficiaries of their rights and obligations under the plan.'" *Smith v. Westvaco Corp.,* 399 F. Supp. 2d 692, 695–96 (D.S.C. 2005) (citation omitted).

Other recent cases have found that the previous regulations applied because the claims in question were filed before January 1, 2002. *See, e.g., DiCamillo v. Liberty Life Assur. Co.,* 287 F. Supp. 2d 616 (D. Md. 2003) ("The 2002 regulations explicitly provide, however, that they do not apply to claims filed before January 1, 2002. Liberty Life contends, and the court agrees, that DiCamillo's claim is not governed by the 2002 regulations because it was initially filed on November 7, 2001"); *Wertheim v. Hartford Life Ins. Co.,* 268 F. Supp. 2d 643, 659 (E.D. Va. 2003) (applying ERISA regulations in effect at the time plaintiff's claim was initially filed).

Prior to 2002, there were some cases interpreting the old regulations that may form a basis for interpreting the current regulations. There have also been cases decided after 2002 relating to claims initially filed before January 1, 2002.

With respect to the notification requirements, a failure to give notice within a reasonable period of time was deemed a denial of a claim and permitted the claimant to pursue internal review procedures. *Sheppard & Enoch Pratt Hosp. v. Travelers Ins. Co.,* 32 F.3d 120 (4th Cir. 1994). Whether a notice of denial of benefits is adequate, consistent with ERISA regulations, was held to be a question of law, subject to de novo review. *See Ellis v. Metro. Life Ins. Co.,* 126 F.3d 228, 234 (4th Cir. 1997). However, substantial compliance with the spirit of the regulation would suffice, for "not all procedural defects will invalidate a plan administrator's decision." *Brogan v.*

*Holland,* 105 F.3d 158, 165 (4th Cir. 1997). Substantial compliance exists where the claimant is provided with "a statement of reasons that, under the circumstances of the case, permitted a sufficiently clear understanding of the administrator's position to permit effective review." *Id.* Yet, in *Ellis,* the Fourth Circuit cautioned that "plan administrators and fiduciaries[] would be well advised to ascertain their compliance with these ERISA procedural requirements." *Id.* at 239. Substantial compliance with the regulations regarding the content of the denial letter was required, and a letter that stated only that the claim was denied, without providing any reasons for the denial, was deemed to be insufficient. *Burdett v. Mees,* 1991 U.S. App. LEXIS 10403, at *11 (4th Cir. 1991). In such a situation, the Fourth Circuit held, the remedy would be to remand the decision back to the claims administrator for a new consideration. *Id.* at *12. In addition, the Fourth Circuit has held that 29 C.F.R. § 2560.503-1 does not direct ERISA plan administrators to provide claimants with a formula for obtaining benefits. *Donnell v. Metro. Life Ins. Co.,* 165 Fed. Appx. 288, 296 (4th Cir. 2006).

The Fourth Circuit has refused to find an abuse of discretion based on ERISA procedural violations absent a causal connection between the procedural defects and the final denial of a claim. *Donnell,* 165 Fed. Appx. at 297. As for the "full and fair review" procedural requirements, the Fourth Circuit has held that while normally a failure to comply with ERISA's proceeds would have required a court to remand the case to the plan administrator for a "full and fair" review, a remand for further action was unnecessary where the evidence clearly shows that the plan abused its discretion. *Weaver v. Phoenix Home Life Mut. Ins. Co.,* 990 F.2d 154, 159 (4th Cir. 1993).

The federal regulations governing appeals authorize limited periods for claimants to file requests for reviews of denied claims. Courts enforce these limits "'because haphazard waiver of time limits would increase the probability of inconsistent results where one claimant is held to a limitation, and another is not. Similarly, permitting appeals well after the time for them has passed can only increase the cost and time of the settlement process.'" *Gayle v. United Parcel Service,* 401 F.3d 222, 226 (4th Cir. 2005) (citation omitted). The regulations do not require that a plan review an appeal for a particular amount of time. *Clark v. Metro. Life Ins. Co.,* 369 F. Supp. 2d 770, 779 (E.D. Va. 2005).

The Fourth Circuit has noted that under the ERISA regulations, once a claimant has filed a lawsuit fiduciaries cannot offer new reasons for a claim determination, other than those they provided a claimant in the claims process. *Thompson v. Life Ins. Co. of N. Am.,* 30 Fed. Appx. 160, 2002 U.S. App. LEXIS 3390 (4th Cir. 2002). It concluded that, "A district court's review is limited to whether the rationale set forth in the initial denial notice is reasonable. A court may not consider a new reason for claim denial offered for the first time on judicial review." *Id.* at *7.

## XII. Cases Interpreting ERISA Statutes of Limitation

For claims that allege a breach of a fiduciary duty, ERISA provides either a six-year or a three-year statute of limitations, hinging on certain acts, omissions, or knowledge. *See* 29 U.S.C. § 1113(a). Typically, except in cases of fraud or concealment, the three-year ERISA statute of limitations begins to run when a plaintiff has knowledge of the alleged breach of a responsibility, duty, or obligation by a fiduciary. 29 U.S.C. § 1113(a)(2): *Shofer v. Stuart Huck Co.,* 970 F.2d 1316 (4th Cir. 1992); *Lamberty v. Premier Millwork & Lumber Co.,* 329 F. Supp. 2d 737, 743 (E.D. Va. 2004).

ERISA does not provide a statute of limitations for denial of benefits claims. As a result, the Fourth Circuit looks to the most analogous state statute of limitations and has found that the statutes of limitations for actions alleging a breach of contract are the most analogous state statutes for denial of benefits claims. *See Cotter v. Eastern Conference of Teamsters Ret. Plan,* 898 F.2d 424, 428 (4th Cir. 1990); *see also Dameron v. Sinai Hosp. of Baltimore, Inc.,* 815 F.2d 975, 981 (4th Cir. 1987). For example, the court has noted that the statute of limitations for a claimant in Virginia is that for breach of a written contract in Virginia: i.e., five years under Virginia Code § 8.01-246. *Christensen v. Northrop Grumman Corp.,* 1997 U.S. App. LEXIS 28565 (4th Cir. 1997); *see also Hughes v. UNUM Provident Corp.,* 2006 U.S. Dist. LEXIS 1400 (M.D.N.C. 2006). However, in at least two cases, courts have noted that benefit claims cases that do not allege a breach of fiduciary duty are analogous to claims "for either negligence or breach of contract." *Shofer,* 970 F.2d 1316; *see also Lippard v. UnumProvident Corp.,* 261 F. Supp. 2d 368, 377 (M.D.N.C. 2003). Yet, in both of these cases, the court adopted state statutes that applied to "civil actions" in general.

In some cases involving denials of benefits, courts have enforced limitation periods that were set forth in the plan. In *Gayle v. United Parcel Service,* 401 F.3d 222 (4th Cir. 2005), the Fourth Circuit enforced a procedure that had a limited appeal period that was mandatory under the plan. In *Payne v. Blue Cross & Blue Shield,* 1992 U.S. App. LEXIS 24357 (4th Cir. 1992), the Fourth Circuit found that a twelve-month limitation period in a health insurance policy was enforceable because it was consistent with a state statute that provided that insurance policies limiting the time within which to bring an action to a period of less than one year are invalid. *See also Koonan v. Blue Cross & Blue Shield of Va.,* 802 F. Supp. 1424, 1425 (E.D. Va. 1992) ("This Court is aware of no public policy of the United States or Virginia which would prevent enforcement of a one year contractual limitation period. Indeed, in Virginia the issue has already been addressed by statute which provides that 'no provision in any insurance policy shall be valid if it limits the time within which an action may be brought to less than one year after the loss occurs or the cause of action accrues.'") (citations omitted). In *Arnold v. Metropolitan Life Insurance Co.,* 2005 U.S. Dist. LEXIS 23240 (W.D. Va. 2005), the court found that the plan's limitation provision—"no lawsuit may be started more than 3 years after the time proof of loss must be given"—was "reasonable and enforceable."

Courts have applied other limitations periods for wrongful discharge claims under ERISA. ERISA sets forth a remedy for plaintiffs who believe they have been wrongfully terminated for filing for benefits. *See* 29 U.S.C. § 1140. District courts have concluded that such a claim under 29 U.S.C. § 1140 is analogous to wrongful discharge under state law and have applied state statute of limitations for wrongful discharge actions. *Malik v. Philip Morris, USA, Inc.,* 2006 U.S. Dist. LEXIS 41046 (E.D. Va. 2006); *Sutter v. First Union Nat'l Bank,* 932 F. Supp. 753 (E.D. Va. 1996);

*Baradell v. Board of Social Servs.,* 970 F. Supp. 489 (W.D. Va. 1997); *Carter v. Times-World Corp.,* 1997 U.S. Dist. LEXIS 10743 (W.D. Va. 1997), *aff'd,* 1998 U.S. App. LEXIS 10497 (4th Cir. 1998).

Looking to the law of the forum state, at least one court has held that a limitation period for breach of a written contract applied to a subrogation action. *Lincoln General Ins. Co. v. State Farm Mut. Auto. Ins. Co.,* 425 F. Supp. 2d 738, 743 (E.D. Va. 2006).

As for when a cause of action accrues for a denial of benefits, the Fourth Circuit has held that an "ERISA cause of action does not accrue until a claim of benefits has been made and formally denied. . . . To hold otherwise would require lay participants and beneficiaries to be constantly alert for 'errors or abuses that might give rise to a claim and start the statute of limitations running.'" *Rodriguez v. MEBA Pension Trust,* 872 F.2d 69, 72 (4th Cir. 1989) (citation omitted); *see also Singleton v. Temporary Disability Benefits Plan,* 2006 U.S. App. LEXIS 12318 (4th Cir. 2006). However, although causes of action for breach of contract typically accrue at the time of the breach and such an instance of a claim under ERISA would be at the time that benefits are denied, the Fourth Circuit has held, in at least one case, that the cause of action accrued at the time when a claimant should have been alerted to an entitlement to benefits that he did not receive. *Cotter v. Eastern Conference of Teamsters,* 898 F.2d 424 (4th Cir. 1990). *See also Arnold, supra,* at *5–7, (where the district court enforced a plan's provision which started the three-year limitation period when "proof of loss must be given)".

In applying the state statute of limitations, courts have applied state principles of tolling to that limitation period. *Shofer,* 970 F.2d at 1320. For example, the Fourth Circuit has held that the commencement of an action in a clearly inappropriate forum, that is, in a court that clearly lacks jurisdiction, will not toll the statute of limitations. *Id.* It has also refused to apply equitable tolling to allow a claimant to bring a late claim based on an argument that the claimant's lawyer's negligence caused her to miss the plan's deadline. *Gayle,* 401 F.3d at 226–27.

## XIII. Subrogation Litigation

In *Great-West Life & Annuity Insurance Co. v. Knudson,* 534 U.S. 204 (2002), the Supreme Court held that insurance companies seeking reimbursement of medical expenses paid on behalf of beneficiaries out of the beneficiaries' settlement with a tortfeasor were not entitled to relief under 29 U.S.C. § 1132(a)(3) because the relief they sought was not equitable in nature. Although not a subrogation case, *Rego v. Westvaco Corp.,* 319 F.3d 140 (4th Cir. 2003), contains a discussion of the *Knudson* decision. There, the Fourth Circuit rejected an employee's claim under 29 U.S.C. § 1132(a)(3) to obtain "appropriate equitable relief" seeking his share of benefits from two employee benefits plans. The employee argued that his claim could be considered a request for equitable restitution or a constructive trust, a type of relief that was typically available in courts of equity. Quoting *Knudson,* the Fourth Circuit found that a claim for equitable restitution must seek "'not to impose personal liability on the defendant, but to restore to the plaintiff particular funds or property in the defendant's possession.'" *Id.* at 145 (citation omitted). A plaintiff, in other words, must argue that "'money or property identified as belonging in good conscience to the plaintiff could clearly be traced to particular funds or property in the defendant's possession.'" *Id.* at 145 (citation omitted). It is only under such circumstances that plaintiffs can proceed in equity with a claim for restitution; other claims for restitution are considered "restitution *at law.*" *Id.* (emphasis in original).

In *Sereboff v. Mid Atlantic Medical Services, Inc.,* 126 S. Ct. 1869 (2006), a case on appeal from the Fourth Circuit, the Supreme Court held that a fiduciary could assert a claim for equitable relief under § 1132(a)(3)(B) for restitution where it sought "specifically identifiable" funds that were within the possession and control of the beneficiary. The plan provided for payment of certain covered medical expenses and contained an "Acts of Third Parties" provision. *Id.* at 1872. This provision applied "when a beneficiary is sick or injured as a result of the act or omission of another person or party," and required a beneficiary who "receives benefits" under the plan for such injuries to "reimburse [the fiduciary]" for those benefits from "[a]ll recoveries from a third party (whether by lawsuit, settlement, or otherwise)." *Id.* The beneficiaries were injured in an automobile accident. *Id.* Pursuant to the plan's coverage provisions, the fiduciary paid their medical expenses. *Id.* The beneficiaries filed a tort action and received a settlement from several third parties, but did not repay the fiduciary. *Id.* at 1872–73. The fiduciary filed suit under 29 U.S.C. § 1132(a)(3) seeking to collect from the beneficiaries the medical expenses it had paid on their behalf. *Id.* at 1873. By stipulation, the beneficiaries agreed to keep a portion of the settlement equal to the medical expenses paid by the fiduciary in an investment account pending the outcome of the litigation. *Id.*

The Supreme Court first noted that the fiduciary sought "specifically identifiable" funds that were within the possession and control of the beneficiaries—that portion of the tort settlement due the fiduciary which had been set aside and preserved in the beneficiaries' investment accounts. *Id.* at 1874. Further, the fiduciary did not simply seek to impose personal liability for a contractual obligation to pay money; rather, it sought its recovery through a constructive trust or equitable lien on a specifically identified fund, not from the beneficiaries' assets generally, as would be the case with a contract action at law. *Id.* The Supreme Court found that the fiduciary had established that the basis of its claim was equitable because equity would allow the fiduciary to "follow" a portion of the recovery into the beneficiaries' hands as soon as the settlement fund was identified, and impose on that portion a constructive trust or equitable lien. *Id.* at 1875. Further, the Supreme Court held that there was no tracing requirement that applied to equitable liens by agreement or assignment. *Id.* at 1875–76. It also observed that the fund over which a lien is asserted need not be in existence when the contract containing the lien provision is executed. *Id.* at 1876. The fiduciary's action to enforce the "Acts of Third Parties" provision qualified as an equitable remedy because it was indistinguishable from an action to enforce an equitable lien established by agreement. *Id.* at 1877.

At the time of this writing, the Fourth Circuit has not cited the *Sereboff* opinion in a subrogation case. In two unpublished decisions before *Sereboff,* the Fourth Circuit had held that when plan administrators seek an equitable lien on particular property in the hands of plan beneficiaries, such a suit would sound in equity and would be authorized under 29 U.S.C. § 1132(a)(3). *Primax Recoveries, Inc. v. Young,* 83 Fed. Appx. 523, 2003 U.S. App. LEXIS 25786 (4th Cir. 2003); *Carpenter v. Wal-Mart Stores, Inc.,* 36 Fed. Appx. 80, 2002 U.S. App. LEXIS 10615 (4th Cir. 2002).

## XIV. Miscellaneous

### A. Unique Substantive or Procedural Rules for ERISA Cases

The Fourth Circuit has held that it is not an abuse of discretion for a plan fiduciary to deny disability pension benefits where conflicting medical reports were presented. *See Ellis v. Metro. Life Ins. Co.,* 126 F.3d 228, 234 (4th Cir. 1997) (finding no abuse of discretion in fiduciary's denial of benefits where claimant's primary medical provider's finding of disability conflicted with reports of an independent panel of medical specialists); *Brogan v. Holland,* 105 F.3d 158, 162–63 (4th Cir. 1997) (affirming district court's grant of summary judgment for trustees where medical evidence was conflicting as to whether plaintiff's stroke occurred during course of employment). Nor is an administrator's acceptance of the opinion of an independent physician consultant rather than those of a claimant's treating physicians in itself an abuse of discretion. *Dwyer v. Metro. Life Ins. Co.,* 4 Fed. Appx. 133, 2001 U.S. App. LEXIS 1541 (4th Cir. 2001); *but see Edmonds v. Hughes Aircraft Co.,* 1998 U.S. App. LEXIS 9419 (4th Cir. 1998) ("disinterested decision makers would [have] give[n] greater weight to the opinions of two treating therapists of long standing (neither of whom were hired in connection with the filing of the claim) over the first impression of another expert, who had conducted a single short interview and whose opinion belies perhaps too great a familiarity with its intended purpose."). A district court has recently noted, "Although a treating physician must accept a patient's subjective complaints, the same is not required of a plan administrator in determining eligibility for benefits." *Williams v. Unum Life Ins. Co. of Am.,* 250 F. Supp. 2d 641, 649 (E.D. Va. 2003).

### B. Unique Approach to Common Policy-Based Defenses

#### *1. Disability*

There are generally two types of disability coverage. "An 'occupational' disability policy provides benefits if the claimant is unable to perform his *regular* job; a 'general' disability policy provides benefits if the claimant is unable to perform *any* job for which he is qualified." *Dewitt v. State Farm Ins. Companies Retirement Plan,* 905 F.2d 798, 802 (4th Cir. 1990) (emphasis in original). The Fourth Circuit has noted: "The difference between the two is substantial." *Id.* District courts have rejected insureds' arguments that being disabled from some, but not all, of their regular duties renders them totally disabled. "When the policy language reads as that at hand, *i.e.,* total disability due to the inability to perform the important duties of regular occupation, the claimant must show his disability 'prevented him from performing all of those duties, not just some of them.'" *Conway v. Paul Revere Life Ins. Co.,* 2002 U.S. Dist. LEXIS 23656, *27 (W.D.N.C. 2002) (citations omitted). Otherwise, the existence of the residual disability portion of the policy would have no meaning:

It is evident that a person who can perform some but not all of his or her important duties has a "Residual Disability" within the meaning of the policy, and that therefore in order to be eligible for total disability payments a person would be required to show that he or she was unable to perform any of those important duties. It is not otherwise possible to give effect to both parts of the contract.

*Id.* at *28 (citations omitted). *See also Provident Life & Accident Ins. Co. v. Cohen,* 423 F.3d 413, 421–22 (4th Cir. 2005).

### 2. Mental Illness

A district court has upheld a twenty-four-month exclusion for mental illness under Georgia law. *Johnson v. Gen. Am. Life Ins. Co.,* 178 F. Supp. 2d 644 (W.D. Va. 2001). It found that the provision was not ambiguous and that the etiology of the mental illness was irrelevant. The court applied the limitation to the plaintiff's depression, even though that depression had an identifiable physical cause. *Id.* Another district court has found that such limitation provisions need not use the terminology from the most current *Diagnostic and Statistical Manual. Kelly-Hicks v. Paul Revere Ins. Co.,* 1998 U.S. Dist. LEXIS 12530 (W.D.N.C., 1998) ("Applying the clause in question to Plaintiff's claim, the Court finds that Plaintiff's diagnosis for anxiety, dissociative and depressive disorder are contained in the plain meaning of the terms 'neurosis' and 'psychoneurosis' as employed in the contract."). *See also Saah v. Contel Corp.,* 1992 U.S. App. LEXIS 27532 (4th Cir. 1992); *Allen v. Unum Life Ins. Co. of Am.,* 289 F. Supp. 2d 745 (W.D. Va. 2003) (upholding thirty-six-month mental illness limitation).

### C. Other Miscellaneous Issues

### 1. ERISA Class Actions

The Fourth Circuit applies an analysis of Rule 23 of the Federal Rules of Civil Procedure to determine whether a class action is appropriate in the context of ERISA claims. In *Gunnells v. Healthplan Servs.,* 348 F.3d 417 (4th Cir. 2003), claims were made against a third-party administrator based on allegations that it mismanaged administration of the plan, created a huge backlog of unpaid claims, did not timely transfer information, and made it impossible to forecast rate increases accurately, resulting in the plan's collapse and failure to pay hundreds, if not thousands, of health care claims. The district court conditionally granted plaintiffs' motion for class certification with respect to their mismanagement claim against the administrator. The Fourth Circuit upheld that certification based on its analysis of Rule 23 of the Federal Rules of Civil Procedure:

> Class actions must meet several criteria. First, the class must comply with the four prerequisites established in Rule 23(a): (1) numerosity of parties; (2) commonality of factual and legal issues; (3) typicality of claims and defenses of class representatives; and (4) adequacy of representation. Fed. R. Civ. P. 23(a). Second, the class action must fall within one of the three categories enumerated in Rule 23(b). . . .

If a lawsuit meets these requirements, certification as a class action serves important public purposes. In addition to promoting judicial economy and efficiency, class actions also "afford aggrieved persons a remedy if it is not economically feasible to obtain relief through the traditional framework of multiple individual damage actions." Thus, federal courts should "give Rule 23 a liberal rather than a restrictive construction, adopting a standard of flexibility in application which will in the particular case 'best serve the ends of justice for the affected parties and promote judicial efficiency.'"

To be sure, Rule 23(b)(3) class actions must meet predominance and superiority requirements not imposed on other kinds of class actions. This is because these suits involve situations where "class-action treatment is not as clearly called for." However, as the Supreme Court has noted, the predominance and superiority requirements in Rule 23(b)(3) do not foreclose the possibility of mass tort class actions, but merely ensure that class certification in such cases "achieve economies of time, effort, and expense, and promote . . . uniformity of decision as to persons similarly situated, without sacrificing procedural fairness or bringing about other undesirable results." For these very reasons, we have expressly "embraced the view that the mass tort action for damages may be appropriate for class action, either partially or in whole."

Furthermore, "[d]istrict courts have wide discretion in deciding whether or not to certify a class and their decisions may be reversed only for abuse of discretion," recognizing, of course, that this "discretion must be exercised within the framework of Rule 23." Our review is particularly deferential in a case like this—involving an interlocutory appeal of a conditional class certification.

*Gunnells* at 423–24 (citations omitted). Several district courts have concluded that claims under ERISA that have an element of misrepresentation or detrimental reliance are not appropriate for class certification:

> To prove an ERISA breach of fiduciary duty based on a misrepresentation, a plaintiff must establish each of the following elements: "(1) the defendant's status as an ERISA fiduciary acting as a fiduciary; (2) a misrepresentation on the part of the defendant; (3) the materiality of that misrepresentation; and (4) detrimental reliance by the plaintiff on the misrepresentation."
>
> In order to prove detrimental reliance, the Plaintiffs would have to establish that each member of the proposed class relied on the Defendants' alleged misrepresentations in making his investment decisions.
>
> * * *
>
> Because individual issues will predominate this litigation, regardless of whether the Plan is considered a 404(c) plan, class certification is inappropriate.

*Wiseman v. First Citizens Bank & Trust Co.*, 215 F.R.D. 507, 510–11 (W.D.N.C. 2003) (citations omitted). *See also Tootle v. Arinc, Inc.*, 2004 U.S. Dist. LEXIS 10629 (D. Md. 2004); *Mick v. Ravenswood Aluminum Corp.*, 178 F.R.D. 90 (S.D.W. Va. 1998). Finally, it should be noted that at least one court has observed that

ERISA's "attorneys' fee provision also undercuts one of the prime reasons for permitting a class action (with all of a class action's attendant complexities), mainly that individuals with claims too small to justify individual lawsuits must be allowed to aggregate their claims." *Doe v. Blue Cross Blue Shield of Md., Inc.,* 173 F. Supp. 2d 398, 406 (D. Md. 2001).

### 2. Jurisdictional Removal

The procedure for removal of a case from state to federal court is governed by 28 U.S.C. § 1446, which provides, in relevant part:

(a) A defendant or defendants desiring to remove any civil action or criminal prosecution from a State court shall file in the district court of the United States for the district and division within which such action is pending a notice of removal signed pursuant to Rule 11 of the Federal Rules of Civil Procedure and containing a short and plain statement of the grounds for removal, together with a copy of all process, pleadings, and orders served upon such defendant or defendants in such action.

(b) The notice of removal of a civil action or proceeding shall be filed within thirty days after the receipt by the defendant, through service or otherwise, of a copy of the initial pleading setting forth the claim for relief upon which such action or proceeding is based, or within thirty days after the service of summons upon the defendant if such initial pleading has then been filed in court and is not required to be served on the defendant, whichever period is shorter.

If the case stated by the initial pleading is not removable, a notice of removal may be filed within thirty days after receipt by the defendant, through service or otherwise, of a copy of an amended pleading, motion, order or other paper from which it may first be ascertained that the case is one which is or has become removable, except that a case may not be removed on the basis of jurisdiction conferred by section 1332 of this title more than 1 year after commencement of the action.

The Fourth Circuit recently reviewed the "framework" of jurisdictional removal of ERISA claims in *King v. Marriott Int'l, Inc.,* 337 F.3d 421, 424–25 (4th Cir. 2003):

Although the plaintiff is generally the "master of his complaint," the federal removal statute allows a defendant to remove certain claims originally brought in state court into federal court. Removal is appropriate, however, only where the civil action is one over which "the district courts of the United States have original jurisdiction."

\* \* \*

A civil action "arising under the Constitution, laws, or treaties of the United States" can be brought originally in federal district court. Under the venerable well-pleaded complaint rule, jurisdiction lies under section 1331 only if a claim, when pleaded correctly, sets forth a federal question; in other words, whether "a case is one arising under the Constitution or a law or treaty of the United States, in the sense of the jurisdictional statute, must be determined from what necessarily appears in the plaintiff's statement of his own claim in the bill or declaration, unaided by anything alleged in anticipation or avoidance of defenses which it is thought the defendant may interpose." Thus, ordinarily courts "look no further than the plaintiff's complaint in determining whether a lawsuit raises issues of federal law capable of creating federal-question jurisdiction under 28 U.S.C. § 1331." In particular, a claim in which the federal question arises only as a defense to an otherwise purely state law action does *not* "arise under" federal law, and hence jurisdiction would not lie under section 1331.

There is one corollary to the well-pleaded complaint rule. "Federal preemption is ordinarily a federal defense to the plaintiff's suit." Therefore, a defendant's raising of the defense of federal preemption is, under the well-pleaded complaint rule, insufficient to allow the removal of the case to federal court. But, in some cases, federal law so completely sweeps away state law that any action purportedly brought under state law is transformed into a federal action that can be brought originally in, or removed to, federal court. The operation of this rule has come to be known as the doctrine of "complete preemption." The Supreme Court recently summarized the doctrine in *Beneficial National Bank v. Anderson.* There, the Court emphasized that the touchstone of complete preemption is "whether Congress intended the federal cause of action" to be "the exclusive cause of action" for the type of claim brought by a plaintiff.

In cases of complete preemption, however, it is misleading to say that a state claim has been "preempted" as that word is ordinarily used. In such cases, in actuality, the plaintiff simply has brought a mislabeled federal claim, which may be asserted under some federal statute. Thus, a vital feature of complete preemption is the existence of a federal cause of action that replaces the preempted state cause of action. Where no discernable federal cause of action exists on a plaintiff's claim, there is no complete preemption, for in such cases there is no federal cause of action that Congress intended to be the exclusive remedy for the alleged wrong.

We have found that ERISA does completely preempt many state law claims. In particular, "when a complaint contains state law claims that fit within the scope of ERISA's § 502 civil enforcement provision, those claims are converted into federal claims, and the action can be removed to federal court."

The absence of a federal cause of action says nothing about whether the state claim is preempted in the ordinary sense: it is entirely within the power of Congress to completely eliminate certain remedies by preempting state actions, while providing no substitute federal action. But in such cases, preemption serves only as a federal defense, the barred claims are not completely preempted, and thus not removable to federal court.

*Id.* (citations omitted) (emphasis in original). The fact that there is concurrent jurisdiction in federal and state court over certain ERISA claims is not a basis to remand a case to state court. *Pearson v. Hartford Comprehensive Employee Benefits Servs. Co.,* 2006 U.S. Dist. LEXIS 41953 (M.D.N.C. 2006).

The usual procedural rules of removal apply in ERISA cases. For example, in cases involving multiple defendants, each must join in the petition for removal. *Stonewall Jackson Mem. Hosp. v. Am. United Life Ins. Co.,* 963 F. Supp. 553, 558 (N.D.W. Va. 1997). Courts have recognized that the party seeking to remove a case to federal court has the burden of establishing federal jurisdiction, and if federal jurisdiction is doubtful, a remand is necessary. *See, e.g., Fair v. Giant of Maryland,* 2006 U.S. Dist. LEXIS 5758 (D. Md. 2006); *Four-County Cmty. Servs. v. FIA Adm'rs, Inc.,* 2003 U.S. Dist. LEXIS 23462 (M.D.N.C. 2003). A district court has noted that the majority of courts look to the whole record brought forward on removal, and not just the complaint, to determine if removal jurisdiction exists; "even under this approach the burden of establishing removal jurisdiction rests upon the party seeking to invoke it." *Potter v. Shoney's, Inc.,* 108 F. Supp. 2d 489, 497 n.11 (M.D.N.C. 1999) (citation omitted). Nor does a plaintiff's failure to object to a notice of removal or file a motion to remand automatically confer removal jurisdiction on a federal court. *Id.*

In the context of ERISA, the Fourth Circuit has held that a plaintiff, who timely filed a motion to remand, had not waived her objection to a defendant's removal of her case to federal court by amending her complaint to explicitly assert a cause of action under Section 502 of ERISA. *King,* 337 F.3d at 425–26.

A district court has ruled that a third-party health plan could not remove a case to federal court based on ERISA. *Sanford v. Premier Millwork & Lumber Co.,* 234 F. Supp. 2d 569 (E.D. Va. 2002). When an employee sued her employer in state court alleging that she paid premiums to her employer for group health insurance coverage and that her employer failed to provide the coverage promised, the employer, in turn, brought in the health plan as a third-party defendant, maintaining that it had a contract with the health plan to provide group coverage and that the health plan breached that contract in its failure to provide coverage. The health plan removed the case to federal court. The district court found that although there was a federal claim such that the court could have original jurisdiction, the health plan could not remove the case to federal court because third-party defendants are not the true defendants in the first instance and are not, therefore, entitled to remove under 28 U.S.C. § 1441(a). *Id.* at 571. The court also rejected the health plan's argument that the claim against it was separate and independent:

> It is clear that the third-party complaint is not separate and independent— the single wrong in this case is the alleged failure to provide promised insurance coverage. The resolution of the third-party claim is intertwined with resolution of the original claim. Therefore, even if third-party defendants can remove under § 1441(c), the third-party claim in the instant case is not separate and independent and the claim cannot form the basis for removal under § 1441(c).

*Id.* at 572. *See also Carroll County Gen. Hosp. v. Rosen,* 174 F. Supp. 2d 384 (Md. 2001).

The concurrent jurisdiction that exists between the state and federal courts for benefit claims brought under 29 U.S.C. § 1132(a)(1)(B) has been noted not to be a justification for remanding an ERISA case to state court. *Schrader v. Trucking Employees of N. Jersey Welfare Fund, Inc.*, 232 F. Supp. 2d 560, 567 (M.D.N.C. 2002). Moreover, a district court has rejected an argument that a plan had waived its right to remove a case to federal court by previously including in its summary plan description a notice to participants that "if you have a claim for benefits which is denied or ignored, in whole or in part, you may file suit in a state or federal court." *Fanney v. Trigon Ins. Co.*, 11 F. Supp. 2d 829, 831–32 (E.D. Va. 1998).

As for the timing of filing a notice of removal, a district court has found that a defendant could remove an ERISA case more than 180 days after service of the initial state court pleading, because the case as originally stated in that pleading was not removable. *Therrell v. Cameron*, 1997 U.S. Dist. LEXIS 20294 (M.D.N.C. 1997). Quoting *Lovern v. Gen. Motors Corp.*, 121 F.3d 160, 162 (4th Cir. 1997), the court stated:

> [O]nly where an initial pleading reveals a ground for removal will the defendant be bound to file a notice of removal within 30 days. Where, however, such details are obscured or omitted, or indeed misstated, that circumstance makes the case "stated by the initial pleading" not removable, and the defendant will have 30 days from the revelation of grounds for removal in an amended pleading, motion, order, or other paper to file its notice of removal.

*Id.* at *19. The court found that in reading the entire complaint, "notice of an ERISA cause of action is at best obscure" because it was not apparent that plaintiffs had provided an employee benefit plan and were making a claim against that plan. *Id.* Moreover, citing *Lovern* again, the court rejected the plaintiffs' argument that the defendants had actual knowledge that the insurance constituted an employee benefit, noting that removal jurisdiction is an objective inquiry, not a subjective one. *Id.* at *20–21. The district court found that the thirty-day clock to remove under 28 U.S.C. § 1446(b) began at the plaintiff's subsequent depositions, which constituted "other papers." *Id.* at *22.

# CHAPTER 5

# Fifth Circuit

JENNIFER M. LAWRENCE
VIRGINIA N. RODDY
KELLY D. SIMPKINS
STEPHEN W. SMITH

## I. What Constitutes an ERISA Plan?

### A. Determining the Existence of an Employee Welfare Benefit Plan

Nearly every Fifth Circuit case that discusses the existence of an ERISA (Employee Retirement Income Security Act of 1974) plan begins the inquiry at the statutory definition of an employee benefit plan. 29 U.S.C. § 1002(1)(3).

The Fifth Circuit has "devised a comprehensive test for determining whether a particular plan qualifies as an employee welfare benefit plan." *Meredith v. Time Ins. Co.*, 980 F.2d 352, 355 (5th Cir. 1993). The three-part inquiry is "whether a plan (1) exists; (2) falls within the safe-harbor provision established by the Department of Labor; and (3) satisfies the primary elements of an ERISA 'employee benefit plan'—establishment or maintenance by an employer intending to benefit employees." *Id.* "If any part of the inquiry is answered in the negative, the submission is not an ERISA plan." *Id.*

In determining whether a plan exists, the Fifth Circuit has stated that it turns to a test devised by the Eleventh Circuit: "whether from the surrounding circumstances a reasonable person could ascertain the intended benefits, beneficiaries, source of financing, and procedures for receiving benefits." *Id.*, citing *Donovan v. Dillingham*, 688 F.2d 1367, 1373 (11th Cir. 1982) (*en banc*) (adopted in *Memorial Hosp. Sys. v. Northbrook Life Ins. Co.*, 904 F.2d 236 (5th Cir. 1990)). Determining whether a plan satisfies the elements of an ERISA plan requires an examination of the definitions of employer and employee and the relationship between the two.

## B. Definition of "Employee" for ERISA Purposes

In *Meredith,* the Fifth Circuit notes that "ERISA simply provides that an employee is 'any individual employed by an employer.'" 980 F.2d at 356, citing 29 U.S.C. § 1002(6). Citing *Nationwide Mutual Insurance Co. v. Darden,* 503 U.S. 318, 323 & 323 n.3 (1992), the Fifth Circuit stated, "In the absence of textual clues, courts should look to the federal common law in order to determine who is an employee." *Provident Life & Accident Ins. Co. v. Sharpless,* 364 F.3d 634, 638 (5th Cir. 2004).

Like the Supreme Court, the Fifth Circuit has also looked to the DOL regulations, including its "interpretation of employee status," to determine whether certain individuals should be treated as participants or beneficiaries under ERISA plans. In March of 2004, the Supreme Court answered the question: "Does the working owner of a business . . . qualify as a 'participant' in a pension plan governed by . . . [ERISA]?" *Yates v. Hendon,* 541 U.S. 1, 6 (2004). "The answer," the Court held, "is yes: If the plan covers one or more employees other than the business owner and his or her spouse, the working owner may participate on equal terms with other plan participants." *Id.* This ruling was consistent with the approach taken by the Fifth Circuit in *Vega v. National Life Insurance Services, Inc.,* 188 F.3d 287 (5th Cir. 1999) (holding that husband and wife owners of a corporation were employees for purposes of ERISA). Furthermore, the Fifth Circuit has had an opportunity to rule on this issue post-*Yates,* and has consistently followed *Yates. See Provident Life & Accident Ins. Co. v. Sharpless,* 364 F.3d 634 (5th Cir. 2004) (court held that Dr. Sharpless, who was a shareholder in a multiple shareholder corporation, was also an employee for purposes of ERISA).

A sole proprietor, however, who purchased insurance for herself and her husband only was held not to be an employer for purposes of ERISA and, therefore, her "plan" was not governed by ERISA. *Meredith,* 980 F.2d 352.

## C. Interpretation of Safe Harbor Regulation

To fall under the "safe harbor" provision and be exempt from ERISA, a plan must meet the four criteria established by the Department of Labor at 29 C.F.R. § 2510.3-1(j): (1) the employer does not contribute to the plan; (2) employee participation is voluntary; (3) the employer's role is limited to collecting and remitting premiums to the insurer, without endorsement of the plan; and (4) the employer receives no profit from the plan. "Given the language of the [safe harbor] regulation, especially the use of the conjunction 'and,' the presence of all four conditions is jointly sufficient to cause the program to be excluded from the definition of a 'group plan.'" *Kidder v. H&B Marine, Inc.,* 932 F.2d 347 (5th Cir. 1991). "Group insurance plans which meet all of these criteria are excluded from ERISA's coverage." *Hansen v. Cont'l Ins. Co.,* 940 F.2d 971 (5th Cir. 1991). Where the employer pays the premium for the employees' coverage under the plan (and thereby negates the first of the four safe harbor conditions), the plan is exempt from the safe harbor regulations. *Tatum v. Special Ins. Servs.,* 2003 WL 22922302 (5th Cir. 2003). The Fifth Circuit has also held that a group accidental insurance policy qualified as an ERISA plan where the employer's brochure endorsed the plan by urging employees to "give the program careful consideration" and the employer employed a full-time employee benefits administrator. *Hansen,* 940 F.2d at 974. However, "the mere fact that coverage flows from the employment relationship is not sufficient to invoke ERISA." *Metoyer v. Am. Int'l Life Assurance of N.Y.,* 296 F. Supp. 2d 745, 750 (S.D. Tex. 2003).

### D. Amount of Employer Involvement Required to Sustain an Employee Welfare Benefit Plan

In *Taggart Corp. v. Life & Health Benefits Administration, Inc.,* 617 F.2d 1208 (5th Cir. 1980), the Fifth Circuit held that an employer's "bare purchase" of an insurance policy does not establish an ERISA plan. In *Memorial Hospital System v. Northbrook Life Insurance Co.,* 904 F.2d 236, 242–43 (5th Cir. 1990), the court distinguished *Taggart* as follows:

> Unlike *Taggart,* the present case does not involve the bare purchase of insurance by a lone employee through a MET [multiple employer trust]. Noffs, a statutory employer, has chosen to provide welfare benefits to all of its full-time employees through the purchase of a group insurance policy. Noffs is solely responsible under the policy for submitting monthly premiums directly to Northbrook by the premium due dates. The fact that Noffs' administrative functions under the policy are minimal is perfectly in keeping with its intent that Northbrook administer the plan as well as insure it. There is, thus, an employer-employee-plan relationship that was lacking in *Taggart.*

In *Kidder v. H&B Marine, Inc.,* 932 F.2d 347, 353 (5th Cir. 1991), the Fifth Circuit concluded that "H&B Construction Inc.'s payment of premiums on behalf of its employees is 'substantial evidence that a plan, fund, or program [was] established.'" *See also Hansen,* 940 F.2d at 977 (5th Cir. 1991).

### E. Treatment of Multiple Employer Trusts and Welfare Agreements

Under ERISA, a multiple employer welfare arrangement (MEWA) includes all arrangements "established or maintained for the purpose of offering or providing" certain benefits "to the employees of two or more employers . . . or to their beneficiaries." 29 U.S.C. § 1002(40)(A). "ERISA does not automatically govern all MEWAs. Congress's notion of a MEWA is broader than its concept of an 'employee benefit plan' . . . The statutory definition of a MEWA encompasses both EWBPs and arrangements 'other than . . . employee welfare benefit plan[s].'" *MDPhysicians & Assoc., Inc. v. State Board of Ins.,* 957 F.2d 178, 181 (5th Cir. 1992). For purposes of ERISA preemption, the question is not whether a particular arrangement is a MEWA, but whether the plan in question meets the statutory definition. *See Meredith v. Time Ins. Co.,* 980 F.2d 352 (5th Cir. 1993). In *MDPhysicians,* the Fifth Circuit concluded that MDPhysicians & Associates, Inc. Employee Benefit Plan, formed by an independent physician practice association, was not an employee welfare benefit plan governed by ERISA, although it was a MEWA. The court could not "locate [MDPhysicians] as an 'employer' within ERISA," and stated:

Absent the protective nexus between the entity providing the benefits and the individuals receiving the benefits, we cannot consider the . . . [Plan] a "group or association of employers" acting indirectly for the Subscribing Employers in relation to the . . . Plan.

. . .

[MDPhysicians] established and maintained the [MDPhysicians] Plan to generate profits. The Subscribing Employers, the entities with economic and representational ties to the individuals that benefited from the . . . Plan, were not involved in the establishment or maintenance of the . . . Plan. We hold that the [MDPhysicians] Plan did not act as a "group or association of employers" in the interest of the Subscribing Employers in relation to the . . . Plan.

957 F.2d at 186.

## II. Preemption

### A. Scope of ERISA Preemption

In 2002 a Fifth Circuit judge ruefully observed, "We have spilled much ink over the last few decades trying to interpret this statute." *Roark v. Humana Inc.,* 307 F.3d 298, 313 (5th Cir. 2002). Most of that ink dealt with preemption. Like many other circuits, the Fifth Circuit has found it difficult to stay in step with the Supreme Court's shifting views of ERISA preemption. In general, the circuit has tended toward a narrower view of ERISA's preemptive scope. Thus, in *Pilot Life Insurance Co. v. Dedeaux,* 481 U.S. 41 (1987), the Supreme Court reversed the Fifth Circuit's holding that state-law contract and tort claims for denial of insurance benefits were not preempted by ERISA. In *Boggs v. Boggs,* 520 U.S. 833 (1997), the Supreme Court reversed a Fifth Circuit finding that ERISA did not preempt Louisiana community property laws affecting pension benefits. And most recently in *Aetna Health Inc. v. Davila,* 542 U.S. 200 (2004), the Supreme Court held that ERISA preempted a suit for HMO negligence under the Texas Health Care Liability Act, contrary to the Fifth Circuit's view.

Occasionally, the Fifth Circuit has failed to anticipate Supreme Court zags toward a more restrictive view of preemption. For example, in *Rush Prudential HMO, Inc. v. Moran,* 536 U.S. 355 (2002), the Supreme Court rejected a preemption challenge to an Illinois statute requiring HMOs to provide independent review of disputes between the primary care physician and the HMO. The Fifth Circuit had reached the opposite conclusion in overturning a similar provision of the Texas Health Care Liability Act. *Corp. Health Ins. Inc. v. Texas Dep't of Ins.,* 215 F.3d 526 (5th Cir. 2000), *vacated and remanded sub nom. Montemayor v. Corp. Health Ins. Inc.,* 536 U.S. 935 (2002).

### B. Complete versus Ordinary Preemption

The Fifth Circuit has repeatedly emphasized the important distinction between complete preemption on the one hand and ordinary preemption, sometimes called "conflict" preemption, on the other. Ordinary preemption is a federal defense to the plaintiff's suit and may arise either by express statutory term or by a direct conflict between the operation of federal and state law. *Arana v. Ochsner Health Plan,* 338 F.3d 433, 459 (5th Cir. 2003) *(en banc).* Because it is merely a defense, ordinary preemption does not provide a jurisdictional basis for removal to federal court. *Id.*

Complete preemption has been described as less a principle of substantive preemption than it is a rule of federal jurisdiction. *McClelland v. Gronwaldt,* 155 F.3d 507, 516 (5th Cir. 1998), *rev'd in part on other grounds; Arana,* 338 F.3d at 440 n.11. State-law claims falling within the scope of the civil enforcement provisions contained in ERISA § 502(a) are completely preempted. *Id.* at 517. The state action thus becomes "transmogrified" into a federal one, giving rise to federal question jurisdiction. *Giles v. NYLCare Health Plans, Inc.,* 172 F.3d 332, 337 (5th Cir. 1999). In order to fall within ERISA § 502(a), two criteria must be met: (1) an employee benefit plan must exist; and (2) the plaintiff must have standing to sue under § 502(a). *Vega v. Nat'l Life Ins. Servs., Inc.,* 188 F.3d 287, 291 (5th Cir. 1999) *(en banc).*

The test for ordinary preemption under ERISA § 514(a) (the "relate to" clause) is different, and calls for an evaluation of the nexus between ERISA and the asserted state-law claim in the context of ERISA's statutory objectives. A state-law claim is subject to ordinary preemption if a two-prong test is met: (1) the state-law claim addresses an area of exclusive federal concern, such as the right to receive benefits under the terms of an ERISA plan; and (2) the claim directly affects the relationships among traditional ERISA entities—the employer, the plan and its fiduciaries, and the participants and beneficiaries. *Smith v. Texas Children's Hosp.,* 84 F.3d 152, 155 (5th Cir. 1996). State-law claims with only a tenuous, remote, or peripheral connection with an ERISA plan will not be preempted under § 514. *Lewis v. Bank of Am.,* 343 F.3d 540, 543 (5th Cir. 2003).

The Fifth Circuit has recognized that the tests for complete and ordinary preemption are not co-extensive, and that cases could arise in which "there may be complete preemption subject matter jurisdiction over a claim that falls within ERISA section 502(a) even though that claim is not conflict-preempted by ERISA section 514." *Arana,* 338 F.3d at 440.

### C. Preemption of Health-Care Benefit Claims

In 1992, the Fifth Circuit ruled that any putative tort claim based on negligence in handling a benefit determination was preempted under ERISA § 514. *Corcoran v. United Health Care, Inc.,* 965 F.2d 1321 (5th Cir. 1992). Later panels have expressed discomfort with the *Corcoran* rule, particularly in the managed-care context, where eligibility and medical treatment decisions are frequently mixed:

> [A]fter *Pegram, Corcoran*'s rule creates perverse incentives for HMO's. If a doctor fails to recommend treatment, the patient may sue the doctor and HMO under state law. If the doctor recommends treatment, and the HMO denies coverage, the patient has no remedy. *Corcoran,* 965 F.2d at 1338. In this circuit, HMO's can escape all liability if they instruct their doctors to recommend every possible treatment and leave the real decision to HMO administrators. It is difficult to believe that one of Congress's goals

in passing ERISA was to shift medical judgments from doctors to plan administrators.

*Roark v. Humana, Inc.,* 307 F.3d 298, 315 (5th Cir. 2002), *reversed sub nom. Aetna Health Inc. v. Davila,* 542 U.S. 200 (2004). The *Roark* decision rested in part on an expansive reading of the Supreme Court's decision in *Pegram v. Herdrich,* 530 U.S. 211 (2000):

> We decline, two years after the [Supreme] Court [in *Pegram*] expressed disbelief that Congress would federalize medical malpractice law under § 502(a)(2), to hold that Congress had done so under § 502(a)(1)(B).

*Roark,* 307 F.3d at 311.

In *Davila,* of course, the Supreme Court limited *Pegram*'s carve-out of mixed eligibility/treatment decisions to the HMO context. The *Davila* reversal initially appeared to check any impetus toward cutting back on the scope of ERISA preemption in the health care arena. *See Mayeaux v. La. Health Serv. & Indem. Co.,* 376 F.3d 410 (5th Cir. 2004) (state-law negligence, unfair trade practice, tortious interference, and defamation claims held preempted as collateral attack on benefit denial).

State-law claims challenging denial of long-term-disability status under both the Texas Insurance Code and common-law duty of good faith were held conflict preempted in *Ellis v. Liberty Life Assurance Co.,* 394 F.3d 262 (5th Cir. 2004), *cert. denied,* 125 S. Ct. 2941 (2005). Even though the Insurance Code provides remedies for unfair practices and bad-faith claim denial by insurers, they do not substantially affect the risk pooling arrangement between the insurer and the insured, and therefore do not qualify for the insurance exemption to ERISA preemption under the Supreme Court's decision in *Kentucky Association of Health Plans, Inc. v. Miller,* 538 U.S. 329, 341–42 (2003).

More recent cases appear to revert to the circuit's pre-*Davila* posture of narrowly construing ERISA preemption. A worker's common-law claim against his employer for negligent maintenance of an unsafe workplace was held not preempted by ERISA, even though the employer maintained an ERISA benefit plan to cover occupational injuries in lieu of participating in the Texas workers' compensation system. *Woods v. Texas Aggregates, L.L.C.,* 2006 U.S. App. LEXIS 19888 (5th Cir. Aug. 3, 2006). The lawsuit's only connection to the ERISA plan was that it sought damages that might also be available in the form of plan benefits. This connection was held insufficient to "relate to" the ERISA plan for purposes of ERISA preemption, in light of earlier circuit precedent. *See Hook v. Morrison Milling Co.,* 38 F.3d 776 (5th Cir. 1994). Also, an employer's state-law claims for breach of contract and misrepresentation against the administrator and stop-loss insurer for its self-insured ERISA benefit plan was held not preempted in *Bank of Louisiana v. Aetna US Healthcare Inc.,* 2006 U.S. App. LEXIS 20105 (5th Cir. August 4, 2006). A Louisiana statute requiring insurance companies to honor assignments of benefit claims made by patients to hospitals survived a preemption challenge in *Louisiana Health Service & Indemnity Co. v. Rapides Healthcare System,* ___ F.3d ___, No. 04-31114, 2006 WL 2361696 (5th Cir. 2006). The court found no conflict preemption because the assignment statute did not create an additional means to enforce payment of benefits under an ERISA plan, but merely transferred the cause of action from the patient to the hospital. Nor was there express preemption under the "relate to" clause of Section 514, in light of ERISA's statutory silence on benefit plan assignments, as well as the Supreme Court's rejection of an "uncritical literalism" in *New York State Conference of Blue Cross & Blue Shield Plans v. Travelers Ins. Co.,* 514 U.S. 645 (1995), and return to a traditional preemption analysis paying more respect to areas of traditional state regulation. The panel decision acknowledged and expressly declined to follow contrary holdings in both the Eighth and Tenth Circuits.

## III. Exhaustion of Administrative Remedies

### A. Is Exhaustion an Absolute Requirement?

The Fifth Circuit adheres to the rule that a party must exhaust available administrative remedies under the plan before bringing suit to recover benefits. *Denton v. First Nat'l Bank of Waco,* 765 F.2d 1295, 1300 (5th Cir. 1985). The exhaustion requirement has been extended to claims that a plan breached its fiduciary duty in connection with a benefit denial. *Simmons v. Willcox,* 911 F.2d 1077, 1081 (5th Cir. 1990). However, fiduciary breach claims that do not seek the distribution of any benefits do not require the exhaustion of administrative remedies. *Milofsky v. Am. Airlines, Inc.,* 442 F.3d 311 (5th Cir. 2006) (*en banc*) (suit to recover losses to 401(k) plan arising from delay in transferring account balances to new plan). Exhaustion is not required for claims of interference with protected rights under ERISA § 510. *Chailland v. Brown & Root Inc.,* 45 F.3d 947 (5th Cir. 1995).

Exhaustion of administrative remedies is not a prerequisite for subject matter jurisdiction, however. *Hager v. NationsBank N.A.,* 167 F.3d 245, 248 n.3 (5th Cir. 1999). Although not specifically required by ERISA, the exhaustion doctrine is a common-law defense "uniformly imposed by the courts in keeping with Congress' intent in enacting ERISA." *Hall v. Nat'l Gypsum Co.,* 105 F.3d 225, 231 (5th Cir. 1997). The purposes of the exhaustion requirement include minimizing frivolous ERISA suits, promoting consistent treatment of benefit claims, providing a nonadversarial dispute resolution process, reducing delay and expense, and creating a clear record of administrative action if litigation ensues. *Id.*

### B. Exceptions to the Exhaustion Requirement

The Fifth Circuit has so far recognized two exceptions to the exhaustion requirement. The first is futility: A claimant need not exhaust administrative remedies when it would be futile to do so. *Denton,* 765 F.2d at 1300. But futility may be shown only when the plan administrator is hostile or biased against the claimant. *McGowin v. ManPower Int'l, Inc.,* 363 F.3d 556, 559 (5th Cir. 2004); *Bourgeois,* 215 F.3d at 479. The mere fact that the claim was initially denied by a high-ranking company official, or even by the same committee that would review an appeal, is insufficient to establish futility. *Denton,* 765 F.2d at 1300; *Bourgeois,* 215 F.3d at 479; *McGowin,* 363 F.3d at 560.

The second recognized exception is denial of meaningful access to the administrative process. *McGowin,* 363 F.2d at 560. For example, in *Hall v. National Gypsum Co.,* the plaintiff overcame the exhaustion defense because the plan had abolished the appeals committee that was supposed to review the plaintiff's claim denial. 105 F.3d at 232. By contrast, in *McGowin* the plaintiff was not denied meaningful access, despite her lack of notice of plan claim procedures, because she never requested the plan documents nor was she told specifically that she could not obtain them. 363 F.3d at 560.

The court generally insists upon strict compliance with the claims procedure provided by the plan. "[A]llowing informal attempts to substitute for the formal claims procedure would frustrate the primary purposes of the exhaustion requirement." *Bourgeois,* 215 F.3d at 480 n.14. This normally includes completion of any internal appeals process. *Denton,* 765 F.2d at 1300.

### C. Consequences of Failure to Exhaust

The remedies imposed for failure to exhaust vary depending on the circumstances. If the plaintiff has filed an initial claim, the case is normally remanded back to the plan for further consideration. *Bourgeois,* 215 F.3d at 482 n.30. If no such claim has been filed, then dismissal is the preferred course. *McGowin,* 363 F.3d at 560 (affirming summary judgment dismissing claims); *Cooperative Benefit Adm'rs, Inc. v. Ogden,* 367 F.3d 323 (5th Cir. 2004) (same).

### D. Minimum Number of Levels of Administrative Review

The Fifth Circuit has not required an ERISA plan to provide more levels of administrative reviews than the statute requires. 29 U.S.C § 1133.

### E. Can a Defendant Waive a Failure-to-Exhaust Defense?

Presumably, like any other affirmative defense, failure to exhaust may be waived if not pleaded, although no reported Fifth Circuit decision has so held. The Fifth Circuit has recognized that under certain circumstances plan defendants may be estopped from raising a failure-to-exhaust defense. *Bourgeois v. Pension Plan for Employees of Santa Fe Int'l Corp.,* 215 F.3d 475, 481 (5th Cir. 2000).

## IV. Standard of Review

### A. Plan Language

The Fifth Circuit has not insisted on any talismanic formula to obtain *Firestone* deference for plan determinations. Language conferring discretionary authority to interpret the plan and decide claims is generally sufficient. However, discretionary authority is not conferred by plan language stating merely that the fiduciary has authority to control and manage the plan. *Cathey v. Dow Chem. Co. Med. Care Program,* 907 F.2d 554 (5th Cir. 1990), *cert. denied,* 111 S. Ct. 964 (1991).

### B. What Standard of Review Applies?

Unlike other circuits, the Fifth Circuit adheres to the view that factual findings by the plan administrator are entitled to review under the arbitrary and capricious standard, even where de novo review would be required for plan interpretation issues under *Meditrust Fin. Servs. Corp. v Sterling Chems., Inc.,* 168 F.3d 211, 213 (5th Cir. 1999); *Pierre v. Conn. Gen. Life Ins. Co.,* 932 F.2d 1552 (5th Cir. 1991), *cert. denied,* 502 U.S. 973 (1993). By the same token, a plan administrator's statutory and legal conclusions unrelated to plan interpretation are always subject to de novo review. *Dial v. NFL Player Supp. Disability Plan,* 174 F.3d 606, 611 (5th Cir. 1999) (no deference owed to administrator's interpretation of state court domestic relations order).

The Fifth Circuit has adopted a two-step process for reviewing a plan administrator's denial of benefits for abuse of discretion. First, did the administrator give the plan the "legally correct" interpretation? In answering this question, the court must consider (1) whether the administrator has given the plan a uniform construction; (2) whether the interpretation is consistent with a fair reading of the plan; and (3) any unanticipated costs resulting from different interpretations. *Wildbur v. ARCO Chem. Co.,* 974 F.2d 631, 637–38 (5th Cir. 1992). The second factor is considered the most important. *Gosselink v. Am. Tel. & Tel., Inc.,* 272 F.3d 722, 727 (5th Cir. 2001).

If the court concludes the administrator's interpretation is legally incorrect, the court must then proceed to determine whether the administrator abused its discretion. Three factors are relevant here: (1) the internal consistency of the plan under the administrator's interpretation; (2) any relevant regulations promulgated by administrative agencies; and (3) the factual background of the determination and any inferences of bad faith. *Id.*

Where a benefit plan provides for binding arbitration of disputes, court review of the arbitration award is limited to the same exceedingly deferential standard of review applied to arbitration awards generally. *Kergosien v. Ocean Energy, Inc.,* 390 F.3d 346 (5th Cir. 2004) (enforcing arbitration award under severance pay plan). In addition to the four narrow statutory grounds under the Federal Arbitration Act, the Fifth Circuit also recognizes manifest disregard of law and contrary to public policy as nonstatutory grounds to challenge an arbitration award. *Id.*

## C. Effect of Conflict of Interest or Procedural Irregularity

The existence of a conflict of interest is another factor to consider in determining whether the administrator abused its discretion. A sliding scale of deference is employed: "The greater the evidence of conflict on the part of the administrator, the less deferential our abuse of discretion standard will be." *Vega v. Nat'l Life Ins. Servs., Inc.,* 188 F.3d 287, 297 (5th Cir. 1999) (*en banc*). Less than full deference is accorded a denial of benefits by an administrator that is also an insurer of the plan, because such an administrator potentially benefits from every denied claim. *Gooden v. Provident Life & Acc. Ins. Co.,* 250 F.3d 329, 333 (5th Cir. 2001). But the "mere fact that benefit claims are decided by a paid human resources administrator who works for the [plan sponsor] does not, without more, suffice to create an inherent conflict of interest." *MacLachlan v. ExxonMobil Corp.,* 350 F.3d 473, 479 n.8 (5th Cir. 2003). Nor is a conflict necessarily created when a plan administrator seeks advice from a corporate benefits attorney regarding historical interpretations of the plan. *Id.* at 480.

The *Wildbur* two-step approach need not be rigidly applied in every case, however. Where an administrator interprets an ERISA plan in a manner that "directly contradicts" the plain meaning of the plan language, an abuse of discretion may be found even if there is no evidence of bad faith or violation of administrative regulations. *Gosselink,* 272 F.3d at 727. This direct-contradiction exception to *Wildbur* is to be used "sparingly and with restraint," however. *Baker v. Metro. Life Ins. Co.,* 364 F.3d 624, 634 (5th Cir. 2004) (Weiner, J., concurring).

### D. Other Factors Affecting Standard of Review

Recently the Fifth Circuit confronted an unusual case in which two ERISA fiduciaries, each with discretionary authority to interpret the plan, disagreed on a benefit claim. *Baker,* 364 F.3d 624. The plan administrator initially granted the claim for enhanced life insurance benefits, but the plan insurer refused to pay, citing certain unmet preconditions. The court here agreed with the plan insurer, because the plan administrator's interpretation directly contradicted the plan language, and hence was arbitrary and capricious. In a concurring opinion, Judge Weiner noted that if the plan administrator had not abused its discretion, the court would have been required to defer to the plan administrator's interpretation, especially given the plan insurer's potential conflict of interest.

The standard of review is not affected by a plan fiduciary's decision to terminate benefits previously granted. In particular, a plan insurer is not required to prove a subsequent and substantial change in medical condition in order to justify a decision terminating disability benefits initially granted six months earlier. *Ellis v. Liberty Life Assurance Co.,* 394 F.3d 262 (5th Cir. 2004), *cert. denied,* 125 S. Ct. 2941 (2005) (upholding termination of benefits based on subsequently acquired medical evidence); *cf. Robinson v. Aetna Life Ins. Co.,* 443 F.3d 389 (5th Cir. 2006) (overturning decision to terminate LTD benefits previously granted, where plan administrator relied on evidence outside administrative record that claimant had no opportunity to contest).

## V. Rules of Plan Interpretation

### A. Application of Federal Common Law

The interpretation of ERISA benefit plans is a matter of federal common law. *Wegner v. Standard Ins. Co.,* 129 F.3d 814, 818 (5th Cir. 1997). Analogous state-law principles may provide guidance, but only to the extent that they are consistent with the congressional policy concerns reflected in ERISA. *Todd v. AIG Life Ins. Co.,* 47 F.3d 1448, 1451 (5th Cir. 1995).

Eligibility for ERISA benefits is "governed in the first instance by the plain meaning of the plan language." *Threadgill v. Prudential Sec. Group, Inc.,* 145 F.3d 286, 292 (5th Cir. 1998). ERISA plans are interpreted from the standpoint of "a person of average intelligence and experience." *Jones v. Ga. Pac. Corp.,* 90 F.3d 114, 116 (5th Cir. 1996), or, more particularly, "the average plan participant." *Tucker v. Shreveport Transit Mgmt., Inc.,* 226 F.3d 394, 398 (5th Cir. 2000); *see* 29 U.S.C. § 1022(a). Plan provisions are to be read "not in isolation, but as a whole." *Dallas*

*County Hosp. Dist. v. Assocs.' Health & Welfare Plan,* 293 F.3d 282, 288 (5th Cir. 2002).

When there is an inconsistency between the terms of the plan and the summary plan description (SPD), the terms of the SPD will control, because "[i]t is the SPD and not the Plan upon which the average beneficiary has relied; the SPD most nearly represents the intention of the parties." *Fallo v. Piccadilly Cafeterias, Inc.,* 141 F.3d 580, 584 (5th Cir. 1998).

The Fifth Circuit has finally acknowledged ERISA estoppel as a cognizable legal theory. *Mello v. Sara Lee Corp.,* 431 F.3d 440 (5th Cir. 2005). Its elements are (1) material misrepresentation; (2) reasonable and detrimental reliance; and (3) extraordinary circumstances. Because estoppel is a legal theory rather than an interpretation of plan terms, court review of a plan decision on that ground is de novo rather than deferential. A party's reliance on a misrepresentation that conflicts with the plain language of plan documents will seldom, if ever, be reasonable. *Mello,* 431 F.3d at 445 (reliance upon repeated oral and written misstatements of monthly benefit amount held unreasonable in light of unambiguous plan language); *High v. E-Systems Inc. Long Term Disability Income & Death Benefit Plan,* 2006 U.S. App. LEXIS 19613 (5th Cir. Aug. 3, 2006) (reliance upon actual receipt of disability benefits not offset by monthly VA benefits is unreasonable in view of conflict with plan terms).

The Fifth Circuit continues to hold that the federal common law of waiver applies to ERISA beneficiary rights. *Guardian Life Ins. Co. v. Finch,* 395 F.3d 238 (5th Cir. 2004) (former spouse waived rights to ex-husband's life insurance, even though the former spouse was still the named beneficiary in plan records); *Manning v. Hayes,* 212 F.3d 866 (5th Cir. 2001). To be effective, the waiver must be a voluntary or intentional relinquishment of a known right. *See High v. E-Systems Inc. Long Term Disability Income & Death Benefit Plan,* 2006 U.S. App. LEXIS 19613 (5th Cir. Aug. 3, 2006) (no waiver by new plan administrator, which discovered and discontinued overpayments initiated by previous administrator).

## B. Application of *Contra Proferentem*

The Fifth Circuit follows the rule of *contra proferentem,* i.e., that ambiguities must be resolved against the drafter, in cases involving insurance benefits under ERISA plans. *Wegner v. Standard Ins. Co.,* 129 F.3d 814, 818 (5th Cir. 1997); *Hansen v. Cont'l Ins. Co.,* 940 F.2d 971, 982 (5th Cir. 1991) (construing SPD that conflicted with underlying life insurance policy). The rule applies even to cases where the plan administrator has been given discretion to interpret the insurance plan. *Rhorer v. Raytheon Eng'rs & Const'rs Inc. Basic Life, Optional Life, Accidental Death & Dependent Life Ins. Plan,* 181 F.3d 635, 642 (5th Cir. 1999) (*contra proferentem* may properly be used under first step of *Wildbur* abuse of discretion review). The Fifth Circuit has not definitively ruled whether the *contra proferentem* doctrine applies to uninsured ERISA benefits. *See, e.g., Weir v. Fed. Asset Disposition Ass'n,* 123 F.3d 281, 286 (5th Cir. 1997) (describing the issue as one of first impression in the circuit, but declining to reach it). A later Fifth Circuit case strongly implies that *contra proferentem* should be confined to insurance contracts because the doctrine would be inconsistent with Congressional intent under ERISA. *Walker v. Wal-Mart Stores, Inc.,* 159 F.3d 938, 940 (5th Cir. 1998). *But see McCall v. Burlington Northern/Santa Fe Co.,* 237 F.3d 506, 512 (5th Cir. 2000) (declaring without analysis that ambiguities in a severance pay SPD "must be resolved in the employee's favor"; citing insurance plan cases).

### C. Other Rules of Plan or Contract Interpretation

Procedural amendments to a benefit plan may legitimately be applied to a pending claim, at least before the claim has initially been ruled on by the administrator. *Vercher v. Alexander & Alexander,* 379 F.3d 222, 226 n.6 (5th Cir. 2004) (*dicta*).

## VI. Discovery

### A. Limitations on Discovery

The Fifth Circuit has not specifically proscribed discovery in ERISA cases. However, its limitations on the evidence a court may consider in reviewing a plan administrator's claim decision implies discovery limitations. In *Vega v. National Life Insurance Services, Inc.,* 188 F.3d 287, 295 (5th Cir. 1999), the Fifth Circuit reaffirmed its longstanding rule that it "will not permit the district court or our own panels to consider evidence introduced to resolve factual disputes with respect to the merits of the claim when the evidence was not in the administrative record." *Id.* at 300; *see also Robinson v. Aetna Life Ins. Co.,* 443 F.3d 389, 395 (5th Cir. 2006) (refusing to consider vocational analysis submitted by insurer because it was not in the administrative record); *see also Bellaire Gen. Hosp. v. Blue Cross Blue Shield,* 97 F.3d 822, 827 (5th Cir. 1996) (district court evaluating whether plan administrator abused his discretion in making factual determination, may consider only evidence available to the plan administrator).

### B. Discovery and Conflict of Interest

The Fifth Circuit recognizes two exceptions to the general rule on admissible evidence: (1) interpreting the terms of the plan; and (2) explaining medical terms and procedures related to a claim. *Gooden v. Provident Life & Accid. Ins. Co.,* 250 F.3d 329, 333 (5th Cir. 2001); *Vega,* 188 F.3d at 299. Arguably, discovery related to those topics is permissible. *See also Arnold v. F.A. Richard & Assocs., Inc.,* 2000 WL 1875905, at *2 (E.D. La. 2000) (court allowed discovery of nonprivileged information on issue of whether conflict of interest existed and to what extent).

## VII. Evidence

### A. Scope of Evidence under Standards of Review

"A long line of Fifth Circuit cases stands for the proposition that, when assessing factual questions, the district court is constrained to the evidence before the plan administrator." *Vega v. Nat'l Life Ins. Servs., Inc.,* 188 F.3d 287, 299 (5th Cir. 1999).

In determining whether an administrator's plan interpretation was an abuse of discretion, the district courts may consider "some evidence other than that contained in the administrative record." *Wildbur v. ARCO Chem. Co.,* 974 F.2d 631, 638 (5th Cir. 1992); *see also Vega,* 188 F.3d at 299 (courts may stray from administrative record to determine whether interpretation was an abuse of discretion).

### B. Evidentiary Value of Social Security Determinations

According to the Fifth Circuit in *Moller v. El Campo Aluminum Co.,* 97 F.3d 85, 88 (5th Cir. 1996), Social Security determinations are relevant to a plan administrator's decision if a plan administrator's general policy is to follow the Social Security Administration's decision when determining eligibility. However, where there is no evidence before the court that a plan administrator relies on or considers decisions by the Social Security Administration when determining whether insureds meet the definition of disabled under a particular plan, the administrator is not bound by the Social Security Administration's determination. *Jones v. Metro. Life Ins. Co.,* No. Civ. 303CV0397H, 2003 WL 22952212, at *5 (N.D. Tex. 2003), aff'd 119 Fed. Appx. 635 (5th Cir. 2005).

### C. Other Evidence Issues

One exception to the general rule is that district courts may consider evidence outside the record to help the court understand medical terminology relating to a claim. *Id.* The plan administrator has the obligation to identify the evidence in the administrative record and the claimant may then contest the completeness of the record. *Id.*

## VIII. Procedural Aspects of ERISA Practice

### A. Methods of Adjudication

The Fifth Circuit has recognized that summary judgment is the appropriate procedural vehicle for resolution of a plan beneficiary's suit. *Barhan v. Ry-Ron, Inc.,* 121 F.3d 198, 201–02 (5th Cir. 1997). Once the motion for summary judgment is filed, a court applies the usual summary judgment rules. *Id.*

### B. Reported ERISA Trials

There is no right to jury trial in an ERISA claim; the plaintiff's request for a jury trial should be stricken. *Calamia v. Spivey,* 632 F.2d 1235, 1237 (5th Cir. 1980); *Sparks v. Life Investors Ins. Co.,* 818 F. Supp. 945, 948 (N.D. Miss. 1993); *but see LeTourneau Lifelike Orthotics & Prosthetics, Inc. v. Wal-Mart Stores, Inc.,* 298 F.3d 348, 349 (5th Cir. 2002) (court tried issue of whether provider was entitled to reimbursement); *Estate of Bratton v. Nat'l Union Fire Ins. Co. of Pittsburgh, PA,* 215 F.3d 516 (5th Cir. 2000) (court tried issue of whether accidental death benefits were due to estate of plan participant); *Gibbs v. Gibbs,* 210 F.3d 491 (5th Cir. 2000) (beneficiary brought ERISA claim for death benefits and court tried claim and insurer's counterclaim for interpleader); *Williams on Behalf of Williams v. Jackson Stone Co.,* 867 F. Supp. 454 (S.D. Miss. 1994) (court could try issue of whether employer breached fiduciary duty).

## IX. Fiduciary Liability Claims

### A. Definition of Fiduciary

ERISA provides for named and de facto fiduciaries. Fiduciary status may be conferred by express designation, pursuant to 29 U.S.C. § 1105(c)(1)(A); or, pursuant to 29 U.S.C. § 1002(21)(A), a person may be a fiduciary with respect to a plan to the extent that "he . . . exercises any authority or control regarding management . . . of [a benefits] plan or . . . its assets"; renders "investment advice for a fee or other compensation, direct or indirect, with respect to any moneys or other property of such plan"; or has "any discretionary authority or discretionary responsibility in administration of a plan." Therefore, a "fiduciary may be defined not only by reference to a particular title . . . but also by considering the authority which a particular person has over an employee benefit plan." *Donovan v. Mercer,* 747 F.2d 304, 308 (5th Cir. 1984). "The term 'fiduciary' is liberally construed in keeping with the remedial purpose of ERISA." *Bannistor v. Ullman,* 287 F.3d 394, 401 (5th Cir. 2002) (citation omitted).

### B. Definition of Fiduciary Duties

ERISA imposes a uniform standard of fiduciary conduct upon fiduciaries of plans regulated by ERISA. Pursuant to 29 U.S.C. § 1104(a)(1)(B):

> A fiduciary shall discharge his duties with respect to a plan solely in the interest of the participants and beneficiaries and . . . for the exclusive purpose of providing benefits to participants and their beneficiaries . . . and . . . defraying reasonable expenses of administering the plan . . . and with the care, skill, prudence, and diligence under the circumstances then prevailing that a prudent man acting in a like capacity and familiar with such matters would use in the conduct of an enterprise of like character and with like aims.

"ERISA does not expressly enumerate the particular duties of a fiduciary, but rather relies on the 'common law of trusts to define the general scope of a fiduciary's responsibilities.'" *Martinez v. Schlumberger,* 338 F.3d 407, 412 (5th Cir. 2003), citing Edward E. Bintz, *Fiduciary Responsibility under ERISA: Is There Ever a Fiduciary Duty to Disclose?* 54 U. PITT. L. REV. 979 (1993).

A more recent line of ERISA fiduciary duty cases decided in the circuits after *Varity Corp. v. Howe,* 516 U.S. 489 (1996), has focused on an employer-administrator's representations (or lack thereof) to employees concerning plan changes or amendments. In *Martinez,* the Fifth Circuit held that an employer-administrator has no fiduciary duty under ERISA to affirmatively disclose whether it is considering amending its benefit plan and that the employer had no duty to disclose to employees that it was considering an early retirement offering. However, the court did note that if an employer "chooses to communicate about the future of a participant's plan benefits, [it] has a fiduciary duty to refrain from misrepresentations." 338 F.3d at 424. The court could not, however, "agree that misrepresentations are actionable only after the company has seriously considered the plan change." *Id.* at 425.

Rather, the court indicated that "the more seriously a plan is being considered, the more likely a representation about the plan is material." *Id.* at 428. Refusing to accept or formulate a bright-line rule to determine whether an employer's alleged misrepresentations are material and, therefore, actionable, the court held "only that the lack of serious consideration does not equate to a free zone for lying." *Id.*

### C. Fiduciary Liability in the Context of Health and Disability Claims

A plaintiff cannot bring a private action for breach of fiduciary duty under § 502(a)(3) of ERISA when the civil enforcement provisions of ERISA provide a possible remedy. *See Estate of Bratton v. Nat'l Union Fire Ins. Co.,* 215 F.3d 516, 526 (5th Cir. 2000); *Rhorer v. Raytheon Eng'rs & Const'rs, Inc.,* 181 F.3d 634, 639 (5th Cir. 1999). If a plaintiff may bring a claim under § 502(a)(1)(B) for benefits allegedly owed under an ERISA plan, he may not bring a claim for breach of fiduciary duty. *Id. See also Tolson v. Avondale Inds.,* 141 F.3d 604, 610 (5th Cir. 1998). Therefore, fiduciary liability does not generally arise in the context of health and disability claims.

### D. Remedies for Breach of Fiduciary Duty

ERISA § 409(a) provides that anyone who breaches a fiduciary duty to a plan shall be personally liable to make good to such plan any losses to the plan resulting from each such breach, and to restore to such plan any profits of such fiduciary that have been made through use of assets of the plan by the fiduciary, and shall be subject to such other equitable or remedial relief as the court may deem appropriate, including removal of such fiduciary.

ERISA § 502(a)(3) authorizes lawsuits for individualized equitable relief for breach of fiduciary obligations. *Varity Corp. v. Howe,* 516 U.S. 489 (1996).

### E. Contribution and Indemnity Claims among Fiduciaries

The Fifth Circuit has not expressly ruled as to whether cofiduciaries can claim indemnification and contribution.

### F. ERISA Claims against Nonfiduciaries

There are no recent Fifth Circuit cases that recognize ERISA claims against nonfiduciaries.

## X. Attorneys' Fees

### A. Criteria for Awarding Attorneys' Fees

Under ERISA, "the court in its discretion may allow a reasonable attorneys' fee and costs of action to either party." 29 U.S.C. § 1132(g)(1). In the Fifth Circuit, a party need not prevail on its underlying claim in order to be eligible for an award of attorneys' fees under 29 U.S.C. § 1132(g)(1). *Gibbs v. Gibbs,* 210 F.3d 491, 503 (5th Cir. 2000); *Todd v. AIG Life Ins. Co.,* 47 F.3d 1448, 1459 (5th Cir. 1995). Rather, such an award, as the statute states, is purely discretionary. *Riley v. Adm'r of Supersaver 401K Capital Accumulation Plan for Employees of Participating AMR Corp. Subsidiaries,*

209 F.3d 780, 782 (5th Cir. 2000); *Todd,* 47 F.3d at 1458; *Salley v. E.I. DuPont de Nemours & Co.,* 966 F.2d 1011, 1016 (5th Cir. 1992). Additionally, the Fifth Circuit will review a district court's decision only for an abuse of discretion. *Id.* Although other circuits have asserted that a presumption exists under ERISA in favor of awarding costs and attorneys' fees, no such presumption exists in the Fifth Circuit. *Todd,* 47 F.3d at 1459; *Harms v. Cavenham Forest Indus., Inc.,* 984 F.2d 686, 694 (5th Cir. 1993).

Once a request for attorneys' fees under 29 U.S.C. § 1132(g)(1) has been made, the Fifth Circuit has generally required that the following five *Bowen* factors be considered in deciding whether to award attorneys' fees to the party under 29 U.S.C. § 1132(g)(1):

1. The degree of the opposing parties' culpability or bad faith;
2. The ability of the opposing parties to satisfy an award of attorneys' fees;
3. Whether an award of attorneys' fees against the opposing party would deter other persons acting under similar circumstances;
4. Whether the parties requesting attorneys' fees sought to benefit all participants and beneficiaries of an ERISA plan or to resolve a significant legal question regarding ERISA itself; and
5. The relative merits of the parties' positions.

*Riley,* 209 F.3d at 781–82; *Todd,* 47 F.3d at 1458; *Iron Workers Local No. 272 v. Bowen,* 624 F.2d 1255, 1266 (5th Cir. 1980).

The Fifth Circuit considers all of the *Bowen* factors as a whole. No one factor individually is entitled to greater weight than any of the others. *Riley,* 209 F.3d at 782. Although the *Bowen* factors are the "nuclei" of concerns that the Fifth Circuit will address in applying 29 U.S.C. § 1132(g)(1), the *Bowen* factors are a "non-exhaustive" list of factors the Fifth Circuit will consider. *Id.* The Fifth Circuit will also consider, on a case-by-case basis, other factors and considerations that it deems relevant. *Id.*

### B. Fees Awarded to Plan Fiduciaries

There is no requirement that a party prevail in order to be eligible for consideration for attorneys' fees. *Gibbs v. General American Life Ins. Co.,* 210 F.3d 491, 503–04 (5th Cir. 2000). The Fifth Circuit has recognized that "either" party may recover attorneys' fees. *See Gibbs,* 210 F.3d at 501 (court may award "reasonable attorneys' fees and costs . . . to *either* party") (quoting 29 U.S.C. § 1132 (g)(1) and supplying the emphasis). In *Tolson v. Avondale Industries,* 141 F.3d 604, 611 (5th Cir. 1998), the Fifth Circuit assessed costs of appeal against the plaintiff to discourage "prosecuting litigation of this ilk." It warned that similar actions "could result in sanctions more stringent than mere assessment of costs, including, without limitation, attorneys' fees and double costs under Federal Rules of Appellate Procedure 38 for frivolously appealing adverse dispositions of the district court." *Id.* In other instances, the Fifth Circuit has been reluctant to affirm the award of attorneys' fees to plan fiduciaries. In *Gibbs,* the Fifth Circuit reversed the award of attorneys' fees to the plan fiduciary, even though the district court found that the plaintiff/appellant acted in bad faith. *Gibbs,* 210 F.3d at 505. *See also Dennard v. Richards Group,* 681 F.2d 306, 319 (5th Cir. 1982) (rejecting suggestion that the Fifth Circuit establish preference in favor of awarding fees to successful plan defendants, because it would discourage plan participants from attempting to vindicate their rights).

### C. Calculation of Attorneys' Fees

The district court must apply a two-step analysis to determine the amount of attorneys' fees. *Todd v. AIG Life Ins. Co.,* 47 F.3d 1448, 1459 (5th Cir. 1995). A district court must first determine whether a party is entitled to attorneys' fees by applying the five factors enumerated in *Bowen. Id.* If the district court concludes that a party is entitled to attorneys' fees, it must then apply the "lodestar" calculation—multiplying the number of hours expended on the matters at issue in the case by a reasonable hourly rate—to determine the amount to be awarded. *Id.* Attorney fees may not be awarded based upon a percentage of the recovery. *Id.; see also Pennsylvania v. Delaware Valley Citizens' Council for Clean Air,* 478 U.S. 546, 564 (1986) (endorsing the lodestar method for calculating attorneys' fees under federal fee-shifting statutes such as ERISA). *Todd,* 47 F.3d at 1459, *citing Salley v. E.I. DuPont de Nemours & Co.,* 966 F.2d 1011, 1016 (5th Cir. 1992).

## XI. ERISA Regulations

In November 2000, the Department of Labor modified ERISA regulations on claims procedure. *See* 65 Fed. Reg. 70,246–301. The revised regulations apply to claims filed after January 1, 2002. *See id.; see also* 29 C.F.R. § 2560.503.1(f)(3). They establish shorter time frames for benefits determinations than those contained in the earlier version of the regulations. *See* 29 C.F.R. § 2560.503-1(f)(3). Appeals of claims filed before the effective date are governed by the old regulations. *Roig v. Limited Long-Term Disability Program,* 2004 WL 325219 (E.D. La. 2004), citing *DiCamillo v. Liberty Life Assurance Co.,* 287 F. Supp. 2d 616, 625 (D. Md. 2003). To date, there are no reported Fifth Circuit cases interpreting or applying the new regulations. However, many cases decided on claims filed prior to January 1, 2002, may form a basis for interpreting current regulations.

Regulations promulgated by the Secretary of Labor under ERISA § 505 are entitled to "considerable" deference as the pronouncements of the agency charged with enforcement and administration of ERISA. *Memorial Hosp. Sys. v. Northbrook Life Ins. Co.,* 904 F.2d 236, 241 n.6 (5th Cir. 1990).

The Fifth Circuit has often resorted to DOL regulations clarifying the statutory definitions of "employee benefit plan," "welfare plan," and "pension plan" in order to resolve coverage disputed under ERISA. *See* 29 C.F.R. pt. 2510 (2003); *Memorial Hosp. Sys.,* 904 F.2d at 241 n.6 (relying upon 29 C.F.R. § 2510-3-1(j) (1987) to support its conclusion that the group health insurance policy at issue was a covered ERISA plan); *Robertson v. Alexander Grant & Co.,* 798 F.2d 868, 870 (5th Cir. 1986) (upholding regulation (29 C.F.R. § 2510.3-3(c)(2) (1985)) excluding partnership plans from ERISA coverage as consistent with ERISA legislative history); *Murphy v. Inexco Oil Co.,* 611 F.2d 570, 575–76 (5th Cir. 1980) (bonus plan consisting of royalty rights held excluded from ERISA coverage under 29 C.F.R. § 2510.3-(2)(c) (1979)). In *Musmeci v. Schwegmann Giant Super Markets, Inc.*, 332 F.3d 339, 346 (5th Cir. 2003), the court rejected the employer's contention that a grocery voucher program fit within the "sales to employees" exclusion of 29 C.F.R. § 2510.3-1(e), because the transactions more closely resembled gifts than sales.

The court also gives appropriate deference to Treasury regulations pertaining to qualification of plans for preferential tax treatment. In *Myers-Garrison v. Johnson & Johnson*, 210 F.3d 425, 430 (5th Cir. 2000), the court gave *Chevron* deference to Treasury regulations covering transitional discount rates for lump-sum distributions under the Retirement Protection Act of 1994. Similar deference was given to a Treasury regulation (§ 1.401(a)-20Q-10(b)) interpreting "annuity starting date" for lump sum termination distributions, as used in 26 U.S.C. § 417. *PBGC v. Wilson N. Jones Mem. Hosp.*, 374 F.3d 362 (5th Cir. 2004).

Nevertheless, when ERISA confers authority upon the Secretary of Labor to issue clarifying regulations, and the Secretary fails to exercise that authority, the court will not necessarily look to IRS tax regulations to fill the void. *Donovan v. Cunningham*, 716 F.2d 1455, 1473 (5th Cir. 1983), *cert. denied*, 467 U.S. 1251 (1984) (ERISA fiduciaries are not required to follow IRS regulations concerning valuation of closely held stock, where Secretary of Labor has not exercised congressionally delegated authority to issue regulations on the subject).

## XII. Cases Interpreting ERISA Statutes of Limitation

Under ERISA, a cause of action accrues, and the statute of limitations begins to run, when a request for benefits is denied. *Craft v. Northbrook Life Ins. Co.*, 813 F. Supp. 464 (5th Cir. 1993), citing *Hogan v. Kraft Foods.*, 969 F.2d 142 at 145 (5th Cir. 1992); *Simmons v. Willcox*, 911 F.2d 1077, 1981 (5th Cir. 1990). Because ERISA does not provide a statute of limitations period for a § 502(a)(1)(B), 29 U.S.C. § 1132(a)(1)(B), claim to enforce plan rights, the Fifth Circuit has addressed the issue by applying the state statute of limitations most analogous to the cause of action raised in each particular action. *Hall v. Nat'l Gypsum Co.*, 105 F.3d 225 (5th Cir. 1997); *Hogan*, 969 F.2d 142.

For instance, in Mississippi, the "catch-all" statute of limitations period set forth in Section 15-1-49 of the Mississippi Code Annotated is most analogous and provides a three-year statute of limitations period for § 502 actions. *Craft*, 813 F. Supp. 464. In Louisiana, § 502 claims are governed by Louisiana's ten-year prescription period. *Hall v. Nat'l Gypsum Co.*, 105 F.3d 225 (5th Cir. 1997). In Texas, § 502 claims are most analogous to an action under state law for breach of contract and are governed by Texas's four-year statute of limitations applicable to breach of contract claims, Section 16.004 of the Texas Civil Practice and Remedies Code. *Stahl v. Exxon Corp.*, 212 F. Supp. 2d 657 (S.D. Tex. 2002); *but see Lopez v. Premium Auto Acceptance Corp.*, 389 F.3d 504 (5th Cir. 2004) (applying two-year statute of limitations to claim for COBRA notice violations in Texas).

Where the action is one for interference with protected rights under ERISA § 510, 29 U.S.C. § 1140, the Fifth Circuit has found § 510 claims to be most analogous to wrongful discharge or employment discrimination claims. *McClure v. Zoecon, Inc.,* 936 F.2d 777 (5th Cir. 1991).

The appropriate statute of limitations for wrongful termination under Mississippi law is the "catch-all" statute of limitations, Section 15-1-49 of the Mississippi Code Annotated. *Banks v. Jockey Intern. Inc.,* 996 F. Supp. 576 (N.D. Miss. 1998). In Louisiana, courts have consistently applied the one-year prescriptive period of article 3492 in wrongful discharge cases. *Franz v. Iolab, Inc.,* 801 F. Supp. 1537 (E.D. La. 1992), citing *Lynn v. Berg Mech., Inc.,* 582 So. 2d 902 (La. App. 2d Cir. 1991); *Arvie v. Century Tel. Enters., Inc.,* 452 So. 2d 392 (La. App. 3d Cir. 1984)). In Texas, a § 510 suit is most similar to a wrongful discharge or employment discrimination claim and, consequently, subject to the two-year prescription period prescribed in Section 16.003 of the Texas Civil Practice and Remedies Code. *McClure v. Zoecon, Inc.,* 936 F.2d 777 (5th Cir. 1991).

Federal common law provides that unambiguous policy deadlines are enforceable. *Jones v. Ga. Pac. Corp.,* 90 F.3d 114, 115–18 (5th Cir. 1996). Although the Fifth Circuit has yet to address this issue in the context of an ERISA case, other circuits have held that where an ERISA plan includes a contractual limitations period, that period is controlling even when it is shorter than the analogous state statutory period. *See Northlake Reg'l Med. Ctr. v. Waffle House Sys. Employee Benefit Plan,* 160 F.3d 1301, 1303–04 (11th Cir. 1998) (finding that employee benefit plan's ninety-day limitation period following administrative appeal was enforceable); *Blaske v. UNUM Life Ins. Co. of Am.,* 131 F.3d 763, 764 (8th Cir. 1997) (finding that three-year limitation period in disability insurance policy was enforceable), *cert. denied,* 525 U.S. 812 (1998); *Doe v. Blue Cross & Blue Shield United of Wis.,* 112 F.3d 869 (7th Cir. 1997) (finding that thirty-nine-month limitation period in employee benefit plan was enforceable).

A person with fiduciary responsibilities to an employee benefit plan may be sued under ERISA § 413, 29 U.S.C. § 1113, for breach of those responsibilities. Section 413 of ERISA prescribes the period within which such suits must be brought. Generally, the limitation period is the shorter of six years from the date of the last action constituting a part of the breach or three years from the date the plaintiff first gains actual knowledge of the breach. In a case of fraud or concealment, however, a more liberal limitation period applies—an action may be commenced up to six years after the date of discovery of the breach.

The Fifth Circuit has held that the three-year limitations period will begin to run only when a plaintiff has "actual knowledge of all material facts necessary to understand that some claim exists, which facts could include necessary opinion of experts, knowledge of a transaction's harmful consequences, or even actual harm." *Babcock v. Hartmarx Corp.,* 182 F.3d 336 (5th Cir. 1999); *Reich v. Lancaster,* 55 F.3d 1034, 1057 (5th Cir. 1995); *Maher v. Strachan Shipping Co.,* 68 F.3d 951, 953–55 (5th Cir. 1995). The test is stringent and requires "specific knowledge of the actual breach" upon which plaintiff sues. *Lancaster,* 55 F.3d at 1057. Mere awareness of a particular event or set of facts later revealed as a breach of fiduciary duty is not actual knowledge of material facts that would make up each of the elements in a complex ERISA claim. *Maher,* 68 F.3d at 954–55 (claimants must have been aware of the process utilized in choosing an investment to have actual knowledge of the resulting fiduciary duty breach). Without more, the six-year limitations period applies and begins to run on the date of the last action that constituted a breach or violation.

## XIII. Subrogation Litigation

In the first of the three cases considered post-*Knudson* the Fifth Circuit held that § 502(a)(3) of ERISA did not authorize the plaintiff's suit. *See Bauhaus USA, Inc. v. Copeland,* 292 F.3d 439 (5th Cir. 2002). Judge Weiner, the author of the majority opinion in two subsequent cases, *Bombardier Aerospace Employee Welfare Benefits Plan v. Ferrer, Poirot & Wansbrough,* 354 F.3d 348 (5th Cir. 2003), and *Cooperative Benefit Administrators v. Ogden,* 2004 WL 811730 (5th Cir. 2004), dissented from the majority opinion in *Bauhaus.* The *Bauhaus* plaintiff, an ERISA plan sponsor and administrator, had filed a complaint for declaratory judgment that under the terms of the plan it was entitled to a portion of the funds a plan participant had received by settlement with a third-party tortfeasor. The district court granted motions to dismiss the action for lack of subject matter jurisdiction, but did not consider the applicability of ERISA § 502(a)(3) because the asserted basis for jurisdiction was ERISA preemption. The Fifth Circuit had indicated that it would not consider the preemption issue until it resolved the issue of whether the plaintiff's action was "authorized" by ERISA. It concluded that the facts in *Bauhaus* were "indistinguishable in principle" from those of *Knudson,* and held that § 502(a)(3) did not authorize Bauhaus's suit. The court discussed *Knudson,* enumerating the similarities between the two cases as follows:

> Both cases involve ERISA-governed employee benefit plans that include reimbursement provisions allowing the plans to recover from any settlement proceeds any amount the plans advanced for medical expenses resulting from third party wrong-doing. Third-party tortfeasors injured the plan beneficiaries in both cases, and the plans advanced funds to the beneficiaries for medical expenses. In both cases, the plan beneficiaries made tort settlements with third-party tortfeasors following suit in state court. In both, the plan administrator or assignee filed suit in the federal district court seeking declaratory relief that it was entitled to repayment of the benefits it had conferred. In the instant case, the settlement proceeds are in the registry of the Mississippi Chancery Court. In *Great-West,* the proceeds of the settlement were placed in a private Special Needs Trust outside the possession and control of the plan beneficiary. Nevertheless, the defendants in this case, like the Knudsons in *Great-West,* are not in possession of the disputed funds, a fact that Justice Scalia found extremely important in *Great-West.*

The Court in *Knudson* characterized the suit in the case as "[a] claim for money due and owing under a contract" and that such a suit is "quintessentially an action at law." In his dissent, Judge Weiner stated that the *Bauhaus* majority erred in "adopting an overly expansive reading" of *Knudson* and in misreading the central principles enunciated by the Supreme Court in *Knudson. Id.* He concluded that the majority "seriously misreads" *Knudson* as holding that "if the disputed funds are not in the defendant's possession, the remedy sought must be legal and not equitable." *Id.* at 450. He noted that the "doctrinal point" was that

> *after* the distribution of funds, the tort victim herself was left without specific, identifiable funds to which the ERISA plan could assert title . . . the [Supreme] Court's test was not whether the money was in the defendant's possession *vel non,* but whether the remedy that the plan sought to impose was legal or equitable; and this distinction turned on *where the money to pay the judgment would come from:* if from the defendant's personal, fungible, and untraceable resources, the remedy sought was legal and proscribed. That was the case in *Great-West Life;* that is not the case in *Bauhaus.*

*Id.* Judge Weiner further distinguished *Bauhaus* from *Knudson,* explaining that Bauhaus claimed entitlement to funds in a state court registry and, therefore, his claim was *"in rem* against funds possessed by a neutral stakeholder," and there was no "danger . . . of the district court's imposing general, personal, contractual liability on anyone." 292 F.3d at 451.

Judge Weiner also found an "important distinction" between the two cases in "the nature of the obligation" sought to be enforced—subrogation in *Bauhaus* and reimbursement or restitution in *Knudson. Id.* Judge Weiner noted that the language in the Great-West plan provided for personal liability of the beneficiary; the Bauhaus plan did not. Furthermore, "unlike garden-variety restitution or reimbursement, subrogation does not require that the contested funds be in the possession of the principal obligor." *Id.* at 452–53. The final point that Judge Weiner made in his dissent was that the Bauhaus claim would have no adequate legal remedy against the funds held in the state court registry. He stated:

> [I]f the district courts are held to lack jurisdiction in cases such as this, ERISA plaintiffs like Bauhaus would have to sue in state court, overcome ERISA preemption, and then contend with a welter of disparate state laws—such as Mississippi's anti-reimbursement doctrine at issue here—that could and likely would defeat the congressional purpose of achieving a nationally uniform set of rules to govern ERISA plans.

292 F.2d at 455.

Following his dissent in *Bauhaus,* Judge Weiner wrote the majority opinion in two Fifth Circuit decisions addressing relief available under ERISA § 502(a)(3). In *Bombardier,* the Fifth Circuit held that § 502(a)(3) authorized an ERISA plan's suit against a law firm for settlement funds held in the law firm's trust account under a "constructive trust" theory. The court found the facts of *Bombardier* "significantly distinguishable" from *Knudson* and *Bauhaus* based upon a "three-part inquiry":

> Does the Plan seek to recover funds (1) that are specifically identifiable, (2) that belong in good conscience to the Plan, and (3) that are within the possession and control of the defendant beneficiary?

*Bombardier,* 354 F.3d at 356.

The third element of the inquiry, the court held, distinguished *Bombardier* from *Knudson*, as follows:

> Here . . . the funds that the Plan is seeking to recover belong to the participant and are simply being held in a bank account in the name of the participant's attorneys, who are indisputably his agent. Unlike the beneficiaries in *Knudson* and *Bauhaus*, the Plan's participant . . . has ultimate control over, and thus *constructive* possession of, the disputed funds. The law firm . . . is legally obligated to disburse the funds . . . the moment [the plan participant] directs their release.

*Id.* at 357.

*Cooperative Benefit Administrators v. Ogden*, the second of Weiner's two majority opinions post-*Knudson*, found no authority under ERISA § 502(a)(3) or federal common law (unjust enrichment) for a claims administrator's suit against a plan participant seeking reimbursement of benefits advanced prior to the receipt by the participant (and her dependents) of Social Security disability benefits. Noting that the relief sought—enforcement of the plan participant's contractual reimbursement obligation—was "precisely the kind of 'legal' remedy that the Supreme Court has held to be beyond § 502(a)(3)'s jurisdictional grant," the court rejected the claim for unjust enrichment, stating:

> As *Mertens* and *Knudson* demonstrate, Congress, in drafting § 502(a)(3) to allow only "equitable relief," specifically contemplated the possibility of extending to plan fiduciaries a right to sue a participant for money damages and chose instead to limit fiduciaries' remedies to those typically available in equity. As ERISA's text "specifically and clearly addresses" the issue . . . there is no "gap" in ERISA on this question and thus no basis for granting . . . a federal common law remedy . . . to pursue . . . money damages. . . .

*Ogden*, 2004 WL 811730, at *6 (citations omitted).

Applying the three-part inquiry advanced in *Bombardier* and distinguishing *Bauhaus*, a Louisiana federal court had concluded that "to the extent the Plan seeks to recover the funds deposited into the registry of the court in this action," the relief is "typically equitable in nature." *Reynolds v. South Central Reg'l Laborers Health & Welfare Fund*, 306 F. Supp. 2d 646, 651 (W.D. La. 2004). However, the remainder of funds allegedly in the hands of the plaintiff's attorney were not recoverable by the plan, since the plaintiff's attorney had not been joined as a defendant in the suit. *Id.*, citing *Great-West Life & Annuity Ins. Co. v. Knudson*, 534 U.S. 204 (2002).

A post-*Knudson* clarification case by the Supreme Court that employs an analysis consistent with *Bombardier* is *Sereboff v. Mid Atlantic Medical Services, Inc.* 126 S. Ct. 1869 (2006). In *Sereboff*, the Court notes the division in the courts of appeal as to whether § 502(a)(3) authorizes recovery of settlement funds held in plan participants' investment account where those funds equal the amount paid under a health insurance plan for the participants' medical expenses. Like the Fifth Circuit in *Bombardier*, the *Sereboff* Court found the *Knudson*-distinguishing fact to be that the funds sought were "specifically identified funds" in the plan participants' possession. In so doing, the Court abrogated Sixth and Ninth Circuit cases that had held otherwise in similar circumstances.

## XIV. Miscellaneous

Judges in Lafayette, Alexandria, and Baton Rouge have adopted variations of an ERISA Case Order designed to streamline ERISA cases. The Order generally requires the parties to file: (1) a joint stipulation that ERISA governs the plan at issue or a summary judgment motion presenting the issue for the court's determination if disputed; (2) a "defendant's response to ERISA Case Order," identifying any discretionary language in the plan documents and stating the defendant's position as to whether state-law claims are preempted, along with a copy of the plan at issue and the complete administrative record; (3) a "plaintiff's response to ERISA Case Order," which requires a statement as to whether the plan vests the administrator with discretionary authority, whether ERISA preempts the state-law claims at issue, and whether the administrative record is complete; and (4) a joint stipulation or dispositive motions on (a) the completeness of the administrative record; (b) the issues as to which counsel cannot agree; and (c) whether the plan vests the administrator with discretionary authority to determine eligibility for benefits and to construe the terms of the plan.

The orders may also state that "absent further order, discovery . . . is limited to subject matter which relates to the administrator's interpretation of the terms of the policy or plan" and that "discovery may not be conducted regarding the factual basis of the plaintiff's medical claim because this court's review is constrained to the evidence in the administrative record as reviewed by the plan administrator." Following completion of the ERISA Case Order, a briefing schedule is entered.

# CHAPTER 6

# Sixth Circuit

ROBERT D. ANDERLE
CRAIG R. CARLSON
LEIGH M. CHILES
KRISTI R. GAUTHIER
S. RUSSELL HEADRICK
MICHAEL SHPIECE

## I. What Constitutes an ERISA Plan?

### A. Determining the Existence of an Employee Welfare Benefit Plan

The Sixth Circuit has adopted a three-step factual test to determine whether a plan is a benefit plan under the Employee Retirement Income Security Act of 1974 (ERISA). "First, we apply the Department of Labor 'safe harbor' regulations to determine whether the program is exempt from ERISA. Second, we determine if a 'plan' existed by inquiring whether 'from surrounding circumstances a reasonable person [could] ascertain the intended benefits, the class of beneficiaries, the source of financing, and the procedures for receiving benefits.' (citation omitted). Third, we ask whether the employer established or maintained the plan with the intent of providing benefits to its employees." *Agrawal v. Paul Revere Life Ins. Co.*, 205 F.3d 297 at 299–300 (6th Cir. 2000), citing *Thompson v. Am. Home Assurance Co.*, 95 F.3d 429, 434–35 (6th Cir. 1996). See also *Kolkowski v. Goodrich Corp.*, 448 F.3d 843 (6th Cir. 2006) (hallmark of an ERISA plan is ongoing administrative program).

### B. Definition of "Employee" for ERISA Purposes

ERISA § 3(6) defines "employee" as any individual employed by an employer. This circular and somewhat meaningless definition has led the Sixth Circuit to adopt the

175

traditional common-law agency principles as a guide to determining whether an individual is considered an "employee" under ERISA. *See Nationwide Mut. Ins. Co. v. Darden,* 503 U.S. 318 (1992) (holding that an insurance agent did qualify as an employee upon application of the agency law definition of employee); *Moore v. Lafayette Life Ins. Co.,* 458 F.3d 416 (6th Cir. 2006) (plaintiff's representation to Social Security Administration that he was an independent contractor was compelling); *Simpson v. Ernst & Young,* 100 F.3d 436 (6th Cir. 1996) (applying the common-law agency test, the court determined that the plaintiff was an employee, rather than a partner, for purposes of the ADA and ERISA); *Johnson v. City of Saline,* 151 F.3d 564 (6th Cir. 1998) (holding that the common-law agency test was appropriate to determine if an individual is an employee in the context of the ADA); *Santino v. Provident Life & Accident Ins. Co.,* 276 F.3d 772 (6th Cir. 2001) (applying common-law agency criteria, the court determined that a physician shareholder was considered an employee under ERISA); *Shah v. Deaconess Hosp.,* 355 F.3d 496, 499 (6th Cir. 2004) ("[W]e apply the common law agency test to determine whether a hired party is an independent contractor or an employee. . . . [W]e have made it clear that we prefer the common law agency analysis").

In *Yates v. Hendon,* 541 U.S. 1, 6 (2004), the Supreme Court held that "the working owner of a business, the sole shareholder and president of a professional corporation, in this case, may qualify as a 'participant' in a pension plan covered by ERISA." The Court explained "ERISA's text contains multiple indications that Congress intended working owners to qualify as plan participants. . . [therefore] there is no cause in this case to resort to common law." *Id.* at 12. "If the plan covers one or more employees other than the business owner and his or her spouse, the working owner may participate on equal terms with other plan participants. Such a working owner, in common with other employees, qualifies for the protections ERISA affords plan participants and is governed by the rights and remedies ERISA specifies." *Id.* at 6.

It is important to note that the Sixth Circuit's view had been that a sole proprietor or sole shareholder of a business is considered an employer, and not an employee, under ERISA, and therefore, is not considered a plan participant. *See Fugarino v. Hartford Life Ins. Co.,* 969 F.2d 178 (6th Cir. 1992); *Agrawal,* 205 F.3d 297. In light of *Yates,* it is yet to be determined how the Sixth Circuit will decide future cases involving individual business owners and their status under ERISA.

### C. Interpretation of Safe Harbor Regulation

The Department of Labor's "safe harbor" regulations provide that an employer-provided insurance plan will be exempt from ERISA if (1) the employer makes no financial contribution to policy premiums; (2) employee participation is voluntary; (3) the employer's sole function is to permit the insurer to publicize the policy to employees and to collect payroll deductions; and (4) the employer receives no consideration from the insurer. 29 C.F.R. § 2510.3-1(j).

In the Sixth Circuit, a plan will be exempt from ERISA if it meets all four criteria established in the safe harbor regulations. *See Thompson,* 95 F.3d at 435. The court has focused on whether employee neutrality is compromised to such an extent that ERISA should provide the governing framework. *Id.* (actions by employer did not give rise to endorsement. "[A] finding of endorsement is appropriate if, upon examining all the relevant circumstances, there is some factual showing on the record of substantial employer involvement in the creation or administration of the plan."); *Fugarino,* 969 F.2d 178 (where employer paid premiums and permitted employees to reimburse it, and also paid for at least one employee's coverage, the plan was not exempt from ERISA); *Arbor Health Care Co. v. Sutphen Corp.,* 1999 U.S. App. LEXIS 8565 (6th Cir. 1999) (plan was not exempt from ERISA because the employer paid 80 percent of the premiums, and "endorsed" the plan by being named as plan administrator); *Nicholas v. Standard Ins. Co.,* 48 Fed. Appx. 557, 29 Empl. Benefits Cas. (BNA) 1570 (6th Cir. 2002) ("Under *Thompson,* when an employer determines which employees will be eligible for coverage, negotiates the terms or benefits of the policy, is named as plan administrator, and provides a summary plan description describing the plan as an ERISA plan, the plan is governed by ERISA." *Id.* at *18, citing *Thompson,* 95 F.3d at 436–37).

### D. Amount of Employer Involvement Required to Sustain an Employee Welfare Benefit Plan

The Sixth Circuit has determined that minimal employer involvement is required for a plan to qualify as an ERISA employee welfare benefit plan. The mere purchase of insurance is sometimes enough to bring the plan under ERISA. *See Arbor Health Care Co.,* 1999 U.S. App. LEXIS 8565 (company "established and maintained the plan" by paying 80 percent of the premiums for covered employees with the intent of providing benefits to them); *Libbey-Owens-Ford Co. v. Blue Cross & Blue Shield Mut. of Ohio,* 982 F.2d 1031 (6th Cir. 1993) (company established an ERISA plan by contracting with insurer to provide benefits to its employees even though it had no administrative responsibilities); *Fugarino,* 989 F.2d 178 (employer established and maintained a plan by purchasing a group health insurance policy for the benefit of its employees); *Int'l Res., Inc. v. N.Y. Life Ins. Co.,* 950 F.2d 294 (6th Cir. 1991) (plan was covered by ERISA where the employer contracted with an agency, chose a plan, all employees were automatically covered, and the employer paid the premiums).

### E. Treatment of Multiple Employer Trusts and Welfare Agreements

The Sixth Circuit has determined that multiple employer trusts are considered employee welfare benefit plans under ERISA if the employer obtains and purchases the insurance coverage for its employees with the intent to provide coverage to its employees. *See Int'l Res., Inc.,* 950 F.2d 294, citing *Donovan v. Dillingham,* 688 F.2d 1367 (11th Cir. 1981).

## II. Preemption

### A. Scope of ERISA Preemption

The Sixth Circuit has interpreted the scope of the ERISA preemption provision very broadly. Consistent with the Supreme Court's directive, the court has given the phrase "relates to" broad meaning such that a state-law claim is preempted if it has connection with or reference to a plan. *See Briscoe v. Fine,* 444 F.3d 478, 497 (6th Cir. 2006) (noting that both the Supreme Court and the Sixth Circuit emphasize the expansiveness of ERISA preemption). The court has explained that ERISA preempts virtually all state-law claims stemming from processing claims for benefits. *Nester v. Allegiance Healthcare Corp.,* 315 F.3d 610, 613 (6th Cir. 2003) (any judicial complaint for recovery of any benefits allegedly due under an employee benefit plan is strictly governed by ERISA); *Caffey v. Unum Life Ins. Co.,* 302 F.3d 576, 582 (6th Cir. 2003); *Cromwell v. Equicor—Equitable HCA Corp.,* 944 F.2d 1272, 1276 (6th Cir. 1991).

More recently, the court has focused on "the kind of relief the plaintiffs seek, and its relation to the pension plan." *Briscoe,* 444 F.3d at 497 (6th Cir. 2006), quoting *Ramsey v. Formica Corp.,* 398 F.3d 421, 424 (6th Cir. 2005). In *Briscoe,* the court also quoted, with approval, a Fourth Circuit decision that identified several areas of ERISA preemption, including state laws that mandate benefit structures or their administration; provide alternative enforcement mechanisms; or bind employers or plan administrators to particular choices or preclude uniform administrative practices. *Id.,* quoting *Coyne & Delany Co. v. Selman,* 98 F.3d 1457, 1468 (4th Cir. 1996). The *Briscoe* court also permitted a state-law claim based on a legal duty independent of the existence of an ERISA plan. *Id.* at 499. *See also Penny/Ohlmann/Nieman, Inc. v. Miami Valley Pension Corp.,* 399 F.2d 692 (6th Cir. 2005) (distinguishing between claims that are and are not preempted; preemption does not extend to state-law claims brought against a nonfiduciary service provider whose professional services for the plan are limited to record-keeping and do not directly touch the plan); *McMurtry v. Wiseman,* No. 1:04-CV-88, 2006 U.S. Dist. LEXIS 58136, at *28 (W.D. Ky. Aug. 16, 2006) (state-law fraud and negligent misrepresentation claims not preempted when claims arose from the defendant's inducement to have the plaintiff join the plan); *Miami Valley Hosp. v. Cmty. Ins. Co.,* No. 3:05-cv-297 2006 U.S. Dist. LEXIS 54627, at *19–20 (S.D. Ohio Aug. 7, 2006) (broad scope of preemption avoided when the plaintiff alleges a violation of a law that simply regulates insurance and does not contend that any term of the plan was violated).

The Sixth Circuit has held a variety of claims to be preempted, including (1) wrongful death, (2) bad faith, (3) improper denial of benefits, (4) malpractice, (5) breach of contract, (6) promissory estoppel, (7) negligent misrepresentation, and (8) unjust enrichment. *Cromwell,* 944 F.2d at 1276; *see also Ackerman v. Fortis Benefits Ins. Co.,* 254 F. Supp. 2d 792, 819 (S.D. Ohio 2003).

In *Marks v. Newcourt Credit Group,* 342 F.3d 444 (6th Cir. 2003), a Sixth Circuit case addressing preemption, the court reiterated that state-law claims are not preempted if their effect on the plan is "merely tenuous, remote or peripheral." The court has provided examples such as employment discrimination claims that merely refer to a clause in a plan summary, or where a plaintiff makes reference to specific, ascertainable damages by citing a life insurance contract. *See id.; Paysource, Inc. v. Triple Crown Fin. Group,* No. 2004-171-WOB, 2005 U.S. Dist. LEXIS 34780, at *12, 16 (E.D. Ky. Aug. 29, 2005) (reference to the cost of covering employee claims was merely a component of damages resulting from defendant's misconduct and not a preempted claim for benefits).

## B. Preemption of Managed-Care Claims

The court addressed malpractice and managed care claims in *Tolton v. American Biodyne, Inc.*, 48 F.3d 937 (6th Cir. 1995). There, plaintiffs brought a wrongful-death action against various health care providers and the decedent's health care plan. Plaintiffs claimed that the claims administrator had negligently refused benefits (inpatient treatment) pursuant to a utilization review. In affirming the grant of summary judgment, the court of appeals held that plaintiffs' claims, including those for medical malpractice and negligent refusal to provide treatment, arose from an allegedly improper denial of benefits and were preempted by ERISA because they related to the benefit plan. *Id.* at 942–43. It did not matter that the claims were based upon a utilization review, because the court found such review to be a "means of processing claims."

## C. Preemption of Malpractice Claims

Several district court decisions from the Sixth Circuit have distinguished *Tolton* and held that certain types of malpractice and/or managed care claims were not "completely preempted" by ERISA and, therefore, not subject to removal. In *Oullette v. The Christ Hosp.*, 942 F. Supp. 1160 (S.D. Ohio 1996), for example, the district court reasoned that plaintiff's claim against Choice Care, alleging that its utilization procedures and financial relationships with the hospital caused the malpractice in question, was not a claim for benefits. The *Oullette* court held that plaintiff's claims did not rest on the terms of the plan because she was not challenging the benefits, but rather on the quality of service she received. *Id.* at 1165. Consequently, her claim that "Choice Care's financial arrangements with the Christ Hospital caused the hospital to commit malpractice" will not, said the court, "require review of Choice Care's utilization review or otherwise demand construction of the Choice Care plan." *Id.; see also Stewart v. Berry Family Healthcenter,* 105 F. Supp. 2d 807 (S.D. Ohio 2000) (claims alleging Anthem's financial incentives induced medical malpractice not completely preempted); *Kendrick v. CNA Ins. Cos.,* 71 F. Supp. 2d 815 (S.D. Ohio 1999) (claim that CNA had negligently performed a physical examination was not a claim for benefits under the plan or to enforce a right to any benefits under the plan and was not completely preempted). Of course, the district courts in these cases held only that the claims were not ERISA claims for benefits and not completely preempted and did not directly address whether the claims would otherwise be preempted, as relating to an employee benefit plan. The Sixth Circuit has not addressed this issue since *Tolton.*

## D. Other Preemption Issues

Prior to the Supreme Court's decision in *Kentucky Association of Health Plans, Inc. v. Miller,* 538 U.S. 329 (2003), courts in the Sixth Circuit held that claims for bad faith are not preserved by the savings clause because the "good faith" requirement is not limited to the insurance industry. *See Schachner v. Blue Cross & Blue Shield of Ohio,* 77 F.3d 889 (6th Cir. 1996); *Little v. Unum Provident Corp.,* 196 F. Supp. 2d 659 (S.D. Ohio 2002). In other pre-*Miller* decisions, the Sixth Circuit held that Michigan's No-Fault Act regulates insurance and is saved from ERISA preemption.

*Am. Med. Security, Inc. v. Auto Club Ins. Ass'n of Mich.*, 238 F.3d 743 (6th Cir. 2001). In *Davis v. Centennial Life Insurance Co.*, 128 F.3d 934 (6th Cir. 1997), however, the court held that Section 3923.14 of the Ohio Revised Code, regarding rescission of an accident or health policy, did not regulate insurance and was preempted. 128 F.3d at 940–42 (statute did not spread the risk).

Although the Sixth Circuit has not directly addressed ERISA's savings clause following *Miller*, several of the district courts have had the opportunity. *See Beard v. Benicorp Ins. Co.*, No. 04-2417B, 2005 U.S. Dist. LEXIS 38500, at *11–13 (W.D. Tenn. Dec. 28, 2005) (Tennessee common law requiring notice to insured of policy termination did not fall into savings clause because it failed *Miller*'s second prong requiring risk-spreading); *Forbes v. CEMEX*, No. 1:03CV67-R, 2005 U.S. Dist. LEXIS 15322, at *6–7 (although Texas and Kentucky insurance statutes regulate insurance, the statutes failed to affect risk-pooling); *Kindel v. Cont'l Cas. Co.*, No. 1:02-CV-879, 2005 U.S. Dist. LEXIS 9878, at *6–7 (Ohio statute requiring exceptions and deductions from indemnity be adequately captioned and clearly set forth fails *Miller*'s second prong and does not regulate "the scope of permissible bargains between insurers and insureds" by mandating the type of benefits that must be provided), quoting *Miller*, 538 U.S. at 338.

In *Husvar v. Rapoport*, 430 F.3d 777 (6th Cir. 2005), the Sixth Circuit emphasized the difference between removal and preemption. Cases are removable only if they fall under ERISA's benefit payment enforcement provision, 29 U.S.C. 1132(a)(1)(B). *Id.* at 781, quoting *Warner v. Ford Motor Co.*, 46 F.3d 531, 535 (6th Cir. 1995). But a state-law claim might still be preempted under the general preemption provision of 29 U.S.C. 1144. In those cases, the claim would be preempted but not removable (unless, of course, there was some other basis for federal jurisdiction). *Id.*

More recently, in *Daimler-Chrysler Corp. v. Cox*, 447 F.3d 967 (6th Cir. 2006), the Sixth Circuit held that the State of Michigan could not require ERISA pension plans to send a prisoner's pension benefits to the warden of the prison, where the warden could garnish up to 90 percent to reimburse the state for the cost of the prisoner's care. The court's decision was based on the state law conflicting with ERISA's anti-alienation provision; it specifically declined to opine on the effect of the general preemption provision. *Id.* at 976. The court noted, however, that the anti-alienation provision did not prevent the garnishment of the prisoner once the plan had paid the benefits. *Id.* at 174, 176.

## III. Exhaustion of Administrative Remedies

### A. Is Exhaustion an Absolute Requirement?

The general rule is that exhaustion of administrative remedies is a requirement to bring suit to recover benefits under 29 U.S.C. § 1132(a)(1)(B) in the Sixth Circuit. *See, e.g., Hill v. Blue Cross & Blue Shield of Mich.*, 409 F.3d 710, 717 (6th Cir. 2005). "Although ERISA is silent as to whether exhaustion of administrative remedies is a prerequisite to bringing a civil action, we have held that the administrative scheme of ERISA requires a participant to exhaust his or her administrative remedies prior to commencing suit in federal court." *Coomer v. Bethesda Hosp., Inc.*, 370 F.3d 499 (6th Cir. 2004), citing *Miller v. Metro. Life Ins. Co.*, 925 F.2d 979, 986 (6th Cir. 1991); *see also Ravencraft v. UNUM Life Ins. Co. of Am.*, 212 F.3d 341, 343 (6th Cir. 2000); *Fallick v. Nationwide Mut. Ins. Co.*, 162 F.3d 410, 418 n.4 (6th Cir. 1998); *Baxter v. C.A. Muer Corp.*, 941 F.2d 451, 453 (6th Cir. 1991). "Application of the administrative exhaustion requirement is [, however,] committed to the discretion of the district court . . . ." *Fallick*, 162 F.3d at 418. Whether exhaustion is required for ERISA statutory claims such as breach of fiduciary duty is an open question. *See Hill*, 409 F.3d at 717. *But see Fallick*, 162 F.3d at 418 n.6 (citing *Richards v. Gen. Motors Corp.*, 991 F.2d 1227 (6th Cir.1993)); *Moeckel v. Caremark RX Inc.*, 385 F. Supp. 2d 668, 679–81 (M.D. Tenn. Aug. 29, 2005).

## B. Exceptions to the Exhaustion Requirement

Both futility and inadequacy of the administrative remedy are recognized by the Sixth Circuit as exceptions to the exhaustion of administrative remedies requirement. *See Coomer,* 370 F.3d at 505; *cf. Hagen v. VPA, Inc.,* 428 F. Supp. 708, 712–13 (W.D. Mich. April 19, 2006) (while equitable tolling might excuse failure to exhaust, district court rejected plaintiff's factual showing as inadequate). However, these claims must be substantial enough for the court to waive the exhaustion requirement. *See Coomer,* 370 F.3d at 505. "The standard for adjudging the futility of resorting to the administrative remedies provided by a plan is whether a clear and positive indication of futility can be made." *Id.,* citing *Fallick,* 162 F.3d at 419. "The Plaintiff must show that 'it is certain that his claim will be denied on appeal, not merely that he has doubts that an appeal will result in a different decision." *Id.,* quoting *Lindemann v. Mobil Oil Corp.,* 79 F.3d 647, 650 (7th Cir. 1996). Futility excused the plaintiff's failure to file a long-term disability claim where the plaintiff's short-term disability claim was denied before onset of long-term disability period and long-term disability policy requires the plaintiff to qualify for short-term disability benefits through the short-term disability maximum benefit period. *Welsh v. Wachovia Corp.,* 2006 WL 1972108 (6th Cir. July 13, 2006) (remanding long-term disability claim to permit exhaustion).

## C. Consequences of Failure to Exhaust

The consequence of bringing suit in the Sixth Circuit without exhausting administrative remedies is that the case will be dismissed, either with or without prejudice, depending upon the circumstances of the case. *See Ravencraft,* 212 F.3d at 344 (court dismissed case without prejudice because case was dismissed solely based on the plaintiff's failure to exhaust administrative remedies); *Baxter,* 941 F.2d at 454 n.1 (court dismissed case with prejudice because dismissal was based on both a loss on the merits and procedural deficiency). *But see Hagen,* 428 F. Supp. 2d at 713–14 (dismissing benefit denial claim with prejudice on the sole ground of failure to exhaust); *cf. Dozier v. Sun Life Assurance of Can.,* 2005 WL 2179386 (E.D. Ky. Sept. 5, 2005) (following dismissal without prejudice for failure to exhaust, the plaintiff attempted exhaustion, but the defendant denied claim as untimely; the defendant's motion for summary judgment based on untimeliness was granted).

## D. Minimum Number of Levels of Administrative Review

No Sixth Circuit case has expressly decided how many levels of administrative review a claimant may be required to exhaust.

## E. Can a Defendant Waive a Failure-to-Exhaust Defense?

The Sixth Circuit has not directly addressed this issue in the ERISA context. In an analogous situation, however, the Southern District of Ohio has held that a defendant may waive exhaustion on administrative review. *See, Newman-Waters v. Blue Cross/Blue Shield of Tenn., Inc.,* 2005 WL 1263026, at *21–23 (E.D. Tenn. May 17, 2005) (holding that a court can exercise discretion to excuse non-exhaustion); *Smith v. Gen. Motors Corp.,* 791 F. Supp. 701, 704 (S.D. Ohio 1992) (defendant may waive review required by collective bargaining agreement, which the court likened to ERISA's requirements).

# IV. Standard of Review

## A. Plan Language

The Sixth Circuit has held that no "magic words" are required for the discretionary grant, but that it must be a "clear grant of discretion." *Perez v. Aetna Life Ins. Co.,* 150 F.3d 550, 555 (6th Cir. 1998) (*en banc*). Interestingly, that case also held that the following language constitutes a clear grant:

> [Aetna] shall have the right to require as part of the proof of claim satisfactory evidence . . . that [the claimant] has furnished all required proofs for such benefits. . . .

*Id.* at 555. Thus, "satisfactory evidence" language will trigger the deferential standard of review.

## B. What Standard of Review Applies?

As provided in *Firestone Tire & Rubber Co. v. Bruch,* 489 U.S. 101 (1989), benefit denials are generally reviewed de novo unless the plan grants discretionary authority, in which case they are reviewed under an "arbitrary and discretionary" standard. *See Yeager v. Reliance Standard Life Ins. Co.,* 88 F.3d 376, 381 (6th Cir. 1996). This deferential standard requires upholding the claim administrator's decision if it has a reasoned explanation, based on the evidence. *Univ. Hosps. of Cleveland v. Emerson Elect. Co.,* 202 F.3d 839, 846 (6th Cir. 2000); *Marquette Gen'l Hosp. v. Goodman Forest Ind.,* 315 F.3d 629, 632 (6th Cir. 2002).

As the Sixth Circuit described this standard in an earlier case,

> The arbitrary and capricious standard is the least demanding form of judicial review of administrative action. . . . When it is possible to offer a reasonable explanation, based on the evidence, for a particular outcome, that outcome is not arbitrary or capricious.

*Davis v. Ky. Finance Cos. Ret. Plan,* 887 F.2d 689, 693 (6th Cir. 1989). *Davis* quoted a remarkable statement from a Seventh Circuit case:

Although it is an overstatement to say that a decision is not arbitrary and capricious whenever a court can review the reasons stated for the decision without a loud guffaw, it is not much of an overstatement.

This standard will apply to both factual determinations as well as to legal conclusions. *Wilkins v. Baptist Healthcare Sys., Inc.,* 150 F.3d 609, 613 (6th Cir. 1998), citing *Rowan v. UNUM Life Ins. Co.,* 119 F.3d 433, 435 (6th Cir. 1997).

However, this deferential review is not a mere rubber stamp of the plan administrator's claim denial. *McDonald v. Western-Southern Life Ins. Co.,* 347 F.3d 161, 172 (6th Cir. 2003), quoting *Hackett v. Xerox Corp. Long-Term Disability Income Plan,* 315 F.3d 771, 774–75 (7th Cir. 2003).

### C. Effect of Conflict of Interest or Procedural Irregularity

The question arises as to whether the review standard changes if the decision maker is operating under some type of a conflict of interest; for example, if the decision maker is paying the claim out of its own account. The Court in *Firestone* recognized this situation and said that a "conflict must be weighed as a factor in determining whether there is an abuse of discretion." 489 U.S. 101 at 115. While some courts have applied a sliding-scale approach in these cases, the Sixth Circuit has steadfastly viewed a conflict as merely a factor in determining whether the claim denial was arbitrary. *Davis,* 887 F.2d at 694; *see also Brown v. Nat'l City Corp.,* 1998 U.S. App. LEXIS 28055 (6th Cir. 1998); *Univ. Hosps.,* 202 F.3d at 846.

Although there are fewer cases, a similar result may apply to the case of procedural irregularities (and those irregularities may be evidence of arbitrariness). *Daniel v. Eaton Corp.,* 839 F.2d 263, 267 (6th Cir. 1988) ("the standard of review is no different whether the appeal is actually denied or is deemed denied"); *Stoll v. Western & Southern Life Ins. Co.,* 64 Fed. Appx. 986, 991, 30 Empl. Benefits Cas. (BNA) 2832 (6th Cir. 2003) (requiring only "substantial compliance with procedural requirements"), *but see Myers v. Iron Workers Dist. Council of S. Ohio & Vicinity Pension Trust,* Case No. 2:04-CV-966, 2005 U.S. Dist. LEXIS 39191 (S.D. Ohio Nov. 7, 2005) (reviewing the administrator's decision de novo, quoting *Univ. Hosps. of Cleveland v. Emerson Elec. Co.,* 202 F.3d 839, 846 n.3 (6th Cir. 2000) ("there is undeniable logic in the view that a plan administrator should forfeit deferential review by failing to exercise its discretion in a timely manner")). Finally, the circuit does not allow substantive remedies for procedural violations. *See, e.g., Lewandowski v. Occidental Chem. Corp.,* 986 F.2d 1006 (6th Cir. 1993); *see also Sanford v. Harvard Indus., Inc.,* 262 F.3d 590 (6th Cir. 2001) (de novo standard applies where an unauthorized party makes the benefit determination; matter remanded to plan administrator).

### D. Other Factors Affecting Standard of Review

The same standard-of-review analysis appears to apply even in the case of an insured plan or an insurance policy. *Libbey-Owens-Ford Co. v. Blue Cross & Blue Shield Mut.,* 982 F.2d 1031 (6th Cir. 1993) (based on ERISA § 3(1), which defines a welfare plan as providing benefits through "insurance or otherwise"). Moreover, since the Sixth Circuit apparently applies the *contra proferentem* rule both to ERISA plans and to the interpretation of insurance policies, it is hard to see what the difference would be. *See Perez,* 150 F.3d at 557 n.7 (adopting *contra proferentem*). It is also unclear how to reconcile *contra proferentem* with the deferential standard.

## V. Rules of Plan Interpretation

### A. Application of Federal Common Law

The Sixth Circuit has determined that Congress expected federal courts to develop federal common law to fill in ERISA's gaps in order to ensure national uniformity. *Auto Owners Ins. Co. v. Thorn Apple Valley, Inc.,* 31 F.3d 371, 374 (6th Cir. 1994). "In situations where the substantive provisions of ERISA are not at issue, federal courts are expected to develop a body of federal common law to resolve claims." *Parker v. Union Planters Corp.,* 203 F. Supp. 2d 888 (W.D. Tenn. 2002). Federal courts develop federal common law by considering the law of the state where it sits, or by reviewing general contract law and developing a federal rule on the issue. *Regents of the Univ. of Mich. v. Employees of Agency Rent-A-Car Ass'n,* 122 F.3d 336, 339 (6th Cir. 1997); *Perez v. Aetna Life Ins. Co.,* 150 F.3d 550, 556 (6th Cir. 1998); *COB Clearinghouse Corp. v. Aetna U.S. Healthcare, Inc.,* 362 F.3d 877 (6th Cir. 2004), *Citizens Ins. Co. of Am. v. MidMichigan Health ConnectCare Network Plan,* 449 F.3d 688 (6th Cir. 2006); *Rehab Inst., Inc. v. Mich. United Food & Commercial Workers Health & Welfare Funds,* 206 U.S. App. LEXIS 10056. Federal courts adopt the rules "that best comport with the interests served by ERISA's regulatory scheme." *Regents of the Univ. of Mich.,* 122 F.3d at 339, quoting *PM Group Life Ins. Co. v. Western Growers Assur. Trust,* 953 F.2d 543, 546 (9th Cir. 1992). If federal courts in the Sixth Circuit employ state law as a guide for creating federal common law, the state law must be in accord with the ERISA provisions. *Swisher-Sherman v. Provident Life & Accident Ins. Co.,* 37 F.3d 1500 (table), 1994 U.S. App. LEXIS 35030 (6th Cir. 1994), citing *Brewer v. Lincoln Nat'l Life Ins. Co.,* 921 F.2d 150, 153 (8th Cir. 1990).

### B. Application of *Contra Proferentem*

*Contra proferentem* requires that an ambiguous provision in a written document be construed against the person who prepared the terms of the document. As a principle of state contract law, *contra proferentem* has not survived ERISA preemption in the Sixth Circuit. In *McMahan v. New England Mutual Life Insurance Co.,* 888 F.2d 426 (6th Cir. 1989), the court held that ERISA preempted Kentucky's law of interpreting ambiguity against the drafter. The court maintained that *contra proferentem* does not "regulate insurance" and therefore does not fall within ERISA's savings clause. *Id.* at 430.

However, in several cases the Sixth Circuit either has referenced *contra proferentem* or suggested *in dicta* that it applies in ERISA cases. In *Tolley v. Commercial Life Insurance Co.,* 14 F.3d 602 (table), 1993 U.S. App. LEXIS 37296 (6th Cir. 1993), the court explained that although ERISA preempts state contract law, *contra proferentem* still may be relevant under federal common law. State case law, although preempted, can be referred to in developing federal common law. *Regents of the Univ. of Mich.,* 122 F.3d at 339. In *Tolley,* the court noted that the federal common law in other circuits required that ambiguous terms in ERISA plans be construed strictly against the drafter. *Tolley,* 14 F.3d at 340. Similarly, in *University Hospitals of Cleveland v. Emerson Electric Co.,* 202 F.3d 839, 847 (6th Cir. 2000), the court noted *in dicta* that if an ERISA plan provision is ambiguous, the court would construe ambiguities against the drafter. *See also Perez,* 150 F.3d at 557 n.7 ("[t]he rule of *contra proferentem* provides that the ambiguous contract provisions in ERISA-governed insurance contracts should be construed against the drafting party"); *Marquette Gen. Hosp.,* 315 F.3d 629 (court noted *contra proferentem,* but found no ambiguity).

In an unreported decision, *Mitchell v. Dialysis Clinic, Inc.,* 18 Fed. Appx. 349, 353 (6th Cir. 2001), the court itself recognized that these various citations to the rule of *contra proferentem* were *in dicta* and that the Sixth Circuit had not clearly established a "rule that would completely contradict the deference paid to an administrator's decision." The court refused to resolve how the rule of *contra proferentem* affects application of the arbitrary and capricious standard, deciding the case on other grounds. Thus, despite the Sixth Circuit's willingness to cite to the rule of *contra proferentem,* its application in cases applying an arbitrary and capricious standard of review remains an open question. *See, e.g., Muse v. Central States, Southeast & Southwest Areas Health & Welfare & Pension Funds,* 227 F. Supp. 2d 873 (S.D. Ohio 2002) (based on the *Mitchell* analysis, the court rejected *contra proferentem*).

Even when relevant, courts apply *contra proferentem* only when the contract is equally susceptible to two reasonable interpretations. *Id; Perez,* 150 F.3d at 556. In applying federal common law rules of contract interpretation, the Sixth Circuit interprets ERISA plan provisions according to their plain meaning. The words in an ERISA provision are read as having an "ordinary and popular" meaning. *Id.* Therefore, in order for the Sixth Circuit to apply *contra proferentem* under federal common law, the ERISA provision must have two reasonable interpretations. *Id.* at 557.

### C. Deference Afforded to an Administrator's Interpretation of a Plan

When the plan grants the plan administrator discretion to construe plan terms, the Sixth Circuit will give deference to the administrator's interpretation. *See Jones v. Metro Ins. Co.,* 385 F.3d 654, 661 (6th Cir. 2004); *Peruzzi v. Summa Med. Plan,* 137 F.3d 431, 433 (6th Cir. 1998). However, the deference is not unlimited. The courts have repeatedly held that deference afforded to the plan administrator does not mean "no review" or merely "rubber stamping" the plan administrator's decision. *McDonald v. Western-Southern Life Ins. Co.,* 347 F.3d 161, 172 (6th Cir. 2003); *Jones,* at 661 (6th Cir. 2004); *Buchanan v. Aetna Life Ins. Co.,* 2006 U.S. App. LEXIS 11046 (6th Cir. 2006). Furthermore, discretion to interpret the plan, for example, will not support adding to the plan terms. *Jones,* at 661 (deference does not include the authority to add eligibility requirements to the plan).

### D. Other Rules of Plan or Contract Interpretation

The Sixth Circuit also has held that principles of estoppel cannot be applied to vary the terms of an unambiguous plan document. *See Marks v. Newcourt Credit Group,*

342 F.3d 444, 456 (6th Cir. 2003). Estoppel may, however, be invoked when the plan terms at issue are ambiguous. *See Sprague v. Gen. Motors Corp.,* 133 F.3d 388 (6th Cir. 1998).

## VI. Discovery

### A. Limitations on Discovery

The Sixth Circuit has held that regardless of the standard of review, a district court's review of a claim decision under ERISA is limited to the record before the administrator. *Perry v. Simplicity Eng'g,* 900 F.2d 963, 966 (6th Cir. 1990); *Wilkins v. Baptist Healthcare Sys., Inc.,* 150 F.3d 609, 615 (6th Cir. 1998). Permitting or requiring district courts to consider evidence from the parties that was not presented to the plan administrator would seriously impair the goal of inexpensive and expeditious resolution of claims. *Id.*

The Sixth Circuit, however, has developed an exception to the general rule prohibiting consideration of matters outside the record, and, consequently, discovery. *See Wilkins,* 150 F.3d at 619; *Vanderklok v. Provident Life & Accident Ins. Co.,* 956 F.2d 610 (6th Cir. 1992). If the plaintiff alleges that the administrator failed to follow proper administrative procedures resulting in a denial of a full and fair opportunity for review, the appropriate remedy is to allow the plaintiff to submit additional evidence to the court. Thus, evidence may be offered in "support of a procedural challenge to the administrator's decision, such as an alleged lack of due process afforded by the administrator or alleged bias on its part," and discovery should be limited to such challenges. *Wilkins,* 150 F.3d at 619; *see also Heffernan v. Unum Life Ins. Co. of Am.,* 2004 U.S. App. LEXIS 11836 (6th Cir. 2004) (court commented that district court had properly authorized discovery to explore a procedural challenge).

For example, in *Vanderklok,* the court held that the administrator's denial letter was defective because it failed to provide the specific reason for denial or to identify the pertinent plan provisions. 906 F.2d at 616–17. Consequently, the plaintiff was denied his opportunity to submit any additional evidence relevant to the claim decision. *Id.* The court remanded the case to the district court and instructed that the plaintiff be permitted to submit additional evidence for review by the court. *Id.*

Similarly, in *Killian v. Healthsource Provident Administrators,* 152 F.3d 514 (6th Cir. 1998), the plaintiff claimed the administrator had improperly rejected additional material provided by the claimant and closed the administrative record. The court explained that the remedy for this procedural failure was to allow in the evidence. However, the court in *Killian* remanded the claim back to the claim administrator for consideration of the plaintiff's submissions.

The Sixth Circuit has not further defined or provided guidance on the extent or type of challenges that will justify consideration of evidence outside the administrative record. *See Schey v. Unum Life Ins. Co. of N. Am.,* 145 F. Supp. 2d 919, 921 (N.D. Ohio 2001). In *Wilkins,* the court identified two possible procedural challenges: lack of due process, and bias on the part of the administrator. However, no case clearly "delineates the circumstances in which such evidence is appropriate." *Bennett v. Unum Life Ins. Co.,* 321 F. Supp. 2d 925 (E.D. Tenn. 2004).

## B. Discovery and Conflict of Interest

While lack of due process may be easy to identify, district courts in the Circuit have struggled to a degree with identifying when allegations of bias and alleged conflicts of interest justify discovery and consideration of evidence outside the record. Consequently, district courts in the Sixth Circuit have addressed these issues on a case-by-case basis. Some district court judges simply have denied requests to conduct discovery, citing the general rule against considering matters outside of the record. *See, e.g., Maxwell v. Ameritech Corp. Inc.,* 7 F. Supp. 2d 905 (E.D. Mich. 1998) (discovery inappropriate on a conflict of interest). Others have denied discovery on conflict of interest or bias if it did not relate to a specific procedural challenge. *Schey,* 145 F. Supp. 2d at 925 (fact that administrator also is payor does not entitle the plaintiff to discovery; the plaintiff must identify specific procedural challenge). Still others have held that even when a procedural challenge or bias is alleged, the plaintiff must come forward with some threshold evidence in order to conduct discovery.

In *Bennett,* 321 F. Supp. 2d 925, the court addressed *Wilkins* and other district court decisions going both ways on whether discovery was appropriate and concluded that a "middle of the road" approach is appropriate, neither prohibiting nor permitting discovery in ERISA cases simply because the fiduciary holds dual, conflicting roles. Rather, where a claimant

> 1) identifies specific procedural challenges concerning a fiduciary's decision to deny or terminate ERISA benefits, and 2) makes an initial showing to the court that he has a reasonable basis to make such procedural challenges, then good cause exists to permit the plaintiff to conduct appropriate discovery.

*Id.* at *18.

In dicta, panels of the Sixth Circuit have twice mildly chastised plaintiff's counsel for failing to pursue discovery on the issues of bias in the hiring of medical experts and the defendant's alleged conflict of interest, which left the court with no evidence to support those contentions. *See Kalish v. Liberty Mut./Liberty Life Ass. Co. of Boston,* 419 F.3d 501, 508 (6th Cir. 2005) (suggesting discovery of statistical evidence to demonstrate correlation between number of times medical reviewer hired and number of claimant-adverse decisions by the reviewer); *Calvert v. Firstar Finance, Inc.,* 409 F.3d 286, 292 n.2 (6th Cir. 2005) (court would have a "better feel for the weight to accord this conflict of interest" if the plaintiff pursued discovery on issue). One court rejected the plaintiff's argument that *Kalish* and *Calvert* implicitly rejected *Bennett*'s requirement that the plaintiff demonstrate a "specific procedural challenge" to obtain discovery. *Bradford v. Metro. Life Ins. Co.,* 2006 WL 1006578 (E. D. Tenn. April 14, 2006).

# VII. Evidence

## A. Scope of Evidence under Standards of Review

The Sixth Circuit has long been of the view that generally a court can consider only evidence in the administrative record. *Perry v. Simplicity Eng'g,* 900 F.2d 963, 966 (6th Cir. 1990). This applies to both de novo review and the deferential review. *Id.* (de novo); *Killian v. Healthsource Provident Adm'rs,* 152 F.3d 514, 522 (6th Cir.

1998); *Univ. Hosps. of Cleveland v. Emerson Elect. Co.*, 202 F.3d 839 (6th Cir. 2000) (arbitrary and capricious).

As set forth in the previous section, however, the majority of the *Wilkins* court set forth an exception to this rule for procedural challenges to the administrator's decision:

> The district court may consider evidence outside of the administrative record only if that evidence is offered in support of a procedural challenge to the administrator's decision, such as an alleged lack of due process afforded by the administrator or alleged bias on its part. This also means that any prehearing discovery at the district court level should be limited to such procedural challenges.

Wilkins v. Baptist Healthcare Sys., Inc., 150 F.3d 609, 619 (6th Cir. 1998).

Thus, discovery can be obtained and evidence introduced on tangential matters such as lack of due process, procedural irregularities, or bias.

### B. Evidentiary Value of Social Security Determinations

Following the decision in *Black & Decker Disability Plan v. Nord,* 538 U.S. 822, the Sixth Circuit has held that an ERISA plan administrator is not bound by a Social Security Administration disability determination when reviewing a benefits claim under an ERISA plan. *See Whitaker v. Hartford Life & Acc. Ins. Co.,* 404 F.3d 947 (6th Cir. 2005) (citing *Hurse v. Hartford Life & Acc. Ins. Co.,* 77 Fed. Appx. 310, 2003 U.S. App. LEXIS 20030 (6th Cir. Sept. 26, 2003)). Additionally, in *Raskin v. Unum Provident Corp.,* No. 03-2270, 2005 U.S. App. LEXIS 1838, at *12–14 (6th Cir. Feb. 3, 2005), the court held that an ERISA administrator making an ERISA determination does not have to follow the Social Security Administration's decision regarding a claimant's right to benefits. Specifically, the court held that benefits determinations under the Social Security Administration follow a different set of procedures from ERISA claims because the procedures are designed to meet the need of efficiently and uniformly administering a large system. Therefore, the Social Security determination would not necessarily change the outcome of this case. *Id.* at *14 (citing *Nord,* 538 U.S. at 832–33).

### C. Other Evidence Issues

Although we have not found any Sixth Circuit case on point, extrinsic evidence could presumably be offered if there was a dispute over the contents of the administrative record. *See Heffernan v. UNUM Life Ins. Co. of Am.,* 101 Fed. Appx. 99 (6th Cir. 2004) (discovery permitted in the trial court limited to resolving a dispute over the contents of the administrative record). At least one district judge, in Michigan, routinely orders the parties to certify the administrative record and bring to him any disputes.

## VIII. Procedural Aspects of ERISA Practice

### A. Methods of Adjudication

In *Wilkins v. Baptist Healthcare System, Inc.,* 150 F.3d 609 (6th Cir. 1998), the Sixth Circuit confirmed that jury trials are not permitted by ERISA, which provides only for equitable relief. *Id.* at 616. It went on to suggest that summary judgment is an inappropriate procedure by which to resolve ERISA benefit claims. Rule 56 of the Federal Rules of Civil Procedure is designed to filter out cases in which there are no factual disputes and, consequently, no need for a factual hearing. *Id.* at 619. However, a factual hearing already has occurred before the administrator in an ERISA benefits case, and, therefore, there is no need to "filter out" cases.

Although the *Wilkins* court did not specify exact procedures for resolving ERISA claims, the court set forth the following steps or guidelines:

1. As to the merits of the action, the district court should conduct a de novo review based solely upon the administrative record, and render findings of fact and conclusions of law accordingly. The district court may consider the parties' arguments concerning the proper analysis of the evidentiary materials contained in the administrative record, but may not admit or consider any evidence not presented to the administrator.
2. The district court may consider evidence outside of the administrative record only if that evidence is offered in support of a procedural challenge to the administrator's decision, such as an alleged lack of due process afforded by the administrator or alleged bias on its part. This also means that any prehearing discovery at the district court level should be limited to such procedural challenges.
3. For the reasons set forth above, the summary judgment procedures set forth in Rule 56 are inapposite to ERISA actions and thus should not be utilized in their disposition.

*Wilkins* at 619.

The court in *Reznick v. Provident Life & Accident Insurance Co.,* 2006 U.S. App. LEXIS 12192 (6th Cir. 2006), held that ERISA cases are not standard "trials on the merits" and therefore, require a different procedural posture before the court.

ERISA cases are appeals from agency determinations rather than trials on the merits, and thus come before the court in a different procedural posture and with a different standard of review than those before us here. *See Wilkins,* 150 F.3d at 618 ("[A] district court should not adjudicate an ERISA action as if it were conducting a standard bench trial under Rule 52").

### B. Reported ERISA Trials

The Sixth Circuit has held that plaintiffs are not entitled to a jury trial under ERISA. However, there are many cases in the Sixth Circuit, particularly prior to *Wilkins,* in which district courts conducted bench trials or styled the method of adjudication as a bench trial. Thus, there are many reported ERISA trials. As set forth below, courts have been inconsistent, even in following *Wilkins,* in how they resolve ERISA claims, and some may conduct or style the adjudication as a bench trial.

### C. Special Procedures for ERISA Benefit Cases

In practice, several district courts have heeded *Wilkins* and established specific procedures for resolving ERISA claims, including (1) requiring the parties' motions to be styled as motions for entry of judgment; and (2) rendering specific findings of fact and conclusions of law. "This Court will follow this procedure making necessary findings of fact and conclusions of law and deciding this case by issuing an order for judgment on the merits." *Lehman v. Executive Cabinet Salary Continuation Plan*, 241 F. Supp. 2d 845, 847 (S.D. Ohio 2003); (citing *Frankenmuth Mut. Ins. Co. v. Wal-mart Assocs.' Health & Welfare Plan*, 182 F. Supp. 2d 612 (E.D. Mich. 2002)). However, other district courts in the Sixth Circuit have resolved ERISA claims using Rule 56, without comment from the Sixth Circuit. *See, e.g., Marks v. Newcourt Credit Group*, 342 F.3d 444 (6th Cir. 2003) (affirming grant of summary judgment); *Hill v. Blue Cross & Blue Shield*, 409 F.3d 710 (6th Cir. 2005); *Kottmyer v. Maas*, 436 F.3d 684 (6th Cir. 2006); *Westside Mothers v. Olszewski*, 2006 Fed. App. 0247P (6th Cir. 2006); *Nester v. Allegiance Healthcare Corp.*, 162 F. Supp. 2d 901, 907–08 (S.D. Ohio 2001) (noting the Sixth Circuit has ignored *Wilkins* and panels of that court have reviewed ERISA claims by conducting summary judgment analyses); *Gieger v. Unum Life Ins. Co. of Am.*, 213 F. Supp. 2d 813, 817 n.1 (N.D. Ohio 2002), citing *Bucks v. Reliance Standard Life Ins. Co.*, 2000 WL 659029, at *3 n.1 (6th Cir. 2000) (it appears *Wilkins* applies only when the administrator does not have discretionary authority).

## IX. Fiduciary Liability Claims

### A. Definition of Fiduciary

The Sixth Circuit applies a functional interpretation of ERISA's definition of "fiduciary," looking to a party's control and authority over a plan rather than formal grants of trusteeship. *Briscoe v. Fine*, 444 F.3d 478, 486 (6th Cir. 2006); *Seaway Food Town, Inc. v. Med. Mut.*, 347 F.3d 610, 616 (6th Cir. 2003); *Hamilton v. Carell*, 243 F.3d 992, 998 (6th Cir. 2001). The Sixth Circuit's functional interpretation follows the Supreme Court's mandate in *Mertens v. Hewitt Assocs.*, 508 U.S. 248, 262 (1993). *See id.* When applying this functional interpretation, courts in the Sixth Circuit ". . . [examine] the conduct at issue to determine whether it constitutes 'management' or 'administration' of the plan, giving rise to fiduciary concerns, or merely a business decision that has an effect on an ERISA plan not subject to fiduciary standards." *Seaway*, 347 F.3d at 617, quoting *Hunter v. Caliber Sys., Inc.*, 220 F.3d 702, 718 (6th Cir. 2000); *Briscoe*, 444 F.3d at 486; *Sengpiel v. B.F. Goodrich Co.*, 156 F.3d 660, 666 (6th Cir. 1998).

In applying a functional interpretation of ERISA's definition of "fiduciary" to parties charged with a breach of fiduciary duty, the threshold question in every case is "not whether the actions of some person employed to provide services under a plan adversely affected a plan beneficiary's interest, but whether that person was acting as a fiduciary (that is, was performing a fiduciary function) when taking the action subject to complaint." *Seaway*, 347 F.3d at 617, quoting *Pegram v. Herdrich*, 530 U.S. 211, 226 (2000). If the conduct at issue is merely a business decision that affects an ERISA plan, without constituting management or administration of the plan, the person's actions are not subject to fiduciary standards with respect to that conduct. *Id.* A party is a fiduciary only insofar as its conduct constitutes a fiduciary function, because, under ERISA, a person may be a fiduciary for some purposes but not for others. *See, e.g., Kuper v. Quantum Chem. Corp.,* 838 F. Supp. 342, 347 (S.D. Ohio 1993), *judgment entered,* 852 F. Supp. 1389 (S.D. Ohio 1994), *aff'd, Kuper v. Iovenko,* 66 F.3d 1447 (6th Cir. 1995).

In *Libbey-Owens-Ford Co. v. Blue Cross & Blue Shield Mut.,* 982 F.2d 1031 (6th Cir. 1993), the court held that an insurance company administrator of a self-insured employee benefit plan was a fiduciary for ERISA purposes, as long as it had discretionary authority regarding claims. *Id.* at 1036; *see also Hill v. Blue Cross & Blue Shield of Mich.,* 409 F.3d 710, 716–17 (6th Cir. 2006) (same). Similarly, in *Guardsmark, Inc. v. Blue Cross & Blue Shield of Tennessee,* 169 F. Supp. 2d 794 (W.D. Tenn. 2001), an insurance company was found to be a fiduciary under ERISA because it administered claims for an employee welfare benefit plan, having the authority to grant or deny any of those claims. However, in *Seaway,* the court found that an insurance company was not a fiduciary under ERISA where group contracts did not authorize it to exercise discretion with respect to any funds resulting from provider discounts, but specifically required the provider to retain such funds for its sole benefit. *Seaway,* 347 F.3d at 619; *see also Mich. Affiliated Healthcare Sys., Inc. v. Lansing Gen. Hosp.,* 139 F.3d 546 (6th Cir. 1998) (claims administrator not a fiduciary where it had no discretion and employer had final discretion to grant or deny claims).

## B. Definition of Fiduciary Duties

The Sixth Circuit has concluded that ERISA's fiduciary duty, codified at 29 U.S.C. § 1104(a)(1), essentially encompasses three components: (1) the duty of loyalty; (2) the "prudent man" duty; and (3) the "exclusive purpose" duty. *See Berlin v. Mich. Bell Tel. Co.,* 858 F.2d 1154, 1162 (6th Cir. 1988); *see also Gregg v. Transp. Workers of Am. Int'l,* 343 F.3d 833, 840 (6th Cir. 2003); *Kuper v. Iovenko,* 66 F.3d 1447, 1458 (6th Cir. 1995). The duty of loyalty is rooted in the statute's "requirement that each fiduciary of a plan must act solely in the interests of the plan's participants and beneficiaries." *Berlin,* 858 F.2d at 1162, quoting *Donovan v. Bierwirth,* 680 F.2d 263, 271 (2d Cir.), *cert. denied,* 459 U.S. 1069, 74 L. Ed. 2d 631, 103 S. Ct. 488 (1982)). Moreover, § 1104(a)(1)(B) expressly requires that a plan fiduciary act "with the skill, prudence, and diligence under the circumstances then prevailing that a prudent man acting in a like capacity would use in conducting an enterprise of like character." *Berlin,* 858 F.2d at 1162. Under the Sixth Circuit's analysis, the prudent-man standard coupled with the duty of loyalty "imposes an unwavering duty on an ERISA trustee to make decisions with a single-minded devotion to a plan's participants and beneficiaries and, in so doing, to act as a prudent person would act in a similar situation." *Id.* Finally, "an ERISA fiduciary must act for the exclusive purpose of providing benefits to plan beneficiaries." *Id.; see also Gregg,* 343 F.3d at 840–41 (ERISA fiduciary duty standard encompasses three components—a duty of loyalty, the prudent-person obligation, and that a fiduciary act for the exclusive purpose of providing benefit plans to employees) (quoting *Bierwirth,* 680 F.2d at 271); *James v. Pirelli Armstrong Tire Corp.,* 305 F.3d 439, 448–49 (6th Cir. 2002) (same); *Krohn v. Huron Mem'l Hosp.,* 173 F.3d 542, 547 (6th Cir. 1999) (same); *Kuper,* 66 F.3d at 1458 (if a fiduciary fails to meet any one of the three components, the fiduciary may be held personally liable for any losses to the plan that result from the fiduciary's breach of duty); *Best v. Londrigan,* 310 F.3d 932, 935 (6th Cir. 2002) (a fiduciary has a duty to act in the interest of the plan's fiduciaries and with skill, care, prudence, and diligence).

### C. Fiduciary Liability in the Context of Health and Disability Claims

The significant Sixth Circuit cases on this issue, including *Libbey-Owens-Ford Co., Guardsmark,* and *Seaway,* are identified above.

### D. Remedies for Breach of Fiduciary Duty

While "the Secretary of Labor and the plan administrator are entitled to seek the full gamut of legal and equitable relief" in enforcing the statute's provisions, "ERISA restricts plan beneficiaries to equitable relief with no recourse to money damages." *Helfrich v. PNC Bank, Ky., Inc.,* 267 F.3d 477 (6th Cir. 2001). Beneficiaries may not recover compensatory or punitive damages. *Id.; see also Del Rio v. Toledo Edison Co.,* 130 Fed. Appx. 746, 750 (6th Cir. 2005) (ERISA "does not afford avenue of redress" for plan beneficiary seeking damages in individual capacity in breach-of-fiduciary-duty claim); *Int'l Union, United Auto., Aerospace, & Agr. Implement Workers of Am. v. Park-Ohio Indus. Inc.,* 661 F. Supp. 1281 (N.D. Ohio 1987) (denying recovery of extracontractual and punitive damages where breach of fiduciary duty under ERISA was found); *Bova v. Am. Cyanamid Co.,* 662 F. Supp. 483 (S.D. Ohio 1987) (granting recovery of benefits owed but not extracontractual or punitive damages); *Varhola v. Doe,* 820 F.2d 809 (6th Cir. 1987) (holding that in an action to recover benefits under 29 U.S.C. § 1132(a)(3), punitive damages are not recoverable).

In addition, the Sixth Circuit appears to be strictly construing the Supreme Court's decision in *Knudson,* limiting remedies to those that are nonmonetary. For example, the court has held that labeling a claim as one for "restitution" will not allow a plaintiff to recover compensatory damages. In *Helfrich,* the court explained that while equitable relief may include restitution, a restitutionary award must focus on the defendant's conduct and wrongfully obtained gain as opposed to the plaintiff's loss. The court looked past the label and held that measuring relief by the plaintiff's loss was the hallmark of money damages, which are not permitted under ERISA. *Id. But see McFadden v. R & R Engine & Mach. Co.,* 102 F. Supp. 2d 458 (N.D. Ohio 2000) (decided before *Helfrich*). Similarly in *Qualchoice Inc. v. Rowland,* 367 F.3d 638 (6th Cir. 2004), the court rejected claims for subrogation and restitution, even though the participant possessed recovery in an identifiable fund, finding that such restitution was a legal remedy. The Supreme Court's decision in *Sereboff v. Mid Atlantic Medical Services, Inc.,* 126 S. Ct. 1869 (2006), however, abrogated *Qualchoice.* In *Sereboff,* a plan filed suit under 29 U.S.C. § 1132(a)(3) to recover from a plan participant more than $70,000 paid by the plan on the participant's behalf after the participant settled a tort lawsuit. The Supreme Court held that though the plan's claim was a subrogation claim, the relief the plan sought was indistinguishable from an action to enforce an equitable lien and was, therefore, permissible under § 1132(a)(3). *Sereboff,* 126 S. Ct. at 1874–76.

## E. Contribution and Indemnity Claims among Fiduciaries

In *McDannold v. Starbank,* 261 F.3d 478 (6th Cir. 2001), the Sixth Circuit acknowledged the split among the circuits regarding whether ERISA fiduciaries could seek contribution from a cofiduciary. *See also May v. Nat'l Bank of Commerce,* 390 F. Supp. 2d 674, 676 (W.D. Tenn. 2004). There, however, the court refused to address the issue, finding it was not ripe due to factual issues that remained outstanding and required remand.

While the Sixth Circuit has not yet issued an opinion determining whether a fiduciary may seek contribution, district courts in the circuit have rejected such claims. *See id.; Williams v. Provident Inv. Counsel Inc.,* 279 F. Supp. 2d 894 (N.D. Ohio 2003); *Roberts v. Taussig,* 39 F. Supp. 2d 1010 (N.D. Ohio 1999) (ERISA does not contain a right of contribution or indemnity).

## F. ERISA Claims against Nonfiduciaries

In the Sixth Circuit, there is some question as to whether officials with nonfiduciary status can be found liable under ERISA. In *McDannold v. Starbank,* 261 F.3d 478 (6th Cir. 2001), the court remanded the case to the trial court, holding that professional advisors who were not fiduciaries of an employee stock ownership plan could still have common liability under ERISA. Specifically, the court held that a cause of action lies under ERISA § 502(a)(3) against a nonfiduciary party-in-interest who knowingly participates in a prohibited transaction. *Id.* at 486 (citing *Harris Trust & Sav. Bank v. Salomon Smith Barney, Inc.,* 530 U.S. 238, 120 S. Ct. 2180, 147 L. Ed. 2d 187 (2000)). Moreover, in *Brock v. Hendershott,* 840 F.2d 339, 342 (6th Cir. 1998), the court allowed a disgorgement of profits against an ERISA nonfiduciary because the nonfiduciary aided and assisted in the breach of a fiduciary duty.

Despite these holdings, there is case law within the Sixth Circuit indicating that a plaintiff's state-law claims are not preempted by ERISA when those claims are brought against nonfiduciaries. *See Smith v. Provident Bank,* 170 F.3d 609, 613 (6th Cir. 1999). In *Penny/Ohlmann/Nieman, Inc. v. Miami Valley Pension Corp.,* 399 F.3d 692 (6th Cir. 2005), the court was faced with a breach of contract claim brought against an entity that provided professional services to ERISA plans. In this instance the court held that ERISA does not preempt state-law claims brought against nonfiduciary service providers in connection with professional services rendered to an ERISA plan. *Id.* at 698–99.

# X. Attorneys' Fees

## A. Criteria for Awarding Attorneys' Fees

To determine whether a party is entitled to an award of attorneys' fees, courts in the Sixth Circuit consider the five *Bowen* factors:

> (1) the degree of the opposing party's culpability or bad faith; (2) the opposing party's ability to satisfy an award of attorney's fees; (3) the deterrent effect of an award on other persons under similar circumstances; (4) whether

the party requesting fees sought to confer a common benefit on all participants and beneficiaries of an ERISA plan or to resolve significant legal questions regarding ERISA; and (5) the relative merits of the parties' positions.

*Sec'y of Dept. of Labor v. King,* 775 F.2d 666, 669 (6th Cir. 1985); *see also Foltice v. Guardsman Prods., Inc.,* 98 F.3d 933, 937 (6th Cir. 1996) ("The five factors . . . have been cited in numerous subsequent cases."). The factors are flexible, developed to give guidance to the district court in exercising its discretion. Of course, in general, a party also must prevail to be awarded fees. *See Cattin v. Gen. Motors Corp.,* 955 F.2d 416, 427 (6th Cir. 1992).

ERISA has been interpreted by the Sixth Circuit as granting substantial discretion to the district courts to grant or deny a request for attorneys' fees. *See Jordan v. Mich. Conf. of Teamsters Welfare Fund,* 207 F.3d 854, 860 (6th Cir. 1998). Awards are reviewed for abuse of discretion. *See Armistead v. Vernitron Corp.,* 944 F.2d 1287, 1304 (6th Cir. 1991); *but see Moon v. Unum Provident Corp.,* No. 05-1974, 2006 U.S. App. LEXIS 16597 (6th Cir. June 29, 2006) (reversed denial-of-fee award).

## B. Fees Awarded to Plan Fiduciaries

The Sixth Circuit has not precluded awarding attorneys' fees to prevailing defendants in ERISA actions. In *Gettings v. Bldg. Laborers Local 310 Fringe Benefits Fund,* 349 F.3d 300 (6th Cir. 2003), the court stated that fees may be awarded to a prevailing defendant and remanded the case to the district court for explicit consideration of the five-factors test. The court instructed the district court to provide a reasoned explanation for its decision granting or denying the award of fees.

## C. Fees Awarded When Plaintiffs Lack Standing

The Sixth Circuit has held that a determination that the plaintiff is not an employee or participant under an ERISA plan does not preclude the district court from awarding attorneys' fees under the statute. In *Moon v. Unum Provident Corp.,* No. 05-1974, 2006 U.S. App. LEXIS 16597 (6th Cir. June 29, 2006), the court rejected the plaintiff's argument that if he was not an employee, he lacked standing, and the court lacked jurisdiction under ERISA, and could not award fees. The court concluded that the plaintiff made at least a colorable claim that he was an employee and therefore an ERISA participant, and his claims were not so insubstantial that they failed to present a federal controversy. *See also Primax Recoveries, Inc. v. Gunter,* 433 F.3d 515, 519–20 (6th Cir. 2006) (district had subject matter jurisdiction to award fees even though the plaintiff failed to state a claim).

## D. Calculation of Attorneys' Fees

The Sixth Circuit has held that district courts must apply the lodestar method (relevant hours times a reasonable hourly rate) in calculating an appropriate fee award. *See Bldg. Serv. Local 47 Cleaning Contractors Pension Plan v. Grandview Raceway,* 46 F.3d 1392, 1401 (6th Cir. 1995). The lodestar method is used regardless of whether there is a fee arrangement. *Id.* There is no requirement in the Sixth Circuit that fee awards be proportional to the damages awarded; however, the fees must be reasonable. *Id.* Although fees generally are not awarded for the administrative process, in at least one case a district court included such fees in its award, based on what it viewed as the defendant's culpable conduct. *See Kohrn v. Citigroup,* No. 3:04 CV 7553, 2006 U.S. Dist. LEXIS 11691 (N.D. Ohio March 21, 2006), 2006 U.S. District LEXIS 11691 (N.D. Ohio 2006).

## XI. ERISA Regulations

In November of 2000, the Department of Labor modified ERISA regulations on claims procedure, applicable to claims filed after January 1, 2002. The current regulations establish shorter time frames for benefits determinations than those contained in the earlier version of the regulations. Appeals of claims filed before the effective date are governed by the old regulations. However, many cases decided on claims filed prior to January 1, 2002, may form a basis for interpreting current regulations.

- **29 C.F.R. § 2509.75-8.** *Briscoe v. Fine,* 444 F.3d 478, 494 (6th Cir. 2006) (third-party administrator is a fiduciary with respect to the plan assets under his control); *Penny/Ohlmann/Nieman, Inc. v. Miami Valley Pension Corp.,* 399 F.3d 692, 700 (6th Cir. 2005) (service provider performing record-keeping services and having no discretionary control over the management of the plan is not a fiduciary); *Six Clinics Holdings Corp. II v. Catcomp Sys., Inc.,* 119 F.3d 393, 402 (6th Cir. 1997) (party that had authority to amend plan was fiduciary); *Flache v. Sun Life Assur. Co.,* 958 F.2d 730 (6th Cir. 1992) (mere payment of claims insufficient to give discretionary control over plan assets); *Loren v. Blue Cross & Blue Shield of Mich.,* 2006 U.S. Dist. LEXIS 53784, at *26–27 (E.D. Mich. Aug. 3, 2006) (a named fiduciary may not delegate to anyone, other than an investment manager, authority or discretion to manage a plan); *Toke v. Hadick,* 2005 U.S. Dist. LEXIS 40703, at *23–25 (S.D. Ohio Oct. 27, 2005) (party providing ministerial functions for the plan and not employed as the plan-defined administrator is not a fiduciary); *In re AEP,* 324 F. Supp. 2d 812, 832–33 (S.D. Ohio 2004) (fiduciary has a duty to monitor those he appoints to make decisions for the plan); *Noble v. Cumberland River Cool Co.,* 26 F. Supp. 2d 958 (E.D. Ky. 1998).
- **29 C.F.R. § 2510.3-1(b).** *Capriccioso v. Henry Ford Health Sys.,* 2000 U.S. App. LEXIS 17535, at *8 (6th Cir. July 17, 2000) (salary continuation policy constituted payroll practice); *Hart v. Reynolds & Reynolds Co.,* 1993 U.S. App. LEXIS 17678 (6th Cir. July 6, 1993) (same); *Langley v. Daimler-Chrysler Corp.,* 407 F. Supp. 2d 897, 912–13 (N.D. Ohio 2005) (where the criteria are otherwise met, the payroll practice exemption still applies even though the employer represented that the plan was covered by ERISA); *Hall v. Group Sickness & Accident Ins. Plan,* 2005 U.S. Dist. LEXIS 40700, at *15 (E.D. Mich. Aug. 19, 2005) (sickness and accident plan paid for out of the general assets of the employer was a payroll practice exempt from ERISA coverage); *Miller v. PPG Indus. Inc.,* 278 F. Supp. 2d 826 (W.D. Ky. 2003)

(vacation benefit program was payroll practice); *Williams v. Great Dane Trailer Tenn. Inc.,* 1995 U.S. Dist. LEXIS 22152, 19 Empl. Benefits Cas. (BNA) 1403 (W.D. Tenn. 1995) (short-term disability benefits constituted payroll practice).

- **29 C.F.R. § 2510.3-1(j).** *Thompson v. Am. Home Assurance Co.,* 95 F.3d 429 (6th Cir. 1996) (court considered employer endorsement of plan); *Nicholas v. Standard Ins. Co.,* 48 Fed. Appx. 557 (6th Cir. 2002); *Gindele v. Am. United Life Ins. Co.,* 2006 U.S. Dist. LEXIS 66750, at *11–12 (E.D. Ky. Sep. 15, 2006) (plan exempted only if it meets all four of the safe harbor criteria; plan failed on three grounds when employers contributed to the fund, participation was not voluntary, and the union created and had substantial involvement in administering the plan); *Doskey v. Unum Life Ins. Co. of Am.,* 2006 U.S. Dist. LEXIS 10319, at *4–6 (N.D. Ohio Feb. 17, 2006) (court found plan endorsed by the employer because of its substantial involvement in the creation and administration of the plan); *Harvey v. Life Ins. Co. of N. Am.,* 404 F. Supp. 2d 969, 976–77 (E.D. Ky. 2005) (court found employer endorsement despite lack of employer involvement in claim processing and eligibility determination when a reasonable employee would believe the employer endorsed the plan and all other factors indicate endorsement); *Oliver v. Sun Life Assurance Co. of Can.,* 417 F. Supp. 2d 865, 867 (W.D. Ky. 2005) (no employer endorsement when employee paid 100 percent of the cost with after-tax dollars and employer made clear that participation was voluntary and that the plan was distinct from the employer-endorsed plan); *Vincent v. Unum Provident Corp.,* 2005 U.S. Dist. LEXIS 9087, at *7 (E.D. Tenn. May 5, 2005) (safe harbor provision did not apply when employee could not prove that he, and not the employer, paid the premiums); *B-T Dissolution, Inc. v. Provident Life & Accident Ins. Co.,* 101 F. Supp. 2d 930 (S.D. Ohio 2000) (questions of fact existed concerning whether employer endorsed plan and paid premiums); *Wausau Benefits v. Progressive Ins. Co.,* 270 F. Supp. 2d 980 (S.D. Ohio 2003) (court found endorsement where employer was plan administrator).
- **29 C.F.R. § 2510.3-3(c)(1).** *Santino v. Provident Life & Accident Ins. Co.,* 276 F.3d 772 (6th Cir. 2001) (joint shareholder a participant); *Talley v. Kan. City Life Ins. Co.,* 2006 U.S. Dist. LEXIS 17168, at *11–12 (E.D. Tenn. Feb 28, 2006) (plan had no employee participants when it covered only husband and wife co-owners); *Melluish v. Provident Life & Accident Ins. Co.,* 2001 U.S. Dist. LEXIS 4595 (W.D. Mich. Feb. 26, 2001) (plaintiff not sole shareholder and not employer).
- **29 C.F.R. § 2520.102-2(a), (b).** *Bolone v. TRW Sterling Plant Pension Plan,* 130 Fed Appx. 761, 766 (6th Cir. 2005) (court would not reach the issue of whether the plan was misleading because there is no substantive remedy available when the plaintiff alleges only procedural violations); *Anderson v. Mrs. Grisson's Salads, Inc.,* 2000 U.S. App. LEXIS 14511, 25 Empl. Benefits Cas. (BNA) 1540 (6th Cir. June 19, 2000) (summary plan description was misleading); *Heady v. Dawn Food Prods., Inc.,* 2003 U.S. Dist. LEXIS 21634 (W.D. Ky. Nov. 25, 2003) (summary plan descriptions must not be misleading).

- **29 C.F.R. § 2560.503-1(b).** *Marks v. Newcourt Credit Group, Inc.,* 342 F.3d 444 (6th Cir. 2003) (administrator substantially complied with procedural requirements).
- **29 C.F.R. § 2560.503-1(g).** *McCartha v. Nat'l City Corp.,* 419 F.3d 437, 446 (6th Cir. 2005) (requirement that participant be notified of the specific reason for benefit denial necessitates more than mere reference to the provision to which participant failed to comply); *Stoll v. Western & Southern Life Ins. Co.,* No. 01-3401, 64 Fed. Appx. 986, 30 Empl. Benefits Cas. (BNA) 2832 (6th Cir. 2003) (failure to provide adequate notice of basis for denial did not alter standard of review); *Seal v. John Alden Life Ins. Co.,* 437 F. Supp. 2d 674, 687 (E.D. Mich. 2006) (notification failed to state plaintiff's right to have claim denial reviewed); *Children's Hosp. Med. Center of Akron v. Grace Mgmt. Servs. Employment Benefit Plan,* 2006 U.S. Dist. LEXIS 62567, at *9–10, 12 (N.D. Ohio Sept. 1, 2006) (plaintiff was entitled to present evidence outside of the administrative record because defendant failed to comply with claims procedures); *Jacobs v. Unum Life Ins. Co.,* 2006 U.S. Dist. LEXIS 10567, at *38–39 (M.D. Tenn. Feb. 21, 2006) (purpose of notification requirements essentially satisfied when the benefit determination letter stated the reason for denial, the specific plan provision at issue, and the information necessary to perfect or appeal, and informed participant that he had access to relevant information); *Neiheisel v. AK Steel Corp.,* 2005 U.S. Dist. LEXIS 4639, at *20, 21 (S.D. Ohio Feb. 17, 2005) (conclusory denial letter that failed to provide additional information necessary to perfect claim did not constitute notification); *Francis v. United Parcel Serv.,* 288 F. Supp. 2d 882 (S.D. Ohio 2003) (written notice of denial not provided); *Parker v. Union Planters Corp.,* 203 F. Supp. 2d 888 (W.D. Tenn. 2002) (plaintiff not provided timely notice of claim denial; defendant did not offer reasonable opportunity for full and fair review).
- **29 C.F.R. § 2560.503-1(h).** *Morrison v. Marsh & McLennon Cos., Inc.,* 2004 U.S. Dist. LEXIS 14096 (E.D. Mich. 2004) (requirement to provide relevant information applies only to participant or beneficiary).
- **29 C.F.R. 2560.503-1(l).** *Kohrn v. Plans Adm'r Comm. of Citigroup,* 2006 U.S. Dist. LEXIS 1092, at *19, 24–25 (N.D. Ohio Jan. 13, 2006) (defendant failed to provide a reasonable claims procedure, and therefore the court deemed that claimant exhausted administrative remedies); *Netzel v. Crowley Am. Transp. Co.,* 2006 U.S. Dist. LEXIS 16603, at *13–14 (E.D. Mich. Feb. 22, 2006) (exhaustion not excused when denial letter complied with ERISA requirements).

## XII. Cases Interpreting ERISA Statutes of Limitation

A claim for breach of fiduciary duty is the only claim for which ERISA establishes a statute of limitations. Pursuant to § 413 of ERISA, 29 U.S.C. § 1113, a claim for breach of fiduciary duty must be brought by the earlier of:

1. Six years after the act that constituted the breach or violation, or if an omission, the last date the breach of violation could have been cured, or;
2. Three years after the plaintiff had actual knowledge of the breach or violation.

*Wright v. Heyne,* 349 F.3d 321, 327 (6th Cir. 2003).

In situations where the defendant hides the breach or violation, and therefore fraud and concealment exist, the plaintiff will have six years from the date she discovers the breach to bring a claim. *Id.*

Given that ERISA does not provide a statute of limitations for claims other than for breach of fiduciary duty, courts are forced to borrow the most analogous state-law statute of limitations applicable to the case. *Meade v. Pension Appeal & Review Comm.,* 966 F.2d 190, 194–95 (6th Cir. 1992); *see also Preston v. John Alden Life Ins. Co.,* 2006 WL 2010763, at *2 (S.D. Ohio July 17, 2006).

For claims concerning benefits, enforcement of plan terms, and failure to provide required information or documentation, the Sixth Circuit generally looks to the analogous state statute of limitations for contract actions. *Santino v. Provident Life & Accident Ins. Co.,* 276 F.3d 772, 776 (6th Cir. 2001).

In general, the statute of limitations for a claim for ERISA benefits begins to run when the claim for benefits has been formally denied. *Stevens v. Employer-Teamsters Joint Council No. 84 Pension Fund,* 979 F.2d 444 (6th Cir. 1992). However, under certain circumstances the courts apply the discovery rule whereby the statute of limitations begins to run when the claimant discovers, or should have discovered, the denial, or was put on notice of the denial. *Mich. United Food & Commercial Workers Union v. Muir Co.,* 992 F.2d 594 (6th Cir. 1993).

## XIII. Subrogation Litigation

In *Qualchoice Inc. v. Rowland,* the Sixth Circuit joined those courts of appeals rejecting claims for subrogation by a plan fiduciary regardless of whether the plan participant possessed any recovery in an identifiable fund. 367 F.3d 638 (6th Cir. 2004). The court held that a plan fiduciary's action to enforce a plan-reimbursement provision is a legal action, regardless of whether the plan participant recovered from another entity and possesses that recovery in an identifiable fund. *Id.* at 648–51. The court explained that its previous decisions following *Great-West Life & Annuity Insurance Co. v. Knudson,* 534 U.S. 204 (2002), had not determined the application of *Knudson* to situations in which the participant recovered money from another entity and held the recovery in an identifiable fund. *Qualchoice,* 367 F.3d at 644–45 (previous decisions applied *Knudson* to reject claims where there was no identifiable fund). The Supreme Court expressly abrogated *Qualchoice* in *Sereboff v. Mid Atlantic Medical Services, Inc.,* 126 S. Ct. 1869 (2006). In *Sereboff,* a plan filed suit under 29 U.S.C. § 1132(a)(3) to recover from a plan participant's tort settlement more than $70,000 paid by the plan on the participant's behalf. The Supreme Court held that though the plan's claim was a subrogation claim, the relief the plan sought was indistinguishable from an action to enforce an equitable lien and was, therefore, permissible under § 1132(a)(3). *Sereboff,* 126 S. Ct. at 1874–76.

## XIV. Miscellaneous

The Sixth Circuit has permitted ERISA plaintiffs to bring class actions in spite of the exhaustion requirement. *See Fallick v. Nationwide Mut. Ins. Co.,* 162 F.3d 410 (6th Cir. 1998) ("where . . . the crux of an ERISA plaintiff's complaint concerns the methodology used to determine benefits, court have recognized that the standing-related provisions of ERISA were not intended to limit a claimant's right to proceed under Rule 23" of the Federal Rules of Civil Procedure). However, class claims must still satisfy Rule 23. For example, in *Sprague v. General Motors Corp.,* 133 F.3d 388 (6th Cir. 1998), the court reversed class certification where the claims were based on representations and individual issues predominated. *Id.* at 398–99.

# CHAPTER 7

# Seventh Circuit

MICHAEL BROWN
MARK D. DeBOFSKY
MARK E. SCHMIDTKE

## I. What Constitutes an ERISA Plan?

### A. Determining the Existence of an Employee Welfare Benefit Plan

The Seventh Circuit has held that there are five statutory criteria required for a plan to constitute an employee welfare benefit plan under the Employee Retirement Income Security Act of 1974 (ERISA):

> (1) A plan, fund or program, (2) established or maintained, (3) by an employer or by an employee organization, or by both, (4) for the purpose of providing medical, surgical, hospital care, sickness, accident, disability, death, unemployment or vacation benefits, apprenticeship or other training programs, day care centers, scholarship funds, pre-paid legal services or severance benefits, (5) to participants or their beneficiaries.

*Ed Miniat, Inc. v. Globe Life Ins. Group,* 805 F.2d 732, 738 (7th Cir. 1986), *cert. denied,* 482 U.S. 915 (1987); *Cler v. Ill. Educ. Ass'n,* 423 F.3d 726, 730 (7th Cir. 2005). The Seventh Circuit also follows the virtually universal rule that a "plan, fund, or program" implies "the existence of intended benefits, intended beneficiaries, a source of financing, and a procedure to apply for and collect benefits." *James v. Nat'l Bus. Sys., Inc.,* 924 F.2d 718, 720 (7th Cir. 1991), citing *Donovan v. Dillingham,* 688 F.2d 1367, 1372 (11th Cir. 1982); *Ed Miniat, Inc.,* 805 F.2d at 739 (citing *Donovan*). For purposes of determining whether a benefit plan is subject to ERISA, its various aspects ought not be unbundled. *Postma v. Paul Revere Life Ins. Co.,* 223

F.3d 533, 538 (7th Cir. 2000). A mere failure to comply with all of ERISA's technical requirements is irrelevant to whether a plan is governed by ERISA. For example, the core technical requirement is that an ERISA plan be in writing. Nevertheless, the Seventh Circuit has held that even where a plan is not in writing, it may
still be governed by ERISA. *See, e.g., Diak v. Dwyer, Costello & Knox,* 33 F.3d
809, 811 (7th Cir. 1994) ("[a] plan need not be in writing to be covered by ERISA
so long as the plan is a reality, meaning something more than a mere decision to
extend benefits"); *James,* 924 F.2d at 720 ("while a plan is not established merely
by the employer's deciding to have a plan, the plan need not be in writing, provided
it is a reality"). All that is required is that its terms can be determined with reasonable definiteness. *Miller v. Taylor Insulation Co.,* 39 F.3d 755, 760 (7th Cir. 1994).
Extending its holdings further, in *Shyman v. Unum Life Ins. Co.,* 427 F.3d 452 (7th
Cir. 2005), the court ruled that a commodity trader was a participant and/or a beneficiary in a benefit plan sponsored by the clearinghouse through which he made his
trades regardless of the fact the plaintiff was an independent contractor. *See also
Ruttenberg v. U.S. Life Ins. Co. in the City of New York,* 413 F.3d 652 (7th Cir.
2005) (same).

### B. Definition of "Employee" for ERISA Purposes

An "employee" in the traditional sense is a person who works in the service of
another person under which the employer has the right to control the details of work
performance. *Ruttenberg v. U.S. Life Ins. Co.,* 413 F.3d 652, 665 (7th Cir. 2005).
Under ERISA, any person employed by an employer is considered an "employee."
29 U.S.C. § 1002(6) (2005). However, fitting within the definition of "employee"
under the common-law definition articulated in *Nationwide Mutual Insurance Co. v.
Darden,* 503 U.S. 318 (1992), does not automatically entitle one to benefits under an
ERISA plan's definition of employee; it only entitles one to standing. *Trombetta v.
Cragin Fed. Bank for Sav. Employee Stock Ownership Plan,* 102 F.3d 1435, 1440
(7th Cir. 1997). The Seventh Circuit has held that "[n]othing in ERISA ... compels
a plan to use the term 'employee' in the same way it is used in the statute....
[B]ecause a plan governed by ERISA need not include all categories of employees,
there is no reason to expect that it would." *Id.*

Former employees are eligible under ERISA if they have a colorable claim to
benefits. *Miller,* 39 F.3d at 758. A working joint shareholder is considered a participant in an ERISA plan where the plan covers the joint shareholder and other
nonowner employees even though no nonowner employees remain covered at the
time of the dispute. *In re Baker,* 114 F.3d 636 (7th Cir. 1997). The Seventh Circuit
went further in both *Shyman,* 427 F.3d 452, and *Ruttenberg,* 413 F.3d 652, where the
court held that commodity traders who were independent contractors were also participants and/or beneficiaries in employee benefit plans sponsored by the clearing-
houses through which the traders cleared their trades. *But see* Department of Labor
amicus brief in *Yates v. Hendon,* 541 U.S. 1 (2004) (arguing that a "beneficiary" of a
plan can be designated as such only by a "participant"). An employer need not provide the same benefits to all of its employees so long as the employer treats similarly situated employees the same. *Rush v. McDonald's Corp.,* 966 F.2d 1104,
1120–21 (7th Cir. 1992).

## C. Interpretation of Safe Harbor Regulation

A district court's finding that a plan is an ERISA plan is a finding of fact that can be reversed only where it is clearly erroneous. *See, e.g., Postma v. Paul Revere Life Ins. Co.*, 223 F.3d 533, 537 (7th Cir. 2000). Among other things, an ERISA plan must be established or maintained by an employer. An employer establishes or maintains an ERISA plan if it enters into a contract with an insurer and pays the premiums. *See, e.g., Brundage-Peterson v. Compcare Health Serv. Ins. Corp.*, 877 F.2d 509, 511 (7th Cir. 1989). An employer may also establish or maintain an insurance policy as part of an ERISA plan where it pays premiums for a time, where the policy is part of a broader benefits package that is financed in whole or in part by the employer, and where the employer carries out some of the administrative functions associated with maintenance of the policy. *Postma*, 223 F.3d at 538. *See also Reber v. Provident Life & Acc. Ins. Co.*, 93 F. Supp. 2d 995 (S.D. Ind. 2000) (finding that law firm employer established or maintained an ERISA plan by its subsidy of the agreement and payment arrangements when the firm wrote checks that purchased the policy, established a system whereby the law firm would pay the premiums, and received refund checks when the policies were cancelled).

The Department of Labor's "safe harbor" regulation, 29 C.F.R. § 2510.3-1(j), provides guidelines for when a plan does not fall under ERISA. A plan might fall outside of regulation under ERISA if:

> (1) No contributions are made by an employer or employee organization;
>
> (2) Participation [in] the program is completely voluntary for employees or members;
>
> (3) The sole functions of the employer or employee organization . . . are . . . to permit the insurer to publicize the program to employees or members, to collect premiums through payroll deductions or dues checkoffs and to remit them to the insurer; and
>
> (4) The employer or employee organization receives no consideration in the form of cash or otherwise in connection with the program, other than reasonable compensation, excluding any profit, for administrative services actually rendered in connection with payroll deductions or dues checkoffs.

29 C.F.R. 2510.3-1(j). A plan is outside of the safe harbor where the employer enters into a contract with an insurer for a group insurance plan and designates which employees are eligible for coverage under the contract. *See, e.g., Postma*, 223 F.3d at 538. A plan is also outside of the safe harbor if the employer helps to defray the costs of the insurance coverage. *Id.*

## D. Amount of Employer Involvement Required to Sustain an Employee Welfare Benefit Plan

See discussion in Section I.C, *supra.*

## E. Treatment of Multiple Employer Trusts and Welfare Agreements

In *Ed Miniat*, 805 F.2d 732, the Seventh Circuit held that an employer's subscription to a multiple employer trust constitutes the establishment of an ERISA welfare plan where the subscription is for the purpose of providing insured welfare benefits to one or more classes of employees. Upon consideration of ERISA statutory language that "any residual assets of a single plan may be distributed to the employer," the court in *Chicago Truck Drivers v. Local 710*, 2005 WL 525427 (N.D. Ill. 2005), held that this language does not prevent compensation from being distributed to three employers when all three employers have made contributions to the plan. *Id.* at *10. In *Chicago Truck Drivers*, the group policy was owned by the employers and the plan was silent with respect to how to treat demutualization compensation. *Id.*

## II. Preemption

### A. Scope of ERISA Preemption

ERISA's preemption provision states that federal law "supersede[s] any and all State laws insofar as they may now or hereafter relate to any employee benefit plan." 29 U.S.C. § 1144(a). A state-law claim relates to an employee benefit plan if it has a connection with or reference to such a plan. *Sembos v. Philips Components*, 376 F.3d 696, 703 (7th Cir. 2004). Relying on Supreme Court authorities such as *Pilot Life Insurance Co. v. Dedeaux*, 481 U.S. 41 (1987), and *Metropolitan Life Insurance Co. v. Taylor*, 481 U.S. 58 (1987), the Seventh Circuit has held that state-law claims such as breach of contract and bad faith are preempted by ERISA and that ERISA's civil enforcement provisions are the exclusive means of remedying a wrongful denial of plan benefits. *See, e.g., Panaras v. Liquid Carbonic Indus. Corp.*, 74 F.3d 786 (7th Cir. 1996) (breach-of-contract claims preempted by ERISA); *Tomczyk v. Blue Cross & Blue Shield United of Wisconsin*, 951 F.2d 771 (7th Cir. 1991), *cert. denied*, 504 U.S. 940 (1992) (bad-faith claims preempted by ERISA). More recently, again following the Supreme Court's refinement of ERISA preemption principles, the Seventh Circuit has identified three categories of state laws that are preempted by ERISA: (1) state laws that mandate employee benefit structures or their administration; (2) state laws that bind employers or plan administrators to particular choices or preclude uniform administrative practices, thereby functioning as a regulation of an ERISA plan itself; and (3) state laws that provide an alternative enforcement mechanism to ERISA. *Trustees of AFTRA Health Fund v. Biondi*, 303 F.3d 765, 775 (7th Cir. 2002).

In *Rush Prudential HMO, Inc. v. Moran*, 536 U.S. 355 (2002), the Supreme Court affirmed a Seventh Circuit decision holding that a state law mandating independent review of a health insurer's medical necessity determination was "saved" from preemption as a state law that regulated insurance under 29 U.S.C. § 1144. In reaching its conclusion, the Supreme Court relied on the fact that the state regulatory scheme at issue provided no new cause of action and authorized no new form of relief, but instead promulgated a procedural rule of the type ERISA does not preempt. *Id.* at 379–80.

### B. Preemption of Managed-Care Claims

In *Rush Prudential HMO, Inc. v. Moran*, 536 U.S. 355 (2002), the Supreme Court upheld a Seventh Circuit decision that a state third-party review law regulated insurance and, consequently, was not preempted by ERISA. As yet, the Seventh Circuit has not specifically addressed the preemptive effect of the Supreme Court's ruling in *Pegram v. Herdrich,* 530 U.S. 211 (2000), which found that mixed eligibility/treatment decisions by an HMO through its physician were not fiduciary decisions regulated by ERISA, as that decision might affect the preemption of managed care and/or medical malpractice claims. *See Klassy v. Physicians Plus Ins. Co.,* 371 F.3d 952, 956 (7th Cir. 2004) (ruling that there was no need to discuss the precise boundaries of *Pegram* because a decision to deny benefits for a proposed surgery was purely an eligibility decision remedied by ERISA).

### C. Preemption of Malpractice Claims

Although *Aetna Health Inc. v. Davila,* 542 U.S. 200 (2004), made clear that efforts to bring malpractice claims against employee benefit plans are preempted by ERISA, the Seventh Circuit has decided a number of cases on that issue. In *Rice v. Panchal,* 65 F.3d 637, 646 (7th Cir. 1995), the court held that a suit against an ERISA health plan insurer alleging vicarious liability for the malpractice of a network physician was not completely preempted by ERISA for removal jurisdiction purposes (i.e., it did not fall within the scope of ERISA's civil enforcement section, 29 U.S.C. § 1132(a)), in part because the claim did not rest on the terms of the ERISA plan and could be resolved without interpreting the ERISA-governed plan. Because the court held that it did not have jurisdiction over the state-law claim, the court did not address whether the vicarious liability claim was preempted by ERISA's preemption provision, 29 U.S.C. § 1144(a), although it acknowledged that this was an issue that the state court would need to resolve on remand. In *Jass v. Prudential Health Care Plan,* 88 F.3d 1482, 1495 (7th Cir. 1996), the court held that a medical malpractice claim against a nurse who worked as a utilization review administrator for an ERISA plan insurer was completely preempted by ERISA and would be recharacterized as a claim for plan benefits under ERISA, 29 U.S.C. § 1132(a)(1)(B). The court also held that a state-law claim of vicarious liability against the plan insurer arising from the alleged negligence of the attending physician's "failure to treat," which extended from the utilization reviewer's refusal to authorize the treatment, was preempted by ERISA 29 U.S..C. § 1144(a) because the vicarious liability claim "relate[d] to" the ERISA health plan. *See also Lehmann v. Brown,* 230 F.3d 916, 920 (7th Cir. 2000) (stating that ERISA does not attempt to specify standards of medical care); *Klassy v. Physicians Plus Ins. Co.,* 371 F.3d 952, 957 (7th Cir. 2004) (finding preemption after recharacterizing a provider's decision regarding an out-of-network doctor as a denial of benefits claim).

### D. Other Preemption Issues

The Seventh Circuit has held that a state-law doctrine of substantial compliance "relates to" an ERISA plan and is preempted. *Metro. Life Ins. Co. v. Johnson,* 297 F.3d 558, 566 (7th Cir. 2002). The Seventh Circuit ruled in *Administrative Committee of the Wal-Mart Stores, Inc. Associates' Health & Welfare Plan v. Varco,* 338 F.3d 680 (7th Cir. 2003), that though the equitable common fund doctrine survived ERISA preemption, plan language explicitly disclaiming the applicability of that doctrine trumps state law.

# III. Exhaustion of Administrative Remedies

## A. Is Exhaustion an Absolute Requirement?

On several occasions, the Seventh Circuit has applied an exhaustion-of-remedies requirement in ERISA benefit disputes. *See, e.g., Stark v. PPM Am.*, 354 F.3d 666 (7th Cir. 2004); *Zhou v. Guardian Life Ins. Co.*, 295 F.3d 677 (7th Cir. 2002); *Gallegos v. Mount Sinai Med. Ctr.*, 210 F.3d 803 (7th Cir. 2000). Exhaustion is favored because the plan's review process may resolve a number of issues, the facts and the administrator's interpretation of the plan may be clarified, and exhaustion encourages private resolution of disputes. *Id.* In addition, the Seventh Circuit is one of the few circuits to also require exhaustion of remedies in matters based on alleged violations of ERISA statutory duties. *See, e.g., Ames v. Am. Nat'l Can Co.*, 170 F.3d 751 (7th Cir. 1999). In the context of class actions under ERISA, the Seventh Circuit has recognized that in some cases, "requiring exhaustion by the individual class members would merely produce an avalanche of duplicative proceedings and accidental forfeitures." *In re Household Int'l Tax Reduction Plan*, 441 F.3d 500, 501 (7th Cir. 2006). However, like other types of ERISA actions, in class action suits the district court has discretion whether or not to require exhaustion of remedies. *Id.*

## B. Exceptions to the Exhaustion Requirement

The Seventh Circuit treats a failure to exhaust internal remedies as an affirmative defense. *Mosley v. Bd. of Educ. of City of Chi.*, 434 F.3d 527, 533 (7th Cir. 2006). Accordingly, in order to avoid the exhaustion requirement once a defendant has satisfied its defense, a plaintiff has the burden of proving that an administrative appeal would be futile or that the plaintiff was not afforded meaningful access to the plan's administrative process. *Gallegos*, 210 F.3d 803. *See also Ruttenberg v. U.S. Life Ins. Co.*, 413 F.3d 652, 662 (7th Cir. 2005). The exhaustion requirement may also be excused if the plaintiff relies to her detriment on written misrepresentations by the plan insurer or the plan administrator. *See, e.g., Bowerman v. Wal-Mart Stores, Inc.*, 226 F.3d 574 (7th Cir. 2000). Exhaustion may also be waived at the discretion of the court. *Salus v. GTE Directories Serv. Corp.*, 104 F.3d 131 (7th Cir. 1997).

## C. Consequences of Failure to Exhaust

Dismissal is an appropriate remedy for a plaintiff's failure to exhaust administrative remedies. *Gallegos*, 210 F.3d 803.

## D. Minimum Number of Levels of Administrative Review

There is nothing unique in the Seventh Circuit regarding this issue.

## E. Can a Defendant Waive a Failure-to-Exhaust Defense?

Since a failure to exhaust is an affirmative defense, defendants can waive the defense. *See Massey v. Helman*, 196 F.3d 727, 734–35 (7th Cir. 2000). However, failure to raise the defense in the answer does not constitute a waiver as long as the defendant asserts the affirmative defense in a subsequent motion to dismiss. *Id.* See discussion in Section III.B, *supra*.

# IV. Standard of Review

## A. Plan Language

The Seventh Circuit has approved specific language that will grant discretion and require application of a deferential review standard: "Benefits under this plan will be paid only if the plan administrator decides in his discretion that the applicant is entitled to them." *Herzberger v. Standard Ins. Co.,* 205 F.3d 327, 331 (7th Cir. 2000). The court reinforced that holding in *Diaz v. Prudential Insurance Co. of America,* 422 F.3d 630 (7th Cir. 2005), where the court explicitly overturned prior rulings that upheld more lenient language in granting discretion.

The court ruled in *Ruiz v. Continental Casualty Co.,* 400 F.3d 986 (7th Cir. 2005), that language conveying discretion could be located in the policy certificate; similarly, in *Semien v. Life Insurance Co. of North America,* 436 F.3d 805 (7th Cir. 2006), the court found discretion from its examination of a series of plan documents that made it clear to the court that the plan sponsor intended a reservation of discretion. However, in *Sperando v. Lorillard Tobacco Co.,* 2006 U.S. App. Lexis 21216 (7th Cir. August 18, 2006), the court held that discretionary language appearing in the certificate but not in the master policy did not grant discretion where the certificate was not incorporated into the master policy.

## B. What Standard of Review Applies?

If an ERISA plan grants discretion to a claim administrator to interpret plan terms or to determine eligibility for plan benefits, the reviewing court will employ the arbitrary and capricious standard of review. *Blickenstaff v. R.R. Donnelley & Sons Co.,* 378 F.3d 669, 677 (7th Cir. 2004). *See also Dabertin v. HCR Manor Care, Inc.,* 373 F.3d 822, 827 (7th Cir. 2004) (recognizing that once the court determines that proper discretion was granted, the review is limited to whether actions pursuant to this discretion were arbitrary and capricious). The plan language that is in effect at the time the claim arises controls whether or not a court will apply an arbitrary and capricious review standard. Thus, even if a plan under which a claimant is initially found disabled did not contain discretionary language, if benefits are subsequently terminated the court applies the language of the plan in existence at the time of the termination. *Hackett v. Xerox Corp. Long-Term Disability Income Plan,* 315 F.3d 771 (7th Cir. 2003).

Where the arbitrary and capricious standard is applicable, a court will not substitute its judgment for that of the claim administrator, but will overturn the claim administrator's decision only if it is "downright unreasonable." *See, e.g., Cozzie v. Metro. Life Ins. Co.,* 140 F.3d 1104 (7th Cir. 1998). Under this standard, the reviewing court will uphold the administrator's decision as long as it has rational support in the record. *Davis v. Unum Life Ins. Co. of Am.,* 444 F.3d 569, 576 (7th Cir. 2006) (finding rational support in the record for a denial of disability benefits where the insurer relied on in-house medical personnel). Nonetheless, the Seventh Circuit has also explained, "deferential review is not no review," and "deference need not be abject." *Gallo v. Amoco Corp.,* 102 F.3d 918, 922 (7th Cir. 1996). In some cases, the plain language or structure of the plan will require the court to pronounce an administrator's determination arbitrary and capricious. *Hess v. Hartford Life & Accident Ins. Co.,* 274 F.3d 456, 461 (7th Cir. 2001). In other cases, the Seventh Circuit has held that a decision will not be overturned under an arbitrary and capricious review standard if (1) it is possible to offer a reasoned explanation, based on the evidence, for a particular outcome; (2) the decision is based on a reasonable explanation of relevant plan documents; or (3) the claim administrator has based its decision on a consideration of the relevant factors that encompass important aspects of the problem. *Militello v. Cent. States,* 360 F.3d at 686.

### C. Effect of Conflict of Interest or Procedural Irregularity

The Seventh Circuit was one of the first jurisdictions to apply a sliding scale analysis to the deferential review standard under ERISA to take into account a claim administrator's conflict of interest. *See, e.g., Van Boxel v. Journal Co. Employees' Pension Trust,* 836 F.2d 1048, 1052 (7th Cir. 1987) ("the arbitrary and capricious standard may be a range, not a point"). *See also Mers v. Marriott Int'l Group Accidental Death & Dismemberment Plan,* 144 F.3d 1014, 1020 n.1 (7th Cir. 1998) ("The arbitrary and capricious standard does not pose an all-or-nothing choice between full deference or none. Courts may vary the deference incrementally to account for the strength or weakness of a specific conflict of interest."). In order for a court to apply less deference in the face of a conflict, the plaintiff has the burden to prove more than a potential conflict (e.g., the "inherent" conflict of an insurer that decides whether or not to pay benefits under a fully insured benefit plan). Rather, the plaintiff must prove that a conflict of interest actually affected the administrator's decision on the plaintiff's claim. *Mers,* 144 F.3d at 1020–21; *Leipzig v. AIG Life Ins. Co.,* 362 F.3d 406, 408–09 (7th Cir. 2004). The Seventh Circuit has pointed out, though:

> When it is "possible to question the fiduciaries' loyalty, they are obliged at a minimum to engage in an intensive and scrupulous independent investigation of their options to insure that they act in the best interests of the plan beneficiaries." *Leigh v. Engle,* 727 F.2d 113, 125–26 (7th Cir. 1984). Seeking independent expert advice is evidence of a thorough investigation, and provided that the fiduciary has investigated the expert's qualifications, has provided the expert with complete and accurate information, and determined that reliance on the expert's advice is reasonably justified under the circumstances, the fiduciary's decision will be respected, despite the conflict of interest. *Howard v. Shay,* 100 F.3d 1484, 1488 (9th Cir. 1996).

*Hightshue v. AIG Life Ins. Co.,* 135 F.3d 1144, 1148 (7th Cir. 1998). Decisions by claim administrators are not cloaked with the same level of authority as administrative agencies, but once an ERISA plan grants a claim administrator discretionary authority, the claim administrator's motivations should not be questioned absent a prima facie showing of some misconduct or conflict of interest. *Semien v. Life Ins. Co. of N. Am.,* 436 F.3d 805, 814 (7th Cir. 2006). Reviewing courts presume a plan and its claim administrator act neutrally unless shown otherwise. *Dougherty v. Ind. Bell Tel. Co.,* 440 F.3d 910, 915–16 (7th Cir. 2006). Therefore, in order for a reviewing court to impose a less deferential standard than the arbitrary and capricious review, the plaintiff must prove with specific evidence an actual bias on the part of the claim administrator that creates a significant conflict. *Id.; see also Davis v. Unum Life Ins. Co. of Am.*, 444 F.3d 569, 575 (7th Cir. 2006) ("We presume neutrality unless a claimant shows by providing specific evidence of actual bias that there is a significant conflict.").

In summary, the Seventh Circuit has been reluctant to find a conflict of interest. Characterizing the inherent conflict of an insurer serving as both the payor of benefits and decision maker as ubiquitous in *Liberty Life Assurance Co.*, 438 F.3d 772 (7th Cir. 2006), the court dismissed allegations of a conflict. Other recent decisions rejecting conflict of interest include *Kobs v. United Wisconsin Insurance Co.*, 400 F.3d 1036 (7th Cir. 2005), *Shyman v. Unum Life Insurance Co.*, 427 F.3d 452 (7th Cir. 2005), and *Davis v. Unum Life Insurance Co. of America*, 2006 U.S. App. LEXIS 8167 (7th Cir. 4/5/2006). The *Davis* ruling also found nothing impermissible about utilizing in-house physicians as the sole basis for terminating benefits under a fully insured long-term disability plan.

### D. Other Factors Affecting Standard of Review

In *Ruiz v. Continental Casualty Co.*, 400 F.3d 986 (7th Cir. 2005), the court held that an insurance certificate is a plan document and that discretionary language in the certificate is sufficient to require an arbitrary and capricious review standard. *See also Shyman v. Unum Life Ins. Co.*, 427 F.3d 452, 455 (7th Cir. 2005) (finding discretion-granting language in the certificate of insurance when the contract declared that the certificate is part of the policy unless it contradicts other clauses).

## V. Rules of Plan Interpretation

### A. Application of Federal Common Law

Principles of federal common law govern the interpretation of ERISA plan terms. *See, e.g., Neuma, Inc. v. Amp, Inc.*, 259 F.3d 864 (7th Cir. 2001); *Hammond v. Fidelity & Guar. Life Ins. Co.*, 965 F.2d 428 (7th Cir. 1992); *Bowles v. Quantum Chem. Co.*, 266 F.3d 622, 633 (7th Cir. 2002) ("Because we have determined that Quantum's severance plan is governed by ERISA, we shall construe the plan in accordance with the federal common law under ERISA and shall apply general rules of contract interpretation."). Federal common law "direct[s] us to interpret ERISA plans in an ordinary and popular sense as would a person of average intelligence and experience." *Neuma*, 259 F.3d at 873. *See also Grun v. Pneumo Abex Corp.*, 163 F.3d 411, 419 (7th Cir. 1998). When interpreting an ERISA plan, the court's first task is to determine whether the plan language is ambiguous or unambiguous. *Kamler v. H/N Telecomm. Servs., Inc.*, 305 F.3d 672, 680 (7th Cir. 2002). Where plan language is unambiguous, a court will not look beyond its "four corners" in interpreting its meaning. *Neuma*, 259 F.3d at 873. Unambiguous provisions in ERISA plan documents must be interpreted in accordance with their plain meaning and enforced as written. *Favre v. Prudential Ins. Co. of Am.*, 2006 WL 449204, at *4 (N.D. Ind. 2006). On the other hand, where plan language is ambiguous, a court may look to extrinsic evidence to determine its intended meaning. *Anstett v. Eagle-Pitcher Indus., Inc.,* 203 F.3d 501 (7th Cir. 2000).

## B. Application of *Contra Proferentem*

Where extrinsic evidence does not resolve the ambiguity, a court may apply the *contra proferentem* rule, which construes ambiguities against the drafter of the contract, under principles of federal common law. *Hall v. Life Ins. Co. of N. Am.,* 317 F.3d 773, 776 (7th Cir. 2003). However, *contra proferentem* is just a tiebreaker, and it does not entitle insureds to prevail simply because lay readers do not know all technical details of the law. *Id.* at 776. Even if extrinsic evidence is not first considered to resolve an ambiguous term, the court can apply *contra proferentem* in circumstances where the plan administrator was not empowered to interpret the contract terms, the parties failed to offer extrinsic evidence, and application of the doctrine would serve its function to prevent traps for the unwary. *Ruttenberg,* 413 F.3d at 666.

## C. Deference Afforded to an Administrator's Interpretation of a Plan

The Seventh Circuit gives "great deference" to an administrator's interpretation of its plan, "including its interpretation of the ambiguous language in the Plan." *Dabertin v. HCR Manor Care, Inc.,* 373 F.3d 822, 833 (7th Cir. 2004) (applying an arbitrary and capricious standard); *see also James v. Gen. Motors Corp.,* 230 F.3d 315, 317 (7th Cir. 2000) (stating that a benefit determination will be found arbitrary and capricious only when "downright unreasonable"). When a plan gives the administrator discretion to interpret it, the court will not merely apply federal common-law principles of contract interpretation, but instead will view the contractual ambiguity through a lens that gives broad discretion to the plan administrator to interpret the plan. *Hess v. Reg-Ellen Mach. Tool Corp.,* 423 F.3d 653, 660 (7th Cir. 2005). Furthermore, deference to the claim administrator's interpretation is especially applicable where the language at issue is ambiguous. *Id.* However, even when applying a deferential standard of review, the court will not apply a "rubber stamp" to a fiduciary's decision. *Hackett v. Xerox Corp. Long-Term Disability Income Plan,* 315 F.3d 771, 774 (7th Cir. 2003). "In some cases, . . . simple common sense will require the court to pronounce an administrator's determination arbitrary and capricious." *Hess v. Hartford Life & Accident Ins. Co.,* 274 F.3d 456, 461 (7th Cir. 2001).

## D. Other Rules of Plan or Contract Interpretation

As do other circuits, the Seventh Circuit eliminates all reference to state common law regarding the interpretation of ERISA plans. *Hammond,* 965 F.2d 428, 430 ("ambiguities in ERISA plans and insurance policies should be resolved by referring to the federal common law rules of contract interpretation"). Applying federal common law, the terms of a contract are to be interpreted "in an ordinary and popular sense as would a [person] of average intelligence and experience." *GCIU Employer Ret. Fund v. Chi. Tribune Co.,* 66 F.3d 862, 865 (7th Cir. 1995) (citing *Phillips v. Lincoln Nat'l Life Ins. Co.,* 978 F.2d 302, 308 (7th Cir. 1992)). The Seventh Circuit will not use extrinsic evidence to add terms to a contract that is plausibly complete without them. *Bidlack v. Wheelabrator Corp.,* 993 F.2d 603, 608 (7th Cir. 1993), *cert. denied,* 510 U.S. 909 (1993). Similarly, extrinsic evidence cannot be used to rebut a motion for summary judgment unless patent or latent ambiguity can be proven. *Cherry v. Auburn Gear, Inc.,* 441 F.3d 476, 481 (7th Cir. 2006).

# VI. Discovery

## A. Limitations on Discovery

In *Perlman v. Swiss Bank Corp. Comprehensive Disability Protection Plan,* 195 F.3d 975 (7th Cir. 1999), the Seventh Circuit criticized a district court for allowing interrogatories and depositions of an administrator's claim personnel regarding their training, thought processes, and "in general who said what to whom" in a case involving an arbitrary and capricious review standard. The court held as follows:

> Deferential review of an administrative decision means review on the administrative record. We have allowed parties to take discovery and present new evidence in ERISA cases subject to *de novo* judicial decisions . . . but never where the question is whether a decision is supported by substantial evidence, or is arbitrary and capricious. . . . [W]hen there can be no doubt that the application was given a genuine evaluation, judicial review is limited to the evidence that was submitted in support of the application for benefits, and the mental processes of the plan's administrator are not legitimate grounds of inquiry any more than they would be if the decisionmaker were an administrative agency.

*Id.* at 981–82. However, the court said that "discovery may be appropriate to investigate a claim that the plan's administrator did not do what it said it did—that, for example, the application was thrown in the trash rather than evaluated on the merits." *Id.* In *Semien v. Life Insurance Co. of North America,* 436 F.3d 805 (7th Cir. 2006), the court reiterated *Perlman*'s prohibition against discovery, allowing it only if the claimant could first present credible evidence of bias or corruption in the review process. If the plaintiff can make a prima facie showing of misconduct or bias, or proves a good-faith basis that such evidence will materialize following limited discovery, then impartiality and a genuine review may be questioned and district courts may allow limited discovery. *Id.* at 813–14.

However, in *Burns v. American United Life Insurance Co.,* 2006 U.S. Dist. LEXIS 20096 (S.D. Ill. 4/17/2006), discovery was permitted when the de novo standard of review applied.

## B. Discovery and Conflict of Interest

At least two district courts in the Seventh Circuit have allowed limited discovery regarding a decision maker's conflict of interest. *Robbins v. Milliman U.S. Long Term Disability Ins. Plan,* 2003 U.S. Dist. LEXIS 17138, at *20 (S.D. Ind. 2003) ("[b]ecause the Seventh Circuit recognizes that the potential conflict or bias of an actual decision maker is a relevant factor to be weighed in evaluating whether the denial of benefits was arbitrary and capricious, under Rule 26(b) information regarding such a potential conflict or bias is discoverable"); *Fowler v. Williams Cos.,* 2005

U.S. Dist. LEXIS 5025, at *6–7 (W.D. Wis. 2005) (allowing limited discovery into the funding of benefits and the manner in which the compensation and promotion opportunities of benefits staff were determined). However, in *Semien v. Life Insurance Co. of North America*, 436 F.3d 805 (7th Cir. 2006), the court disallowed discovery even as to bias.

## VII. Evidence

### A. Scope of Evidence under Standards of Review

Where an arbitrary and capricious review standard is applicable, a court's review is limited to the evidence that was before the claim administrator at the time of its final decision, and the court acts in the capacity of a reviewing court. *See, e.g., Semien v. Life Ins. Co. of N. Am.*, 436 F.3d 805 (7th Cir. 2006); *Militello v. Cent. States*, 360 F.3d at 686; *Perlman v. Swiss Bank Corp. Comprehensive Disability Protection Plan*, 195 F.3d 975 (7th Cir. 1999); *Casey v. Uddeholm Corp.*, 32 F.3d 1094, 1098–99 & n.4 (7th Cir. 1994). Under the arbitrary and capricious standard of review, the court does not consider whether the decision maker reached the correct conclusion or whether it relied on proper authority; the only relevant inquiry is whether the decision was completely unreasonable. *Kobs v. United Wisc. Ins. Co.*, 400 F.3d 1036, 1039 (7th Cir. 2005). Because this standard of review is deferential, the reviewing court can consider only evidence that was before the decision maker at the time of its final decision. *Militello*, 360 F.3d at 686.

A claim that the terms of a plan violate ERISA is a legal issue subject to de novo review. *Silvernail v. Ameritech Pension Plan*, 439 F.3d 355, 357 (7th Cir. 2006). Additionally, where the de novo review standard is applicable because no discretion has been granted to the claim administrator, a court has discretion to limit its review to the administrative record or, alternatively, to admit additional evidence where such evidence is necessary for the court to conduct an adequate review of the claim administrator's decision. *Casey v. Uddeholm Corp.*, 32 F.3d 1094, 1098–99 & n.4 (7th Cir. 1994). *See also Wilczynski v. Kemper Nat'l Ins. Cos.*, 178 F.3d 933, 938 n.14 (7th Cir. 1999).

In *Perlman*, 195 F.3d 975, the Seventh Circuit acknowledged a willingness to allow parties additional discovery and present new evidence in ERISA cases subject to de novo review, but stated it has "never [done so] where the question is whether a decision is supported by substantial evidence, or is arbitrary and capricious." *Id.* at 982. Although "discovery may be appropriate to investigate a claim [regardless of the standard of review] that the plan administrator did not do what it said it did . . . when there can be no doubt that the application was given a genuine evaluation, judicial review is limited to the evidence that was submitted in support of the application for benefits, and the mental processes of the plan's administrator are not legitimate grounds of inquiry . . . " *Id.* Thus, even in a case governed by an arbitrary and capricious review standard, a court may consider additional evidence to resolve a dispute over the makeup of the administrative record. *Cf. Militello v. Cent. States*, 360 F.3d at 686–88. In administrative proceedings, a claim administrator is not bound by formal evidentiary rules in determining whether or not to admit specific evidence. *See, e.g., Karr v. Nat'l Asbestos Workers Pension Fund,* 150 F.3d 812 (7th Cir. 1998).

## B. Evidentiary Value of Social Security Determinations

Determinations and decisions made by the Social Security Administration and other plan administrators are instructive, but are not binding in ERISA actions. *See, e.g., Tegtmeier v. Midwest Operating Eng'rs,* 390 F.3d 1040 (7th Cir. 2004); *Anderson v. Operative Plasterers' & Cement Masons' Int'l. Assoc.,* 991 F.2d 356 (7th Cir. 1993). The Seventh Circuit has also discussed the possibility of applying judicial estoppel principles where a disability plan actively pursues a claimant's Social Security claim. *See, e.g., Ladd v. ITT Corp.,* 148 F.3d 753, 755–56 (7th Cir. 1998).

# VIII. Procedural Aspects of ERISA Practice

## A. Methods of Adjudication

Most ERISA benefit disputes in the Seventh Circuit have been decided by summary judgment. However, more recently, there has been less consistency. Some district judges in the Southern District of Indiana prefer "paper bench trials" (i.e., where the parties submit the administrative record, plan documents, and written argument). One district in the Seventh Circuit highly recommends adjudication through trial on the papers, contending that such a method eliminates problems of nondecision, unnecessary litigation, additional costs, and unnecessary delay. *See Crespo v. Unum Life Ins. Co. of Am.,* 294 F. Supp. 2d 980, 991–92 (N.D. Ill. 2003) (finding trial on the papers beneficial because it is certain to result in a decision for one party rather than present the risk of a nondecision; it does not require a remand for a new trial if reversed on appeal; and it does not require complex mental gymnastics such as drawing particular inferences in favor of one party). Nonetheless, in *Coles v. LaSalle Partners Inc. Disability Plan,* 287 F. Supp. 2d 896 (N.D. Ill. 2003), the court refused to conduct a paper trial absent the parties' stipulation, and the court denied cross-motions for summary judgment, finding that a genuine issue of material fact precluded the entry of either motion for summary judgment. *Id.*

## B. Reported ERISA Trials

Because ERISA provides only equitable remedies, there is no right to a jury trial. *Mathews v. Sears Pension Plan,* 144 F.3d 461, 468 (7th Cir. 1998). *Hess v. Hartford Life & Accident Insurance Co.,* 274 F.3d 456, 461 (7th Cir. 2001), supported the resolution of ERISA cases by a trial on the papers. Such a procedure was also followed in *LaBarge v. Life Insurance Co. of North America,* 2001 WL 109527 (N.D. Ill. 2001), and in *Deal v. Prudential Insurance Co. of America,* 263 F. Supp. 2d 1138 (N.D. Ill. 2003). Moreover, in *Crespo v. Unum Life Insurance Co. of America,* 294 F. Supp. 2d 980 (N.D. Ill. 2003), the court recommended a trial on the papers due to the unsuitability of summary judgment as a means of resolving ERISA benefit disputes.

## IX. Fiduciary Liability Claims

### A. Definition of Fiduciary

Fiduciaries are defined by the ERISA statute. 29 U.S.C. § 1002(21)(A). Fiduciary status under ERISA is to be liberally construed in a way consistent with ERISA's policies and objectives. *Smith v. Aon Corp.,* 2006 WL 1006052, at *4 (N.D. Ill. 2006). A person can be deemed a fiduciary either by assumption of the fiduciary duties or by express designation in the applicable ERISA plan documents. *Id.* Applying the statutory definition, the Seventh Circuit has held that discretionary authority with respect to the administration of a plan is a sine qua non of fiduciary status under ERISA. *See, e.g., Pohl v. Nat'l Benefits Consultants, Inc.,* 956 F.2d 126, 128 (7th Cir. 1991). Management or control of plan assets also results in fiduciary status. *See, e.g., Peoria Union Stock Yards Co. Ret. Plan v. Penn Mut. Life Ins. Co.,* 698 F.2d 320, 327 (7th Cir. 1983) A health plan third-party administrator that has no authority to make final claims decisions is not a fiduciary. *See, e.g., Klosterman v. Western Gen. Mgmt., Inc.,* 32 F.3d 1119, 1123 (7th Cir. 1994). There is no per se rule that prevents professionals who give advice to an ERISA plan from becoming fiduciaries. *Pappas v. Buck Consultants, Inc.,* 923 F.2d 531, 538 (7th Cir. 1991). Whether a consultant has exercised the degree of influence over a plan to constitute a fiduciary is a fact sensitive analysis. *Id.* Finally, the court held in *Wallace v. Reliance Standard Life Insurance Co.,* 318 F.3d 723 (7th Cir. 2003), that a disability insurer is not necessarily a fiduciary under ERISA where it has not been granted discretion to make benefit eligibility determinations. Some contend that the latter holding may be altered by *Aetna Health v. Calad,* 2004 U.S. Lexis 4571 (2004).

### B. Definition of Fiduciary Duties

Fiduciaries have a duty not to mislead plan participants or misrepresent the terms or administration of a plan. *Schmidt v. Sheet Metal Workers' Nat'l Pension Fund,* 128 F.3d 541, 546 (7th Cir. 1997); *Anweiler v. Am. Elec. Power Serv. Corp.,* 3 F.3d 986, 991 (7th Cir. 1993); *Peoria Union Stock Yards Co. Ret. Plan v. Penn Mut. Life Ins. Co.,* 698 F.2d 320, 326 (7th Cir. 1983) (lying is inconsistent with the duty of loyalty owed by all fiduciaries). A fiduciary also has a duty to administer a plan in accordance with its terms. *See, e.g., Swaback v. Am. Info. Techs. Corp.,* 103 F.3d 535 (7th Cir. 1996). However, a fiduciary can wear two hats, and when a fiduciary is not performing an ERISA-regulated discretionary function, its actions are not subject to ERISA's fiduciary provisions. For example, where an employer amends or terminates a benefit plan, the employer is not acting in a fiduciary capacity and decisions to amend or terminate the plan are not regulated by ERISA's fiduciary requirements. *See, e.g., Baker v. Kingsley,* 387 F.3d 649 (7th Cir. 2004); *Ames v. Am. Nat'l Can Co.,* 170 F.3d 751 (7th Cir. 1999).

### C. Fiduciary Liability in the Context of Health and Disability Claims

A person who is not a fiduciary cannot be held liable for a breach of fiduciary duties under ERISA. *See, e.g., Tegtmeier v. Midwest Operating Eng'rs,* 390 F.3d 1040, 1047 (7th Cir. 2004). A person is a fiduciary only when performing discretionary functions. *See, e.g., Beach v. Commonwealth Edison Co.,* 382 F.3d 656, 658 (7th Cir. 2004). Where a plaintiff claims that a plan was amended to deprive him of health benefits, such a claim is not cognizable under ERISA because amendment of a health plan is not regulated by ERISA's fiduciary duty provision. *Dade v. Sherwin-Williams Co.,* 128 F.3d 1135 (7th Cir. 1997).

## D. Remedies for Breach of Fiduciary Duty

Remedies for violation of ERISA's fiduciary duty provision are limited to the remedies available under ERISA's civil enforcement section, 29 U.S.C. § 1132(a). For example, although a participant or beneficiary can bring a cause of action for breach of fiduciary duties under § 1132(a)(3), remedies under that subsection are limited to injunctive and/or equitable remedies. Damages, whether compensatory or punitive, are not available. *See, e.g., Harsch v. Eisenberg,* 956 F.3d 651 (7th Cir. 1992); *but see Clair v. Harris Trust & Savings Bank,* 190 F.3d 495, 498 (7th Cir. 1999) (recognizing that equity sometimes awards monetary relief and restitution can take the form of an equitable remedy, therefore an award of unpaid benefits is permissible under ERISA). The remedy for a plaintiff who has sued to overturn a denial of benefits under an ERISA plan should focus on what is required in each case to fully remedy defects in the claim review process given the status quo prior to the denial or termination of benefits. *Schneider v. Sentry Group Long Term Disability Plan,* 422 F.3d 621, 629 (7th Cir. 2005). Reinstatement of long-term disability benefits is appropriate to claimants who were receiving benefits and who, but for the decision maker's arbitrary and capricious conduct, would have continued to receive benefits, or where there is no evidence in the record to support a termination or denial of benefits. *Id.; Quinn v. Blue Cross & Blue Shield Assoc.,* 161 F.3d 472, 477 (7th Cir. 1998). However, where a court or agency fails to make proper findings or reasoning, the proper remedy is to remand for further findings or explanations, unless it is clear that it would be unreasonable for the claim administrator to deny the application for benefits on any ground. *Quinn,* 161 F.3d at 477.

## E. Contribution and Indemnity Claims among Fiduciaries

Older cases may suggest the possibility of contribution and indemnification claims among cofiduciaries under ERISA. *Alton Mem'l v. Metro. Life Ins. Co.,* 656 F.2d 245, 250 (7th Cir. 1981); *Free v. Briody,* 732 F.2d 1331, 1337 (7th Cir. 1984). More recent cases, however, note that the status of contribution among cofiduciaries is "still unsettled" at the circuit level. *Lumpkin v. Envirodyne Indus.,* 933 F.2d 449, 464 n.10 (7th Cir. 1991); *see also Donovan v. Robbins,* 752 F.2d 1170, 1178 (7th Cir. 1985) (following *Alton* and *Free* without deciding the issue). Some district courts have rejected the principle, finding no statutory basis for contribution among fiduciaries. *See, e.g., Mut. Life Ins. Co. v. Yampol,* 706 F. Supp. 596, 600 (N.D. Ill. 1989); *Plumbers Local 93 Health & Welfare & Pension Fund, Journeymen Training Fund & Apprenticeship Training Fund v. Dipietro Plumbing Co.,* 1999 U.S. Dist. LEXIS 6913, at *13–15 (N.D. Ill. 1999). One district court has relied on traditional trust law principles to uphold a right to contribution. *Daniels v. Bursey,* 329 F. Supp. 2d 975, 979 (N.D. Ill. 2004).

### F. ERISA Claims against Nonfiduciaries

The Seventh Circuit follows *Harris Trust & Savings Bank v. Salomon Smith Barney Inc.*, 530 U.S. 238 (2000), which reversed a Seventh Circuit decision and held that ERISA authorizes a cause of action for restitution from nonfiduciary parties in interest who engage in prohibited transactions under 29 U.S.C. § 1106(a). *Sprague v. Cent. States, Se. & Sw. Areas Pension Fund*, 269 F.3d 811, 817–18 (7th Cir. 2001) (finding no liability for a nonfiduciary employer where the employer was not obligated to contribute to an ERISA plan). According to one district court, in order to successfully plead a claim against a nonfiduciary under 29 U.S.C. § 1132(a)(3), a plaintiff must prove that a fiduciary violated a substantive provision of ERISA and that the nonfiduciary knowingly participated in the conduct that constituted the violation. *Daniels v. Bursey*, 313 F. Supp. 2d 790, 807–08 (N.D. Ill. 2004). Once a participant or beneficiary establishes that a particular transaction is prohibited under § 1106, the plaintiff can seek injunctive and/or equitable relief for the violation under § 1132(a)(3) against parties in interest. *Keach v. U.S. Trust Co., N.A.*, 244 F. Supp. 2d 968, 975 (C.D. Ill. 2003).

## X. Attorneys' Fees

### A. Criteria for Awarding Attorneys' Fees

The Seventh Circuit applies a "substantially justified" test as well as a five-factor test in determining whether attorneys' fees should be shifted to the opposing party under ERISA's fee-shifting provision. Under the five-factor test, a district court evaluates the merits of a fee request based on consideration of the following: (1) the degree of the opposing party's culpability or "bad faith"; (2) the ability of the opposing party to satisfy a fee award; (3) the degree that an award would deter other persons acting under similar circumstances; (4) the amount of benefit conferred on all plan members; and (5) the relative merits of the parties' positions. *Fritcher v. Health Care Serv. Corp.*, 301 F.3d 811, 819 (7th Cir. 2002). Under the "substantially justified" test, the district court determines whether the opposing party's position was substantially justified or taken in bad faith. *Lowe v. McGraw-Hill Cos., Inc.*, 361 F.3d 335, 339 (7th Cir. 2004). If the losing party's position was taken in good faith and between the realm of nonfrivolous and meritorious, an award of attorneys' fees will be denied to the successful party. *Herman v. Cent. States, Se. & Sw. Areas Pension Fund*, 423 F.3d 684, 695 (7th Cir. 2005). Both tests essentially posit the same inquiry: Was the losing party's position justified in good faith, or was that party simply out to harass its opponent? *Id.* An award of fees is discretionary with the district court and is reviewable only for abuse of discretion. *See, e.g., Helfrich v. Carle Clinic Ass'n, P.C.*, 328 F.3d 915, 919 (7th Cir. 2003). However, when a district court denies attorneys' fees on the basis of interpreting and applying a principle of law, the reviewing court will employ the de novo standard. *See Moriarty v. Svec*, 429 F.3d 710, 717 (7th Cir. 2005) (citing *Jaffe v. Redmond*, 142 F.3d 409, 412–13 (7th Cir. 1998)). When fees are properly awarded in the district court under the authority of a fee-shifting statute, they are automatically awarded on appeal where the underlying judgment is affirmed. *Id.*

The Seventh Circuit recognizes a modest presumption in favor of attorneys' fees awards for prevailing plaintiffs. *Fritcher v. Health Care Serv. Corp.*, 301 F.3d 811 (7th Cir. 2002); *Bowerman v. Wal-Mart Stores, Inc.*, 226 F.3d at 592. A fee request was found premature in *Ravensloot v. Administrative Committee of Baxter International, Inc.*, 2004 U.S. Dist. LEXIS 11572 (N.D. Ill. 2004), based on the fact that the court remanded the case rather than ordered the payment of benefits. *See also Carugati v. Long Term Disability Plan*, 2002 U.S. Dist. Lexis 4774 (N.D. Ill. 2002); *Quinn v. Blue Cross & Blue Shield Assoc.*, 161 F.3d 472, 479 (7th Cir. 1998) (prevailing party is entitled to a modest presumption to be awarded reasonable attorneys' fees, but having the case remanded does not make a plaintiff a prevailing party in the truest sense of the term).

### B. Fees Awarded to Plan Fiduciaries

Fee awards to prevailing defendants are unavailable in the absence of frivolousness or claims pursued in bad faith. *Harris Trust & Savings Bank v. Provident Life & Acc. Ins. Co.*, 57 F.3d 608 (7th Cir. 1995); *Senese v. Chi. Area Int'l Bhd. of Teamsters Pension Fund*, 237 F.3d 819, 826 (7th Cir. 2001).

### C. Calculation of Attorneys' Fees

The Seventh Circuit applies a lodestar formula in determining the amount of fees to be awarded, based on a calculation of the reasonable number of hours multiplied by a reasonable hourly rate for the work performed. *S..rk v. PPM Am., Inc.*, 354 F.3d 666, 674 (7th Cir. 2004). One important factor in determining the reasonableness of a fee award is the degree of success obtained in relation to the other goals of the lawsuit. *Linda v. Rice Lake Area School Dist.*, 417 F.3d 704, 708 (7th Cir. 2005). Although the district court is entitled to wide discretion and substantial deference upon review, it must demonstrate that it has considered the proportionality of the fee award to the total damages award (including settlement offers), and it must provide an explanation of the hourly rate used. *Moriarty*, 429 F.3d at 717. Fees are not awarded for work that is excessive, redundant, or unnecessary. *Id.* A district court can also reduce fees for time spent litigating claims on which the party seeking fees did not succeed to the extent those claims are distinct from the claims on which the party did succeed. *Id.* Where a defendant is entitled to fees, the defendant can recover the amount of fees incurred in producing a defense to the plaintiff's allegations. *Helfrich*, 328 F.3d at 919.

## XI. ERISA Regulations

In *Schneider v. Sentry Group Long Term Disability Plan*, 422 F.3d 621 (7th Cir. 2005), the Seventh Circuit reiterated its holding in *Halpin v. W.W. Grainger, Inc.*, 962 F.2d 685 (7th Cir. 1992), that the Department of Labor's ERISA claim regulations (29 C.F.R. §2560.503-1) are mandatory. Thus, the plan's failure to substantially comply with proper procedures for terminating benefits necessitated restoration of the status quo ante reinstatement of long-term disability benefits until proper procedures could be implemented. The primary procedural violation in *Schneider* was the claim administrator's failure to draft a proper denial letter. Similarly, in *Halpin* the issue was whether a claim administrator "substantially complied" with DOL claim procedure regulations in terminating the claimant's long-term disability benefits. The court held that the regulations require articulation of the reasons for the denial and that a full and fair review requires that claimants be given an opportunity to examine the evidence on which the decision was based. Because of the claim administrator's failure to substantially comply with the claim regulations, the Seventh Circuit vacated the claim administrator's decision, ordered the reinstatement of disability benefits, and remanded the matter to the claim administrator for further review in accordance with the regulations.

## XII. Cases Interpreting ERISA Statutes of Limitation

Because ERISA itself does not contain a statute of limitations for benefit claims, a reviewing court must apply the most analogous state statute of limitations. *See, e.g., Daill v. Sheet Metal Workers' Local 73,* 100 F.3d 62, 65 (7th Cir. 1996). In *Daill,* the Seventh Circuit held that the most analogous state statute of limitations in an ERISA benefit claim under 29 U.S.C. § 1132(a)(1)(B) was Illinois' ten-year limitations period for suits pertaining to written contracts. The court also held that federal common law governs the accrual date and that the action accrued in a suit for pension benefits when the claim was denied. *Id. See also Jenkins v. Local 705, Int'l Bhd. of Teamsters Pension Plan,* 713 F.2d 247, 254 (7th Cir. 1983).

In *Doe v. Blue Cross & Blue Shield United of Wisconsin,* 112 F.3d 869 (7th Cir. 1997), the court held that where an ERISA plan contains a contractual limitations period that is shorter than the otherwise applicable state statutory period, the contractual limitations period is enforceable so long as it is reasonable and even though state law expressly forbids contractual periods that are shorter than statutory periods of limitation. *Id.* at 874–75. In that case, a thirty-nine-month contractual limitations period in a health benefit plan that ran from the date that services for which benefits were sought were rendered to the participant was reasonable where the participant's claim for benefits was finally denied nearly a year and a half before the contractual period ended. *Id.* at 875. The court also held that in appropriate cases, estoppel and tolling principles can apply to prevent or delay application of a contractual limitations period. *Id.* at 875–77. Similarly, the equitable doctrine of laches is an available defense in an ERISA case and can be used to shorten the applicable state statute of limitations. *Teamsters & Employers Welfare Trust of Ill. v. Gorman Bros. Ready Mix,* 283 F.3d 877, 881 (7th Cir. 2002).

## XIII. Subrogation Litigation

The leading post-*Knudson* decision in the Seventh Circuit is *Administrative Committee of the Wal-Mart Stores, Inc. Associates' Health & Welfare Plan v. Varco,* 338 F.3d 680 (7th Cir. 2003), which held that so long as identifiable funds are in defendant's possession, it is permissible to seek restitution. A suit to impose a constructive trust, on funds in defendant's possession, is an equitable claim and therefore permissible under ERISA. *Bon Secours Health Systems, Inc. v. Coultthurst,* 2005 WL 1528267, *2 (N.D. Ill. 2005). Moreover, because the plan in *Varco* explicitly excluded giving any credit for attorneys' fees incurred by the defendant in securing a tort recovery, the court ruled that the common fund doctrine did not apply. In contrast, if a plan is silent about the payment of attorneys' fees and costs, the common fund doctrine may apply. *Primax Recoveries, Inc. v. Sevilla,* 324 F.3d 544 (7th Cir. 2003). Another important ruling is *Trustees of the AFTRA Health Fund v. Biondi,* F.3d 765 (7th Cir. 2002), which held that a plan's claim that the plan participant committed fraud against the plan is not preempted by ERISA and the plan has the right to sue for reimbursement of plan benefits fraudulently obtained.

## XIV. Miscellaneous

### A. Unique Approach to Common Policy-Based Defenses

In *Hawkins v. First Union Corp.,* 326 F.3d 914 (7th Cir. 2003), the court rejected several arguments advanced by the insurer to support a denial of long-term disability benefits for a claimant with fibromyalgia. The court ruled that a consultant's opinion that the majority of people with fibromyalgia are capable of working is the "weakest possible evidence," and that individualized consideration is required. The court also held that the fact the insured worked after his diagnosis is a tribute to his courage and determination; the court recognized that many people work as long as they possibly can before surrendering to this condition. Finally, the court ruled that the ability to perform some housework and to use the Internet does not necessarily mean the claimant can work.

In *Leipzig v. AIG Life Insurance Co.,* 362 F.3d 406 (7th Cir. 2004), the court was unpersuaded that a claimant's risk of adverse medical consequences due to the effect of stress on an underlying cardiac condition justified an award of long-term disability benefits under a deferential standard of review. The court cited examples of well-known people who had serious heart conditions but continued to work (e.g., Vice President Cheney, Justice Stevens).

### B. Other Miscellaneous Issues

The question of whether a court should remand or reinstate disability benefits after reversing the insurer's determination was discussed at length in *Hackett v. Xerox Corp. Long-Term Disability Income Plan,* 315 F.3d 771 (7th Cir. 2003), where the court held that when benefits had been paid for a period of time, the usual course of action is to reinstate benefits, while in initial benefit claims, the usual course of action is to remand the case to the insurer.

The Seventh Circuit has also held that a choice-of-forum provision in the ERISA Rights section of a summary plan description stating that a benefit claim can be filed in state or federal court does not waive the plan's right to remove a benefit claim to federal court. *Cruthis v. Metro. Life Ins. Co.,* 356 F.3d 816, 819 (7th Cir. 2004).

## C. Interpretation of Safe Harbor Regulation

The Eighth Circuit has not considered the Department of Labor's "safe harbor" regulation at 29 C.F.R. § 2510.3-1(j). However, the Northern District of Iowa has addressed the safe harbor regulation three times.

In *Bonestroo v. Continental Life & Accident Co.,* 79 F. Supp. 2d 1041 (N.D. Iowa 1999), the court held that the safe harbor regulation did not apply in light of the employer's extensive endorsement of the policy. The court made the following findings concerning endorsement: (1) the employer chose the insurer and entered into a written contract with it as the employer's group insurer; (2) employees could not independently subscribe to a policy; (3) benefits were conditioned on acceptance of the employer's continued contract with the insurer; (4) coverage ceased when the employee ceased working for the employer; (5) the employer determined employee eligibility for coverage and dictated the permitted benefits; (6) the employer was responsible for notifying employees if the policy covered them; (7) the employer was liable for all premium payments; and (8) the employer was designated as trustee. *Id.* at 1048.

In *Van Natta v. Sara Lee Corp,* 2006 WL 1793543 (N.D. Iowa 2006), the court held that the safe harbor provision did not apply because the employer's involvement in the program extended beyond collecting premiums and was more than advisory in nature. More specifically, the court found that: (1) the employer had the sole discretionary authority to adopt rules and procedures to effectuate efficient administration of the plan; (2) the employer had discretion to determine which employees were eligible for coverage and which benefits employees could obtain; and (3) the employer was responsible for paying premiums or other charges due on account of any plan benefits as well as paying benefits on behalf of the employees. *Id.* at *6.

However, the Northern District of Iowa considered and applied the safe harbor provision in *Merrick v. Northwestern Mutual Life Insurance Co.,* 2001 WL 34152095 (N.D. Iowa 2001). In *Merrick,* the court found that: (1) the insurance contract was made between the individual employee and the insurer; (2) the employee was listed as both the insured and the owner on each of the relevant policies; (3) employees could independently subscribe with the insurer; (4) employees determined the extent of their coverage under the individual policies and the insurer's relationship with the employer bore no consequence to the extent of disability coverage under the individual policies; (5) the policies were completely portable when an employee ceased working for the employer; and (6) there was no evidence that the employer played any role in keeping employees apprised of their continued coverage eligibility under the individual policies. *Id.* at *12.

Expanding on one of the safe harbor factors, the *Merrick* court offered this test to establish employer endorsement: Would an objectively reasonable employee interpret the employer's actions as exercising control over the plan or insinuating that the plan was part of the employer's general benefits package? *Id.* at *10. Employer neutrality vis-à-vis the plan's operation is the crucial inquiry. *Id.* at *10–14. Thus, if the employer acts merely as an "honest broker" between its employees and the insurer, it does not endorse the plan: "As long as the employer merely advises employees of the availability of the plan, accepts payroll deductions, passes them on to the insurer, and performs other ministerial tasks that assist the insurer in publicizing the program, it will not be deemed to have endorsed the program under the regulation." *Id.* at *10.

### D. Amount of Employer Involvement Required to Sustain an Employee Welfare Benefit Plan

The Eighth Circuit does not require the employer to play "any role in the administration of the plan" for the arrangement to be an ERISA plan, if the employer established the plan, since "the statute simply provides that the [plan] must be 'established or maintained by the employer.' " *Robinson v. Linomaz,* 58 F.3d 365, 368 (8th Cir. 1995) (finding establishment of an ERISA plan where employer purchased insurance policy to protect all full-time employees and their families).

### E. Treatment of Multiple Employer Trusts and Welfare Arrangements

A multiple employer welfare arrangement (MEWA) or similar arrangement is an employee welfare benefit plan, established or maintained for the purpose of offering or providing certain benefits to the employees of two or more employers or their beneficiaries. *Forbes v. Lathers, Plasterers & Cabinet Makers Ins. Trust,* 2006 WL 1072030, at *3 (D. Minn. 2006) (citing 29 U.S.C. §1002(40)(A)). MEWAs do not include plans established or maintained pursuant to collective bargaining agreements. *Id.*

The Eighth Circuit has seldom dealt with multiple employer trusts or MEWAs and it has provided little guidance in determining whether a plan constitutes a MEWA. *See Fuller v. Ulland,* 76 F.3d 957 (8th Cir. 1996) (while court acknowledged that MEWAs are covered by ERISA, it declined to reach preemption issue and remanded to district court). *See also State of Minn. by Ulland v. Int'l Ass'n of Entrepreneurs of Am.,* 858 F. Supp. 937, 939 (D. Minn. 1994) (29 U.S.C. § 1144(b)(6) specifically subjects MEWAs to limited regulation and control by state authorities, and cause of action to enjoin the trust from practicing in Minnesota did not fall within the scope of civil enforcement provisions at 29 U.S.C. § 1132(a)).

## II. Preemption

### A. Scope of ERISA Preemption

#### 1. State-Law Claims

Applying *Pilot Life Insurance Co. v. Dedeaux,* 481 U.S. 41, 52 (1987), the Eighth Circuit has consistently held that state-law causes of action are completely preempted by ERISA when they "arise from the administration of benefits." *Fink v. Dakotacare,* 324 F.3d 685, 689 (8th Cir. 2003). More specifically, state-law claims are preempted if the claims "relate to" an employee benefit plan governed by ERISA. *Daley v. Marriott Int'l, Inc.,* 415 F.3d 889, 894 (8th Cir. 2005) (citing 29 U.S.C. §1144(a)).

In determining whether a state law "relates to" an ERISA plan, the Eighth Circuit follows the test set forth by the Supreme Court in *California Division of Labor*

*Standards Enforcement v. Dillingham Construction,* 519 U.S. 316, 324 (1997): A state law "relates to" an ERISA plan if it has a connection with, or reference to, such a plan. *Johnston v. Paul Revere Life Ins. Co.,* 241 F.3d 623, 630 (8th Cir. 2001). A state law that "premises a cause of action on the existence of an ERISA plan" relates to an ERISA plan. *Howard v. Coventry Health Care of Iowa, Inc.,* 293 F.3d at 446.

In addition, when making the "relates to" determination, district courts are to look to the objectives of the ERISA statute and to the nature of the effect of the state law on ERISA plans. *Johnston,* 241 F.3d at 630, citing *Dillingham,* 519 U.S. at 325. The Eighth Circuit has endorsed several factors for analyzing the effect of the state law on ERISA plans: (1) whether the state law negates an ERISA plan provision; (2) whether the state law affects relations between primary ERISA entities; (3) whether the state law impacts the structure of ERISA plans; (4) whether the state law impacts the administration of ERISA plans; (5) whether the state law has an economic impact on ERISA plans; (6) whether preemption of the state law is consistent with other ERISA provisions; and (7) whether the state law is an exercise of traditional state power. *Eckelkamp v. Beste,* 315 F.3d 863, 870 (8th Cir. 2002).

### 2. Savings Clause

Under the "savings clause," a state law that regulates insurance is "saved" from ERISA preemption. *Daley,* 415 F.3d at 894. The Eighth Circuit applies the common-sense test set forth by the Supreme Court in determining whether a state law regulates insurance so as to come within the purview of the savings clause (29 U.S.C. § 1144 (b)(2)(A)). *Howard v. Coventry Health Care of Iowa, Inc.,* 293 F.3d at 446 (citing *UNUM Life Ins. Co. of Am. v. Ward,* 526 U.S. 358, 367 (1999)). In addition, a state law will be held to regulate insurance for purposes of the Savings Clause if it falls within the reference to the business of insurance in the McCarran-Ferguson Act, 15 U.S.C. §§ 1011–15. *Id.* (citing *Metro. Life Ins. Co. v. Mass.,* 471 U.S. 724, 742–43 (1985)).

In applying the common sense test, the claim "*must* not just have an impact on the insurance industry, but must be specifically directed toward that industry." *Id.* at 446 (emphasis added). In applying the McCarran-Ferguson test, the Eighth Circuit considers three factors from the Act itself: "*first,* whether the practice has the effect of transferring or spreading a policyholder's risk; *second,* whether the practice is an integral part of the policy relationship between the insurer and the insured; and *third,* whether the practice is limited to entities within the insurance industry." *Id.* (affirming district court's dismissal of claims for tortious breach of a statute, breach of contract, violation of public policy, and bad faith as preempted, and holding that bad-faith claims under Iowa law were not saved by 29 U.S.C. § 1144 (b)(2)(A)).

### B. Preemption of Managed-Care Claims

ERISA preempts claims against managed care providers stemming from the denial of medical treatment. *Shea v. Esensten,* 107 F.3d 625, 627–28 (8th Cir. 1997). *See also Kuhl v. Lincoln Nat'l Health Plan of Kansas City, Inc.,* 999 F.2d 298, 301–02 (8th Cir. 1993) (action against HMO for delay in authorizing surgery held preempted).

## C. Preemption of Malpractice Claims

ERISA preempts medical malpractice claims against plan administrators where the "essence of the claim rests on the denial of benefits." *See Thompson v. Gencare Health Sys., Inc.*, 202 F.3d 1072, 1073 (8th Cir. 2000) (ERISA preempted claim of surviving spouse of employee health plan participant alleging that administrator committed medical malpractice by failing to provide certain treatment for participant's breast cancer); *Hull v. Fallon*, 188 F.3d 939 (8th Cir. 1999) (ERISA preempted health insurance plan participant's medical malpractice claim against plan administrator and vicarious liability claim against plan for administrator's alleged negligence).

## D. Other Preemption Issues

In *Prudential Insurance Co. of America v. National Park Medical Center, Inc.*, 154 F.3d 812, 825 (8th Cir. 1998), the Eighth Circuit affirmed an order enjoining enforcement of an Arkansas "any willing provider" statute. The district court subsequently dissolved the injunction, relying on the opinion in *Kentucky Association of Health Plans v. Miller*, 538 U.S. 329 (2003), which held that a Kentucky "any willing provider" statute was not preempted. On appeal, the Eighth Circuit affirmed dissolution of the injunction as it related to insured ERISA and non-ERISA plans. *Prudential Ins. Co. of Am. v. Nat'l Park Med. Ctr., Inc.*, 413 F.3d 897, 907 (8th Cir. 2005). However, the court went on to hold that ERISA preempts the Arkansas statute to the extent it relates to self-funded ERISA plans, and reversed the district court's dissolution of the injunction against such plans. *Id.* The court also held that ERISA completely preempts the civil penalties provision of the statute as applied to suits that could have been brought under 29 U.S.C. §1132(a)(1)(B). *Id.* at 907–08.

# III. Exhaustion of Administrative Remedies

## A. Is Exhaustion an Absolute Requirement?

When an ERISA plan clearly requires exhaustion, a claimant's failure to exhaust her administrative remedies bars her from seeking relief in federal court. *Norris v. Citibank, N.A. Disability Plan (501)*, 308 F.3d 880, 884 (8th Cir. 2002). This rule applies if the claimant has notice of the review procedure, even if the denial of benefits letter fails to provide explicit notice of the exhaustion requirement and even if the plan document describes a review procedure that is permissive rather than mandatory. *Wert v. Liberty Life Assurance Co. of Boston, Inc.*, 447 F.3d 1060, 1065–66 (8th Cir. 2006).

## B. Exceptions to the Exhaustion Requirement

### 1. Futility Exception

ERISA plan beneficiaries are not required to exhaust administrative remedies if they can demonstrate that exhaustion "would be wholly futile." *Burds v. Union Pac. Corp.*, 223 F.3d 814, 817 n.4 (8th Cir. 2000). Under the futility exception, the claim accrues at the time it became futile to apply for benefits. *Union Pac. R.R. v. Beckham*, 138 F.3d 325, 332 n.4 (8th Cir. 1998).

## 2. Denial of Meaningful Access to Procedures

The claimant may be excused from exhausting administrative remedies if the employer fails to provide the claimant with meaningful access to the plan's administrative claims procedure. *See Back v. Dancka Corp.*, 335 F.3d 790, 792 (8th Cir. 2003) (claimant's failure to exhaust administrative remedies excused because employer failed to inform claimant of necessity of seeking an internal remedy).

## 3. Rapid and Life-Threatening Illness

Claimants seeking treatment for "rapid, life-threatening illnesses" need not exhaust administrative procedures before bringing a lawsuit to compel coverage under an ERISA plan. *See Henderson v. Bodine Aluminum, Inc.*, 70 F.3d 958, 962 (8th Cir. 1995) (reversing district court's denial of injunctive relief and remanding where the claimant had breast cancer and made a showing of likely success on the merits, and the plan covered high-dose chemotherapy for other types of cancer).

## C. Consequences of Failure to Exhaust

Where a claimant fails to exhaust administrative remedies that are clearly required under an ERISA plan, his claim for relief is barred. *Layes v. Mead Corp.*, 132 F.3d 1246, 1252 (8th Cir. 1998). However, if time remains to exhaust administrative remedies, the district court can stay the action or dismiss without prejudice pending exhaustion. *See Galman v. Prudential Ins. Co. of Am.*, 254 F.3d 768, 769 (8th Cir. 2001) (staying case pending exhaustion); *Painter v. Golden Rule Ins. Co.*, 121 F.3d 436, 440 (8th Cir. 1997) (granting motion for voluntary dismissal without prejudice in declaratory judgment action brought by administrator that had not exhausted policy's procedure for an independent determination of what is medically necessary). The district court may also have discretion to remand to the plan fiduciary to permit the beneficiary to exhaust administrative procedures if the time to do so has not expired. *Cf. Welsh v. Burlington Northern, Inc., Employee Benefits Plan*, 54 F.3d 1331, 1340 (8th Cir. 1995) (holding that a district court is not required to remand a case to the administrator, especially when remand would be a useless formality).

## D. Minimum Number of Levels of Administrative Review

The Eighth Circuit does not require an ERISA plan to provide a minimum number of administrative reviews. One district court has observed that nothing in ERISA requires plan administrators to allow limitless appeals. *Fogerty v. Hartford Life & Accident Ins. Co.*, 2003 WL 22076589, at *8 (D. Minn. 2003).

## E. Can a Defendant Waive a Failure-to-Exhaust Defense?

Although the Eighth Circuit has not addressed the issue, the district court for the District of North Dakota has held that an administrator can waive a failure-to-exhaust defense. *See Spagnolia v. Dakota Neurosurgical Assocs., P.C.*, 2003 WL 23101775, at *5 (D.N.D. Dec. 19, 2003) (administrator waived its failure-to-exhaust defense by making exhaustion a discretionary requirement and by failing to comply with other procedural requirements).

## IV. Standard of Review

### A. Plan Language

A plan document must contain "explicit discretion-granting language." *McKeehan v. Cigna Life Ins. Co.,* 344 F.3d 789, 793 (8th Cir. 2003). The discretion-granting language varies by plan. *See, e.g., Groves v. Metro. Life Ins. Co.,* 438 F.3d 872, 874 (8th Cir. 2006) (where summary plan description provides that plan administrator "has discretionary authority to determine eligibility for benefits" and appoints claim administrator "to process and pay claims for these benefits in accordance with the terms of the Plan," claim administrator has discretionary authority); *Hutchins v. Champion Int'l Corp.,* 110 F.3d 1341, 1344 (8th Cir. 1997) ("sole, absolute and uncontrolled discretion" confers discretion); *Cash v. Wal-Mart Group Health Plan,* 107 F.3d 637, 641 (8th Cir. 1997) ("the administrative committee discretionary authority" confers discretion); *Birdsell v. UPS of Am., Inc.,* 94 F.3d 1130, 1133 (8th Cir. 1996) ("the exclusive right and discretion to interpret the terms and conditions of the plan, and to decide all matters arising in its administration and operation, including questions pertaining to eligibility for, and the amounts of benefits to be paid by the plan" confers discretion).

Phrases such as "to be considered disabled," "as long as the definition of total disability is satisfied," and "proof of loss," however, "read like a typical insurance policy" and "do not trigger the deferential ERISA standard of review." *Brown v. Seitz Foods, Inc.,* 140 F.3d 1198, 1200 (8th Cir. 1998), quoting *Ravenscraft v. Hy-Vee Employee Benefit Plan & Trust,* 85 F.3d 398, 402 n.2 (8th Cir. 1996); *see also Walke v. Group Long-Term Disability Ins.,* 256 F.3d 835, 839 (8th Cir. 2001) (provision that benefits would be paid if claimant "submits satisfactory proof of total disability to us" insufficient to confer discretionary authority).

### B. What Standard of Review Applies?

The Eighth Circuit recognizes three standards of review.

#### 1. Abuse of Discretion

"Under the traditional abuse of discretion standard, the plan administrator's decision to deny benefits will stand if a reasonable person could have reached a similar decision." *Woo v. Deluxe Corp.,* 144 F.3d 1157, 1162 (8th Cir. 1998). To determine whether a decision was reasonable, a court evaluates whether the administrator's decision is supported by substantial evidence, meaning "more than a scintilla but less than a preponderance." *Woo,* 144 F.3d at 1162, quoting *Donaho v. FMC Corp.,* 74 F.3d 894, 900 n.10 (8th Cir. 1996) (quotation omitted). A decision "will be deemed reasonable if a reasonable person *could* have reached a similar decision, given the evidence before him, not that a reasonable person *would* have reached that decision." *Clapp v. Citibank, N.A. Disability Plan (501),* 262 F.3d 820, 828 (8th Cir. 2001) (emphasis in original), quoting *Cash v. Wal-Mart Group Health Plan,* 107 F.3d 637, 641 (8th Cir. 1997). A court "will not disturb a decision supported by a reasonable explanation 'even though a different reasonable interpretation could have been made.'" *Clapp,* 262 F.3d at 828.

Some courts employ a five-factor test in determining reasonableness: (1) whether the administrator's interpretation is consistent with the goals of the plan; (2) whether the interpretation renders any language in the plan meaningless or internally inconsistent; (3) whether the administrator's interpretation conflicts with the substantive or procedural requirements of the ERISA statute; (4) whether the administrator has interpreted the relevant terms consistently; and (5) whether the interpretation is contrary to the clear language of the plan. *Torres*, 405 F.3d at 680, citing *Shelton v. ContiGroup Cos., Inc.*, 285 F.3d 640, 643 (8th Cir. 2002). Although all factors are to be considered, "significant weight should be given to [] a misinterpretation of unambiguous language in the plan." *Lickteig v. Bus. Men's Assurance Co. of Am.*, 61 F.3d 579, 585 (8th Cir. 1995).

## *2. De Novo*

Where a plan document does not grant the administrator discretion, a court makes its own determination as to whether the claimant is entitled to benefits within the meaning of the plan. *See Donatelli v. Home Ins. Co.*, 992 F.2d 763, 765 (8th Cir. 1993) (when "discretion is lacking, the district court conducts a de novo review that is not limited to the fiduciary's explanation of its denial"). De novo review applies to both fact determinations and plan interpretations. *Riedl v. Gen. Am. Life Ins. Co.*, 248 F.3d 753, 756 n.2 (8th Cir. 2001).

## *3. Sliding Scale*

Where the court finds a conflict of interest or procedural irregularity, the administrator's decision may be reviewed under the sliding scale standard of review. *Woo v. Deluxe Corp.,* 144 F.3d 1157 (8th Cir. 1998). However, heightened scrutiny of a decision otherwise reviewed under the abuse of discretion standard is proper only where the claimant produces "material probative evidence demonstrating that (1) a palpable conflict of interest or serious procedural irregularity existed, which (2) caused a serious breach of the plan administrator's fiduciary duty to [the claimant]." *Clapp*, 262 F.3d at 827 (8th Cir. 2001), quoting *Barnhart v. UNUM Life Ins. Co. of Am.*, 179 F.3d 583, 588 (8th Cir. 1999).

In practice, the effect of a conflict of interest or procedural irregularity is muted by the claimant's inability to demonstrate that it had "some connection to the substantive decision reached." *Woo*, 144 F.3d at 1161–62. This causation requirement presents a "considerable hurdle for plaintiffs." *Barnhart v. UNUM Life Ins. Co. of Am.*, 179 F.3d 583, 588 (8th Cir. 1999). "The evidence offered by the claimant must give rise to 'serious doubts as to whether the result reached was the product of an arbitrary decision or the plan administrator's whim.'" *Barnhart*, 179 F.3d at 589, quoting *Layes v. Mead Corp.*, 132 F.3d 1246, 1250 (8th Cir. 1998). *See also Torres v. UNUM Life Ins. Co. of Am.*, 405 F.3d 670, 679 (8th Cir. 2005) ("[W]e are aware of only two cases that have satisfied the second part of the *Woo* test.").

## C. Effect of Conflict of Interest or Procedural Irregularity

If the claimant establishes a causal connection to the benefits decision, "the evidence supporting the plan administrator's decision must increase in proportion to the seriousness of the conflict or procedural irregularity." *Woo v. Deluxe Corp.,* 144 F.3d 1157, 1162 (8th Cir. 1998). For example, in *Woo,* the court determined that the administrator's "egregious conduct" required that the record contain "evidence bordering on a preponderance to uphold [its] decision." *Id.*

### 1. Conflict of Interest

In *Armstrong v. Aetna Life Insurance Co.,* 128 F.3d 1263, 1265 (8th Cir. 1997), the claim analyst's receipt of remuneration for benefit denials constituted a financial conflict of interest, resulting in de novo review of the claim decision.

Where the alleged financial conflict is the result of the insurer acting as the administrator, the result is less certain. *Torres v. UNUM Life Ins. Co. of Am.,* 405 F.3d 670, 678 (8th Cir. 2005) (collects cases). Some decisions hold that this "dual role" creates a conflict of interest that may be rebutted. *Schatz v. Mut. of Omaha Ins. Co.,* 220 F.3d 944, 948–49 (8th Cir. 2000) ([T]he conflict may "be negated by ameliorating circumstances, such as equally compelling long-term business concerns that militate against improperly denying benefits despite the dual role.").

Others opinions provide that it is wrong to presume a financial conflict of interest where the administrator is also the insurer. *See McGarrah v. Hartford Life Ins. Co.,* 234 F.3d 1026, 1030 (8th Cir. 2000). In *Farley v. Ark. Blue Cross & Blue Shield,* 147 F.3d 774 (8th Cir. 1998), the Eighth Circuit expressed reluctance to imply a financial conflict of interest:

> ERISA specifically contemplates the utilization of fiduciaries that may not be entirely neutral. . . . When considered in isolation, an insurer's desire to maintain competitive insurance rates could be construed as a conflict of interest. However, a benefits determination includes equally compelling long-term business concerns that encourage insurers to make these determinations in a fair and consistent manner, thus negating any indicia of bias. In the long run, an insurer that routinely denies valid claims for benefits would have difficulty retaining current customers and attracting new business.

147 F.3d at 776–77. Even if a conflict is found, the burden is on the claimant to establish that it "has some connection to the substantive decision reached to trigger a departure from the abuse of discretion standard." *Torres,* 405 F.3d at 679. *See also Kolosky v. UNUM Life Ins. Co. of Am.,* 2006 WL 1379633, at *2 (8th Cir. 2006) (claimant must establish a "causal connection between the presumed conflict of interest and [administrator]'s benefits eligibility decision").

### 2. Procedural Irregularity

This analysis focuses on alleged inadequacies in the administration of a claim. "In determining whether procedural irregularities occurred, we consider whether the plan administrator's decision was made without reflection or judgment, such that it was the product of an arbitrary decision or the plan administrator's whim." *Parkman v. Prudential Ins. Co.,* 439 F.3d 767, 772 n.5 (8th Cir. 2006). For example, it is a procedural irregularity where the administrator (1) relies on an in-house physician rather than a specialist to review a disability claim involving an uncommon medical condition, *Woo v. Deluxe Corp.,* 144 F.3d 1157, 1161 (8th Cir. 1998); (2) fails to respond in writing to a claimant's appeal, *McGarrah v. Hartford Life Ins. Co.,* 234 F.3d 1026, 1030–31 (8th Cir. 2000); (3) fails to address adequately the medical evidence provided by the claimant's treating physicians, *Morgan v. UNUM Life Ins. Co. of Am.,* 346 F.3d 1173, 1176 (8th Cir. 2003); (4) fails to obtain medical records after it led the claimant to believe it would; *Harden v. Am. Express Fin. Corp.,* 384 F.3d 498, 500 (8th Cir. 2004); (5) fails to consider the effects of medication on a claimant's ability to work; *Torres v. UNUM Life Ins. Co. of Am.,* 405 F.3d 677–78 (8th Cir. 2005); or (6) never issues a written decision. *Buttram v. Cent. States, Se. & Sw. Areas Health & Welfare Fund,* 76 F.3d 896, 900 (8th Cir. 1996).

It is *not* a procedural irregularity where the administrator (1) declines to obtain an independent medical examination, *Torres,* 405 F.3d at 670; (2) refuses to utilize a cardiologist or rheumatologist to review the claimant's complex medical condition where a treating physician declines to render an opinion on disability, *Clapp v. Citibank, N.A. Disability Plan (501),* 262 F.2d 820, 828 (8th Cir. 2001); (3) fails to independently verify the accuracy of data submitted by the claimant, *Sahulka v. Lucent Techs., Inc.,* 206 F.3d 763, 769 (8th Cir. 1999); (4) relies on the opinions of in-house physicians who review the claimant's treatment records, *Kolosky v. UNUM Life Ins. Co. of Am.,* 2006 WL 1379633, at *2 (8th Cir. 2006).

As with a conflict of interest, even if the claimant establishes a procedural irregularity, he must also show that it caused a serious breach of the administrator's duty. *See, e.g., McGarrah v. Hartford Life Ins. Co.,* 234 F.3d 1026, 1030–31 (8th Cir. 2000) (while the administrator's failure to respond to the claimant's appeal letter was a serious procedural irregularity, heightened scrutiny under the abuse of discretion standard was not justified, because the claimant failed to provide evidence linking the procedural irregularity to the ultimate benefits decision). *But see Morgan v. Contractors, Laborers, Teamsters & Eng'rs Pension Plan,* 287 F.3d 716, 723 (8th Cir. 2002) (withholding relevant information from claimant and basing decision on preconceptions was a procedural irregularity that resulted in a serious breach of fiduciary duty); *Harden,* 384 F.3d at 500 (leading claimant to believe that administrator was considering information not in its possession was a serious procedural irregularity justifying less deferential review and remand to administrator).

### D. Other Factors Affecting Standard of Review

Failure to comply with regulatory requirements may constitute a serious procedural irregularity. For example, in *Mansker v. TMG Life Insurance Co.,* the administrator denied coverage for medical expenses. 54 F.3d 1322, 1327 (8th Cir. 1995). It argued that if the claimant was covered under the plan, remand was appropriate so it could determine whether the expenses incurred were "medically necessary, reasonable, and customary." The Eighth Circuit disagreed, holding that the administrator's failure to render a decision on this issue during its administration of the claim resulted in a loss of discretion. *Id.* at 1327–29. *See also Janssen v. Minneapolis Auto Dealers Benefit Fund,* 447 F.3d 1109, 1113 (8th Cir. 2006) (failure to provide an adequate explanation for the benefit denial (29 C.F.R. § 2560.503-1(g)(1)(ii)) or the right to appeal (29 C.F.R. § 2560.503-1(g)(1)(iv)) are procedural irregularities).

In *McGarrah v. Hartford Life Insurance Co.*, the administrator failed to acknowledge the claimant's request for an appeal of the initial benefits denial (and thus failed to make a decision within the prescribed time limits). 234 F.3d 1026, 1029 (8th Cir. 2000). The claimant did not submit additional information in his request for an appeal. The Eighth Circuit held that while the failure to acknowledge the appeal was a serious procedural irregularity, heightened scrutiny was not justified because of the administrator's thorough investigation in making its initial claim determination. *See also Tillery v. Hoffman Enclosures Inc.*, 280 F.3d 1192, 1199 (8th Cir. 2002) (claimant's "failure to offer any analysis explaining how the untimely notice so infected the decision making process as to render the decision to deny suspect" fails to satisfy the second prong of *Woo* analysis).

In *Seman v. FMC Corp. Retirement Plan for Hourly Employees*, the claimant appealed the initial benefits denial and, like *McGarrah*, the administrator declined to make any decision. However, unlike *McGarrah*, the claimant provided additional information for consideration on appeal. *Seman*, 334 F.3d 728, 733 (8th Cir. 2003). The Eighth Circuit held that where the administrator fails to make a decision on the initial application for benefits, remand to the administrator for a decision is appropriate. However, where the administrator makes an initial determination, receives information from the claimant in conjunction with an appeal, and fails to decide the appeal, the de novo standard of review was appropriate in reviewing its benefit decision. *Id.*

In addition, regardless of whether the delay or failure to respond affects the standard of review, it may excuse the claimant from exhausting her administrative remedies. *See Phillips-Foster v. UNUM Life Ins. Co. of Am.*, 302 F.3d 785, 796 (8th Cir. 2002) (administrator's failure to meet claim deadlines under 29 C.F.R. § 2560.503 (1997) resulted in a "deemed denial" giving claimant the "right to bring a civil action to have the merits of [her] application determined. . . .").

## V. Rules of Plan Interpretation

### A. Application of Federal Common Law

Plan interpretation is subject to the principles of federal common law. *Brewer v. Lincoln Nat'l Life Ins. Co.*, 921 F.2d 150, 153 (8th Cir. 1990); *Mansker v. TMG Life Ins. Co.*, 54 F.3d 1322, 1327 (8th Cir. 1995).

### B. Application of *Contra Proferentem*

*Contra proferentem* does not apply in ERISA cases. *Brewer v. Lincoln Nat'l Life Ins. Co.*, 921 F.2d 150, 153 (8th Cir. 1990).

### C. Deference Afforded to an Administrator's Interpretation of a Plan

Generally, under the abuse of discretion standard, the administrator's interpretation is entitled to deference. *See Hutchins v. Champion Int'l Corp.*, 110 F.3d 1341, 1344 (8th Cir. 1997) ("Under an abuse of discretion standard we do not search for the best or preferable interpretation of a plan term: it is sufficient if the [administrator]'s interpretation is consistent with a commonly accepted definition.").

In some cases, courts employ apply a five-factor test in determining whether the administrator's plan interpretation is reasonable under the abuse of discretion standard. *See* Section IV.B.1, *supra; see also Cash v. Wal-Mart Group Health Plan,* 107 F.3d 637, 641 (8th Cir. 1997); *Finley v. Special Agents Mut. Benefit Ass'n, Inc.,* 957 F.2d 617, 621 (8th Cir. 1992). Where an administrator evaluates facts to determine the plan's application to a particular case, the substantial evidence test governs the court's review. *Donaho v. FMC Corp.,* 74 F.3d 894, 899 n.9 (8th Cir. 1996).

## D. Other Rules of Plan or Contract Interpretation

### 1. Ordinary Meaning

"[U]nless the plan language specifies otherwise, courts should construe any disputed language 'without deferring to *either* parties' interpretation.'" *Brewer v. Lincoln Nat'l Life Ins. Co.,* 921 F.2d 150, 153–54 (8th Cir. 1990) (emphasis in original), quoting *Wallace v. Firestone Tire & Rubber Co.,* 882 F.2d 1327, 1329 (8th Cir. 1989).

The administrator is required to furnish plan descriptions that are written in a manner calculated to be understood by the average plan participant. *Brewer,* 921 F.2d at 154, citing 29 U.S.C. § 1022(a)(1). As a result, the terms of an ERISA plan "should be accorded their ordinary, and not specialized, meanings." *Brewer,* 921 F.2d at 154; *see also Mansker v. TMG Life Ins. Co.,* 54 F.3d 1322, 1327 (8th Cir. 1995) (applying interpretation of "arising out of employment" used by Arkansas courts in workers' compensation cases contrary to ERISA "because legal definition is not consistent with what an average plan participant would understand the words to mean"). In ERISA cases, ordinary meaning is determined by the dictionary definition of a word and the context in which it is used. *Hutchins v. Champion Int'l Corp.,* 110 F.3d 1341, 1344 (8th Cir. 1997). Where an ERISA plan is ambiguous, a court may consider extrinsic evidence. *Barker v. Ceridian Corp.,* 122 F.3d 628, 638 (8th Cir. 1997).

### 2. Vesting of Benefits

While ERISA mandates vesting of pension benefits, Congress did not require vesting of employee welfare benefit plans (EWBPs). *Stearns v. NCR Corp.,* 297 F.3d 706, 711 (8th Cir. 2002). Vesting of EWBPs is not presumed and is determined by a review of the plan documents. *Barker v. Ceridian Corp.,* 122 F.3d 628, 632–33 (8th Cir. 1997). Absent a contractual agreement to the contrary, an employer may unilaterally modify or terminate an EWBP at any time. *Stearns,* 297 F.3d at 711; *Hutchins v. Champion Int'l Corp.,* 110 F.3d 1341, 1343 (8th Cir. 1997). Whether vesting of benefits occurs is a legal issue governed by ERISA. *John Morrell & Co. v. United Food & Commercial Workers Int'l Union,* 37 F.3d 1302, 1303 (8th Cir. 1994). The claimant has the burden of establishing vested benefits. *Stearns,* 297 F.3d at 711.

An agreement to vest must be written and incorporated into the ERISA plan itself. *See Barker,* 122 F.3d at 633; *United Paperworkers Int'l Union v. Jefferson Smurfit Corp.,* 961 F.2d 1384, 1386 (8th Cir. 1992). Accordingly, the payment of ongoing benefits may be modified or terminated, depending on the plan language. *See, e.g., Hutchins,* 110 F.3d at 1345–46 (because the plan did not contain language that limited the ability of the administrator to terminate or amend benefits once a participant was already entitled to receive them, administrator could terminate claimant's receipt of long-term disability benefits); *Hughes v. 3M Retiree Med. Plan,* 281 F.3d 786, 792–93 (8th Cir. 2002) (reservation of rights provision in plan otherwise devoid of vesting language defeats claim by participants that their welfare benefits vested for life); *Blessing v. Deere & Co.,* 985 F. Supp. 899, 903 (S.D. Iowa. 1997) (the plan in effect at the time benefits are terminated or denied is the plan governing the scope of the review of the administrator's decision).

# VI. Discovery

## A. Limitations on Discovery

The scope of discovery is determined by the standard of review.

### 1. Abuse of Discretion Standard of Review

Under the abuse of discretion standard, discovery is generally limited to the administrative record compiled by the administrator up to the time of the final benefits decision. *Milone v. Exclusive Healthcare, Inc.,* 244 F.3d 615, 618 (8th Cir. 2001), citing *Sahulka v. Lucent Techs., Inc.,* 206 F.3d 763, 769 (8th Cir. 2000). *See, e.g., Barnhart v. UNUM Life Ins. Co. of Am.,* 179 F.3d 583 (8th Cir. 1999) (district court properly excluded claimant's affidavit and Social Security Administration determination from consideration at motion for summary judgment); *Maune v. I.B.E.W., Local No. 1, Health & Welfare Fund,* 83 F.3d 959, 963 (8th Cir. 1996) (order denying discovery process where district court was limited to review of evidence before the administrator); *Davidson v. Prudential Ins. Co. of Am.,* 953 F.2d 1093, 1095 (8th Cir. 1992) (refusing to reopen administrative record to allow additional evidence because the claimant had the burden to submit all relevant information before the administrator made its final benefits determination).

However, discovery may be permitted to determine whether the administrator fully developed the record. *Larson v. Minn. Chamber Bus. Services,* 114 F. Supp. 2d 867, 870–71 (D. Minn. 2000).

### 2. De Novo Standard of Review

Generally, "additional evidence gathering" under de novo review is discouraged to "ensure expeditious judicial review of ERISA benefit decisions and to keep district courts from becoming substitute plan administrators." *Brown v. Seitz Foods, Inc.,* 140 F.3d 1198, 1200 (8th Cir. 1998), quoting *Cash v. Wal-Mart Group Health Plan,* 107 F.3d 637, 641–42 (8th Cir. 1997). *See also* Section VII.B, *infra. But see Weber v. St. Louis Univ.,* 6 F.3d 558, 561 (8th Cir. 1993) (district court erred in declining to permit the administrator to conduct discovery under the de novo review where onset of claimant's disability was necessary "to sustain a verdict for either [party]").

## B. Discovery and Conflict of Interest

Discovery may be permitted under the abuse of discretion standard to establish a procedural irregularity or conflict of interest. In *Farley v. Ark. Blue Cross & Blue Shield,* however, the court suggested that discovery was not boundless:

A palpable conflict of interest or serious procedural irregularity will ordinarily be apparent on the face of the administrative record or will be stipulated to by the parties. Thus, the district court will only rarely need to permit discovery and supplementation of the record to establish these facts. We note, however, that conducting limited discovery for the purpose of determining the appropriate standard of review does not run afoul of the general prohibition on admitting evidence outside the administrative record for the purpose of determining benefits.

147 F.3d 774, 776 n.4 (8th Cir. 1998); *see also Brown v. Seitz Foods, Inc.,* 140 F.3d 1198, 1200–01 (8th Cir. 1998) (allowing limited discovery for the purpose of determining the appropriate standard of review does not violate the general prohibition on admitting evidence outside the administrative record).

# VII. Evidence

## A. Scope of Evidence under Standards of Review

Under the abuse of discretion standard, evidence not presented to the administrator is generally inadmissible. *See Maune v. I.B.E.W., Local No. 1, Health & Welfare Fund,* 83 F.3d 959, 963 (8th Cir. 1996) (district court's stay of discovery affirmed). In *Rittenhouse v. UnitedHealth Group Long Term Disability Ins. Plan,* __ F.3d __, 2007 WL 517739 (8th Cir. 2007), the Eighth Circuit considered whether the administrator abused its discretion in failing to consider evidence submitted by the claimant after the appeal determination. In that case, the claimant's submissions included a report containing results of a test conducted just after the appeal and records from his treating physicians *Id.* at *4. The district court admitted this evidence and determined that the administrator abused its discretion in denying benefits. *Id.*

The Eighth Circuit reversed and help that the district court erred in accepting the post appeal evidence. Initially, the court reasoned that the claimant had failed to show "good cause" why evidence should be admitted, although the "good cause" exception is generally considered in cases utilizing the de novo standard of review. *Id.* The court further reasoned that:

> ERISA's administrative appeal process is not indefinite. Once the claimant has had a "full and fair review," the process is complete, and the administrator may close the record and issue a final decision.

*Id.* at *5; *see also Davidson v. Prudential Ins. Co. of Am.,* 933 F.2d 1093, 1096 (8th Cir. 1992) ("the administrative [review] process must end at some point," i.e., after a "full and fair review").

However, district courts may consider evidence outside the administrative record in limited circumstances. *See, e.g., Barnhart v. UNUM Life Ins. Co. of Am.,* 179 F.3d 583, 588 (8th Cir. 1999) (*en banc*), citing *Woo v. Deluxe Corp.,* 144 F.3d 1157, 1160 (8th Cir. 1998) (claimant may present "material, probative evidence demonstrating that (1) a palpable conflict of interest or a serious procedural irregularity existed, which (2) caused a serious breach of the plan administrator's fiduciary duty to her"); *Barham v. Reliance Standard Life Ins. Co.*, 441 F.3d 581, 585 n.1 (8th Cir. 2006) (plan need not have been in the administrative record to be considered by the court in determining the standard of review); *Koons v. Aventis Pharms., Inc.*, 367 F.3d 768, 780 (8th Cir. 2004) (court may consider additional evidence where administrative record is disputed); *Welsh v. Burlington Northern, Inc., Employee Benefit Plan*, 54 F.3d 1331 (8th Cir. 1995) (district court permitted to consider additional evidence necessary to make an informed judgment where plan made no factual determination in denying benefits).

With respect to de novo review, consideration of evidence outside the administrative record is discouraged to "ensure expeditious judicial review of ERISA benefit decisions and to keep district courts from becoming substitute plan administrators." *Brown*, 140 F.3d at 1200; *Ferrari v. Teachers Ins. & Annuity Ass'n*, 278 F.3d 801, 807 (8th Cir. 2002) (*en banc*).

District courts applying de novo review may look beyond the administrative record for "good cause," but only if consideration is necessary for adequate review of the fiduciary's decision. *Donatelli v. Home Ins. Co.*, 992 F.2d 763, 765 (8th Cir. 1993); *Koons v. Aventis Pharms., Inc.*, 367 F.3d at 780. Good cause may exist where the claimant did not receive an opportunity to supplement the administrative record during the initial benefit determination and appeal. *See Ferrari*, 278 F.3d at 807; *Birdsell v. UPS of Am., Inc.*, 94 F.3d 1130, 1133 (8th Cir. 1996). *See also Bernards v. United of Omaha Life Ins. Co.*, 987 F.2d 486 (8th Cir. 1993) (expedient clarification of the experimental nature of medical treatment for a terminally ill patient is good cause). However, good cause is not established where a claimant fails to take advantage of an opportunity to supplement the record. *Brown*, 140 F.3d at 1201.

### B. Evidentiary Value of Social Security Determinations

Although a Social Security Administration determination is not binding, it is admissible evidence to support an ERISA claim for long-term disability benefits. *Riedl v. Gen. Am. Life Ins. Co.*, 248 F.3d 753, 759 (8th Cir. 2001), citing *Duffie v. Deere & Co.*, 111 F.3d 70, 74 n.5 (8th Cir. 1997); *see also Walden v. Eaton Corp.*, 170 Fed. Appx. 435, 436, 2006 WL 550890, at *1 (8th Cir. 2006) (employer justifiably relied on denial letter from Social Security Administration as proof of claimant's work activities). However, the Social Security Administration's determination is not admissible where it was not part of the administrative record. *See Barnhart*, 179 F.3d at 590 (court properly refused to consider Social Security benefits letter that was not before administrator at time of benefits determination); *Glick v. Coop. Benefit Adm'rs, Inc.*, 2002 WL 1194786, at *1 (8th Cir. 2002) (rejecting claimant's argument that administrative record should be supplemented by record of Social Security Administration hearing conducted two years after closure of administrative record on claimant's claim for long-term disability benefits); *but see Harden v. Am. Express Fin. Corp.*, 384 F.3d 498, 500 (8th Cir. 2004) (reversing summary judgment for administrator and remanding to reopen administrative record, obtain Social Security records, and make new determination of claim, where administrator obtained authorizations for, and led claimant to believe it was considering, certain Social Security medical documents but did not obtain the documents and therefore omitted them from the administrative record).

## C. Other Evidence Issues

In cases where the administrative record is not in dispute, it is presumed that the record reflects the evidence that was before the administrator or committee. *White v. HealthSouth Long-Term Disability Plan,* 320 F. Supp. 2d 811, 820 (W.D. Ark. 2004). However, when there is a dispute over the composition of the administrative record, district courts will make their own determination whether the disputed evidence was actually offered to the administrator, and even whether it was timely offered. *See Fogerty v. Hartford Life & Accident Ins. Co.,* 2003 WL 22076589, at *8 (D. Minn. 2003) (court found that evidence was not part of administrative record and declined to find good cause to consider it because it was not offered until after record was closed). *See also Taylor by Taylor v. Kawneer Co. Comprehensive Med. Expense Plan for Salaried Employees,* 898 F. Supp. 667, 673 (W.D. Ark. 1995) (court considered both a letter from claimant's attorney to a worker in employer's personnel department confirming attorney's understanding regarding claimant's coverage and an affidavit from same worker in order to adjudge equitable estoppel claim that the attorney's letter had provided plan with knowledge of a relevant issue).

# VIII. Procedural Aspects of ERISA Practice

## A. Methods of Adjudication

Most ERISA cases in the Eighth Circuit are resolved by summary judgment. Some courts have also considered motions for judgment on the administrative record, but as yet no such motion has been granted in a reported case. *See Chronister v. Baptist Health,* 442 F.3d 648 (8th Cir. 2006) (affirming district court's denial of "motion for judgment on the ERISA record" and remand to re-open the administrative record and to make a new determination of the claim for long-term disability benefits based on fibromyalgia); *Atkinson v. Prudential Ins. Co.,* 2006 WL 1663832 (E.D. Ark. 2006) (denying cross motions for judgment on the record and remanding for determination of eligibility for benefits).

## B. Reported ERISA Trials

There is no right to a jury trial of ERISA cases in the Eighth Circuit. *In re Vorpahl,* 695 F.2d 318 (8th Cir. 1982); *see also Houghton v. Sipco, Inc.,* 38 F.3d 953, 957 (8th Cir. 1994) (no jury trial for alleged deprivation of severance and retirement medical benefits); *Langlie v. Onan Corp.,* 192 F.3d 1137, 1141 (8th Cir. 1999) (no jury trial for alleged violation of 29 U.S.C. § 1140); *King v. Hartford Life & Accident Ins. Co.,* 414 F.3d 994, 1010 (8th Cir. 2005) (parties acknowledged that there is no right to jury trial in action for benefits under ERISA and consented to trial before magistrate judge). There have been several reported ERISA bench trials within the Eighth Circuit. *See, e.g., Koons v. Aventis Pharms., Inc.,* 367 F.3d 768 (8th Cir. 2004).

## C. Special Procedures for ERISA Benefit Cases

There are no special procedures for ERISA benefit cases in the Eighth Circuit.

# IX. Fiduciary Liability Claims

## A. Definition of Fiduciary

Discretion is the "benchmark for fiduciary status under ERISA" pursuant to the explicit wording of 29 U.S.C. § 1002(21). *Johnston v. Paul Revere Life Ins. Co.*, 241 F.3d 623, 632 (8th Cir. 2001) (quoting *Maniace v. Commerce Bank of Kansas City*, 40 F.3d 264, 267 (8th Cir. 1994)).

In *Harold Ives Trucking Co. v. Spradley & Coker, Inc.*, the Eighth Circuit considered whether a third-party administrator (TPA) was a fiduciary. The TPA determined in consultation with an excess-insurance carrier that rehabilitation services provided to the claimant would not be reimbursed by the plan because the provider was not a "covered facility." 178 F.3d 523, 525 (8th Cir. 1999). The TPA reversed its decision and reimbursed the claimant for the services. The administration agreement between the employer and the TPA provided that the TPA would exercise ministerial duties only, and have no discretionary authority. *Id.* at 526. The employer/plan brought an action against the TPA for breach of fiduciary duty and breach of the administration contract. *Id.* at 525.

The court cited 29 U.S.C. § 1002(21)(A) (1994) for the definition of a fiduciary. "[A] person is a fiduciary with respect to the plan if (i) he exercises any discretionary authority or discretionary control respecting management of such plan or exercises any authority or control respecting management or disposition of its assets. . . ." *Id.* at 525–26. The TPA was held to have acted as a fiduciary because it had exercised discretionary authority in contravention of the administration agreement. *Id.* at 526. Fiduciaries can take many different forms. *See, e.g., Prudential Ins. Co. of Am. v. Doe*, 140 F.3d 785, 789–90 (8th Cir. 1998) (insurer with sole responsibility to interpret plan and to review and decide claims); *FirsTier Bank, N.A. v. Zeller*, 16 F.3d 907 (8th Cir. 1994) (trustee of profit-sharing plan); *Martin v. Feilen*, 965 F.2d 660 (8th Cir. 1992) (controlling stockholders, directors, and accountants who exercised effective control over the plan's assets); *Olson v. E.F. Hutton & Co.*, 957 F.2d 622, 627 (8th Cir. 1992) (account broker whose investment advice served as primary basis for plan's investment decisions).

However, professionals who merely provide services to an employee benefits plan are not fiduciaries unless they transcend the normal role and exercise discretionary authority. *See Johnston v. Paul Revere Life Ins. Co.*, 241 F.3d 623, 632 (8th Cir. 2001) (broker); *Kerns v. Benefit Trust Life Ins. Co.*, 992 F.2d 214 (8th Cir. 1993) (broker who informed employees of impending termination of health insurance coverage); *Consol. Beef Ind., Inc. v. N.Y. Life Ins. Co.*, 949 F.2d 960, 964–65 (8th Cir. 1991) (insurance company and its salesman who sold annuities to plan); *Anoka Orthopaedic Assoc., P.A. v. Lechner*, 910 F.2d 514, 517 (8th Cir. 1990) (attorney and benefits consultant).

## B. Definition of Fiduciary Duties

Pursuant to 29 U.S.C. § 1104, a fiduciary must discharge his duties (1) for the exclusive purpose of providing benefits to participants and their beneficiaries and defraying reasonable expenses of the plan; (2) with the care, skill, prudence, and diligence under the circumstances then prevailing that a prudent person acting in a like capacity and familiar with such matters would use in the conduct of an enterprise of a like character and with like aims; (3) by diversifying the investments of the plan so as to minimize the risk of large losses, unless under the circumstances it is clearly prudent not to do so; and (4) in accordance with the documents and instruments governing the plan.

Congress included these provisions in order to make the law of trusts applicable to plans and to eliminate "such abuses as self-dealing, imprudent investing, and misappropriation of plan funds." *Boyle v. Anderson,* 68 F.3d 1093, 1102 (8th Cir. 1995) (citing *Fort Halifax Packing Co. v. Coyne,* 482 U.S. 1, 15, 107 S. Ct. 2211, 2219, 96 L. Ed. 2d 1 (1987)). The prudent-person standard in 29 U.S.C. § 1104 is an objective standard that focuses on the fiduciary's conduct preceding the challenged decision. *Roth v. Sawyer-Cleator Lumber Co.,* 16 F.3d 915, 917 (8th Cir. 1994). Thus the prudent-person standard is not concerned with results; rather, it is a test of how the fiduciary acted viewed from the perspective of the time of the challenged decision and not from the "vantage point of hindsight." *Id.* at 918. To say a decision is objectively reasonable requires taking into account everything that the fiduciary should have known at the time of the decision. *Id.* at 919.

One district court has held that it is not enough for a plaintiff bringing a breach of fiduciary duty claim merely to show that the fiduciary failed to act in accordance with the plan documents; the plaintiff must also show that such failure amounted to a failure to discharge the duties "with the care, skill, prudence, and diligence under the circumstances then prevailing that a prudent man acting in a like capacity and familiar with such matters would use in the conduct of an enterprise of a like character and with like aims." *Cossey v. Assocs.' Health & Welfare Plan,* 363 F. Supp. 2d 1115, 1139 (E.D. Ark. 2005).

## C. Fiduciary Liability in the Context of Health and Disability Claims

Fiduciary duties apply to the consideration of health and disability claims. *See, e.g., Knieriem v. Group Health Plan, Inc.,* 434 F.3d 1058, 1061 (8th Cir. 2006) (individual health plan participant was permitted to seek equitable remedies for breach of fiduciary duty in his individual capacity, but affirmed dismissal of his breach of fiduciary duty claim that essentially sought damages).

As in other types of ERISA cases, the issue of breach of fiduciary often arises in health and disability cases in the context of standard of review, as a breach of fiduciary duty can lead to less-deferential review. *See, e.g., Kolosky v. UNUM Life Ins. Co. of Am.,* 2006 WL 1379633, at *1 (8th Cir. 2006) (less deferential review than abuse of discretion review applies where claimant presents material, probative evidence demonstrating that (1) palpable conflict of interest or serious procedural irregularity existed, which (2) caused serious breach of plan administrator's fiduciary duty).

## D. Remedies for Breach of Fiduciary Duty

ERISA provides a cause of action for breach of fiduciary duty under 29 U.S.C. §1109(a) and personal liability where a fiduciary breaches his or her duty. *Conley v. Pitney Bowes,* 176 F.3d 1044, 1047 (8th Cir. 1999).

An individual plan participant, in his individual capacity, may seek equitable remedies for breach of fiduciary duty under 29 U.S.C. § 1132(a)(3)(B). *Knieriem v. Group Health Plan, Inc.,* 434 F.3d 1058, 1061 (8th Cir. 2006). However, recovery in such cases is limited to "classic" equitable remedies such as injunctive, restitutionary, or mandamus relief, and does not extend to compensatory damages. *Id.* Restitution can be either equitable or compensatory, and the distinction lies in the origin of the award sought. *Id.* Equitable restitution seeks to punish the wrongdoer by taking his ill-gotten gains. *Id.* Compensatory damages, on the other hand, focus on the plaintiff's loss and seek to recover in money the value of the harm done. *Id.* Therefore, regardless of the label attached to the remedy in a particular case, the court looks to the origin of the relief sought to determine whether it is equitable or compensatory. *Id.* If the relief requested is compensatory damages, it is not recoverable under § 1132(a)(3)(B). *Id.* Moreover, a claim for breach of fiduciary duty under § 1132(a)(3) may be raised only when other remedies are not available to the complaining party. *Taylor v. Liberty Life Assurance Co. of Boston,* 2005 WL 1654521, at *1 (W.D. Mo. 2005) (citing *Varity Corp. v. Howe,* 516 U.S. 489, 116 S. Ct. 1065, 134 L. Ed. 2d 130 (1996)).

Individual plan participants have no right of action for recovery of extra-contractual compensatory or punitive damages for breach of a fiduciary duty. *Brant v. Principal Life & Disability Ins. Co.,* 6 Fed. Appx. 533, 535, 2001 WL 432235, at *1 (8th Cir. 2001).

A plan participant may recover a loss to the plan for breach of fiduciary duty under 29 U.S.C. § 1132(a)(2). *Harley v. Minn. Mining & Mfg. Co.,* 413 F.3d 866, 872 (8th Cir. 2005) (Bye, J. concurring). *See also Conley v. Pitney Bowes,* 176 F.3d 1044, 1047 (8th Cir. 1999) (plan participant stated no claim for breach of fiduciary duty for restoration of his long-term disability benefits because recovery under 29 U.S.C. § 1109(a) provides relief only to the plan, not to individual beneficiaries); *Roth v. Sawyer-Cleator Lumber Co.,* 16 F.3d 915, 920 n.4 (8th Cir. 1994) ("a fiduciary who breaches his duty is liable to the plan—not the beneficiaries individually . . . to get money out of a plan, the beneficiaries must make a claim for benefits").

A fiduciary may recover damages for breach of fiduciary duty from another fiduciary under 29 U.S.C. § 1132(a)(2). *See Harold Ives Trucking Co. v. Spradley & Coker, Inc.,* 178 F.3d 523 (8th Cir. 1999) (employer permitted to recover monetary damages from its third-party administrator).

## E. Contribution and Indemnity Claims among Fiduciaries

The Eighth Circuit offers no analysis for contribution or indemnity among fiduciaries, but does permit breach of fiduciary duty claims between fiduciaries. *See Harold Ives Trucking Co. v. Spradley & Coker, Inc.,* 178 F.3d 523 (8th Cir. 1999) (employer permitted to recover monetary damages from its third-party administrator). District courts in the Eight Circuit have split on whether to allow claims for contribution. *See W. Auto Supply Co. v. Nw. Mut. Life Ins. Co.,* 1994 WL 520910, at *1 (W.D. Mo.

1994) ("ERISA does not expressly create the right to contribution . . . [but] the court finds that sufficient authority exists to support the theory that the right of contribution has become part of the federal common law surrounding the rights and remedies under ERISA."); *but see Center Physicians Inc. Profit Sharing Trust v. PaineWebber Group Inc.*, 1996 WL 622470, at *2 (E.D. Mo. 1996) (denying motion for leave to amend to add contribution claim because the Eighth Circuit has not yet decided whether ERISA permits a contribution or indemnity claim and other circuits have reached different conclusions on the issue).

### F. ERISA Claims against Nonfiduciaries

A nonfiduciary is not liable for damages under ERISA. *Fink v. Union Cent. Life Ins. Co.*, 94 F.3d 489, 493 (8th Cir. 1996). "Appropriate equitable relief" can be obtained from a nonfiduciary "party in interest" pursuant to 29 U.S.C. § 1132(a)(3). *Harris Trust & Sav. Bank v. Salomon Smith Barney, Inc.*, 530 U.S. 238, 241, 120 S. Ct. 2180, 2184 (2000). However, the Eighth Circuit has not yet addressed such a claim. One district court has held that a claimant may seek restitution under § 1132(a)(3) from a nonfiduciary service provider who knowingly participated in a fiduciary's breach of duty. *Clark v. Ameritas Inv. Corp.*, 408 F. Supp. 2d 819, 831 n.3 (D. Neb. 2005) (citing *Harris Trust & Sav. Bank*, 530 U.S. 238).

## X. Attorneys' Fees

### A. Criteria for Awarding Attorneys' Fees

In *Lawrence v. Westerhaus*, 749 F.2d 494, 496 (8th Cir. 1984), the Eighth Circuit adopted a five-factor test to determine whether to award attorneys' fees under 29 U.S.C. § 1132(g). Those factors are (1) the degree of culpability or bad faith of the opposing party; (2) the ability of the opposing party to pay attorneys' fees; (3) whether an award of attorneys' fees against the opposing party might have a future deterrent effect under similar circumstances; (4) whether the parties requesting attorneys' fees sought to benefit all participants and beneficiaries of a plan or to resolve a significant legal question regarding ERISA itself; and (5) the relative merits of the parties' positions. *Lawrence*, 749 F.2d at 496; *Seitz v. Metro. Life Ins. Co.*, 433 F.3d 647, 652 (8th Cir. 2006).

The five factors are neither exclusive nor to be mechanically applied. *Martin v. Ark. Blue Cross & Blue Shield*, 299 F.3d 966, 972 (8th Cir. 2002). The *Martin* court noted that when considering the second factor (ability to pay), the district court should consider fundamental differences in plan-funding mechanisms. *Id.* "Ordering large fee payments from an employee-funded plan might actually hurt the plan participants by increasing costs, contrary to the statutory purpose of ERISA." *Id.* A district court "may consider any and all facts it deems relevant" when deciding whether to award attorneys' fees. *Id.* The court need not consider all of the factors in every case. *Christianson v. Poly-America, Inc. Med. Benefit Plan*, 412 F.3d 935, 941 (8th Cir. 2005).

There is no presumption that a prevailing claimant is entitled to an award of attorneys' fees. *Martin*, 299 F.3d at 971–72, overruling *Landro v. Glendenning*

*Motorways, Inc.,* 625 F.2d 1344, 1356 (8th Cir. 1980). Where the plan cooperates by expediting the exhaustion of administrative remedies, agrees to a stipulated record for the district court, agrees to a simultaneous briefing schedule, and does not appeal the district court's adverse ruling, the district court does not abuse its discretion by refusing to award attorneys' fees to the prevailing claimant. *Id.* at 973. In that case, the court suggested that plan participants were better served by rejecting the claimants' attorneys' fee request. *Id.* ("A plan that understands it may avoid attorney fees if it acts appropriately and quickly is more likely to do so.").

### B. Fees Awarded to Plan Fiduciaries

The district court has discretion to award attorneys' fees to a plan fiduciary. *See, e.g., Baker v. Greater Kansas City Laborers Welfare Fund,* 716 F. Supp. 1229 (W.D. Mo. 1989) (trustees awarded attorneys' fees for defending frivolous claims). The Eighth Circuit has upheld an attorneys' fee award to a plan trustee from the plan where the plan specifically provided for such relief in all lawsuits except those "where it is finally determined that the Trustee has breached its duties." *FirsTier Bank, N.A. v. Zeller,* 16 F.3d 907, 913 (8th Cir. 1994).

### C. Calculation of Attorneys' Fees

In addition to the Supreme Court's lodestar formula, which is the starting point for determining the amount of a reasonable fee in ERISA cases within the Eighth Circuit, *Hensley v. Eckerhart,* 461 U.S. 424, 433 (1983) (number of hours reasonably expended on the litigation multiplied by a reasonable hourly rate), district courts also consider the amount of the recovery and the results obtained by the lawsuit. *Griffin v. Jim Jamison, Inc.,* 188 F.3d 996, 997 (8th Cir. 1999). In cases where a fee award is appropriately made to a prevailing claimant, district courts, in calculating the award, may also consider the number of lawyers who had previously declined to represent the claimant before he or she found counsel to prosecute the case, whether the claimant obtained relief from each of the defendants, and the extent of the relief obtained against any particular defendant. *Id.* at 997–98. District courts have discretion to decide on a case-by-case basis which factors to explicitly consider. *Id.*

A reduced fee is appropriate if the claimant's relief, however significant, is limited in comparison to the scope of the litigation as a whole. *Delcastillo v. Odyssey Res. Mgmt., Inc.,* 431 F.3d 1124 (8th Cir. 2005); *Geissal v. Moore Med. Corp.,* 338 F.3d 926 (8th Cir. 2003). As to the hourly rate, a reasonable attorney's fee should be consistent with market rates and practices in the community. *West v. Aetna Life Ins. Co.,* 188 F. Supp. 2d 1096, 1099 (N.D. Iowa 2002). A prevailing claimant may not recover attorneys' fees incurred in pre-administrative proceedings. *Parke v. First Reliance Standard Life Ins. Co.,* 368 F.3d 999, 1011 (8th Cir. 2004).

## XI. ERISA Regulations

"Full and fair review [of a denial of ERISA plan benefits] includes the right to review all documents, records, and other information relevant to the claimant's claim for benefits, and the right to an appeal that takes into account all comments, documents, records, and other information submitted by the claimant relating to the claim." *Abram v. Cargill, Inc.,* 395 F.3d 882, 886 (8th Cir. 2005) (citing 29 C.F.R. § 2560.503-1(h)(2000)). "The persistent core requirements of full and fair review include 'knowing what evidence the decision-maker relied upon, having an opportunity to address the accuracy and reliability of that evidence, and having the decision-maker consider the evidence presented by both parties prior to reaching and rendering a decision.'" *Id.* (citation omitted). *See also Janssen v. Minneapolis Auto Dealers Benefit Fund,* 447 F.3d 1109, 1113 (8th Cir. 2006) (failure to provide an adequate explanation for the benefit denial (29 C.F.R. § 2560.503-1(g)(1)(ii)) or right to appeal (29 C.F.R. § 2560.503-1(g)(1)(iv)) are procedural irregularities and constitute violation of the plan). Plan procedures cannot be "full and fair" without a meaningful dialogue between plan administrators and their beneficiaries. *Abram,* 395 F.3d at 886 (citation omitted). ERISA plans must include a "reasonable opportunity to appeal from an 'adverse benefit determination' to allow full and fair review of the contested claim." *Price v. Xerox Corp.,* 445 F.3d 1054, 1056 (8th Cir. 2006) (citing 29 C.F.R. § 2560.503-1(h)(1)).

To be "full and fair," claimants must have at least 180 days after an "adverse benefit determination" to file an administrative appeal. *Id.* (citing 29 C.F.R. §§ 2560.503-1(h)(3)(i), (h)(4)). The regulations also permit, but do not require, plans to mandate a second internal appeal of a denial before a claimant may sue." *Id.* (citing §§ 2560.503-1(c)(2), (d)). The regulations, however, do not mandate a specified time period for this appeal, and require instead only enough time for a "full and fair" review. *Id.* at 1057 (citing §§ 2560.503-1(1)(b), (h)(2)).

## XII. Cases Interpreting ERISA Statutes of Limitation

District courts must consider the most analogous state-law statute of limitations. *Adamson v. Armco, Inc.,* 44 F.3d 650, 652 (8th Cir. 1995). However, a contractual limitations period shorter than the applicable state law may be effective. *Weyrauch v. Cigna Life Ins. Co. of N.Y.,* 416 F.3d 717, 720 n.2 (8th Cir. 2005).

The characterization of a claim for statute of limitations purposes is a question of federal law. *Johnson v. State Mut. Life Assurance Co. of Am.,* 942 F.2d 1260, 1262 (8th Cir. 1991). Claim accrual is also governed by federal law. *Abdel v. U.S. Bancorp,* 457 F.3d 887, 880 (8th Cir. 2006). A cause of action for benefits under ERISA accrues when an administrator "formally denie[s] an applicant's claim for benefits or when there has been a repudiation by the fiduciary which is clear and made know to the beneficiary." *Id.,* quoting *Cavegn v. Twin City Pipe Trades Pension Plan,* 223 F.3d 827, 829–30 (8th Cir. 2000). *Cf. Weyrauch,* 416 F.3d at 721 (under Minnesota law, statute of limitations period for claim for disability benefits does not accrue until disability ends).

In practice, the applicable limitations period varies depending on the jurisdiction, type of benefit, and panel considering the case. *See Abdel,* 457 F.3d at 880 (Minnesota's two-year statute of limitations applies to claim for disability benefits); *Weyrauch,* 416 F.3d at 720 (Minnesota's three-year statute of limitations applies to claim for disability benefits); *Shaw v. McFarland Clinic, P.C.,* 363 F.3d 744, 748

(8th Cir. 2004) (Iowa's general ten-year statute of limitations applies to claims for denial of preauthorization of surgery); *Mead v. Intermec Techs. Corp.*, 271 F.3d 715 (8th Cir. 2001) (Iowa's two-year statute of limitations applies to claim for short-term disability benefits); *Anderson v. John Morrell & Co.*, 830 F.2d 872, 877 (8th Cir. 1987); (South Dakota's six-year statute of limitations applies to claim for health benefits); *Duchek v. Blue Cross & Blue Shield of Neb.*, 153 F.3d 648, 650 (8th Cir. 1998) (Nebraska's five-year statute of limitations applies to claim for medical benefits); *Minn-Kota Ag Prods., Inc. v. Carlson*, 2004 WL 1486328 (N.D. 2004) (North Dakota's three-year statute of limitations applies to action for breach of fiduciary duty under 29 U.S.C. § 1113); *Wilkins v. Hartford Life & Accident Ins. Co.*, 299 F.3d 945, 948–49 (8th Cir. 2002) (three-year statute of limitations period applies over Arkansas' five-year statute of limitations for actions on written contracts because Arkansas law provided for shorter limitations period, three years was reasonable, and the plan expressly adopted the shorter limitation period); *Harris v. Epoch Group, L.C.*, 357 F.3d 822, 825 (8th Cir. 2004) (Missouri's ten-year statute of limitations applies to claim for disability benefits).

## XIII. Subrogation Litigation

Only equitable remedies, such as constructive trust, injunction, and restitution, are available to recover overpayment under ERISA. *N. Am. Coal Corp. v. Roth*, 395 F.3d 916, 917 (8th Cir. 2005). Legal remedies for recovery of overpayment are not authorized under 29 U.S.C. § 1132(a)(3). *Id.* at 917–18. In *Dillard's Inc. v. Liberty Life Assurance Co. of Boston*, 2006 WL 1997164 (8th Cir. 2006), the claimant asserted that the administrator was precluded from obtaining judgment against him in the amount of overpaid benefits because its claim sought monetary, rather than equitable relief, under ERISA. *Id.* at *5–6. The court disagreed, holding that seeking repayment from "a specifically identified fund—all overpayments resulting from the payment of social security benefits"—was sufficient to satisfy the requirements of *Sereboff v. Mid Atlantic Medical Services, Inc.*, 126 S. Ct. 1969 (2006). *Id.* at *6.

## XIV. Miscellaneous

### A. Unique Approach to Common Policy-Based Defenses

#### 1. Mental/Nervous Limitation

The terms of the plan should be accorded their ordinary, and not specialized, meanings. *Brewer v. Lincoln Nat'l Life Ins. Co.*, 921 F.2d 150, 154 (8th Cir. 1990). In applying this principle to the mental/nervous limitation, courts should consider how laypersons, rather than experts, would define mental illnesses and not limit the mental illness definition to diseases with a nonorganic origin. *Brewer*, 921 F.2d at 154. As a result, "regardless of the cause of [the claimant's] disorder, a disease which manifests itself in terms of mood swings and aberrant behavior is a 'mental illness' within the meaning of the policy." *Id.; see also Stauch v. Unisys Corp.*, 24 F.3d 1054, 1056 (8th Cir. 1994) ("depression, fatigue, irritability, sleeplessness, poor appetite and impaired concentration and memory" subject to mental illness limitation in policy);

*Walke v. Group Long-Term Disability Ins.,* 256 F.3d 835, 841 (8th Cir. 2001) (fatigue, anxiety, dizziness, and tachycardia were subject to mental illness limitation).

## 2. Total Disability versus Residual Disability

The Eighth Circuit recognizes the distinction between total and residual (or partial) disability benefits in ERISA plans. In *McOsker v. Paul Revere Life Insurance Co.,* the Eighth Circuit enforced a residual disability provision that it viewed as less than clear:

> It is evident to us that a person who can perform some but not all of his or her important duties has a "Residual Disability" within the meaning of the policy, and that therefore in order to be eligible for total disability payments a person would be required to show that he or she was unable to perform any of those important duties. We believe that it is not otherwise possible to give effect to both parts of the contract.

279 F.3d 586, 588 (8th Cir. 2002). *See also Bond v. Cerner Corp.,* 309 F.3d 1064, 1068 (8th Cir. 2002) (in order to give partial disability language its intended effect, the claimant was not totally disabled where he was able to perform some of the substantial duties of his occupation).

## 3. Preexisting-Condition Exclusion

Preexisting-condition exclusions are enforceable in ERISA-regulated policies under the abuse of discretion standard. *See, e.g., Wise v. Kind & Knox Gelatin, Inc.,* 429 F.3d 1188, 1191 (8th Cir. 2005) (medical benefits); *Marshall v. UNUM Life Ins. Co.,* 13 F.3d 282, 284–85 (8th Cir. 1994) (long-term disability benefits).

The preexisting-condition exclusion is also applicable in cases considered under the de novo review standard. *See, e.g., Davolt v. Executive Comm. of O'Reilly Auto.,* 206 F.3d 806 (8th Cir. 2000) (exclusion applied under either standard of review to long-term disability benefits); *Armstrong v. Aetna Life Ins. Co.,* 128 F.3d 1263 (8th Cir. 1997) (disability benefits).

## 4. Burden of Proof

Where the plan requires the claimant to provide "proof" of entitlement to benefits, he has the burden of substantiating his claim. *Sahulka v. Lucent Techs., Inc.,* 206 F.3d 763, 768 (8th Cir. 2000); *see also Ferrari v. Teachers' Ins. & Annuity Ass'n,* 278 F.3d 801, 806 (8th Cir. 2002) (fault for claimant's failure to submit documentation that might have affected the administrator's decision lies with claimant himself); *Torres v. UNUM Life Ins. Co. of Am.,* 405 F.3d 670, 678 (8th Cir. 2005) ("UNUM was not required to articulate a theory for Torres's inability to perform his job, but rather to consider the evidence Torres submitted to determine whether it proved him disabled.").

## 5. Basis for Denial Not Considered by Administrator

Under the de novo standard of review, courts may consider a basis for denial first raised in the litigation. "[I]t is entirely proper for a trial court to consider 'policy provisions [that] clearly may . . . be the basis for such a denial' even if those provisions were not 'specified as the basis for the [original] denial of coverage.'" *Weber v. Saint Louis Univ.,* 6 F.3d 558, 560 (8th Cir. 1993), quoting *Farley v. Benefit Trust Life Ins. Co.,* 979 F.2d 653, 660 (8th Cir. 1992). Under the abuse of discretion standard, courts exclude reasons for denial of benefits raised for the first time in litigation. *See King v. Hartford Life & Accident Ins. Co.,* 414 F.3d 994, 1000 (8th Cir. 2005) ("[T]he benefit plan must articulate its reasons for denying benefits when it notifies the participant or beneficiary of an adverse decision . . . .").

## B. Certification of Class Actions

The Eighth Circuit offers little authority concerning certification of class actions in ERISA cases. In *Parke v. First Reliance Standard Life Insurance Co.,* 368 F.3d 999 (8th Cir. 2004), a beneficiary sought to certify a class seeking to enjoin an adminis-trator from terminating long-term disability benefits without, as the beneficiary alleged, requesting or receiving evidence that the allegedly disabling condition had improved. The Eighth Circuit affirmed the district court's denial of class certifica-tion, reasoning that the question of whether the administrator breached its obliga-tions to the members of the class required "a case-by-case determination" and that the claimant had an adequate remedy at law. *Id.* at 1006.

# CHAPTER 9

# Ninth Circuit

FREDERIC ESRAILIAN
HORACE GREEN
LINDA M. LAWSON
JOANNE RYAN
KATHERINE SOMERVELL

## I. What Constitutes an ERISA Plan?

### A. Determining the Existence of an Employee Welfare Benefit Plan

A plan may be created under the Employee Retirement Income Security Act of 1974 (ERISA) without an intentional plan adoption if "from the surrounding circumstances a reasonable person can ascertain the intended benefits, a class of beneficiaries, the source of financing, and procedures for receiving benefits." *Carver v. Westinghouse Hanford Co.,* 951 F.2d 1083, 1086 (9th Cir. 1991). The Ninth Circuit has held that an ERISA plan exists if the following requirements are met:

> (1) A "plan, fund or program" (2) established or maintained (3) by an employer or by an employee organization, or both (4) for the purpose of providing medical, surgical, hospital care, sickness, accident, disability, death, unemployment, or vacation benefits . . . (5) to the participants or their beneficiaries.

*Kanne v. Conn. Gen. Life Ins. Co.,* 867 F.2d 489, 491–92 (9th Cir. 1988), *cert. denied,* 492 U.S. 906 (1989); *Steen v. John Hancock Mut. Life Ins. Co.,* 106 F.3d 904, 917 (9th Cir. 1997).

Severance plans are not governed by ERISA, because they provide a one-time benefit that does not require ongoing administration. *Velarde v. PACE Membership Warehouse,* 105 F.3d 1313 (9th Cir. 1997); *Delaye v. Agripac, Inc.,* 39 F.3d 235 (9th Cir. 1994). Other exempted plans include employee benefit plans provided by governmental entities or as part of a church plan. 29 U.S.C. § 1003(b). There are exceptions to this exemption, though. A plan that covers governmental employees but that is not established or maintained by a governmental entity will not qualify for the ERISA exemption. *See Sarraf v. Standard Ins. Co.,* 102 F.3d 991, 993 (9th Cir. 1996) (finding that Orange County Employees Association plan is governed by ERISA and that ERISA covers benefit funds managed by employee or employer organizations); *but see Silvera v. Mut. Life Ins. Co. of N.Y.,* 884 F.2d 423, 426 (9th Cir. 1989) (finding that a city managed or established benefit plan qualifies as a government plan and is exempt from ERISA coverage).

### B. Definition of "Employee" for ERISA Purposes

Inclusion under ERISA will be extended to those individuals who were treated as common-law employees regardless of whether they were denominated as independent contractors. *Vizcaino v. Microsoft Corp.,* 120 F.3d 1006, 1010 (9th Cir. 1997) (applying the "objective manifestation theory of contracts" in order to discern the reasonable meaning of an employee benefit agreement) (citation omitted). Similarly, the Ninth Circuit has stated that "when Congress uses the word 'employee,' courts 'must infer, unless the statute otherwise dictates, that Congress means to incorporate the established meaning' of the word." *Vizcaino,* 120 F.3d at 1009, quoting *Nationwide Mut. Ins. Co. v. Darden,* 503 U.S. 318, 322 (1992).

With respect to plans that cover partners or shareholders in addition to employees, the Ninth Circuit has held that while such persons are not "participants" under the plan, they do qualify as "beneficiaries," thus rendering their claims under the plan subject to ERISA. *Peterson v. Am. Life & Health Ins. Co.,* 48 F.3d 404 (9th Cir.), *cert. denied,* 516 U.S. 942 (1995). Where, however, the owner's plan is for the sole benefit of the owner, is separate and distinct from any plan covering employees, and was not created contemporaneously with the employee plan, the owner's policies will *not* be subject to ERISA. *LaVenture v. Prudential Ins. Co. of Am.,* 237 F.3d 1042 (9th Cir. 2001). More recently, the Supreme Court has held that a working owner of a company who was also the sole shareholder and president could qualify as a "participant" so long as the plan covers one or more employees other than himself and his spouse. *Raymond B. Yates, M.D., P.C. Profit Sharing Plan v. Hendon,* 541 U.S. 1 (2004).

### C. Interpretation of Safe Harbor Regulation

The Ninth Circuit has required that *all four* "safe harbor" criteria outlined by the Department of Labor must be met in order to exempt a plan from ERISA. *Kanne v. Conn. Gen. Life Ins. Co.,* 867 F.2d 489, 493 (9th Cir. 1988); *Stuart v. UNUM Life Ins. Co. of Am.,* 217 F.3d 1145, 1153 (9th Cir. 2000). Thus, each of the following factors must be established: (1) no contributions are made by an employer or employee organization; (2) participation in the program is completely voluntary for employees or members; (3) the sole functions of the employer or employee organization with respect to the program are, without enforcing the program, to permit the insurer to publicize the program to employees or members, to collect premiums through payroll deductions or dues check-off, and to remit them to the insurer; and (4) the employer or employee organization receives no consideration in the form of cash or otherwise in connection with the program, other than reasonable compensation, excluding a profit, for administrative services actually rendered in connection with payroll deductions or dues check-offs.

### D. Amount of Employer Involvement Required to Sustain an Employee Welfare Benefit Plan

Unless *all four* safe harbor regulations are met, the Ninth Circuit considers the employer's involvement in a group insurance plan significant enough to constitute an "employee benefit plan" subject to ERISA. *Kanne,* 867 F.2d at 492 (state-law claims against insurer were preempted by ERISA where only one of the above-mentioned conditions was not met; the failure of any one of the conditions "would prevent the exclusion of the insurance plan from ERISA coverage"); *see also Qualls By & Through Qualls v. Blue Cross of Cal., Inc.,* 22 F.3d 839 (9th Cir. 1994); *Stuart v. UNUM Life Ins. Co. of Am.,* 217 F.3d 1145 (9th Cir. 2000).

### E. Treatment of Multiple Employer Trusts and Welfare Agreements

An employer can establish an ERISA plan by subscribing to a multiple employer trust or multiple employer welfare arrangement. *Credit Managers Ass'n v. Kennesaw Life & Accident Ins.,* 809 F.2d 617, 625 (9th Cir. 1987) (noting that "each employer who subscribed to [the multiple employer trust] thereby established its own individual ERISA plan").

## II. Preemption

### A. Scope of ERISA Preemption

In *Pilot Life Ins. Co. v. Dedeaux,* 481 U.S. 41 (1987), the Supreme Court held that state-law claims relating to the improper handling of claims under an employee benefit plan are not saved from federal preemption by the savings clause. It thus held that Mississippi's bad-faith law was preempted because it was derived from tort and contract principles and was not aimed solely at the insurance industry. *Id.* Thus, under *Pilot Life,* ERISA preempts state common-law claims for relief for breach of the covenant of good faith and fair dealing. *See, e.g., Bast v. Prudential Ins. Co. of Am.,* 150 F.2d 1003 (9th Cir. 1998).

Following the Supreme Court's decision in *Pilot Life,* the Ninth Circuit reconsidered a case questioning whether ERISA preempted a section of the California Code. *Kanne v. Conn. Gen. Life Ins. Co.,* 867 F.2d 489, 491 (9th Cir. 1989). Section 790.03(h) dealt with unfair insurance practices and created a private right of action. *Id.* Plaintiff argued that Section 790.03(h) was not preempted because it was a law regulating insurance. *Id.* The Ninth Circuit agreed that the law regulated insurance but held that under *Pilot Life* the private right of action given to beneficiaries under

Section 790.03(h) was preempted by ERISA. *Id.* The circuit relied on the *Pilot Life* opinion, which made clear that Congress intended ERISA's enforcement provision to be the sole method by which plan beneficiaries and participants could bring actions. *Id.*

In *Greany v. Western Farm Bureau Life Insurance Co.,* 973 F.2d 812, 819 (9th Cir. 1992), the plaintiff brought suit against his health insurance company for, among other things, violating Montana's unfair claims-settlement-practice statutes. The Ninth Circuit held that the Montana statutes did not regulate insurance but were civil enforcement provisions and, thus, preempted by ERISA. *Id.*

The Ninth Circuit has also applied *Pilot Life* to find that ERISA preempts wrongful death claims arising from the improper denial of plan benefits. In *Spain v. Aetna Life Insurance Co.,* 11 F.3d 129, 132 (9th Cir. 1993), the Ninth Circuit held that ERISA preempted the plaintiffs' wrongful death action because the plaintiffs sought damages for improper administration of benefit claims. There, Spain suffered from cancer and required a three-part medical procedure, which the defendant, the administrator of Spain's employee benefit plan, originally approved. *Id.* at 131. After the first two parts of the procedure had been completed, the defendant withdrew its authorization for the third part. *Id.* The plaintiffs brought a wrongful death suit, alleging that the delay caused by the defendant's denial of benefits negligently caused Spain's death. *Id.* Because the plaintiffs' wrongful death action involved a denial of benefits and thus improper processing of claims, their action was preempted by ERISA. *Id.*

An issue that created a raging debate a few years ago was whether the Supreme Court's decision in *UNUM Life Insurance Co. of America v. Ward,* 526 U.S. 358 (1999), heralded a retreat from prior decisions holding that bad-faith claims are preempted. The Ninth Circuit examined this possible discrepancy between *Pilot Life* and *Ward* in *Elliot v. Fortis Benefits Insurance Co.,* 337 F.3d 1138, 1142 (9th Cir. 2003). First, the Ninth Circuit noted the Supreme Court's decision in *Kentucky Association of Health Plans, Inc. v. Miller,* 538 U.S. 329 (2003), and considered the new requirements that must be met in order for a state law to be deemed a law that regulates insurance. A state law is regarded as one that regulates insurance if it is "specifically directed toward entities engaged in insurance" and "substantially affects the risk pooling arrangement between the insurer and the insured." *Elliot,* 337 F.3d at 1142. In *Elliot,* a plan participant brought suit against the plan administrator for violating Montana's Unfair Trade and Practice Act (UTPA), specifically a provision dealing with misrepresentations in insurance policies and with good faith in effectuating settlements of claims. *Id.* at 1141.

The circuit considered three facets of *Pilot Life* that indicated that claims were preempted: (1) "claims processing laws are not specifically directed at insurance companies if bad-faith claims can be made in another setting"; (2) "claims processing laws do not affect the risk-pooling arrangement"; and (3) "all state private causes of action for claim processing are preempted by ERISA's enforcement provision." *Elliot,* 337 F.3d at 1144. In applying these rules, the circuit found that the UTPA did not satisfy the requirements for exemption. *Id.* However, the circuit noted that decisions subsequent to *Pilot Life* have cast doubt on whether these three indicators are still valid. *Id.*

One of the subsequent decisions that challenged *Pilot Life* was *Ward,* 526 U.S. 358. There, the court took a more lenient approach in deciding whether the law was "specifically directed" to insurance companies, looking at the law "by its very terms" rather than generally. *Elliot,* 337 F.3d at 1145. Thus, the circuit found that, under the *Ward* approach, the UTPA was sufficiently directed toward insurance companies. The *Ward* court also may have broadened the concept of risk pooling, making it possible for a court to find that the UTPA affected risk spreading.

With only a few exceptions, most courts of appeal and district courts have taken the opposite view. In *Jabour v. Cigna Healthcare of California Inc.,* 162 F. Supp. 2d 1119, 1127–28 (C.D. Cal. 2001), the district court held that the Ninth Circuit view is that ERISA preempts claims for tortious breach of the implied covenant of good faith and fair dealing because it is not a claim specifically directed to the insurance industry, as required by ERISA's savings clause and that nothing in the *Ward* case detracts from *Pilot Life* or opens the door to state-law bad-faith claims.

The Ninth Circuit in *Glaubach v. Regence Blueshield,* 2006 U.S. App. LEXIS 7251, 2006 WL 711523 (9th Cir. 2006), issued an unpublished opinion affirming the district court's ruling that the plaintiff's claim was not preempted by ERISA's civil enforcement remedy, 29 U.S.C. § 1132(a). The insurer argued that ERISA preempted the plaintiff's claim concerning a violation of a provision in the Washington Insurance Code that prohibited certain unfair insurance practices. *Id.* at *5. The court held that the statutory claims did not challenge the denial of benefits provided under the terms of her policy. *Id. See also Cleghorn v. Blue Shield,* 408 F.3d 1222, 1225–26 (9th Cir. 2005). The court also stated that the plaintiff did not assert any causes of action asserting improper processing of claims following *Pilot Life,* 481 U.S. at 52, 56, and *Elliot v. Fortis Benefits Insurance Co.,* 337 F.3d at 1147. *Id.* Therefore, the court ruled the claim was not preempted since the plaintiff did not seek recovery of benefits due under the terms of her plan. *Id.*

### B. Preemption of Managed-Care Claims

In *Rutledge v. Seyfarth, Shaw, Fairweather & Geraldson,* 201 F.3d 1212, 1216 (9th Cir. 2000), the Ninth Circuit stated that it has "not arrived upon a single, precise rule that universally determines whether ERISA preempts a state law." Rather, following the Supreme Court's decision in *New York Conference of Blue Cross & Blue Shield Plans v. Travelers Insurance Co.,* 514 U.S. 645 (1995), the circuit has used a variety of compatible tests in preemption cases. *Rutledge,* 201 F.3d 1212. The circuit created these different tests in an effort to maintain broad preemption as mandated by the ERISA statute while not intruding upon areas that have traditionally been governed by state law. *Id.* The effect of these new tests has been a narrowing of the scope of ERISA's preemption.

In *Miniance v. Pacific Maritime Association (PMA),* 2005 U.S. Dist. LEXIS 40708, 2005 WL 2230149 (N.D. Cal. 2005), the district court considered whether a dispute over a death benefit payment under a secured executive benefit plan (SEBP) to a decedent's widow of more than $9 million was preempted by ERISA. The plaintiff, an insurance broker, alleged state-law tort causes of actions after being terminated from his employment for his role in allegedly altering the SEBP without the board's approval. *Id.* at *5. After PMA removed the case to federal court, PMA filed cross actions against the insurance broker asserting claims for breach of contract, breach of fiduciary duty, and negligence. *Id.* at *21. PMA was seeking damages for wrongful payment of benefits to the decedent's widow under the SEBP. *Id.* The court found that PMA's claims were not preempted because there were no claims filed against the SEBP plan administrator; the state-law claims would not affect the "uniform regulatory regime over employee benefit plans," as the defendants are not ERISA fiduciaries; and the agreement entered into by the parties created a legal duty outside of duties regulated by ERISA. *Id.* at *26. *See also Rutledge,* 201 F.3d 1212.

In *Arizona State Carpenters Pension Trust Fund v. Citibank,* 125 F.3d 715, 723 (9th Cir. 1997), the circuit recognized that there were limits to ERISA's preemptive sweep. Relying on *Travelers,* the Ninth Circuit established three areas in which Congress intended for ERISA to preempt state laws. *Arizona State Carpenters,* 125 F.3d at 723. ERISA preempts state laws that (1) "mandate employee benefit structures or their administration"; (2) "bind employers or plan administrators to particular choices or preclude uniform administrative practice"; and (3) provide "alternate enforcement mechanisms for employees to obtain ERISA plan benefits." *Id.,* quoting *Travelers,* 514 U.S. at 655–61. The circuit concluded that state laws are not preempted if they "fall outside of these three areas. . . , arise from state laws of general application, do not depend upon ERISA, and do not affect the relationships between the principal ERISA participants." *Id.* at 724.

The Ninth Circuit used a similar "relationship" approach in *Geweke Ford v. St. Joseph's Omni Preferred Care Inc.,* 130 F.3d 1355, 1358 (9th Cir. 1997). The relationship test maintains that when state laws infringe upon an ERISA relationship, they are preempted. ERISA relationships do not include those that are common to all other commercial entities, such as the relationship between the plan and its own employees or its insurers and creditors. Rather, state laws are preempted only if they intrude upon ERISA-governed relationships. *Id.* In *Geweke Ford,* an employer brought suit against its third-party plan administrator and excess liability insurance company for failure to perform their contractual duties. *Id.* at 1357. The Ninth Circuit held that contract law, not ERISA, affected the relationship between the plaintiff and the third-party administrator. *Id.* at 1359. Likewise, the relationship between the plaintiff and the insurance company was like that of any commercial entity and, thus, not preempted by ERISA. *Id.*

In *Blue Cross of California v. Anesthesia Care Associates Medical Group, Inc.,* 187 F.3d 1045, 1052 (9th Cir. 1999), the Ninth Circuit examined 29 U.S.C. § 1144(a), which states that ERISA preempts "any and all State laws insofar as they may now or hereafter relate to any employee benefit plan" governed by ERISA. The circuit relied on the Supreme Court's definition of "relate to" as set forth in *California Division of Labor Standards Enforcement v. Dillingham Construction,* 519 U.S. 316, 324 (1997), finding that a law "relates to" an employee benefit plan if it has a reference to or connection with the plan. *Blue Cross,* 187 F.3d at 1052. In *Blue Cross,* a fee dispute arose between Blue Cross and physicians who participated in its medical care plan. *Id.* at 1049. Blue Cross argued that the providers' claims were preempted by ERISA because higher payments to providers would impose economic burdens on ERISA plans. *Id.* at 1052. The Ninth Circuit held that the economic impact of the claims was not sufficiently related to ERISA for preemption to occur. *Id.*

Similarly, the circuit utilized the "relates to" test in *Providence Health Plan v. McDowell,* 361 F.3d 1243, 1247 (9th Cir. 2004), defining the terms "reference to" and "connected with" as applied to ERISA plans. A sufficient reference exists when the state-law claim relies on an ERISA plan and such a plan is essential to the law's operation. *Id.* A claim is connected with an employee benefit plan if the action affects an ERISA relationship, i.e., the relationship test. *Id.*

In *Associated Builders & Contractors of Southern California, Inc. v. Nunn,* 356 F.3d 979, 981 (9th Cir. 2004), plaintiffs sought an injunction to prevent the State of California from amending regulations that established minimum wages for apprentices, arguing that the provisions were preempted by ERISA. The Ninth Circuit found that the amendments did not act exclusively on ERISA plans nor were ERISA plans essential to their operation. *Id.* at 984. Thus, the amendments did not have a sufficient reference to employee benefit plans. *Id.* Likewise, the amendments were not connected with ERISA plans because apprentice regulations have traditionally been an area of state concern and thus the amendments did not deal with ERISA-governed relationships. *Id.*

The Ninth Circuit in *Oregon Columbia Brick Masons Joint Apprenticeship Training Comm. v. Gardner,* 448 F.3d 1082 (9th Cir. 2006), followed *Travelers, Dillingham,* and *Nunn* in ruling that an Oregon statute that promoted apprentice training programs by establishing a registration system for programs that met specified criteria was not preempted by ERISA. Two apprenticeship training programs submitted applications to register with the governing council. *Id.* at 1084. The council rejected their applications for registration as apprenticeship training programs, concluding that appellants did not offer programs that satisfied any unmet needs of the existing programs. *Id.* The Ninth Circuit held that Oregon's needs requirement was indifferent to funding, and attendant ERISA coverage, of apprenticeship programs because it did not distinguish between funded and unfunded plans. *Id.* at 1087. *See also Dillingham,* 519 U.S. 328; *see also Nunn,* F.3d at 984. Therefore, the Ninth Circuit affirmed the district court's ruling that the Oregon statute's needs requirement did not refer to ERISA, nor did it have an impermissible connection to ERISA. *Id.* at 1091.

## C. Preemption of Malpractice Claims

A significant battleground for managed care organizations (MCOs) in recent years arises out of the sometimes subtle distinction between coverage or benefit determination decisions, i.e., the availability of benefits under a managed care plan, and the quality of decisions regarding medical care provided to a plan participant. In this regard, courts have tended to distinguish between state laws and/or claims involving quality of care (not preempted under ERISA) and those involving administration of a benefit plan (preempted).

In *Cleghorn v. Blue Shield,* 408 F.3d 1222 (9th Cir. 2005), the plaintiff was a participant in his employer's ERISA health plan offered by Blue Shield of California. *Id.* at 1223. The plaintiff sought and received emergency medical services, for which Blue Shield denied reimbursement. *Id.* The plaintiff sued Blue Shield in California state court, asserting state-law causes of action and alleging that Blue Shield had violated an emergency care provision in Section 1371.4(c) of the California Health and Safety Code. *Id.* Blue Shield removed the action to federal court on the grounds that the plaintiff's state-law causes of action were completely preempted by ERISA. *Id.* at 1224. The district court held that the plaintiff's claims were preempted by ERISA. *Id.* When the plaintiff declined to amend his complaint to allege an ERISA claim, the district court dismissed his complaint for failure to state a claim. *Id.*

On appeal, the Ninth Circuit affirmed the judgment of the district court, following the principles set forth in both *Pilot Life* and *Elliot* by stating that the refusal of Blue Shield to reimburse the plaintiff for the emergency medical care he received falls under Blue Shield's administration of ERISA-regulated benefit plans. *Cleghorn,* 408 F.3d at 1226; *see also Aetna Health Inc. v. Davila,* 542 U.S. 200, 208–210 (2004); *Pilot Life Ins. Co. v. Dedeaux,* 481 U.S. 41, 54 (1987) (noting that the "policy choices reflected in the inclusion of certain remedies and the exclusion of others under the federal scheme would be completely undermined if ERISA-plan participants and beneficiaries were free to obtain remedies under state law that Congress rejected in ERISA."); *Elliot v. Fortis Benefits Ins. Co.,* 337 F.3d 1138, 1147 (9th Cir. 2003) (holding that an action "which seeks non-ERISA damages for what are essentially claim processing causes of action clearly falls under the § 1132 preemption exemplified by Pilot Life."); *Dishman v. UNUM Life Ins. Co.,* 269 F.3d 974, 983 (9th Cir. 2001) (ruling that "claimants simply cannot obtain relief by dressing up an ERISA benefits claim in the garb of a state law tort.").

The Ninth Circuit, in *Bui v. AT&T, Inc.,* 310 F.3d 1143 (9th Cir. 2003), held that ERISA did not preempt a malpractice claim brought by the widow of a plan participant against his employer and a direct services provider with which his employer had contracted to provide emergency medical advice and evacuation services to enrollees working abroad. There, the plaintiff alleged that the direct services provider caused her husband's death by negligently advising him to stay in Saudi Arabia where the decedent was working and by failing to evacuate him when his medical condition became serious. The court stated, "Medical malpractice is one traditional field of state regulation that several circuits have concluded Congress did not intend to preempt." *Id.* at 1147. The court then held that state-law standards for medical malpractice apply equally to service providers treating ERISA and non-ERISA beneficiaries. If a claim involves a medical decision made in the course of treatment, ERISA does not preempt it; but if a claim involves an administrative decision made in the course of administering an ERISA plan, ERISA preempts it. *Id.* at 1149.

The court did note that had the failure to evacuate the decedent resulted from an administrative decision, ERISA would preempt this claim, but found no evidence in the record suggesting that the failure was in any way administrative.

In *Satterly v. Life Care Centers of America, Inc.,* 61 P.3d 468 (Ariz. App. Div. 1, 2003), the Arizona Court of Appeals distinguished *Bui* and affirmed the lower state court decision to dismiss the plaintiffs' tort and contract claims due to ERISA preemption. The defendant entered into a group service agreement with an insurance company to provide health insurance for the defendant's employees. *Id.* at 470. The plan provided that the defendant would pay the monthly premiums with deductions from the employee payroll and with its own contributions. *Id.* After failure to remit insurance payments, the plaintiffs filed a class action suit alleging state-law claims of breach of contract, breach of fiduciary duty, fraud, negligent misrepresentation, conversion, accounting, and negligence. *Id.* at 470–71. After the defendant moved to dismiss the action under ERISA, the plaintiffs cited *Bui* as authority in arguing that ERISA does not preempt their state-law contract and tort claims. *Id.* at 472. The appeals court held that unlike in *Bui,* the plaintiffs' claims did not involve any allegation of negligent medical advice or treatment. *Id.* Rather, the claims focused on the administrative failure to remit premiums to the insurer, an obligation not only required by the terms of the plan agreement, but also part of the administration of an ERISA plan. *Id.*

Several other courts have held that ERISA does not preempt negligence claims that involve quality of care and are unrelated to benefit determinations. *See, e.g., Crum v. Health Alliance-Midwest, Inc.,* 1999 WL 284785 (C.D. Ill. 1999); *Moreno v. Health Partners Plan,* 4 F. Supp. 2d 888 (D. Ariz. 1998); *Roessert v. Health Net,* 929 F. Supp. 343 (N.D. Cal. 1996).

The Supreme Court case *Pegram v. Herdrich,* 530 U.S. 211 (2000), although not a preemption case, added substantial fuel to the debate over ERISA preemption of claims against MCOs. In the context of litigation against MCOs the critical issue is whether plaintiffs may avoid ERISA preemption altogether any time an MCO denies benefits on the basis that the treatment sought was not medically necessary. Although not an ERISA preemption case either, *Palmer v. Superior Court,* 103 Cal. App. 4th 953, 968 (2002), discussed the "closely intertwined nature of health insurance coverage decisions and medical necessity diagnostic decisions." In *Palmer,* the defendant was a medical provider under contract with an HMO to provide utilization review services of medical claims. *Id.* at 959. The HMO denied Palmer's benefits after the defendant suggested that there was a "lack of medical necessity." *Id.* The court held that the defendant, in making the "lack of medical necessity" decision, was acting as a health care provider even though the defendant's decision would have financial coverage consequences. *Id.* at 969.

## D. Other Preemption Issues

### 1. State Independent Review Statutes

In contrast to the independent review statutes that create no new cause of action or ultimate form of relief, California Civil Code § 3428, known as the Managed Care Insurance Accountability Act of 1999, affirmatively imposes liability on the MCO that fails to furnish covered benefits. In relevant part, Section 3428 places on an MCO a "duty of ordinary care" to provide the necessary medical care to subscribers and enrollees, where such medical care is provided for under a plan.

The statute provides, among other things, that the MCO will be liable for all harm caused by the failure to exercise ordinary care: "(1) where the failure results in the denial, delay or modification of care recommended for or furnished to the subscriber or enrollee"; and "(2) the subscriber or enrollee suffers substantial harm."

CAL. CIV. CODE § 3428(a)(1) and (2). The statute further provides that managed care entities are not health care providers under California law. CAL. CIV. CODE § 3428(d).

In enacting this statute, the California legislature has attempted to circumvent ERISA preemption by declaring that managed care entities, for the purposes of California Civil Code § 3428, are "engaged in the business of insurance . . . as that term is defined for the purposes of the McCarran-Ferguson Act." *See* 1999 Cal. Stat. 536 § 1, 2 (S.B. 21).

Whether California Civil Code § 3428 will withstand preemption under ERISA remains to be seen. One district court has already determined that claims based on alleged violations of California Civil Code § 3428 are indeed preempted. *Lagomarsino v. Aetna US Healthcare, Inc.*, No. CV 03-2741-GAF (C.D. Cal. August 20, 2003). There, the court rejected the plaintiff's contention that their claims were saved from preemption because California Civil Code § 3428 regulates the business of insurance. The court applied the two-prong test enunciated in *Kentucky Association of Health Plans, Inc. v. Miller*, 538 U.S. 329 (2003), and held that the statute does not affect the risk-pooling arrangement between insurer and insured as would, for example, California's notice-prejudice rule, which requires an insurer to expand its time limit to accept proofs of claim. Instead, the court held that California Civil Code § 3428 "merely provides for a standard of conduct ('ordinary care') in arranging for services and benefits already called for by the policy." The court also held that California Civil Code § 3428 added a state-law remedy as an alternative to ERISA's remedial scheme, a result not allowed under *Pilot Life*, 481 U.S. at 57. This ruling was on appeal, but the Ninth Circuit dismissed the appeal for failure to prosecute.

### 2. Bad-Faith Claims

In *Bast,* the plaintiff offered an interesting yet unpersuasive argument as to why his insurance bad-faith claim should not be preempted by ERISA. *Bast v. Prudential Ins. Co. of Am.,* 150 F.2d 1003, 1008 (9th Cir. 1998). The plaintiff argued that he was not suing the plan, but was suing his insurance company as a business in Washington for violating the state insurance code. *Id.* The Ninth Circuit found that the plaintiff's bad-faith claims related to the defendant's actions as an employee benefit administrator, not as an insurance company. Thus, the claims were not exempt from ERISA under the savings clause.

In *Ritchie v. Cox Enters. Long Term Disability Plan Co.,* 2006 U.S. Dist. LEXIS 14536, 2006 WL 798871 (D. Ariz. 2006), the district court followed *Bast* and dismissed the plaintiff's bad-faith action against the plan administrator for denial of disability benefits on the basis that ERISA provides the exclusive remedial scheme.

## III. Exhaustion of Administrative Remedies

### A. Is Exhaustion an Absolute Requirement?

Claimants must exhaust administrative remedies before filing a lawsuit for benefits. *Dishman v. UNUM Life Ins. Co. of Am.,* 269 F.3d 974, 984 (9th Cir. 2001) (finding that federal courts have authority to enforce exhaustion requirement); *Diaz v. United Agric. Employee Welfare Benefit Plan,* 50 F.3d 1478 (9th Cir. 1995); *Amato v.*

*Bernard,* 618 F.2d 559 (9th Cir. 1980). Where a suit for ERISA plan benefits is filed before the claims administrator has issued its final administrative appeal decision, the suit is subject to dismissal. Some plans have multiple levels of mandatory appeals that must be exhausted before suit can be filed.

### B. Exceptions to the Exhaustion Requirement

Where the administrative route of appeal is futile or the available remedy inadequate, the Ninth Circuit has found that the district court has discretion to waive the administrative exhaustion requirement. *Amato v. Bernard,* 618 F.2d 559, 568 (9th Cir. 1980); *see also Dishman v. UNUM Life Ins. Co. of Am.,* 269 F.3d 974, 984 (9th Cir. 2001). "Bare assertions of futility are insufficient to bring a claim within the futility exception, which is designed to avoid the need to pursue an administrative review that is demonstrably doomed to fail." *Diaz v. United Agric. Employee Welfare Benefit Plan,* 50 F.3d 1478, 1485 (9th Cir. 1995). Also, a plan's failure to establish and follow reasonable claims procedures may result in administrative remedies being deemed exhausted under 29 C.F.R. § 2560.503-1(l).

### C. Consequences of Failure to Exhaust

In general, a failure to exhaust administrative remedies will bar a claimant from bringing a claim in federal court and will warrant dismissal of the complaint. *See Amato v. Bernard,* 618 F.2d 559, 566–68 (9th Cir. 1980).

### D. Minimum Number of Levels of Administrative Review

There is no minimum other than as set forth by regulation. 29 C.F.R. § 2560.503-1.

### E. Can a Defendant Waive a Failure-to-Exhaust Defense?

The Ninth Circuit has not addressed this issue.

## IV. Standard of Review

### A. Plan Language

In order for the abuse of discretion standard to apply, the plan language must unambiguously confer discretion upon the administrator. A requirement that the claimant produce "satisfactory proof" is insufficient to confer discretion. *Kearney v. Standard Ins. Co.,* 175 F.3d 1084, 1090 (9th Cir. 1999). The Ninth Circuit has stated in no uncertain terms that "unless plan documents unambiguously say in sum or substance that the plan Administrator or fiduciary has authority, power, or discretion to determine eligibility or to construe the terms of the plan, the standard of review will be de novo." *Sandy v. Reliance Standard Life Ins. Co.,* 222 F.3d 1202, 1206 (9th Cir. 2000). Recently, the Ninth Circuit held that wording "granting the power to interpret plan terms and to make final benefits determinations" is sufficient to confer discretion on the plan administrator. *Abatie v. Alta Health & Life Ins. Co.,* 2006 U.S. App. LEXIS 20829 (9th Cir. August 15, 2006). For a grant of discretionary authority to be effective it must be in plan documents; grants contained in the summary plan description alone are not sufficient. *Grosz-Salomon v. Paul Revere Life Ins. Co.,* 237 F.3d 1154 (9th Cir. 2001).

## B. What Standard of Review Applies?

The district court will review the denial de novo unless the plan language grants to the administrator the power to interpret plan terms and make final benefits determinations. If such language is present, the court reviews the decision for abuse of discretion. *Abatie v. Alta Health & Life Ins. Co.,* 2006 U.S. App. LEXIS 20829 (9th Cir. August 15, 2006). An exception lies in circumstances where the administrator's procedural violations are so flagrant as to alter the substantive relationship between the employer and the employee, thereby causing substantive harm to the beneficiary. *Gatti v. Reliance Standard Life Ins. Co.,* 415 F.3d 978, 985 (9th Cir. 2005). In such cases, the court will conduct a de novo review, notwithstanding the grant of discretion.

Under the abuse of discretion standard of review, an administrator's decision must be upheld unless it is not grounded on any reasonable basis. *Horan v. Kaiser Steel Ret. Plan,* 947 F.2d 1412, 1417 (9th Cir. 1991). A court may not substitute its own judgment for that of the administrator unless the administrator's decision was clearly erroneous, or if the administrator rendered its decision without any explanation, or construed provisions of the plan in a way that conflicts with the plain language of the plan. *Eley v. Boeing Co.,* 945 F.2d 276, 279 (9th Cir. 1991); *Taft v. Equitable Life Assurance Soc.,* 9 F.3d 1469, 1473 (9th Cir. 1993). *See also Boyd v. Bert Bell/Pete Rozelle NFL Players Retirement Fund,* 410 F.3d 1173 (9th Cir. 2005). The Ninth Circuit has noted that in the context of ERISA claims the abuse of discretion standard is the same as the "arbitrary and capricious" standard of review. *Taft,* 9 F.3d at 1471 n.2.

However, in determining whether the administrator abused its discretion, the court must take into account the nature, extent, and effect of any conflict of interest that may appear in the record, as well as evidence of procedural violations or irregularities. *Abatie v. Alta Health & Life Insurance Co.,* 2006 U.S. App. LEXIS 20829 (9th Cir. August 15, 2006). Such evidence may heighten judicial scrutiny. While the court explicitly rejected the "sliding scale" approach, it did hold that in each instance the district court shall determine how much weight to give to the administrator's decision, after consideration of the factors set forth above. To the extent that *Atwood v. Newmont Gold Company, Inc.,* 45 F.3d 1317 (9th Cir. 1995) and other cases formerly held that claimants were required to produce "material, probative evidence, beyond the mere fact of the apparent conflict, tending to show that the fiduciary's self-interest caused a breach of the administrator's fiduciary obligations to the beneficiary" in order to obtain a more favorable standard of review, such cases are overruled by *Abatie.*

Under the de novo standard of review, the court does not give deference to the administrator's decision, but instead reviews the evidence and makes its own determination as to the ultimate issue (e.g., whether the plaintiff is disabled under the terms of the policy). *Kearney v. Standard Ins. Co.,* 175 F.3d 1084, 1095 (9th Cir. 1999).

## C. Effect of Conflict of Interest or Procedural Irregularity

The existence of a conflict of interest is a factor to be weighed in determining whether an administrator has abused its discretion. *Abatie v. Alta Health & Life Insurance Co.,* 2006 U.S. App. LEXIS 20829 (9th Cir. August 15, 2006), citing *Fire-*

*stone Tire & Rubber Co. v. Bruch*, 489 U.S. 101 (1989). The effect on the standard of review depends on the extent to which the conflict affected the decision. The Ninth Circuit has repeatedly held that the mere fact that the administrator is both the decision maker and the payor (an "apparent" or "inherent" conflict) is insufficient to create a conflict of interest that alters the standard of review. *Lang v. Long-Term Disability Plan*, 125 F.3d 794, 799 (9th Cir. 1997); *Bendixen v. Standard Ins. Co.*, 185 F.3d 939, 943 (9th Cir. 1999); *Atwood v. Newmont Gold Co.*, 45 F.3d 1317, 1322 (9th Cir. 1999). In *Abatie*, the court stated that "[t]he level of skepticism with which a court views a conflicted administrator's decision may be low if a structural conflict of interest is unaccompanied, for example, by any evidence of malice, of self-dealing, or of a parsimonious claims-granting history." Conversely, courts may give less deference to the claims decision where there is evidence of inconsistent reasons for denial (*Lang*, 125 F.3d at 797); or where the administrator fails to adequately investigate a claim or to ask the claimant for necessary evidence (*Booton v. Lockheed Med. Benefit Plan*, 110 F.3d 1461, 1463–64 (9th Cir. 1997)); or where the administrator fails to credit a claimant's reliable evidence (*Black & Decker Disability Plan v. Nord*, 538 U.S. 822, 834 (2003)); or has repeatedly denied benefits to deserving participants by interpreting plan terms incorrectly or by making decisions against the weight of evidence in the record (*Abatie*, 2006 U.S. App. LEXIS 20829).

A violation of procedural requirements is another factor to be taken into account by the court in determining the weight to give to the administrator's decision. Ordinarily, a procedural violation does not divest the administrator of the discretion granted by the terms of the plan. *Gatti v. Reliance Standard Life Ins. Co.*, 415 F.3d 978, 985 (9th Cir. 2005). However, de novo review is appropriate in cases where the violations are so flagrant as to alter the substantive relationship between employer and employee. *Id.* at 985. One example is *Blau v. Del Monte Corp.*, 748 F.2d 1348 (9th Cir. 1984), *abrogated on other grounds recognized by Dytrt v. Mountain State Tel. & Tel. Co.*, 921 F.2d 889, 894 n.4 (9th Cir. 1990). In *Blau*, the administrator failed to disclose details of the plan to employees and provided no claims procedure. In the absence of such flagrant conduct, procedural irregularities are matters to be weighed in deciding whether an administrator has abused its discretion. *Abatie*, 2006 U.S. App. LEXIS 20829, citing *Fought v. Unum Life Ins. Co.*, 379 F.3d 997 (10th Cir. 2004).

The judge may consider evidence outside the administrative record to determine the extent to which the administrator's decision was tainted by a conflict of interest. *Abatie*, 2006 U.S. App. LEXIS 20829; *Tremain*, 196 F.3d 970. In situations where the administrator has engaged in a procedural irregularity that has affected the administrative review, the court will reconsider the claim denial after providing the claimant the opportunity to submit additional evidence. *Abatie*, citing *VanderKlok v. Provident Life & Accident Ins. Co.*, 956 F.2d 610, 617 (6th Cir. 1992).

## D. Other Factors Affecting Standard of Review

### *1. Timeliness*

Failure to timely issue a claims decision may also be sufficient to warrant de novo review. *See Jebian v. Hewlett Packard*, 349 F.3d 1098, 1109 n.8 (9th Cir. 2003).

Subsequent case law, however, limits *Jebian* to its facts, specifically the fact that the plan language included a "deemed denied" clause that cut off the administrator's discretion. Where the plan fails to comply with ERISA's procedural guidelines, the claimant is afforded the right to bring suit, but the administrator does not automatically lose discretion otherwise granted under the terms of the plan. *Gatti v. Reliance Standard Life Ins. Co.,* 415 F.3d 978, 983 (9th Cir. 2005). This is consistent with the Ninth Circuit's prior holding that no substantive remedies are available for procedural violations of ERISA unless the procedural violations rise to a level that "alter[s] the substantive relationship between employer and employee." *Id.* at 984–85, citing *Blau v. Del Monte Corp.,* 748 F.2d 1348 (9th Cir. 1984).

The Ninth Circuit has also created a "good faith" exception to the *Jebian* rule. Where even though a claim is "deemed denied" under the terms of the plan at issue, an exception to the loss of discretion exists for administrators who are "engaged in a good faith attempt to comply with its deadlines." *See LaMantia v. Voluntary Plan Administrators, Inc.,* 401 F.3d 1114, 1122 (9th Cir. 2005).

### 2. Discretionary Clauses

On February 26, 2004, in a letter opinion issued by the Department of Insurance of the State of California, General Counsel Gary M. Cohen stated, "Discretionary clauses render the contract 'fraudulent or unsound insurance' within the meaning of [California Insurance Code] § 10291.5. Although the contract contains the insurer's promise to pay benefits under the stated conditions, the discretionary clause makes those payments contingent on the *unfettered discretion* of the insurer, thereby nullifying the promise to pay and rendering the contract potentially illusory." Ltr. Op. per Cal. Ins. Code § 12921.9: Discretionary Clauses (Feb. 26, 2004) (emphasis added). The letter opinion further states that discretionary clauses "effectively shield insurers who deny meritorious claims." *Id.*

Immediately following the letter opinion, on February 27, 2004, the California Department of Insurance issued notice to "All Disability Insurers Doing Business in California" that "The Insurance Commissioner withdraws any approval of the forms listed below for the reason that the forms contain Discretionary Clauses." The Department of Insurance also specifically withdrew approval of policy forms issued by The Hartford, Unum Life Insurance Company of America, Provident Life and Accident Insurance Company, and Metropolitan Life Insurance Company. Unum Life and The Hartford requested administrative review; by order dated March 18, 2005, an administrative law judge upheld the Department of Insurance's withdrawal of approval. Subsequently, in an October 2005 meeting with a number of disability carriers, the Department of Insurance indicated its intention to require a number of modifications to disability policy firms, including but not limited to the elimination of any language purporting to grant discretion in claims review.

The Hartford filed an action seeking a writ of mandate and declaratory/injunctive relief in the San Francisco Superior Court. On June 8, 2006, the court issued a statement of decision denying writ of mandate and upholding the Department of

Insurance's actions. In November 2005, the Association of California Life & Health Insurance Companies (ACLHIC), America's Health Insurance Plans, the American Council of Life Insurers, and the California Chamber of Commerce filed suit in Sacramento County Superior Court, seeking an order preventing the Department of Insurance from banning discretionary language and from requiring other modifications to disability policy forms. The parties in the ACLHIC matter reached a settlement in July 2006 under which both sides agreed to adopt the final determination with respect to discretionary language from the *Hartford v. Garadmendi* matter. The parties also agreed to further administrative review and consideration of policy language containing "additional benefit triggers" (i.e., other preconditions to payment of benefits besides the existence of a disabling illness or injury, such as actual loss of income, appropriate care, or a requirement that the claimant actually be precluded from working).

The courts, in the interim, have held for the most part that the letter opinion and the withdrawal of approval of discretionary language apply only prospectively, and do not affect policies that are currently in force. *See Boyd v. Aetna Life Ins. Co.,* 2006 U.S. Dist. LEXIS 47263 (C.D. Cal. 2006); *Lundquist v. Cont'l Cas. Co.,* 394 F. Supp. 2d 1230 (C.D. Cal. 2005); *Williston v. Norwood Promotional Prod. Inc. Long Term Disability Plan,* 2005 U.S. Dist. LEXIS 40732 (C.D. Cal. 2005); *Moskowite v. Everen Capital Corp. Group Disability Income Plan,* 2005 U.S. Dist. LEXIS 20842 (N.D. Cal. 2005); *Mitchell v. Aetna Life Ins. Co.,* 359 F. Supp. 2d 880 (C.D. Cal. 2005); *Firestone v. Acuson Corp. Long Term Disability Plan,* 326 F. Supp. 2d 1040 (N.D. Cal. 2004); *Washington v. Standard Ins. Co.,* 2004 U.S. Dist. LEXIS 22975 (N.D. Cal. 2004); *Horn v. Provident Life & Accident Ins. Co.,* 351 F. Supp. 2d 954 (N.D. Cal. 2004). *Contra, Fenberg v. Cowden Auto. Long Term Disability Plan,* 2004 U.S. Dist. LEXIS 22927 (N.D. Cal. 2004).

# V. Rules of Plan Interpretation

## A. Application of Federal Common Law

Federal courts apply federal common law when faced with issues of insurance policy interpretation. *Padfield v. AIG Life Ins. Co.,* 290 F.3d 1121, 1125 (9th Cir. 2002). Under federal common law the *Padfield* court stated, "[W]e interpret terms in ERISA insurance policies in an ordinary and popular sense as would a person of average intelligence and experience. As we develop federal common law to govern ERISA suits, we may borrow from state law where appropriate, and [be] guided by the policies expressed in ERISA and other federal labor laws." *Id.* (internal quotations and citation omitted).

## B. Application of *Contra Proferentem*

The court may apply *contra proferentem* only where the court is reviewing the decision de novo; if the plan gives the administrator discretion to interpret the terms of the plan, application of the principle of *contra proferentem* is not appropriate. *See Winters v. Costco Wholesale Corp.,* 49 F.3d 550 (9th Cir. 1995).

### C. Deference Afforded to an Administrator's Interpretation of a Plan

Deference is given to the administrator's interpretation only where the plan language expressly confers such discretion. Under the de novo standard the court applies common law and renders its own decision on the appropriate interpretation. *See Padfield v. AIG Life Ins. Co.,* 290 F.3d 1121, 1125 (9th Cir. 2002); *Winters v. Costco Wholesale Corp.,* 49 F.3d 550 (9th Cir. 1995).

### D. Other Rules of Plan or Contract Interpretation

The Ninth Circuit has applied the *ejusdem generis* cannon of construction in one recent ERISA case. *See Shaver v. Operating Eng'r Local 428 Pension Trust Fund,* 332 F.3d 1198 (9th Cir. 2003).

The Ninth Circuit has been silent on the effect of plan amendments on pending claims. In other contexts, however, it has held that so long as it is contemplated in the plan, federal law does not prohibit an employer from altering the package of medical benefits that it provides its employees, but only from interfering with an employee's use of the benefits provided. *See, e.g., Serrato v. John Hancock Mut. Life Ins. Co.,* 31 F.3d 882, 884 (9th Cir. 1994) (health care benefits not vested under ERISA); *Joanou v. Coca-Cola Co.,* 26 F.3d 96, 98 (9th Cir. 1994) (employers providing employees with ERISA-qualified welfare plans "remain free to unilaterally *amend* or *eliminate* such plans without considering the employees' interests.") (emphasis in original).

# VI. Discovery

## A. Limitations on Discovery

When reviewing the determination of a plan administrator under the deferential abuse of discretion standard, the Ninth Circuit has held that courts are generally limited to reviewing evidence in the administrative record before the administrator at the time of its decision. *Abatie v. Alta Health & Life Ins. Co.,* 2006 U.S. App. LEXIS 20829 (9th Cir. August 15, 2006); *Taft v. Equitable Life Assurance Soc.,* 9 F.3d 1469, 1471–72 (9th Cir. 1993). However, the court has discretion to consider evidence outside of the administrative record for the limited purpose of evaluating the nature, extent, and effect of any conflict of interest. *Abatie,* citing *Doe v. Travelers Ins. Co.,* 167 F.3d 53, 57 (1st Cir. 1999). *Abatie* does not address the issue of what discovery, if any, claimants will be allowed to take in order to obtain such evidence. Under the former *Atwood* standard, courts allowed limited discovery to explore a potential conflict of interest.

A number of courts have rejected complete limitations on discovery. In *Alford v. DCH Found. Group LTD Plan,* 144 F. Supp. 2d 1183 (C.D. Cal. 2001), *aff'd on other grounds,* 311 F.3d 955 (9th Cir. 2002), the court held that discovery would be allowed to show conflict of interest but not to show that the decision was an abuse of discretion. *Accord, Medford v. Metro. Life Ins. Co.,* 244 F. Supp. 2d 1120 (D. Nev. 2003). The court discussed the dual goals of obtaining justice for the parties and prompt and fair claims settlement procedures and adopted the analysis of the court in *Waggoner v. UNUM Life Insurance Co.,* 238 F. Supp. 2d 1179 (S.D. Cal. 2002). Limited discovery relevant to the following was allowed:

1.  Whether a conflict of interest existed;
2.  If there was such a conflict, whether it affected the decision of denial; and
3.  The neutrality of the medical providers defendant relied on in denying benefits.

### B. Discovery and Conflict of Interest

*Abatie* expressly allows courts to consider evidence from outside the record concerning a potential conflict of interest. 2006 U.S. App. LEXIS 20829. However, since plaintiffs no longer have the burden of demonstrating that the potential conflict materially affected the claims decision as was the case before *Abatie (see, e.g., Tremain v. Bell Industries,* 196 F.3d 970, 976–77 (9th Cir. 1999)) the availability and necessity for discovery into the nature and extent of the conflict is an open question. In *Futamura v. UNUM Life Insurance Co. of America,* 305 F. Supp. 2d 1181 (W.D. Wa. 2004), the district court considered several motions to strike supplemental declarations. In *Futamura,* the plaintiff brought a cause of action against his employee benefit plan administrator, UNUM, after he was denied disability benefits. *Id.* at 1184.

UNUM moved to strike the supplemental declaration of a former UNUM employee who had no knowledge of the plaintiff's specific case but provided information regarding incentives given to employees based on high claim denial rates. *Id.* at 1188–89. The district court held that the evidence, although not part of the administrative record, was relevant to the alleged conflict of interest and could be admitted to supplement the record. *Id.* at 1189. *Abatie's* holding that a plan's history of misinterpreting plan terms and/or making decisions contrary to the weight of the evidence is relevant to the amount of deference to be granted to the decision at issue suggests that such evidence is both discoverable and admissible.

Similarly, UNUM moved to strike the declarations of two doctors who issued reports relating to the plaintiff's health history. *Futamura,* 305 F. Supp. 2d at 1191. Because this evidence was not part of the administrative record and was included only to illustrate that UNUM abused its discretion rather than to demonstrate a conflict of interest, the court granted UNUM's motion to strike.

# VII. Evidence

### A. Scope of Evidence under Standards of Review

The Ninth Circuit has held that the district court's determination as to whether an administrator abused its discretion is limited to reviewing the evidence in the administrative record before the administrator at the time of its decision. *Abatie,* 2006 U.S. App. LEXIS 20829; *Taft v. Equitable Life Assurance Soc.,* 9 F.3d 1469, 1471–72 (9th Cir. 1993). In most circumstances, ERISA cases under de novo review should be limited to the administrative record where possible. District courts may look beyond the record "only when circumstances clearly establish that additional evidence is necessary to conduct an adequate de novo review of the benefit decision." *Thomas v. Oregon Fruit Prods. Co.,* 228 F.3d 991, 997 (9th Cir. 2000); *Kearney v.*

*Standard Ins. Co.,* 175 F.3d 1084, 1095 (9th Cir. 1999); *Mongeluzo v. Baxter Travenol,* 46 F.3d 938, 944 (9th Cir. 1995).

### B. Evidentiary Value of Social Security Determinations

The Ninth Circuit has found that eligibility for social security disability does not necessarily mean a person is eligible for ERISA disability benefits. *Madden v. ITT Long Term Disability Plan for Salaried Employees,* 914 F.2d 1279, 1286 (9th Cir. 1990) (stating that "if [this] argument were correct, ERISA fiduciaries would be stripped of all administrative discretion, as they would be required to follow the Department of Health and Human Services' decisions regarding social security benefits, even where the Plan determines benefits under different standards or the medical evidence presented is to the contrary").

The Supreme Court recently overturned the Ninth Circuit's importation of Social Security's treating physician rule to ERISA cases. *See Black & Decker Disability Plan v. Nord,* 538 U.S. 822 (2003) (holding that "ERISA does not require plan administrators to accord special deference to the opinions of treating physicians" in determining whether an employee is disabled).

### C. Other Evidence Issues

No other significant evidence issues have arisen in the Ninth Circuit.

## VIII. Procedural Aspects of ERISA Practice

### A. Methods of Adjudication

The Ninth Circuit has held that under the abuse of discretion standard of review, a motion for summary judgment is "the conduit to bring the legal question before the district court, and the usual tests of summary judgment, such as whether a dispute of material fact exists, do not apply." *Bendixen v. Standard Ins. Co.,* 185 F.3d 939, 942 (9th Cir. 1999).

De novo cases may be resolved by motion for summary judgment only if there is no genuine issue of material fact in dispute. *Tremain v. Bell Industries,* 196 F.3d 970 (9th Cir. 1999).

### B. Reported ERISA Trials

If a question of fact exists, the court will hold a bench trial on the record. The Ninth Circuit has clarified that the trial court judge "will be asking a different question as he reads the evidence [than on summary judgment], not whether there is a genuine issue of material fact, but instead whether [the plaintiff] is disabled within the terms of the policy. In a trial on the record, but not on summary judgment, the judge can evaluate the persuasiveness of conflicting testimony and decide which is more likely true." *Kearney v. Standard Ins. Co.,* 175 F.3d 1084, 1094 (9th Cir. 1999). "Although Rule 43(a) [of the Federal Rules of Civil Procedure] requires that 'testimony' be taken in open court, the record should be regarded as being, in the nature of exhibits, in the nature of documents, which are routinely a basis for findings of fact even though no one reads them aloud." *Id.*

# IX. Fiduciary Liability Claims

## A. Definition of Fiduciary

Under ERISA, a person is a plan fiduciary to the extent he or she (1) exercises discretionary authority or control over plan management or control over management or disposition of plan assets, (2) renders investment advice regarding plan assets for a fee or other compensation or has authority to do so, or (3) has any discretionary authority or responsibility in plan administration. 29 U.S.C. § 1002(21)(A).

## B. Definition of Fiduciary Duties

An ERISA fiduciary has a basic duty to act "solely in the interest" of plan participants and fiduciaries, and for the "exclusive purpose" of providing benefits and defraying reasonable expenses of plan administration. 29 U.S.C. § 1104(a). A fiduciary is required to discharge these duties (1) with the care, skill, and diligence of a prudent person; (2) by diversifying investments to minimize the risk; and (3) in accordance with the plan documents. § 1104(a)(1)(B).

## C. Fiduciary Liability in the Context of Health and Disability Claims

An ERISA plan administrator has a fiduciary duty to provide timely notification to employees of the termination of an employee welfare benefit plan. *Peralta v. Hispanic Bus. Inc.,* 419 F.3d 1064, 1072 (9th Cir. 2005) (administrator breached fiduciary duty in failing to notify employees that long-term disability plan had terminated).

## D. Remedies for Breach of Fiduciary Duty

An ERISA fiduciary will also be liable to the extent he engages in any "prohibited transactions." 29 U.S.C. § 1106. There are two types of prohibited transactions identified by ERISA: (1) transactions with a party in interest (defined as another fiduciary, a person providing services to the plan, an employer of the employees covered by the plan, or a spouse or child of the foregoing); (2) self-dealing on the part of the fiduciary by using plan assets for his own interest or for his own account. *Id.*

## E. Contribution and Indemnity Claims among Fiduciaries

Unlike some other circuits, the Ninth Circuit does *not* recognize claims for contribution or indemnity among breaching ERISA fiduciaries. *Call v. Sumitomo Bank of Cal.,* 881 F.2d 626 (9th Cir. 1989); *Kim v. Fujikawa,* 871 F.2d 1427 (9th Cir. 1989). However, in certain circumstances, e.g., where cofiduciary was the one who improperly calculated and paid benefits, an indemnity claim may be proper under 29 U.S.C. § 1132(a)(8). *See Younberg v. Bekins, Co.,* 930 F. Supp. 1396 (E.D. Cal. 1996).

## F. ERISA Claims against Nonfiduciaries

A nonfiduciary does not subject itself to liability simply by participating in a breach of trust by fiduciaries. *See Batchelor v. Oak Hill Med. Group,* 870 F.2d 1446 (9th Cir. 1989); *Nieto v. Ecker,* 845 F.2d 868 (9th Cir. 1988). The Ninth Circuit has even rejected an argument to hold a nonfiduciary liable when that individual was a knowing participant in the breach of fiduciary. *Mertens v. Hewitt Assoc.,* 948 F.2d 607

(9th Cir. 1991). Nonfiduciaries may, however, be liable for equitable relief if they are a "party in interest" and engaged in prohibited conduct. *See Call v. Sumitomo Bank of Cal.,* 881 F.2d 626 (9th Cir. 1989); *see also Concha v. London,* 62 F.3d 1493 (9th Cir. 1995) (subject to liability under ERISA § 406); *Steen v. John Hancock Mut. Life Ins. Co.,* 106 F.3d 904 (9th Cir. 1997) (subject to liability as set forth in ERISA § 406).

## X. Attorneys' Fees

### A. Criteria for Awarding Attorneys' Fees

In an ERISA action, a court may use its discretion in awarding reasonable attorneys' fees and costs. 29 U.S.C. § 1132(g). In *Hummell v. Rykoff,* 634 F.2d 446, 453 (9th Cir. 1980), the Ninth Circuit set forth five factors for courts to use as guidelines in exercising this discretion: (1) the degree of the opposing parties' culpability or bad faith; (2) the ability of the opposing parties to satisfy an award of fees; (3) whether an award of fees against the opposing parties would deter others from acting under similar circumstances; (4) whether the parties requesting fees sought to benefit all participants and beneficiaries of an ERISA plan or to resolve a significant legal question regarding ERISA; and (5) the relative merits of the parties' positions. *Hummell,* 634 F.2d at 453.

In applying the *Hummell* factors, courts must keep in mind that the purpose of ERISA is to protect participants in employee benefit plans; thus, the factors should be liberally construed to serve that purpose. *McElwaine v. US West, Inc.,* 176 F.3d 1167, 1172 (9th Cir. 1999). Furthermore, it is not required that each of the factors be supportive of awarding fees. *Id.* at 1774. Rather, the *Hummell* factors should be viewed as a balancing test. *Id.*

While the presence of the first factor, bad faith by the opposing party, justifies an award of fees, it is not required. *Smith v. CMTA-IAM Pension Trust,* 746 F.2d 587, 590 (9th Cir. 1984). In *Smith,* the parties settled a dispute regarding pension benefits but could not reach an agreement concerning attorneys' fees. *Id.* at 589. The plaintiff's motion for fees was denied, and he appealed. *Id.* The Ninth Circuit noted that there was no bad faith on either side, so the first factor of the *Hummell* test was not decisive. *Id.* at 590. The second factor, the ability of the parties to satisfy an award of fees, was relevant to the court. *Id.* In considering the limited resources usually available to employees bringing suits under ERISA, the Ninth Circuit held that, absent special circumstances that would make an award of fees unjust, a prevailing ERISA employee plaintiff should ordinarily receive attorneys' fees from a defendant. *Id.* The Ninth Circuit reaffirmed this "special circumstances" rule in *Canseco v. Construction Laborers Pension Trust of Southern California,* 93 F.3d 600, 609 (9th Cir. 1996), in which the court awarded attorneys' fees to prevailing retirees in a suit to recover pension benefits.

Several recent district court cases have followed the *Smith* decision and awarded attorneys' fees to the prevailing beneficiary. For example, in *Broderick v. Prudential Insurance Co. of America,* 2005 U.S. Dist. LEXIS 21471 (C.D. Cal. 2005), the district court followed the principles set out in *Smith* regarding awarding attorneys' fees to the prevailing beneficiary by stating, "As a general rule, ERISA employee plaintiffs should be entitled to a reasonable attorney's fee if they succeed on any significant issue in litigation which achieves some of the benefit the parties sought in bringing suit." *Id.* at 2, citing *Smith,* 746 F.2d at 590. The court in *Broderick* also followed the rationale stated in the *Smith* decision that the court must "'keep at the forefront ERISA's remedial purposes that should be liberally construed in favor of protecting participants in employee benefit plans.'" *S.A. McElwaine v. U.S. West, Inc.,* 176 F.3d 1167, 1172 (9th Cir. 1999), quoting *Smith,* 746 F.2d at 589. Finally, in *Broderick,* the court also applied the "special circumstances" rule, where a successful ERISA participant "should ordinarily recover an attorney's fee unless special circumstances would render such an award unjust." *Id.*

In *McElwaine,* the plaintiff brought a claim against her former employer to recover pension benefits that were withheld from her and other retirees due to a calculation error. 176 F.3d 1167 at 1169. Because the employer made no promise to remedy the situation, the plaintiff filed suit. *Id.* Five months later, the employer made a commitment to compensate the beneficiaries, but the plaintiff continued to pursue litigation until her case was dismissed nearly a year later. *Id.* The trial court denied the plaintiff attorneys' fees, and she appealed. *Id.* In applying the *Hummell* factors, the Ninth Circuit noted that the employer may have acted in bad faith in not informing the plaintiff that it intended to pay the beneficiaries, making it necessary for her to file suit. *Id.* at 1174. Looking at the other factors, the court determined that the employer could easily pay the fee, that a fee award would serve as a deterrent for future employers, and that the plaintiff's action benefited many beneficiaries. *Id.* Thus, the Ninth Circuit held that the *Hummell* factors supported awarding the plaintiff reasonable fees. *Id.*

In *Honolulu Joint Apprenticeship & Training Committee of United Association v. Foster,* 332 F.3d 1234, 1236 (9th Cir. 2003), the plaintiff operated an apprenticeship program that trained individuals for free on the condition that they work for a union employer after completion of the program. The plaintiff brought suit against the defendant, a former apprentice, after he notified them that he was working for a nonunion employer. *Id.* The Ninth Circuit affirmed the district court's summary judgment in favor of the defendant and the denial of the defendant's attorneys' fee request. *Id.* The Ninth Circuit applied the *Hummell* factors and found that the plaintiff had not acted in bad faith; both parties were equally able to pay the fees (the defendant was being represented by a nonunion organization); there was no need for deterrence in this case; the defendant did not seek to benefit others; and neither side was relatively more meritorious. Further, the court held that awarding the defendant fees would not serve the remedial purpose of ERISA because the defendant had already received four years of training for free.

Since 2004, the Ninth Circuit has issued two unpublished opinions affirming the district courts' application of the *Hummell* factors when determining if an award of attorneys' fees and costs to the prevailing party were justified. *See Mizell v. Paul Revere Ins. Co.,* 155 Fed. Appx. 254 (9th Cir. 2005) (district court did not abuse discretion in denying attorneys' fees to Hartford as the prevailing party); *King v. GE Fin. Assurance Co.,* Fed. Appx. 995 (9th Cir. 2005) (district court properly determined that all of the *Hummell* factors weighed in favor of granting prevailing insured attorneys' fees).

While there are no recent Ninth Circuit published opinions affecting the *Hummell* decision, the district courts continue to apply the *Hummell* factors in determining whether to award attorneys' fees. In *Gunn v. Reliance Standard Life Insurance Company,* 407 F. Supp. 2d 1162 (C.D. Cal. 2006), the court weighed in on whether to grant attorneys' fees after the court determined the insured was entitled to benefits under the plan after the administrator terminated benefits. *Id.* First, the insured presented some evidence of the administrator's bad faith in the review of his claim for benefits. *Id.* at 1164. Second, there was no indication that the administrator would have been unable to satisfy an award of fees. *Id.* Third, the court determined that an award of fees was appropriate to deter others from acting in similar circumstances, which is almost always favored when the insured is the prevailing party. *Id.* Fourth, an award of fees was favored because the insured helped establish precedent regarding a plaintiff's right to discovery in an ERISA case by successfully defending a motion for a protective order in which the administrator sought to preclude the insured from deposing the administrator's reviewing physician. *Id.* Finally, the fifth *Hummell* factor favored an award of fees since the beneficiary obtained all the benefits he sought and prevailed. *Id.* at 1165. As a result, the court awarded fees to the prevailing insured. *See also Broderick v. Prudential Ins. Co. of Am.,* 2005 U.S. Dist. LEXIS 21471 (C.D. Cal. 2005).

### B. Fees Awarded to Plan Fiduciaries

In *Carpenters Southern California Admin. Corp. v. Russell,* the Ninth Circuit held that the *Hummell* criteria for awarding attorneys' fees should be applied to both prevailing plaintiffs and defendants. 726 F.2d 1410, 1416 (9th Cir. 1984). However, the court noted that in most cases, the *Hummell* factors would not lead to favorable decisions for defendants because plaintiffs are usually less culpable and are less likely to be able to pay for fees. *Id. See also Marquardt v. N. Am. Car Corp.,* 652 F.2d 715, 720–21 (7th Cir. 1981). In addition, making a plaintiff pay fees likely has little deterrent value. *Carpenters Southern California Admin. Corp.* 726 F.2d at 1416. Plaintiffs are already deterred by the knowledge that, should they bring a frivolous suit and not prevail, they will have to pay their own attorneys' fees. *Id.*

Shortly after the *Russell* decision was handed down, the Ninth Circuit affirmed the district court's decision to award attorneys' fees to a prevailing defendant. *Operating Engineers Pension Trust v. Gilliam,* 737 F.2d 1501, 1506 (9th Cir. 1984). In *Gilliam,* the plaintiffs, Trust Funds, had "substantial ability to pay the fees" and met several of the other *Hummell* factors. *Id.*

In *Huntsinger v. Shaw Group, Inc.,* 2006 U.S. Dist. LEXIS 12621, 2006 WL 572134 (D. Or. 2006), however, the District of Oregon was faced with this issue when deciding whether to award attorneys' fees to a prevailing defendant after the plaintiff, as an individual and as a representative of the decedent's estate, filed a complaint for recovery of life insurance benefits. After weighing the *Hummell* factors, and keeping in mind the considerations expressed in *Marquardt,* the court concluded that an award of attorneys' fees to the prevailing the defendant was inappropriate. *Id.*

The Ninth Circuit once again affirmed a defendant's award of attorneys' fees in *Paddack v. Morris,* 83 F.2d 844, 847 (9th Cir. 1986). In *Paddack,* the plaintiff, trust funds, brought suit against the defendant, a small business owner, to recover unpaid contributions. *Id.* at 845. The trial court ruled in favor of the defendant and awarded her attorneys' fees. On appeal, the Ninth Circuit considered the five *Hummell* factors and determined that the plaintiff trust funds had possibly acted in bad faith and were in a much better position to pay the funds, and that awarding fees would deter trust funds from bringing tenuous claims. *Id.* at 847. Thus, the trial court did not err in its conclusion to award fees. *Id.*

In *Shockley v. Alyeska Pipeline Service Co.,* 130 F.3d 403, 405 (9th Cir. 1997), the Ninth Circuit affirmed an order imposing attorneys' fees on noncommercial defendants. Shockley, a participant in the defendant's pension plan, was unmarried and had five children at the time of his death. *Id.* Because the plan provided benefits only to spouses of employees who died before they were retired, Shockley's children were ineligible for benefits. *Id.* Shockley's estate brought suit against the defendant fiduciary to recover benefits. *Id.* The district court entered summary judgment in favor of the defendant and awarded the defendant 10 percent of its requested attorneys' fees. *Id.* On appeal, the Ninth Circuit denied the district court's contention that the court disfavored awarding attorneys' fees against ERISA plaintiffs. *Id.* at 408. The Ninth Circuit maintained that the "playing field is level" and that courts must apply the *Hummell* factors without bias. *Id.* The court then applied the factors and determined that the estate's inability to pay was the fault of plaintiff's personal representative, and thus inconclusive. The court also found that there was no merit in trying to gain benefits that had been explicitly excluded. Finally, it found that, in order to prevent overdeterrence, a 10 percent award of fees to the fiduciary was appropriate.

In *Plumbing & Air Conditioning Contractors of Central & North Arizona v. Plumbing & Air Conditioning Contractors of Arizona, Tuscan Area,* 2005 U.S. Dist. LEXIS 31664, 2005 WL 3273565 (D. Ariz. 2005), the District Court of Arizona followed the ruling in *Shockley* after finding in favor of trust fund defendants and awarding attorneys' fees and expenses. The court ruled that plaintiffs acted in an erroneous and unreasonable manner by forcefully litigating a case without merit, that both sides of the litigation would be adversely affected by attorneys' fees, and that an award of attorneys' fees would deter others from acting in such an unreasonable manner. *Id.*

In an unreported case, the district court in *Epstein v. Unum Life Insurance Co. of America,* 2004 WL 2418310 (C.D. Cal. 2004), awarded attorneys' fees to a benefits administrator after weighing the *Hummell* factors. The plan participant stopped working as a result of alleged chronic fatigue disorder and fibromyalgia. *Id.* at 1. Despite the plaintiff's contention that she was resigned to staying in her house at all times, the plaintiff was videotaped leaving her residence to run errands and take her daughter to school. She was also seen pushing her daughter up a hill in a stroller. *Id.* The plaintiff filed suit after the defendant terminated benefits. *Id.* The court ruled in the defendant's favor after holding a bench trial, and the defendant sought attorneys' fees. *Id.* The court awarded the defendant attorneys' fees after concluding that the plaintiff brought the suit in bad faith; that the award of attorneys' fees in favor of the defendant would deter others from bringing similar groundless suits; and that the relative merits of the parties' positions weighed in the defendant's favor. *Id.* at 4.

Finally, in another unpublished case, the Ninth Circuit ordered the plaintiff's attorney in an ERISA action to pay attorneys' fees and costs. *Sommer v. UNUM Life Ins. Co. of Am.,* 35 Fed. Appx. 489 (9th Cir. 2002). In *Sommer,* the plaintiff brought the same claim against the defendant three times. *Id.* In *Sommer I,* the district court entered summary judgment in favor of the defendant and the decision was affirmed on appeal. In *Sommer II,* the district court dismissed the case for lack of jurisdiction because *Sommer I* was still pending before the Ninth Circuit. *Id.* In *Sommer III,* the district court dismissed the claim on *res judicata* grounds, and imposed Federal Rule of Civil Procedure sanctions and attorneys' fees against the plaintiff's attorney. *Id.* On appeal, the Ninth Circuit held that while an ERISA suit must be brought by a participant, beneficiary, or fiduciary in an ERISA plan, attorneys' fees can be assessed against anyone. Because the *Hummell* factors supported imposing attorneys' fees on the plaintiff's attorney, the Ninth Circuit affirmed the lower court decision.

### C. Calculation of Attorneys' Fees

In *D'Emanuele v. Montgomery Ward & Co. Inc.,* 904 F.2d 1379, 1383 (9th Cir. 1990), the Ninth Circuit adopted the lodestar/multiplier approach for calculating attorneys' fees in ERISA cases. The lodestar amount is calculated by multiplying the number of hours the attorney reasonably spent on the litigation by a reasonable hourly rate. *Id.*

While the lodestar amount is presumed to be a reasonable calculation of attorneys' fees, in rare cases courts may use a multiplier to increase or decrease the lodestar amount. *Id.* In such cases, district courts must explain their specific reason for using a multiplier. *Id.* In *Kerr v. Screen Extras Guild,* 526 F.2d 67, 70 (9th Cir. 1975), the Ninth Circuit adopted several guidelines to be considered in determining reasonable attorneys' fees. These factors include (1) the time and labor required, (2) the novelty and difficulty of the questions involved, (3) the skill requisite to perform the legal services properly, (4) the preclusion of other employment by the attorney due to acceptance of the case, (5) the customary fee, (6) whether the fee is fixed or contingent, (7) time limitations imposed by the client or the circumstances, (8) the amount involved and the results obtained, (9) the experience, reputation, and ability of the attorney, (10) the "undesirability" of the case, (11) the nature and length of the professional relationship with the client, and (12) awards in similar cases. *Id.* Several of these factors are subsumed in the lodestar calculation; the other *Kerr* factors may be taken into account in deciding whether to modify the lodestar amount. *D'Emanuele,* 904 F.2d at 1382.

In *Fleming v. Kemper National Services, Inc.,* 373 F. Supp. 2d 1000 (N.D. Cal. 2005), the district court ruled in favor of the participant. In determining attorneys' fees, the court reviewed declarations of the attorneys and clerks working on the matter and considered defendants' request to lower the respective rates. *Id.* at 1013. Upon review, the court awarded fees based on the market rate of ERISA attorneys in the San Francisco Bay Area, and reduced work that the court considered unreasonable. *Id.*

Further, in *Cann v. Carpenter's Pension Trust Fund for Northern California,* 989 F.2d 313, 318 (9th Cir. 1993), the Ninth Circuit held that courts may not use a multiplier to reflect the additional risk of taking a contingent-fee case. The Ninth Circuit found that there was no relevant distinction between the ERISA fee provision and other statutory fee provisions for which the Supreme Court had held that contingency multipliers were not permitted. *Id.; see also City of Burlington v. Dague,* 505 U.S. 557 (1992). In *McElwaine v. US West Inc.,* 176 F.3d 1167, 1173 (9th Cir. 1999), the Ninth Circuit reaffirmed its decision to prohibit contingency multipliers.

In *Van Gerwen v. Guarantee Mutual Life Co.,* 214 F.3d 1041, 1044 (9th Cir. 2000), the Ninth Circuit considered the use of a multiplier to reflect the quality of representation. Because the attorney had performed poorly, the district court reduced the lodestar amount by 25 percent. *Id.* The Ninth Circuit held that, instead of using a multiplier, the quality of representation should have been taken into account when determining the hourly rate for the lodestar calculation. *Id.* at 1046. Courts may use multipliers only in rare circumstances where the quality of the attorney's performance cannot be fully reflected in the hourly rate. *Id.* at 1947. In such cases, courts must explain their reason for using the multiplier. *Id.*

The district court in *Opeta v. American Bankers Life Assurance Co.,* 2005 U.S. Dist. LEXIS 21464 (C.D. Cal. 2005), followed *Cann* and *Van Gerwen* by stating that once the court finds the plaintiff is entitled to recover attorneys' fees, it engages in a two-step process to determine what amount is reasonable. *Id.* at 7. First, the court determines the lodestar amount. *Id.* (citing *McElwaine v. U.S. West Inc.,* 176 F.3d 1167, 1173 (9th Cir. 1999)). The court then must determine whether or not to adjust the lodestar amount by looking at the factors discussed in *Kerr v. Screen Extras Guild,* 526 F.2d 67, 70 (9th Cir. 1975). *Id.* The *Opeta* court reiterated that the court should adjust the reasonable hours and reasonable rate in the lodestar calculation, instead of adjusting the lodestar at a later point based on subsumed Kerr factors. *Id.* at 8. (citing *Morales v. City of San Rafael,* 96 F.3d 359, 363–64 (9th Cir. 1996)).

In class action suits where plaintiffs secure a common fund, courts may use either the lodestar method or a percentage-of-the-fund method in calculating fees. *Fischel v. Equitable Life Assurance Soc'y of the U.S.,* 307 F.3d 997, 1006 (9th Cir. 2002). Courts have the discretion to decide which method should be applied and may compare the two methods when deciding what amount of fees is reasonable. *Id.* Although the Ninth Circuit has established a 25 percent benchmark in percentage-of-the-fund cases, this figure may be unreasonable in certain cases and can thus be adjusted upward or downward. *Id.* Factors to consider include the length of time before a settlement was reached and whether members of the class object to the fees requested by their attorney. *Id.*

Additionally, in common funds cases, courts may use a contingency multiplier to reflect the risk of nonpayment. *Fischel,* 307 F.3d at 1008. Because attorneys' fees come out of the plaintiff's award in common fund cases, there is no concern that a contingency multiplier will financially burden defendants. *Id.* While district courts have the discretion to decide whether or not to use the risk multiplier, they abuse this discretion if they fail to apply it in cases where (1) attorneys expect to be compensated for the extra risk should they prevail, (2) their hourly rate does not reflect the risk, and (3) there is evidence that the case is risky. *Id.* Risk should be assessed at the time the attorney agreed to pursue the claim. *Id.* at 1009. A district court also abuses its discretion if it fails to apply the multiplier after the attorney establishes that the plaintiffs would have had substantial difficulty securing counsel without an adjustment for the risk. *Id.* at 1008 n.8. Thus, although a district court has discretion to decide whether or not to use a risk multiplier, this discretion is subject to several strict guidelines.

The number of hours a court can use in calculating fees is also subject to restriction. Although ERISA requires beneficiaries to exhaust internal administrative procedures before filing a civil action, the Ninth Circuit has held that prevailing parties may not recover attorneys' fees incurred during these administrative proceedings. *Cann v. Carpenter's Pension Trust Fund for N. Cal.,* 989 F.2d 313, 317 (9th Cir. 1993). The court noted that, under the American rule, courts may *not* award attorneys' fees absent a statutory exception. *Id.* A textual examination of ERISA led to the conclusion that attorneys' fees could only be awarded in "actions" brought in a court of law. *Id.* at 316. The court also considered the Supreme Court's decisions in *Pennsylvania v. Delaware Valley Citizens Council,* 478 U.S. 546, 559 (1986), and *Sullivan v. Hudson,* 490 U.S. 877 (1989), in which the Court held that the word "action" was meant to include administrative proceedings. *Id.* The Ninth Circuit distinguished the ERISA provision from the Supreme Court decisions on the grounds that both those cases involved administrative proceedings that occurred after the court action and were held before governmental agencies. *Id.* In ERISA cases, administrative proceedings must occur before a claim is filed and are part of a private claims process. *Id.* Thus, the Ninth Circuit held that in ERISA cases, courts have no discretion to award fees for administrative procedures. *Id.*

In *Dishman v. UNUM Life Insurance Co. of Am.,* 269 F.3d 974, 987 (9th Cir. 2001), the Ninth Circuit held that *Cann* did not necessarily prevent plaintiffs from recovering fees for work done before a complaint was filed. In *Dishman,* the defendant insurance company cancelled the plaintiff's disability payments without properly investigating the plaintiff's situation. *Id.* at 978. The Ninth Circuit affirmed the district court's judgment in favor of the plaintiff and awarded full attorneys' fees. *Id.* at 979. The court distinguished *Dishman* from *Cann* on the basis that the work performed prior to filing the complaint was devoted to preparing for litigation, not to exhausting administrative procedures. *Id.* at 988.

In *Gunn v. Reliance Standard Life Insurance Company,* 407 F. Supp. 2d 1162, 1165 (C.D. Cal. 2006), the court followed the determination in *Dishman* and found that 1.2 hours spent by plaintiff's counsel in meeting with the plaintiff before the complaint was filed was regarding possible litigation, and therefore compensable.

## XI. ERISA Regulations

Most of the case law in the Ninth Circuit concerning ERISA regulations has focused on the timing and content of the denial letter. Although the regulations were revised and the current version of 29 C.F.R. § 2560.503-1 applies only to claims made after 2002, both the previous and current versions require that the denial letter provide specific reasons for the denial and a description of any additional information necessary for the claimant to perfect his or her claim. *Compare* 29 C.F.R. § 2560.503-1(f) (former version) *with* 29 C.F.R. § 2560.503-1(g) (current version). In contrast, only former § 2560.503-1(h) provided that a claim would be "deemed denied" if the administrator did not timely issue a decision. Although the current version of the regulation no longer contains a "deemed denied" provision, the effect of such language is still being litigated.

In *Jebian v. Hewlett Packard Employee Benefits Plan,* 349 F.3d 1098 (9th Cir. 2003), the Ninth Circuit examined the effect of the administrator's failure to issue a decision on the plaintiff's claim within the timeline set by the pre-2002 regulations. Former 29 C.F.R. § 2560.503-1(h) provided that if the administrator did not issue a decision within sixty days, or request an extension before the expiration of sixty days, the claim would be "deemed denied." Although the plan granted the administrator sufficient discretion to warrant application of the abuse of discretion standard of review, the Ninth Circuit held that the administrator's failure to issue a decision before the "deemed denied" deadline rendered the abuse of discretion standard inapplicable: "Deemed denials are not exercises of discretion. They are therefore undeserving of deference under *Firestone* and a de novo standard of review applies." *Id.* at 1105. Courts have applied the same rationale where the plan contains similar "deemed denied" language even if the claim is governed by the new version of the regulation, which no longer has that provision. *Mindt v. Prudential,* 322 F. Supp 2d 1150 (D. Or. 2004).

Subsequent case law, however, limits *Jebian* to its facts, specifically the fact that the plan language included a "deemed denied" clause that cut off the administrator's discretion. Where the plan fails to comply with ERISA's procedural guidelines, the claimant is afforded the right to bring suit, but the administrator does not automatically lose discretion otherwise granted under the terms of the plan. *Gatti v. Reliance Standard Life Ins. Co.,* 415 F.3d 978, 983 (9th Cir. 2005). This is consistent with the Ninth Circuit's prior holding that no substantive remedies are available for procedural violations of ERISA unless the procedural violations rise to a level that "alter[s] the substantive relationship between employer and employee." *Id.* at 984–85, citing *Blau v. Del Monte Corp.,* 748 F.2d 1348 (9th Cir. 1984).

The Ninth Circuit has also created a "good faith" exception to the *Jebian* rule. Even where a claim is "deemed denied" under the terms of the plan at issue, an exception to the loss of discretion exists for administrators who are "engaged in a good faith attempt to comply with its deadlines." *LaMantia v. Voluntary Plan Administrators, Inc.,* 401 F.3d 1114, 1122 (9th Cir. 2005). In *LaMantia,* the court held that the plan's decision to grant the claimant's request for additional time to submit information beyond the plan's "deemed denied" deadlines constituted a basis for granting such a "good faith" exception. *Id.* at 1123–24.

As noted above, several courts have interpreted the regulations setting forth the level of specificity required in a denial letter. In *Kearney v. Standard Insurance Co.,* 175 F.3d 1084 (9th Cir. 1999), the Ninth Circuit concluded that the administrator did not fail to comply with the regulation's requirement that the denial letter provide the claimant with notice of any additional evidence necessary to perfect his claim. The court noted that the plaintiff's claim did not fail because there was insufficient evidence; instead, the plaintiff's claim failed because the administrator reviewed the totality of the evidence in the record and concluded that it did not support the plaintiff's claimed disability. In *Jordan v. Northrop Grumman,* 370 F.3d 869, 881 (9th Cir. 2004), the Ninth Circuit noted that the administrator had not failed to comply with the specificity requirement where the evidence the claimant could have produced would have made no difference to the claim determination.

Because the purpose of the regulations is to require that the denial letter provide sufficient information to allow the claimant to understand the basis for the administrator's decision, conclusory statements that do not give reasons for the denial do not satisfy the specificity requirement. *Lee v. Cal. Bankers Pension Trust,* 154 F.3d 1075 (9th Cir. 1998) (holding that conclusory statements did not satisfy requirement of 29 C.F.R. § 2560.503-1(f)). Ambiguous denial letters are similarly insufficient. In *Olive v. American Express LTD Plan,* 183 F. Supp. 2d 1191 (C.D. Cal. 2002), the court noted that the denial letter did not clearly state whether the plaintiff's claim was considered procedurally deficient as a result of missing medical records or substantively deficient because the claimant's medical condition was not disabling, or both. The letter's failure to unambiguously and clearly articulate the procedural or medical reasons for the denial did not meet the specificity required by the regulations. However, ERISA does not require the administrator to address every piece of evidence in order to comply with the "specificity" requirement. *Abatie v. Alta Health & Life Ins. Co.,* 421 F.3d 1053, 1064 (9th Cir. 2005), *review granted,* 2006 U.S. App. LEXIS 2827 (Feb. 6, 2006).

If additional information is needed, the administrator must ask for it. In *Booton v. Lockheed,* 110 F.3d 1461 (9th Cir. 1997), the administrator issued its decision on the plaintiff's claim apparently based solely on information provided in the postoperative report. Although the plan's physician consultant opined that the patient's x-rays would be helpful to make a determination as to whether the procedure was medically necessary, the administrator neither requested nor obtained the x-rays. The Ninth Circuit held that the administrator had abused its discretion—and failed to comply with the applicable regulation—by failing to request the information necessary to make its decision. The court stated: "If the plan is unable to make a rational decision on the basis of the materials submitted by the claimant, it must explain what else it needs. If ERISA plan administrators want to enjoy the deference to which they are statutorily entitled, they must comply with these simple, commonsense requirements embodied in the regulations and our caselaw." *Id.* at 1464.

## XII. Cases Interpreting ERISA Statutes of Limitation

In *Wetzel v. Cadillac Group Long Term Disability Insurance Program,* 222 F.3d 643, 648 (9th Cir. 2000), the Ninth Circuit held that California's four-year statute of limitations for suits on written contract was the applicable statute of limitations for an ERISA cause of action based on a claim for benefits under a written contractual policy. *See also Mogck v. UNUM Life Ins. Co. of Am.,* 292 F.3d 1025, 1028 (9th Cir. 2002). In so holding, the *Wetzel* court overruled *Nikaido v. Centennial Life Insurance Co.,* 42 F.3d 557 (9th Cir. 1994). In *Nikaido,* the Ninth Circuit held that California Insurance Code § 10350.11 provided the appropriate three-year statute of limitations.[1]

*Wetzel* also overruled *Nikaido* on the issue of accrual, holding that California Insurance Code § 13050.11 did not supply the appropriate rule for determining when the statute of limitations in an ERISA action commences. *Wetzel,* 222 F.3d at 649. Rather, the Ninth Circuit reiterated its decision in *Northern California Retail Clerks Unions & Food Employers Joint Pension Trust v. Jumbo Markets Inc.,* 906 F.2d 1371 (9th Cir. 1990). In *Northern California,* the court held that, in a federal action, federal law determines the point at which the cause of action accrues. *Id.* at 1372. Under federal law, this point occurs when a person knows or has reason to know of the injury that is the basis of the action. *Id.* Thus, in an ERISA action, the statute of limitations begins to accrue at the time benefits are denied or when the plaintiff has reason to know they are denied. *Wetzel,* 222 F.3d at 649.

In *Wetzel,* the plaintiff was a participant in an employee welfare benefit plan that provided the plaintiff with disability insurance. *Id.* at 645. In 1991, Wetzel submitted a claim for long-term disability and began receiving monthly benefits. *Id.* at 646. On August 5, 1992, the plaintiff received a letter from the plan administrator stating that it viewed the plaintiff's disability as psychiatric in nature and would pay benefits only through July 30, 1993. The letter also informed the plaintiff that if he disagreed with the decision, he could supply additional information for review. *Id.* The Ninth Circuit held that because the letter invited the plaintiff to provide further information, the plaintiff could have reasonably believed that his benefits had not yet been finally denied. *Id.* at 650. Thus, the plaintiff's cause of action did not accrue at that time. *Id.*

Often, a letter denying benefits is sufficient to commence the statute of limitations. In *Rodoloff v. Provident Life & Accident Insurance Co.,* 2002 WL 32072401 (S.D. Cal. 2002), the district court held that the plaintiff's action began to accrue on the date that the plaintiff received the original letter denying benefits despite the fact that the plaintiff appealed the denial.

The Ninth Circuit interpreted the four-year statute in *LaMantia v. Voluntary Plan Administrators, Inc.,* 401 F.3d 1114, 1117 (9th Cir. 2005). Defendant granted the plaintiff short-term disability benefits, which terminated on May 8, 1997. *Id.* The plaintiff filed claim for long-term disability benefits, which was denied on May 14, 1997. *Id.* The plaintiff appealed the defendant's denial of benefits on June 10, 1997. *Id.* An agreement was reached to extend the time for determination to allow the plaintiff to file additional medical reports. *Id.*

Shortly thereafter, the plaintiff's counsel sent a copy of a medical report with a letter informing the defendant that an additional medical report would be forthcoming. *Id.* On October 3, 1997, the plaintiff's counsel sent a letter confirming an agreement that the appeal review would not conclude until the plaintiff obtained and submitted a report. *Id.* No report was submitted and there was no communication for at least two years. *Id.* Plaintiff's counsel claimed that a letter with additional medical reports eventually was sent on July 15, 1999, and the plan claimed that it never received it. *Id.* On August 4, 2000, the defendant received a letter from the plaintiff's counsel inquiring about the status of her appeal and referring to the July 15, 1999, letter. *Id.* The defendant responded the next month by stating that it had not received the July 15, 1999, letter and requested that this information be forwarded. *Id.* The reports were again submitted, and after nearly a year the defendant still had not rendered a final decision. *Id.* The defendant finally sent a letter reaffirming the initial denial of long-term disability benefits. *Id.* The plaintiff then filed a complaint on October 17, 2001, alleging a claim for disability benefits pursuant to the ERISA. *Id.*

The defendant argued that the action was untimely since the language of the plan stated the claimant must file a lawsuit challenging a denial of benefits "within four (4) years after the occurrence of the loss for which a claim is made." *Id.* at 1118. The district court held that the complaint was timely, following the ruling in *Wetzel* that "an ERISA cause of action accrues either at the time benefits are actually denied, or when the insured has reason to know that the claim has been denied." *Id.* (citing *Wetzel,* 222 F.3d at 649). On appeal, the Ninth Circuit agreed with the district court's conclusion, but the opinion differed in that the appeals court held the defendant was estopped from even claiming statute of limitations as a defense. *Id.* at 1119. The court followed the general rule that a defendant will be estopped from setting up a statute-of-limitations defense when its own prior representations or conduct could have caused the plaintiff to allow the statute to expire. *See Allen v. A.H. Robins Co., Inc.,* 725 F.2d 1365, 1371–72 (9th Cir. 1985); *Doe v. Blue Cross & Blue Shield United of Wis.,* 112 F.3d 869, 875–77 (7th Cir. 1997). The court stated, "[T]he totality of [defendant's] representations and conduct between September 1997 and August 2001 estopped the Plan from asserting either limitations defense." *Id.*

The Ninth Circuit has often addressed the continuing-violation theory of the statute of limitations. In *Phillips v. Alaska Hotel & Restaurant Employee Pension Fund,* 944 F.2d 509, 520 (9th Cir. 1991), the Ninth Circuit rejected the district court's application of the continuing-violation theory in determining when the limitations period commenced. In *Phillips,* nonvested participants in an employee pension fund brought action against their employer. *Id.* at 512. In determining the date at which the statute of limitations began to run, the district court held that each time the employer decided not to relax the vesting rules, a new breach occurred and the limitation period began anew. *Id.* at 520. The Ninth Circuit reversed the decision, holding that the statute of limitations began to run at the earliest date at which the plaintiff had knowledge of a breach. *Id.*

The Ninth Circuit also rejected the continuing-violation theory in *Pisciotta v. Teledyne Industries Inc.,* 91 F.3d 1326, 1332 (9th Cir. 1996). There, the plaintiffs brought a cause of action against their former employer after the employer put a freeze on medical insurance payments. *Id.* at 1328. The plaintiffs contended that a new cause of action accrued each time they should have received reimbursements for insurance premiums. *Id.* at 1332. The Ninth Circuit rejected this argument and held that a cause of action accrued on the date that the plaintiffs first learned of the freeze. *Id.*

In *Nikaido,* the Ninth Circuit applied the rolling-accrual rule under California Insurance Code § 13050.11, holding that for each month the claimant was disabled and the company did not make payments, a new cause of action accrued. 42 F.3d at 560. In overruling *Nikaido,* the Ninth Circuit confirmed that the rolling-accrual rule or continuing-violation theory is not applicable to ERISA cases. *Wetzel,* 222 F.3d. at 649. Rather, a cause of action accrues at the time a claimant first learns that his benefits have been denied or when he has reason to know they have been denied. *Id.*

The Ninth Circuit recently issued a decision concerning whether ERISA's statute of limitations may bar a claim for pension benefits notwithstanding a plan's failure to fulfill its disclosure and review obligations under ERISA § 503, 29 U.S.C. § 1133. *Chuck v. Hewlett Packard Co.,* 2006 WL 2052288 (9th Cir. 2006). In *Chuck,* the plan administrator calculated pension benefits for the claimant in 1978 and 1979. *Id.* at *1. In 1980, however, the plan recalculated benefits lowering the claimant's benefits based on a gap in employment between 1972 through 1974. *Id.* at *1. The plan pre-selected the claimant to receive a lump sum payment that was irrevocable. *Id.* The claimant wrote a letter contending that he should have received benefits under the initial calculations. *Id.* The claimant was aware that the plan would contend that he was not eligible for any further pension benefits, and soon afterward received a lump sum payment of $3,269.06, which the plan viewed as a full and complete distribution of the claimant's benefits under the plan. *Id.* at *2. Then, in late 1991 and early 1992, the claimant wrote a series of letters requesting additional benefits under the plan's initial calculation. *Id.* The plan administrator replied indicating that the claimant was not entitled to any further benefits under the plan. *Id.* For the next several years and again starting in 2001, the claimant continued to request further benefits and asked for plan documentation. *Id.* The plan administrator repeatedly denied his request for further benefits, and never provided the claimant with plan documentation. *Id.*

The claimant filed a complaint in 2003, alleging damages under ERISA for denial of benefits and breach of fiduciary duty. *Id.* The plan moved for summary judgment asserting that the claimant's claim was barred under the statute of limitations. *Id.* The district court ruled in favor of the plan stating that ERISA's statute of limitations barred the claimant's benefits claim and related fiduciary duty claims, and that consequently he lacked standing under ERISA to bring his claims for plan documents and information. *Id.* The Ninth Circuit affirmed the decision, stating, "At the heart of this case, we are faced with an issue of first impression in this circuit: whether ERISA's statute of limitations may bar a claim for benefits notwithstanding a plan's failure to fulfill its disclosure and review obligations under ERISA § 503, 29 U.S.C. § 1133. We hold that a plan's material violation of § 1133 is a factor that militates strongly against a finding that the statute of limitations has begun to run against a claimant, but that a compelling showing of circumstances in this case nevertheless indicates that [plaintiff's] benefits claim is time-barred." *Id.* at *1. The court went on to explain that even though the plan did not provide adequate justification for its denial of benefits, with a reasonable opportunity for review, the claimant had knowledge of the denial of claim for benefits, which triggered the limitation period. *Id.* at *7. Specifically, the court opined that the claimant was aware of the plan's decision denying further benefits no later than March of 1992, which foreclosed the claimant from any reasonable belief that the plan had not finally denied benefits. *Id.*

## XIII. Subrogation Litigation

The Ninth Circuit has long held that claims for reimbursement by a health insurer are "not cognizable" under ERISA because the relief sought is not properly equitable.

*FMC Medical Plan v. Owens,* 122 F.3d 1258 (9th Cir. 1997); *Reynolds Metal Co. v. Ellis,* 202 F.3d 1246 (9th Cir. 2000). Immediately after the Supreme Court's decision in *Great-West Life & Annuity Insurance Co. v. Knudson,* 534 U.S. 204 (2002), the Ninth Circuit held in *Westaff v. Arce,* 298 F.3d 1164 (9th Cir. 2002), that the plan's claims for declaratory relief and specific performance were not cognizable under ERISA even though the disputed funds were placed into a joint escrow account pending determination of to whom the money was owed. The Ninth Circuit took this position even further, holding in *Providence Health Plan v. McDowell,* 361 F.3d 1243 (9th Cir. 2004), that an insurer's attempt to enforce a plan reimbursement provision is not preempted by ERISA and is appropriately brought as a state-law claim for breach of contract. The Ninth Circuit's longstanding position on this issue has recently been impliedly overruled by the Supreme Court's decision in *Sereboff v. Mid Atlantic Medical Services, Inc,* 126 S. Ct. 1869 (2006). In *Sereboff,* the Supreme Court held that the plan could bring an ERISA action under 29 USC § 1132(a)(3) for reimbursement under an equitable lien or constructive trust theory where the funds that the plan seeks to recover are identifiable and owned by the beneficiary. The Ninth Circuit has not addressed this issue post-*Sereboff.*

## Note

1. CAL. INS. CODE § 10350.11 provides:

*Limitation of actions on policy*

A disability policy shall contain a provision which shall be in the form set forth herein. Legal Actions: No action at law or in equity shall be brought to recover on this policy prior to the expiration of 60 days after written proof of loss has been furnished in accordance with the requirements of this policy. No such action shall be brought after the expiration of three years.

# CHAPTER 10

# Tenth Circuit

MICHAEL S. BEAVER
TRENT A. HOWELL
DAVID N. KELLEY
SCOTT M. PETERSEN

## I. What Constitutes an ERISA Plan?

### A. Determining the Existence of an Employee Welfare Benefit Plan

Interpreting 29 U.S.C. §§ 1002(1), the Tenth Circuit has set forth five elements that must be considered to determine whether an ERISA (Employee Retirement Income Security Act of 1974) plan exists: "(1) A 'plan, fund, or program' (2) established or maintained (3) by an employer . . . (4) for the purpose of providing benefits . . . (5) to participants or their beneficiaries." *Peckham v. Gem State Mut. of Utah,* 964 F.2d 1043, 1047 (10th Cir. 1992), quoting *Donovan v. Dillingham,* 688 F.2d 1367, 1371 (11th Cir. 1982); *accord Gaylor v. John Hancock Mut. Life Ins. Co.,* 112 F.3d 460, 464 (10th Cir. 1997).

A "plan, fund, or program" under ERISA is established if "'from the surrounding circumstances a reasonable person can ascertain the intended benefits, a class of beneficiaries, the source of financing, and the procedures for receiving benefits.'" *Peckham,* 964 F.2d at 1047; *Hemphill v. Unisys Corp.,* 855 F. Supp. 1225 (D. Utah 1994). In *Peckham,* the Tenth Circuit held that the policy constituted a "plan, fund, or program" covered by ERISA based solely on policy or plan language at issue. *Peckham,* 964 F.2d at 1047–48. However, where a reasonable person cannot ascertain the intended benefits of the plan, it will not be an ERISA-governed plan. *Siemon v. AT&T Corp.,* 117 F.3d 1173 (10th Cir. 1997).

"An important factor in determining whether a plan has been established is whether the employer's purchase of the policy is an expressed intention by the employer to provide benefits on a regular and long-term basis." *Gaylor,* 112 F.3d at 464; *see Lettes v. Kinam Gold, Inc.,* 3 Fed. Appx. 783 (10th Cir.), *cert. denied,* 533 U.S. 929 (2001) ("'golden parachute' agreement which was unfunded, contingent on a one-time event that might never happen, and expressly limited to a narrow time period . . . did not constitute an employee welfare benefit 'plan' within ERISA's ambit"); *Averhart v. USWest Mgmt. Pension Plan,* 46 F.3d 1480 (10th Cir. 1994) (employer's activities in relation to group insurance policy are evidence of a plan). A formal written plan is not a prerequisite for establishing or maintaining a plan. *Lohmann v. Green Bay Packaging, Inc.,* 39 F.3d 1192 (10th Cir. 1994).

### B. Definition of "Employee" for ERISA Purposes

For the purpose of determining whether an ERISA plan exists, the plan must provide benefits to at least one employee. *Sipma v. Mass. Cas. Ins. Co.,* 256 F.3d 1006, 1010 (10th Cir. 2001), citing *Slamen v. Paul Revere Life Ins. Co.,* 166 F.3d 1102, 1104 (11th Cir. 1999); *see also* 29 C.F.R. § 2510.3-3(b) (excluding from the definition of "employee welfare benefit plan" any plan "under which no employees are participants covered under the plan"). Whether an individual is an employee is a question of fact. *Marvel v. United States,* 719 F.2d 1507, 1515 (10th Cir. 1983). In *Herr v. Heiman,* 75 F.3d 1509, 1512–13 (10th Cir. 1996), the court applied a common-law twelve-factor test to determine whether a worker qualifies as an employee for ERISA purposes. *Id.,* citing *Nationwide Mut. Ins. Co. v. Darden,* 503 U.S. 318, 323 (1992).

In *Sipma,* the court distinguished a shareholder/employee of a corporation from the corporation itself holding that a shareholder could also be an employee of the corporation for ERISA purposes. *Sipma,* 256 F.3d at 1010 (noting that Colorado common law and common law generally treat a corporation as a distinct entity from its shareholders). However, where the shareholder is the sole shareholder of the corporation, he cannot be counted as an employee for the purpose of determining whether a plan exists. *Id.* at 1012.

The Tenth Circuit has not determined whether individual business owners may be plan participants under ERISA.

### C. Interpretation of Safe Harbor Regulation

Plans that meet each of the four "safe harbor" factors are excluded from ERISA coverage. *Gaylor,* 112 F.3d at 463; *Peckham v. Gem State Mut. of Utah,* 964 P.2d 1043, 1045 (10th Cir. 1992) (reviewing as a whole, and holding to be an ERISA plan, "group policies" that provided single employee medical benefits paid for by the employer but also additional family medical coverage if elected and paid for by the employee). However, simply because the plan is not excluded under the safe harbor provisions does not compel the conclusion that it is an ERISA plan. *Gaylor,* 112 F.3d at 463.

## D. Amount of Employer Involvement Required to Sustain an Employee Welfare Benefit Plan

A plan is "established or maintained" by the employer where it is "part of an employment relationship." *Peckham,* 964 F.2d at 1049, citing *Massachusetts v. Morash,* 490 U.S. 107 (1989). The Tenth Circuit has defined this as follows:

> [W]e determine whether the plan is part of an employment relationship by looking at the degree of participation by the employer in the establishment or maintenance of the plan. An employer's mere purchase of insurance for its employees does not, without more, constitute an ERISA plan. An important factor in determining whether a plan has been established is whether the employer's purchase of the policy is an expressed intention by the employer to provide benefits on a regular and long-term basis.

*Sipma v. Mass. Cas. Ins. Co.,* 256 F.3d 1006, 1012 (10th Cir. 2001), quoting *Gaylor,* 112 F.3d at 464. "While merely purchasing insurance is insufficient to establish an ERISA plan, the purchase of a group policy or multiple policies covering a class of employees offers substantial evidence that a plan . . . has been established." *Id.* (internal quotation marks omitted).

### E. Treatment of Multiple Employer Trusts and Welfare Agreements

A multiple employer trust is not itself an employee-benefit plan. *Peckham,* 964 F.2d at 1047 n.4. The employer who subscribes to such a trust must show that it has created a separate employee-benefit plan in connection with the subscription. *Id.*

Multiple employer welfare arrangements that are not fully insured may not be used to escape state insurance regulations that would otherwise be applicable, such as those governing workers' compensation. *Fuller v. Norton,* 86 F.3d 1016 (10th Cir. 1996).

# II. Preemption

## A. Scope of ERISA Preemption

ERISA's preemption provision, 29 U.S.C. § 1144, preempts state laws to the extent that they "relate to" an employee-benefit plan, but saves from preemption any state law that "regulates insurance, banking or securities." Whether a state law regulates insurance is, in turn, determined by a two-part test articulated by the Supreme Court in *Kentucky Association of Health Plans, Inc. v. Miller,* 538 U.S. 329, 341–42 (2003): (1) "[T]he state law must be specifically directed toward entities engaged in insurance;" and (2) it "must substantially affect the risk pooling arrangement between the insurer and the insured."

The Tenth Circuit's usual approach to determining whether a state law "relates to" an employee benefit plan is that it frequently focuses upon whether the law "affect[s] the relations among the principal ERISA entities, the employer, the plan, the plan fiduciaries and the beneficiaries." *David P. Coldesina, D.D.S., P.C.,*

*Employee Profit Sharing Plan & Trust v. Estate of Simper,* 407 F.3d 1126, 1136 (10th Cir. 2005); *Woodworker's Supply, Inc. v. Principal Mut. Life Ins. Co.,* 170 F.3d 985, 990 (10th Cir. 1999). "[A]ctions that affect the relations between one or more of these plan entities and an outside party . . . escape ERISA preemption." *Id.* Similarly, "a claim only falls within ERISA's civil enforcement scheme when it is based solely on legal duties created by ERISA or the plan terms, rather than some other independent source." *David P. Coldesina, D.D.S., P.C., Employee Profit Sharing Plan & Trust,* 407 F.3d at 1137.

The Tenth Circuit draws a substantive distinction between state-law claims that are expressly preempted and those that are conflict-preempted. Only state-law claims that are the subject of conflict preemption can be removed to federal court based on the "complete preemption" doctrine, under which state laws that would impose remedies in conflict with ERISA are converted to federal claims, even where no federal claim is expressly stated. *Felix v. Lucent Techs., Inc.,* 387 F.3d 1146 (10th Cir. 2004). Thus, where a plaintiff's claim is arguably subject to express preemption under 29 U.S.C. § 1144, but it is not subject to conflict preemption, a federal district court is without jurisdiction to assess the claim of express preemption, and the action must be remanded to state court. *Id.,* 387 F.3d at 1158.

### B. Preemption of Managed-Care Claims

The Tenth Circuit has considered cases involving managed-care decisions denying benefits for various procedures. The court has held that such claims are preempted. *E.g., Cannon v. Group Health Serv. of Okla.,* 77 F.3d 1270 (10th Cir. 1996) (denial of coverage for autologous bone-marrow transplant; claim for wrongful death preempted).

### C. Preemption of Malpractice Claims

In *Pacificare of Oklahoma, Inc., v. Burrage,* 59 F.3d 151 (10th Cir. 1995), the court considered whether a claim of medical malpractice, asserted vicariously against a health maintenance organization, was preempted by ERISA. The court found that such malpractice claims are premised upon "laws of general application—not specifically targeting ERISA plans—that involve traditional areas of state regulation and do not affect relations among the principal ERISA entities." *Id.* at 154. Thus, medical malpractice claims do not "relate to" employee benefit plans, and are not preempted. *Id.* Of course, to be distinguished are claims premised upon the denial of certain kinds of care under managed-care arrangements; such claims are preempted. *See Cannon,* 77 F.3d 1270.

### D. Other Preemption Issues

#### 1. Bad-Faith Breach of Insurance Contract

The Tenth Circuit applied the two-part *Miller* test in *Kidneigh v. UNUM Life Insurance Co. of America,* 345 F.3d 1182 (10th Cir. 2003), *cert. denied,* 540 U.S. 1184 (2004), finding that ERISA preempts a Colorado state-law claim for bad-faith breach of insurance contract. First, the court found that such claims are not "specifically directed" at insurers, for purposes of the *Miller* test, because they are founded upon general principles of contract and tort law. *Id.* at 1186–87. Second, the court held that bad-faith claims do not "substantially affect the risk pooling arrangement" between insurers and insureds, in that such claims merely provide additional remedies in the event of a breach of an insurance contract. *Id.* at 1187. In addition, however, the Tenth Circuit held that bad-faith claims would be preempted in any event because they purport to provide remedies in addition to ERISA's exclusive remedial scheme. *Id.* at 1185–86. In reaching these conclusions, the court drew heavily upon pre-*Miller* decisions, including *Pilot Life Insurance Co. v. Dedeaux*, 481 U.S. 41 (1985). In so doing, the court affirmed its previous rulings that bad-faith laws of various other states are preempted. *See Conover v. Aetna US Healthcare, Inc.*, 320 F.3d 1076 (10th Cir. 2003) (Oklahoma bad-faith law preempted); *Moffett v. Halliburton Energy Servs., Inc.*, 291 F.3d 1227 (10th Cir. 2002) (Wyoming bad-faith law preempted); *Kelley v. Sears, Roebuck & Co.*, 882 F.2d 453 (10th Cir. 1989) (Colorado bad-faith law preempted).

Prior to the Tenth Circuit's ruling in *Kidneigh*, several district courts within the Tenth Circuit had held, joining a small handful of other district courts around the United States, that state-law bad-faith claims were no longer preempted after the Supreme Court's ruling in *UNUM Life Insurance Co. of America v. Ward*, 526 U.S. 358 (1999). *See, e.g., Colligan v. UNUM Life Ins. Co. of Am.*, 2001 WL 433742 (D. Colo. 2001); *Lewis v. Aetna U.S. Healthcare, Inc.*, 78 F. Supp. 2d 1202 (N.D. Okla. 1999). The Tenth Circuit's ruling in *Moffett* expressly rejected this argument, and in any event the argument is completely foreclosed by the court's more recent ruling in *Kidneigh*.

### 2. State Claims-Handling Statutes

Claims based upon state statutes that would purport to govern the handling, timing, or payment of claims, such as state unfair-practices statutes, are also preempted. *Kidneigh*, 345 F.3d 1182, 1188–89 (Colorado unfair-claims-practices statute preempted); *Moffett*, 291 F.3d 1227, 1236 (Wyoming statute, mandating deadline for claim response and imposing attorneys' fees for violation, preempted); *Gaylor v. John Hancock Mut. Life Ins. Co.*, 112 F.3d 460, 465–66 (10th Cir. 1997) (Oklahoma statute providing bad-faith remedy preempted); *Kelley*, 882 F.2d 453, 456 (claim premised upon Colorado insurance statutes preempted). State laws affecting assignability of benefits may also be preempted. *St. Francis Reg'l Med. Ctr. v. Blue Cross & Blue Shield of Kan., Inc.*, 49 F.3d 1460 (10th Cir. 1995).

### 3. State Laws Construing Insurance Contracts

The Tenth Circuit has found a number of state laws relating to the construction of insurance contracts not to be preempted. State-law "notice-prejudice" rules are not preempted, and may require a "choice of laws" analysis to determine which states' rule to apply. *Dang v. UNUM Life Ins. Co. of Am.*, 175 F.3d 1186 (10th Cir. 1999). State-law "substantial compliance" doctrines are not preempted. *Peckham v. Gem State Mut. of Utah*, 964 F.2d 1043 (10th Cir. 1992); *see also Klover v. Antero Healthplans*, 64 F. Supp. 2d 1003 (D. Colo. 1999). State-law rules interpreting accidental-death clauses may not be preempted. *Winchester v. Prudential Life Ins. Co. of Am.*, 975 F.2d 1479 (10th Cir. 1992).

### 4. Other State-Law Claims by Participants

Other than with respect to medical malpractice, state-law claims by participants and beneficiaries are preempted because they "relate to" an employee-benefit plan and are not saved from ERISA preemption because they do not regulate insurance. *See, e.g., Pitman v. Blue Cross & Blue Shield of Okla.*, 24 F.3d 118 (10th Cir. 1994) (tortious breach of contract claim preempted); *Kelso v. Gen. Am. Life Ins. Co.*, 967 F.2d 388 (10th Cir. 1992) (misrepresentation claim preempted); *Settles v. Golden Rule Ins. Co.*, 927 F.2d 505 (wrongful-death claim preempted); *Straub v. Western Union Tel. Co.*, 851 F.2d 1262 (10th Cir. 1988) (breach of contract and negligent misrepresentation claims preempted); *Mein v. Pool Co. Disabled Int'l Employee Long Term Disability Benefit Plan*, 989 F. Supp. 1337 (D. Colo. 1998) (state claims for intentional infliction of emotional distress, intentional interference with property interest, and breach of fiduciary duty preempted).

### 5. Claims by Health Care Providers Based upon Precertification

Claims by employee-benefit plan participants based upon notions of estoppel are typically not allowed. *Straub v. Western Union Tel. Co.*, 851 F.2d 1262 (10th Cir. 1988). However, where a health plan gives erroneous certification of coverage for treatment to a healthcare provider, and the provider relies to its detriment, an estoppel claim by the provider against the plan is not preempted. *Hospice of Metro Denver, Inc. v. Group Health Ins. of Okla., Inc.*, 944 F.3d 752 (10th Cir. 1991). This holding is premised upon the notion that such a claim does not involve relations between principal ERISA entities. *Id.* at 756. The Tenth Circuit has not decided a case in which the health care provider had also taken an assignment of benefits from the participant (which would place the provider in the shoes of the participant, thereby making the provider a "principal ERISA entity" by assignment). However, one district court within the Tenth Circuit has addressed this issue. In *Northern Utah Healthcare Corp. v. BC Life & Health Ins. Co.*, 2006 WL 2559817 (D. Utah Sept. 6, 2006), a hospital obtained several certifications of coverage before providing substantial medical services. It also obtained an assignment of benefits from the plan participant, and before commencing litigation attempted to collect from the insurer as assignee. However, once the hospital sued, it asserted claims based only on the confirmations of coverage it had received from the insurer, and asserted no claims based upon its status as assignee. The district court held that because the hospital had elected to pursue only its claims based on precertification, its assignee status was irrelevant. The court allowed the hospital's state-law claims, consistent with *Hospice of Metro Denver*, 944 F.3d 752.

### 6. Claims by Employers against Insurers and Service Providers

Employers frequently retain outside consultants, accountants, and other professionals to render advice about the creation and administration of employee benefit plans. Sometimes insurers provide advice on such subjects directly to employers. A claim by the employer for negligence or professional malpractice arising out of that relationship is not preempted. *Airparts Co., Inc. v. Custom Benefit Servs. of Austin, Inc.,* 28 F.3d 1062 (10th Cir. 1994). A claim for fraud in connection with the "sale" of a benefit plan to an employer by an insurer is not preempted with respect to conduct occurring before the plan was actually created. *Woodworkers Supply, Inc. v. Principal Mut. Life Ins. Co.,* 170 F.3d 985 (10th Cir. 1999). Similarly, a claim of negligent supervision against a service provider was not preempted where the service provider failed to take action that might have prevented the theft of plan assets by another service provider. *David P. Coldesina, D.D.S., P.C., Employee Profit Sharing Plan & Trust v. Estate of Simper,* 407 F.3d 1126, 1137–38 (10th Cir. 2005). However, a claim against a service provider that is based solely upon its derivative, or vicarious, liability for the actions of an ERISA-governed party (such as a plan fiduciary) would be preempted. *Id.* at 1138–39.

## III. Exhaustion of Administrative Remedies

### A. Is Exhaustion an Absolute Requirement?

The Tenth Circuit requires that a plan participant exhaust his or her remedies under the relevant employee-benefit plan before commencing an action for benefits under ERISA. "[E]xhaustion of administrative (i.e., company- or plan-provided) remedies is an implicit prerequisite to seeking judicial relief." *Held v. Mfrs. Hanover Leasing Corp.,* 912 F.2d 1197, 1206 (10th Cir. 1990). This "aligns with ERISA's overall structure of placing primary responsibility for claim resolution on fund trustees." *McGraw v. Prudential Ins. Co. of Am.,* 137 F.3d 1253, 1263 (10th Cir. 1998). "Otherwise, premature judicial interference with the interpretation of a plan would impede those internal processes which result in a completed record of decision making for a court to review." *Id.*

### B. Exceptions to the Exhaustion Requirement

Two grounds for avoiding the exhaustion requirement have been recognized within the Tenth Circuit: (1) "when resort to administrative remedies would be futile" and (2) "when the remedy provided is inadequate." *McGraw,* 137 F.3d 1253, 1263. The first exception "is limited to those instances where resort to administrative remedies would be clearly useless." *Id.* (citation and internal quotes omitted). To utilize the futility exception, the claimant must prove that the claim would be denied on appeal, not just that he or she thinks that the appeal is unlikely to result in a different decision. *Getting v. Fortis Benefits Ins. Co.,* 5 Fed. Appx. 833 (10th Cir. 2001). The second exception requires "proof of a lack of access to an internal review procedure." *Id.*

### C. Consequences of Failure to Exhaust

Where a plaintiff fails to exhaust administrative remedies, the district court should dismiss the action for "lack of subject matter jurisdiction based upon the doctrine of ripeness." *Schwob v. Standard Ins. Co.,* 37 Fed. Appx. 465, 469 (10th Cir. 2002). *But see Getting v. Fortis Benefits Ins. Co.,* 5 Fed. Appx. 833 (10th Cir. 2001) (affirming summary judgment against the plaintiff for failure to exhaust remedies). The Tenth

Circuit upheld dismissal of a claim originally brought in state law and later removed on ERISA preemption grounds even where the claimant originally brought claims for fraud and breach of contract. The court held that the exhaustion requirement applies even though the claimant does not initially assert ERISA claims. *Karls v. Texaco, Inc.,* 139 Fed. Appx. 29, 2005 WL 1189828 (10th Cir. 2005).

### D. Minimum Number of Levels of Administrative Review

No Tenth Circuit case has expressly decided how many levels of administrative review a claimant may be required to exhaust. However, in *Getting v. Fortis Benefits Ins. Co.,* 5 Fed. Appx. 833 (10th Cir. 2001), the court found a failure to exhaust where the plaintiff did not avail herself of a third level of review contained in the relevant benefit plan. Further, in *Schwob v. Standard Ins. Co.,* 37 Fed. Appx. 465 (10th Cir. 2002), the court applied the exhaustion requirement to post-appeal consideration of the plaintiff's claim. In *Schwob,* the plaintiff continued to submit additional medical information to the insurer even after it had denied her appeal of a claim denial. The insurer agreed to review the additional medical information and reopen the claim. Under these circumstances, the court held that the plaintiff was required to exhaust the remedy provided by the reopening of her claim.

### E. Can a Defendant Waive a Failure-to-Exhaust Defense?

The Tenth Circuit has not expressly decided whether the exhaustion defense can be waived, but in *Schwob,* 37 Fed. Appx. at 469, the court held that the district court should have dismissed a complaint *sua sponte* for failure to exhaust, finding that the district court lacked subject-matter jurisdiction under such circumstances. A defense of lack of subject-matter jurisdiction is not waivable. *See First State Bank & Trust Co. v. Sand Springs State Bank,* 528 F.2d 350 (10th Cir. 1976).

## IV. Standard of Review

### A. Plan Language

The Tenth Circuit has been "comparatively liberal in construing language to trigger the more deferential standard of review under ERISA." *Nance v. Sun Life Assurance Co. of Can.,* 294 F.3d 1263, 1268 (10th Cir. 2002). Courts within the Tenth Circuit do not require "any magic words, such as 'discretion,' 'deference,' 'construe' or 'interpret'" in order to find discretionary authority invested in the plan decision maker. *Gust v. Coleman Co.,* 740 F. Supp. 1544, 1550 (D. Kan. 1990), *aff'd,* 936 F.2d 583 (10th Cir. 1991) (table).

Words suggesting that plan decision makers must exercise judgment have consistently been found by the court to convey discretionary authority. In *Charter Canyon Treatment Center v. Pool Co.,* 153 F.3d 1132, 1135 (10th Cir. 1998), the court found it sufficient that the plan decision maker had "the exclusive right to interpret the Medical Plan and to decide all matters arising thereunder." In *Dycus v. Pension Benefit Guaranty Corp.,* 133 F.3d 1367, 1369 (10th Cir. 1998), the plan decision maker had discretionary authority where it had power "to decide all questions concerning the application or interpretation of the provisions of the plan." Similarly, in *Arfsten v. Frontier Airlines, Inc. Ret. Plan for Pilots,* 967 F.2d 438, 440 (10th Cir. 1992), discretion was found where the decision makers were authorized "to construe the Plan and to determine all questions of fact that may arise thereunder." Likewise, in *Pratt v. Petroleum Production Management, Inc. Employee Savings Plan & Trust,* 920 F.2d 651, 658 (10th Cir. 1990), it was enough to convey discretionary authority that the decision maker was empowered to "construe and interpret the Plan in accordance with uniform rules and regulations consistently applied to all Participants, . . . decide the eligibility of any persons to be covered under the Plan in accordance with the Plan, . . . [and] determine the right of any person to a benefit, in accordance with the Plan."

Similarly, in the context of managed care, plan language providing that a physician or other decision maker must exercise judgment as to covered medical care will convey discretionary authority. In *McGraw v. Prudential Insurance Co. of America,* 137 F.3d 1253, 1259 (10th Cir. 1998), the health insurance policy provided that "[t]o be 'needed,' the [health] service or supply must be determined by [the administrator] to meet all of these tests." (emphasis omitted). Likewise, in *Chambers v. Family Health Plan Corp.,* 100 F.3d 818, 825 (10th Cir. 1996), it was enough to confer discretion that a procedure would be considered experimental "in the judgment of the [administrator]." *See also McGee v. Equicor-Equitable HCA Corp.,* 953 F.2d 1192, 1200 (10th Cir. 1992) (arbitrary and capricious standard applied to "the plan physician's exercise of medical judgment.").

Words to the effect that the plan decision maker's determinations are final also have been found to convey discretionary authority. In *Millensifer v. Retirement Plan for Salaried Employees of Cotter Corp.,* 968 F.2d 1005, 1010 (10th Cir. 1992), the court found discretionary authority where, according to the governing plan instrument, the decision maker

> shall have the power to construe the plan, to supply any omissions therein, to reconcile and correct any errors or inconsistencies, and to make equitable adjustments for any mistakes or errors made in the administration of the plan, and all such actions or determinations made in good faith shall not be subject to review by anyone.

According to the court, the phrase that insulated plan decisions from further review "may not be enforceable, but it certainly indicates an intention to vest as much discretion as possible" in the decision maker. *Id.* at n.2. Likewise, in *Winchester v. Prudential Life Insurance Co. of America,* 975 F.2d 1479, 1483 (10th Cir. 1992), the court found discretionary authority in language stating that the insurer, "as Claims Administrator, determines the benefits for which an individual qualifies under the Benefit Plan," and that "the insurance company has the exclusive right to interpret the provisions of the Plan, [and] its decision is conclusive and binding."

A recurring issue among the appellate courts is whether the requirement of "proof satisfactory to the decision maker," or a similar phrase, conveys discretionary authority. In *Nance v. Sun Life Assurance Co. of Canada,* 294 F.3d 1263, 1267–68 (10th Cir. 2002), the Tenth Circuit held that such language does convey discretionary authority sufficient to invoke deferential judicial review. It is important to note that under the Tenth Circuit's analysis, the plan must actually provide that proof must be satisfactory not just generally but specifically to the decision maker. *Id.* "[L]anguage in other plans that requires only submission of satisfactory proof, without reference to who must be satisfied," does not convey discretionary authority. *Id.* at 1268.

## B. What Standard of Review Applies?

### *1. Abuse of Discretion or Arbitrary and Capricious Standard*

Where the terms of a governing employee-benefit plan confer discretionary authority upon a plan decision maker to interpret the plan or determine entitlement to benefits, the courts employ a deferential abuse of discretion standard of review. *Firestone Tire & Rubber Co. v. Bruch,* 489 U.S. 101, 115 (1989). The abuse of discretion standard is the same as, and often referred to as, the arbitrary and capricious standard of review. *Chambers v. Family Health Plan Corp.,* 100 F.3d 818, 825 n.1 (10th Cir. 1996).

The Tenth Circuit has stated that "this standard is a difficult one for a claimant to overcome." *Nance v. Sun Life Assurance Co. of Canada,* 294 F.3d 1263, 1269 (10th Cir. 2002). Under the arbitrary and capricious standard of review, the plan administrator's decision may not be set aside if it is based upon "a reasonable interpretation of the plan's terms . . . made in good faith." *Averhart v. USWest Mgmt. Pension Plan,* 46 F.3d 1480, 1485 (10th Cir. 1994). An interpretation or decision under this standard having "*any reasonable basis* will be upheld; it need not be the only logical or even the best decision." *Rademacher v. Colo. Ass'n of Soil Conservation Dists. Med. Benefit Plan,* 11 F.3d 1567, 1570 (10th Cir. 1993) (emphasis added); *see also Woolsey v. Marion Labs., Inc.,* 934 F.2d 1452, 1460 (10th Cir. 1991) (administrator's decision "need only be sufficiently supported by the facts within [its] knowledge to counter a claim that it was arbitrary or capricious" and the court "will not substitute [its] judgment for the judgment of the [administrator] unless the actions of the [administrator] are not grounded on any reasonable basis"). Perhaps the best summary of the Tenth Circuit's view of deference under the arbitrary and capricious standard is found in *Kimber v. Thiokol Corp.,* 196 F.3d 1092, 1098 (10th Cir. 1999) (citations omitted):

> When reviewing under the arbitrary and capricious standard, "[t]he Administrator['s] decision need not be the only logical one nor even the best one. It need only be sufficiently supported by facts within [his] knowledge to counter a claim that it was arbitrary or capricious." . . . The reviewing court "need only assure that the administrator's decision fall[s] somewhere on a continuum of reasonableness—even if on the low end."

Except where a conflict of interest may otherwise require (see discussion below), a claim decision is not arbitrary and capricious if it is supported by substantial evidence. *Sandoval v. Aetna Life & Cas. Ins. Co.,* 967 F.2d 377, 382 (10th Cir. 1992). "Substantial evidence is such evidence that a reasonable mind might accept as adequate to support the conclusion reached by the decisionmaker. Substantial evidence requires more than a scintilla but less than a preponderance." *Id.* (quotation marks, brackets, and citation omitted).

In particular circumstances, failure of a claim decision maker to investigate—that is, to request particular evidence—may render a decision arbitrary and capricious. *Gaither v. Aetna Life Ins. Co.,* 388 F.3d 759, 807 (10th Cir. 2004). The general rule remains that "nothing in ERISA requires plan administrators to go fishing for evidence favorable to a claim when it has not been brought to their attention that such evidence exists." *Id.* at 804. However, as a limited exception (or in the court's terms, "narrow principle"), a fiduciary cannot ignore "readily available information" when (1) the evidence in the record suggests that the information might confirm the beneficiary's theory of entitlement and (2) the fiduciary has little or no evidence in the record to refute that theory. *Id.* at 807.

### 2. De Novo Standard

Where de novo review is required, the courts determine "not whether the fiduciaries' interpretation of the contract was arbitrary or capricious, but only whether it was correct." *Pratt v. Petroleum Prod. Mgmt., Inc. Employee Sav. Plan & Trust,* 920 F.2d 651, 658 (10th Cir. 1990).

### C. Effect of Conflict of Interest or Procedural Irregularity

The Tenth Circuit has adopted a "sliding scale" approach to considering a decision maker's conflict of interest when applying the arbitrary and capricious standard. *Chambers v. Family Health Plan Corp.,* 100 F.3d 818, 826–27 (10th Cir. 1996). However, where the plaintiff demonstrates an "inherent" conflict, a "serious" conflict, a "proven" conflict, or a serious procedural irregularity, the scale "slides" in a prescribed way: The burden of proof shifts to the defendant to show that its decision was reasonable, and neither arbitrary nor capricious. *Fought v. UNUM Life Ins. Co. of Am.,* 379 F.3d 997 (10th Cir. 2004).

An "inherent" conflict may exist in cases where an insurance company that both funds benefits and decides claims is put in the position of determining whether an insured loss has occurred. *Id.* at 1006; *see also Adamson v. UNUM Life Ins. Co. of Am.,* 455 F.3d 1209, 1213 (10th Cir. 2006). But such an apparent conflict may not alone trigger a shift in the burden of proof, because this situation was "never meant to [create] an ipso facto conclusive presumption to be applied without regard to the facts of the case—including the solvency of the insurer or the nature or size of the claim." *Id.* at 1213. As to the existence of a "serious" or "proven" conflict of interest, it is the burden of the plaintiff to establish it, based upon factors such as "whether (1) the plan is self-funded; (2) the company funding the plan appointed and compensated the plan administrator; (3) the plan administrator's performance review or level of compensation were linked to the denial of benefits; and (4) the provision of benefits had a significant economic impact on the company administering the plan." *Wolberg v. AT&T Broadband Pension Plan,* 2005 WL 23683, at *4 (10th Cir. 2005) (unpublished).

Where the plaintiff fails to establish an "inherent," "proven," or "serious" conflict, and where no serious procedural irregularity exists, a "standard" conflict (i.e., an apparent but less serious conflict) may still be considered by the court in determining whether the plan decision maker acted arbitrarily or capriciously. Such a conflict is considered as a factor in the overall analysis. *E.g., Wolberg,* 2005 U.S. App. LEXIS 197, at *12; *Fought,* 379 F.3d 997, 1005; *see also Kimber v. Thiokol Corp.,* 196 F.3d 1092, 1098 (10th Cir. 1999) ("the mere fact that the plan administrator was also a Thiokol employee is not enough per se to demonstrate a conflict.").

### D. Other Factors Affecting Standard of Review

"[W]hen substantial violations of ERISA deadlines result in the claim's being automatically deemed denied on review, the district court must review the denial de novo, even if the plan administrator has discretionary authority to decide claims." *Gilbertson v. Allied Signal, Inc.,* 328 F.3d 625, 631 (10th Cir. 2003). This is because "deemed denied . . . decisions are not exercises of discretionary power." *Id.* at 632. However, substantial compliance with ERISA's claims regulations will preserve deferential review. *Id.* at 634–35. A claim decision maker is in substantial compliance with ERISA deadlines if its delay is (1) "inconsequential" and (2) in the context of an ongoing, good-faith exchange of information between the administrator and the claimant. *Finley v. Hewlett-Packard Co. Employee Benefits Org. Income Prot. Plan,* 379 F.3d 1168, 1174 (10th Cir. 2004) (citing *Gilbertson,* 328 F.3d at 635).

An example of "inconsequential" delay is when the decision maker fully evaluated a claim at initial submission, did not timely dispose of the administrative appeal, but was not at that time faced with any "meaningful new evidence . . . or significant new issues." *Id.* at 1174–75. In that situation, the decision maker's initial denial and statement of reasons can effectively be applied, and an arbitrary and capricious review remains proper. *Id.*

A typical example of "ongoing, good-faith exchange" sufficient to preserve deferential review, notwithstanding noncompliance with ERISA deadlines, would be where the decision maker considers additional information submitted by the claimant relatively late in the claim process, where the parties continue to engage in a "meaningful dialogue" concerning the claim. *Gilbertson,* 328 F.3d at 634–35.

Whether the "deemed denied" doctrine continues to apply to benefit claims filed after 2001 is uncertain. *Gilbertson* and *Finley* both interpreted and applied the "deemed denied" provision of 29 C.F.R. § 2560.503-1(h)(4) (1999). That regulation was amended to strike the "deemed denied" clause. 29 C.F.R. § 2560.503-1(h)(4) (2002). The amended form applies to claims filed under employee benefits plan, generally, on or after January 1, 2002, *see* 29 C.F.R. § 2560.503-1(o)(1) (2002), and to claims filed under a group health plan on or after the first day of the first plan year beginning on or after July 1, 2002, but in no event later than January 1, 2003. 29 C.F.R. § 2560.503-1(o)(2). Hence, in *Finley,* the Tenth Circuit "specifically reserve[d] the question of whether this decision and our decision in *Gilbertson* apply to the regulations, as amended." *Id.*

Another factor is where the claim decision maker "fails to gather or examine relevant evidence." *Kimber v. Thiokol Corp.,* 196 F.3d 1092, 1097 (10th Cir. 1999). However, this does not necessarily shift the burden of the claimant to produce evidence in support of his or her claim. "If a plan participant fails to bring evidence to the attention of the administrator, the participant cannot complain of the administrator's failure to consider this evidence." *Sandoval v. Aetna Life & Cas. Ins. Co.,* 967

F.2d 377, 381 (10th Cir. 1992). Deference is reduced only where a decision maker had evidence but failed to consider it, or where the decision maker completely fails to obtain any relevant medical records. *See, e.g., McGraw v. Prudential Ins. Co. of Am.,* 137 F.3d 1253, 1262–63 (10th Cir. 1998).

Deference can also be reduced based upon "a plan's inconsistencies in handling an applicant's claims." *Kimber,* 196 F.3d at 1097. Deference may also be reduced on account of failure to provide an adequate claim-review procedure or failure to provide notice to a claimant of his or her appeal rights. *Sage v. Automation, Inc. Pension Plan & Trust,* 945 F.2d 885, 893–95 (10th Cir. 1988) (finding that deficiencies did not justify overturning decision unfavorable to claimants; "[n]ot every procedural defect will upset the decision of plan representatives").

## V. Rules of Plan Interpretation

### A. Application of Federal Common Law

As a matter of federal common law, the Tenth Circuit has applied "standard tenets of contract construction" to interpret ERISA plan documents. *Pirkheim v. First UNUM Life Ins.,* 229 F.3d 1008, 1010 (10th Cir. 2000); *see also Member Servs. Life Ins. Co. v. Am. Nat'l Bank & Trust Co. of Sapulpa,* 130 F.3d 950, 954 (10th Cir. 1997), *cert. denied,* 523 U.S. 1139 (1998); *Chiles v. Ceridian Corp.,* 95 F.3d 1505, 1515 (10th Cir. 1996). Thus, in interpreting plan terms, the court examines the plan documents as a whole and, if they are unambiguous, construes them as a matter of law. *Admin. Comm. of the Wal-Mart Assocs. Health & Welfare Plan v. Willard,* 393 F.3d 1119 (10th Cir. 2004); *Allison v. Bank One-Denver,* 289 F.3d 1223, 1233, *amended on denial of reh'g* (10th Cir. 2002); *Pirkheim,* 229 F.3d at 1010 n.2; *Chiles,* 95 F.3d at 1511. If plan terms are ambiguous, the court may look at extrinsic evidence to interpret the plan. *Capital Cities/ABC, Inc. v. Ratcliff,* 141 F.3d 1405, 1411 (10th Cir.), *cert. denied,* 525 U.S. 873 (1998). In so doing, the objective is to ascertain and carry out the true intentions of the party based on the manner in which a reasonable person in the position of a general participant, and not the litigating participant, would have understood the contract terms. *Wal-Mart,* 393 F.3d at 1123; *McGee v. Equicor-Equitable HCA Corp.,* 953 F.2d 1192, 1202 (10th Cir. 1992).

In a de novo review case, when the evidence is equivocal regarding the parties' intent on type of health coverage to be provided under a new ERISA benefits plan, the Tenth Circuit has construed ambiguity in favor of the beneficiaries. *See, e.g., Deboard v. Sunshine Min. & Refining Co.,* 208 F.3d 1228, 1243 (10th Cir. 2000).

### B. Application of *Contra Proferentem*

The doctrine of *contra proferentem* does not apply in a case involving the arbitrary and capricious standard of review. *Kimber v. Thiokol Corp.,* 196 F.3d 1092, 1100 (10th Cir. 1999); *see also Lefler v. United HealthCare of Utah, Inc.,* 72 Fed. Appx. 818, 826 (10th Cir. 2003). While language from the *Kimber* decision suggests that the doctrine of *contra proferentem* would be applicable in a de novo case, the Tenth Circuit recently noted in a footnote that it had not reached the decision of whether the doctrine of *contra proferentem* applies in a de novo review case. *Andrews v. Blue*

*Cross Blue Shield of Neb.,* 165 Fed. Appx. 650, 2006 WL 259673 (10th Cir. 2006). Even if the doctrine applies, however, before employing, the courts should first seek to interpret the disputed language given "its common and ordinary meaning as a reasonable person in the position of the [plan] participant, not the actual participant, would have understood the words to mean." *Id.* If the language of the plan is ambiguous as viewed through this prism, the court "may look at extrinsic evidence." *Id.*

### C. Deference Afforded to an Administrator's Interpretation of a Plan

Under the arbitrary and capricious standard of review, the plan administrator's interpretation of the plan is entitled to deference if the plan gives the administrator deference to determine eligibility or interpret terms of the plan. *Wagner-Harding v. Farmland Indus. Inc. Employee Ret. Plan,* 26 Fed. Appx. 811, 815 (10th Cir. 2001) (plan gave authority to determine eligibility for benefits and construe terms of plan); *Arfsten v. Frontier Airlines, Inc. Ret. Plan for Pilots,* 967 F.2d 438, 440–41 (10th Cir. 1992) (decisions of retirement board were due deference where plan authorized them to construe plan and determine all questions of fact that might arise thereunder). *See also Adamson v. UNUM Life Ins. Co. of Am.,* 455 F.3d 1209, 1212 (10th Cir. 2006) (administrator's decision "will be upheld so long as it is predicated on a reasoned basis. . . . [T]here is no requirement that the basis relied upon be the only logical one or even the superlative one."); *Trujillo v. Cyprus Amax Minerals Co. Ret. Plan Comm.,* 203 F.3d 733, 736 (10th Cir. 2000) (under this standard of review, the court of appeals will not set aside the decision if it was based on a reasonable interpretation of the plan's terms and was made in good faith); *Caldwell v. Life Ins. Co. of N. Am.,* 287 F.3d 1276, 1282 (for purposes of determining whether denial of ERISA benefits was an arbitrary and capricious decision, substantial evidence is such evidence that a reasonable mind might accept as adequate to support the conclusion reached by the decision maker); *Kimber,* 196 F.3d at 1098 (when reviewing under the arbitrary and capricious standard, "[t]he Administrator decision need not be the only logical one nor even the best one. It need only be sufficiently supported by facts within [his] knowledge to counter a claim that it was arbitrary or capricious. The decision will be upheld unless it is not grounded on any reasonable basis.") (internal citations and quotation marks omitted); *accord Alves v. Silverado Foods, Inc.,* 6 Fed. Appx. 694, 700 (10th Cir. 2001).

However, if the administrator has a proven conflict of interest in making the challenged decision, the level of deference that the court affords the administrator's decision diminishes in direct relation to any conflict. *Siemon v. AT&T Corp.,* 117 F.3d 1173, 1177 (10th Cir. 1997); *see also Pitman v. Blue Cross & Blue Shield of Okla.,* 217 F.3d 1291, 1296 (10th Cir. 2000) (nonexhaustive factors that may affect such an administrator's conflict include whether (1) the plan is self-funded; (2) the company funding the plan appointed and compensated the plan administrator; (3) the plan administrator's performance reviews or level of compensation were linked to the denial of benefits; and (4) the provision of benefits had a significant economic impact on the company administering the plan). The Tenth Circuit will not find a conflicted administrator's decision "presumptively void." *Chambers v. Family Health*

*Plan Corp.,* 100 F.3d 818, 826–27 (10th Cir. 1996). Where an "inherent," "serious," or "proven" conflict of interest exists, the burden may shift to the defendant to establish that its interpretation was reasonable. *Fought v. UNUM Life Ins. Co. of Am.,* 379 F.3d 997, 1006 (10th Cir. 2004); *see also DeGrado v. Jefferson Pilot Fin. Ins. Co.,* 451 F.3d 1161 (10th Cir. 2006) (under circumstances, administrator bore the burden of proving that its interpretation of the terms of the policy was reasonable).

## D. Other Rules of Plan or Contract Interpretation

### 1. Summary Plan Descriptions

In this process of plan interpretation, a summary plan description (SPD) is considered part of the plan documents, which must be considered as a whole. *Chiles v. Ceridian Corp.,* 95 F.3d 1505 (10th Cir. 1996). For purposes of determining whether terms are ambiguous, the relative clarity of an SPD is viewed against the special obligation imposed by ERISA §§ 1022(a) (requiring that an SPD be written in a manner clearly calculated to be understood by the average plan participant) and 1022(b) (requiring inclusion in SPD of "circumstances which may result in disqualification, ineligibility or denial or loss of benefits," as well as "the remedies available under the plan for the redress of claims which are denied in whole or in part"). *Haymond v. Eighth Dist. Elec. Benefit Fund,* 36 Fed. Appx. 369, 372–73 (10th Cir. 2002). Thus considered, an SPD establishing two separate limitations periods was found ambiguous, and the fund, as drafter of the SPD, was made to "bear the consequences of this inaccuracy." *Id.* On the same principles, terms of the SPD were held to control over conflicting terms of the plan, based on the view that SPDs best reflect expectations of the parties to an ERISA plan. *Chiles,* 95 F.3d at 1515; *Semtner v. Group Health Serv. of Okla., Inc.,* 129 F.3d 1390, 1393 (10th Cir. 1997).

### 2. Effect of Plan Amendments

Finally, questions may arise as to what effect plan amendments have on pending claims. No plan amendment can operate to deprive a beneficiary of a vested welfare benefit. *Chiles,* 95 F.3d at 1510. But since welfare benefit plans are exempt from vesting requirements that ERISA imposes on pensions benefits, a plan administrator generally remains able to amend terms prospectively. *Welch v. UNUM Life Ins. Co. of Am.,* 382 F.3d 1078, 1083 (10th Cir. 2004); *Pitman v. Blue Cross & Blue Shield of Okla.,* 217 F.3d 1291, 1297 n.6 (10th Cir. 2000). Benefits under a welfare benefit plan vest, if at all, under the terms of the plan itself. *Member Servs. Life Ins. Co. v. Am. Nat'l Bank & Trust Co. of Sapulpa,* 130 F.3d 950, 954 (10th Cir. 1997), *cert. denied,* 523 U.S. 1139 (1998). In making this assessment, the court will apply general principles of contract interpretation. *Id.* Thus, if the plan so provides, a plan sponsor retains the discretionary right to change benefits of all long-term disability plan participants, including those who had already qualified for long-term disability benefits. *Welch,* 382 F.3d at 1085–86; *Chiles,* 95 F.3d at 1512–13. *But see Member Servs.,* 130 F.3d at 954–56 (under a medical insurance policy, benefits had vested after medical expenses were both incurred and paid, and subsequent amendments purporting to exclude such expenses were ineffective).

# VI. Discovery

## A. Limitations on Discovery

The Tenth Circuit has not addressed the scope of discovery in a published decision, but has discussed the matter in an unpublished decision involving deferential review and conflict of interest. *See infra.* District courts within the circuit have observed that, because of the narrow scope of review and admissibility in 29 U.S.C. § 1132(a)(1)(B) claims, the only information that a plaintiff may obtain from the defendant is "the information which was available and presented to the plan administrator at the time of the administrator's decision." *Spangler v. UNUM Life Ins. Co. of Am.,* 38 F. Supp. 2d 952, 954 (N.D. Okla. 1999) (deferential review case, interpreting Tenth Circuit decisions in *Sandoval v. Aetna Life & Cas. Ins. Co.,* 967 F.2d 377 (10th Cir. 1992); *Chambers v. Family Health Plan Corp.,* 100 F.3d 818 (10th Cir. 1996); and *Kaus v. Standard Ins. Co.,* 1998 WL 778055 (10th Cir. Nov. 5, 1998)); *see also Hemphill v. Unisys Corp.,* 855 F. Supp. 1225, 1239 (D. Utah 1994) (deferential review case, denying plaintiff's request for discovery and witness testimony that was not a part of the evidence considered by the administrator in denying the claim); *Caldwell v. Life Ins. Co. of N. Am.,* 165 F.R.D. 633, 637 (D. Kan. 1996) (de novo review case, finding "plaintiff is not entitled to pursue discovery that he could or should have presented to the administrator before arriving at the district court level. . . . Subjecting a party to such discovery constitutes annoyance and oppression. It also imposes undue burden and expense upon it"); *see also Lovelace v. Scientific Drilling Int'l Long Term Disability Plan,* No. 01-CV-1056-D (D. Wyo.) (Order Ruling on Plaintiff's Motion for Reconsideration (July 19, 2002) at 8, n.3); *Avery v. UNUM,* 02-CV-193-WPJ (D.N.M.) (Order Denying Plaintiff's Request for Limited Discovery on ERISA Claim (June 11, 2002)); *Shearer v. Western Gas Res., Inc.,* No. 02-CV-081-D (D. Wyo.) (Order Ruling on Defendants' Motion to Prohibit Discovery Pursuant to ERISA (September 12, 2002)); *Finn v. UNUM,* 02-MK-1303 (D. Colo.) (July 25, 2003 Order re Motions in Limine) (order limiting evidentiary scope to administrative record in ERISA case, pp 4–5). Once that administrative record has been provided, a plaintiff should be denied the opportunity to conduct further discovery. *See Spangler,* 38 F. Supp. 2d at 954. *See also Avery v. UNUM,* 02-CV-193-WPJ (D.N.M.) (de novo review case, denying discovery based on plaintiff's failure to "come forward with a compelling reason to warrant departure from the general rule precluding discovery outside of the administrative record.").

## B. Discovery and Conflict of Interest

In *Kaus v. Standard Ins. Co.,* 1998 WL 778055 (10th Cir., Nov. 5, 1998), the district court entered summary judgment for Standard, and the plaintiff on appeal complained that discovery should have first been allowed regarding, inter alia, Standard's conflict of interest in concurrently funding and administering claims under the plan. The Tenth Circuit affirmed summary judgment, as well as the district court's denial of discovery. In so doing, the court favorably cited *Farley v. Arkansas Blue Cross & Blue Shield,* 147 F.3d 774, 776 n.4 (8th Cir. 1998) (recognizing that conflict of interest will usually be apparent on face of administrative record and thus district court rarely needs to permit discovery); *Trombetta v. Cragin Fed. Bank for Sav. Employee Stock Ownership Plan,* 102 F.3d 1435, 1438 n.1 (7th Cir. 1996) (holding district court properly barred discovery) and *Maune v. Int'l Bhd. of Elec. Workers, Local No. 1, Health & Welfare Fund,* 83 F.3d 959, 963 (8th Cir. 1996) (affirming district court's order refusing discovery).

Further, the Tenth Circuit has recently favorably cited a district court decision for the point that, in a sliding-scale review, "where [the claim administrator's] conflict of interest is apparent, further discovery is not required." *Fought v. UNUM Life Ins. Co. of Am.,* 379 F.3d 997, 1004 (10th Cir. 2004) (quoting *Spangler,* 38 F. Supp. 2d at 955–56) (internal quotation marks omitted). On the other hand, in a subsequent unpublished decision, the Tenth Circuit stated that the burden of proof was shifted to the insurer in *Fought* because it "resisted discovery on [its] conflict." *Grosvenor v. Qwest Commc'ns Int'l,* 2006 WL 2076804 (10th Cir. 2006). The Tenth Circuit has more recently held that "some proof (supplied by the claimant) must identify a conflict that could plausibly jeopardize the plan administrator's impartiality" before a finding of inherent conflict can justify a shifting of the burden of proof. *Adamson v. UNUM Life Ins. Co. of Am.,* 455 F.3d 1209, 1213 (10th Cir. 2006). These more recent decisions raise at least a possible argument that limited discovery as to the extent of a conflict should be allowed.

# VII. Evidence

## A. Scope of Evidence under Standards of Review

### 1. Arbitrary and Capricious Review

Under the arbitrary and capricious standard of review, the court's review is limited to evidence and arguments that were presented during the claim and appeal process. *See, e.g., DeGrado v. Jefferson Pilot Fin. Ins. Co.,* 451 F.3d 1161, 1176 (10th Cir. 2006); *Chambers v. Family Health Plan Corp.,* 100 F.3d 818, 823–24 (10th Cir. 1996); *Sandoval v. Aetna Life & Cas. Ins. Co.,* 967 F.2d 377, 380–81 (10th Cir. 1992) ("In effect, a curtain falls when the fiduciary completes its review, and for purposes of determining if substantial evidence supported the decision, the district court must evaluate the record as it was at the time of the decision."). The Tenth Circuit has noted that important policy reasons underlie this limited scope of review:

> A primary goal of ERISA was to provide a method for workers and beneficiaries to resolve disputes over benefits inexpensively and expeditiously. Permitting or requiring district courts to consider evidence from both parties that was not presented to the plan administrator would seriously impair the achievement of that goal.

*Sandoval,* 967 F.2d at 380.

### 2. De Novo Review and Evidence beyond the Administrative Record

In a case involving de novo review, the evidence is also generally limited to the administrative record. *Hall v. UNUM Life Ins. Co. of Am.,* 300 F.3d 1197, 1201 (10th Cir. 2002). The court may allow supplementation of the claim record "when circumstances clearly establish that additional evidence is necessary to conduct an adequate . . . review of the benefit decision." But the Tenth Circuit has emphasized, "it is the unusual case in which the district court should allow supplementation of the record." *Id.* Such exceptional circumstances may include:

> claims that require consideration of complex medical questions or issues regarding the credibility of medical experts; the availability of very limited administrative review procedures with little or no evidentiary record; the necessity of evidence regarding interpretation of the terms of the plan rather than specific historical facts; instances where the payor and the administrator are the same entity and the court is concerned about impartiality; claims which would have been insurance contract claims prior to ERISA; and circumstances in which there is additional evidence that the claimant could not have presented in the administrative process.

*Id.* at 1203, citing *Quesinberry v. Life Ins. Co. of N. Am.,* 987 F.2d 1017, 1027 (4th Cir. 1993). However, the trial court retains discretion to reject extrarecord evidence even in the few circumstances where such evidence may be appropriate. The party seeking to supplement the record bears the burden of establishing how the evidence is necessary to the de novo review. And the court will not admit any extrarecord evidence unless the party seeking its admission first "demonstrate[s] that it could not have been submitted to the plan administrator at the time the challenged decision was made." *Id.*

Applying these standards, *Hall* held that "conflict of interest" evidence was inadmissible where the plaintiff had failed to show how particular additional evidence would be relevant to the conflict or would address a particular shortcoming in the record or decision-making process purportedly caused by the conflict. *Id.* at 1206. In contrast, the trial court had not erred in admitting evidence of surgeries the plaintiff underwent after her administrative claim had closed, because (1) the plaintiff had been unable to submit such evidence to the administrator prior to its final decision, and (2) the plaintiff's willingness to undergo such surgeries corroborated her claim of severe, unrelenting, disabling pain. *Id.* at 1205–07.

### B. Evidentiary Value of Social Security Determinations

Another type of evidence that claimants commonly offer to support their disability claims is a favorable Social Security determination. In an unpublished decision, the Tenth Circuit has stated that a Social Security finding of disability does not "compel" a plan administrator to grant disability benefits. *Wagner-Harding v. Farmland Indus. Inc. Employee Ret. Plan,* 26 Fed. Appx. 811, 817 (10th Cir. 2001). The court refused to give the Social Security process such effect because "those proceedings are entirely different and separate from a claim under ERISA, with different parties, different evidentiary standards, and different bodies of law governing their outcomes." *Id.*

Similarly, when the Social Security decision was "based in large part" on evidence of a different impairment than that upon which the plaintiff sought plan benefits, the trial court does not err by refusing to consider it as part of a de novo review. *Gilbertson v. AlliedSignal, Inc.,* 172 Fed. Appx. 857, 862 (10th Cir. 2006).

The court reached a different result in *Wilcott v. Matlack, Inc.,* 64 F.3d 1458 (10th Cir. 1995), which affirmed a trial court's reliance on a participant's Social Security award as "conclusive proof" of total disability. However, in *Wilcott,* this effect arose simply from terms of the plan, which read "Notwithstanding the above [provisions regarding substantiation of total disability], the awarding of a primary Social Security Disability Benefit will be accepted by the Trust as proof of total disability and the continuation of such Social Security Disability Benefit will be accepted as proof of a continuing total disability." *Id.* at 1461.

Apart from these decisions, there is limited discussion in published district court decisions regarding the effect to be given to a claimant's successful application for Social Security disability. In *Eye v. Metropolitan Life Insurance Co.,* 202 F. Supp. 2d 1204, 1211 (D. Kan. 2002), the court generally followed the rationale of *Wagner-Harding,* but criticized the claim administrator for failing to address the Social Security disability award during the claim process. The court remarked: "Although the standards between the two disability benefits are different and an award of Social Security disability benefits does not dispose of the issue of benefits under the Plan, MetLife should have considered this fact when it made its determination." *Id. But see Sparkman v. Prudential Ins. Co. of Am.,* 427 F. Supp. 2d 1117, 1125 (D. Utah 2006) (plaintiff "fail[ed] to provide any evidence that the Social Security Administration's disability determination in any way mirrors the relevant definition of 'total disability' under his policy.").

### C. Other Evidence Issues

The Tenth Circuit's recent imposition of an enhanced standard of review where an "inherent" conflict of interest exists (see Section IV.C, *supra*) requires in such situations that the claim decision maker prove its determination was not arbitrary or capricious. *Fought,* 379 F.3d 997 (10th Cir. 2004). The Tenth Circuit has indicated that where such a conflict exists, "the administrator best promotes the purposes of ERISA by obtaining an independent evaluation," especially where medical information is conflicting (although the court stopped short of requiring independent evaluation, suggesting that such measures be considered on a case-by-case basis). *Id.* at 1015.

## VIII. Procedural Aspects of ERISA Practice

### A. Methods of Adjudication

Motions, rather than trial, typically resolve ERISA § 502(a)(1)(B) cases involving the arbitrary and capricious standard of review. *See, e.g., Hickman v. Gem Ins. Co.,* 299 F.3d 1208 (10th Cir. 2002) (affirming summary judgment for HMO on class action claims for denied benefits); *Nance v. Sun Life Assurance Co. of Can.,* 294 F.3d 1263, 1275 (10th Cir. 2002) (affirming summary judgment for administrator in case involving arbitrary and capricious review of decision to deny benefits). The Tenth Circuit has generally approved this practice in *dicta,* while outlining how a benefits claim should proceed:

In short, the issue presented by this case could normally be handled by the
expedient of summary judgment. When the trial court is presented with the
evidence that was considered by the trustees, if it is substantial enough to
support the trustees' decision, the trustees' motion for summary judgment
should be granted. If the evidence does not support the trustees' decision, a
remand to them may be proper or, in the extreme case, an order requiring
payment of retirement benefits to the applicant-plaintiff may be appropriate.
Further, if a plaintiff can present evidence of factors not considered by the
trustees which should have been, and which raise a material issue of fact,
summary judgment should be foregone in favor of a trial.

*Carter v. Cent. States, SE & SW Areas Pension Plan,* 656 F.2d 575, 576 (10th Cir.
1981). Courts have debated whether motions to affirm or overturn an ERISA claim
decision are, in fact, for "summary judgment." *See Clausen v. Standard Ins. Co.,* 961
F. Supp. 1446, 1455 (D. Colo. 1997) (ERISA § 502(a)(1)(B) case to be handled as
an administrative appeal, and summary judgment is an "inappropriate vehicle for
evaluating the arbitrariness and capriciousness of an administrator's denial of disability benefits under ERISA") (citing discussion in *Olenhouse v. Commodity Credit
Corp.,* 42 F.3d 1560, 1579 n.31 (10th Cir. 1994)). But this debate has not changed
the result. *See, e.g., id.* (resolving case on motion, notwithstanding court's objections
to use of Federal Rules of Civil Procedure Rule 56 process).

Similarly, benefits cases involving the de novo standard of review often resolve
on motion. *See, e.g., Devers v. Quivira,* 35 F. Supp. 2d 1282, 1287–88 (D. Kan.
1998) (ruling on cross-motions for summary judgment); *Lund v. UNUM Life Ins. of
Am.,* 19 F. Supp. 2d 1254, 1259–60 (D. Utah 1996) (accord).

## B. Reported ERISA Trials

Benefit claims as well as claims for breaches of fiduciary duty and other statutory
violations are equitable in nature and no right to a jury trial exists. *Adams v. Cyprus
Amax Minerals Co.,* 149 F.3d 1156 (10th Cir. 1998) (no jury trial for 29 U.S.C.
§ 1132(a)(1)(B) claim); *Bonnell v. Bank of Am.,* 284 F. Supp. 2d 1284, 1289 (D.
Kan. 2003); *Conover v. Aetna US Healthcare, Inc.,* 167 F. Supp. 2d 1317, 1322
(N.D. Okla. 2001); *see Millsap v. McDonnell Douglas Corp.,* 368 F.3d 1246 (10th
Cir. 2004) (analyzing and rejecting claim for back pay under ERISA as "Section
502(a)(3), by its terms, only allows for *equitable* relief.").

In certain cases, the court may proceed in a manner similar to that of a bench
trial under Rule 52 of the Federal Rules of Civil Procedure. *See, e.g., Hall v. UNUM
Life Ins. Co. of Am.,* 300 F.3d 1197, 1200 (10th Cir. 2002). In *Hall v. UNUM,* the
trial court denied the defendant's "motion for judgment on the administrative
record" on the plaintiff's ERISA § 502 claim. *Id.* at 1200. The court proceeded to a
bench trial and in the process allowed presentation of evidence including "enormous
amounts of testimony and evidentiary materials outside of the administrative record,
including depositions, Hall's medical records and the testimony of several witnesses." *Id.* at 1204. While *Hall* does not typify the scope of evidence that should be
allowed at trial of an ERISA de novo review,[1] it demonstrates that the trial court

may proceed to bench trial if it considers evidence outside of the administrative record necessary to conduct the de novo review.

Other reported ERISA decisions reaching a bench trial have generally involved claims apart from ERISA § 502(a)(1)(B). *See, e.g., Greene v. Safeway Stores, Inc.,* 98 F.3d 554, 556 (10th Cir. 1996) (trial court allowed concurrent presentation of evidence on plaintiff's claims under ERISA § 510 and Age Discrimination in Employment Act, then ruled upon ERISA claim); *Hockett v. Sun Co., Inc.,* 109 F.3d 1515, 1518 (10th Cir. 1997) (fiduciary duty case); *Ershick v. United Mo. Bank of Kansas City,* 948 F.2d 660 (10th Cir. 1991) (ERISA §§ 404 and 406 claims).

### C. Special Procedures for ERISA Benefit Cases

There are no reported cases establishing special procedures for ERISA benefit cases within the Tenth Circuit. However, a number of district judges within the circuit routinely impose special procedures in ERISA benefit cases, including early briefing of conflict of interest issues, early filing of a stipulated claim record, and limited discovery.

The Tenth Circuit has articulated several circumstances under which the district courts should remand claims to the plan decision maker before engaging in final judicial review. In *Rekstad v. U.S. Bancorp,* 451 F.3d 1114 (10th Cir. 2006), the decision maker had refused to consider certain nonmedical affidavits from the claimant's family and friends regarding her alleged inability to work. The court found that it was arbitrary and capricious for the decision maker to have failed to consider this evidence. *Id.* at 1121. However, rather than simply reverse the decision, the court ordered that the claim be remanded to the decision maker so that it could consider this evidence. *Id.* As support for its decision, the court stated that "[t]his is not a case where it is so clear-cut that it was unreasonable . . . to deny benefits." *Id.* Thus, the court was unable to determine whether substantial evidence supported a denial decision, requiring the remand. *Id.*

In *DeGrado v. Jefferson Pilot Financial Insurance Co.,* 451 F.3d 1161 (10th Cir. 2006), the Tenth Circuit found remand to be the proper remedy where the decision maker had "fail[ed] to make adequate findings or to explain adequately the grounds of its decision." *Id.* at 1175 (citation omitted). On the other hand, where "but for the plan administrator's arbitrary and capricious conduct, the claimant would have continued to receive benefits," or where "there was no evidence in the record to support a termination or denial of benefits," simple reversal of the decision would be appropriate. *Id.* at 1175–76.

## IX. Fiduciary Liability Claims

### A. Definition of Fiduciary

29 U.S.C. § 1002(21)(A) defines a fiduciary as follows:

> a person is a fiduciary with respect to a plan to the extent (i) he exercises any discretionary authority or discretionary control respecting management of such plan or exercises any authority or control respecting management or

disposition of its assets, (ii) he renders investment advice for a fee or other compensation, direct or indirect, with respect to any moneys or other property of such plan, or has any authority or responsibility to do so, or (iii) he has any discretionary authority or discretionary responsibility in the administration of such plan.

The Tenth Circuit, like other circuits, views fiduciary status in a functional way, recognizing that one may be a fiduciary either by being "named in the plan instrument" or through the fiduciary functions performed. *See Maez v. Mountain States Tel. & Tel., Inc.*, 54 F.3d 1488, 1498 (10th Cir. 1995); *Hockett v. Sun Co., Inc.*, 109 F.3d 1515, 1522 (10th Cir. 1997). Thus, the Tenth Circuit applies the definitions based on the functions at issue. *See, e.g., Reich v. Stangl*, 73 F.3d 1027, 1029 (10th Cir. 1996). Plan management or administration confers fiduciary status only to the extent that the party exercises discretionary authority or control. *David P. Coldesina, D.D.S., P.C., Employee Profit Sharing Plan & Trust v. Estate of Simper*, 407 F.3d 1126 (10th Cir. 2005). The court also stated that discretion exists where a party has the power of free decision or individual choice. *Id.*

On the other hand, where a party has "any authority of control" over the management of disposition of plan assets, this is sufficient to render fiduciary status. *Id.*

## B. Definition of Fiduciary Duties

The duties of an ERISA fiduciary are not limited to those enumerated in the statute. Rather, the Tenth Circuit looks to the "law of trusts to define the general scope" of a fiduciary's responsibility and authority. *Ershick v. United Mo. Bank of Kansas*, 948 F.2d 660, 666 (10th Cir. 1991); *Reich v. Stangl*, 73 F.3d 1027, 1029 (10th Cir. 1996); *Horn v. Cendant Operations, Inc.*, 2003 WL 21513210, at *5 (10th Cir. 2003). Additionally, these duties can extend beyond a fiduciary's termination. *Allison v. Bank One-Denver*, 289 F.3d 1223 (10th Cir. 2002).

## C. Fiduciary Liability in the Context of Health and Disability Claims

In the Tenth Circuit, claims for benefits under 29 U.S.C. § 1132(a)(1)(B) are generally appropriate only against the ERISA plan or a fiduciary of the plan. *Moore v. Berg Enters., Inc.*, 1999 WL 1063823, at *3 (10th Cir. 1999), *aff'g Moore v. Berg Enters., Inc.*, 3 F. Supp. 2d 1245, 1248 (D. Utah 1998). The Tenth Circuit has been less than careful in its use of labels for ERISA claims fiduciaries. It is not uncommon for the Tenth Circuit to refer to the entity that both makes the claims determination and also pays the claim as the "plan administrator" instead of the more appropriate "claim fiduciary." *See, e.g., Fought v. UNUM Life Ins. Co. of Am.*, 379 F.3d 997 (10th Cir. 2004) (referring to the insurance company that administers claims and is also the payor of those claims as the "plan administrator"). Nonetheless, benefit claims may be maintained against plan fiduciaries who are responsible for making claims determinations in the insured plan setting. *Id.; Pitman v. Blue Cross & Blue Shield of Okla.*, 24 F.3d 118 (10th Cir. 1994); *Ray v. UNUM Life Ins. Co. of Am.*, 314 F.3d 482 (10th Cir. 2002); *Roach v. Prudential Ins. Brokerage, Inc.*, 2003 WL 1880641 (10th Cir. 2003).

### D. Remedies for Breach of Fiduciary Duty

Following the statute, the Tenth Circuit recognizes that the usual remedy for breach of fiduciary duty under 29 U.S.C. §§ 1109 and 1132(a)(2) is to make the breaching fiduciary personally liable to the plan for the losses resulting from the breach. *Reich v. Stangl,* 73 F.3d 1027, 1029 (10th Cir. 1996). A causal connection between the breach and the loss is a necessary element to a fiduciary breach claim. *Allison v. Bank One-Denver,* 289 F.3d 1223, 1239 (10th Cir. 2002).

Rescission or other, alternative, equitable relief may also be an appropriate remedy for fiduciary breach under § 1132(a)(2). *See Gorman v. Carpenters' & Millwrights' Health Benefit Trust Fund,* 410 F.3d 1194, 1201 (10th Cir. 2005); *Eaves v. Penn,* 587 F.2d 453, 461–62 (10th Cir. 1978) (approving the "alternative remedy of restoring plan participants to the position in which they would have occupied but for the breach of trust").

Claims seeking individual benefits for breach of fiduciary duty under 29 U.S.C. § 1132(a)(2) are not allowed, because that section authorizes relief only on behalf of a plan. *Walter v. Int'l Ass'n of Mach. Pension Fund,* 949 F.2d 310, 317 (10th Cir. 1991); *see Moore v. Berg Enters., Inc.,* 3 F. Supp. 2d 1245, 1246 (D. Utah 1998) ("[A plaintiff] cannot obtain relief pursuant to § 1104(a) inasmuch as he seeks to recover benefits for himself only and that section provides only for plan wide relief."), *aff'd,* 201 F.3d 448 (10th Cir. 1999). This has been the result even after *Varity Corp. v. Howe,* 516 U.S. 489 (1996). *See Lefler v. United HealthCare of Utah, Inc.,* 2003 WL 21940936, at *6 (10th Cir. 2003); *Mein v. Pool Co. Disabled Int'l Employee Long Term Disability Benefit Plan,* 989 F. Supp. 1337, 1350–51 (D. Colo. 1998); *Lenhart v. Air Am., Inc.,* 2003 WL 23355737, at *4 (D. Utah 2003).

Finally, claims under 29 U.S.C. § 1132(a)(3) are not appropriate, even when pled in the alternative, if the plaintiff can state a claim for relief under 29 U.S.C. § 1132(a)(1)(B). *See Moore,* 1999 WL 1063823, at *2 n.2 ("[Plaintiff] is not entitled to repackage his . . . denial of benefits claim as a claim for breach of fiduciary duty . . . and seek relief under section 1132(a)(3)" (citation omitted)); *Lefler,* 2003 WL 21940936, at *6 ("We agree with the district court that consideration of a claim under 29 U.S.C. § 1132(a)(3) is improper when the Class, as here, states a cognizable claim under 29 U.S.C. § 1132(a)(1)(B). . . ."), *aff'g Lefler v. United HealthCare of Utah, Inc.,* 162 F. Supp. 2d 1310, 1325 (D. Utah 2001) ("The court, likewise, concludes that, because plaintiffs had the right to pursue their viable claim under Section 1132(a)(1)(B), regardless of the outcome, plaintiffs may not maintain their claims for breach of fiduciary duties under Section 1132(a)(3).").

Even in circumstances where relief under § 1132(a)(3) might be allowed, such relief cannot be monetary; it is limited to traditional forms of equitable relief, such as injunction, mandamus, and restitution. *Callery v. U.S. Life Ins. Co. in the City of New York,* 392 F.3d 401, 404, & 409 (10th Cir. 2004); *Millsap v. McDonnell Douglas Corp.,* 368 F.3d 1246, 1251 (10th Cir. 2004). Compensatory damages are not authorized by this remedial provision. *Id.* at 1254; *see also LaFoy v. HMO Colo.,* 988 F.2d 97 (10th Cir. 1993) (compensatory and other forms of extracontractual damages not allowed).

### E. Contribution and Indemnity Claims among Fiduciaries

An agreement to indemnify a fiduciary with respect to negligent acts is valid and enforceable. *Allison v. Bank One-Denver,* 289 F.3d 1223, 1239–42 (10th Cir. 2002). Indemnification as to intentional acts is not available. *Id.*

### F. ERISA Claims against Nonfiduciaries

Although there is little Tenth Circuit case law on the subject, in *Reich v. Stangl,* 73 F.3d 1027, 1031 (10th Cir.), *cert. denied,* 519 U.S. 807 (1996), a case decided years prior to the U.S. Supreme Court's decision in *Harris Trust & Savings Bank v. Salomon Smith Barney, Inc.,* 530 U.S. 238 (2000), the court held that the Secretary of Labor could bring an "equitable action" against a nonfiduciary "party in interest" under 29 U.S.C. §§ 1106 and 1132(a)(5) for participating in an alleged fiduciary breach.

## X. Attorneys' Fees

### A. Criteria for Awarding Attorneys' Fees

A decision whether to award fees is made upon consideration of five factors: (1) the degree of the opposing party's culpability or bad faith; (2) the ability of the opposing party to satisfy an award of fees and costs; (3) whether an award of fees and costs against the opposing party would deter others from acting under similar circumstances; (4) whether the party requesting fees sought to benefit all participants and beneficiaries of an ERISA plan or to resolve a significant legal question regarding ERISA; and (5) the relative merits of the parties' positions. *Thorpe v. Ret. Plan of the Pillsbury Co.,* 80 F.3d 439 (10th Cir. 1996). These factors are not necessarily exhaustive or exclusive, and other factors might be considered where appropriate. *Moothart v. Bell,* 21 F.3d 1499 (10th Cir. 1994).

Fees are not automatically awarded in favor of a prevailing plaintiff. *See, e.g., Thorpe,* 80 F.3d 439. Even where fees are awarded, the award should be limited to issues or claims on which the plaintiff prevailed. *Deboard v. Sunshine Mining & Ref. Co.,* 208 F.3d 1228 (10th Cir. 2000); *Sage v. Automation, Inc. Pension Plan & Trust,* 845 F.2d 885 (10th Cir. 1988).

The district court must explain its decision to award fees in favor of a prevailing plaintiff. *Pratt v. Petroleum Prod. Mgmt., Inc. Employee Sav. Plan & Trust,* 920 F.2d 651 (10th Cir. 1990). The district court's failure to do so will normally result in a remand of the fee issue. *Id.* However, the district court's resolution of the attorneys' fee issue does not necessarily have to take all of the above-enumerated factors into account. *Rademacher v. Colo. Ass'n of Soil Conservation Dists. Med. Benefit Plan,* 11 F.3d 1567 (10th Cir. 1993). A reduction in fees based upon duplicative or unnecessary efforts should be explained by the district court. *Bartlett v. Martin Marietta Operations Support, Inc. Life Ins. Plan,* 38 F.3d 514 (10th Cir. 1994).

### B. Fees Awarded to Plan Fiduciaries

The Tenth Circuit has not addressed the circumstances under which an award of fees against a plaintiff should be granted or denied.

### C. Calculation of Attorneys' Fees

To determine the amount of a fee award under ERISA, the district court "arrives at a lodestar figure by multiplying the hours counsel reasonably spent on the litigation by a reasonable hourly rate and then determines whether the lodestar figure is subject to upward or downward adjustment." *Boilermaker-Blacksmith Nat'l Pension Fund v. Ace Polyethylene Bag Co.*, 2002 WL 372868, at *1 (D. Kan. 2004). The burden is on the party seeking an award of fees to show that the hours claimed are reasonable. *Id.* The reasonable hourly rate "is calculated by examining the prevailing market rates of the relevant community," and thus, "in setting a rate of compensation for the hours reasonably expended, the Court should consider what lawyers of comparable skill or experience practicing in the area in which the litigation occurs would charge for their time." *LaSelle v. Pub. Serv. Co. of Colo.*, 988 F. Supp. 1348, 1351 (D. Colo. 1997). The lawyer's customary rate charged to clients is a relevant, but not conclusive, factor. *Id.*

A reduction may be made to the lodestar amount to account for work on claims or issues as to which the party seeking fees did not succeed. *DeBoard v. Sunshine Mining & Ref. Co.*, 208 F.3d 1228, 1244–45 (10th Cir. 2000). Reductions may be made to the lodestar amount based upon duplicative work. *LaSelle*, 988 F. Supp. 1348, 1353. Fees for work on the prelitigation "administrative phase" of a benefits claim are not recoverable. *Id.* at 1352.

## XI. ERISA Regulations

In November of 2000, the Department of Labor modified ERISA regulations on claims procedure. The revised regulations, which apply to claims filed after January 1, 2002, establish shorter time frames for benefits determinations than those contained in the earlier version of the regulations. *See* 29 C.F.R. § 2560.503-1(f)(3). Appeals of claims filed before the effective date are governed by the old regulations. However, many cases decided on claims filed prior to January 1, 2002, may form a basis for interpreting current regulations.

Common areas of litigation in the Tenth Circuit are the notice and "full and fair review" requirements of 29 U.S.C. § 1133 and the accompanying claims procedure regulations at 29 C.F.R. § 2560.503-1. "[R]eceiving a full and fair review requires knowing what evidence the decision maker relied upon, having an opportunity to address the accuracy and reliability of the evidence, and having the decision maker consider the evidence presented by both parties prior to reaching and rendering his decision." *Sandoval v. Aetna Life & Cas. Ins. Co.*, 967 F.2d 377, 382 (10th Cir. 1992) (citation omitted); *see* Sage v. Automation, Inc. Pension Plan & Trust, 845 F.2d 885, 893–94 (10th Cir. 1988); *Redding v. AT&T Corp.*, 1997 U.S. App. LEXIS 23037, at *18–19 (10th Cir. 1997) (approving the proposition that "the opportunity to submit documentary evidence, consideration of evidence submitted, and explanation of evidence relied upon satisfied full and fair review requirements of 29 U.S.C. § 1133(2)"). "Substantial compliance with the requirements of § 1133 is sufficient." *Hickman v. Gem Ins. Co., Inc.*, 299 F.3d 1208, 1215 (10th Cir. 2002).

If a court determines that the entity responsible for providing the full and fair review has violated one of the regulation's requirements, the court must nevertheless determine whether the violation caused a "substantive violation" of the requirements or caused the claimant a "substantive harm." *Hickman*, 299 F.3d at 1215. "In other words, if after judicial review, it appears the administrator or fiduciary was correct in its decision, the court will uphold that decision even in light of a violation of Section 1133." *Id.; see Sage*, 845 F.2d at 895 (where "the merits of the [claims administrator's decision] have been correctly resolved, no purpose would be served by a further, but procedurally correct, review of [plaintiff's] claims by the [administrator]."); *Macklin v. Ret. Plan for Employees of Kan. Gas & Elec. Co.*, 1996 WL 579940, at *3 (10th Cir. 1996) ("[P]rocedural defects in the claims process do not necessarily require that a plan's determination be overturned. So long as the claimant has an opportunity to be heard, a plan determination that is not otherwise arbitrary and capricious will be upheld despite procedural irregularities.").

If the court determines a substantive violation or harm to have occurred, the general procedure in the Tenth Circuit is to remand the matter back to the decision maker with instructions to remedy the violation. *Caldwell v. Life Ins. Co. of N. Am.*, 287 F.3d 1276, 1288 (10th Cir. 2002); *Stegelmeier v. Doug Andrus Distrib. Inc.*, 2004 WL 736831, at *12 (D. Utah 2004). If the case "is so clear cut" that the decision maker had no basis for denying the claim, then remand would not be appropriate. *Caldwell*, 287 F.3d at 1288.

As described in Standard of Review, Section IV, *supra,* where a claim is "deemed denied" by virtue of a claim decision maker's failure to render a determination within the deadlines prescribed by ERISA claim regulations, the court may impose the de novo standard of review, notwithstanding a grant of discretionary authority to the decision maker.

## XII. Cases Interpreting ERISA Statutes of Limitation

ERISA has no statute of limitations that governs claims under 29 U.S.C. § 1132. *Wright v. S.W. Bell Tel. Co.*, 925 F.2d 1288 (10th Cir. 1991); *Trustees of Wyo. Laborers Health & Welfare Plan v. Morgen & Oswood Const. Co., Inc. of Wyo.*, 850 F.2d 613 (10th Cir. 1988); *Moore v. Berg*, 1999 U.S. App. LEXIS 20481 (10th Cir. 1999). In *Moore*, the court indicated that a court must therefore look to either the "most analogous" state statute of limitations, "or if the plan itself contains a limitations period, to the plan if the contractual limitations period is reasonable." *Id.* at *6. *See also Lang v. Aetna Life Ins. Co.*, 1999 WL 1021170 (10th Cir. 1999) (applying Utah insurance code three-year statute of limitations for claim brought to recover payments allegedly due under disability insurance policy); *Trustees of Wyo.*, 850 F.2d 613 ("When Congress has not established a time limitation for a federal cause of action, the settled practice has been to adopt a local time limitation as federal law if it is not inconsistent with federal law or policy to do so. Characterization of the nature of the claim for the purpose of determining the applicable statute of limitations is, therefore, a question of federal law.") (internal quotations and citations omitted); *Held v. Mfrs. Hanover Leasing Corp.*, 912 F.2d 1197 (10th Cir. 1990) ("Although this case arguably provides an ideal context for considering whether adoption of an ERISA limitation period makes more sense than searching for an analogous state statute, we believe that inquiry is foreclosed to this panel by this circuit's decision in *Trustees of the Wyoming*"); *Woods v. Halliburton Co.*, 2002 WL 31379873 (10th Cir. 2002) (applying Oklahoma two-year statute of limitations for discrimination claims). The particular statute of limitations and when that period begins to run may vary based on the specific ERISA cause of action involved. *Wright*, 925 F.2d 1288 (10th Cir. 1991).

# XIII. Subrogation Litigation

In *Administrative Committee of the Wal-Mart Associates Health & Welfare Plan v. Willard*, 393 F.3d 1119 (10th Cir. 2004), the Tenth Circuit addressed the viability of plan subrogation claims after the Supreme Court's decision in *Great-West Life & Annuity Ins. Co. v. Knudson*, 534 U.S. 204 (2002). The key facts as addressed by the Tenth Circuit were whether the plan seeks to recover funds "(1) that are specifically identifiable, (2) that belong in good conscience to the plan, and (3) that are within the possession and control of the defendant beneficiary." *Id.* at 1122. The first factor is satisfied where funds were placed in a reserve bank account and the funds had not been dissipated, or where settlement proceeds are placed in a trust account by the beneficiary's law firm. *Id.* at 1122. The funds "belong in good conscience to the plan" where the plan contains express, unambiguous reimbursement provisions. *Id.* at 1123. Such a provision may be found through interpreting the plan documents. *Id.* The Tenth Circuit held that the language giving the administrators the right to "recover or subrogate" and giving "first priority with respect to its right to reduction, reimbursement, and subrogation" was sufficient such that the funds belonged to the plan. *Id.* Finally, the funds must be in the plan beneficiary's possession for a reimbursement claim to be considered equitable. *Id.* at 1124. In *Wal-Mart,* where the funds were placed in the court's registry by agreement of the parties after negotiation between the tortfeasor and the victim, this constituted sufficient control to satisfy the third prong of the analysis. *Id.* at 1124–25.

# XIV. Miscellaneous

## A. Unique Substantive or Procedural Rules for ERISA Cases

As described above, the Tenth Circuit employs a unique two-tiered approach to the adjustment of the standard of review based upon a conflict of interest. *See* Standard of Review, Section IV, *supra.* Further, within the Tenth Circuit, a court may impose de novo review, even where arbitrary and capricious review would otherwise be required, if the claim decision maker fails to make a determination with respect to a claim such that the claim is "deemed denied" under ERISA regulations. *See* ERISA Regulations, Section XI, *supra.*

## B. Unique Approach to Common Policy-Based Defenses

An insurer bears the burden of proving that a claim falls within the terms of an exclusionary clause. *Fought v. UNUM Life Ins. Co. of Am.,* 379 F.3d 997, 1007 (10th Cir. 2004). Further, "[e]xclusions must be interpreted narrowly." *Id.*

A preexisting condition exclusion, therefore, must be interpreted narrowly. Unless plan language requires otherwise, the courts will look to whether the condition allegedly requiring exclusion is in fact the proximate cause of the disability or medical care involved. *Id.* at 1189–91.

"Medical necessity," as that term is used in health plans, may not be interpreted to require that a particular treatment or procedure will actually result in improvement of a condition. It is enough that the treatment or procedure will maintain the patient's condition, or prevent deterioration. *McGraw v. Prudential Ins. Co. of Am.,* 137 F.3d 1253 (10th Cir. 1998).

# Note

1. The *Hall* process stemmed from the trial court's view that it "was required by law to admit evidence outside of the administrative record." *Id.* at 1204–05. This conclusion, the Tenth Circuit held, was error. *Id.* And while not all of the evidence admitted at trial was taken up for consideration on appeal, the court emphasized that "it is the unusual case in which the district court should allow supplementation of the record." *Id.* at 1203.

# CHAPTER 11

# Eleventh Circuit

RUSSELL BUHITE
H. SANDERS CARTER JR.
NIKOLE M. CROW
TIFFANY D. DOWNS
MAGGIE MARRERO-LADIK
DOUGLAS L. OPPENHEIMER
ANTHONY H. PELLE
AARON E. POHLMANN
JOELLE C. SHARMAN

## I. What Constitutes an ERISA Plan?

### A. Determining the Existence of an Employee Welfare Benefit Plan

The Eleventh Circuit has held that there are five elements necessary to establish the existence of an employee welfare benefit plan under the Employee Retirement Income Security Act of 1974 (ERISA): "(1) a plan, fund, or program (2) established or maintained (3) by an employer or by an employee organization, or by both, (4) for the purpose of providing . . . benefits . . . (5) to participants or their beneficiaries." *Anderson v. UnumProvident Corp.,* 369 F.3d 1257 (11th Cir. 2004) (quoting *Donovan v. Dillingham,* 688 F.2d 1367, 1371 (11th Cir. 1982) (*en banc*)). *See also* 29 U.S.C. § 1002(1).

At a minimum, a "plan, fund, or program" under ERISA "implies the existence of intended benefits, intended beneficiaries, a source of financing, and a procedure to apply for and collect benefits." *Donovan,* 688 F.2d at 1371. Thus, a "plan, fund, or program" exists "if from the surrounding circumstances a reasonable person can ascertain the intended benefits, a class of beneficiaries, the source of financing, and procedures for receiving benefits." *Williams v. Wright,* 927 F.2d 1540, 1543 (11th Cir. 1991) (quoting *Donovan,* 688 F.2d at 1373).

The "established or maintained" requirement "is designed to ensure that the plan is part of an employment relationship. . . ." *Anderson,* 369 F.3d at 1263. Whether the plan is part of an employment relationship is determined by "the degree of participation by the employer in the establishment or maintenance of the plan." *Id.* A plan is "established" when there is "some degree of implementation by the employer going beyond a mere intent to confer a benefit." *Butero v. Royal Maccabees Life Ins. Co.,* 174 F.3d 1207, 1214 (11th Cir. 1999) (citing *Whitt v. Sherman Int'l Corp.,* 147 F.3d 1325, 1331 (11th Cir. 1998)).

While acknowledging that ERISA "excludes public employees covered by government health plans from [the statute's] employee benefit plan provisions," the Eleventh Circuit has not yet addressed the scope of the "governmental plan" exemption. *Brett v. Jefferson County, Ga.,* 123 F.3d 1429, 1435–36 (11th Cir. 1997); 29 U.S.C. § 1002(32). District courts in the circuit are divided on whether plans established and maintained by regional hospital authorities are "governmental plans." *Compare Germaine v. Unum Life Ins. Co. of Am.,* 2004 WL 2624873, at *8 (N.D. Ga. Sept. 23, 2004) (a hospital authority, under Georgia law, is not a county, a municipal corporation, or a political subdivision of the state when it acts as an employer), *with Williams-Mason v. Reliance Standard Life Ins. Co.,* 2006 WL 1687760, at *4 (S.D. Ga. Jun. 16, 2006) (hospital authorities, under Georgia law, are "instrumentalities" of the state).

## B. Definition of "Employee" for ERISA Purposes

An insurance policy that provides benefits only to a business owner, but not to at least one employee, is not governed by ERISA. *Slamen v. Paul Revere Life Ins. Co.,* 166 F.3d 1102, 1104 (11th Cir. 1999). A plan falls within the ambit of ERISA only if it "covers ERISA participants because of their employee status in an employment relationship, and an employer or employee organization is the person that establishes or maintains the plan, fund, or program." *Id.* (quoting *Donovan,* 688 F.2d at 1373). "Thus, in order to establish an ERISA employee welfare benefit plan, the plan must provide benefits to at least one employee, not including an employee who is also the owner of the business in question." *Id.*

An employee's status as a shareholder of a corporation does not make him an "owner" of that business so as to "preclude him from being a beneficiary under [an] ERISA plan." *Engelhardt v. Paul Revere Life Ins. Co.,* 139 F.3d 1346, 1351 (11th Cir. 1998). Once a plan has been established by the inclusion of at least one employee as a plan participant, "a sole shareholder is a 'beneficiary,' within the meaning of [ERISA], when he is entitled to benefits from a benefits plan which otherwise qualifies as an ERISA plan." *Gilbert v. Alta Health & Life Ins. Co.,* 276 F.3d 1292, 1302 (11th Cir. 1998).

## C. Interpretation of Safe Harbor Regulation

The Department of Labor's "safe harbor" regulation provides that group insurance offered to workers through their place of employment is not an ERISA plan if the insurance program satisfies four criteria: "(1) No contributions are made by an employer or employee organization; (2) Participation [in] the program is completely voluntary for employees. . .; (3) The sole functions of the employer . . . with respect to the program are, without endorsing the program, to permit the insurer to publicize the program to employees or members, to collect premiums through payroll deductions or dues checkoffs and to remit them to the insurer; and (4) The employer . . . receives no consideration in the form of cash or otherwise in connection with the program. . . ." *Butero,* 174 F.3d at 1213 (quoting 29 C.F.R. § 2510.3-1(j)). "To fall within the safe harbor regulations, the insurance program must satisfy all four statutory criteria," and "[i]n conducting its inquiry, the Court must focus on how an objectively reasonable employee would view the totality of the circumstances." *Stern v. Provident Life & Accident Ins. Co.,* 295 F. Supp. 2d 1321, 1325 (M.D. Fla. 2003).

Endorsement of the plan may be evidenced by the employer's distribution of an employee benefits handbook describing the benefits available to employees under the plan, listing the eligibility requirements, establishing enrollment conditions of the plan, listing the employer as the sponsor of the plan, containing a statement of ERISA rights, and listing an officer as the agent for service of process for claims based on the plan. *Belknap v. Hartford Life & Accident Ins. Co.,* 389 F. Supp. 2d 1320, 1324 (M.D. Fla. 2005).

## D. Amount of Employer Involvement Required to Sustain an Employee Welfare Benefit Plan

No single act by the employer in itself is determinative, but seven factors may be relevant in determining whether a plan has been established: "(1) the employer's representations in internally distributed documents; (2) the employer's oral representations; (3) the employer's establishment of a fund to pay benefits; (4) actual payment of benefits; (5) the employer's deliberate failure to correct known perceptions of a plan's existence; (6) the reasonable understanding of employees; and (7) the employer's intent." *Anderson,* 369 F.3d at 1263 (quoting *Butero,* 174 F.3d at 1215). The purchase of insurance by an employer constitutes "substantial evidence" of the existence of a plan, even if it does not by itself "conclusively establish" a plan. *Donovan,* 688 F.2d at 1373.

"[T]here is no requirement that the employer play any role in administering the plan in order for it to be deemed an ERISA employee welfare benefit plan." *Randol v. Mid-West Nat'l Life Ins. Co. of Tenn.,* 987 F.2d 1547, 1550 n.5 (11th Cir. 1993). "Thus, a commercially purchased insurance policy under which the procedures for receiving benefits are all dictated by the insurance carrier can constitute a plan for ERISA purposes." *Id.* (citing *Donovan,* 688 F.2d at 1374). However, the disjunctive "established or maintained" dictates that if a plan was not "established" by an employer, it nevertheless may qualify as an ERISA plan if it is "maintained" by an employer. *Anderson,* 369 F.3d at 1265; *Randol,* 987 F.2d at 1551 n.6. For example, if the employer "began to involve itself more in the payment of benefits, changed the critical terms of the policy, or performed all the administrative functions associated with the maintenance of the plan, those would be actions on the part of the employer which could 'maintain,' rather than establish the plan as an employee welfare benefits plan." *Anderson,* 369 F.3d at 1265.

Standing alone, the decision by an employer to purchase insurance coverage for employees, the requirement that all employees be covered, or the payment of the premiums by the employer do not conclusively establish the plan. *Stefansson v. Equitable Life Assurance Soc'y of the U.S.,* 2005 WL 2277486, at *8 (M.D. Ga. Sept. 19, 2005). However, taken together, they provide substantial evidence that a plan was established under 29 U.S.C. § 1002(1). *Id.*

### E. Treatment of Multiple Employer Trusts and Welfare Agreements

The Eleventh Circuit has acknowledged that an employer or employee organization that subscribes to a multiple employer trust to provide health insurance to its employees or members may be said to have established or maintained an ERISA plan, but beyond this, the court has not had occasion to address the application of ERISA to such trusts or welfare agreements. *See Randol,* 987 F.2d at 1551.

## II. Preemption

### A. Scope of ERISA Preemption

The world of ERISA preemption has changed dramatically over the years as a result of the U.S. Supreme Court's decisions in *Pilot Life Ins. Co. v. Dedeaux,* 481 U.S. 41 (1987), *Unum Life Ins. Co. of Am. v. Ward,* 526 U.S. 358 (1999), and *Kentucky Association of Health Plans, Inc. v. Miller,* 538 U.S. 329 (2003). Specific causes of action have been found to be preempted within the Eleventh Circuit before and after these landmark decisions.

Regardless of whether *Pilot Life, Ward,* or *Miller* apply, the Eleventh Circuit follows *Perkins v. Time Ins. Co.,* 898 F.2d 470 (5th Cir. 1990), for the proposition that claims are not preempted by ERISA when the state-law claim is brought against a non-ERISA entity, such as an independent insurance agent or agency. In *Morstein v. National Insurance Services, Inc.,* 93 F.3d 715 (11th Cir. 1996), claims were brought against an insurance agent and his agency for fraudulent inducement and negligence. The insurance agent and agency were not ERISA entities, which were identified as the employer, the plan, the plan fiduciaries, and the beneficiaries under the plan. Therefore, the Eleventh Circuit concluded that the claims were not preempted, "as they do not have a sufficient connection with the plan to 'relate to' the plan." *Id.* at 724. *See also Lordmann Enters. v. Equicor, Inc.,* 32 F.3d 1529 (11th Cir. 1994) (where the Eleventh Circuit held that a negligent misrepresentation claim against a health insurer by a home health agency was not preempted); *Skilstaf, Inc. v. Adminition, Inc.,* 66 F. Supp. 2d 1210 (M.D. Ala. 1999) (where the district court determined that an employer's state-law claims against a third-party administrator were not preempted, citing *Morstein*). *But see Jones v. LMR Int'l, Inc.,* 367 F. Supp. 2d 1346 (M.D. Ala. 2005) (*Skilstaf* distinguished because claims were claim-related).

Soon after *Pilot Life,* the Eleventh Circuit determined that Florida's bad-faith statute, Florida Statute § 624.155, was preempted because it regulated insurance as a matter of common sense and because it did not meet all of the McCarran-Ferguson factors required to be saved from preemption. *Anschultz v. Conn. Gen. Life Ins. Co.,* 850 F.2d 1467 (11th Cir. 1988). *See also Swerhun v. Guardian Life Ins. Co. of Am.,* 979 F.2d 195 (11th Cir. 1992).

Lower courts in the Eleventh Circuit continue to rely on *Pilot Life* to preempt statutory bad-faith laws, even though they are specifically directed to the insurance industry, because these statutes are rooted in the common law of contract and tort. *Walker v. Southern Co. Servs., Inc.,* 279 F.3d 1289 (11th Cir. 2002); *Gilbert v. Alta Health & Life Ins. Co.,* 276 F.3d 1292 (11th Cir. 2001).

In *Revells v. Metropolitan Life Insurance Co.,* 261 F. Supp. 2d 1359 (M.D. Ala. 2003), one of the few post-*Miller* ERISA preemption decisions, the district court considered whether Alabama's state claims for breach of contract and bad-faith failure to pay disability benefits were preempted. First, the court dismissed, "as specious," the plaintiff's claim that preemption was an issue of fact. *Id.* at 1364. The court reiterated the familiar preemption analysis, as follows:

> The civil enforcement provisions of ERISA . . . provide the exclusive remedy available to recover benefits due under employee welfare benefit plans. *Pilot Life Ins. Co. v. Dedeaux,* 481 U.S. 41 (1987). Any common law or statutory claim of a person seeking to recover ERISA plan benefits is preempted. 29 U.S.C. § 1144(a); *Metropolitan Life Ins. Co. v. Taylor,* 481 U.S. 58 (1987). Federal law completely preempts an area, converts state law claims into federal claims and provides a basis for federal jurisdiction where the state law (1) is preempted, and (2) falls within a federal enforcement scheme. *See Brown v. Conn. Gen. Life Ins. Co.,* 934 F.2d. 1193, 1196 (11th Cir. 1991). The law is well settled that state law claims relating to ERISA-governed employee welfare benefit plans are displaced by federal law. *Id.* "The preemption provision of ERISA provides that it 'shall supersede any and all state laws insofar as they may now or hereafter relate to any employment plan' covered by ERISA." *Variety Children's Hosp., Inc. v. Century Med. Health Plan, Inc.,* 57 F.3d 1040, 1042 (11th Cir. 1995).

*Id.* at 1364.

The court concluded that the plaintiff's claims for breach of contract and bad faith "related to" the employee welfare benefit plan because they were based on the defendant's failure to pay the disability benefits and because the court would have to evaluate the terms of the policy to ascertain whether the benefits are due. However, the plaintiff also argued that the bad-faith claim was "saved" pursuant to *Unum v. Ward.* The court rejected this argument on the basis that *Ward* did not address bad-faith claims and because "prior and subsequent Supreme Court precedent" established that bad-faith laws did not "regulate insurance." *Pilot Life,* 481 U.S. at 50. The court also cited Miller in support of this analysis.[1]

## B. Preemption of Managed-Care Claims

Although the U.S. Supreme Court's decision in *Aetna v. Davila,* 542 U.S. 200 (2004), effectively mooted most issues that might arise, there are several earlier cases of interest in the Eleventh Circuit that were inconsistent with *Davila.*

In *Rivers v. Health Options Connect, Inc.,* 96 F. Supp. 2d 1370 (S.D. Fla. 2000), the care provider's physician-administrator reviewed the claimant's clinical information and made a "medical" decision that further hospitalization was not "medically necessary." The court determined that this claim was not sufficient to trigger complete preemption, although it acknowledged that the federal defense could be asserted in state court. Also, in *Hammerich v. Aetna U.S. Healthcare, Inc.,* 209 F. Supp. 2d 1282 (M.D. Fla. 2002), the plaintiff claimed injury due to Aetna's delay in informing him of positive results of a colorectal cancer screening test. The court determined that the claims were not preempted by ERISA and remanded because the complaint did not "seek benefits or to enforce or clarify rights under the plan." *Id.* at 1285.

In contrast, the court in *Lane v. Health Options, Inc.,* 221 F. Supp. 2d 1301 (S.D. Fla. 2002), determined that the failure to approve a recommended treatment procedure but authorizing a "lower quality" procedure "directly attack[ed] defendant's administrative functions and the 'quality of benefits' rather than the quality of care received." *Id.* at 1305. Complete preemption was found, so the defendant's motion to dismiss was granted and remand was denied.

## C. Preemption of Malpractice Claims

Although *Davila* specifically dealt with claims against the insurers for negligently handling coverage decisions, it has been used as a basis for vacating pre-*Davila* decisions denying complete preemption that involved medical malpractice claims. For example, in *Land v. CIGNA,* 339 F.3d 1286 (11th Cir. 2003), the court vacated and remanded to the district court its denial of the insured's motion to remand and the granting of the HMO's motion to dismiss. The Eleventh Circuit held that the insured's claim for failure to diagnose and authorize proper care causing the loss of his finger was a mixed decision of eligibility and treatment but that such a claim was not within the scope of ERISA's civil enforcement provisions. However, *Davila* was decided while a petition for writ of certiorari was pending. The Supreme Court, 124 S. Ct. 2903 (2004), vacated and remanded. Upon instructions from the U.S. Supreme Court and based on its decision in *Davila,* the 11th Circuit held that a plaintiff's state-law malpractice claims were preempted by ERISA. *Land v. CIGNA Healthcare of Florida,* 381 F.3d 1274 (11th Cir. 2004). The court stated: "After carefully reviewing *Davila* we find that Land's state law malpractice claim against his health maintenance organization ("HMO") was preempted . . ." and was thus removable to federal court. *Id.* at 1276.[2] This holding would make it difficult for insureds to argue that, in the Eleventh Circuit, *Davila* does not apply to pure malpractice claims.

## D. Other Preemption Issues

Issues of preemption also affect jurisdictional and procedural aspects of an ERISA case. Whether a complaint initially filed in state court can be removed (and then potentially dismissed) notwithstanding the well-pleaded complaint rule depends on whether the claims asserted at the time of the removal are "super preempted" or "defensively preempted." *Butero v. Royal Maccabees Life Ins. Co.,* 174 F.3d 1207 (11th Cir. 1999); *Whitt v. Sherman Int'l Corp.,* 147 F.3d 1325 (11th Cir. 1998). In *Butero,* the court established a four-part test for determining ERISA super preemption: (1) a relevant ERISA plan exists, under which (2) a plaintiff with standing is suing (3) an ERISA entity for (4) "compensatory relief akin to that available under [29 U.S.C.] § 1132(a); often this will be a claim for benefits due under a plan." *Butero* at 1212. Whereas super or complete preemption is a matter of federal jurisdiction, defensive preemption provides only an affirmative defense to state-law claims. In *Ervast v. Flexible Products Co.,* 346 F.3d 1007 (11th Cir. 2003), the court analyzed the plaintiff's claim alleging breach of fiduciary duty and negligence resulting from the employer's failure to disclose material information that would have affected the plaintiff's decision to liquidate his account in the employee stock ownership plan (ESOP). The court decided that these claims failed the "akin to that available under § 1132(a)" prong of the *Butero* test and remanded to state court so the ERISA preemption defense could be considered as an affirmative defense, rather than as a basis for federal jurisdiction. *See also Engelhardt v. Paul Revere Life Ins. Co.,* 139 F.3d 1346 (11th Cir. 1998).

However, as extensively described in such lower-court opinions as *Wilson v. Coman,* 284 F. Supp. 2d 1319 (M.D. Ala. 2003), and *York v. Ramsay Youth Services of Dothan,* 313 F. Supp. 2d 1275 (M.D. Ala. 2004), there is significant controversy over the analysis set forth by the Eleventh Circuit in *Butero* versus the analysis employed by a prior panel in *Franklin v. QHG of Gadsden, Inc.,* 127 F.3d 1024 (11th Cir. 1997), and *Hall v. Blue Cross & Blue Shield of Alabama,* 134 F.3d 1063 (11th Cir. 1998). In *Franklin,* the court employed defensive preemption analysis in the context of a complete preemption argument. However, the *Wilson* court felt constrained to try to follow *Franklin* due to the prior panel rule providing that "only a decision by this court sitting *en banc* or the United States Supreme Court can overrule a prior panel decision." *United States v. Machado,* 804 F.2d 1537, 1543 (11th Cir. 1986). Based on this, the *Wilson* court denied the motion to remand. In order to avoid confusion created by *Butero* and *Franklin,* the court in *York* applied both tests and (somewhat conveniently) found the plaintiff's claims subject to complete preemption regardless of whether the *Butero* or *Franklin* tests were applied. *York,* 313 F. Supp. 2d at 1283. Although *Butero* is probably the better-reasoned case, the prior-panel rule requires that *Franklin* be addressed. *See also Cotton v. Mass. Mut. Life Ins. Co.,* 18 Fla. L. Weekly Fed. C324a (11th Cir., Mar. 16, 2005).

In *Autonation, Inc. v. United Healthcare Insurance Co.,* 423 F. Supp. 2d 1265 (S.D. Fla. 2006), the court dismissed based on conflict preemption two state-law counts by a plan sponsor/employer against a claim administrator, but allowed breach of fiduciary claims to remain.

In *Jones v. LMR International. Inc.*, 2006 WL 2097075 (11th Cir. 2006), the court upheld dismissal of state-law claims on preemption grounds on a terminated plan, and included preemption of claims against a non-ERISA entity because to not preempt them might affect the claims against the ERISA entities.

## III. Exhaustion of Administrative Remedies

### A. Is Exhaustion an Absolute Requirement?

The Eleventh Circuit has "repeatedly held that plaintiffs must exhaust their administrative remedies under a covered benefits plan prior to bringing an ERISA claim in federal court." *Variety Children's Hosp., Inc. v. Century Med. Health Plan, Inc.*, 57 F.3d 1040, 1042 (11th Cir. 1995). Further, a plaintiff's complaint must allege exhaustion, recite facts showing that administrative remedies have been exhausted, or plead impossibility of exhaustion. *Id.; Byrd v. MacPapers, Inc.*, 961 F.2d 157, 161 (11th Cir. 1992). The exhaustion requirement applies both to ERISA claims arising from the substantive provisions of the statute and to ERISA claims arising from the plan. *See Springer v. Wal-Mart Assoc. Group Health Plan*, 908 F.2d 897, 899 (11th Cir. 1990); *Mason v. Cont'l Group, Inc.*, 763 F.2d 1219 (11th Cir. 1985).

The Eleventh Circuit has recognized these "compelling considerations" for the exhaustion requirement: (1) reduction of the number of frivolous lawsuits; (2) minimization of the cost of resolving disputes; (3) enhancement of the administrators' "ability to carry out their fiduciary duties expertly and efficiently by preventing premature judicial intervention in the decisionmaking process"; and (4) availability of "prior fully considered actions" by the administrator to assist the courts. *Mason*, 763 F.2d at 1227. Moreover, the exhaustion requirement is consistent with Congressional intent that plans "provide intrafund review procedures." *Id.*

### B. Exceptions to the Exhaustion Requirement

The Eleventh Circuit "strictly enforce[s] an exhaustion requirement on plaintiffs bringing ERISA claims in federal court with certain caveats reserved for exceptional circumstances." *Perrino v. Southern Bell Tel. & Tel. Co.*, 209 F.3d 1309, 1315 (11th Cir. 2000). In *Curry v. Contract Fabricators, Inc. Profit Sharing Plan*, 891 F.2d 842, 846 (11th Cir. 1990), *abrogated on other grounds by Murphy v. Reliance Standard Life Ins. Co.*, 247 F.3d 1313 (11th Cir. 2001), the court recognized that there are exceptions to the exhaustion requirement, "the most familiar examples perhaps being when resort to the administrative route is futile or the remedy inadequate." In such cases, the district court has discretion to excuse the requirement. *Counts v. Am. Gen. Life & Accident Ins. Co.*, 111 F.3d 105, 108 (11th Cir. 1997).

However, in *Counts*, the Eleventh Circuit declined to create an additional exception where the benefits termination letter did not comply with the notice requirements of ERISA. *Id.* at 108. The court held that "the consequence of an inadequate benefits termination letter is that the normal time limits for administrative appeal may not be enforced against the claimant. . . . Thus, the usual remedy is not excusal from the exhaustion requirement, but remand to the plan administrator for an out-of-time appeal." *Id.*

Similarly, in *Perrino,* 209 F.3d at 1316–17, the court declined to recognize a new exception to the exhaustion doctrine based on "noncompliance with ERISA's technical requirements," where the administrative scheme would have been available to plaintiffs if they had invoked it. *Id.* at 1317. The court held that "the exhaustion requirement . . . should not be excused for technical violations of ERISA that do not deny plaintiffs meaningful access to an administrative remedy procedure through which they may receive an adequate remedy." *Id.*

Conversely, in *Watts v. BellSouth Telecomm., Inc.,* 316 F.3d 1203, 1204 (11th Cir. 2003), the court created an additional exception to the exhaustion requirement where the plaintiff's failure to exhaust her administrative remedies was the result of language in the summary plan description that the plaintiff "reasonably interpreted as meaning that she could go straight to court with her claim." *Id.* at 1204.

### C. Consequences of Failure to Exhaust

The Eleventh Circuit has "held a number of times that a claimant's failure to exhaust the administrative remedies that an ERISA plan provides for challenging the denial of a benefits claim ordinarily bars her from pursuing that claim in court." *Watts,* 316 F.3d at 1204 (citing *Counts*). Thus, "[o]rdinarily, if a plan participant failed to take advantage of an available administrative appeal by pursuing it in compliance with a reasonable filing deadline, . . . that bars federal court review of her claim." *Id.* at 1206. The Eleventh Circuit has upheld the grant of summary judgment in favor of the defendant when the plaintiff failed to exhaust. *See, e.g., Perrino,* 209 F.3d at 1319; *Counts,* 111 F.3d at 109; and *Mason,* 763 F.2d at 1227. In *Springer,* 908 F.2d at 902, the court remanded the case with instructions to dismiss the lawsuit for failure to exhaust. In *Variety Children's Hosp.,* 57 F.3d at 1042, the court upheld the district court's decision to dismiss the case without prejudice subject to the plaintiff's exhaustion of administrative remedies.

### D. Application to Claims for Breach of Fiduciary Duty

In an unpublished decision, the Eleventh Circuit upheld the dismissal of a class action alleging breach of fiduciary duties for failure to exhaust administrative remedies. *Bickley v. Caremark RX, Inc.,* 2006 WL 1746928 (11th Cir. June 27, 2006). There, the plaintiffs sued the third-party administrator of their employer's self-funded prescription drug benefits plan without first exhausting the administrative remedies provided by the plan.

The named plaintiff in *Bickley* argued on appeal: (1) "that the district court should have excused his failure to exhaust the administrative remedies because an administrative remedy was not available for his claims of breach of fiduciary duty"; (2) "that the administrative scheme set out in the Plan was limited solely to claims for benefits"; and (3) "that the Plan explicitly provided that a participant who alleges violations of fiduciary duty may file suit in federal court." *Id.* at *2.

With regard to the argument that the plan provided that participants could file suit in federal court, the Eleventh Circuit held that "[t]his Plan language . . . merely recites plan participants' general rights under ERISA and does not excuse a participant from satisfying the exhaustion requirement." *Id.* at *3. Further, the court found the argument that administrative remedies were limited to claims for benefits unpersuasive, because the plan contained language advising participants to contact the employer/plan administrator, which had discretion to "resolve all interpretive, equitable and other questions that shall arise in the operation and administration of this Plan." *Id.* Thus, had the plaintiffs followed the proper procedure, the employer/plan administrator could have responded to their claims, and indeed would have had a duty under the plan to consider pursuing a breach of fiduciary duty claim on the plan's behalf. *Id.*

Finally, the court rejected the argument that the futility exception should have been applied by the district court, because "bare allegations of futility are no substitute for the 'clear and positive' showing of futility required before suspending the exhaustion requirement." *Id.* at *4 (quoting *Springer,* 908 F.2d at 901) (punctuation omitted).

## IV. Standard of Review

### A. Plan Language

In reviewing an ERISA benefits decision in the Eleventh Circuit, the court must evaluate whether the administrator's decision was "wrong." *Williams v. BellSouth Telecomm., Inc.,* 373 F.3d 1132, 1138 (11th Cir. 2004). "Wrong," according to the Eleventh Circuit, "describe[s] the conclusion a court reaches when, after reviewing the plan documents and disputed terms de novo, the court disagrees with the claims administrator's plan interpretation." *HCA Health Servs. of Ga., Inc., v. Employers Health Ins. Co.,* 240 F.3d 982, 994 n.23 (11th Cir. 2001).

If the court determines that the decision was "de novo wrong," it then must determine whether the plan afforded the administrator the requisite discretion to make the decision. *Williams,* 373 F.3d at 1138. If the discretion exists, then the court simply determines whether "reasonable" grounds supported the benefits decision. *Id.*

The existence of discretion in an ERISA plan thus affects the level of scrutiny applied to the benefits decision. Courts must look to all of the plan documents to determine whether the plan affords sufficient discretion in deciding whether to apply a deferential standard of review. *Cagle v. Bruner,* 112 F.3d 1510, 1517 (11th Cir. 1997). But at least in one case, the court found that a grant of discretion in the summary plan description was insufficient unless it also was set out in the group policy. *Shaw v. Conn. Gen. Life Ins. Co.,* 353 F.3d 1276, 1283–84 (11th Cir. 2003) (applying de novo review, notwithstanding an unambiguous grant of discretion contained in the summary plan description, where the group policy had not been amended to contain the discretionary language, despite specific procedures which would have allowed the amendment). *But see Curran v. Kemper Nat'l Servs., Inc.,* 2005 WL 894840 (11th Cir. Mar. 16, 2005) (declining to follow *Shaw).*

The language must clearly, unambiguously, and expressly provide discretion to avoid the default de novo review. *Kirwan v. Marriott Corp.,* 10 F.3d 784, 788 (11th Cir. 1994). *Compare Guy v. Se. Iron Workers' Welfare Fund,* 877 F.2d 37, 38–39 (11th Cir. 1989) (applying the deferential standard of review where the plan afforded the administrator "full and exclusive authority to determine all questions of coverage and eligibility" and "full power to construe the provisions"), *with Baker v. Big Star Div. of the Grand Union Co.,* 893 F.2d 288, 292 (11th Cir. 1989) (applying the de novo standard of review where the plan conferred upon the administrator only the authority to make initial eligibility determinations "according to the terms of the plan," but not final decisions on appeal). *See also Tippitt v. Reliance Standard Life Ins. Co.,* 2006 WL 2105986 (11th Cir. 2006) (requirement that insured submit "satisfactory proof of Total Disability to us" grants discretionary authority to claims administrator); *Curran,* 2005 WL 894840, at *3 ("We have held that this type of language, requiring that proof be satisfactory or acceptable to the administrator, is sufficient to convey discretion and to apply the arbitrary and capricious standard of review."); *Sorrells v. Sun Life Assurance Co. of Can.,* 85 F. Supp. 2d 1221, 1229–30 (S.D. Ala. 2000) (plan's use of the term "satisfactory" in the proof of claim requirements "contemplate[d] a review of the submitted evidence for evaluation by defendant, and clearly, such a review and evaluation require[d] the exercise of discretion"); *accord Morency v. Rudnick & Wolfe Staff Group Long Term Disability Ins. Plan,* 2001 WL 737531, at *2–3 (M.D. Fla. Jan. 31, 2001) (same).

## B. What Standard of Review Applies?

There are three distinct standards of review under ERISA in the Eleventh Circuit: (1) the de novo standard, (2) the arbitrary and capricious standard, and (3) the heightened arbitrary and capricious standard.

Courts typically apply de novo review unless the plan expressly grants discretionary authority to make eligibility determinations or to construe the plan's terms. *Williams v. BellSouth Telecomm., Inc.,* 373 F.3d 1132, 1137 (11th Cir. 2004); *Kirwan v. Marriott Corp.,* 10 F.3d 784, 788 (11th Cir. 1994); *Jett v. Blue Cross & Blue Shield of Ala.,* 890 F.2d 1137, 1139 (11th Cir. 1989). A de novo review "offers the highest scrutiny (and thus the least judicial deference) to the administrator's decision. In fact, [the court] accord[s] no deference there, since, no judgment/discretion was exercised in making the determination (*i.e.,* there is no discretion to which [the court] would defer)." *Williams,* 373 F.3d at 1137.

Where the plan grants discretion to the administrator to make plan decisions, courts typically review the propriety of those decisions under the arbitrary and capricious (i.e., abuse of discretion) standard. *Id.* Courts employ this standard "to avoid judicial second guessing/intrusion by according the most judicial deference (and thus, the least judicial scrutiny)." *Id.*

A third standard of review applies where the plan affords the administrator discretion, but the administrator also is the entity that pays benefits under the plan. In that situation, courts apply "heightened arbitrary and capricious" review. *Id.; HCA Health Servs. of Ga., Inc. v. Employers Health Ins. Co.,* 240 F.3d 982, 993 (11th Cir. 2001). This review contemplates "a level of deference (and conversely, scrutiny) somewhere between what is applied under the de novo and 'regular' arbitrary and capricious standards." *Williams,* 373 F.3d at 1137.

The Eleventh Circuit has established the following six-step approach, which incorporates all three levels of review, in reviewing "virtually all" ERISA benefit denials, whether based on plan interpretations or factual determinations:

1. Apply the de novo standard to determine whether the claim administrator's benefits-denial decision is "wrong" (i.e., the court disagrees with the administrator's decision); if it is not, then end the inquiry and affirm the decision.
2. If the administrator's decision in fact is "de novo wrong," then determine whether he was vested with discretion in reviewing claims; if not, end judicial inquiry and reverse the decision.
3. If the administrator's decision is "de novo wrong" and he was vested with discretion in reviewing claims, then determine whether "reasonable" grounds supported it (hence, review his decision under the more deferential arbitrary and capricious standard).
4. If no reasonable grounds exist, then end the inquiry and reverse the administrator's decision; if reasonable grounds do exist, then determine if he operated under a conflict of interest.
5. If there is no conflict, then end the inquiry and affirm the decision.
6. If there is a conflict of interest, then apply heightened arbitrary and capricious review to the decision to affirm or deny it.

*Williams,* 373 F.3d at 1138 (footnotes omitted).

## C. Effect of Conflict of Interest

If a court determines that the fiduciary's benefits decision was wrong but reasonable, it then must determine whether the fiduciary acted under a conflict of interest in making the decision. Arguably, the most straightforward case is one where the plan fiduciary making the benefit decision also is the insurance company responsible for paying claims. When that happens, the traditional arbitrary and capricious standard of review "must be contextually tailored." *Brown v. Blue Cross & Blue Shield of Ala.,* 898 F.2d 1556, 1564 (11th Cir. 1990). The reason is that because the insurance company pays claims from its own assets, it may operate under a conflict of interest when making claim decisions, in that it incurs a "direct, immediate expense as a result of benefit determinations favorable to [p]lan participants." *Id.* at 1561, quoting *DeNobel v. Vitro Corp.,* 885 F.2d 1180, 1191 (4th Cir. 1989).

In Brown, the Eleventh Circuit clarified that:

> [W]hen a plan beneficiary demonstrates a substantial conflict of interest on the part of the fiduciary responsible for benefits determinations, the burden shifts to the fiduciary to prove that its interpretation of plan provisions committed to its discretion was not tainted by self-interest.

*Id.* at 1566. Thus, under *Brown*'s burden-shifting presumption, an inherently conflicted fiduciary must show that its claim decision was not affected by any self-interest. Unfortunately, the Eleventh Circuit has not clarified what a conflicted plan administrator must do to meet this burden.

Other district courts within the Eleventh Circuit, however, have held that an administrator can discharge its burden by showing that the opinions and evidence upon which it relied were as objectively reliable as the conflicting opinions and evidence offered by the participant. *See, e.g., Tookes v. Metro. Life Ins. Co.,* 2006 WL 870313, at *12 (N.D. Ga. Mar. 31, 2006); *Norwood v. State Farm Mut. Auto. Inc.*

*Co.,* 2006 WL 218183, at *10 (N.D. Ga. Jan. 27, 2006); *Wise v. Hartford Life & Accident Ins. Co.,* 360 F. Supp. 2d 1310, 1323 (N.D. Ga. 2005); *but cf. Richards v. Hartford Life & Accident Ins. Co.,* 2005 WL 2888214, at *3 (11th Cir. Nov. 3, 2005) (skipping the conflict-of-interest prong in dicta by noting that even if the decision was de novo wrong, it still would have been upheld as reasonable).

While these courts did not specify what type of evidence is considered "reliable," a district court within the Eleventh Circuit has suggested that short-shrift or otherwise incomplete reviews are unreliable and, therefore, do not dispel inferences of taint. *Lake v. UNUM Life Ins. Co. of Am.,* 50 F. Supp. 2d 1243, 1255 (M.D. Ala. 1999) (administrator did not discharge its burden of showing that its decision was free from self-interest where it did not explain why it ignored evidence from the participant's treating physicians in deciding to terminate disability benefits).

## V. Rules of Plan Interpretation

### A. Application of Federal Common Law

Courts have the authority "to develop a body of federal common law to govern issues in ERISA actions not covered by the act itself." *Kane v. Aetna Life Ins. Co.,* 893 F.2d 1283, 1285 (11th Cir. 1990). In some circumstances, it may be necessary to refer to state law to determine a proper plan interpretation. For example, ERISA provides no guidelines for determining the proper application of accidental death policy where there may be a relevant state law that includes a presumption against suicide. Although ERISA requires a claimant to prove entitlement, the court in *Horton v. Reliance Standard Life Ins. Co.,* 141 F.3d 1038 (11th Cir. 1998), permitted incorporation of the presumption against suicide and an affirmative presumption of accidental death into federal common law. Also, in *Kobold v. Aetna U.S. Healthcare,* 258 F. Supp. 2d 1317 (M.D. Fla. 2003), the court invoked federal common law to establish a possible agency relationship between the group health insurer and the employer, depending on whether plaintiff could establish the requisite factual basis.

These courts stated that a rule should become part of ERISA's common law where it would further ERISA's scheme and goals, which are (1) protection of the interest of employees and their beneficiaries in employee benefit plans; and (2) uniformity in the administration of employee benefit plans. *See also Buce v. Allianz Life Ins. Co.,* 247 F.3d 1133 (11th Cir. 2001).

### B. Application of *Contra Proferentem*

The Eleventh Circuit adheres to the rule of *contra proferentem* to resolve ambiguities against insurers in insurance contracts regulated by ERISA. In *Lee v. Blue Cross/Blue Shield of Alabama,* 10 F.3d 1547 (11th Cir. 1994), the court determined that a health policy that provided benefits for "medically necessary" services but excluded dental and orthodontic services was ambiguous because it did not address medically necessary dental or orthodontic services. However, the lower court's order granting the insured's motion for summary judgment was reversed because the appellate court determined that it applied an erroneous standard of review. *See also Jones v. Am. Gen. Life & Accident Ins. Co.,* 370 F.3d 1065 (11th Cir. 2004); *Florence*

*Nightingale Nursing Servs., Inc. v. Blue Cross & Blue Shield of Ala.*, 41 F.3d 1476 (11th Cir. 1995) (*contra proferentem* applies to insured and self-funded ERISA plans); *Dahl-Eimers v. Mut. of Omaha Life Ins. Co.*, 986 F.2d 1379 (11th Cir. 1993).

## C. Deference Afforded to an Administrator's Interpretation of a Plan

Note the interplay between rules of interpretation and standard of review analysis. For example, in *contra proferentem* analysis, a claimant's interpretation will be considered correct, if an ambiguity is found to exist. However, if the relevant standard of review is arbitrary and capricious, the claimant does not necessarily prevail because the court must still overcome the principle of trust law that a trustee's interpretation will not be disturbed if it is reasonable. If the administrator's interpretation is reasonable, then the wrong but reasonable interpretation is entitled to deference even if the claimant's interpretation is also reasonable. *Vickers v. Guardian Life Ins. Co.*, 204 F. Supp. 1326 (M.D. Fla. 2002); *HCA Health Servs. of Ga., Inc. v. Employers Health Ins. Co.*, 240 F.3d 982 (11th Cir. 2001).

As noted in Standard of Review, Section IV, *supra*, in cases where a conflict of interest arises the Eleventh Circuit applies a heightened standard of review. In applying this standard, the court first evaluates the claim administrator's interpretation of the plan to determine whether it was "wrong," as it would do under the regular arbitrary and capricious standard. *HCA Health Servs.*, 240 F.3d at 993. "Wrong" is the word used by the Eleventh Circuit "to describe the conclusion a court reaches when, after reviewing the plan documents and disputed terms de novo, the court disagrees with the claims administrator's plan interpretation." *Id.* at 994 n.23. If the court determines that the plan administrator's interpretation was "wrong," the court then must determine whether "the claimant has proposed a 'reasonable' interpretation of the plan to rival the plan administrator's interpretation." *Id.* at 994. Even if the court determines that the claimant's interpretation was reasonable, the administrator may still prevail if the court determines that its interpretation was also reasonable. *Id.*

Under the heightened standard, if the claimant has proposed a reasonable interpretation to rival the plan administrator's interpretation, "the burden shifts to [the plan administrator] to prove that its interpretation of the plan is not tainted by self-interest," i.e., that its determination was not arbitrary and capricious. *Id.* "[A] wrong but apparently reasonable interpretation is arbitrary and capricious if it advances the conflicting interest of the fiduciary at the expense of the affected [participant] . . . unless the fiduciary justifies the interpretation on the ground of its benefit to the class of all participants and beneficiaries." *Brown v. Blue Cross & Blue Shield of Ala.*, 898 F.2d 1556, 1566–67 (11th Cir. 1990).

In addition, there is no distinction in the Eleventh Circuit between plan interpretations and factual determinations made by an administrator where the heightened standard of review is applied due to conflict of interest. *Torres v. Pittston Co.*, 346 F.3d 1324 (11th Cir. 2003). *See also Paramore v. Delta Air Lines, Inc.*, 129 F.3d 1446 (11th Cir. 1997). Therefore, even factual determinations will be reviewed on the same heightened level of scrutiny as plan interpretations where there is a conflict of interest.

### D. Other Rules of Plan or Contract Interpretation

Anti-assignment clause in plan documents precludes a claim by the health care provider suing as the participant's assignee. *Physicians Multispecialty Group v. Health Care Plan of Horton Homes, Inc.*, 371 F.3d 1291 (11th Cir. Ga. 2004), *cert. denied*, 543 U.S. 1002, 125 S. Ct. 620.

## VI. Discovery

### A. Limitations on Discovery

With the seminal *Brown v. Blue Cross & Blue Shield of Alabama*, 898 F.2d 1556 (11th Cir. 1990) decision, and its framework for heightened arbitrary and capricious review in situations involving a conflict of interest, litigants have been confronted with developing proof on a number of additional analytical steps toward final resolution in an ERISA benefits case. The *Brown* decision introduced consideration of whether the administrator's apparent conflict of interest affected the decision and, more basically, whether a conflict of interest existed in the first place. The Eleventh Circuit recently determined that the heightened arbitrary and capricious standard of review announced in *Brown* applies "regardless of whether the decision turns on findings of fact or on interpretations of plan terminology." *See Torres v. Pittston Co.*, 346 F.3d 1324, 1334 (11th Cir. 2003).

### B. Discovery and Conflict of Interest

In the Eleventh Circuit, the issue as to the scope of discovery in ERISA cases depends largely upon the standard of review chosen by the court in light of plan documents and the role of the ERISA fiduciary. With mandatory Federal Rule of Civil Procedure 26 disclosures, some ERISA cases proceed to trial without any formal discovery while other cases can involve extensive deposition testimony.

In cases governed by the de novo standard of review, courts in the Eleventh Circuit permit discovery beyond the administrative record because in such cases the court may permit testimony and the introduction of evidence at trial beyond the record. *See Moon v. Am. Home Assurance Co.*, 888 F.2d 86, 89 (11th Cir. 1989); *Whatley v. CNA Ins. Co.*, 189 F.3d 1310, 1312 (11th Cir. 1999); *Shaw v. Conn. Gen'l Life Ins. Co.*, 353 F.3d 1276, 1284, fn. 6 (11th Cir. 2003).

Since the *Brown* decision, litigants in the Eleventh Circuit have focused upon conducting discovery on a number of issues relevant to the appropriate standard of review, the extent of the record, and issues pertaining to conflict. The first issue to be considered prior to the court's review of the claims decision is to find out exactly what were "the facts as known to the administrator at the time the decision was made." *See Jett v. Blue Cross & Blue Shield of Ala., Inc.*, 890 F.2d 1137 (11th Cir. 1999); *Buckley v. Metro. Life*, 115 F.3d 936, 941 (11th Cir. 1997). Courts in this circuit have allowed discovery as it pertains to the "facts known" if there is a legitimate issue raised that the claims file does not contain all such facts. *See Burks v. Am. Cast Iron Pipe Co.*, 212 F.3d 1333, 1337 (11th Cir. 2000); *Cerrito v. Liberty Life Assurance Co. of Boston*, 209 F.R.D. 663 (M.D. Fla. 2002).

As to the conflict of interest analysis for standard of review, this does not necessarily permit broad discovery. One court has held that the scope of discovery in such an ERISA case is limited to that which focuses on evidence relevant to the "self-interest process." *Featherston v. Metro. Life Ins. Co.,* 223 F.R.D. 647, 657 (N.D. Fla. 2004). *But see Miller v. Bank of Am. Corp.,* 401 F. Supp. 2d 1372, 1379 (N.D. Ga. 2005) (in heightened review case, the plaintiff was entitled to conduct discovery to obtain information that might enable him to refute any evidence that carrier's interpretation of the plan was not tainted by self-interest). In the *Miller* case, the court permitted discovery into the carrier's routine practice for deciding claims, but not the particulars of individual claims. *Id.* at 1380.

Courts in this circuit have also permitted discovery, even in instances in which an arbitrary and capricious standard applies, so as to enable the court to evaluate "(1) the exact nature of the information considered by the fiduciary in making the decision; (2) whether the fiduciary was competent to evaluate the information in the administrative record; (3) how the fiduciary reached its decision; and (4) whether given the nature of the information in the record, it was incumbent upon the fiduciary to seek outside technical assistance in reaching a fair and full review of the claim." *Cerrito,* 209 F.R.D. at 664; *Woodward v. Reliance Std. Life Ins. Co.,* 2003 W.L. 1798519 (N.D. Fla. 2003); *Crume v. Metro. Life Ins. Co.,* 388 F. Supp. 2d 1342, 1344–45 (M.D. Fla. 2005), *aff'd,* 387 F. Supp. 2d 1212 (M.D. Fla. 2005).

As a result of these decisions, it is not uncommon to see experienced ERISA litigators in this circuit serving discovery requesting not merely the claim file and the summary plan description, but copies of telephone messages, emails, treatises, medical summaries, dictionaries, periodicals, and other texts used with regard to the claim. It is also quite common to see interrogatories or requests for admissions to the defendant aimed at establishing whether the claim decision maker operated under an apparent conflict of interest based upon paying benefits out of its own assets. Aimed at determining this issue, litigants question whether the plan was or was not funded by stop-loss insurance or other policy, whether it was reimbursed by the employer for claims, whether a trust fund was established by the employer, whether any premium rebates were given to an employer based upon loss history, or more basically, whether anyone other than the insurer played any role in making the decision to deny benefits. *See Mazzacoli v. Cont'l Cas. Co.,* 322 F. Supp. 2d 1376 (M.D. Fla. 2004) (permitting discovery beyond record an issue of extent of employer's delegation of fiduciary responsibilities and the claim handling process).

Discovery may also be permitted in this circuit on preliminary issues such as standing to sue and whether or not the ERISA "safe harbor" provision applies. In *Kobold v. Aetna U.S. Healthcare, Inc.,* 258 F. Supp. 2d 1317, 1322 (M.D. Fla. 2003), the court noted that discovery would be permitted bearing upon whether the plaintiff could bring an action as someone who was or could become eligible to receive a plan benefit. *See Willett v. Blue Cross & Blue Shield of Ala.,* 953 F.2d 1335, 1342 (11th Cir. 1992). In the *Kobold* case, the plaintiff was an employee of ADP but the fiduciary apparently failed to process his application for benefits. The plaintiff claimed standing as someone who would have received benefits had the application been processed correctly. Therefore, the court concluded that "if, through discovery, the plaintiff is able to show that he met his obligation under the plan by applying for benefits on two occasions, he will satisfy the second prong of the test . . . [for standing]." *Kobold,* 258 F. Supp. 2d at 1322.

Limited discovery relating to the district court's jurisdiction has been used frequently in determining if the safe harbor provision (29 C.F.R. § 2510.3-1(j)) applies. In *Wilson v. Coman,* 284 F. Supp. 2d 1319 (M.D. Ala. 2003), the court permitted six weeks of discovery on issues relating to the court's jurisdiction prior to deciding a motion to remand based upon the ERISA safe harbor provision. *Id.* at 1322. Typically such discovery would include depositions of alleged plan sponsor representatives and requests for production or admissions as to documents disseminated to employees. *Id.* at 1323. n.3. *See also Gray v. New York Life Ins. Co.,* 879 F. Supp. 99, 100 (N.D. Ala. 1995). The court may also deem it necessary to stay consideration of a pending motion to remand a case to state court on safe harbor grounds so as to allow discovery on the factors set forth in 29 C.F.R. § 2510.3-1(j). *See Thomas v. Burlington,* 763 F. Supp. 1570, 1576 (S.D. Fla. 1991).

In breach of fiduciary duty claims, parties have been permitted to conduct discovery on who operated as an ERISA fiduciary regarding the plan. *Kobold,* 258 F. Supp. 2d at 1322. Depositions have also been taken in such cases on the issue of whether the fiduciary fulfilled its obligations. *See Useden v. Acker,* 947 F.2d 1563, 1572 (11th Cir. 1991); *Justice v. Bankers Trust Co,* 607 F. Supp. 527, 533 (N.D. Ala. 1985); *Hamilton v. Allen Bradley Co.,* 244 F.3d 819, 827, n.1 (11th Cir. 2001); *Donovan v. Nellis,* 528 F. Supp. 538, 542 (N.D. Fla. 1981); *Dairy Fresh Corp. v. Poole,* 108 F. Supp. 2d 1344, 1352 (S.D. Ala. 2000); *Byars v. Coca Cola Co.,* 2004 WL 1595399, at *9 (N.D. Ga. 2004). Discovery has also been permitted in such a case to enable the claimant to develop evidence as to the amount of accrued benefits and on the issue of attorneys' fees following a finding of breach. *Chambers v. Kaleidoscope, Inc. Profit Sharing Plan & Trust,* 650 F. Supp. 359, 378 (N.D. Ga. 1986).

## VII. Evidence

### A. Scope of Evidence under Standards of Review

#### 1. De Novo Standard of Review

The evidence that will be admissible in an ERISA trial in the Eleventh Circuit also depends upon the standard of review to be applied by the court to the benefits decision. A district court in this circuit conducting a de novo review of an administrative denial of benefits is not limited to the facts available at the time of the administrator's determination, and it may consider facts developed in discovery and expert testimony. *See Kirwan v. Marriott Corp.,* 10 F.3d 784, 789 (11th Cir. 1994); *Moon v. Am. Home Assurance Co.,* 888 F.2d 86, 89 (11th Cir. 1989) (on summary judgment, court reviewed affidavits and Social Security claim materials as well as medical records). *GIW Indus., Inc. v. Trevor, Stewart, Burton & Jackson,* 895 F.2d 729, 731 (11th Cir. 1990) (one-day bench trial included expert testimony), *Levinson v. Reliance Standard Life Ins. Co.,* 245 F.3d 1321 (11th Cir. 2000) (trial court admitted expert, lay, and medical testimony). In an arbitrary and capricious standard case, however, the evidence that the court may consider for purposes of reviewing the decision to deny benefits or interpret plan terms is limited to the administrative records and only those facts presented to the administrator at the time of the claim. *Jett v. Blue Cross & Blue Shield,* 10 F.3d 1547 (11th Cir. 1994); *Broom v. Bell South Telephone, Inc.,* 73 F. Supp. 2d 1308 (M.D. Fla. 1999); *Stvartak v. Eastman Kodak Co.,* 945 F. Supp. 1532, 1534 (M.D. Fla. 1996); *Daniels v. Hartford Life & Accident Ins. Co.,* 898 F. Supp. 909, 912 (N.D. Ga. 1995).

In a case decided under the heightened scrutiny applicable where a conflict exists due to benefits being paid out of the funds of the claim fiduciary (often an insurance company), the court will first review the entire administrative record and the disputed plan terms to determine whether the decision to deny benefits was right or wrong. *See HCA Health Servs. of Ga. v. Employers Health Ins. Co.,* 240 F.3d 982, 993 (11th Cir. 2001). The court is still not supposed to review evidence beyond the administrative record or permit additional testimony at trial unless there remains some issue as to whether there is in fact a conflict of interest and whether defendant can remove the "taint" of the apparent conflict of interest. *Id.* In such case, the court may permit the defendant to present evidence as to the funding of the plan, the lack of any claim denial incentives (or conversely the plaintiff may introduce countering evidence), the decisions benefit to the plan as a whole, or statistical evidence tending to negate the operation of any conflict in the determination of the claim. *Brown v. Blue Cross & Blue Shield of Ala.,* 898 F.2d 1556, 1568-69 (11th Cir. 1990); *HCA Health Servs.,* 240 F.3d at 1005. The weight of such evidence at trial is open to question, however, because typically once a court determines there is a conflict of interest it has been more inclined to find in favor of the participant or beneficiary and against the plan insurer without getting into a detailed analysis of the evidence introduced to purge the taint of an asserted conflict. *See HCA Health Servs,* 240 F.3d at 1005; *Lake v. UNUM Life Ins. Co.,* 50 F. Supp. 2d 1243, 1256 (M.D. Ala. 1999) (court analyzed stated reasons for claims decision in denial letters on issue of "taint of self interest."); *Brown v. Bellsouth Telecomms., Inc.,* 73 F. Supp. 2d 1308, 1324 (M.D. Fla. 1999) (primarily analyzing reasons for defendant's decision on "taint" issue); *Calhoun v. Complete Health, Inc.,* 860 F. Supp. 1494 (S.D. Ala. 1994) (rejecting administrator's proof of consistent plan interpretation as evidence that determination was not infected by self-interest). If the carrier purges the taint of self-interest, the court will then examine whether the "wrong" claim decision was nevertheless "reasonable." *HCA Health Servs.,* 240 F.3d at 994.

### 2. Deferential Standard of Review

When applying a deferential standard of review, the Eleventh Circuit has held that the admissible evidence is limited to the administrative record, i.e., the evidence on which the administrator based the benefits decision. *See Jett v. Blue Cross & Blue Shield of Ala.,* 890 F.2d 1137 (11th Cir. 1990). Even the more stringent, heightened arbitrary and capricious standard "requires [the court] to look only to the facts known to [the fiduciary] at the time the decision was made to deny" the claim. *Lee v. Blue Cross/Blue Shield of Ala.,* 10 F.3d 1547, 1549 (11th Cir. 1994).

This rule has been somewhat eroded, however, by several district court cases. *See, e.g., Cerrito v. Liberty Life Assurance Co.,* 209 F.R.D. 663 (M.D. Fla. 2002);

*Lake v. Hartford Life & Accident Ins. Co.,* 218 F.R.D. 260 (M.D. Fla. 2003); *Fish v. Unum Life Ins. Co. of Am.,* 229 F.R.D. 699 (M.D. Fla. 2005); *see also Miller v. Bank of Am. Corp.,* 401 F. Supp. 2d 1372 (N.D. Ga. 2005). As the court acknowledged in *Fish,* the Eleventh Circuit "has never squarely addressed the issue of the limits of discovery in ERISA cases," and "[c]ourts throughout Florida have addressed this issue differently." 229 F.R.D. at 701.

A number of district courts have allowed some discovery, premised at least in part on the notion that the conflict of interest prong of the heightened standard requires the introduction of evidence beyond the administrative record. *See, e.g., Featherston v. Metro. Life Ins. Co.,* 223 F.R.D. 647, 658 (N.D. Fla. 2004) (the "specific areas of inquiry set forth in [*Cerrito*]" would "only constitute permissible discovery to the extent that each factor is relevant in determining whether the administrator's decision was infected with its own self-interest"); *Miller,* 401 F. Supp. 2d at 1379 ("Given the analysis required by *Brown* [*v. Blue Cross & Blue Shield, Inc.,* 898 F.3d 1556 (11th Cir. 1990),] the court rejects MetLife's arguments and parts with those district court decisions holding or suggesting that no documents or evidence outside of the administrative record and plan documents should be considered when applying the heightened arbitrary and capricious standard of review.").

Other district courts have concluded that resolution of the conflict of interest prong need not expand the record. In *Wise v. Hartford Life & Accident Insurance Co.,* 360 F. Supp. 2d 1310 (N.D. Ga. 2005), the court considered how to apply the "burden-shifting approach" of the heightened arbitrary and capricious standard of review with respect to a wrong but reasonable claim decision. The court concluded that a conflicted fiduciary could prevail "[b]y demonstrating that it chose to follow what it reasonably perceived as equally or more objectively reliable data," *id.* at 1323, and that "when evaluating the objective reliability of conflicting evidence, the factual opinions and evidence considered should, as in the context of assessing the 'reasonableness' of the administrator's decision, be limited to those before the administrator at the time it made the challenged decision." *Id.* at 1325. *See also Tookes v. Metro. Life Ins. Co.,* 2006 WL 870313, at *15 (N.D. Ga. Mar. 31, 2006); *Norwood v. State Farm Mut. Auto. Ins. Co.,* 2006 WL 218183, at *10 (N.D. Ga. Jan. 27, 2006).

### B. Other Evidence Beyond the Administrative Record

Where a court in an ERISA case finds that the plan language at issue is ambiguous, the issue is one of contract interpretation and extrinsic evidence going to the issue of intent is admissible to resolve the ambiguity. *See Adams v. Thiokol Corp.* 231 F.3d 837, 844 (11th Cir. 2000) (heightened arbitrary and capricious review case).

### C. Evidentiary Value of Social Security Determinations

This circuit has held that Social Security benefits determinations may be considered in the course of the court's review of the plan administrator's denial of benefits. *See Kirwan v. Marriott Corp.,* 10 F.3d 784, 789 (11th Cir. 1994); *Whatley v. CNA Ins. Co.,* 189 F.3d 1310, 1314 (11th Cir. 1999). The court will not apply any particular weight to the decision but will likely analyze the administrator's consideration of the Social Security determination in arriving at its decision to deny benefits. *See Paramore v. Delta Air Lines, Inc.,* 129 F.3d 1446, 1452 n.5 (11th Cir. 1997).

### D. Treating Physician Rule

Following *Black & Decker Disability Plan v. Nord,* 538 U.S. 822, 825–28 (2003), the Eleventh Circuit held in *Shaw v. Connecticut General Life Insurance Co.,* 353 F.3d 1276, 1287 (11th Cir. 2003), that it was error for the district court to give "special weight to the opinions of [plaintiff's] treating physicians." *See also Jett v. Blue Cross & Blue Shield of Ala., Inc.,* 890 F.2d 1137, 1140 (11th Cir. 1989) (rejecting the treating physician rule in ERISA cases).

## VIII. Procedural Aspects of ERISA Practice

### A. Methods of Adjudication

Counsel for ERISA participants and beneficiaries, as well as defense counsel in benefits cases, typically make use of Federal Rule of Civil Procedure 56 summary judgment motions in order to resolve the cases short of a bench trial or, at a minimum, to resolve important legal issues such as the standard of review applicable in the case and the admissibility of evidence. However, the prevalence of summary judgments granted in this context varies somewhat with the applicable standard of review in this circuit.

In cases governed by the arbitrary and capricious standard of review, that is, where the plan document has conferred unquestionable discretion on the administrator to determine entitlement to benefits or to construe plan terms, the courts have been more willing to entertain summary judgment as an expedient way of resolving the case. *HCA Health Servs. of Ga. v. Employers Health Ins. Co.,* 240 F.3d 982 (11th Cir. 2001); *Lee v. Blue Cross/Blue Shield,* 10 F.3d 1537 (11th Cir. 1994); *Seales v. Amoco Corp.,* 82 F. Supp. 2d 1312 (M.D. Ala. 2000) (summary judgment granted in breach of fiduciary duty claim analyzed under arbitrary and capricious standard). In these cases, the court will typically review a stipulated administrative record along with the parties' briefs and make a ruling without the necessity of a hearing or a bench trial. In such cases, as explained below, a court will not introduce any additional evidence, so it makes sense for the litigants and the court to address these issues on summary judgment.

Summary judgment has also been utilized frequently by the district courts in the Eleventh Circuit when addressing cases that present a heightened scrutiny based upon an asserted conflict of interest. *See Buce v. Allianz Life Ins. Co.,* 247 F.3d 1133, 1136 (11th Cir. 2001) (granting in part motion for summary judgment); and *Krebs v. Aviation Constructors, Inc.,* 2006 WL 1208048 (11th Cir. 2006). Courts in such cases have still been able to rule on summary judgment motions based upon the administrative record, perhaps supplemented through deposition or other testimony regarding the completeness of the record, the respective roles of the employer and/or plan administrator, and the funding of the plan.

In cases governed by the de novo standard of review, it is not uncommon for counsel to file motions for summary judgment in this circuit, but a ruling granting summary judgment is much more difficult to obtain. *See Kirwan v. Marriott Corp.,* 10 F.3d 784, 788 (11th Cir. 1994); *Whatley v. CNA Ins. Co.,* 189 F.3d 1310 (11th Cir. 1999); *Moon v. Am. Home Assurance Co.,* 888 F.2d 86, 89 (11th Cir. 1989). Because the court is not required to limit its review in such cases to the record before the administrator, and may consider facts developed through discovery and other documentation found relevant, it is more likely that the court could find an issue of fact preventing summary judgment in such cases. *Kirwan,* 10 F.3d at 790; *Moon,* 888 F.2d at 89.

Accordingly, while summary judgment practice is very common in ERISA benefits litigation in the Eleventh Circuit, the success of such a motion will often be determined by the appropriate standard of review. Even if a court does find an issue of fact, however, it is not uncommon that the district judge will at least determine the appropriate standard of review to be applied at the bench trial. Summary judgment motions remain an important tool, therefore, to litigants in this Circuit in these types of cases, not only for narrowing the issues but also for purposes of a potential settlement of these cases short of bench trial.

### B. Reported ERISA Trials

The Eleventh Circuit has consistently held that there is no right to a jury trial in ERISA benefits cases. *See Blake v. UnionMutual Stock Life Ins. Co.,* 906 F.2d 1525, 1526 (11th Cir. 1990); *Chilton v. Savannah Foods & Ind., Inc.,* 814 F.2d 620, 623 (11th Cir. 1987); *Howard v. Parisian,* 807 F.2d 1560 (11th Cir. 1987); *Shaw v. Conn. Gen. Life Ins. Co.,* 353 F.3d 1276 (11th Cir. 2003). While there have been some attempts to get around these rulings, no litigants have to date been successful and these holdings are uniformly followed despite some rulings from other states.

A number of cases have proceeded to bench trial in the district courts in the Eleventh Circuit on ERISA benefits cases. *See Ogden v. Blue Bell Creameries U.S.A., Inc.,* 348 F.3d 1284 (11th Cir. 2003); *Buce v. Allianz Life Ins. Co.,* 247 F.3d 1133 (11th Cir. 2001); *Smith v. Am. Int'l Life Assurance Co.,* 50 F.3d 956 (11th Cir. 1995); *Wimbush-Bowles v. GTE Service Corp.,* 2004 WL 392918 (11th Cir. 2004), *cert. denied,* 543 U.S. 1121 (2005); *GIW Indus., Inc v. Trevor, Stewart, Burton & Jacobsen, Inc.,* 895 F.2d 729 (11th Cir. 1990). Typically, such a bench trial merely involves the presentation of trial briefs by the respective lawyers to the court along with a stipulated administrative record regarding the claim denial and testimony if the matter is reviewed de novo. *See Alford v. Blue Cross & Blue Shield of Ala.,* 910 F. Supp. 560, 561 (N.D. Ala. 1995). The "trial" in an arbitrary and capricious case would ordinarily consist of a hearing before a judge in which each lawyer would present arguments from the trial brief and as to the law and interpretation of the facts in the administrative record. *See Schindler v. Metro. Life Ins. Co.,* 141 F. Supp. 2d 1073, 1075 (M.D. Fla. 2001). However, sometimes courts in the circuit allow live testimony as to certain issues even in an arbitrary and capricious case. *See Lipsey v. Union Underwear Pension Plan,* 146 Fed. Appx. 326, 35 Empl. Benefits Cas. 2310 (11th Cir. 2005). Trials often resemble a hearing on a motion for summary judgment, as typically all of the materials have previously been presented to the court, with the difference being that the court is not reviewing to determine whether there exists an issue of fact and one side is entitled to judgment as a matter of law based upon the lack of any issue of fact under Federal Rule of Civil Procedure 56 analysis. After bench trial, many district courts ask the parties to submit post-trial briefs with proposed findings of fact and conclusions of law. *See Newell v. Prudential Ins. Co.,* 904 F.2d 644, 648 (11th Cir. 1990); *Herman v. Reinecke Agency,* 37 F. Supp. 2d 1338, 1339 (M.D. Fla. 1998). The court's determination is thus governed by the appropriate standard of review applicable to the case.

### C. Special Procedures for ERISA Benefit Cases

The procedural aspects of ERISA litigation in the Eleventh Circuit do not differ substantially from the experience of other litigants across the country regarding prosecuting and defending such cases in the federal courts. Courts in the Eleventh Circuit have been perhaps less proactive in establishing special rules governing the pretrial and trial procedures utilized in these types of cases.

## IX. Fiduciary Liability Claims

### A. Definition of Fiduciary

#### 1. Employers

Unlike other circuits where an employer is not allowed to be designated as a co-plan administrator for the purposes of ERISA liability, in the Eleventh Circuit an employer will be regarded as a fiduciary, even if it is not designated as such in the plan document, if it exercises "sufficient decisional control over the claim process." In *Hamilton v. Allen-Bradley Co.,* 244 F.3d 819 (11th Cir. 2001), summary judgment for the employer was vacated and remanded for further determinations because the facts supported a fiduciary duty claim against a party who acted as a co-administrator of the plan. The court's determination was based on the fact that the employer had effectively acted as a gate-keeper to the claims made on the insured disability plan by fielding eligibility questions from participants and processing their claims. Employees could not file a benefit claim directly with Unum, the insurer of the plan, but were required to go through the employer's human resources department when they sought to apply for disability benefits. The court determined that under these circumstances, the employer was deemed accountable for fiduciary responsibility under ERISA and could be held liable if a trier of fact found its actions to have been wrongful.

ERISA does not, however, prevent an employer from acting in accordance with its interests as employer when not administering the plan or investing its assets. In *Phillips v. Amoco Oil Co.,* 799 F.2d 1464 (11th Cir. 1986), *cert. denied,* 481 U.S. 1016 (1987), the court held that the defendant employer was not acting in its ERISA fiduciary capacity when it negotiated an agreement to sell its business operations, even if such sale affected contingent and nonvested future retirement benefits of its employees. Relevant to that determination was the fact that the sale agreement had no effect on the vested retirement benefits earned under the plan and the defendant had continued to fulfill its obligations in that regard.

ERISA fiduciary status is not omnipresent in a person who serves in multiple capacities. In the Eleventh Circuit, a person assumes fiduciary status under ERISA only when and to the extent that they function in their capacity as plan fiduciaries, not when they conduct business that is not regulated by ERISA. In *Local Union 2134, United Mine Workers of America v. Powhatan Fuel, Inc.,* 828 F.2d 710, 713–14 (11th Cir. 1987), the court vacated judgment entered against the president of the corporate plan sponsor after determining that the defendant had served in two distinct roles. The court concluded that the defendant's decision to pay business expenses instead of health insurance premiums, in an attempt to keep the corporation from financial collapse, was a business decision made in his capacity as president of the corporation, not as fiduciary of an ERISA plan. The court did not dismiss the fiduciary claim, however, and remanded it for fact determinations as to whether this defendant had made misrepresentations regarding the status of the health plan. *See also Gelles v. Skrotsky,* 983 F. Supp. 1398, (M.D. Fla. 1997), *aff'd,* 189 F.3d 484 (11th Cir. 1999) (where defendants' decisions, which affected the plan, were found not to be in breach of their fiduciary duties to the plan because they were business decisions performed in that capacity).

Fiduciary status has been conferred to an employer as a basis for standing to bring an ERISA action against other co-fiduciaries even when the employer has delegated most of the administration functions and discretion over claims determination to other entities. In *Hope Center, Inc. v. Well America Group, Inc.,* 196 F. Supp. 2d 1243, 1247–48 (S.D. Fla. 2002), the court found that the plaintiff employer exercised enough discretionary authority over the plan so as to characterize it as a fiduciary permitting it to sue under 29 U.S.C. § 1132(a)(2) and (3) for losses caused to the plan due to unpaid health benefit claims. In that case, the employer submitted evidence to establish that it exercised its fiduciary duty by: (1) engaging the services provided by the defendant, the Well America Group (WAG) for the administration of the plan; (2) permitting WAG to appoint a third-party claims administrator; (3) exercising its right to terminate the plan for cause; (4) providing employees with forms and information about the plan; (5) assisting employees who were experiencing problems with their coverage under the plan; (6) maintaining a file of all unpaid claims and calling medical providers on behalf of plan beneficiaries; (7) employing efforts on behalf of the plan beneficiaries to obtain claims itemizations from the medical providers and forwarding them to WAG for processing; and (8) terminating the plan upon learning that WAG was under investigation by the State of Florida.

Even when an employer holds fiduciary status in regard to the plan and to its participants, it will not be considered a fiduciary with respect to other co-fiduciaries, such as the insurance carrier covering the plan benefit. *See First National Life Ins. Co. v. Sunshine-Jr. Food Stores, Inc.,* 960 F.2d 1546 (11th Cir. 1992), *cert. denied,* 506 U.S. 1079 (1993) (where the court declined to find the defendant plan sponsor an ERISA fiduciary in regard to the claimant insurer).

## 2. Corporate Officers

No ERISA fiduciary status will be conferred on a corporate officer who is not involved in or is responsible for the management or administration of an employee benefit plan. *See Smith v. Delta Air Lines Inc.,* 422 F. Supp. 2d 1310, 1326 (N.D. Ga. 2006) (where fiduciary breach claims were dismissed against the members of the administrative committee, even though the committee was the named fiduciary in the plan documents, because the members exercised no discretion on investment decisions over the plan assets). But *in dicta,* this court stated that it was possible for fiduciary liability to attach to corporate officers who fail to disclose material information regarding the financial health of the company or for appointing imprudent members to the committee that oversees the investment decisions concerning plan assets.

In *Local Union 2134,* 828 F.2d 710 at 712–13, the court dismissed an ERISA fiduciary claim against the secretary-treasurer of the corporate plan sponsor after determining that his duties in such capacity were "purely ministerial." The court based its determination on the fact that this particular defendant had no authority or control over the disbursement of funds toward the health plan.

Also, corporate officers are not to be held personally liable for unpaid employer contributions unless the plan agreement contains "clear contractual language or a clearly shared intent of the parties" in that regard. In *ITPE Pension Fund v. Hall,* 334 F.3d 1011, 1013 (11th Cir. 2003), an ERISA plan brought a fiduciary claim against the general manager and the president of the employer, seeking to hold them personally liable for unpaid contributions to a retirement fund. The defendants argued that they could not be held liable for breach of fiduciary duty over the claimed contributions because, since they were unpaid, they were not yet "held" or "acquired" by the fund, and therefore, could not be considered assets of the fund. The court found that fiduciary liability could not be imposed on these officers under ERISA if the unpaid employer contributions could not be deemed to be "assets" of the fund within the meaning of 29 U.S.C. § 1002(21)(A). The court, however, vacated the summary judgment entered for the defendants and remanded the case for determinations as to whether the parties intended unpaid employer contributions to be assets of the fund. In a previous suit, the ITPE Fund had obtained judgment against the employer, H & R Services, for the amount of contributions owed, but the judgment went uncollected, and the ITPE Fund then decided to file suit directly against the main shareholders of the corporation.

## 3. Insurers

Insurers can be conferred fiduciary status either by designation in the plan document or by its actions in the administration of plan benefits. However, an insurer will not be regarded as an ERISA fiduciary for merely selling its products to a plan. *See Cotton v. Mass. Mut. Life Ins. Co.,* 402 F.3d 1267, 1278 (11th Cir. 2005) (involving life insurance policies purchased from the defendant through a "wealth-op deferred compensation agreement" entered into by the plaintiffs with their employer).

In the Eleventh Circuit, an insurer can be assessed fiduciary liability for breaches incurred by other parties, such as the employer or a third-party administrator, if the insurer had knowledge of the breach and failed to take reasonable steps to remedy it or otherwise took affirmative action to conceal the breach. In *Willett v. Blue Cross & Blue Shield,* 953 F.2d 1335 (11th Cir. 1992), the court held that the plan's insurer could be held liable for the employer's failure to inform participants that their health coverage had lapsed due to nonpayment of premiums, even though the main responsibility for this notification had been delegated to the employer. In that case, the court vacated judgment and remanded the case for the trier of fact to determine whether the insurer could have been imputed knowledge of the breach since there was conflicting evidence suggesting that the insurer had received multiple calls from participants and medical providers inquiring about coverage after the lapse date and the insurer had then misrepresented the availability of coverage.

Notwithstanding the above, in the Eleventh Circuit an insurance company will not be deemed an ERISA "fiduciary" if its function is limited to the performance of administrative functions and claims processing within a framework of rules established by an employer, especially when the claims processor has not been granted the authority to review benefits denials and make the ultimate decisions regarding eligibility. *See Baker v. Big Star Div. of the Grand Union Co.,* 893 F.2d 288, 290 (11th Cir. 1989), citing *Howard v. Parisian, Inc.,* 807 F.2d 1560, 1564–65 (11th Cir. 1987).

### 4. Third-Party Plan Administrators

A plan administrator who merely performs claims processing, investigatory, and record keeping duties is not a fiduciary under ERISA. In *Baker v. Big Star Div. of the Grand Union Co.,* 893 F.2d 288, 290 (11th Cir. 1989), the court declined to find fiduciary status on Connecticut General, a plan administrator who processed claims and disbursed benefit payments pursuant to plan terms under an administrative services agreement with Grand Union. Relevant to the court's decision was the fact that Connecticut General did not contract to provide Grand Union with insurance benefits for Grand Union employees and that Grand Union reserved the right to review any and all claim denials. Based on these facts, the court concluded that Grand Union did no more than "rent" the claims processing department of Connecticut General to review claims and determine the amount payable in accordance with the terms and conditions of the plan.

However, a third-party claims administrator will hold ERISA fiduciary status if it exercises discretion in the allocation of available funds, if its actions serve to conceal the plan's financial distress, or if the administrator makes disbursement of benefits that exceed those contemplated in the terms of the plan. *See Autonation Inc. v. United Healthcare Ins. Co.,* 423 F. Supp. 2d 1265, 1272–73 (S.D. Fla. 2006) (fiduciary breach claim was sustained against insurer, which served as plan administrator to self-funded health plan, because it paid out more benefits than afforded by the plan). *See also Hope Center, Inc. v. Well America Group, Inc.,* 196 F. Supp. 2d 1243, 1248 (S.D. Fla. 2002) (where the court found SMA, a third-party claims administrator, to have been a fiduciary to the plan because it exercised discretion in its decision to pay administrative fees before paying benefit claims and it did not promptly notify plan participants and beneficiaries of the financial problems affecting the plan).

### 5. Banks

The Eleventh Circuit Court acknowledges that a bank, like any other organization, could conceivably assume ERISA fiduciary status if it exercises discretionary power over a plan's assets. However, the court has followed the approach adopted by the Ninth Circuit to hold that no such liability will attach to an entity that assumes discretionary authority or control over plan assets if that discretion is sufficiently limited by a pre-existing framework of policies, practices, and procedures. In *Useden v. Acker,* 947 F.2d 1563, 1574–75 (11th Cir. 1991), *cert. denied,* 508 U.S. 959 (1993), the court affirmed summary judgment for the defendant bank determining that the powers it had exercised, as a secured commercial lender, over the assets of an ERISA profit sharing plan did not give rise to the amount and nature of discretionary control under which fiduciary responsibility is premised. In that case, the defendant bank had issued a short-term loan to the plan. The plan defaulted on the loan and consequently, the bank acquired and sold the plan assets that had been pledged to guarantee the loan. The court noted that although the rights given to the Bank under the loan agreement created an "authority" over the plan assets, they were remedies typical of arm's length commercial loan agreements and were limited by a fixed framework—the statutory and common law, the terms of the loan, and the dictates of banking industry custom.

### 6. Legal Counsel

The Eleventh Circuit court has also been reluctant to extend fiduciary status under ERISA to attorneys who provide legal services to the plan or to its participants. The standard adopted in this Circuit inquires whether the attorney has "departed from the usual functions of a law firm or otherwise (has) effectively or realistically controlled the Plan." *Useden,* 947 F.2d at 1577–78, also involved ERISA fiduciary claims against a law firm that served as outside counsel to the plan on an as-requested basis. The court rejected the plaintiff's contention that Greenberg, Traurig had acted outside the usual professional function of attorneys by providing business and financial advice in regard to a loan taken out by the plan. The court further held that the commingling of legal advice with incidental business observations, especially when this advice is proffered to businesspersons of some sophistication, will not automatically confer fiduciary status on attorneys and thus expose them to ERISA liability. The court supported its conclusion by reasoning that ERISA does not contemplate an allocation of liability that will deter consultants such as attorneys from assisting plans.

The *Useden* rationale was upheld in an unusual case brought against the attorney of a plan participant who handled a personal injury case. In *Chapman v. Klemick,* 3 F.3d 1508, 1510–11 (11th Cir. 1993), *cert. denied,* 510 U.S. 1165 (1994), an ERISA plan sought to impose fiduciary status on an attorney who had obtained an insurance settlement for an accident involving a plan participant. The plan had obtained from the participant a subrogation agreement to recover the medical benefits disbursed by the plan in relation to the participant's treatment of injuries arising from the accident. The plan was unsuccessful in collecting its subrogation claim from the attorney holding the settlement funds through an ERISA action since the court determined that the attorney could not be conferred fiduciary status under the *Useden* standard. In reaching that conclusion, the court reflected on the fact that the attorney had rendered professional services, not to the plan, but to an individual beneficiary, in connection to a matter unrelated to the plan. The court's decision was also based on the determination that the settlement funds obtained through the personal injury claim did not constitute "plan assets" by the mere existence of a contractual claim for reimbursement.

### 7. Investment Advisors

Investment advisors with authority to manage the funds of a plan will be held accountable for the fiduciary duties established by ERISA. In *GIW Industries, Inc. v. Trevor, Stewart, Burton & Jacobsen, Inc.,* 895 F.2d 729, 731 (11th Cir. 1990), the court imposed fiduciary liability on the investment manager hired by the plan sponsor to strategize and adopt an investment plan for the retirement fund. Relevant, although not dispositive to the ruling, was the fact that the plan sponsor had delegated to the defendant sole authority over the investment of the retirement fund.

### 8. Plan Participants

Plan participants cannot be deemed fiduciaries, even if designated as such, if they do not meet the definitional standard for an ERISA fiduciary. In *Herman v. Nations-Bank Trust Co.,* 126 F.3d 1354, 1367–68 (11th Cir. 1997), the court held that the participants of the Polaroid ESOP plan could not be considered ERISA fiduciaries with regard to the disposition of unallocated shares because they did not knowingly exercise control over these plan assets. That case involved an action brought by the Secretary of Labor against the plan trustee, NationsBank, for failing to exercise independent judgment in responding to competing tender offers for ESOP's shares. The Bank's defense was based on the contention that the disposition of the unallocated shares was directed by the participants by virtue of a mirror voting provision, where their action or inaction regarding stocks offered would control the disposition of unallocated shares with respect to tender offers. In rejecting NationsBank's contention that the plan participants were the fiduciaries responsible for the manner unallocated shares were disposed of, the court stated that ESOP participants are not fiduciaries with regard to unallocated shares when they are not given notice that their action or inaction with regard to their allocated shares will control the disposition of the unallocated shares. The implication of the notice that NationsBank had sent to the Polaroid participants was that they controlled only their allocated shares and in no way informed them that they could be held liable to the plan for their individual choices.

### B. Fiduciary Liability—Generally

The Eleventh Circuit court has defined fiduciary liability under ERISA as an obligation to the plan and its beneficiaries to act prudently and unselfishly in regard to the administration of assets of the plan. *See Ironworkers Local No. 272 v. Bowen,* 695 F.2d 531 (11th Cir. 1983). Five threshold elements are necessary to impose fiduciary liability under ERISA in the Eleventh Circuit. First, the conduct charged must arise from an explicit duty, under the terms of the plan or the statutory provisions. The court is adamant against finding implied duties from the statute. *See Henderson v. Transamerica Occidental Life Ins. Co.,* 263 F.3d 1171 (11th Cir. 2001); *ITPE Pension Fund v. Hall,* 334 F.3d 1011 (11th Cir. 2003); *Barnes v. Lacy,* 927 F.2d 539 (11th Cir. 1991). Second, the duty must be owed to the plan or to its beneficiaries, not to other fiduciaries. *See First Nat'l Life Ins. Co. v. Sunshine-Jr. Food Stores, Inc.,* 960 F.2d 1546 (11th Cir. 1992). Third, the action upon which the fiduciary action is premised must be wrongful or negligent. *See Hamilton v. Allen-Bradley Co.,* 244 F.3d 819 (11th Cir. 2001); *Willett v. Blue Cross & Blue Shield,* 953 F.2d 1335 (11th Cir. 1992). Fourth, the fiduciary breach must cause a detriment to the plan's assets or impair the rights of a beneficiary under the terms of the plan or the statute. *See ITPE Pension Fund; Chapman v. Klemick,* 3 F.3d 1508 (11th Cir. 1993). Finally, the person charged should have actual or constructive knowledge of its fiduciary status, being aware of its potential liability and of its power to exercise discretion over the plan's assets. *See Herman v. NationsBank Trust Co.,* 126 F.3d 1354 (11th Cir. 1997).

In regard to the discretion element, the court has pronounced that in order for a fiduciary to have the power of decision or choice, the person must know that he can decide an issue and be aware of the choices he has. A person cannot exercise the power of choice or individual judgment unless he is aware of his ability to do so. To "exercise" is to "make effective in action," and a person must have knowledge of his authority or power to control in order to exercise control. In order for a fiduciary to exercise discretion, the fiduciary must engage in conscious decision-making or knowledgeable control over assets. *See Herman,* 126 F.3d at 1365.

No fiduciary duty is owed under ERISA to the participants of a "top hat" benefit plan; that is, one that is unfunded and is maintained by an employer primarily for the purpose of providing deferred compensation for a select group of management or highly compensated employees. *See* 29 U.S.C.A. § 1101(a)(1); *Holloman v. Mail-Well Corp.,* 443 F.3d 832, 842 (11th Cir. 2006) (involving a retirement benefits plan).

An ERISA participant has a right to accurate information, and a plan administrator's withholding of information may give rise to a cause of action for breach of fiduciary duty. *See Jones v. Am. Gen. Life & Accident Ins. Co.,* 370 F.3d 1065, 1071–72 (11th Cir. 2004) (reinstating a fiduciary duty claim against an employer who misrepresented to employees the extent of their life insurance coverage under an ERISA plan).

A fiduciary will not be held liable for misrepresentation if it makes no untrue statements to its participants. In *Barnes v. Lacy,* 927 F.2d 539, 543 (11th Cir. 1991), *cert. denied,* 502 U.S. 938 (1991), the court reversed judgment entered against the employer imposing fiduciary liability for alleged misrepresentations regarding the amendment of an early retirement plan. In that case, a number of participants complained that the plan sponsor amended the plan to offer a second and more beneficial offer for early retirement to its participants. The claimants alleged that the employer had breached its fiduciary duties by misrepresenting, at the time of inception of the plan, that it was "a one-time offer" and by failing to notify its intention to amend the plan in the future to provide additional offers. The court held that no fiduciary liability could attach to the employer when there was no evidence in the record to maintain that any of its statements were untrue at the time they were made. The court noted in its opinion that the lower court placed an unreasonable burden upon the employer to predict the future and unintended events.

No fiduciary liability can attach when the plan sponsor complies with the disclosure rules mandated by Congress in the statute. In *Barnes,* 927 F.2d at 543, the court rejected the contention that the plan sponsor was liable for failing to notify participants that it was intending to reserve a right to amend the plan, since such reservation had been published in the summary plan document. The court held that no additional notification was necessary to comply with the fiduciary responsibilities prescribed by the statute.

An employer does not incur in fiduciary breach for failing to disclose in its plan description the possibility that sale of the business might result in the loss of future benefits. In *Phillips v. Amoco Oil,* 799 F.2d 1464, 1471–72 (11th Cir. 1986), the court found that the employer had complied with the disclosure requirements under ERISA by notifying employees in the plan document that terminated employees would not be entitled to full benefits. Since a "terminated employee" was defined in the plan summary as one who had not retired from the company, then it was logical to conclude that any event causing an employee to leave the company prior to retirement would result in the receipt of less than full benefits.

Fiduciaries may be held liable for amendments to the plan if such action is taken for the sole benefit of a party other than the plan and is carried out without careful and impartial investigation as to the repercussions of the amendment or the consideration of alternative means to achieve the professed objective. In *Deak v. Masters, Mates & Pilots Pension Plans,* 821 F.2d 572, 581 (11th Cir. 1987), *cert. denied,* 484 U.S. 1005 (1988), the court affirmed judgment for the plan participants who brought a class action suit against the trustees of a plan since the evidence did not show that the amendment they had promulgated was "rationally related to the financial integrity of the Plan" and instead operated to unjustifiably discriminate among plan participants.

A fiduciary will be liable for impeding the prosecution of an ERISA claim in the plan's behalf if he or she has no legitimate justification for its action. In *Ironworkers Local No. 272 v. Bowen,* 695 F.2d 531, 534 (11th Cir. 1983), the court found that three management trustees of the plan sponsor had breached their fiduciary duties under ERISA by refusing to authorize a suit containing charges of willful misconduct against them and effectively deadlocking the board. The court noted that the defendants did not conduct an independent investigation into the allegations of misconduct and its refusal to vote in favor of the legal action occurred even after their own attorney had advised them that a suit without allegations of fraud or conspiracy would be a nullity due to the indemnity provisions of the trust agreement.

Even a fiduciary who passively acts to allow other co-fiduciaries to prevent the prosecution of an action to be pursued for the benefit of the plan will be subject to personal liability under ERISA. In *Ironworkers Local No. 272,* 695 F.2d at 535, the court found that a trustee who had not voted to block the lawsuit had also incurred in fiduciary breach since he had participated in the meetings concerning the motion to file a suit that would have included himself as a defendant, and if he had stepped down from the board, the lawsuit would have not been blocked.

Failure to comply with an arbitrator's directive is automatically deemed a breach of fiduciary duty under ERISA, unless the directive was ambiguous. *See id.* at 535.

An ERISA fiduciary may also serve as an officer, employee, agent, or other representative of a union or employer, as long as exercise of the multiple functions do not cause him or her to violate the general fiduciary duties required under ERISA. In *Evans v. Bexley,* 750 F.2d 1498, 1499 (11th Cir. 1985), the court found that a trustee of an employee benefit plan did not violate ERISA by merely serving in a position with an employee organization that requires him to represent such entity in the collective bargaining negotiations that determine the funding of the plan. In reaching this determination, the court noted that in those negotiations, the bargaining representative represents either the employer or the employees, and to require him to consider only the best interests of the plan at the negotiation table would be to require him to breach the trust of his constituents.

The fiduciary provisions of ERISA are not implicated in the sale of a business merely because some plan benefits may terminate. *See Phillips v. Amoco Oil Co.,* 799 F.2d at 1471 (where no fiduciary liability was found to attach the plan sponsor for having sold the business and therefore causing a limitation on the employees' contingent and nonvested future retirement benefits).

An investment manager may be found liable for the losses sustained by the plan's assets if they are the result of a negligent investment strategy. In *GIW Industries, Inc. v. Trevor, Stewart, Burton & Jacobsen, Inc.,* 895 F.2d 729, 731–32 (11th Cir. 1990), the plan's investment manager was found to have incurred in fiduciary breach for failing to investigate the particular cash flow requirements of the fund he was hired to manage. Because of this oversight, the investment strategy adopted by the defendant limited the fund's liquidity and the plan's ability to pay the necessary amount of retirement benefits to participants. The lack of adequate liquidity in the investments made by the defendant impaired the plan's ability to pay out benefits and forced it to take a loss in the fund's value by having to prematurely sell long-term investments. Relevant to the liability determination was the fact that the investment manager had at its disposition information on the plan's historical cash flow needs that would have allowed him to determine what the anticipated withdrawal patterns of the fund would be. Yet, the defendant never obtained this information, nor read relevant plan documents prior to investing the fund's assets.

### C. Fiduciary Liability in the Health and Disability Claims

In addition to misrepresentations, a fiduciary can be found liable in relation to the administration of an ERISA plan for withholding claim forms and delaying the forwarding of information and/or forms to the insurers covering the benefits. In *Hamilton v. Allen-Bradley Co.,* 244 F.3d 819, 827 (11th Cir. 2001), the claimant employee lost her disability coverage under the plan policy because her claim was untimely filed. She claimed that her loss was caused by the employer's representation that she was not eligible for this coverage, its concealment of the insurance company information, and its delay in providing her with the necessary forms to file the claim. The participant was not allowed to contact the insurer directly, but had to process her claim through her employer's human resources department. The employer disputed the allegations, but acknowledged it had no evidence to show when the participant had requested the claim forms and when they had been provided to her. The circuit court determined that the employer could be held liable for fiduciary breach if the trier of fact was to find that the claimant's allegations were true and that the employer's actions were wrongful.

A fiduciary is not liable, however, for failing to provide forms or information that have not been properly requested according to 29 U.S.C. § 1024(b)(4). In *Hamilton,* 244 F.3d at 827, the court noted that the employer could not be held liable for failing to provide the participant claim forms that were not requested in writing.

The Eleventh Circuit allows an ERISA fiduciary to delegate to another party some or all of its fiduciary responsibilities, but cautions that such delegation is not absolute and the delegating fiduciary does not shield itself from liability arising out of a fiduciary breach under 29 U.S.C. § 1105(a) and (c)(2). Liability under those circumstances depends on the co-fiduciary's knowledge of the breach and its disposition to take timely and reasonable remedial action to counter the breach. Liability may also be independently imposed on the delegating fiduciary for concealment of the breach. In *Willett v. Blue Cross & Blue Shield,* 53 F.2d 1335, 1341–42 (11th Cir. 1992), the court held that the plan's health insurer could be held liable for the employer's failure to inform participants of the lapse in coverage, despite the fact that the main responsibility for this notification had been delegated to the employer. The court concluded that even if the employer bore the primary responsibility in regard to the notification of a lapse of coverage to the plan participants, the insurer would also be held liable if it had knowledge of the breach and did not take reasonable steps to remedy it. The insurer could also be found liable for concealment of the breach if it made affirmative misrepresentations to the plan participants leading them to believe coverage was still in place.

Following the decision in *Evans v. Bexley,* the court in *Local Union 2134,* 828 F.2d 710 at 714, determined that the defendant's decision to pay company bills other than the insurance premiums to maintain the employees' health plan was not a fiduciary breach since the defendant made the decision not in the capacity of fiduciary of the health plan but as president of the corporation.

A fiduciary breach claim premised solely on the wrongful denial of plan benefits will not prevail in the Eleventh Circuit if the claimant can assert a remedy for such conduct under 29 U.S.C. § 1132(a)(1)(B). *See Katz v. Comprehensive Plan of Group Ins.,* 197 F.3d 1084, 1089 (11th Cir. 1999) (where plan beneficiary's fiduciary claim was dismissed because claimant had an adequate remedy under § 1132(a)(1)(B) to address the merits of her life benefits claim).

However, in a recent decision, the Eleventh Circuit court addressed the reach of its ruling in *Katz,* and cautioned that a plan beneficiary may bring an action under

§ 1132(a)(3) when the allegations in the complaint cannot sustain a benefit claim under § 1132(a)(1)(B). *See Jones v. Am. Gen. Life & Accident Ins. Co.,* 370 F.3d 1065, 1073–74 (11th Cir. 2004) (where fiduciary claim was allowed, despite the fact that the relief sought was essentially the equivalent to plan benefits, because the claimants conceded that they were not entitled to the disputed life benefits under the terms of the plan).

A plan administrator does not incur in fiduciary breach by having its own employee make determinations as to the medical necessity of benefits claimed. In *Newell v. Prudential Insurance Co. of America,* 904 F.2d 644, 649–50 (11th Cir. 1990), the court held that Prudential did not violate ERISA as a matter of law by allowing a medical doctor employed by the insurer to make decisions concerning medical necessity of inpatient care. The court recognized that both the doctor employee and the insurer were considered fiduciaries of the plan under which the claimant was insured, but rejected the argument that this coverage procedure constituted a prohibitive transaction involving an impermissible conflict of interest.

An ERISA fiduciary can be charged a civil penalty under 29 U.S.C. § 1132(c) for noncompliance with COBRA provisions as long as the fiduciary is considered the plan administrator. In *Vincent v. Wells Fargo Guard Services, Inc.,* 44 F. Supp. 2d 1302, 1305 (S.D. Fla. 1999), the court determined that it could not hold the defendant employer liable under § 1132(c) for its one-year delay in notifying the plan administrator of the plaintiff's termination in employment (or "qualifying event" under COBRA) because the employer was not acting as the administrator of the plan and this civil penalty provision is reserved for plan administrators.

Employers have no affirmative fiduciary obligation to help plan participants with the pursuit of their benefit claims. In *Henderson v. Transamerica Occidental Life Insurance Co.,* 263 F.3d 1171 (11th Cir. 2001), the court declined to find cause finding the employer liable for fiduciary breach under ERISA for the plaintiff's allegation that it did not do enough to help him with his travel accident group insurance claims. Relevant to this decision was the fact that the employer had delegated full authority over the claims determination process to the insurance carrier covering the disputed benefit, had made claim forms available, filled in the employer sections of those forms, forwarded information from the plaintiff to the insurers, and made its own employment and timekeeping records available to those same insurers.

The Eleventh Circuit imposes on ERISA fiduciaries an affirmative obligation to notify plan participants and beneficiaries of a plan's financial problems that are apparent to them. In *Hope Center, Inc. v. Well America Group, Inc.,* 196 F. Supp. 2d 1243, 1249 (S.D. Fla. 2002), the claims administrator defendant was found to have incurred in fiduciary breach since it had been aware of the plan's financial troubles since February 2000, but had failed to notify this jeopardy to participants and beneficiaries until June 2002. *See also McNeese v. Health Plan Mktg., Inc.,* 647 F. Supp. 981, 985–86 (N.D. Ala. 1986) (failure to notify participants of employer's delinquent contributions to pension fund); and *Chambers v. Kaleidoscope, Inc. Profit Sharing Plan & Trust,* 650 F. Supp. 359, 377 (N.D. Ga. 1986) (same).

Fiduciary liability will attach to a plan administrator that causes undue delay in the processing of a claim, in the appeal's process, or in the payment of benefits. In *Flint v. ABB, Inc.*, 337 F.3d 1326, 1331 (11th Cir. 2003), *cert. denied*, 124 S. Ct. 1507 (2004), the court did not find fiduciary breach because the evidence showed that the defendant had followed the appeal's process according to the plan's provisions and ERISA regulations, and had determined to reinstate disability benefits to the participant retroactively.

When the terms of the plan or group policy insuring the plan benefits requires provision of evidence to establish the continuation of a disability, the plan fiduciaries are not under an obligation to give the participant or beneficiary advance notice before suspending the payment of benefits due to noncompliance with the evidence requirement, unless the plan provides otherwise. *See Flint*, 337 F.3d at 1331 n.3 (where the court declined to find the plan administrator liable for having suspended long-term disability coverage without previous notice to the participant when he failed to provide proof of continued disability).

In *Autonation Inc. v. United Healthcare Ins. Co.*, 423 F. Supp. 2d 1265, 1272–73 (S.D. Fla. 2006), the court validated the plan sponsor's fiduciary liability claim against the plan administrator that paid out benefits in excess of the plan's terms.

## D. Remedies

In *GIW Industries, Inc. v. Trevor, Stewart, Burton & Jacobsen, Inc.*, 895 F.2d 729, 733–34 (11th Cir. 1990), the court imposed on the defendant fiduciary, an investment manager, personal liability for the difference between the actual value of the fund's assets and the value it would have had if an adequate portfolio for the particular plan's needs would have been adopted. The court deemed appropriate the reliance on the claimant's expert witness model portfolio since the defendant did not present any evidence to contend the appropriateness of that model.

In *Hope Center*, 196 F. Supp. 2d at 1249–50, an action brought by a plan sponsor under § 1132(a)(2) to recover losses incurred by a self-funded plan due to fiduciary breaches, the court imposed on the defendant plan administrators joint and personal liability for the total amount of outstanding health benefit claims. In rendering its judgment, the court explained that this award did not stem from the damages sustained by the plan beneficiaries, but responded to the injury caused to the financial integrity of the plan as a result of the fiduciary breaches incurred by the plan administrators.

In *Willett*, 53 F.2d at 1342, the appeals court concluded that if the insurer was found liable for the plan sponsor's failure to inform plan beneficiaries about their suspension in medical coverage due to nonpayment of premiums, then it would have to respond for that breach under § 1132(a)(1) or under § 1132(a)(3). In this case, which predates *Varity v. Howe*, 516 U.S. 489 (1996), the court referred that "the beneficiaries may seek compensation from Blue Cross for any injuries they suffered as a result of Blue Cross' (the insurer) alleged failure to cure Mays' (the plan sponsor) breach," without making any further pronouncements as to the kind of the remedy that may be sought under § 1132(a)(1) or under § 1132(a)(3) for this type of breach. In *Varity*, the Supreme Court held that § 1132(a)(3)—the "catchall provision"—allows individualized equitable relief when no other ERISA remedy is available to a plan beneficiary to redress an injury caused by a fiduciary's violation to the terms of the plan or the statute.

The Eleventh Circuit court's definition of "appropriate equitable relief" under § 1132 (a)(3) and (5) for fiduciary and party in interest liability clearly encompasses the fruits of a prohibited transaction. *See Herman v. S.C. Nat'l Bank*, 140 F.3d 1413, 1422 (11th Cir. 1998), *cert. denied*, 525 U.S. 1140 (1999).

Reinstatement may be an appropriate equitable remedy under § 1132(a)(3) and the *Varity* ruling, as long as the claimants have no other remedy under ERISA to address their injury. In *Seales v. Amoco Corp.*, 82 F. Supp. 2d 1312, 1324 (M.D. Ala.), *aff'd*, 245 F.3d 795 (11th Cir. 2000), the plaintiffs sought to have their participation in the plan reinstated, so as to receive the correct retirement benefit, since the plan administrator had breached its fiduciary duties by concealing to them a mistake made in the payment of the benefit. The court recognized that reinstatement may be a suitable remedy in some instances under *Varity*, but concluded that it was an inappropriate remedy for the plaintiffs to be seeking in this case since they had recourse for their claim under § 1132(a)(1)(B) and the remedies sought for the breach of fiduciary duty claim seemed to be exactly the same as the remedies requested for the claim for benefits.

In similar fashion to other circuits, the Eleventh Circuit has extended the Supreme Court's reasoning in *Massachusetts Mutual Life Ins. Co. v. Russell*, 473 U.S. 134 (1985), holding that the statutory limitation of remedies available under § 1132(a)(3) to those of an equitable nature precludes extra-contractual remedies, which are legal in nature. *See McRae v. Seafarers' Welfare Plan*, 920 F.2d 819, 822 (11th Cir. 1991); *Bishop v. Osborn Transp., Inc.*, 838 F.2d 1173, 1174 (11th Cir. 1988), *cert. denied*, 488 U.S. 832 (1988); *Amos v. Blue Cross-Blue Shield of Ala.*, 868 F.2d 430, 431 (11th Cir. 1989), *cert. denied*, 493 U.S. 855 (1989); *United Steelworkers of Am. v. Connors Steel Co.*, 855 F.2d 1499, 1509 (11th Cir. 1988), *cert. denied*, 489 U.S. 1096 (1989). *See also Westcott v. Thomas*, 819 F. Supp. 1056, 1063 (M.D. Fla. 1993) (where a prayer for relief asking the defendants to "make good" generally to the plaintiff for any losses he experienced as a result of their alleged breaches was deemed an impermissible request for extra-contractual damages under ERISA); and *Seales v. Amoco Corp.*, 82 F. Supp. 2d 1312, 1324 (M.D. Ala.) (where the court denied the plaintiffs' claim for compensatory and punitive damages in a fiduciary breach action).

The Eleventh Circuit court maintains that punitive and compensatory damages are not available under § 1132(a)(3) since they do not constitute "equitable relief." *See Bishop*, 838 F.2d 1173; *First Nat'l Life Ins. Co. v. Sunshine-Jr. Food Stores, Inc.*,

960 F.2d 1546, 1551–52 (11th Cir. 1992) (where the court declined to award compensatory damages to the insurance carrier covering the ERISA plan benefits for loss in profits caused by the plan sponsor's failure to maintain a 75 percent enrollment in the policy because such remedy was not available under § 1132(a)(3)).

The Eleventh Circuit court has not yet decided the issue as to whether § 1132(a)(3) allows an award of interest for the delayed payment of plan benefits caused by a fiduciary breach. In *Flint v. ABB, Inc.,* 337 F.3d 1326, 1329, 1331 (11th Cir. 2003), the court did not reach the merits of a claim for interest on the retroactive payment of disability payments since it found that the defendants had not incurred in a fiduciary breach. The court did recognize, however, that such remedy may be available to a participant or beneficiary through § 1132(a)(1)(B) if the terms of the plan provide for it.

### E. Contribution and Indemnity

Although the Eleventh Circuit courts have not yet addressed the issue of contribution or of indemnification among co-fiduciaries under ERISA, their pronouncements on cases imposing joint liability on several fiduciaries may support the availability of such a claim under principles of federal common law. In the *Hope Center* decision, for example, the district court did not entertain a claim for contribution among the defendants, but it did provide that the judgment against one of the plan administrators (SMA) be reduced by any damages paid by the other plan administrator charged (WAG) pursuant to an earlier order imposing liability on the latter party, since it would "be inequitable to permit the plaintiff to recover more than its contractual damages due under the Plan." 196 F. Supp. 2d at 1250 n.4.

### F. Liability of Nonfiduciaries

Like other circuits, the Eleventh Circuit court has held that a nonfiduciary may be held liable under 29 U.S.C. § 1132(a)(5) for benefiting from the participation in an impermissible transaction with an ERISA fiduciary and will be required to disgorge ill-gotten assets from the ERISA plan. *See Herman v. S.C. Nat'l Bank,* 140 F.3d 1413, 1421 (11th Cir. 1998), *cert. denied,* 525 U.S. 1140 (1999).

## X. Attorneys' Fees

### A. Criteria for Awarding ERISA Fees

The Eleventh Circuit follows established ERISA case law derived from 29 U.S.C. § 1132(g)(1) in allowing reasonable attorneys' fees and costs to the prevailing party within the discretion of the court. *See Freeman v. Cont'l Ins. Co.,* 996 F.2d 1116, 1119 (11th Cir. 1993). ERISA allows the court to award fees to either party. *Dixon v. Seafarers' Welfare Plan,* 878 F.2d 1411, 1412 (11th Cir. 1989).

The statute itself does not prescribe the criteria for discretionary fee award, nor does the legislative history offer guidance. *Nachwalter v. Christie,* 805 F.2d 956, 961 (11th Cir. 1986). Therefore, the Eleventh Circuit has guided the district courts' discretion by enumerating five factors for the courts to consider when deciding a motion for attorneys' fees under the statute:

> (1) The degree of the opposing parties' culpability or bad faith; (2) the ability of the opposing parties to satisfy an award of attorneys' fees; (3) whether an award of attorneys' fees against the opposing parties would deter other persons acting under similar circumstances; (4) whether the parties requesting attorneys' fees sought to benefit all participants and beneficiaries of an ERISA plan or to resolve a significant legal question regarding ERISA itself; and (5) the relative merits of the parties' positions.

*Nachwalter,* 805 F.2d at 961–62; *McKnight v. Southern Life & Health Ins. Co.,* 758 F.2d 1566 (11th Cir. 1985); *Freeman,* 996 F.2d at 1119; *Iron Workers Local No. 272 v. Bowen,* 624 F.2d 1255 (5th Cir. 1980). No one factor is determinative but the list is provided to guide district courts in the Eleventh Circuit in exercising their discretion in this regard. *Id.* at 1266. The weight to be given each factor depends upon the circumstances of each case, but together these factors are a nuclei of concerns that a court should address. *Freeman,* 996 F.2d at 1119. No presumption in favor of awarding fees exists under ERISA. *Wright v. Hanna Steel Corp.,* 270 F.3d 1336, 1344 (11th Cir. 2001). Although the courts may award fees to either party, adherence to ERISA policy "often counsels against charging fees against plan beneficiaries." *Nachwalter,* 805 F.2d at 962. Nevertheless, courts in this circuit have, on occasion, awarded fees to the prevailing defendant. *See Nelson v. Liberty Life Assurance Co. of Boston,* 2005 WL 1181885 (M.D. Fla. 2005). The district court in its fee ruling should set forth findings as to satisfaction of the enumerated factors. *Iron Workers Local No. 272,* 624 F.2d 1255. Appellate review of the decision is for abuse of discretion. *Wright v. Hanna Steel Corp.,* 26 Empl. Benefits. Cas. 2737 (11th Cir. 2001).

The "bad faith" element of the test has been the subject of differing interpretations in the courts. Nevertheless, it has been the most often cited and determinative factor in these decisions with most fee denials turning on lack of the carrier's bad faith. *See First Nat'l Life Ins. Co. v. Sunshine-Jr. Food Stores, Inc.,* 960 F.2d 1546, 1554 (11th Cir. 1992); and *Freeman v. Cont'l Ins. Co.,* 996 F.2d 1116, 1120 (11th Cir. 1993). It has been held, however, that a showing of bad faith is not required for an award of fees if the balance of the other factors warrants them. *See Wright* at 1345.

The Eleventh Circuit has recognized the importance of this factor but has recently found bad faith under circumstances that diverge slightly from those recognized in other circuits. Error should not be equated with bad faith. *Dixon v. Seafarers' Welfare Plan,* 878 F.2d 1411 (11th Cir. 1989). In *National Company's Health Plan v. St. Joseph's Hospital,* 929 F.2d 1558 (11th Cir. 1991), the court found bad faith sufficient to justify an award of fees when the defendant had previously interpreted its own plan and promised the plaintiff certain benefits but later, changed its position to deny the plaintiff the promised benefits. In *Curry v. Contract Fabricators, Inc. Profit Sharing Plan,* 891 F.2d 842 (11th Cir. 1991), the court found bad faith where the plan misrepresented facts regarding a waiting period for benefits and then later retaliated against the claimant for accepting a job with a competitor by fraudulently denying him benefits. *Id.* at 849. Repeated failure to pay claims after a settlement agreement and contempt hearing was found to constitute bad faith supporting a fee award in *Tyler v. Ploof Truck Lines, Inc.,* 1999 WL 961262 (M.D. Ala. 1999). In *Bishop v. Osborn Transp., Inc.,* 687 F. Supp. 1526 (N.D. Ala. 1988), the court found bad faith supporting the award of fees where Osborn intentionally altered an employee's discharge date so as to avoid paying benefits. 687 F. Supp. at 1529. One court found culpable conduct supporting an award when the claim fiduciary relied upon a paper review of disability and disregarded treating physician reports of disability. *Blankenship v. SmithKline Beecham Corp.,* 2004 WL 3554969 (S.D. Fla. 2004).

The Eleventh Circuit has denied fees when it declined to find bad faith due to what it deemed as the administrator's "arguable basis for its decision." *Florence Nightingale Nursing Servs. Inc.,* 41 F.3d 1476, 1485 (11th Cir. 1995) (plausibility of defendant's position negated any finding of bad faith); *see also Hogarth v. Life Ins. Co. of North Am.,* 898 F. Supp 891 (S.D. Fla. 1995) (no bad faith where defendant's delays were due in part to lack of cooperation by insured's physician). Equating "bad faith" with "culpable conduct," meaning "blameable" or "at fault," at least one court has held that this factor is not met merely because the losing party has taken a position that did not prevail in litigation. *See Hoover v. Bank of Am. Corp.,* 2005 WL 1074290 (M.D. Fla. 2005), *report and recommendation adopted by* 2005 WL 1073919 (M.D. Fla. 2005). By contrast, in *Wright v. Hanna Steel Corp.,* 270 F.3d 1336 (11th Cir. 2001), the court affirmed fees even in the absence of a finding of bad faith in a case where the district court found that the defendant had acted carelessly in providing COBRA notices and in retroactively canceling insurance coverage for the claimant without notice. *Id.* at 1344.

Regarding the "ability to pay" factor, this Circuit requires that the party seeking fees offer specific proof of the opposing party's ability to satisfy the attorneys' fees award. *See Dixon v. Seafarers' Welfare Plan,* 878 F.2d 1411 (11th Cir. 1989) (absence of any evidence of either party's ability to satisfy award of attorneys' fees found to constitute sufficient grounds for upholding denial of fee award). In *Tyler,* 1999 WL 961262, the court found this prong satisfied when the plaintiff submitted an affidavit that the defendant's operation included 600 drivers, 650 tractors, and over 1,800 trailers and nine office locations. Often, however, this issue is not in dispute when a corporate defendant is involved. *See e.g., Montgomery v. Metro. Life Ins. Co.,* 2006 WL 1455684 (N.D. Ga. 2006).

The next factor requires consideration of the deterrent effect of an award. The fee applicant must generally present direct evidence to support deterrence of the conduct at issue. The circuit has found the factor satisfied where it could be argued that the award of fees would encourage an employer to furnish accurate summary plans. *McKnight v. Southern Life & Health Ins. Co.,* 758 F.2d 1566, 1572 (11th Cir. 1985)

When the award of attorneys' fees was found to be the only way to impose damages for bad-faith conduct, in the absence of state insurance bad-faith law in the

ERISA context, a district court in this circuit concluded that such an award would serve as a deterrent. *Tyler,* 1999 WL 961262. Similarly, in *Bishop v. Osborn Transp., Inc.,* 687 F. Supp. 1526 (N.D. Ala. 1988), the court found that because Eleventh Circuit ERISA case law prohibited the award of punitive damages, the best way to deter future culpable conduct was to award fees. *Id.* at 1529. In *Clarke v. Unum Life Ins. Co.,* 14 F. Supp. 2d 1351 (S.D. Ga. 1998), the court agreed with the plaintiff that awarding fees would deter others from denying untimely claims without investigating the reasons for the denial. *Id.* at 1358.

The Eleventh Circuit has noted that the plaintiff must "seek to resolve a significant legal question regarding ERISA or seek directly to benefit all beneficiaries under the plan" to satisfy the "benefit to the plan" prong of the test. *Dixon v. Seafarers' Welfare Plan,* 878 F.2d 1411 (11th Cir. 1989); *Freeman v. Cont'l Ins. Co.,* 996 F.2d 116, 119 (11th Cir. 1993). If, on the other hand, the plaintiff merely seeks individual benefits so as to protect his own interests, this prong is not satisfied. *Dixon,* 878 F.2d at 1413.

In *Clarke,* 14 F. Supp. 2d at 1358, the court found that the plaintiff raised a unique issue in regard to the administration of ERISA plans: the legal suffering of mental illnesses an excuse for untimely notice. Therefore, the fourth prong was satisfied by resolution of what the courts concluded was a "significant legal question."

As to the relative merits of the parties' positions, where there appears to be no bad faith and all other factors are neutral, courts have considered this factor at least "especially helpful." *Smith v. Miller Brewing Co. Health Benefits Program,* 860 F. Supp. 855, 857 (M.D. Ga. 1994). However, it has been suggested that when the decision depends entirely on the relative merits of the parties' arguments, a party's position must be extremely weak to justify an award of attorneys' fees based on this factor alone. *See Plumbers & Steamfitters Local 150 v. Vertex Const.,* 932 F.2d 1443, 1453 (11th Cir. 1991); *First Nat'l Life Ins. Co. v. Sunshine-Jr. Food Stores, Inc.,* 960 F.2d 1546, 1554 (11th Cir. 1992). At least one district court in the circuit has observed that "this factor turns on the degree of disparity and the merits of the parties' positions; that is, whether the losing party's position was so insubstantial that equity should compensate the winning party with an award of attorney's fees." *See Blank v. Bethlehem Steel Corp.,* 738 F. Supp. 1380, 1383 (M.D. Fla. 1990). In an unusual decision, after evaluating the Iron Workers' factors and concluding that the fee decision involved close questions, the court in *Smith v. Miller Brewing* awarded fees but reduced the amount available to account for the relative merits of the parties' positions. 860 F. Supp. at 857.

## B. Fees Awarded to Plan Fiduciaries

Where the claimant is a fiduciary, the court should also consider the additional factor of whether the party would violate fiduciary duties by not bringing suit. *Iron Workers Local No. 272,* 624 F.2d at 1266. However, legal fees are not awardable to a breaching fiduciary, even if the actions taken were in good faith and did not cause loss to the plan. *Martin v. Walton,* 773 F. Supp. 1524 (S.D. Fla. 1991).

## C. Settling Parties and Fees

On rare occasions, courts in this circuit have even awarded ERISA prevailing party fees to settling plaintiffs. *See Sabina v. Am. Gen. Life Ins. Co.,* 856 F. Supp. 651, 656 (S.D. Fla. 1992) (after an injunction was entered, the defendant agreed to settle by paying the extended benefits sought in the complaint and the court retained jurisdiction as to fees); *see also Thomas v. CSX Corp.,* 2005 WL 2756214 (M.D. Fla. 2005) (whereby settlement plaintiff ultimately received the short-term benefits he sought).

## D. Prelitigation Fees

Historically, courts have denied recovery of fees for taking an ERISA matter through the administrative process before bringing suit. *See Anderson v. Proctor & Gamble Co.,* 220 F.3d 449 (6th Cir. 2000). However, in a recent case, *Kamlet v. Hartford Life & Accident Ins Co.,* 2006 WL 1819406 (11th Cir. 2006), the court may have upheld an award for fees that included pre-suit time. The decision on this issue is far from clear from the opinion. In that case, the parties had a dispute as to the proper amount of deductions from benefits. Eventually, the parties came to an agreement as to the amount and to make it retroactive. Kamlet then demanded attorneys' fees for the administrative efforts and Hartford refused. Apparently, the settlement then fell apart and Kamlet sued in federal court for benefits and fees. After the plaintiff prevailed on the merits in the trial court, he sought fees that seem to have included pre-suit time. Hartford argued that the plaintiff could have settled the matter pre-suit and that his attorney filed suit merely to receive fees. It also argued that courts have not awarded pre-suit fees in an ERISA case. The court distinguished cases where the parties settled during the administrative process and admonished Hartford for not tendering the benefits at issue to the plaintiff or the registry of the court. Instead, it opted to dispute liability and litigate the whole case. The court then analyzed the fee claim according to the traditional factors and upheld the district court's award of fees to the plaintiff, which may have included the administrative-level fees. What is confusing is that at the end of the opinion, the Eleventh Circuit panel states that "based on our consideration of all five factors, we conclude that the district court did not abuse its discretion in awarding attorneys' fees to Kamlet for the litigation." 2006 WL 1819406 at **4. The decision promises to provide fodder for further argument on this issue.

## E. Calculation of Attorney's Fees

Regarding the amount of proper attorneys' fees, the Eleventh Circuit follows the lodestar approach in determining a reasonable fee awardable on ERISA matters by multiplying the number of hours reasonably expended on the cases times a reasonable hourly rate. *See Loranger v. Stierheim,* 3 F.3d 356 (11th Cir. 1993). In such issues, the applicant bears the burden of proof. *Norman v. Housing Auth. of City of Montgomery,* 836 F.2d 1292, 1303 (11th Cir. 1988). Thus, the applicant must also show that the requested hourly rate is in accordance with the prevailing market rates.

*Id.* A downward adjustment from the lodestar is appropriate only if the prevailing party was only partially successful. *Resolution Trust Corp. v. Hallmark Bldrs., Inc.,* 996 F.2d 1144 (11th Cir. 1993).

The award of a contingency fee multiplier in ERISA matters has been specifically rejected by the Eleventh Circuit. *See Murphy v. Reliance Standard Life Ins. Co.,* 247 F.3d 1313 (11th Cir. 2001).

### F. Class Action Fees

On at least one occasion, a district court in the Eleventh Circuit has addressed the application for attorneys' fees in an ERISA class action case involving a common fund. After the court reiterated that the starting point in setting attorneys' fees under the lodestar method is to determine the lodestar figure, that is, the number of hours reasonably expended on litigation multiplied by the reasonable hourly rate, the court examined whether the fee should be adjusted upward or downward. The court determined that an attorneys' fees award in an ERISA class action that resulted in a tentative settlement with the creation of a common fund, was subject to enhancement by 67 percent to represent the contingent nature of class counsel's fee. *Bowen v. South Trust Bank of Ala.,* 760 F. Supp. 889, 899 (M.D. Ala. 1991). The continuing validity of the decision is subject to question following the Eleventh Circuit's rejection of the award of a multiplier in ERISA matters in *Murphy. See Solutia Inc. v. Forsberg,* 221 F. Supp. 2d 1280 (N.D. Fla. 2002) (no multiplier given employer/defendant's previous agreement to pay reasonable attorneys' fees of retiree/plaintiff and recent prohibition of multipliers based on contingencies in ERISA cases). Nevertheless, it is likely that the Eleventh Circuit would approve the recovery of ERISA attorneys' fees (without a multiplier) in a class action case upon application and the appropriate set of facts triggering the factors set forth in the *Iron Workers* decision.

## XI. ERISA Regulations

- **29 C.F.R. § 2510.3 (2005)—Employee Benefit Plan Defined**: In *Slamen v. Paul Revere Life Ins. Co.,* 166 F.3d 1102 (11th Cir. 1999), the insured successfully appealed the district court's denial of his motion to remand after the conclusion of the bench trial. The Eleventh Circuit reversed the denial of the motion to remand on the basis that there was no ERISA plan where the insured was the sole shareholder and there were no others covered. The court held that, in order to establish an ERISA employee welfare benefit plan, the plan must provide benefits to at least one employee, not including an employee who is also the owner of the business in question. *See Williams v. Wright,* 927 F.2d 1540 (11th Cir. 1991).

  In *Gilbert v. Alta Health & Life Ins. Co.,* 276 F.3d 1292 (11th Cir. 2001), the court held that a sole shareholder is a beneficiary within the meaning of 29 U.S.C. § 1002(8) when he is entitled to benefits from a benefits plan that otherwise qualifies as an ERISA plan. The court found that there was an ERISA plan because it covered employees besides the sole shareholder and his wife. Therefore, an ERISA plan existed of which he could be a beneficiary. *Gilbert* at 1303.

In 2000, the Department of Labor modified ERISA regulations on claims procedure. The revised regulations, which apply to claims filed after January 1, 2002, establish shorter time frames for benefits determinations than those contained in the earlier version of the regulations. *See* 29 C.F.R. § 2560.503-1(f)(3).

However, many cases decided under the old regulations may form a basis for interpreting current regulations.

Issues about whether the new or old regulations apply will diminish over time. See *Parness v. Metro. Life,* 291 F. Supp. 2d 1347 (S.D. Fla. 2003), for a case involving an appeal after the new regulations became effective.

- **29 C.F.R. § 2510.3-1(b)(2) (2005)—Payroll Practices**: In *Stern v. IBM Corp.,* 326 F.3d 1367 (11th Cir. 2003), the court determined that IBM's "payroll practice" of compensating, from its general assets, employees who were physically or mentally unable to perform their duties or otherwise absent for medical reasons, was not an "employee benefit welfare plan." Therefore, it reversed an order of the district court denying remand and granting summary judgment to IBM.

- **29 C.F.R. § 2510.3-1(j) (2005)—"Safe Harbor"**: In *Butero v. Royal Maccabees Life Ins. Co.,* 174 F.3d 1207 (11th Cir. 1999), the court determined that a life insurance policy was not excepted from the definition of "employee welfare benefit plan" under ERISA's safe harbor regulations where employer did more than simply permit insurer to publicize program and collect premiums; in addition, employer picked insurer, decided on key terms such as portability and amount of coverage, deemed certain employees ineligible to participate, incorporated policy terms into self-described summary plan description for its cafeteria plan, and retained power to alter compensation reduction for tax purposes. However, the court held that a plan not protected by the safe harbor regulations is not necessarily an ERISA plan. The requirements of *Donovan v. Dillingham,* 688 F.2d 1367 (11th Cir. 1982), must still be satisfied. *See also Anderson v. UnumProvident Corp.,* 2004 WL 1067788 (May 13, 2004), *Randol v. Mid-West Nat'l Life Ins. Co.,* 987 F.2d 1547 (11th Cir. 1993).

Failure to satisfy any one of the four safe harbor provisions closes the exemption and exposes a group insurance programs, if it otherwise qualifies, to ERISA. *Belknap v. Hartford Life,* 389 F. Supp. 2d 1320 (M.D. Fla. 2005).

In *Smith v. Jefferson Pilot Life Ins. Co.,* 14 F.3d 562 (11th Cir. 1994), and in *Glass v. United of Omaha,* 33 F.3d 1341 (11th Cir. 1994), the court determined that a type of coverage could not be severed from the benefits package that was otherwise an ERISA plan in order to try to qualify for safe harbor protection from application of ERISA. In Smith, the insured argued that the coverage for dependants for which the insured fully paid, could come within the safe harbor provisions and, in *Glass,* the insured argued that the life insurance protection element of the benefits package could be severed from the rest of the benefits in order to avoid ERISA preemption. The court rejected both arguments.

- **29 C.F.R. § 2560.503-1(b)(2) & (f) (2005)—Notice of Claim Procedure & Denial of Benefits**: In *Perrino v. Southern Bell,* 209 F.3d 1309 (11th Cir. 2000), the insured argued that he should not be barred from pursuing his claim because the employer failed to comply with the ERISA regulations requiring that the claims and appeal procedure be clearly set forth. The court required the insured to exhaust administrative remedies, finding that the insurer's noncompliance was "exceedingly technical." *Perrino* at 1317.

    In *Counts v. American General Life & Accident Insurance Co.,* 111 F.3d 105 (11th Cir. 1997), the court also required the insured to exhaust administrative remedies where a letter terminating disability benefits was not technically in compliance with the ERISA regulations because the letter "substantially complied" with the requirements that the reasons for termination be sufficiently clear to permit effective review.

- **29 C.F.R. § 2560.503(1)(e)(2) (1999)—Deemed Denied**: In *Torres v. Pittston Co.,* 346 F.3d 1324 (11th Cir. 2003), the insured sued the plan administrator and insurer for denying disability benefits after a work-related automobile accident. After grant of the administrator and insurer's motions for summary judgment, the insured appealed and argued, among other things, that the "deemed denied" claim should be reviewed de novo rather than under the arbitrary and capricious standard or the heightened arbitrary and capricious standard. The lower court had ruled that the insurer's late response excused the insured from having to exhaust administrative remedies. After noting that it could not tell why the district court did not rule on the applicable standard of review for the deemed denial, the circuit court remanded to the district court for further determination of the applicable standard of review. The "Deemed Denied" provision was omitted from the 2002 regulations.

    A number of cases have addressed the issue of the appropriate standard of review when, under the 2002 regulation, participants have attempted to use a late appeal response or other ERISA regulation violation to change the standard to de novo. *See Brucks v. Coco-Cola Co.,* 391 F. Supp. 2d 1193 (N.D. Ga. 2005); *Stefansson v. Equitable Life Assurance Society,* 2005 WL 2277486 (M.D. Ga. 2005); *Hamall-Desai v. Fortis,* 370 F. Supp. 2d 1283 (N.D. Ga. 2004); and *Segar v. Reliastar,* 2005 WL 2249905 (N.D. Fla.).

## XII. Cases Interpreting ERISA Statutes of Limitation

In the context of an ERISA claim, the Eleventh Circuit has adopted the rule that a cause of action does not become an enforceable demand until a claim is denied. Thus, under ERISA, a cause of action does not accrue until an application for benefits is denied. *Paris v. Profit Sharing Plan for Employees of Howard B. Wolf, Inc.,* 637 F.2d 357 (5th Cir. 1981) (*Paris* is binding in the Eleventh Circuit by virtue of *Bonner v. City of Prichard, Ala.,* 661 F.2d 1206 (11th Cir. 1981)).

Like those in most other circuits, courts in the Eleventh Circuit borrow the forum state's statute of limitations for the most closely analogous action if it is not inconsistent with federal law or policy to do so and there is not a more closely analogous federal statute of limitations. *Harrison v. Digital Health Plan,* 183 F.3d 1235 (11th Cir. 1999); *Byrd v. MacPapers, Inc.,* 961 F.2d 157 (11th Cir. 1992); *Northlake Reg'l Med. Ctr. v. Waffle House Sys. Employee Benefit Plan,* 160 F.3d 1301 (11th Cir. 1998).

Federal courts have almost uniformly held that a suit for ERISA benefits pursuant to 29 U.S.C. § 1132(a)(1)(B) is most analogous to breach of contract claims for statute of limitations purposes. *Harrison,* 183 F.3d at 1240.

In Florida, a § 1132(a)(1)(B) claim was held not barred based on that state's five-year statute of limitations for bringing an action based on breach of contract. *Hoover v. Bank of Am. Corp.,* 286 F. Supp. 2d 1326 (M.D. Fla. 2003). In *Blue Cross & Blue Shield of Ala. v. Sanders,* 138 F.3d 1347 (11th Cir. 1998), the court held that a fiduciary's action to enforce a reimbursement provision pursuant to § 1132(a)(3) is most closely analogous to a simple contract action brought under Alabama law and applied its six-year statute of limitations for simple contract actions. The Eleventh Circuit also enforced an ERISA plan's ninety-day limitation period rather than looking to state law and barred a claim against the plan after it determined that the ninety-day limitation was reasonable in the context of a claim asserted against the plan. Northlake, 160 F.3d at 1303.[3]

## XIII. Subrogation Litigation

The Eleventh Circuit has not ruled on any subrogation case since *Great-West Life & Annuity Insurance Co. v. Knudson,* 534 U.S. 204 (2002). However, district courts in the Eleventh Circuit have done so. The claims in those cases fall into two categories: (1) subrogation claims regarding recovery of medical benefits, and (2) reimbursement claims regarding overpaid disability benefits.

Neither the Eleventh Circuit nor any district courts within the circuit have issued a decision since *Sereboff v. Mid Atlantic Medical Services, Inc.,* 126 S. Ct. 1869 (2006), in which the Supreme Court distinguished *Knudson* and ruled that an administrator's claim to recover tort settlement proceeds from a plan beneficiary on whose behalf it had paid medical expenses was a claim for equitable relief under 29 U.S.C. § 1132(a)(3). Unlike the insurer in *Knudson,* which sought funds that were not in possession of the plan beneficiaries, the Supreme Court noted that the administrator in *Sereboff* was seeking identifiable tort settlement funds within the beneficiaries' possession and control, as the funds had been placed in a separate account distinct from the beneficiaries' general assets.

### A. Subrogation Claims

The district courts in the Eleventh Circuit are split on whether subrogation claims are appropriate. Some courts have denied subrogation claims.

In *Popowski v. Parrott,* 403 F. Supp. 2d 1215 (N.D. Ga. 2004), the fiduciary and third-party administrator sought reimbursement or restitution through the imposition of a constructive trust, an equitable lien, or other appropriate equitable mechanism to recover identifiable assets of a personal injury settlement between the plan participant and third-party tortfeasors. The court dismissed the claim because the settlement proceeds had not been segregated into an identifiable amount or location, but rather were placed directly in the participant's checking or savings account. The court reasoned that the Eleventh Circuit seemed to approve this analysis in *Flint v. ABB, Inc.*, 337 F.3d 1326, 1330 n.2 (11th Cir. 2003), where it discussed "appropriate equitable relief" under 29 U.S.C. § 1132(a)(3) by stating that "the law of unjust enrichment is concerned solely with enrichments that are unjust independently of wrongs and contracts."

Likewise, in *Blue Cross Blue Shield of S.C. v. Carillo*, 372 F. Supp. 2d 628 (N.D. Ga. 2005), the administrator sought reimbursement from the beneficiaries' settlement with a third-party tortfeasor for medical costs paid on their behalf under the terms of the plan. Noting that the circuits were split on whether a subrogation claim was permissible, and that the Eleventh Circuit had not ruled on the issue, the court applied the minority view of the circuits and dismissed the claim. The court ruled that regardless of whether the claim was styled as one for a constructive trust, for equitable restitution, or for an equitable lien, it simply sought to enforce a provision of the plan that would require the beneficiaries to pay money. The court added that such a claim was not equitable in nature and was not "appropriate equitable relief" for purposes of § 1132(a)(3). Alternatively, the court stated that even if it followed the majority approach of the circuits, the claim still would be dismissed because the administrator did not seek the recovery of specific, identifiable funds, but instead sought recovery of funds that had been commingled into various checking accounts and spent for the most part.

Other courts have allowed subrogation claims. In *Space Gateway Support v. Prieth*, 371 F. Supp. 2d 1364 (M.D. Fla. 2005), the court ruled that a plan fiduciary stated a claim for equitable relief by seeking equitable restitution in the form of a constructive trust on that portion of the settlement proceeds in the participant's possession, and by seeking an equitable lien on any property or account to which the settlement proceeds had been converted. Applying the approach adopted by the majority of circuits and by some district courts within the Eleventh Circuit, the court reasoned that the administrator had satisfied the three-part inquiry whether the plan sought to recover funds (1) that were specifically identifiable, (2) that belonged in good conscience to the plan, and (3) that were within the possession and control of the defendant beneficiary.

The court in *Prieth*, however, denied the fiduciary's claim for unjust enrichment under federal common law, following the Eleventh Circuit's restrictive interpretation of the availability of federal common-law remedies under ERISA. *See, e.g., Sanson v. Gen. Motors Corp.*, 966 F.2d 618 (11th Cir. 1992); *First Nat'l Life Ins. Co. v. Sunshine-Jr. Food Stores, Inc.*, 960 F.2d 1546 (11th Cir. 1992); *McRae v. Seafarers' Welfare Plan*, 920 F.2d 819 (11th Cir 1991).

Similarly, in *Culp, Inc. v. Cain*, 414 F. Supp. 2d 1118 (M.D. Ala. 2006), the plan and its third-party administrator sued a participant for reimbursement of health care benefits after the participant settled a tort claim, and the court ruled that plaintiffs were entitled to reimbursement. Distinguishing *Knudson*, the court reasoned that the settlement proceeds in *Knudson* were never in the possession of the beneficiaries, whereas the settlement proceeds in Culp were paid directly to the participant or her lawyers on her behalf. The court concluded that because the participant was in actual or constructive possession of the settlement proceeds, the action for restitution was equitable and proper under § 1132(a)(3). The court noted that should the plaintiffs seek to impose personal liability on the participant, the claim would fall outside the reach of ERISA.

## B. Reimbursement Claims

District courts within the Eleventh Circuit are split on whether reimbursement claims for overpaid disability benefits are permissible.

In *Eldridge v. Wachovia Corp. Long-Term Disability Plan,* 383 F. Supp. 2d 1367 (N.D. Ga. 2005), the plan and its claim administrators filed a counterclaim, asserting claims for restitution, unjust enrichment, and specific performance of the plan's offset provision. Noting a split among the circuits regarding whether *Knudson* permitted claims for restitution under 29 U.S.C. § 1132(a)(3), the absence of an Eleventh Circuit decision, and a split among the district courts within the Eleventh Circuit as to whether restitution claims brought pursuant to provisions in ERISA plans were cognizable under § 1132(a)(3), the court dismissed the restitution claim. Even under the more lenient approach adopted by some courts, the court reasoned that a claim for restitution, in order to constitute a claim for equitable relief, must seek specifically identifiable property that is within control or possession of the beneficiary. The court concluded that the administrators had not alleged the existence of any specified, identifiable funds presently controlled or possessed by the beneficiary, or even suggested that the beneficiary preserved or otherwise segregated the duplicate benefits.

Likewise, the court in *Eldridge* dismissed the administrators' claim for unjust enrichment under federal common law. The court observed that neither the Supreme Court nor the Eleventh Circuit had ruled on whether a claim for unjust enrichment under federal common law could be asserted, but that there was a split among the other circuits. Although several district courts within the Eleventh Circuit had recognized common-law actions for unjust enrichment in ERISA cases, the court noted that the Eleventh Circuit had expressed hesitancy to create federal common-law remedies under ERISA and had refused to infer an unjust enrichment claim based on contractual obligations. *See, e.g., Fick v. Metro. Life Ins. Co.,* 347 F. Supp. 2d 1271 (S.D. Fla. 2004); *but see Space Gateway Support v. Prieth,* 371 F. Supp. 2d 1364 (M.D. Fla. 2005).

In *Unum Life Insurance Co. of America v. O'Brien,* 2004 WL 2283559 (M.D. Fla. Oct. 4, 2004), the court denied the administrator's claim for unjust enrichment pursuant to § 1132(a)(3) to recover overpaid disability benefits. The court, however, allowed a claim for unjust enrichment under federal common law because ERISA did not provide an explicit remedy, and the purpose of ERISA would be furthered by applying such a remedy. The court explained that it would be difficult to believe that Congress intended beneficiaries to be rewarded for overpayments to which they were not entitled.

## XIV. Miscellaneous

### A. ERISA Class Actions

The Eleventh Circuit has certified a number of class actions in ERISA cases and has appeared to analyze these types of cases no differently than any other putative class claims. In *Piazza v. Ebsco Industries, Inc.*, 273 F.3d 1341 (11th Cir. 2001), the court addressed the appropriateness of class certification in an ERISA action brought by a former employee and participant in the plan against the employer, directors' and certain trustees and fiduciaries of the plan complaining of the employer's stock buyback. Citing traditional class action case law, the court addressed the requirements for class action certification: numerosity, commonality, typicality, and adequacy of representation. The court ultimately found that a former employee whose professional malpractice claims against accountants who allegedly undervalued the employer's stock, which the ERISA plan sold back to the employer, could not be an adequate class representative for other employees alleging malpractice. The court also found that the class representative did not have standing to assert claims relating to conduct before he became an employee with regard to the ERISA breach of fiduciary duty claims and did not have standing to raise a claim for alleged breaches occurring after his retirement.

Significantly, the defendants contended that because Piazza was not individually injured by the plan's 1994 sale of the Ebsco stock, his only ERISA claim was "for appropriate relief" to the plan for alleged breaches of fiduciary duty. Because such a claim was brought on behalf of the plan itself only, any recovery will benefit the plan and, indirectly the members of the class. Defendants argued that allowing individuals to opt out of the class action and pursue their own suits under § 1132(a)(2) would require the defendants to defend against multiple suits, each asserting what is actually one claim belonging to the plan. Therefore, defendants argued that the requirements of Rule 23(b)(1) were met because "inconsistent or varying adjudications with respect to individual members of the class" on the claim would "establish incompatible standards of conduct" for them. The court agreed and found that the district court had abused its discretion to certify the § 1132(a)(2) claim under Rule 23(b)(3).

In *Hudson v. Delta Air Lines Inc.*, 90 F.3d 451 (11th Cir. 1996), certain retirees brought a class action against the airline based on alleged ERISA violations and a pendant breach of contract claim. The Eleventh Circuit reviewed the district court's denial of the motion for class certification and dismissal of pendant state claims for lack of jurisdiction on the interlocutory appeal. The court upheld the district court's denial of class certification by agreeing that commonality was not satisfied with regard to allegations that the employer misled retirees as the claims were not susceptible to class-wide proof.

The court in *Specialty Cabinets & Fixtures Inc. v. American Equitable Life Insurance Co.*, 140 F.R.D. 474 (S.D. Ga. 1991), conditionally certified a class action brought by beneficiaries who sought to recover unpaid benefits and for damages for breach of fiduciary duties, for settlement purposes only. The court concluded that all four factors for class certification had been met. In *Jones v. American General Life*

*& Accident Insurance Co.,* 213 F.R.D. 689 (S.D. Ga. 2002), the court certified class claims by a retiree on behalf of a class seeking to enjoin a successor employer from canceling life insurance for retirees. The court certified the injunctive class with respect to a breach of conduct claim regarding the termination of life insurance coverage but refused to certify the injunctive class with respect to promissory estoppel claims.

## B. Removal of ERISA Cases

Courts in the Eleventh Circuit typically approve removal of ERISA matters as a matter of course and have found that benefit actions are an exception to the well-pleaded complaint rule for removal. *Whitt v. Sherman Int'l Corp.,* 147 F.3d 1325, 1329–30 (11th Cir. 1998).

## Notes

1. Another post-*Miller* decision is *Anderson v. UnumProvident Corp.,* 369 F.3d 1257 (11th Cir. 2004) (breach of contract, fraud, suppression, and bad-faith claims preempted).

2. *See also Krasny v. Aetna Life Ins. Co. d/b/a Aetna Healthcare,* 147 F. Supp. 2d 1300 (M.D. Fla. 2001) (complete preemption applied to claim that involved both treatment and coverage); *Garrison v. Ne. Ga. Med. Ctr.,* 66 F. Supp. 2d 1336 (N.D. Ga. 1999) (complete preemption applied to claim that cesarean section was denied due to economic factors).

3. The author acknowledges the valuable assistance of Amy Deruelle in the preparation of this section.

# CHAPTER 12

# D.C. Circuit

JAMES L. MARKETOS
GLENN MERTEN
ROBIN SANDERS

## I. What Constitutes an ERISA Plan?

### A. Determining the Existence of an Employee Welfare Benefit Plan

Not every grant of an employee benefit is governed by the Employee Retirement Income Security Act of 1974 (ERISA). The statute's focus is "on the administrative integrity of the benefit plans—which presumes that some type of administrative activity is taking place," and applies only "with respect to benefits whose provision by nature requires an ongoing administrative program to meet the employer's obligation." *Young v. Washington Gas Light Co.,* 206 F.3d 1200, 1203 (D.C. Cir. 2000), quoting *Fort Halifax Packing Co. v. Coyne,* 482 U.S. 1, 11, 15 (1987) (decided in context of a corporate restructuring plan, which included a retirement incentive program that provided for a one-time, lump-sum payment triggered by a single event and required no ongoing administration of the benefit). "[W]hether a benefit is regulated by ERISA turns on the nature and extent of the administrative obligations that the benefit imposes on the employer." *Id.,* quoting with favor *Belanger v. Wyman-Gordon Co.,* 71 F.3d 451, 454 (1st Cir. 1995) ("[A]n employee benefit may be considered a plan for purposes of ERISA only if it involves the undertaking of continuing administrative and financial obligations by the employer to the behalf of employees or their beneficiaries.").

Is the existence of an ERISA plan jurisdictional or, instead, is it a substantive element of a plaintiff's claim for relief? The district court is *Gray v. Am. Acad. of*

*Achievement,* 2005 U.S. Dist. LEXIS 4646 (D.D.C. Mar. 21, 2005), held that "[t]o create federal jurisdiction under ERISA, a plaintiff must allege facts that show the establishment of a plan of the type covered by ERISA." *Id.* at *3, citing *Young v. Washington Gaslight Co.,* 206 F.3d 1200 (D.C. Cir. 2000). In *Gray,* a "split dollar" insurance policy and its surrounding agreements—which obligated the defendant employer to pay lump sums, premiums, and deficit contributions during and after plaintiff's employment, but did not require ongoing administrative obligations (particularly none of a discretionary nature)—were found not to amount to an ERISA plan. The district court therefore dismissed the complaint "on jurisdictional grounds." *Id.* at *1. Although the case was appealed, it was voluntarily dismissed before the D.C. Circuit could address the relevant jurisdictional issue. *See Gray v. Am. Acad. of Achievement,* 2006 U.S. App. LEXIS 9327 (D.C. Cir. April 5, 2006) (ordering supplemental briefs addressing the impact of *Arbaugh v. Y & H Corp.,* 126 S.Ct. 1235 (Feb. 22, 2006) on *Young*).

### B. Definition of "Employee" for ERISA Purposes

ERISA defines "employee" merely as "any individual employed by an employer." 29 U.S.C. § 1002(6) (1999). The statute provides no further guidance. Instead, "one must look to common-law rules of agency to determine employee status." *Holt v. Winpisinger,* 811 F.2d 1532, 1538 (D.C. Cir. 1987). In *Holt,* the court relied on the Restatement (Second) of Agency § 220(2) (1958), which lists ten factors to be considered when differentiating between an employee and an independent contractor:

1. the extent of control which, by the agreement, the master may exercise over the details of the work;
2. whether or not the one employed is engaged in a distinct occupation or business;
3. the kind of occupation, with reference to whether, in the locality, the work is usually done under the direction of the employer or by a specialist without supervision;
4. the skill required in the particular occupation;
5. whether the employer or the workman supplies the instrumentalities, tools, and the place of work for the person doing the work;
6. the length of time for which the person is employed;
7. the method of payment, whether by the time or by the job;
8. whether or not the work is a part of the regular business of the employer;
9. whether or not the parties believe they are creating the relation of master and servant; and
10. whether the principal is or is not a business.

*Id.* at 1541 n.54. Of the ten factors, the *Holt* court found "the right of one party to control not only the result to be achieved by the other, but also the means and manner of performing the task assigned, [to be] the most critical factor in ascertaining whether an employment relationship exists." *Id.* at 1539. In *Mayeske v. International Association of Fire Fighters,* 905 F.2d 1548, 1553 (D.C. Cir. 1990), the court confirmed that *Holt* sets the "standard for distinguishing between employees and independent contractors," but noted that *Community for Creative Non-Violence v. Reid,* 490 U.S. 730, 109 S. Ct. 2166, 104 L. Ed. 2d 811 (1989), influenced its approach to the *Holt* common-law test. Unlike *Holt,* which held that the "control over details" factor is the most critical factor, *Mayeske* acknowledged that the "*Reid* Court's analysis makes clear that 'the hiring party's right to control the manner and means by which the product is accomplished' deserves separate analysis but 'is not dispositive.'" *Mayeske,* 905 F.2d at 1554, quoting *Reid,* 109 S. Ct. at 2178–79. *Reid* involved a copyright dispute between a sculptor who had prepared a commissioned work and the commissioning organization. The sculptor's claim to copyright ownership depended on whether the sculptor was an employee of the commissioning organization. After applying the same common-law test outlined in *Holt,* the court concluded that the sculptor was an independent contractor. The court found that the sculptor did not control the details of his work, but determined that the other factors outweighed this finding.

## C. Interpretation of Safe Harbor Regulation

To date, no reported D.C. Circuit cases have addressed the "safe harbor" regulation.

## D. Amount of Employer Involvement Required to Sustain an Employee Welfare Benefit Plan

ERISA does not specifically state what constitutes a "plan" within the meaning of the statute. However, the Supreme Court has made clear that ERISA does not govern every grant of an employee benefit. The Court noted that ERISA's focus was "on the administrative integrity of benefit plans—which presumes that some type of administrative activity is taking place." *Fort Halifax Packing Co. v. Coyne,* 482 U.S. 1, 15 (1987), and concluded that the statute applies only "with respect to benefits whose provision by nature requires an ongoing administrative program to meet the employer's obligation." *Id.* at 11. Accordingly, "whether a benefit is regulated by ERISA turns on the nature and extent of the administrative obligations that the benefit imposes on the employer." *Young v. Washington Gas Light Co.,* 206 F.3d 1200, 1203 (D.C. Cir. 2000). In *Young,* after applying the test set forth in *Fort Halifax Packing,* the court concluded that the Washington Gas "Voluntary Separation Pay Window Program" was not a qualified plan under ERISA because the administrative responsibilities imposed upon Washington Gas were "not the kinds of administrative decisions that require ERISA's protection." *Id.* at 1204. "Washington Gas was only required to make the straightforward factual determination of whether the employee had met each of the conditions specified in the Program, such as the requirements that the employee submit an election form and meet certain length-of-service criteria, and then to calculate the amount of the separation payment by multiplying the employee's base pay rate by fifty-two." *Id.* The court acknowledged that the program also required Washington Gas to perform one discretionary act, but concluded that "the exercise of this limited discretionary right . . . did not create a need for an ongoing administration benefit; therefore, it did not bring the Program under ERISA." *Id.*

### E. Treatment of Multiple Employer Trusts and Welfare Agreements

The D.C. Circuit has not had occasion to address the treatment of multiple employer trusts and welfare agreements.

## II. Preemption

### A. Scope of ERISA Preemption

ERISA provides broadly for the preemption of "all State laws insofar as they may now or hereafter relate to any employee benefit plan described in section 1003(a) of this title," 29 U.S.C. § 1144(a), subject to certain exceptions. *See Greater Washington Bd. of Trade v. District of Columbia*, 948 F.2d 1317, 1321–22 (D.C. Cir. 1991) (ERISA establishes as an area of exclusive federal concern the subject of every state law that "relates to" an employee benefit plan governed by ERISA), *aff'd*, 506 U.S. 125 (1992). "State law" in this context includes common law as well as statutory law. *Nat'l Rehab. Hosp. v. Manpower Int'l, Inc.*, 3 F. Supp. 2d 1457, 1459 n.4 (D.D.C. 1998). "[E]ven general common law causes of action, such as breach of contract, which were not specifically intended to apply to benefit plans covered by ERISA, will nonetheless be preempted insofar as they affect ERISA-protected rights." *Bd. of Trs. of the Hotel & Rest. Employees Local 25 v. Madison Hotel, Inc.*, 97 F.3d 1479, 1486–87 (D.C. Cir. 1996). *See also Moore v. Blue Cross & Blue Shield of the Nat'l Capital Area*, 70 F. Supp. 2d 9, 18–19 (D.D.C. 1999); *Psychiatric Inst. of Washington, D.C., Inc. v. Conn. Gen. Life Ins. Co.*, 780 F. Supp. 24, 28–29 (D.D.C. 1992).

An exception is found in the savings clause for "any law of any State which regulates insurance, banking, or securities." 29 U.S.C. § 1144(b)(2)(A). Under *Pilot Life Ins. Co. v. Dedeaux*, 481 U.S. 41 (1987), the Supreme Court described the test by which courts are to determine whether a state law "regulates insurance" within the meaning of the ERISA saving clause. Courts are to take a "common-sense view" of the term "regulates insurance" and look to three factors the court previously identified for determining whether an activity comes within the "business of insurance" as that term is used in the McCarran-Ferguson Act. The three factors are: (1) whether the practice has the effect of transferring or spreading a policyholder's risk; (2) whether the practice is an integral part of the policy relationship between the insurer and the insured; and (3) whether the practice is limited to entities within the insurance industry. *Id.* at 48–49.

In analyzing whether the ERISA saving clause applies, satisfaction of the second and third McCarran-Ferguson Act factors will suffice, at least where these factors weigh heavily in favor of saving the state law, and rote application of the first factor would "work unreasoned mischief" against the broad purpose of the saving clause. *O'Connor v. UNUM Life Ins. Co. of Am.*, 146 F.3d 959 (D.C. Cir. 1998) (saving from ERISA preemption applicability of California's common-law notice-prejudice rule in case involving question of timeliness of proof of disability claim). In *O'Connor*, the parties agreed that the rule of state law in question related to an employee benefit plan covered by ERISA, so the only dispute was whether the savings clause applied. *Id.* at 962. *O'Connor* expressly adopted the reasoning of *Cisneros v. UNUM Life Ins. Co. of Am.*, 134 F.3d 939 (9th Cir. 1998), *id.* at 962, and expressly rejected the argument that a state law regulates insurance within the meaning of the ERISA savings clause only if all three McCarran-Ferguson factors favor that characterization. *Id.* at 963.

The district court acknowledges the "tenuous and peripheral" exception to ERISA preemption: "Certain 'state actions may affect employee benefit plans in too tenuous, remote or peripheral a manner to warrant a finding that the law "relates to" the plan.'" *Nat'l Rehab. Hosp. v. Manpower Int'l, Inc.,* 3 F. Supp. 2d 1457, 1459 (D.D.C. 1998), quoting *Shaw v. Delta Airlines, Inc.,* 463 U.S. 85, 100 (1983). In the absence of guidance from the D.C. Circuit, the district court in the *Manpower* case adopted the reasoning of the Fifth and Eighth Circuits in concluding that ERISA did not preempt a state-law contract action against an ERISA plan administrator and an ERISA claims processor where the action was based on incorrect verifications of coverage for a nonparticipant in the plan. *Id.* at 1459–60, citing *Mem'l Hosp. Sys.,* 904 F.2d 236 (5th Cir. 1990) (two-factor test: preemption only where (1) state-law claims address areas of exclusive federal concern, such as right to receive benefits under terms of an ERISA plan, and (2) claims directly affect relationship among traditional ERISA entities, i.e., employer, plan, fiduciaries, participants, and beneficiaries), and *Home Health, Inc. v. Prudential Ins. Co. of Am.,* 101 F.3d 600 (8th Cir. 1997) (seven-factor test: whether state law (1) contradicts ERISA, (2) affects relations between traditional ERISA entities, (3) impacts the structure of ERISA plans, (4) impacts the administration of ERISA plans, (5) economically impacts ERISA plans, (6) could be preempted consistently with other ERISA provisions and the policy behind ERISA, and (7) is an exercise of traditional state power).

An earlier district court decision distinguished between claims for wrongdoing by ERISA plan personnel or its contractors in the course of administering the plan, which are preempted by ERISA, and claims for wrongdoing in the nature of fraud in the inducement committed not by the plan but by third parties such as the employer and the insurance carrier, which ERISA does not preempt. *Johnson v. Antioch Univ.,* 1992 U.S. Dist. LEXIS 4931 (D.D.C. 1992). In *Johnson,* a former university employee alleged five common-law claims against her former employer and the insurer of the university's long-term disability benefits plan for misrepresenting the coverage available in light of her preexisting medical condition. Guided by the two-factor analysis set out in *Sommer Drug Stores v. Corrigan Enterprises, Inc.,* 793 F.2d 1456, 1467–68 (5th Cir. 1986), the district court held that claims alleging breach of fiduciary duty and breach of contract were sufficiently related to the relevant employee benefit plan to be preempted by ERISA § 514(a), but that claims alleging misrepresentation, gross negligence, and promissory estoppel were not preempted as they were within the exercise of traditional state authority and their resolution would not affect relations among the principal ERISA entities (employer, plan, fiduciaries, and beneficiaries). *Johnson,* at *10–13.

ERISA's preemptive shadow will fall over state-law claims even where the allegations of the complaint fail to state ERISA claims for plan benefits, breach of fiduciary duty, or violation of specific ERISA provisions. A state-law claim will be preempted if it "relates to" an ERISA plan, which may be the case when the claim "is premised on the existence of a plan and when a court must focus its inquiry on the plan in order to resolve the claim" or when the state-law claim "duplicates, supplements, or supplants the ERISA civil enforcement remedy." *Stewart v. Nat'l Educ. Ass'n,* 404 F. Supp. 2d 122, 136–39 (D.D.C. 2005) (dismissing on preemption grounds state-law claims for breach of contract, breach of fiduciary duty, tortious interference with contractual relations, failure of express trust, and unjust enrichment).

An action originally commenced in the D.C. Superior Court and subsequently removed to the district court, alleging discriminatory termination under the D.C. Human Rights Act and common-law tort claims, but which sought damages valued in part based on the loss of ERISA-related health, life, and disability benefits, was not preempted by ERISA. *Schultz v. Nat'l Coalition of Hispanic Mental Health & Human Servs. Orgs.,* 678 F. Supp. 936 (D.D.C. 1988) (remanding to Superior Court). The district court held that ERISA does not preempt claims to recover the value of fringe benefits lost when employment is improperly terminated. In *dicta,* the court observed that ERISA would preempt claims for ERISA benefits per se, or for improper processing of ERISA benefits, or for a termination effected to avoid providing ERISA-covered benefits, or to keep such benefits from vesting, "or for some other reason whose impropriety is directly connected to the ERISA-covered plan." *Id.* at 937–38.

## B. Preemption of Managed-Care and Malpractice Claims

A common-law medical malpractice claim is not preempted by ERISA if the only connection of the claim to an ERISA plan is the defendant physician's employment by a health maintenance organization to which the plaintiff subscribed. *Edelen v. Osterman,* 943 F. Supp. 75 (D.D.C. 1996) (remanding removed action to state court). In the absence of D.C. Circuit guidance, *Edelen* relied on cases from the Third, Tenth, and Seventh Circuits and the district of Maryland. *Edelen* distinguished between claims alleging negligent health care by an HMO physician (not preempted by ERISA) and claims alleging an improper denial of plan benefits by an HMO itself, such as a refusal to precertify a subscriber for surgery or in-patient hospital care (preempted by ERISA).

## C. Other Preemption Issues

Where an initial ERISA-based lawsuit is settled by written agreement, subsequent claims for breach of the settlement agreement are preempted by ERISA, particularly where enforcement of the settlement will require the adjudication of substantive federal-law issues over which federal courts have exclusive jurisdiction under ERISA. *Bd. of Trs. of the Hotel & Rest. Employees Local 25 v. Madison Hotel, Inc.,* 97 F.3d 1479 (D.C. Cir. 1996) (fiduciaries' action for breach of agreement settling earlier claim against hotel-employer to recover delinquent contributions to ERISA employee benefit funds).

ERISA does not divest a Railway Labor Act arbitration panel of its exclusive jurisdiction to interpret collectively bargained agreements. *Air Line Pilots Ass'n, Int'l v. Northwest Airlines, Inc.,* 444 F. Supp. 1138 (D.D.C. 1978).

## III. Exhaustion of Administrative Remedies

### A. Is Exhaustion an Absolute Requirement?

It is well established that, barring exceptional circumstances, plaintiffs seeking a determination of rights under their pension plans pursuant to ERISA must exhaust available remedies under their ERISA-governed plans before they may bring suit in federal court. Because ERISA itself does not specifically require the exhaustion of remedies available under pension plans, courts have applied this requirement as a matter of judicial discretion. Much like the exhaustion doctrine in the context of judicial review of administrative agency action, the exhaustion requirement in the ERISA context serves several important purposes. By preventing premature judicial interference with a pension plan's decision-making processes, the exhaustion requirement enables plan administrators to apply their expertise and exercise their discretion to manage the plan's funds, correct errors, make considered interpretations of plan provisions, and assemble a factual record that will assist the court reviewing the administrators' actions. Indeed, the exhaustion requirement may render subsequent judicial review unnecessary in many ERISA cases because a plan's own remedial procedures will resolve many claims. *Commc'ns Workers of Am. v. Am. Tel. & Tel. Co.*, 40 F.3d 426, 428, 431–32 (D.C. Cir. 1994). *See also Boivin v. US Airways, Inc.*, 2006 U.S. App. LEXIS 10875 *passim* (D.C. Cir. May 2, 2006) (ERISA pension benefits case).

Similarly, administrative remedies must be exhausted before the denial of long-term disability benefits under a welfare benefit plan can be challenged under ERISA. *Hunter v. Metro. Life Ins. Co.*, 251 F. Supp. 2d 107, 110–11 (D.D.C. 2003) (following the rationale expressed in *Communications Workers of America*). In *Hunter*, the claimant filed suit prior to the completion of the plan administrator's review process. *Hunter*'s concise explanation of why administrative remedies had not been exhausted is informative:

> Plaintiff's argument suggests a misunderstanding of both the exhaustion requirement and the communications she received from MetLife. MetLife's notice of the termination of LTD benefits beginning on September 6 was the *initial* determination of the claim. It does not reflect a determination based on a review and, therefore, is not sufficient to exhaust the administrative remedies provided by the Plan. Moreover, the November 7, 2001, letter from MetLife is not a rejection of the claim after completion of a review but an interim notice that LTD benefits could not be reinstated, based on the information submitted, without such a review. The letter confirms that the claim was referred for an "independent review" at that time. Plaintiff was not advised of the results of this review until April 5, 2002. Thus, the review process provided for in the Plan was not exhausted when plaintiff filed suit on January 23, 2002. Further, even to date plaintiff has failed to exhaust administrative remedies. Rather, she pursued an opportunity for further appeal as provided for in MetLife's April 5 letter, and as part of this appeal, she submitted 4,000 additional documents. This appeal process, however,

has not been completed because plaintiff refused to have an [independent medical examination]. This amounts to a failure to exhaust.

*Id.* at 111–12 (emphasis in original; record references omitted).

Exhaustion of administrative remedies is not required for a claim under ERISA § 510 alleging breach of the statute's substantive guarantees (e.g., wrongful termination), but exhaustion is required as to a claim under § 503 for breach of entitlement to plan benefits. *Garvin v. Am. Ass'n of Retired Persons,* 1992 U.S. Dist. LEXIS 2013, at *9–12 (D.D.C. 1992) (holding as to § 510 claims, *dictum* as to § 503 claims).

### B. Exceptions to the Exhaustion Requirement

The general rule in the District of Columbia is that the exhaustion requirement may be waived in only the most exceptional circumstances. The court has recognized a discretionary exception to the exhaustion requirement where resort to administrative remedies would be futile because of the certainty of an adverse decision. The futility exception is quite restricted and has been applied only when resort to administrative remedies is clearly useless. *Commc'ns Workers of Am. v. Am. Tel. & Tel. Co.,* 40 F.3d 426, 432 (D.C. Cir. 1994) (ERISA pension plan); *Hunter v. Metro. Life Ins. Co.,* 251 F. Supp. 2d 107, 111 n.4 (D.D.C. 2003) (ERISA welfare benefit plan).

For cases involving a statutory violation of ERISA, the district court for the District of Columbia found that the exhaustion requirement did not apply. *Coleman v. Pension Benefit Guar. Corp.,* 94 F. Supp. 2d 18, 22–23 (D.D.C. 2000) (relying upon *Zipf v. Am. Tel. & Tel. Co.,* 799 F.2d 889, 891 (3d Cir. 1986), and *Amaro v. Cont'l Can Co.,* 724 F.2d 747, 752 (9th Cir. 1984)); *see also Greer v. Graphic Commc'ns Int'l Union Officers,* 941 F. Supp. 1, 3 (D.D.C. 1996) (same); *Garvin v. Am. Ass'n of Retired Persons,* 1992 WL 693382, at *3–4 (D.D.C. 1992) (same); *Rauh v. Coyne,* 744 F. Supp. 1186, 1191–92 (D.D.C. 1990) (same). The court reached this decision based on the lack of indication in ERISA's statutory language and the legislative history that Congress intended the exhaustion requirement to apply to these claims. *See Coleman,* 94 F. Supp. 2d at 22 n.5.

Exhaustion is not required when efforts to obtain information on administrative appeals from the plan administrator prove fruitless. *Jeffries v. Greater Se. Cmty. Hosp. Group Term Life Ins. Plan,* 2005 U.S. Dist. LEXIS 38824, at *9–10 (D.D.C. Dec. 30, 2005) ("plaintiffs had no reason to believe that further appeals to administrative remedies would be fruitful").

### C. Consequences of Failure to Exhaust

When a disability claimant commences an ERISA-based action without giving the insurer a chance to complete its review of a claim denial, the claimant cannot establish either that she was denied a fair opportunity for review of the claim or that the insurer's processing of the claim denial prejudiced her. *Heller v. Fortis Benefits Ins. Co.,* 142 F.3d 487, 491 (D.C. Cir. 1998) (claimant filed ERISA-based action two days after insurer offered, in writing and by telephone, to treat documents sent by claimant in response to the insurer's claim denial as an appeal of insurer's benefits determination).

A claim for denial of long-term disability benefits under a welfare benefit plan will be dismissed without prejudice in order to allow the plaintiff to exhaust the available administrative remedies, unless the opportunity for pursuing administrative remedies has been foreclosed, making dismissal with prejudice appropriate. *Hunter v. Metro. Life Ins. Co.*, 251 F. Supp. 2d 107, 112 n.10 (D.D.C. 2003).

### D. Minimum Number of Levels of Administrative Review

No D.C. Circuit case has expressly decided how many levels of administrative review a claimant may be required to exhaust.

### E. Can a Defendant Waive a Failure-to-Exhaust Defense?

In the ERISA context, the D.C. Circuit has not addressed this issue. However, in other contexts, the D.C. Circuit has found that a defendant can waive a failure-to-exhaust defense. *See, e.g., Bowden v. U.S.*, 106 F.3d 433, 438–39 (D.C. Cir. 1997).

## IV. Standard of Review

### A. Plan Language

The standard of review turns on whether the ERISA benefit plan confers discretionary authority on the plan fiduciary. "[A] denial of benefits challenged under § 1132(a)(1)(B) is to be reviewed under a de novo standard unless the benefit plan gives the administrator or fiduciary discretionary authority to determine eligibility for benefits or to construe the terms of the plan." *Firestone Tire & Rubber Co. v. Bruch*, 489 U.S. 101, 111, 115 (1989). To determine whether an ERISA benefit plan confers discretion, the court first reviews the plan documents themselves: "'It . . . need only appear on the face of the plan documents that the fiduciary has been given [the] power to construe disputed or doubtful terms—or to resolve disputes over benefits eligibility—in which case the trustee's interpretation will not be disturbed if reasonable.'" *Block v. Pitney Bowes, Inc.*, 952 F.2d 1450, 1453–54 (D.C. Cir. 1992), quoting *De Nobel v. Vitro Corp.*, 885 F.2d 1180, 1187 (4th Cir. 1989) (internal quotations omitted). The district court in *Moore v. Blue Cross & Blue Shield of the Nat'l Capital Area* followed *Block*:

> The D.C. Circuit has declared that there are no special words of art required to invoke the deferential standard of review; rather, the Court should focus on the character of the authority exercised by the administrator under the plan. It need only appear on the face of the plan documents that the fiduciary has been given the power to construe disputed or ambiguous terms or to resolve disputes over benefits eligibility. Therefore, language giving the administrator power "to interpret or construe" the plan or "to make final and binding" decisions, triggers deferential review.

*Moore v. Blue Cross & Blue Shield of the Nat'l Capital Area*, 70 F. Supp. 2d 9, 20 (D.D.C. 1999), citing *Block*, 952 F.2d at 1452–54.

The mere authority to deny a claim does not by itself confer discretion to determine eligibility for benefits. *Mobley v. Cont'l Cas. Co.*, 383 F. Supp. 2d 80, 85

(D.D.C. 2005), *reconsideration denied,* 405 F. Supp. 2d 42 (D.D.C. 2005). Use of the word "discretion" will not by itself result in deferential review, but will do so if it truly reflects the character of the authority granted to the plan administrator. In *Buford v. Unum Life Insurance Co. of America,* 290 F. Supp. 2d 92 (D.D.C. 2003), the employee welfare benefit plan stated: "When making a benefit determination under the policy, UNUM has discretionary authority to determine [the insured's] eligibility for benefits and to interpret the terms and provisions of the policy." The district court observed that "[i]n determining whether a plan grants discretionary authority to the administrator or fiduciary, . . . a reviewing court must focus on more than whether the word 'discretion' is invoked in the plan language; instead, 'what counts . . . is the character of the authority exercised by the administrators under the plan.'" *Id.* at 97, quoting *Block,* 952 F.2d at 1453–54.

A benefits plan requiring the insured to "submit proof of disability" does not confer discretion on the plan administrator to determine eligibility for benefits within the meaning of *Firestone,* and the insurer's classification of a disability (bipolar disorder) as mental rather than physical is therefore subject to de novo review. On such review, the parties are free to supplement the existing record by, among other things, submitting current medical evidence regarding bipolar disorder. *Fitts v. Fed. Nat'l Mortgage Ass'n,* 236 F.3d 1, 4–6 (D.C. Cir. 2001) (distinguishing, with evident disfavor, case upholding deferential review based on plan language requiring insured to submit "satisfactory" proof of eligibility for benefits), *rev'g* 77 F. Supp. 2d 9 (D.D.C. 1999).

The *Fitts* court rejected the disability insurer's argument that the insurance policy, which required submission of proof of disability, necessarily gave the insurer discretion because it must evaluate the legitimacy of the proof submitted. Virtually all insurance policies require proof of eligibility for benefits, and if this requirement sufficed to confer discretion, then, reasoned the court, *Firestone*'s exception would swallow its rule and render the standard of review deferential in almost every case. *Id.* at 5.

The *Fitts* court also rejected the insurer's alternative argument that the benefits plan in question technically designated Fannie Mae's Benefit Plans Committee as the plan administrator, which was to "be afforded the maximum deference allowed by law" in all of its "decisions, interpretations [and] determinations," and that the Committee could delegate its authority to outside consultants and companies, including matters involving discretion. The court found no evidence that the Committee had delegated any discretionary authority to the insurer. Furthermore, no decision or determination by Fannie Mae was in issue, and the parties agreed that Fannie Mae had exercised no discretion with regard to the eligibility determination. *Id.* at 5–6.

The *Fitts* court noted that "the de novo standard might theoretically permit this court [i.e., the D.C. Circuit] to perform the necessary review," but declined to do so, pointing to the intensely factual nature of the underlying classification dispute, and remanded the case to the district court. *Id.* at 6 (noting fact issues on whether existing record establishes that bipolar disorder is physical, whether current medical research supports claimant, whether there is a current medical consensus on nature of bipolar disorder, and whether certain of claimant's evidence is admissible). In a case decided after *Fitts,* the district court determined that the result would be the same under either standard of review and therefore declined to decide whether a benefit plan requiring the claimant to submit "due proof" of loss was sufficient to invoke deferential review under the arbitrary and capricious standard. *Craighill v. Cont'l Cas. Co.,* 2003 U.S. Dist. LEXIS 19222, at *9–11 (D.D.C. 2003).

Plan language requiring "due written proof of loss" is more problematical. The requirement of some proof of eligibility does not by itself confer discretion, but the requirement of "due" proof of loss may leave an ambiguity on the face of the policy about whether the plan intended to confer discretion on the administrator, which ambiguity will be resolved against the plan administrator. *Mobley v. Cont'l Cas. Co.,* 383 F. Supp. 2d 80, 85–88 (D.D.C. 2005) (applying de novo review and observing that D.C. Circuit has not considered whether the words "due written proof" are alone sufficient to confer discretion and that results in other circuits are mixed), *reconsideration denied,* 405 F. Supp. 2d 42 (D.D.C. 2005).

## B. What Standard of Review Applies?

"Courts clearly have the authority to construe the language of the contract de novo where the denial of benefits does not involve any discretionary authority on the part of the plan administrator. However, when a fiduciary exercises discretionary powers to deny benefits or construe the terms of a plan, a deferential standard of review must be employed." *Moore v. Blue Cross & Blue Shield of the Nat'l Capital Area,* 70 F. Supp. 2d 9, 20 (D.D.C. 1999), citing *Firestone,* 489 U.S. at 111, 115, and *Germany v. Operating Eng'rs Trust Fund of Washington, D.C.,* 789 F. Supp. 1165, 1167 (D.D.C. 1992). Where the deferential standard applies, a plan administrator's decision is not an abuse of discretion if it is reasonable:

> When applied to the fiduciary responsibilities of ERISA trustees, [the deferential] standard requires a choice between reasonable alternatives, or a reasonable interpretation of the plan. . . . However, it is for the trustees, not the courts, to chose [*sic*] between two reasonable alternatives. . . . The courts may substitute their judgment for that of the trustee only if the trustee's actions are not grounded on any reasonable basis.

*Block,* 952 F.2d at 1454 (citations and internal quotations omitted).

On deferential review, "[a] decision will be found to be reasonable if it is the result of a deliberate, principled reasoning process and if it is supported by substantial evidence. . . . Substantial evidence means more than a scintilla but less than a preponderance. . . . In taking into account the potential conflict of interest in this case, the Court will also consider in its review whether [the insurer's] decision strayed outside the bounds of reasonableness to become an abuse of discretion." *Buford v. Unum Life Ins. Co. of Am.,* 290 F. Supp. 2d 92, 99–100 (D.D.C. 2003) (citations and internal quotation marks omitted).

## C. Effect of Conflict of Interest or Procedural Irregularity

The D.C. Circuit has yet to address how to apply the standard of review when there is a potential or actual conflict of interest. The district court, however, has observed that the mere presence of a conflict of interest does not automatically activate de novo review, and that no court has shown a willingness to reverse a plan administrator's decision without some evidence that self-interested behavior affected the administrator's decision. In obeisance to *Firestone,* the district court, while recognizing the presence of a potential conflict of interest, will review the insurer's decision for abuse of discretion, bearing in mind any inconsistency the plaintiff points out as a factor in determining whether there was an abuse of discretion. *Buford v. Unum Life Ins. Co. of Am.,* 290 F. Supp. 2d 92, 98 (D.D.C. 2003); *Hamilton v. AIG Life Ins. Co.,* 182 F. Supp. 2d 39, 44 & n.3 (D.D.C. 2002).

The district court has noted three different approaches among the circuit courts in dealing with the presence of a conflict of interest. *Hamilton,* 182 F. Supp. 2d at 43 n.3 (noting "sliding scale," "presumptively void," and refusal to apply any form of heightened review in absence of evidence of actual conflict of interest as three approaches). In declining to alter the level of deference given to the insurance company's eligibility determination, the *Hamilton* court found unconvincing the plaintiffs' two arguments for dramatically decreasing the deference shown to the insurer in determining whether it abused its discretion. *Id.* at 46, citing and quoting *Fitts,* 77 F. Supp. 2d at 20 n.6 ("The potential conflict of interest, however, does not call for abrogation of the arbitrary and capricious standard, where, as here, the challenged decision would have been reasonable if made by a decision maker with no conflict of interest.").

One argument made in *Hamilton* for decreasing the level of deference was that the insurer consistently denied claims of the sort in question (autoerotic asphyxiation), demonstrating that the insurer was self-interestedly committed to denying such claims regardless of their merits. This argument was unconvincing because the consistent denial of autoerotic asphyxiation claims was based on the insurer's belief that the policy-based exception from coverage for intentionally self-inflicted injury barred payment of autoerotic asphyxiation claims. The district court observed that "[i]f language is added so as to exclude certain claims, then a consistent policy of denial based on that contract language is properly characterized as adherence to the contracts' terms rather than as self-dealing behavior." *Id.* at 44–45, citing *Brown v. Blue Cross & Blue Shield of Ala.,* 898 F.2d 1556, 1568 (11th Cir. 1990) (noting that "uniformity of construction" and the "internal consistency of a plan under the fiduciary's interpretation" are evidence that the plan administrator's decision was not an abuse of discretion). Other evidence that the insurer's decision was not an abuse of discretion was that the decision was made after twice obtaining an outside legal opinion on the deniability of plaintiffs' claim and after obtaining the opinion of an independent forensic expert order to evaluate the validity of the contentions of the plaintiffs' expert. *Id.* at 45, citing *Hightsue v. AIG Life Ins. Co.,* 135 F.3d 1144, 1148 (7th Cir. 1998) (finding that reliance on outside experts is evidence of good-faith behavior by a conflicted insurance company).

The *Hamilton* plaintiffs' second argument was that the insurer's internal reversal of its initial determination to pay the claim demonstrated that the superior officer, who made the reversal, wanted to deny the claim regardless of its merits. After observing that an insurer's inconsistent treatment of the same facts suggests a commitment to denying benefits despite facts indicating benefits should be granted, the district court found that the insurer did not consider the same set of facts in an inconsistent fashion, but rather considered two different sets of facts at two different times. *Id.* at 45 ("It is not self-dealing behavior for an insurance company to change its mind on the basis of new information."). The court also recognized that "there is a significant difference between an internal disagreement among employees over the merits of a claim prior to any final claims decision . . . and an insurance company's decision to reverse its previous final decision to award benefits." *Id.* n.5.

A conflict of interest can be implied from the circumstances. In *Hamilton v. AIG Life Ins. Co.,* 182 F. Supp. 2d 39, 43 n.3 (D.D.C. 2002), the district court followed *Fitts v. Fed. Nat'l Mortgage Ass'n,* 77 F. Supp. 2d 9, 20 (D.D.C. 1999), *rev'd on other grounds,* 236 F.3d 1 (D.C. Cir. 2001), in observing that administrators of insurance plans operate under a conflict between their role as fiduciaries, which requires them to act in the best interests of their policyholders, and their status as insurance companies paying benefits out of their own pockets, which gives them an incentive to deny policyholder claims. 182 F. Supp. 2d at 43–44. *See also Moore v. Blue Cross & Blue Shield of the Nat'l Capital Area,* 70 F. Supp. 2d 9, 20 n.5 (D.D.C. 1999) (observing that the conflict of interest factor must be weighed "where . . . the Plan administers itself . . . by dispensing benefits it must also pay for.").

### D. Other Factors Affecting Standard of Review

In applying the deferential standard of review, courts in the D.C. Circuit follow the four-factor test introduced in *Donovan v. Carlough,* 576 F. Supp. 245, 249 (D.D.C. 1983), *aff'd,* 753 F.2d 166 (D.C. Cir. 1985); *see also Germany v. Operating Eng'rs Trust Fund of Washington, D.C.,* 789 F. Supp. 1165, 1167–68 (D.D.C. 1992) (applying the four *Carlough* factors); *Ret. & Sec. Program for Employees of Nat'l Rural Coop. Ass'n. v. Oglethorpe Power,* 712 F. Supp. 223, 227 (D.D.C. 1989) (finding the *Carlough* factors consistent with the Supreme Court's holding in *Bruch*); *Foltz v. U.S. News & World Report,* 663 F. Supp. 1494, 1514 (D.D.C. 1987) (applying the four *Carlough* factors). The four *Carlough* factors are (1) whether the plan administrator's interpretation is contrary to the language of the plan; (2) whether the plan administrator's interpretation is consistent with the plan's purposes; (3) whether the interpretation is consistent with the specific purpose of determining eligibility for the benefit in question; and (4) whether the interpretation is consistent with prior interpretations by the plan administrator and whether the claimant had notice of the plan administrator's interpretation. The application of these factors is not formulaic. The weight given to each will vary according to the context of the case. *Costantino v. Washington Post Multi-Option Benefits Plan,* 404 F. Supp. 2d 31, 42 (D.D.C. 2005).

If deferential review is allowed because a plan sponsor has discretionary authority to determine eligibility for benefits or to construe the terms of the plan, then the same standard of review will apply if the plan clearly allows the plan sponsor to delegate its discretionary authority to a third-party plan administrator and there is evidence that such a delegation has actually been made. *Costantino v. Washington Post Multi-Option Benefits Plan,* 404 F. Supp. 2d 31, 38–41 (D.D.C. 2005).

Any deference owed to discretionary decisions of plan officials does not extend to decisions that discriminate among plan participants in violation of the plain terms of the plan. *Wagener v. SBS Pension Benefit Plan—Nonbargained Program,* 407 F.3d 395, 396, 402–03 (D.C. Cir. 2005) ("An interpretation of the Plan that rests on impermissible discrimination is clearly unreasonable and, therefore, it fails whether we apply *de novo* review or a deferential standard of review.").

## V. Rules of Plan Interpretation

*See generally Psychiatric Inst. of Washington, D.C. v. Conn. Gen. Life Ins. Co.,* 780 F. Supp. 24 (D.D.C. 1992) (plan administrator's interpretation of ambiguous plan provision).

### A. Application of Federal Common Law

After a bench trial, the district court made the following observations in upholding a claim of federal common-law estoppel against an ERISA health plan administrator: "ERISA, of course, preempts plaintiffs' state-law promissory estoppel claim, but preemption does not mean that all common law concepts are automatically inapplicable in an ERISA context. To the contrary, Congress expected that a federal common law of rights and obligations under ERISA-regulated plans would develop. . . . Federal courts have the authority to apply common law principles in order to deal with rights and obligations under ERISA that are not governed by the act itself. . . . Although the [plaintiffs'] state-law promissory estoppel claim as such may be preempted by ERISA, they have proved a state of facts working an estoppel as a matter of federal common law governing actions preempted but not specifically addressed by ERISA." *Moore v. Blue Cross & Blue Shield of the Nat'l Capital Area,* 70 F. Supp. 2d 9, 26–27 (D.D.C. 1999) (citations and internal quotations omitted).

The *Moore* court also noted that once it is determined that the state-law claims are preempted, the court may recharacterize the state-law claims as ones arising under ERISA. *Id.* at 27 n.15, citing *Psychiatric Inst. of Washington, D.C., Inc.,* 780 F. Supp. at 31; *Murphy v. Wal-Mart,* 928 F. Supp. 700, 707 (E.D. Tex. 1996). The court also noted that a majority of federal circuits that have addressed the issue have approved, at least under certain circumstances, the use of estoppel in ERISA cases. *Id.* at 27 n.16.

The district court identified five elements of an equitable estoppel claim: (1) the party to be estopped misrepresented material facts; (2) the party to be estopped had actual or constructive knowledge of the true facts; (3) the party to be estopped intended that the misrepresentation be acted upon or had reason to believe that the party asserting estoppel would rely on it; (4) the party asserting the estoppel did not know, nor should have known, the true facts; and (5) the party asserting the estoppel reasonably and detrimentally relied on the misrepresentation. *Id.* at 31. Commenting on the scope of an ERISA fiduciary's responsibility to disclose material information to beneficiaries, the district court observed: "Refraining from imparting misinformation is only part of the fiduciary's duty. Once [the plaintiff] presented his predicament, [the fiduciary] was required to do more than simply not misinform, [it] also had an affirmative obligation to inform—to provide complete and correct material information on [plaintiff's] status and options." *Id.* at 32, quoting *Eddy v. Colonial Life Ins. Co. of Am.,* 919 F.2d 747, 751 (D.C. Cir. 1990).

The *Moore* court's rationale for recognizing a federal common-law action for estoppel under ERISA was that it prevents both the detriment to the insured who relied on the misleading representation and the unjust enrichment of the party to be estopped. The claim also effectuates Congress's intent to promote the interest of employees and their beneficiaries in employee benefit plans. *Id.* at 27. The court observed that any distinction between the doctrines of promissory estoppel and equitable estoppel "is not significant for purposes of whether the estoppel principles are appropriately part of the federal common law applicable to ERISA actions." *Id.* at 27 n.17. While estoppel cannot be used to enlarge or extend the coverage specified in an ERISA plan, estoppel is appropriate when the provisions of the plan are ambiguous and representations are made involving an oral interpretation of the ambiguous provisions. When these conditions are met, there is no conflict with the requirement that ERISA benefit plans be maintained pursuant to a written instrument (*see* 29 U.S.C. § 1102(a)(1)), as an oral interpretation of an ambiguous plan provision does not modify or extend coverage that is not otherwise conferred by the written instrument. *Moore,* 70 F. Supp. 2d at 27 nn.17 & 18.

In the district court's view, a claim alleging the failure of an express trust or a resulting trust has no support in the federal common law of ERISA. The court reasoned that although the source of ERISA's fiduciary rules is the common law, "Congress, when it enacted ERISA, made even more exacting requirements than those found in the common law of trusts relating to employee benefit trust funds." *Stewart v. Nat'l Educ. Ass'n,* 404 F. Supp. 2d 122, 134–35 & n.7 (D.D.C. 2005).

## B. Application of *Contra Proferentem*

In the ERISA context, the doctrine of *contra proferentem,* which is that ambiguous terms in an insurance contract will ordinarily be construed against the insurer, applies. *See Craighill v. Cont'l Cas. Co.,* 2003 U.S. Dist. LEXIS 19222, n.5 (D.C. 2003). The doctrine was recently applied in a long-running case about whether bipolar disorder falls within a disability plan's two-year limitation of benefits for "mental illness." *Fitts v. Unum Life Ins. Co. of Am.,* 2006 U.S. Dist. LEXIS 9235 (D.D.C. Feb. 23, 2006). Significantly, while the D.C. Circuit has not yet determined whether *contra proferentem* applies in the ERISA context, the district embraced its applicability based on an earlier district court case and "the vast majority of circuit courts that have found the doctrine applicable in ERISA cases" as a matter of federal common law. *Id.* at *10 n.5 (citing *Germany v. Operating Eng'rs Trust Fund,* 789 F. Supp. 1165, 1169–70 (D.D.C. 1992), and cases from the 1st, 2d, 3d, 4th, 5th, 7th, 8th, 9th, and 11th Circuits)). The *Fitts* court evaluated the conflicting definitions of "mental illness" offered by the parties as well as the three-way split among the courts for defining the term (symptom-based analysis, cause-based analysis, and treatment-based analysis) and held that the term is ambiguous because of the lack of consensus and the prevalence of different definitions. *Id.* at *12–25. Applying the rule of *contra proferentem* required construing the ambiguous term "strictly against [the insurer] and in a manner that is reasonable and most favorable to [the claimant]. *Id.* at 24.

## C. Deference Afforded to an Administrator's Interpretation of a Plan

In the scheme of ERISA, a benefit plan that confers discretionary authority on the plan fiduciary with regard to eligibility benefits "may only have its decisions judicially reviewed under the arbitrary and capricious standard." *Sampson v. Citibank*, 53 F. Supp. 2d 13, 16 (D.D.C. 1999). Review under the arbitrary and capricious standard is "deferential and limited to deciding whether it was reasonable." *Id.* at 16. This means that the "Court must not overturn a decision found to be reasonable, even if an alternative decision could have been considered reasonable." *Id.* at 16–17 (citing *Block,* 952 F.2d at 1452).

## D. Other Rules of Plan or Contract Interpretation

ERISA's requirement that terms in benefits plans "be written in a manner calculated to be understood by the average plan participant," 29 U.S.C. § 1022(a)(1), means that those terms "should be given the meaning normally attributed to them by a person of average intelligence and experience." *Hamilton v. AIG Life Ins. Co.,* 182 F. Supp. 2d 39, 49 (D.D.C. 2002) (evaluating whether partial strangulation accompanying autoerotic asphyxiation is an "injury"). While an expert's definition of a contract term is not controlling, the court can rely on expert opinion as a way of determining a term's ordinary meaning. *Fitts v. Unum Life Ins. Co. of Am.,* 2006 U.S. Dist. LEXIS 9235, at *9 (D.D.C. Feb. 23, 2006) (citing *Kunin v. Benefit Trust Life Ins. Co.,* 910 F.2d 534, 536 (9th Cir. 1990)).

When interpreting an employee benefit plan, the summary plan description should be considered part of the plan documents. *See Brubaker v. Metro. Life Ins. Co.,* 2005 U.S. Dist. LEXIS 39816, at *7 (D.D.C. Sept. 26, 2005); *Guyther v. DOL Fed. Credit Union,* 193 F. Supp. 2d 127, 130 (D.D.C. 2002) (noting that summary plan descriptions "often control over conflicting language in plan agreements anyway because (it is thought) employees actually read the summaries."). Where a discrepancy arises between the summary plan description and the plan, the language of the summary plan description governs in ERISA disputes. *See Brubaker,* at *7–8; *Whiteman v. Graphic Commc'ns Int'l Union Supplemental Ret. & Disability Fund,* 871 F. Supp. 465, 466–67 (D.D.C. 1994) (citing cases from the 4th, 5th, 6th, and 11th Circuits).

Unless a plaintiff shows that an employer controls the administration of an ERISA plan or exercises some discretion or plays some role in the determination of the plaintiff's claim, that employer is not a proper party to a suit arising under ERISA. *Hunter v. Metro. Life Ins. Co.,* 251 F. Supp. 2d 107, 112–13 (D.D.C. 2003); *Craighill v. Cont'l Cas. Co.,* 2003 U.S. Dist. LEXIS 19222, at *8–9 (D.D.C. 2003).

Employers and plan sponsors do not act in a fiduciary capacity when they modify, adopt, or amend plans. *Hartline v. Sheet Metal Workers' Nat'l Pension Fund,* 286

F.3d 598 (D.C. Cir. 2002) (*per curiam*) (changes to plan affected determination of benefits); *Systems Council EM-3, Int'l Bhd. of Elec. Workers, AFL-CIO v. AT&T Corp.,* 159 F.3d 1376, 1379–80 (D.C. Cir. 1998) (changes split pension and welfare plans into two and reallocated assets between plans).

# VI. Discovery

## A. Limitations on Discovery

Entitlement to discovery depends directly on the standard of review. At least in cases where the deferential standard applies, the rule is clear: no discovery is permissible where the discovery probes into the plan administrator's factual determinations. *Hunter v. Metro. Life Ins. Co.,* 2002 U.S. Dist. LEXIS 26615 (D.D.C. 2002) (parties agreed deferential standard applied). In *Hunter,* the claimant sought discovery in the form of depositions, production of documents, and answers to interrogatories, all designed to determine the basis for the insurer's denial of benefits. *Id.* at * 2. Noting that the D.C. Circuit has not addressed the issue, the district court followed the rationale of *Perlman v. Swiss Bank Corp. Comprehensive Disability Protection Plan,* 195 F.3d 975, 981–82 (7th Cir. 1999), to conclude that "where review is limited to the arbitrary and capricious standard, the discovery that plaintiff seeks here is not justified." 2002 U.S. Dist. LEXIS 26615, at *4. In the absence of any showing that the discovery sought by the claimant related to the administrator's interpretation of the policy (as opposed to the administrator's factual determinations), the district court did not have occasion to consider whether to follow the distinction to this effect made in *Southern Farm Bureau Life Insurance Co. v. Moore,* 993 F.2d 98 (5th Cir. 1993), but appeared to disfavor it.

The rule is much less clear where review is de novo, and the D.C. Circuit has not yet had occasion to comment on the question. Reluctantly venturing a generalization, the district court in *Fitts v. Federal National Mortgage Association,* 204 F.R.D. 1, 3 (D.D.C. 2001), observed that courts have not allowed the same kind of discovery in ERISA cases as in non-ERISA cases, and that in ERISA cases "courts have searched for a close connection between the information sought and the issues presented."

In *Fitts,* objections to an ERISA claimant's discovery requests were sustained on relevancy and burdensomeness grounds. The claimant sought three broad categories of discovery from her former employer (Fannie Mae) and from the ERISA plan administrator (an insurance company): (1) documents explaining how they derived the physical versus nonphysical disorder classification on which they relied in denying her claim for long-term disability benefits; (2) documents explaining how they applied the physical/nonphysical distinction in handling other claims for long-term disability benefits; and (3) documents from legal proceedings involving the physical/nonphysical distinction. *Id.* at 2. The district court aptly summarized its task as follows: "I must weigh the possibility that a damaging admission by [the insurance company] is contained in their files is only theoretical and that it may have precious little probative force, even if found, against the cost and expense involved in searching for it. Ultimately, I must also allow for the emerging consensus among the courts that discovery in ERISA cases should be less than what is ordinarily required." *Id.* at 5.

As to relevancy, the discovery demands were objectionable even under the standard of Rule 26(a) of the Federal Rules of Civil Procedure. The *Fitts* court reasoned that a decision by the insurer to pay benefits on a nonphysical disorder claim in another case "casts no light whatsoever on the scientific validity of [the insurance company's conclusion in the present case] that plaintiff's bipolar disorder fits within the exclusion of the Fannie Mae policy." *Id.* at 4. Likewise, the opinion of a claimant's expert witness in another case "has absolutely nothing to do with the scientific validity of the specific conclusion reached by [the insurance company's] physicians in this case" that bipolar disorder is a mental illness. *Id.* The district court acknowledged that a contrary conclusion by the same insurer in another case about whether bipolar disorder is a mental illness within the policy exclusion might possibly be relevant and would be admissible as a nonhearsay admission by a party opponent. But such a statement was likely to have little probative value and could therefore be excluded from evidence under Rule 403 of the Federal Rules of Evidence, and could also be excluded as collateral if establishing its probative value required (as was likely) a detailed examination of its source in the other case. *Id.*

As to burdensomeness, the court was satisfied by the insurance company's showing that the identification of responsive documents would require the manual examination of nearly 60,000 active long-term disability policies, up to 86,000 open long-term disability claim files, and 2,400 lawsuit files, many of which were in the physical possession of the insurance company's outside counsel. *Id.* at 3, 5. The theoretical possibility that there might be a probative and damaging admission somewhere in this vast quantity of documents did not justify the expense and time it would take to find it. *Id.* at 5 ("That there is a needle in a haystack does not make searching the haystack worthwhile.").

Like several other courts, the District Court for the District of Columbia has held that an attorney advising a plan fiduciary about matters of plan administration represents the trust's beneficiaries, not the fiduciary personally. *Washington-Baltimore Newspaper Guild, Local 35 v. Washington Star Co.,* 543 F. Supp. 906 (D.D.C. 1982). Thus, communications regarding plan fiduciaries and counsel regarding plan administration are discoverable in litigation brought by participants or beneficiaries. *Id.* at 909. However, when an employer who is also a plan fiduciary seeks counsel solely in its capacity as employer, such communications are protected. *Everett v. USAir Group, Inc.,* 165 F.R.D. 1 (D.D.C. 1995) (when an employer seeks legal counsel solely in its role as employer regarding issues other than plan administration, the employer is the client and may assert attorney-client privilege).

## B. Discovery and Conflict of Interest

Discovery (by way of document requests, interrogatories, requests for admissions, and a Rule 30(b)(6) deposition) into the internal practices of the insurance company administrator of an ERISA employee benefit plan is available to prove a conflict of interest in a case involving denial of long-term disability benefits. *Pulliam v. Cont'l Cas. Co.,* 2003 U.S. Dist. LEXIS 10010 (D.D.C. 2003). Based on cases from the Third, Eighth, and Ninth Circuits and the district of Oregon, discovery was deemed relevant to the issue of the appropriate standard of review. The district court's rulings were shaped by two Ninth Circuit authorities holding that a plan administrator's failure to follow its internal procedures for denying benefit claims and the existence of procedural irregularities are evidence of a conflict of interest. *Id.* at *8 (citing *Hensley v. Northwest Permanente Ret. Plan & Trust*, 258 F.3d 986, 996 (9th Cir. 2001); *Friedrich v. Intel Corp.*, 181 F.3d 1105, 1110 (9th Cir. 1999)).

The particular relevancy rulings in *Pulliam* are worth noting. Documents containing information about incentive-type compensation (including bonuses) for which claim reviewers and supervisors were eligible beginning from the month the claimant suffered a disabling stroke were deemed relevant to the conflict of interest issue; but information about non-incentive-type compensation was deemed not relevant. Premium invoices and premium adjustment reports identifying the plan participants were deemed relevant; bills and premium payments for the plan were not. Documents relating to policies and procedures for handling claims and for evaluating oral statements were deemed relevant. An interrogatory seeking the identity and role of all individuals involved in the appeal of the claim denial was deemed relevant. So were interrogatories seeking facts supporting the insurer's contention that the plaintiff was not employed by the employer or covered under the policy on the relevant date. So were interrogatories seeking information underlying the insurer's contention that the claimant was not disabled. Also relevant was Rule 30(b)(6) deposition testimony regarding all persons involved in processing the plaintiff's claim (including members of the appeals committee) and their respective roles and functions, their education and training in processing long-term disability insurance claims, their incentive-based financial compensation, and the criteria for obtaining each type of incentive-based compensation (particularly any criteria related to claims savings, i.e., denials, terminations, or reductions in payout). Their respective caseloads and non-incentive-based compensation were deemed not relevant. *Id.* at *11–23.

## VII. Evidence

### A. Scope of Evidence under Standards of Review

"Courts review ERISA-plan benefit decisions on the evidence presented to the plan administrators, not on a record later made in another forum." *Heller v. Fortis Benefits Ins. Co.*, 142 F.3d 487, 493 (D.C. Cir. 1998), quoting *Block v. Pitney-Bowes, Inc.*, 952 F.2d 1450, 1455 (D.C. Cir. 1992). On de novo review, a relevant inquiry is whether resolution is appropriate by summary judgment under Federal Rule of Civil Procedure 56, which turns on whether there is a genuine issue as to any material fact, or by the making of findings of fact and conclusions of law under Federal Rule of Civil Procedure 52. *See Mobley v. Cont'l Cas. Co.*, 383 F. Supp. 2d 80, 88–89 (D.D.C. 2005), *reconsideration denied*, 405 F. Supp. 2d 42 (D.D.C. 2005). Courts will also consider whether the record presented is "an accurate compilation of what was before [the plan administrator] at the time of the decision under review." *Id.* at 88 n.4. In this connection, *Mobley* cited numerous issues relating to the content and comprehensibility of the administrative record. *Id.* at 88 & n.4 (no "formal administrative record" lodged with the court; no proffer that exhibits attached to motion for summary judgment comprised entirely of evidence before plan administrator at time of decision on claim for benefits under review; some documents illegible; some documents referred to conversations, raising question whether administrator considered conversations as well as memoranda thereof).

The D.C. Circuit has not had occasion to comment on whether evidence on deferential review is limited to the administrative record. On de novo review in a case involving a dispute over the proper classification of bipolar disorder (mental illness versus physical disability), the parties were free to supplement the existing record by, among other things, submitting current medical evidence regarding bipolar disorder. *Fitts v. Fed. Nat'l Mortgage Ass'n,* 236 F.3d 1, 6 (D.C. Cir. 2001). On remand, the district court recognized a split among the circuits as to the scope of de novo review on the merits of ERISA cases. *Fitts v. Fed. Nat'l Mortgage Ass'n,* 204 F.R.D. 1, 3 n.2 (D.D.C. 2001) (denying motion to compel discovery citing *Luby v. Teamsters Health, Welfare & Pension Funds,* 944 F.2d 1176, 1183–85 (3d Cir. 1991) (court free to limit de novo review to record or to receive further evidence to enable full exercise of informed and independent judgment); *Miller v. Metro. Life Ins. Co.,* 925 F.2d 979 (6th Cir. 1991) (evidence not presented to plan administrator not to be considered on de novo review); *Donatelli v. Home Ins. Co.,* 992 F.2d 763, 765 (8th Cir. 1993) (on de novo review, evidence not presented to plan administrator can be introduced on good cause shown); and *Quesinberry v. Life Ins. Co. of N. Am.,* 987 F.2d 1017, 1025 (4th Cir. 1993) (de novo standard allows examination of evidence not before administrator where necessary for adequate review by district court)).

### B. Evidentiary Value of Social Security Determinations

*Block v. Pitney Bowes, Inc.,* 952 F.2d 1450 (1992), is the only D.C. Circuit case to address the evidentiary value of Social Security determinations. In *Block,* the court afforded no weight to the Social Security Administration's benefit award. The court reasoned that because the Social Security award relied at least in part on medical information never submitted to the plan committee, the Social Security determination should be afforded no weight because "courts review ERISA-plan benefit decisions on the evidence presented to the plan administrators, not on the record later made in another forum." *Id.* at 1455.

### C. Other Evidence Issues

#### 1. Denial Notices

The D.C. Circuit has adopted the "substantial compliance" test to determine whether denial notices comply with ERISA § 1133 and the corresponding DOL regulation. Technical noncompliance will be excused as long as the notice substantially complies with the statute and regulation. In assessing whether a notice substantially complies, the circuit court considers not just the notice itself, but all communications between the insurer and the claimant, making the substantial compliance determination on a case-by-case basis and assessing the information provided by the insurer in the context of the beneficiary's claim. *White v. Aetna Life Ins. Co.,* 210 F.3d 412, 414 (D.C. Cir. 2000), citing *Heller v. Fortis Benefits Ins. Co.,* 142 F.3d 487, 493 (D.C. Cir. 1998). The consequence of an inadequate benefits denial letter is that the normal time limits for administrative appeal may not be enforced against the claimant. *Id.* at 416, quoting *Counts v. Am. Gen. Life & Accident Ins. Co.*, 111 F.3d 105, 108 (11th Cir. 1997). Lack of prejudice from the notice's deficiencies is no justification for refusal to consider a beneficiary's claim. *Id.* at 418. In *White*, the circuit court declined to consider whether the insurer's failure to communicate an important reason for denying a claim has any consequence beyond estopping the insurer from relying on that reason in considering a claimant's appeal, as the insurer did not raise the point until oral argument. *Id.* at 419. The circuit court also admonished that "[i]n view of *Heller* and the decision we reach today, it would be in the best interest of all concerned for insurers to disclose *in writing* all information required by the regulations." *Id.* (emphasis in original).

### 2. Federal Common Law; Remedies

ERISA allows a remedy in restitution where there has been an unjust enrichment. Awards of restitution will be reviewed only for abuse of discretion. *Heller v. Fortis Benefits Ins. Co.*, 142 F.3d 487, 494–95 (D.C. Cir. 1998). Unjust enrichment and quasi-contract encompass three elements: The plaintiff must show that (1) he had a reasonable expectation of payment; (2) the defendant should reasonably have expected to pay; and (3) society's reasonable expectations of person and property would be defeated by nonpayment. *Id.* at 495, quoting *Provident Life & Accident Ins. Co. v. Waller*, 906 F.2d 985, 993–94 (4th Cir. 1990). Even though a benefits plan did not expressly provide for restitution, neither did the plan expressly prohibit such recovery; and the insurer's written notice that its payment of benefits could not be deemed an admission of liability effectively notified the claimant that the insurer expected reimbursement of benefits for which the claimant was not eligible. *Id.*

Following *Massachusetts Mutual Life Insurance Co. v. Russell*, 473 U.S. 134, 144 (1985), and cases from the Fourth, Fifth, Seventh, and Eleventh Circuits, the district court has held that there is no private right of action by an ERISA plan beneficiary for extracontractual compensatory or punitive damages. *Moore v. Blue Cross & Blue Shield of the Nat'l Capital Area*, 70 F. Supp. 2d 9, 37–38 (D.D.C. 1999).

## VIII. Procedural Aspects of ERISA Practice

### A. Methods of Adjudication

ERISA cases in the D.C. Circuit are often resolved on summary judgment. *See Chao v. Day*, 436 F.3d 234 (D.C. Cir. 2006) (affirming grant of summary judgment on the basis that the relevant ERISA plan's insurance broker breached his fiduciary duties); *Heller v. Fortis Benefits Ins. Co.*, 142 F.3d 487 (D.C. Cir. 1998) (affirming the grant of summary judgment for insurer as to both the denial of benefits and restitution of erroneously paid benefits); *May v. Shuttle, Inc.*, 129 F.3d 165 (D.C. Cir. 1997) (affirming grant of summary judgment as to ERISA claim for interference with pension rights); *Francis v. Rodman Local 201 Pension Fund*, 367 F.3d 937 (D.C. Cir. 2004) (affirming grant of summary judgment for pension fund in claim for benefits); *Allied Pilots Ass'n v. Pension Benefit Guar. Corp.*, 334 F.3d 93 (D.C. Cir. 2003) (affirming grant of summary judgment to government in action for injunction to stop termination of retirement plan or reinstate plan if already terminated); *Fuller v. AFL-CIO*, 328 F.3d 672 (D.C. Cir. 2003) (affirming summary judgment for plan trustees in claim for denial of benefits); *Bd. of Trs. of the Hotel & Rest. Employees Local 25 v. JPR, Inc.,* 136 F.3d 794 (D.C. Cir. 1998) (affirming in part and denying in part the district court's ruling on fees and costs recoverable by the trustees after the district court awarded summary judgment to the trustees in an action for delinquent contributions); *Andes v. Ford Motor Co.,* 70 F.3d 1332 (D.C. Cir. 1995) (affirming grant of summary judgment to defendant in action claiming that decision of defendant to sell subsidiary, and resulting loss of early retirement benefits, constituted a violation of ERISA); *Hamilton v. AIG Life Ins. Co.,* 182 F. Supp. 2d 39 (D.D.C. 2002) (granting administrator's motion for summary judgment on claim for denial of benefits). When warranted, the D.C. Circuit Court of Appeals has not been hesitant to reverse grants of summary judgment. *See, e.g., Fitts v. Fed. Nat'l Mortgage Ass'n,* 236 F.3d 1 (D.C. Cir. 2001) (reversing grant of summary judgment as to ERISA claims involving eligibility for and denial of benefits); *White v. Aetna Life Ins. Co.,* 210 F.3d 412 (D.C. Cir. 2000) (reversing grant of summary judgment for plan administrator on claim for denial of benefits on grounds that administrator failed to comply with ERISA notice requirements); *O'Connor v. UNUM Life Ins. Co. of Am.,* 146 F.3d 959 (D.C. Cir. 1998) (reversing grant of summary judgment for insurer on claim for failure to pay benefits); *Commc'ns Workers of Am. v. Am. Tel. & Tel. Co.,* 40 F.3d 426 (D.C. Cir. 1994) (reversing grant of summary judgment for plaintiffs on grounds that plaintiffs did not exhaust administrative remedies).

Courts do not limit summary judgment to judgment for defendants, but may, in appropriate circumstances, grant summary judgment to ERISA plaintiffs. *See Flynn v. R.C. Tile,* 353 F.3d 953 (D.C. Cir. 2004) (affirming grant of summary judgment for trustee plaintiffs in action to recover unpaid contributions to fund from unincorporated entity); *Nat'l Shopmen Pension Fund v. Burtman Iron Works, Inc.,* 148 F. Supp. 2d 60 (D.D.C. 2001) (granting in part and denying in part plaintiffs' motion for summary judgment on claim for past-due contributions). In ERISA actions, parties often bring cross-motions for summary judgment. *See Allied Pilots Ass'n v. Pension Benefit Guar. Corp.,* 334 F.3d 93 (D.C. Cir. 2003) (cross-motions for summary judgment; defendants' motion granted); *Buford v. Unum Life Ins. Co. of Am.,* 290 F. Supp. 2d 93 (D.D.C. 2003) (cross-motions for summary judgment on claim for benefits; defendant's motion granted); *Fuller v. AFL-CIO,* 328 F.3d 672 (D.C. Cir. 2003) (cross-motions for summary judgment on claim for benefits; defendants' motion granted).

## B. Reported ERISA Trials

There have been several reported ERISA trials in the District of Columbia. *See Moore v. Blue Cross & Blue Shield of the Nat'l Capital Area,* 70 F. Supp. 2d 9 (D.D.C. 1999) (granting plaintiffs' request for a declaratory judgment, and recognizing defendants' subrogation rights); *Eddy v. Colonial Life Ins. Co. of Am.,* 919 F.2d 747 (D.C. Cir. 1990) (reversing the judgment of the district court after trial that insurer did not breach fiduciary duty); *Holt v. Winpisinger,* 811 F.2d 1532 (D.C. Cir. 1987) (reversing the judgment of the district court after a bench trial as to plaintiff's eligibility); *Teamsters Local 639-Employers Pension Trust v. United Parcel Serv., Inc.,* 752 F. Supp. 500 (D.D.C. 1990) (after trial, district court held that trust failed to show underpayment of contributions); *Ret. & Sec. Program for Employees of the*

*Nat'l Rural Elec. Coop. Ass'n v. Oglethorpe Power Corp. Ret. Income Plan,* 712 F. Supp. 223 (D.D.C. 1989) (judgment for plaintiff after bench trial in declaratory judgment action); *Foltz v. U.S. News & World Report, Inc.,* 865 F.2d 364 (D.C. Cir. 1989) (affirming the judgment of the district court for defendants after a bench trial).

### C. Special Procedures for ERISA Benefit Cases

Other than as discussed, the D.C. Circuit offers no special procedures for ERISA benefit cases.

## IX. Fiduciary Liability Claims

### A. Definition of Fiduciary

Whether an individual or entity is a fiduciary under ERISA is dependent on the function(s) they perform with respect to the plan. *See Hunter v. Metro. Life Ins. Co.,* 251 F. Supp. 2d 107, 112 (D.D.C. 2003) ("'In ERISA, Congress took a functional approach towards defining who would be treated as a fiduciary.'" (quoting *Brink v. DeLasio,* 496 F. Supp. 1350, 1374 (D. Md. 1980), *aff'd in part, rev'd in part on other grounds,* 667 F.2d 420 (4th Cir. 1981))). The D.C. Circuit recently held that a person or entity is a fiduciary under ERISA to the extent he or she exercises any discretionary authority or discretionary control over the management of a plan *or* exercises authority or control over plan assets. *See Chao v. Day,* 436 F.3d 234, 235 (D.C. Cir. 2006); 29 U.S.C. § 1002(21)(A). The D.C. Circuit views the legislature's inclusion of a disjunctive clause in ERISA's definition of a fiduciary (§ 3(21)(A)) as creating two different circumstances by which an individual or entity may be a fiduciary to an ERISA plan. *Chao,* 436 F.3d at 235–36. Specifically, in the D.C. Circuit a person or entity can be an ERISA fiduciary by either having discretion over a plan's management or having control over plan assets. *Id.* at 235–36.

However, just because an individual or entity is a fiduciary because he, she, or it has discretion over the management of an ERISA plan does not necessarily mean that he, she or it is a fiduciary for every facet of the plan. The scope of a fiduciary's role is limited to how that individual or entity functions within the plan. *Systems Council EM-3 v. AT&T Corp.,* 159 F.3d 1376, 1379 (D.C. Cir. 1998). *See also Hartline v. Sheet Metal Workers' Nat'l Pension Fund,* 134 F. Supp. 2d 1, 10 (D.D.C. 2000) ("a party is subject to ERISA's fiduciary standards only when it acts in a fiduciary capacity" (quoting *Systems Council EM-3*)). Further, when an individual or entity performs incidental, purely ministerial, nondiscretionary, or "settlor" functions for a plan, that individual or entity is not a fiduciary and not subject to ERISA's fiduciary duties with respect to those nonfiduciary functions. *Eaton v. D'Amato,* 581 F. Supp. 743, 745 (D.D.C. 1980). *See also Adams v. Pension Benefit Guar. Corp.,* 332 F. Supp. 2d 231, 237 (D.D.C. 2004) (when an employer or other plan sponsor undertakes to adopt, modify, or terminate a plan, it is doing so as a plan settlor and is not acting as an ERISA fiduciary).

The D.C. Circuit and District Court for the District of Columbia have confirmed that the following actions, among others, constitute fiduciary functions under ERISA: managing and utilizing plan assets, administering plan investments, and granting or denying plan benefits. *See Systems Council EM-3,* 159 F.3d at 1380; *Hunter v. Metro. Life Ins. Co.,* 251 F. Supp. 2d 107, 112–13 (D.D.C. 2003). Each of these functions may require a party to make a discretionary determination with respect to plan management and/or give the fiduciary control over plan assets.

## B. Definition of Fiduciary Duties

The fiduciary duties and responsibilities enumerated in ERISA § 404 have been interpreted by the D.C. Circuit as incomplete and subject to judicial supplementation pursuant to federal common-law trust principles. *Eddy v. Colonial Life Ins. Co. of Am.,* 919 F.2d 747, 750 (D.C. Cir. 1990). "ERISA requires a [plan] fiduciary to act 'solely in the interest' of a plan's participants and beneficiaries, and to discharge his duties 'with the care, skill, prudence, and diligence . . . that a prudent man acting in a like capacity and familiar with such matters would use in the conduct of an enterprise of a like character. . . ." *Fink v. Nat'l Sav. & Trust Co.,* 772 F.2d 951, 955 (D.C. Cir. 1985), quoting 29 U.S.C. § 1104(a)(1)(B). *See also Stewart v. Nat'l Educ. Ass'n,* 404 F. Supp. 2d 122, 132 (D.D.C. 2005); *Chao v. Trust Fund Advisors,* No. Civ. A. 02-559(GK), 2004 WL 444029, at *2 (D.D.C. 2004) ("Under ERISA, a fiduciary is held to the prudent person standard of case . . .").

Generally, a fiduciary may be held accountable for a breach of fiduciary duty for "materially mislead[ing] those to whom the duties of loyalty and prudence . . . are owed." *Eddy,* at 750, quoting *Berlin v. Mich. Bell Tel. Co.,* 858 F.2d 1154, 1163 (6th Cir. 1988). In order for an ERISA plaintiff to successfully establish a claim for breach of fiduciary duty based upon a fiduciary's alleged failure to disclose, the claimant must show that the fiduciary possessed material information not known to the claimant and that the fiduciary failed to disclose such information. *See Barry v. Trs. of the Int'l Assoc. Full-Time Salaried Officers & Employees of Outside Local Unions & District Counsel's (Iron Workers) Pension Plan,* 404 F. Supp. 2d 145, 154 (D.D.C. 2005).

## C. Fiduciary Liability in the Context of Health and Disability Claims

Under ERISA, fiduciaries owe the same general standards of loyalty and prudence regardless of whether an ERISA plan is a health and disability plan or a pension plan. *See Eaton v. D'Amato,* 581 F. Supp. 743, 747–48 (D.D.C. 1980) (after determining that defendants were fiduciaries for plaintiff's welfare and pension plans, the court analyzed defendants' potential liability under ERISA § 409(a)). The D.C. Circuit has not specifically discussed whether an ERISA fiduciary owes any additional fiduciary duties in the context of health and disability plans.

## D. Remedies for Breach of Fiduciary Duty

When an ERISA fiduciary breaches any of its fiduciary duties to the plan, the fiduciary may be held personally liable *to the plan* under ERISA § 409(a). *Fink,* 772 F.2d at 955; 29 U.S.C. § 1109(a). The remedies available to the plan due to a fiduciary's breach range from monetary, based on either losses incurred by the plan because of the fiduciary's breach or profits earned by the fiduciary as a result of the breach, to equitable or remedial relief, as deemed appropriate by the court. *See id.* The D.C. Circuit interprets ERISA § 409(a) as providing "broad authority under [ERISA] to fashion remedies for redressing any breach and for protecting the interests of participants and beneficiaries." *Crawford v. La Boucherie Bernard Ltd.,* 815 F.2d 117, 119 (D.C. Cir. 1987).

Although monetary relief for a breach of fiduciary duty can only be awarded to a plan, an individual plan participant and/or beneficiary may obtain "appropriate equitable relief" against a fiduciary by way of ERISA § 502(a)(3). Individual equitable relief is permissible under § 502(a)(3) for a breach of fiduciary duty, so long as the requested relief is subject to the limitations set forth in *Great-West Life & Annuity Ins. Co. v. Knudson,* 534 U.S. 204 (2002), and *Sereboff v. Mid Atlantic Medical Services, Inc.,* 126 S. Ct. 1869 (2006).

### E. Contribution and Indemnity Claims among Fiduciaries

With respect to the scope of one's liability for breaching ERISA's fiduciary duties, the District Court for the District of Columbia expressly rejected imposing theories of indemnification and contribution. In *International Brotherhood of Painters & Allied Trades Union & Industry Pension Plan v. Duval,* 1994 WL 903314 (D.D.C. 1994), the court adopted the position that because Congress created a comprehensive remedial scheme for breaches of ERISA's fiduciary duties and since Congress was undoubtedly aware that the issues of indemnification and contribution would arise among ERISA fiduciaries, the fact that Congress remained silent on the issue is evidence that no such rights are appropriate. *Id.* at *3.

### F. ERISA Claims against Nonfiduciaries

Each of the remedies afforded under ERISA for a breach of fiduciary duty are also recoverable against cofiduciaries and nonfiduciaries that participate in a fiduciary breach. However, such relief against nonfiduciaries is limited to situations where nonfiduciaries "*knowingly* participate in a breach of trust." *Fink,* 772 F.2d at 958 (emphasis added). *See also Barry,* 404 F. Supp. 2d at 156–57 (D.D.C. 2005) (in order for a nonfiduciary to be subjected to liability under ERISA § 502(a)(3), a claimant must establish that the nonfiduciary had 'actual and constructive knowledge of the circumstances that rendered the transaction unlawful.'" (quoting *Harris Trust & Savings Bank v. Salomon Smith Barney, Inc.,* 530 U.S. 238 (2000))).

## X. Attorneys' Fees

### A. Criteria for Awarding Attorneys' Fees

Consistent with all other circuit courts of appeals, the Court of Appeals for the District of Columbia follows the following five-factor test for determining whether a party in an ERISA § 502 action should be awarded attorneys' fees:

- The losing party's culpability or bad faith;
- The losing party's ability to satisfy a fee award;
- The deterrent effect of such an award;
- The value of the victory to plan participants and beneficiaries, and the significance of the legal issue involved; and
- The relative merits of the parties' positions.

*See Eddy v. Colonial Life Ins. Co.,* 59 F.3d 201, 206 (D.C. Cir. 1995), quoting *Hummell v. S.E. Rykoff & Co.,* 634 F.2d 406, 453 (9th Cir. 1980), and citing *Eaves v. Penn,* 587 F.2d 453, 464 (10th Cir. 1978). However, this five-factor test is "neither exclusive nor quantitative, thereby affording leeway to the district courts to evaluate and augment them on a case-by-case basis." *Eddy,* 59 F.3d at 206. *See also Risteen v. Youth for Understanding,* No. Civ. A. 02-0709(JDB), 2003 WL 22011766, at *2 (D.D.C. Aug. 19, 2003).

The D.C. Court of Appeals has rejected the presumption that prevailing plaintiff plan participants are entitled to fee awards. *Eddy,* 59 F.3d at 206. In practice, however, the district court has been quite willing to award attorneys' fees to such prevailing plaintiffs. *See Eddy v. Colonial Life Ins. Co.,* 844 F. Supp. 790 (D.D.C. 1994), *remanded,* 59 F.3d 201 (D.C. Cir. 1995).

The district court's discretion in awarding fees is given broad deference on appeal to the Court of Appeals for the D.C. Circuit. *See Bd. of Trs. of the Hotel & Rest. Employees Local 25 v. JPR, Inc.,* 136 F.3d 794, 798 (D.C. Cir. 1998) ("Clearly the district court is most familiar with the interstices of the litigation, and we accord its decisions considerable deference"). Appellate review of attorneys' fees decisions "is confined to correcting errors of law and remedying abuses of discretion." *Id.*

## B. Fees Awarded to Plan Fiduciaries

In the non-delinquent contribution context, the District Court for the District of Columbia has been reluctant to grant awards to prevailing fiduciaries. *See Buford v. UNUM Life Ins. Co.,* 290 F. Supp. 2d 92 (D.D.C. 2003) (attorneys' fee award to employer not appropriate where participant did not bring disability claim in bad faith; there was no need to deter plaintiffs in similar situations from bringing suit against insurers; and the relative merits of the parties' positions did not so clearly favor insurer that award of fees and costs was warranted).

In the delinquent contribution context, awards of attorneys' fees are regularly made to fiduciaries seeking overdue contributions. *Flynn v. Thibodeaux Masonry, Inc.,* 2004 WL 722651 (D.D.C. 2004) (piercing corporate veil to hold controlling shareholder personally liable for corporation's ERISA liability from its failure to contribute to pension fund); *Nat'l Stabilization Agreement of the Sheet Metal Industry v. Commercial Roofing & Sheet Metal,* 655 F.2d 1218 (D.C. Cir. 1981) (fee award under ERISA § 502(g)(2) to trustees of joint labor-management trust fund for delinquent contribution action against employer); *Int'l Painters & Allied Trades Indus. Pension Fund v. R.W. Amrine Drywall Co., Inc.,* 239 F. Supp. 2d 26 (D.D.C. 2002) (same).

## C. Calculation of Attorneys' Fees

The method of calculating a reasonable attorneys' fee award under ERISA § 502(g) in the D.C. Circuit is to multiply the hours reasonably expended in the litigation by a reasonable hourly fee, producing the "lodestar" amount. *Bd. of Trs. of the Hotel & Rest. Employees Local 25 v. JPR, Inc.,* 136 F.3d 794, 801 (D.C. Cir. 1998). This lodestar amount may then be adjusted by a multiplier "in certain 'rare' and 'exceptional' cases." *Id.* A party awarded fees is entitled to the market value of the services, rather than the actual rate that may have been charged, if different. *Id.* at 800–01 ("The party must both 'offer evidence to demonstrate [her] attorney's experience, skill, reputation, and the complexity of the case' and 'produce data concerning the prevailing market rates in the relevant community for attorneys of reasonably comparable skill, experience, and reputation.'") (citation omitted). "In setting the market rate, the district court should consider what rate would be commensurate with the attorney's skill and experience, and with the quality of the attorney's work." *Id.* at 801.

## XI. ERISA Regulations

ERISA and its corresponding regulations set certain minimum requirements for the claims procedures that plans are required to follow in processing benefits claims brought by participants and beneficiaries. *See* ERISA § 503; 29 C.F.R. § 2560.503-1. Plan administrators are required to provide procedures for processing claims for benefits made by participants and beneficiaries, including consideration of such claims, notification of the plan's benefit determination, and internal plan appeal and review procedures. Failure by a plan to adhere to those procedures may serve as a basis for successfully challenging a denial of benefits. Conversely, failure by a participant to exhaust these procedures may preclude the party from pursuing his or her claims in court. (See Exhaustion of Administrative Remedies, Section III, *supra.*) The regulations regarding claims procedures were revised effective January 1, 2002, and apply to benefit claims filed after that date. The previous regulations apply to claims filed prior to 2002.[1] The revised regulations establish shorter time frames, additional disclosure requirements, and new standards for making claims decisions. 29 C.F.R. § 560.503-1. The DOL has published guidance in a question-and-answer format that is available at http://www.dol.gov/ebsa/faqs/faq_claims_proc_reg.html.

At least one district court in the D.C. Circuit has held that the disclosure requirements in the regulations must be strictly applied. In *Hurley v. Life Insurance Co. of North America*, Civil Action No. 05-252 (CKK), 2006 WL 1883406 (D.D.C. July 9, 2006), the court held that providing all documents "collected, reviewed, and/or relied upon" in the course of a benefits determination does not satisfy the regulation's requirement to disclose all documents "submitted, considered or generated" in connection with the determination. *Id.* at *5. The court noted that the regulation requires disclosure of all relevant information, "without regard to whether such document, record or other information was relied upon in making the benefit determination[,]" and ordered to defendants to produce all "e-mails, notes, internal memorandum, or other documents that were generated during Defendants' review or decision making process[.]" *Id.* at *5–6.

In 2003, the Supreme Court confirmed in *Black & Decker Disability Plan v. Nord,* 538 U.S. 822 (2003), that the regulations regarding claims procedures do not require deference to the opinions of treating physicians. *Id.* at 831. In doing so, the Court rejected the claimant's attempt to incorporate the "treating physician rule" applicable to Social Security disability determinations into ERISA disability claims. *Id.* at 829. The Court noted that while the regulations governing Social Security disability claims expressly provide for deference to the treating physician, the ERISA regulations, which were revised more than nine years after the Social Security Administration instituted the treating physician rule, include no such requirement. *Id.* at 831. *See also Mobley v. Cont'l Cas. Co.,* 405 F. Supp. 2d at 42, 47–48 (D.D.C. 2005) (refusing to accord deference to the claimant's treating physician).

In *Aetna Health Inc. v. Davila,* 542 U.S. 200 (2004), the Supreme Court noted that the ERISA regulations governing claims procedures "apply equally to health benefit plans and other plans, and do not draw distinctions between medical and nonmedical benefits determinations. Indeed, the regulations strongly imply that benefits determinations involving medical judgments are, just as much as any other benefits determinations, actions by plan fiduciaries." *Id.* at 220.

The D.C. Circuit, like its sister circuits, has adopted the "substantial compliance" test when determining whether a denial notice has complied with ERISA § 503 and the claims-procedures regulations. *See White v. Aetna Life Ins. Co.,* 210 F.3d 412, 414 (D.C. Cir. 2000) (deciding whether the insurer satisfied the requirements of 29 C.F.R. § 2560.503-1(f), citing *Heller v. Fortis Benefits Ins. Co.,* 142 F.3d 487, 493 (D.C. Cir. 1998)); *Block v. Pitney Bowes Inc.,* 705 F. Supp. 20, 24 (D.D.C. 1989) (ERISA Regulation 29 C.F.R. § 2560.503-1(f) requires the employer to state the reasons for its actions). In determining whether there has been substantial compliance, the court will consider "not just the notice itself, but all communications between the insurance company and the claimant." *Id.,* citing *Heller,* 142 F.3d at 493. Courts make this determination on a case-by-case basis and assess the information provided by the insurer in the context of the beneficiary's claim. *Id.* (citations omitted). In *White,* the court stated that insurers must substantially comply with Congress and the Department of Labor requirement that "insurance companies [are] to give claimants specific reasons for denying benefits, to cite relevant plan provisions, to specify additional information needed, and to describe how to appeal." *Id.* at 418; *see also Heller,* 142 F.3d at 492–93 (must follow Department of Labor's regulations for claims handling and the time limits contained therein). The court further advised insurance companies that "they could avoid expensive litigation for themselves and claimants and conserve judicial resources by strictly complying with the Labor Department's regulations." *Id.* at 419.

The district court has interpreted the DOL's bulletins and regulations relating to fiduciary duty and found that investment advisors and corporate entities can be fiduciaries under ERISA. *See Bell v. Executive Comm. of United Food & Commercial Workers Pension Plan for Employees,* 191 F. Supp. 2d. 10, 14 (D.D.C. 2002) (citations omitted). The district court, relying in part on ERISA's regulations, has determined that partners, as beneficiaries, have standing to sue under ERISA. *See Krooth & Altman v. N. Am. Life Assurance Co.,* 134 F. Supp. 2d 96, 100 (D.D.C. 2001). In reaching this finding, the court found that even though the partners were not participants of the ERISA plan, they were "beneficiaries" of the plan with standing to bring suit. The district court also has examined the proper application of the Department of Labor's regulations regarding the scope of a plan fiduciary's investment duties. *Chao v. Trust Fund Advisors,* No. Civ. A. 02-559(GK), 2004 WL 444029 (D.D.C. Jan 20, 2004).

In *Raymond B. Yates, M.D., P.C. Profit Sharing Plan v. Hendon,* 541 U.S. 1330 (2004), the Supreme Court resolved a circuit split regarding whether a working owner may qualify as a participant in an employee benefit plan covered by ERISA. *Id.* at 1338. The Court, correcting the Sixth Circuit's interpretation of DOL regulation 29 C.F.R. § 2510.3-3, held that the regulation imposes no barrier to working owner participation in an ERISA plan. *Id.* at 18–23. In *Central Laborers' Pension Fund v. Heinz,* 541 U.S. 739 (2004), the Court also noted that IRS regulations regarding the anti-cutback rule apply with equal force to similar ERISA provisions.

In *Stewart v. National Education Association,* 404 F. Supp. 2d 122 (D.D.C. 2005), the district court relied on a DOL advisory opinion regarding the proper treatment of the proceeds of demutualization. In addition, in *Risteen v. Youth for Understanding, Inc.,* 245 F. Supp. 2d 1 (D.D.C. 2002), the district court examined the regulations governing COBRA continuation coverage.

The district court has also interpreted regulations applying to the Pension Benefit Guaranty Corporation (PBGC), denying a preliminary injunction requiring the PBGC to immediately correct benefit calculations that participants claimed were in error. *See Boivin v. US Airways, Inc.,* 297 F. Supp. 2d 110, 112–13 (D.D.C. 2003). On appeal, the D.C. Circuit declined to reach the merits of the dispute, holding instead that pursuant to PBGC regulations, the plan participants had failed to exhaust their administrative remedies. *Boivin v. US Airways, Inc.,* 446 F.3d 148 (D.C. Cir. 2006). In addition, the district court reviewed PBGC regulations regarding withdrawal liability and common control in *I.A.M. National Pension Fund v. TMR Realty Co., Inc.,* 431 F. Supp. 2d 1, 11–14 (D.D.C. 2006).

In another case involving the PBGC, the district court stated that Congress implicitly granted the PBGC authority to "promulgate regulations to restricting benefit increases attributable to plan amendments on an amendment-by-amendment basis." *Brown v. Pension Benefit Guar. Corp.,* 821 F. Supp. 26, 29 (D.D.C. 1993). Noting that the regulations were not at issue, the district court recognized the authority of the PBGC to interpret any conflicting policies that may arise. *See id.* at 31–32 (citations omitted).

In the year before *Brown,* the D.C. Circuit addressed the PBGC's construction of ERISA's provision regarding the scope of guarantee of benefits that were "nonforfeitable." *Page v. Pension Benefit Guar. Corp.,* 968 F.2d 1310 (D.C. Cir. 1992). The court reversed the district court's decision that PBGC's interpretation was based on the plain meaning of ERISA and found instead that its decision that participants did not qualify for guaranteed benefits was not "'a reasonable accommodation of the policies underlying ERISA.'" *Id.* at 297, quoting *Rettig v. Pension Benefit Guar. Corp.,* 744 F.2d 133, 156 (D.C. Cir. 1984).

## XII. Cases Interpreting ERISA Statutes of Limitation

The applicable statutes of limitation for ERISA claims will depend on the nature of the claim brought. ERISA § 413 provides a limitations period for suits alleging a breach of fiduciary duty. 29 U.S.C. § 1113. Actions for nonfiduciary duty claims, such as those under ERISA §§ 502(a)(1)(B), 502(a)(3), or 510, are subject to the most analogous state limitations period. If a case is transferred pursuant to 28 U.S.C. § 1404(a), the statute of limitations of the transferor state will continue to apply. *In re UMWA Employee Benefit Plans Litig.*, 854 F. Supp. 914 (D.D.C. 1994).

For fiduciary breach claims, there is a general six-year statute of limitations from when the breach or violation occurred; if defendant can show that the plaintiff had actual knowledge, the plaintiff must bring the claim in three years from the date of actual knowledge. *See Larson v. Northrop Corp.*, 1992 WL 249790, at *3 (D.D.C. 1992). If, however, the plaintiff can show fraudulent concealment, then the plaintiff has six years from the date the breach or violation was discovered. *Id.* The D.C. Circuit rejected the argument that the discovery rule applies to non-fraud-based breach of fiduciary duty claims, finding "[that] the limitations period in § 1113(1)(A) is six years—double that in § 1113(2) where the statute of limitations is triggered by actual knowledge of the breach or violation—suggests a judgment by Congress that when six years has passed after a breach or violation, and no fraud or concealment occurs, the value of repose will trump other interests, such as a plaintiff's right to seek a remedy." *See Larson v. Northrop Corp.*, 21 F.3d 1164, 1172 (D.C. Cir. 1994).

When a plaintiff seeks to establish fraudulent concealment under 29 U.S.C. § 1113, in addition to satisfying the requirements of Rule 9(b) of the Federal Rules of Civil Procedure, the plaintiff must show "'(1) that defendants engaged in a course of conduct designed to conceal evidence of their alleged wrong-doing and (2) that [the plaintiffs] were not on actual or constructive notice of that evidence, despite (3) their exercise of diligence.'" *Larson*, 21 F.3d at 1172, quoting *Foltz v. U.S. News & World Report, Inc.*, 663 F. Supp. 1494 (D.D.C. 1987), *aff'd*, 865 F.2d 364 (D.C. Cir.), *cert. denied*, 490 U.S. 1108 (1989). In order to satisfy the first element, a plaintiff must demonstrate that the defendant engaged in "active concealment," undertaking "some 'trick or contrivance' to 'exclude suspicion and prevent inquiry.' Such concealment must rise to something 'more than merely a failure to disclose.'" *Id.*, quoting *Schaefer v. Arkansas Med. Soc'y*, 853 F.2d 1487, 1491 (8th Cir. 1988) (citation omitted).

Courts apply the most analogous state statute of limitations to nonfiduciary claims, such as actions brought under ERISA §§ 502(a)(1)(B), 502(a)(3), and 510. *See Connors v. Hallmark & Son Coal Co.*, 935 F.2d 336, 341 (D.C. Cir. 1991); *Zarate v. Metro. Wash. Renaldialysis Center of Cap. Hill*, 1987 WL 1395729, at *1 (D.D.C. 1987). Claims brought under § 502(a)(1)(B) are claims challenging the denial of benefits and have been characterized as a breach of contract action. *See Connors*, 935 F.2d at 341 (D.C. Cir. 1991) (applying the District of Columbia's three-year statute of limitations); *Zarate*, 1987 WL 1395729, at *1 (same); *see also In re UMWA Employee Benefit Plans Litig.*, 854 F. Supp. 914, 915–16 (D.D.C. 1994) (for ERISA delinquency actions brought under § 515, "the state statute of limitations selected is typically the limitations period for contract claims"). Claims brought under § 502(a)(3) are for equitable relief to enforce the terms of the plan in question, to enjoin violations of the plan and to obtain redress for such violations. ERISA § 510 provides for an independent cause of action against employers who interfere with an employee's ERISA rights, and ensures plan participants and beneficiaries the right to claim plan benefits without interference or fear of reprisal. Section 510 claims often are characterized as wrongful discharge or employment discrimination claims. *Walker v. Pharmaceutical Research & Mfrs. of Am.*, Civil Action No. 04-1991 (RMU), 2006 WL 1982311, at *4 (D.D.C. July 17, 2006). In the District of Columbia, wrongful discharge claims have a three-year statute of limitations, while employment discrimination claims are subject to a one-year limitations period. *Id.* Although the D.C. Circuit has not yet addressed the applicable statute of limitations for a § 510 claim, at least one district court case has held that the most analogous limitations period is a discrimination claim under the District of Columbia Human Rights Act. *Watts v. Parking Mgmt.*, No. Civ. A. 02-2132 CKK, 2006 WL 627153, at *3–4 (D.D.C. March 12, 2006).

When a plaintiff contests a denial of benefits under the plan, the limitations period will normally begin at when the denial occurs because that is when the plaintiff experienced injury. *Connors*, 935 F.2d at 342 (noting that the "limitations period commenced at the time of injury, even if the plaintiff protests that she did not in fact become aware of the injury when it occurred"). In addition, the statute of limitations can begin to run "when the fiduciary clearly and unequivocally repudiates the beneficiary's benefits claim." *Walker*, 2006 WL 1982311, at *3. Although the D.C. Circuit has not discussed repudiation as a trigger for accrual of ERISA claims, the court in *Walker* noted that the repudiation concept is consistent with the law of trusts, which is used to construe ERISA. *Id.* at *3 n.4 (holding that the statute of limitations on a benefits claim "begins to run when the beneficiary first learns that she is considered an independent contractor and is therefore not entitled to benefits, regardless of whether she later files a formal claim for benefits").

In determining when the claim begins to accrue, courts will examine federal law. *See id.* at 341. In *Connors,* the court applied the discovery rule, which the court determined was "consistent with Congress' intent in ERISA to provide 'broad remedies' and 'to remove jurisdictional and procedural obstacles which in the past appear to have hampered effective . . . recovery of benefits due to participants.'" *Id.* at 343, quoting S. REP. NO. 127, 93d Cong., 1st Sess. 35 (1973), 1974 U.S.S.C.A.N. 4639, 4871; *see also Flynn v. Pulaski Constr. Co., Inc.*, No. Civ. A. 02-02336, 2006 WL 47304, at *9–10 (D.D.C. Jan 6, 2006) (applying the discovery rule and holding that "the claim accrues when the Plaintiffs discovered, or 'with due diligence should have discovered the injury'"); *Trs. of the United Assoc. Full-Time Salaried Officers & Employees of Local Unions, Dist. Councils, State & Provincial Ass'n Pension Plan v. Steamfitters Local Union 395,* 641 F. Supp. 444, 446 (D.D.C. 1986) (applying fraudulent concealment doctrine to claim brought under § 502 that was subject to D.C.'s three-year statute of limitations for breach of contract actions).

## XIII. Subrogation Litigation

Furter, in *Moore v. Capitalcare, Inc.,* 461 F.3d 1 (D.C. Cir. 2006), the D.C. Circuit analyzed the Supreme Court's holding in *Sereboff* in the context of a subrogation claim brought pursuant to a federal common law make whole theory. During the appeal, the appellants dropped their challenge to the lower court's issuance of an equitable lien under § 502(a)(3) because "the *Sereboff* court has made the decision that, where the fund is identifiable, the remedy is equitable." *Id.* at 8. However, notwithstanding this fact, plaintiffs attempted to have the lien reversed on the basis that the injured plaintiff had not been made whole by a prior settlement. The Court held that based on the applicable plan language, which "unabiguously establishe[d] a plan priority to any third party recovery the beneficiary obtains regardless of whether the beneficiary has been made whole by the recovery," it need not decide whether to adopt the make whole doctrine a default rule in the D.C. Circuit. *Id.* at 10. In reaching this conclusion, the Court recognized that there is asplint amongts the circuits on this issue.

In *Primax Recoveries, Inc. v. Lee,* 260 F. Supp. 2d 43 *(D.D.C. 2003),* the court denied the insured's motion to dismiss the plan administrator's ERISA claim for a medical expense reimbursement that the insured recovered from a third-party tortfeasor. Defendant Lee suffered personal injuries in an automobile accident that required medical treatment over a two-and-a-half year period with a total cost of $90,000. *See id.* at 45. Lee and the third-party tortfeasor settled their lawsuit for $450,000. After the settlement was reached, the plan brought an action against Lee pursuant to § 502(a)(3) of ERISA, claiming that the plan was entitled to reimbursement based on the reimbursement clause contained in Lee's health plan. The plaintiff contended that any benefits the defendant received were conditioned upon the plan's right of reimbursement and that the defendant breached this contractual provision when she did not reimburse the plan.

In its complaint, the plan expressly stated that it sought restitution and characterized the relief as equitable. The defendant relied on *Knudson* in arguing that the plaintiff's subrogation claim was legal in nature and thus ERISA did not confer subject matter jurisdiction upon the court. *See id.* at 47. The defendant further argued that the plaintiff's reimbursement claim was an action to impose personal liability on the defendant for a sum of money, which should be precluded under *Knudson*'s interpretation of ERISA. *See id.* at 48. The plaintiff disagreed and argued that the relief sought was "'money or property belonging in good conscience to the plaintiff [that can] clearly be traced to particular funds or property in the defendant's possession.'" *Id.*, quoting *Knudson,* 534 U.S. at 213. Relying on *Knudson,* the district court denied the defendant's motion to dismiss because "the Court [could not] conclude that the funds sought are so far dispersed that they no longer are traceable to defendant" when the funds were being held in trust by defendant's prior attorney. *Id.* The court relied on post-*Knudson* cases and denied the motion, because the plaintiff's claim "seem[ed] to be a claim for restitution in equity (not in law)." *Id.*, citing *IBEW-NECA Sw. Health & Benefit Fund v. Douthitt,* 211 F. Supp. 2d 812 (N.D. Tex. 2002); *Bauer v. Gylten,* 2002 WL 664034 (D.N.D. 2002); *Great-West Life & Annuity Ins. Co. v. Brown,* 192 F. Supp. 2d 1376 (M.D. Ga. 2002); *see also Health Cost Controls of Ill., Inc. v. Washington,* 187 F.3d 703, 710 (7th Cir. 1999), *cert. denied,* 528 U.S. 1136 (2000).

In *Sereboff v. Mid Atlantic Medical Services,* 126 S. Ct. 1869 (2006), the Supreme Court clarified its opinion in *Knudson,* and vindicated the district court's decision in *Primax.* The Court reiterated that *Knudson* did not bar all restitution claims under ERISA § 502(a)(3), but only those that sought legal relief under the guise of restitution. *Id.* at 1874. The Court further held that a restitution claim seeking "specifically identifiable funds" was appropriate under § 502(a)(3). *Id.*

## Note

1. Cases decided on claims filed prior to January 1, 2002, may form a basis for interpreting current regulations.

# TABLE OF CASES

# INDEX

Exhaustion of administrative remedies
requirement, *continued*
failure to exhaust, 7, 38–39, 67, 114–15,
158, 181, 206, 227, 257, 285–86, 315,
362–63
minimum levels of administrative review,
7–8, 39, 67–68, 115, 158, 182, 206,
227, 257, 286, 363
and statute of limitations, 57
Expedited procedures, 129

Failure to exhaust administrative remedies,
7, 38–39, 67–68, 114–15, 158, 181,
206, 227, 257, 285–86, 315, 362–63
Federal common law
agency test, 176, 222, 356
application of in plan interpretation,
11–12, 41, 74–75, 119, 160–61, 184,
209–10, 232, 261, 291, 319, 368–69
contribution and indemnity plans among
cofiduciaries, 51
enforceability of policy deadlines, 169
made whole doctrine, 386
statute of limitations, 218
unambiguous policy deadlines, 169
unjust enrichment, 352, 375
waivers, 161
Federal preemption. *See* Preemption
Federal Rules of Civil Procedure
Rule 23, 199
Rule 56, 45, 189, 190, 326, 373
Fibromyalgia, 219
Fiduciaries
attorneys' fees awarded to, 20–21, 53, 85,
137, 166–67, 194, 217, 242, 268–70,
302, 345, 380
contribution claims, 19, 51, 83–84,
134–35, 165, 193, 215, 240–41, 265,
302, 342, 379
definition/status of, 17, 49, 81–82,
129–31, 164, 190–91, 214, 238, 265,
299–300, 328–34, 377–78
disagreements between, 160
DOL regulations, 195
duties, 17–18, 21–22, 49–51, 82, 131–32,
164–65, 191–92, 214, 239, 265, 300, 378
health and disability claim context, 18,
50, 82–83, 132–33, 165, 192, 214–15,
239, 265, 300, 337–40, 378
HMOs as, 103

improper delegation of discretionary
authority, 41
indemnity claims, 19, 51, 83–84, 134–35,
165, 193, 215, 240–41, 265, 302,
342, 379
liability of, 17–19, 23, 49–51, 81–84,
129–35, 164–65, 190–93, 214–15,
238–41, 265–66, 299–302, 328–42,
377–79
malpractice claims against outside
actuaries, 37
multiple functions of, 336
reimbursement of, 143
removal of, 134
termination of, 300
*See also* Breach of fiduciary duty;
Discretionary authority
Florida
bad-faith statute, 311
statute of limitations, 350
Form 5500, filing of, 64
Former employees, 202
Fraud, 65, 285
Fraudulent concealment, 28, 384
"Full and fair review," 86–87, 140, 242–43,
303–4
Futility exception, 112, 157, 181, 206, 226,
257, 285, 316, 362

"Golden parachute" agreements, 280
Good cause
for de novo review, 17
for discovery, 43, 187
for evidence outside record, 43–44, 47,
235–36, 237
Government plans, 63, 248, 308
Grocery voucher programs, 168
Group insurance plans
discretionary clauses, 74
exclusion from ERISA coverage, 32–33,
95–96, 152–53
outside of safe harbor regulation, 203
purchase of and plan establishment, 2,
31–32, 281

Handbooks, employee, 2, 309
*See also* Summary plan descriptions (SPD)
Health and disability claims, fiduciary liability
in, 18, 50, 82–83, 132–33, 165, 192,
214–15, 239, 265, 300, 337–40, 378